# The Use of Force

# THE USE OF FORCE
## Military Power and International Politics

### SIXTH EDITION

edited by
## Robert J. Art
and
## Kenneth N. Waltz

ROWMAN & LITTLEFIELD PUBLISHERS, INC.
*Lanham • Boulder • New York • Toronto • Oxford*

ROWMAN & LITTLEFIELD PUBLISHERS, INC.

Published in the United States of America
by Rowman & Littlefield Publishers, Inc.
A wholly owned subsidiary of the Rowman & Littlefield Publishing Group, Inc.
4501 Forbes Boulevard, Suite 200, Lanham, Maryland 20706
http://www.rowmanlittlefield.com

P.O. Box 317, Oxford OX2 9RU, United Kingdom

British Library Cataloguing in Publication Information Available

**Library of Congress Cataloging-in-Publication Data**

The use of force : military power and international politics / edited by Robert J. Art
and Kenneth N. Waltz—6th ed.
    p.   cm.
    Includes bibliographical references.
    ISBN 0-7425-2556-2 (cloth : alk. paper)—ISBN 0-7425-2557-0 (pbk. : alk. paper)
    1. International relations.   2. War.   3. Intervention (International law)   I. Art,
Robert J.   II. Waltz, Kenneth Neal, 1924–
JZ1310.U83   2003
327.1'17—dc21                                                            2003046650

Printed in the United States of America

♾™ The paper used in this publication meets the minimum requirements of
American National Standard for Information Sciences—Permanence of Paper
for Printed Library Materials, ANSI/NISO Z39.48–1992.

# Brief Contents

# Detailed Contents

# Preface

In the sixth edition of this book, we have retained the perspective of the first five editions. We have continued to emphasize the relation between military strategy and foreign policy. The selections reprinted here are of two types. Some treat general principles guiding the direct use of force; others deal with specific applications of force and, in doing so, illustrate the general principles. In choosing selections, we have continued to keep the same four questions in mind that motivated us to publish the first edition: (1) What role has the threatened or actual use of military force played in international politics? (2) How has military power changed in the past one hundred years? (3) How have the changes in the instruments of force affected the use of force? (4) What are the implications of the recent profound changes in the structure of international politics?

This edition retains the basic structure of the fifth edition but contains fourteen new selections. We have kept the first two parts largely as they were in the fifth edition, but have added three new articles (George, O'Hanlon, and Burg), omitting three from the previous edition to make room for them. The major changes come in the last part, which has eleven new selections and a section on terrorism. This edition, like the other five, combines classic pieces with contemporary analyses, thereby yielding historical perspective on current issues.

All the selections reprinted in this volume have been edited by removing portions of the text and some or all of the footnotes. For several selections, titles have been changed from their original forms. Full acknowledgments for all thirty-two chapters can be found at the end of the volume.

We hope that beginning and advanced students will find that this edition, as previous editions, helps them understand the dilemmas that political and military leaders face when they have to resort to the use of force.

# PART I

## STRATEGIES FOR THE USE OF FORCE

MILITARY POWER PLAYS a crucial role in international politics because states coexist in a condition of anarchy. If a state is attacked, it has to defend itself with whatever means it can muster. Because no authoritative agency can be called on to resolve disputes among states, leaders find it convenient, and often-times necessary, to threaten the use of force or actually to employ it. Though its importance varies from era to era, military power brings some order to international politics and helps make and enforce the rules of the game.

There are two general questions to ask about the use of force. First, what are the ways in which states can and do use military power? Second, what effects has the nuclear revolution had on the ways that military power can be used?

The essays in the first section of Part I address the first question. Robert Art shows how and why military power is a fungible instrument of statecraft—one that is useful for a wide range of purposes. Barry Posen examines the factors that influence the strategies that states adopt for using force and devises a set of propositions about the determinants of grand strategy. Stephen Van Evera analyzes the offense–defense balance and shows when war is likely to occur and when it is not. Alexander George lays out the logic and requirements of coercive diplomacy—the resort to threats to use force or to limited use of force in order to get an adversary to change its behavior. Brian Jenkins examines the psychology of terrorists and the ways in which they use force.

The essays in the second section assess the effects of the nuclear revolution on the political utility of military power. McGeorge Bundy believes that nuclear weapons give only one advantage to states that have them—to prevent others from using theirs. No other political, diplomatic, or military benefit is gained. Robert Jervis and Kenneth Waltz argue to the contrary. Jervis asserts that the effects of nuclear weapons on international politics are powerful and pervasive, and Waltz argues that nuclear weapons are a force for peace, making not only nuclear but also major conventional wars less likely between states that possess them or enjoy their protection.

# 1

# The Fungibility
# of Force

ROBERT J. ART

## FORCE AND ANARCHY

In anarchy, force is integral to foreign policy because military power can be wielded not only forcefully but also "peacefully." The forceful use of military power is physical: a state harms, cripples, or destroys the possessions of another state. The peaceful use of military power is intimidating: a state threatens to harm, cripple, or destroy, but does not actually do so. To use military power forcefully is to wage war; to use it peacefully is to threaten war. Only when diplomacy has failed is war generally waged. Mainly in the hope that war can be avoided are threats usually made. For any given state, war is the exception, not the rule, in its relations with other countries, because most of the time a given state is at peace, not war. Consequently, states use their military power more frequently in the peaceful than in the forceful mode.

When used forcefully, the effects of military power are easy to identify. A state unleashes its military forces, and it either achieves its objectives or fails to. The adversary is defeated and coerced; or it remains victorious and unbowed; or the battle is fought to a draw. Used in war, force is a blunt instrument, but it can achieve decisive results if wielded properly. When used peacefully, states employ their military power in more subtle, and therefore in less well-defined ways. Used peacefully, military power is held at the ready, and its exact influence on political outcomes becomes more difficult to trace. The war-waging use of military power is akin to a powerful flood: it washes away all before it. The peaceful use of military power is akin to a gravitational field among large objects in space: it affects all motion that takes place, but it produces its effects imperceptibly. The effects

3

of floods are dramatic and easy to pinpoint; those of gravity seem more mundane and are harder to discern. A flood demonstrates its effects by its presence; a gravitational field, by its absence. Most of the time the effect of military power looks more like gravity than a flood; therefore, the usefulness of military power should not be equated simply with its physical use. Short of waging war or playing chicken in a crisis, then, military power shapes outcomes more by its peacetime presence than by its forceful use. Thus, to focus only on the physical use of military power is to miss most of what most states do most of the time with the military power at their disposal.

The peaceful use of military power may be less decisive than its wartime use, but that does not mean the peacetime effects are insignificant. To the contrary: the peaceful use of military power explains why it remains central to statecraft. Lurking behind the scenes, unstated but explicit, lies the military muscle that gives meaning to the posturing of the diplomats. Especially for great powers, but for the lesser ones, too, military power undergirds the other instruments of statecraft. Diplomacy is the striking of compromises by states with differing perspectives and clashing interests. There are many factors that go into the fashioning of diplomatic agreements, but central to each is fear about the consequences of failure. Fear of failure, combined with the knowledge that force can be used if agreement is not reached, help produce agreement. It is the ultimate ability of each state to use its military instrument that disciplines the diplomats. In this fashion the threat to use force plays the same role in bargaining among nations that the threat to strike plays in labor-management negotiations. The threat of either a destructive war or a prolonged strike represents a catastrophic breakdown that the parties would prefer to avoid. The fear of breakdown, together with the desire to avoid it, work to prevent it. Environments where nothing exists to prevent catastrophic breakdowns from occurring, other than the will of the parties, are called permissive realms. In such realms, the fear of failure becomes an essential ingredient for success.

In permissive realms the threat of breakdown need not be made explicit, but can be left implicit and still be effective. The threat to use force (or to strike) need not be articulated because all parties understand that it is an integral part of the situation. The threat cannot be disowned. The right to strike is an inherent feature of collective bargaining; similarly, the right of every state to resort to force is part and parcel of international politics.

In permissive realms, moreover, threats often can be more effective if left implicit. When one state makes an explicit threat, it raises the pressure on the state against which the threat has been directed to follow suit. Threat spawns counterthreat and, in turn, another threat, and so on. Voluntary agreement may be stymied in this escalatory process because threats stiffen the bargainers and harden their positions. Implicit threats, on the other hand, have a better chance of avoiding the escalatory dynamic and can more easily produce agreement, but only if the desire of both parties to avoid breakdown is strong. Whether explicit or implicit, threats remain an integral feature of statecraft, and it is these threats that produce the gravitational effect of military power. That in turn imparts to the other instruments of statecraft more "punch" than they would otherwise have. In short, in a permissive realm like anarchy, where implicit threats inhere, force bolsters diplomacy. . . .

Coercion, therefore, is to a political framework what a political framework is to a market: the necessary, but not the sufficient precondition for its effective functioning. An efficient market depends upon the expectation by its participants that the rules governing their economic interactions will be stable and fair. It is the political framework in which markets exist that provides these rules. Without such a framework, markets function poorly. If, for example, seizure of assets is arbitrary and frequent, private investment will be discouraged. If a state can alter the prices of goods at will, investments will be skewed. If no punishment exists for stock-market fraud, then either fraud will become rampant, or would-be buyers of stock will need to hire their own stock-fraud screeners. To function well, then, free markets must be embedded in a political framework that enforces the rules for stable economic exchanges. As the British historian E. H. Carr put it: "The science of economics presupposes a given political order, and cannot be profitably studied in isolation from politics."

Similarly, the study of politics cannot be profitably studied in isolation from coercion. Political structures, domestic or international, cannot exist apart from it. Within a state, if any group can get its way through the use of force, then public order will break down, might will make right, mafiosos will replace government, and constant warfare will ensue until lines are drawn, power balances are established, and uneasy peaces ensue. When the coercive power of government breaks down, force becomes privatized. When force is privately held, it creates gangsterism; when publicly held, it creates government. It is a state's legitimate monopoly on the use of force that creates the bedrock condition for a stable domestic political order.

Thinking about the role that coercion plays in domestic affairs therefore helps us to understand why it plays an even larger role in a permissive realm like international politics. If force is an important element in politics within nations, then it must be all the more so for politics among nations. When interests clash domestically, matters usually do not get out of hand, because all sides know that there is the ultimate discipline of forceful coercion by the state. When interests clash internationally, reasonableness, persuasion, and logic carry much less weight than they do domestically, because there is no central government standing in the background to enforce them. Instead, there are separate states, each of which possesses its own coercive power, although in varying amounts. International politics is not gangsterism, but it resembles it in at least one respect: all states have the need to be privately armed because there is no legitimate, public coercive authority above them. As Kenneth Waltz aptly put it: "In politics force is said to be the ultima ratio. In international politics force serves, not only as the ultima ratio, but indeed as the first and constant one." In domestic politics force has been subjected to central governmental control; in international politics it has not. Consequently, states in anarchy cannot dispense with something that even national governments cannot do without. . . .

## POWER ASSETS: COMPARISONS AND CONFUSIONS

So far, I have argued that force is integral to statecraft because international politics is anarchic. By itself, that fact makes force fungible to a degree. Exactly how fungible an instrument is military power, however, and how does it compare in this regard to the other power assets a state wields? In this section, I answer these questions. First, I make a rough comparison as to the fungibility of the main instruments of statecraft. Second, I present a counterargument that force has little fungibility and then critique it.

### Comparing Power Assets

Comparing the instruments of statecraft according to their fungibility is a difficult task. We do not have a large body of empirical studies that systematically analyze the comparative fungibility of a state's power assets. The few studies we do have, even though they are carefully done, focus on only one or two instruments, and are more concerned with looking at assets within specific issue areas than with comparing assets across issue areas. As a consequence, we lack sufficient evidence to compare power assets according to their fungibility. Through a little logic, however, we can provide some ballpark estimates.

Consider what power assets a state owns. They include: population—the size, education level, and skills of its citizenry; geography—the size, location, and natural resource endowment of the state; governance—the effectiveness of its political system; values—the norms a state lives by and stands for, the nature of its ideology, and the extent of its appeal to foreigners; wealth—the level, sources, and nature of its productive economy; leadership—the political skill of its leaders and the number of skillful leaders it has; and military power—the nature, size, and composition of its military forces. Of all these assets, wealth and political skill, look to be the most versatile; geography and governance, the least versatile, because both are more in the nature of givens that set the physical and political context within which the other assets operate; values and population, highly variable, depending, respectively, on the content of the values and on the education and skill of the populace; and military power, somewhere between wealth and skill, on the one hand, and geography and governance, on the other hand, but closer to the former than to the latter. In rank order, the three most fungible power assets appear to be wealth, political skill, and military power.

Economic wealth has the highest fungibility. It is the easiest to convert into the most liquid asset of all, namely, money, which in turn can be used to buy many different things—such as a good press, top-flight international negotiators, smart lawyers, cutting-edge technology, bargaining power in international organizations, and so on. Wealth is also integral to military power. A rich state can generate more military power than a poor one. A state that is large and rich can, if it so chooses, generate especially large amounts of military power. The old mercantilist insight that wealth generates power (and vice versa) is still valid.

Political skill is a second power asset that is highly fungible. By definition, skilled political operators are ones who can operate well in different policy realms because they have mastered the techniques of persuasion and influence. They are equally adept at selling free-trade agreements, wars, or foreign aid to their citizens. Politically skillful statesmen can roam with ease across different policy realms. Indeed, that is what we commonly mean by a politically skillful leader—one who can lead in many different policy arenas. Thus, wealth and skill are resources that are easily transferable from one policy realm to another and are probably the two most liquid power assets.

Military power is a third fungible asset. It is not as fungible as wealth or skill, but that does not make it illiquid. Military power possesses versatility because force is integral to politics, even when states are at peace. If force is integral to international politics, it must be fungible. It cannot have pervasive effects and yet be severely restricted in its utility. Its pervasive effects, however, can be uniformly strong, uniformly weak, or variable in strength. Which is the case depends on how military power affects the many domains, policy arenas, and disparate issues that come within its field. At the minimum, however, military power is fungible to a degree because its physical use, its threatened use, or simply its mere presence structure expectations and influence the political calculations of actors. The gravitational effects of military power mean that its influence pervades the other policy realms, even if it is not dominant in most of them. Pervasiveness implies fungibility.

In the case of military power, moreover, greater amounts of it increase its fungibility. Up to a reasonable point, more of it is therefore better than less.[1] It is more desirable to be militarily powerful than militarily weak. Militarily powerful states have greater clout in world politics than militarily weak ones. Militarily strong states are less subject to the influence of other states than militarily weak ones. Militarily powerful states can better offer protection to other states, or more seriously threaten them, in order to influence their behavior than can militarily weak ones. Finally, militarily powerful states are more secure than militarily weak ones. To have more clout, to be less subject to the will of others, to be in a stronger position to offer protection or threaten harm, and to be secure in a world where others are insecure—these are political advantages that can be diplomatically exploited, and they can also strengthen the will, resolve, and bargaining stance of the state that has them. Thus, although military power ranks behind wealth and skill in terms of its versatility, it can be a close third behind those two, at least for those great powers that choose to generate large amounts of it and then to exploit it.

### Conflating Sufficiency and Fungibility

The view argued here—that military power possesses a relatively high degree of fungibility—is not the conventional wisdom. Rather the commonly accepted view is that put forward by David Baldwin, who argues that military power is of restricted utility. Baldwin asserts:

Two of the most important weaknesses in traditional theorizing about international politics have been the tendency to exaggerate the effectiveness of military power resources and the tendency to treat military power as the ultimate measuring rod to which other forms of power should be compared.[2]

Baldwin's view of military power follows from his more general argument that power assets tend to be situationally specific. By that he means: "What functions as a power resource in one policy-contingency framework may be irrelevant in another." If assets are situationally or domain specific, then they are not easily transferable from one policy realm to another. In fact, as Baldwin argues: "Political power resources . . . tend to be much less liquid than economic resources"; and although power resources vary in their degree of fungibility, "no political power resource begins to approach the degree of fungibility of money."

For Baldwin, two consequences flow from the domain-specific nature of power resources. First, we cannot rely on a gross assessment of a state's overall power assets in order to determine how well it will do in any specific area. Instead, we must assess the strength of the resources that it wields in that specific domain. Second, the generally low fungibility of political power resources explains what Baldwin calls the "paradox of unrealized power": the fact that a strong state can prevail in one policy area and lose in another. The reason for this, he tells us, is simple: the state at issue has strong assets in the domain where it prevails and weak ones where it does not.

On the face of it, Baldwin's argument is reasonable. It makes intuitive sense to argue, for example, that armies are better at defeating armies than they are at promoting stable exchange rates. It also makes good sense to take the position that the more carefully we assess what specific assets a state can bring to bear on a specific issue, the more fine-tuned our feel will be of what the state can realistically accomplish on that issue. To deny that all power assets are domain specific to a degree is therefore absurd. Equally absurd, however, are the positions that all assets are domain specific to the same degree, and that a gross inventory of a state's overall power assets is not a reliable, even if only a rough, guide to how well the state is likely to do in any given domain. Assets are not equal in fungibility, and fine-tuning does not mean dramatically altering assessments.

What does all this mean for the fungibility of military power? Should we accept Baldwin's view about it? I argue that we should not. To see why, let us look in greater detail at what else he has to say.

Baldwin adduces four examples that purport to demonstrate the limited versatility of military power.³ The examples are hypothetical, but are nonetheless useful to analyze because they are equivalent to thought experiments. These are the examples:

> Possession of nuclear weapons is not just irrelevant to securing the election of a U.S. citizen as UN secretary-general; it is a hindrance.
>
> . . . the owner of a political power resource, such as the means to deter atomic attack, is likely to have difficulty converting this resource into another resource that would, for instance, allow his country to become the leader of the Third World.
>
> Planes loaded with nuclear weapons may strengthen a state's ability to deter nuclear attacks but may be irrelevant to rescuing the *Pueblo* [a U.S. destroyer seized by the North Koreans in early 1968] on short notice.
>
> The ability to get other countries to refrain from attacking one's homeland is not the same as the ability to "win the hearts and minds of the people" in a faraway land [the reference is to the Vietnam War].⁴

Seemingly persuasive at first glance, the examples are, in fact, highly misleading. A little reflection about each will show how Baldwin has committed the cardinal error of conflating the insufficiency of an instrument with its low fungibility, and, therefore, how he has made military power look more domain specific in each example than it really is.

Consider first the United Nations case. Throughout the United Nation's history, the United States never sought, nor did it ever favor, the election of an American as secretary-general. If it had, money and bribes would have been of as little use as a nuclear threat. The Soviet Union would have vetoed it, just as the United States would have vetoed a Soviet national as secretary-general. Neither state would have countenanced the appointment of a citizen from the other, or from one of its client states. The reason is clear: the Cold War polarized the United Nations between East and West, and neither superpower was willing to allow the other to gain undue influence in the institution if they could prevent it. Therefore, because neither superpower would have ever agreed on a national from the other camp, both sought a secretary-general from the ranks of the unaligned, neutral nations. This explains why Cold War secretaries-general came from the unaligned Scandinavian or Third World nations (Dag Hammarskjold from Sweden; U Thant from Burma, for example), particularly during the heyday of the Cold War. This arrangement, moreover, served both superpowers' interests. At those rare times when they both agreed that the United Nations could be helpful, UN mediation was made more effective because it had a secretary-general who was neutral, not aligned.

Finally, even if America's military power had nothing to do with electing secretaries-general, we should not conclude that it has nothing to do with America's standing within the institution. America's preeminence within the United Nations has been clear. So, too, is the fact that this stems from America's position as the world's strongest nation, a position deriving from both its economic and military strength. Thus, although nuclear weapons cannot buy secretary-general elections, great military power brings great influence in an international organization, one of whose main purposes, after all, is to achieve collective security through the threat or use of force.

The Third World example is equally misleading. To see why, let us perform a simple "thought experiment." Although a Third World leader who had armed his state with nuclear weapons might not rise automatically to the top of the Third World pack, he or she would become a mighty important actor nonetheless. Think of how less weighty China and India, which have nuclear weapons, would be viewed if they did not possess them; and think of how Iraq, Iran, or Libya, which do not have them, would be viewed if they did. For the former set of states, nuclear weapons add to their global political standing; for the latter set, their mere attempts to acquire them have caused their prominence to rise considerably. By themselves, nuclear weapons cannot buy the top slot, in the Third World or elsewhere. Neither economic wealth, nor military power, nor any other power asset alone, can buy top dog. That slot is reserved for the state that surpasses the others in all the key categories of power. Although they do not buy the top position, nuclear weapons nevertheless do significantly enhance the international influence of any state that possesses them, if influence is measured by how seriously a state is taken by others. In this particular case, then, Baldwin is correct to argue that nuclear weapons are not readily convertible into another instrumental asset. Although true, the point is irrelevant: they add to the ultimate resource for which all the other assets of a state are mustered—political influence.

The *Pueblo* example is the most complex of the cases, and the one, when reexamined, that provides the strongest support for Baldwin's general argument. Even when reexamined, this strong case falls far short of demonstrating that military power has little fungibility.

The facts of the *Pueblo* case are straightforward. On 23 January 1968, North Korea seized the U.S.S. *Pueblo*, an intelligence ship that was fitted with sophisticated electronic eavesdropping capabilities and that was listening in on North Korea, and did not release the ship's crew members until 22 December 1968, almost a year after they had been captured. North Korea claimed the ship was patrolling inside its twelve-mile territorial waters limit; the United States denied the claim because its radio "fix" on the *Pueblo* showed that it was patrolling fifteen and a half nautical miles from the nearest North Korean land point. Immediately after the seizure, the United States beefed up its conventional and nuclear forces in East Asia, sending 14,000 Navy and Air Force reservists and 350 additional aircraft to South Korea, as well as moving the aircraft carrier U.S.S. Enterprise and its task force within a few minutes' flying time of Wonsan, North Korea. Some of the aircraft sent to South Korean bases and those on the Enterprise were nuclear capable. According to President Johnson, several military options were considered but ultimately rejected:

mining Wonsan harbor; mining other North Korean harbors; interdicting coastal shipping; seizing a North Korean ship, striking selected North Korean targets by air and naval gunfire. In each case we decided that the risk was too great and the possible accomplishment too small. "I do not want to win the argument and lose the sale," I consistently warned my advisers.[5]

The American government's denial, its military measures, and its subsequent diplomatic efforts, were to no avail. North Korea refused to release the crew. In fact, right from the outset of the crisis, the North Korean negotiators made clear that only an American confession that it had spied on North Korea and had intruded into its territorial waters would secure the crew's release. For eleven months the United States continued to insist that the *Pueblo* was not engaged in illegal activity, nor that it had violated North Korea's territorial waters. Only on 22 December, when General Gilbert Woodward, the U.S. representative to the negotiations, signed a statement in which the U.S. government apologized for the espionage and the intrusion, did North Korea release the crew. The American admission of guilt, however, was made under protest: immediately before signing the statement, the government disavowed what it was about to sign; and immediately after the signing, the government disavowed what it had just admitted.

Although the facts of the *Pueblo* case are straightforward, the interpretation to be put on them is not. This much is clear: neither nuclear weapons, nor any of America's other military assets, appear to have secured the crew's release. Equally clear, however, is that none of its other assets secured the crew's release either. Should we then conclude from this case that military power, diplomacy, and whatever other assets were employed to secure the crew's release have low fungibility? Clearly, that would be a foolish conclusion to draw. There was only one thing that secured the crew's release: the public humiliation of the United States. If nothing but humiliation worked, it is reasonable to conclude that humiliation either was, or more likely, quickly became North Korea's goal. When an adversary is firmly fixed on humiliation, military posturing, economic bribes, diplomatic pressure, economic threats, or any other tool used in moderation is not likely to succeed. Only extreme measures, such as waging war or economic blockade, are likely to be successful. At that point, the costs of such actions must be weighed against the benefits. One clear lesson we can draw from the *Pueblo* case is that sometimes there are tasks for which none of the traditional tools of statecraft are sufficient. These situations are rare, but they do on occasion occur. The *Pueblo* was one of them.

There is, however, a second and equally important point to be drawn from this example. Although it is true that America's military power did not secure the crew's release, nevertheless, there were other reasons to undertake the military buildup the United States subsequently engaged in. Neither the United States nor South Korea knew why the North had seized the *Pueblo*. President Johnson and his advisors, however, speculated that the seizure was related to the Tet offensive in Vietnam that began eight days after the *Pueblo*'s capture. They reasoned that the *Pueblo*'s seizure was deliberately timed to distract the United States and to frighten the South Koreans. Adding weight to this reasoning was the fact that the *Pueblo* was not an isolated incident. Two days earlier, thirty-one special North Korean agents infiltrated into Seoul and got within one half mile of the presidential palace before they were overcome in battle. Their mission was to kill President Park. The United States feared that through these two incidents, and perhaps others to come, North Korea was trying to divert American military resources from Vietnam to Korea and to make the South Koreans sufficiently nervous that they would bring their two divisions fighting in Vietnam back home.

The *Pueblo*'s seizure thus raised three problems for the United States: how to get its crew and ship back; how to deter the North from engaging in further provocative acts; and how to reassure the South Koreans sufficiently so that they would keep their troops in South Vietnam. A strong case could be made that the last two tasks, not the first, were the primary purposes for the subsequent American military buildup in East Asia. After all, the United States did not need additional forces there to pressure the North militarily to release the crew. There were already about 100,000 American troops in East Asia. A military buildup, however, would be a useful signal for deterrence of further provocations and reassurance of its ally. Until (or if) North Korea's archives are opened up, we can not know whether deterrence of further provocation worked, because we do not know what additional plans the North had. What we do know is that the reassurance function of the buildup did work: South Korea kept its divisions in South Vietnam. Thus, America's military buildup had three purposes. Of those, one was achieved, another was not, and the third we cannot be certain about. In sum, it is wrong to draw the conclusion that the *Pueblo* case shows that force has little fungibility, even though military posturing appears not to have gotten the crew released.

Baldwin's final example is equally problematic if the point is to show that military power has little fungibility. Yes, it is true that preventing an attack on one's homeland is a different task than winning the hearts and minds of a people in a distant land. Presumably, however, the point of the example is to argue that the latter task is not merely different from the former, but also more difficult. If this is the assertion, it is unexceptionable: compelling another government to change its behavior has always been an inherently more difficult task than deterring a given government from attacking one's homeland. Not only is interstate compellence more difficult than interstate deterrence, but intrastate compellence is more difficult than interstate compellence. The ability of outside parties to force the adversaries in a civil war to lay down their arms and negotiate an end to their dispute is a notoriously difficult task, as the Chinese civil war in the 1940s, the Vietnamese civil war in the 1960s, and the Bosnian civil war in the 1990s all too tragically show. It is an especially difficult task in a situation like Vietnam, where the outside power's internal ally faces an adversary that has the force of nationalism on its side. (Ho Chi Minh was Vietnam's greatest nationalist figure of the twentieth century and was widely recognized as such within Vietnam.) It is hard to prevail in a civil war when the adversary monopolizes the appeal of nationalism. Equally important, however, it is hard to prevail in a civil war without resort to force. The United States could not have won in Vietnam by force alone, but it would have had no chance at all to win without it.

No thoughtful analyst of military power would therefore disagree with the following propositions that can be teased out of the fourth example: (1) military power works better for defense than for conquest; (2) military power alone cannot guarantee pacification once conquest has taken place; (3) military power alone is not sufficient to compel a populace to accept the legitimacy of its government; and (4) compellence is more difficult than deterrence. These are reasonable statements. There is, however, also a fifth that should be drawn from this example: (5) when an outside power arrays itself in a civil war on the wrong side of nationalism, not only will force be insufficient to win, but so, too, will nearly all the other tools of statecraft—money, political skill, propaganda, and so on. In such cases military power suffers from the same insufficiency as the other instruments. That makes it no more, but no less, fungible than they are.

All four of Baldwin's examples demonstrate an important fact about military power: used alone, it cannot achieve many things. Surely, this is an important point to remember, but is it one that is peculiar to military power alone or that proves that it has little fungibility? Surely not. Indeed, no single instrument of statecraft is ever sufficient to attain any significant foreign-policy objective—a fact I shall term "task insufficiency." There are two reasons for this. First, a statesman must anticipate the counteractions that will be undertaken by the states he is trying to influence. They will attempt to counter his stratagems with those of their own; they will use different types of instruments to offset the ones he is using; and they will attempt to compensate for their weakness in one area with their strength in another. A well-prepared influence attempt therefore requires a multi-instrumental approach to deal with the likely counters to it. Second, any important policy itself has many facets. A multifaceted policy by necessity requires many instruments to implement it. For both reasons, all truly important matters require a statesman to muster several, if not all, the instruments at his disposal, even though he may rely more heavily on some than on others. In sum, in statecraft no tool can stand alone.

For military power, then, as for the other instruments of statecraft, fungibility should not be equated with sufficiency, and insufficiency should not be equated with low fungibility. A given instrument can carry a state part of the way to a given goal, even though it cannot carry the state all the way there. At one and the same time, an instrument of statecraft can usefully contribute to attaining many goals and yet by itself be insufficient to attain any one of them. Thus, careful consideration of Baldwin's examples demonstrates the following: (1) military power was not sufficient to achieve the defined task; (2) none of the other traditional policy instruments were sufficient either; and (3) military power was of some value, either for the defined task or for another task closely connected to it. What the examples did not demonstrate is that states are unable to transfer military power from one policy task to another. Indeed, to the contrary: each showed that military power can be used for a variety of tasks, even though it may not be sufficient, by itself, to achieve any of them.

## HOW FORCE ACHIEVES FUNGIBILITY

If military power is a versatile instrument of statecraft, then exactly how does it achieve its fungibility? What are the paths through which it can influence events in other domains?

There are two paths. The first occurs through the spill-over effects that military power has on other policy domains; the second, through the phenomenon of "linkage politics." In the first case, military power encounters military power, but from this military encounter ensues an outcome with significant consequences for nonmilitary matters. In the second case, military power is deliberately linked to a nonmilitary issue, with the purpose of strengthening a state's bargaining leverage on that issue. In the first case, force is used against force; in the second, force is linked with another issue. In both cases, military power becomes fungible because it produces effects outside the strictly military domain. I explain how each path works and illustrate both with examples.

### Spill-Over Effects

A military encounter, whether peaceful or forceful, yields a result that can be consequential to the interactions and the outcomes that take place in other domains. This result, which I term the "spill-over effect," is too often forgotten.[6] Military-to-military encounters do not produce only military results—cities laid waste, armies defeated, enemies subdued, attacks prevented, allies protected. They also bring about political effects that significantly influence events in other domains. Military power achieves much of its fungibility through this effect: the political shock waves of a military encounter reverberate beyond the military domain and extend into the other policy domains as well. The exercise of successful deterrence, compellence, or defense affects the overall political framework of relations between two states. Because all policy domains are situated within this overarching framework, what happens in the latter affects what happens in the former. Spill-over effects define with more precision why force acts akin to a gravitational field.

A spill-over effect can be understood either as a prerequisite or a by-product. As a prerequisite, the result produced by the act of force checking force creates something that is deliberate and viewed as essential in order to reach a given outcome in another domain. As a by-product, the encounter produces something in another domain that may be beneficial but is incidental or even unintended. Of course, what is by-product and what is prerequisite hangs on what outcomes are valued in that other domain. Two examples will illustrate how the spill-over effect works and how it manifests itself either as a prerequisite or a by-product.

### Examples: Banking and Cold War Interdependence

The first example has to do with banks; the second, with recent history. The banking example demonstrates the role force plays in solvency; the historical example, the role that U.S. military power played in creating today's economic interdependence.

First, the banking example. Begin with this question: why do we deposit our money in a bank? The answer is: we put our money in a bank because we think we can take it out whenever we want. We believe the money is there when we want it. In short, we believe the bank to be solvent.

Solvency is usually thought of solely in economic terms: a bank is solvent because it has enough assets to meet its financial liabilities if they are called.[7] Solvency, however, is a function, not simply of finances, but of physical safety. A bank's solvency depends on the fact both that its assets exceed its liabilities (its balance sheet is in the black) and that its assets are physically secure (not easily stolen). Physical security is therefore as important to a bank's solvency as its liquidity, even though we generally take the former for granted when we reside in a stable domestic order. If the banks within a state could be robbed at will, then its citizens would not put their money in them. A state makes banks physically secure by using its military power to deter and defend against would-be robbers and to compel them to give back the funds if a robbery takes place (assuming they are caught and the funds recovered). Through its use of its legitimate monopoly on the use of force, a state seeks to neutralize the threat of forcible seizure. If the state succeeds in establishing the physical security of its banks, it produces one of the two prerequisites required for a bank's solvency.

In sum, in a well-ordered state, public force suppresses private force. The effect of this suppression is to create a generalized stability that sets the context within which all societal interactions take place. This effect spills over into numerous other domains and produces many manifestations, one of which is confidence about the physical security of banks. This confidence can be viewed as a by-product of the public suppression of private force, as a prerequisite to banking solvency, or, more sensibly, as both.

A good historical example of the spill-over effect of military power is the economic interdependence produced among the free world's economies during the Cold War. In a fundamental sense, this is the banking analogy writ large. The bank is the free-world economies, the potential robber is the Soviet Union, and the provider of physical safety is the United States.

During the Cold War era, the United States used its military power to deter a Soviet attack on its major allies, the Western Europeans and the Japanese. American military power checked Soviet military power. This military-to-military encounter yielded a high degree of military security for America's allies, but it also produced several by-products, one of the most important of which was the creation of an open and interdependent economic order among the United States, Western Europe, and Japan. Today's era of economic interdependence is in no small part due to the exercise of American military power during the Cold War. A brief discussion will show how American military power helped create the economic interdependence from which much of today's world benefits.

America's forty-year struggle with the Soviets facilitated economic integration within Western Europe and among Western Europe, North America, and Japan. Obviously, American military power was not the sole factor responsible for today's interdependence among the major industrialized nations. Also crucial were the conversion of governments to Keynesian economics; their overwhelming desire to avoid the catastrophic experience of the Great Depression and the global war it brought in its wake; the lesson they learned from the 1930s about how noncooperative, beggar-thy-neighbor policies ultimately rebound to the disadvantage of all; the willingness of the United States to underwrite the economic costs of setting up the system and of sustaining it for a time; the acceptance by its allies of the legitimacy of American leadership; the hard work of the peoples involved; and so on. Important as all these factors were, however, we must remember where economic openness first began and where it subsequently flourished most: among the great powers that were allied with the United States against the Soviet Union.

How, then, did the Soviet threat, and the measures taken to counter it, help produce the modern miracle of economic interdependence among America's industrial allies?; and how, exactly, did America's military power and its overseas military presence contribute to it? There were four ways.

First, the security provided by the United States created a political stability that was crucial to the orderly development of trading relations. As I discussed at the outset of this chapter, markets do not exist in political vacuums; rather, they work best when embedded in political frameworks that yield predictable expectations. American military power deployed in the Far East and on the European continent brought these stable expectations, first, by providing the psychological reassurance that the Europeans and the Japanese needed to rebuild themselves and, second, by continuing to provide them thereafter with a sense of safety that enabled their economic energies to work their will. Indeed, we should remember that the prime reason NATO was formed was psychological, not military: to make the Europeans feel secure enough against the Soviets so that they would have the political will to rebuild themselves economically. The initial purpose of NATO is the key to its (and to the United States–Japan defense treaty) long-lasting function: the creation of a politically stable island amidst a turbulent international sea.

Second, America's provision of security to its allies in Europe and in the Far East dampened their respective concerns about German and Japanese military rearmament. The United States's presence protected its allies not only from the Soviets, but also from the Germans and the Japanese. Because German and Japanese military power was contained in alliances that the United States dominated, and especially because American troops were visibly present and literally within each nation, Germany's and Japan's neighbors, while they did not forget the horrors they suffered at the hands of these two during the Second World War, nevertheless, were not paralyzed from cooperating with them. The success of the European Common Market owes as much to the presence of American military power on the continent of Europe as it does to the vision of men like Monnet. The same can be said for the Far East. America's military presence has helped "oil the waters" for Japan's economic dominance there.

Third, America's military presence helped to dampen concerns about disparities in relative economic growth and about vulnerabilities inherent in interdependence, both of which are heightened in an open economic order. Freer trade benefits all nations, but not equally. The most efficient benefit the most; and economic efficiencies can be turned to military effect. Interdependence brings dependencies, all the greater the more states specialize economically. Unequal gains from trade and trade dependencies all too often historically have had adverse political and military effects. Through its provision of military protection to its allies, the United States mitigated the security externalities of interdependence and enabled the Germans and the Japanese to bring their neighbors (America's allies) into their economic orbits without those neighbors fearing that German or Japanese military conquest or political domination would follow. With the security issue dealt with, the economic predominance of the Germans and Japanese was easier for their neighbors to swallow.

Finally, America's military presence fostered a solidarity that came by virtue of being partners against a common enemy. That sense of solidarity, in turn, helped develop the determination and the good will necessary to overcome the inevitable economic disputes that interdependencies bring. The "spill-over" effects of military cooperation against the Soviets on the political will to sustain economic openness should not be underestimated, though they are difficult to pinpoint and quantify. Surely, however, the sense of solidarity and good will that alliance in a common cause bred must have had these spill-over effects. Finally, the need to preserve a united front against the common enemy put limits on how far the allies, and the United States, would permit their economic disputes to go. The need to maintain a united political–military front bounded the inevitable economic disputes and prevented them from escalating into a downward-spiraling economic nationalism. Political stability, protection from potential German and Japanese military resurgence, the dampening of concerns about relative gains and dependencies, and the sense of solidarity—all of these were aided by the American military presence in Europe and the Far East.

## Linkage Politics

The second way force exerts influence on other domains of policy is through the power of linkage politics. In politics, whether domestic or foreign, issues are usually linked to one another. The link can be either functional or artificial. If two issues are linked functionally, then there is a causal connection between them: a change in one produces a change in the other. The price of the dollar (its exchange -rate value) and the price of oil imports, for example, are functionally linked, because the global oil market is priced in dollars. (Not only that, oil can only be bought with dollars.) A decline in the value of the dollar will increase the cost of a given amount of oil imported to the United States. Similarly, a rise in the value of the dollar will decrease the cost of a given amount of imported oil. As long as oil remains priced in dollars, the functional tie between exchange rates and energy cannot be delinked. Moreover, as the oil-dollar example illustrates, functional linkages generally have corresponding spill-over effects. That is, weakness on one issue (a weaker dollar) produces more weakness on the other (more money spent on energy imports); and strength on one (a stronger dollar) produces greater strength on the other (cheaper energy imports). Thus, functional linkages produce causal effects that either magnify a state's weakness or add to its strength.

When two issues are linked artificially, there is no causal connection between them. A change in one does not automatically produce a change in the other. Instead, the two issues become linked because a statesman has made a connection where none before existed. Usually, but not always, this will be done to gain bargaining leverage. By making a link between two heretofore unconnected issues, statesmen try to bring about politically what is not produced functionally. They make a link in order to compensate for weakness on a given issue. Their method is to tie an issue where they are weak to an issue where they are strong. Their goal is to produce a more desirable outcome in the weak area either by threatening to do something undesirable in the strong area, or by promising to do something beneficial there. If they can make the connection stick, then the result of an artificial linkage is a strengthening of a state's overall position. Unlike a functional linkage, where weakness begets weakness and strength begets strength, in an artificial linkage, strength offsets weakness. Thus, an artificial linkage is a bargaining connection that is made in the head of a statesman, but it is not any less real or any less effective as a result. I provide an example of a bargaining linkage below.

Whether functional or artificial, issue linkages have a crucial consequence for both the analysis and the exercise of state power . . . [B]ecause issues are connected, domains cannot be wholly delinked from one another. If they cannot be delinked, then we should not view them in isolation from one another. Therefore, any explanation of an outcome in a given domain that is based only on what goes on in that domain will always be incomplete, if not downright wrong. In sum, issue linkages limit the explanatory power of a domain-restricted analysis.

Bargaining linkages in particular make state assets more fungible than they might otherwise be. Linkage politics is a fact of international political life. We should not expect otherwise. Statesmen are out to make the best deals they can by compensating for weakness in one area with strength in others. Powerful states can better engage in these compensatory linkages than can weak ones. They are stronger in more areas than they are weak; consequently, they can more easily utilize their leverage in the strong areas to make up for their deficit in the weak ones. Great powers are also better able to shift assets among issue areas in order to build positions of bargaining strength when necessary. They can, for example, more easily generate military power when they need to in order to link it to nonmilitary tasks. Therefore, because powerful states can link issues more easily than can weaker ones, can compensate for deficiencies better, can generate more resources and do so more quickly when needed, and can shift assets around with greater ease, how powerful a state is overall remains an essential determinant to how successful it is internationally, irrespective of how weak it may be at any given moment on any specific issue in any particular domain. In sum, linkage politics enhances the advantages of being powerful and boosts the fungibility of force by enabling it to cross domains. . . .

### Examples: Deficits, Petrodollars, and Oil Prices

. . . Three . . . brief examples show the range of state goals that can be served by constructing such linkages.

The first involves the relation between America's large and continuing balance-of-payments deficits and its global alliance system. Throughout most of the Cold War era, the United States ran annual large balance-of-payments deficits. Historically, no nation has been able to buy more abroad than it sells abroad (import more than it exports) in as huge a volume and for as long a period as has the United States. There were many reasons why it was able to, ranging from the liquidity that deficit dollars provided, which enabled world trade to grow, to general confidence in the American economy, which caused foreigners to invest their dollar holdings in the United States. Part of the reason that foreigners continued to take America's continuing flow of dollars, however, was an implicit, if not explicit, tradeoff: in return for their acceptance of American I.O.U.'s (deficit dollars), the United States provided the largest holders of them (the Germans, the Japanese, and the Saudis) military protection against their enemies. America's military strength compensated for its lack of fiscal discipline.

A second example involves the recycling of petrodollars. After the oil price hikes of the 1970s, the OPEC producers, especially its Persian Gulf members, were accumulating more dollars than they could profitably invest at home. Where to put those dollars was an important financial decision, especially for the Saudis, who were generating the largest dollar surpluses. There is strong circumstantial evidence that the Saudis agreed to park a sizable portion of their petrodollars in U.S. Treasury bills (T-bills) in part because of an explicit American proposal "to provide a security umbrella for the Gulf." As David Spiro notes: "By the fourth quarter of 1977, Saudi Arabia accounted for 20 percent of all holdings of Treasury notes and bonds by foreign central banks." The Saudis also continued to agree to price oil in dollars rather than peg it to a basket of currencies. Although there were clear financial incentives for both Saudi decisions, the incentives are not sufficient to explain Saudi actions. The Kuwaitis, for example, never put as many of their petrodollars in the United States, nor as many in T-bills, as did the Saudis. Moreover, an internal U.S. Treasury study concluded that the Saudis would have done better if oil had been pegged to a basket of currencies than to dollars. Indeed, OPEC had decided in 1975 to price oil in such a basket, but never followed through. As with the IEA example, America's provision of security to the Saudis was an important, even if not sufficient, ingredient in persuading them both to price oil in dollars and then to park them in the United States. Both decisions were of considerable economic benefit to the United States. Parking Saudi dollars in T-bills gave the American government "access to a huge pool of foreign capital"; pricing oil in dollars meant that the United States "could print money to buy oil." Military power bought economic benefits.

A third example, again involving the Saudis, concerns the link between American military protection and the price of oil. The Saudis have a long-term economic interest that dictates moderation in oil prices. With a relatively small population and with the world's largest proven oil reserves, their strategy lies in maximizing revenue from oil over the long term. It is therefore to their advantage to keep the price of oil high enough to earn sizable profits, but not so high as to encourage investment in alternative energy sources. Periodically, Saudi Arabia has faced considerable pressure from the price hawks within OPEC to push prices higher than its interest dictates. American military protection has strengthened Saudi willingness to resist the hawks.

A specific instance of this interaction between U.S. protection and Saudi moderation, for example, occurred in the fall of 1980, with the onset of the Iran-Iraq war. Iraq attacked Iran in September, and the two countries proceeded to bomb one another's oil facilities. The initial stages of the war removed about four million barrels of oil per day from world markets and drove the price of oil to its highest level ever ($42 dollars per barrel). As part of their balancing strategy in the Gulf, this time the Saudis had allied themselves with Iraq and, fearing Iranian retaliation against their oil fields, asked for American military intervention to deter Iranian attacks on their oil fields and facilities. The United States responded by sending AWACS aircraft to Saudi Arabia and by setting up a joint Saudi–American naval task force to guard against Iranian attacks on oil tankers in the Gulf. In return, the Saudis' increased their oil production from 9.7 million barrels per day (mbd) to 10.3, which was the highest level it could sustain, and kept it there for the next ten months. Saudi actions had a considerable effect on oil prices. . . .

As in the other cases, in this instance, American military power alone was not sufficient to cause Saudi actions to lower oil prices, but it was essential because during this turbulent period Saudi decisions on how much oil they would pump were not determined solely by economic factors. True, the Saudis, against the desires of the price hawks, which included the Iranians, had been pumping more oil since 1978 in order to lower oil prices. The Saudis had also violated their long-term strategy in March 1979, however, when they decided to cut oil production by 1 mbd, primarily to appease Iran, a move that triggered a rapid increase in oil prices. This pumping decision followed a political decision to move diplomatically away from the United States. Only a few months later, however, the conflict within the Saudi ruling family between an American- versus an Arab-oriented strategy was resolved in a compromise that led to a political reconciliation with the United States; and this political decision was followed by another to increase oil production by 1 mbd, starting 1 July 1979. Before the Iran-Iraq war, then, Saudi pumping decisions were affected by political calculations about their security, in which the strategic connection with the Americans played a prominent role. If this was true in peacetime, surely it was so in wartime, too. The military protection announced by the Americans on September 30, 1980 was a necessary condition for the Saudi increase in oil production that followed in October. Again, military power had bought an economic benefit.

In sum, these . . . examples— . . . America's ability to run deficits, petrodollar recycling, and moderate oil prices—all illustrate just how pervasive bargaining linkages are in international politics and specifically how military power can be linked politically to produce them. In all . . . cases, military power was not sufficient. Without it, however, the United States could not have produced the favorable economic outcomes it had achieved.

## NOTES

1. Exactly where this point is, is difficult to define. One could argue that more military power is reasonable up until the point where other states begin to worry and take counteractions. One could argue that more amounts of offensive power will worry other states more quickly than more amounts of defensive power. One could futhermore argue that the point where reasonable becomes unreasonable is more dependent on the perceived intentions of the state than on its military capability. These are all "reasonable" points. In this chapter, I cannot settle the debate between "aggressive" and "defensive" realists, nor can I show how to distinguish between offense-and-defense dominant worlds. More military power will buy a state more options if other states either do not counter the powerful state, or are unable to keep up with its pace of arming. Offensive military power is more threat-

ening than defensive military power (if the two can be distinguished) and probably more fungible. Defensive military power therefore has less fungibility than offensive power, unless, of course, a militarily powerful state decides to spread its defensive power over another state. I contest none of these points. What I do maintain, however, is that the military instrument possesses more fungibility for the militarily powerful state than for the militarily weak one. In this regard, the fungibility of force argument applies most particularly to the great powers and especially to the American superpower.

2. David Baldwin, *Paradoxes of Power* (New York: Blackwell, 1989), 151–52. Baldwin first developed his argument in his "Power Analysis and World Politics," *World Politics* 31, no. 1 (January 1979): 161–94, which is reprinted in this volume of his previously published essays.

3. In fairness to Baldwin, these examples were not fully developed, but consist of only a sentence or two. Nevertheless, they are fair game because Baldwin used them as illustrations of his more general point about the limits to the utility of military power. The fact that he did not develop them further led him astray, in my view. He was trying to show with them that military power is less effective than commonly thought. I reinterpret these examples to show how versatile military power in fact is. Neither Baldwin nor I, however, can put a number on the fungibility of military power, and I certainly agree with him that "no political power resource begins to approach the degree of fungibility of money" (quoted in Baldwin, *Paradoxes of Power*, 135).

4. Baldwin, *Paradoxes of Power*, 133, 134, 135.

5. Lyndon Baines Johnson, *The Vantage Point: Perspectives of the Presidency, 1963–1969* (New York: Holt, Rinehart, Winston, 1971), 536.

6. I have borrowed this term from Ernst Haas, even though I am using it differently than he does. He used the phrase to describe the effects that cooperation on economic matters among the states of Western Europe could have on their political relations. He argued that cooperation on economic matters would spill over into their political relations, induce greater cooperation there, and lead ultimately to the political integration of Western Europe. See Ernst Haas, *Beyond the Nation State: Functionalism and International Organization* (Stanford, CA: Stanford University Press, 1964), 48.

7. Solvency is to be distinguished from liquidity. A bank can be solvent but not liquid. Liquidity refers to the ability of a bank to meet all its liabilities upon demand. Most banks are not able to do so, however, if all the demands are called at the same time. The reason is that many assets of any given bank are tied up in investments that cannot be called back on short notice, but take time to convert into cash. The function of a central bank is to solve the liquidity problem of a nation's banking system by providing the liquidity in the short term in order to prevent runs on a bank.

# 2

# The Sources of Military Doctrine

BARRY R. POSEN

## MILITARY ORGANIZATIONS AND MILITARY DOCTRINE

### Hypotheses—Offense, Defense, and Deterrence

Most soldiers and many civilians are intuitively attracted to the offense as somehow the stronger form of war. Clausewitz, often misconstrued as the apostle of the offensive, was very mindful of the advantages of a defensive strategy. He called defense "the stronger form of war." However, every aspect of his work that *could be taken* as offensive advocacy has been so taken. What accounts for such systematic misinterpretation?

*Uncertainty Reduction*

Military organizations will generally prefer offensive doctrines because they *reduce uncertainty* in important ways.

1. The need for standard scenarios encourages military organizations to prefer offensive doctrines. In order to have a set of SOPs[1] and programs, they must plan for a "standard scenario." Once SOPs and programs have been tailored to such a scenario, the organization, in order to be "fought"—used in combat—must be used with those SOPs and programs. If the organization is to be "fought" successfully, it must respond to command in predictable ways. Commanders must have orders to give that generate predictable responses. Thus, it is strongly in the interests of a military organization to impose its "standard scenario" on the adversary through offensive action before the adversary does the same to it.

2. Warfare is an extremely competitive endeavor. Its most successful practitioners strive for even the smallest advantages. Thus, military organizations seem

to prefer offensive doctrines not only because they appear to guarantee the side on the offense its standard scenario, but because they also *deny* the enemy his standard scenario. A military organization prefers to fight its own war and *prevent* its adversary from doing so. Taking the offensive, exercising the initiative, is a way of structuring the battle. The advantages seen to lie with surprise are more than psychological. An organization fighting the war that it planned is likely to do better than one that is not. For example, in the Arab attack on Israel in 1973, Egyptian and Syrian preparations were aimed at imposing an uncongenial style of warfare on Israel.

Defensive warfare might also seem to allow an organization to structure the battle. However, the defending organization is often in a reactive position, improvising new programs to cope with the adversary's initiative. If the defending organization is, for whatever reasons, a fast learner, it may rapidly improvise countermeasures that destroy the offender's programs. (The Israel Defense Forces achieved this with their Suez Canal crossing in 1973.) This leaves both organizations fighting a battle of improvisation which both would probably prefer to avoid. Victory goes to the most flexible command structure. Generally, however, professional soldiers appear to believe that striking the first blow is beneficial because, at least initially, it reduces the attacker's necessity to improvise and the defender's ability to improvise. This military judgment may reflect an implicit understanding that military organizations are not fast learners, precisely because they are the structured systems portrayed earlier. The perceived advantage of taking the offensive is thus magnified.

3. Because predicting whose national will can be broken first is a political task, not susceptible to the analytical skills of a military organization, military organizations dislike deterrent doctrines. Punishment warfare, conventional or nuclear, tends not to address an adversary's capabilities, but his will. Calculating in advance of a war whose will is likely to break first is inherently somewhat more difficult for a military organization than devising plausible scenarios for destroying enemy capabilities. Calculations of enemy determination demand an entirely different set of skills than those commanded by a military organization. Calculations about military outcomes are at least somewhat susceptible to "engineering" criteria; calculations of relative will are not. However, this argument may be a weak one. There are more powerful reasons why military organizations do not favor deterrent doctrines.

4. Military organizations will prefer offensive doctrines because they help increase organizational size and wealth. Size and wealth help reduce internal uncertainty by increasing the rewards that the organization can distribute to its members. Size and wealth help reduce external uncertainty by providing a buffer against unforeseen events such as huge losses or partial defeats.

While the offensive allows the attacking force to be more certain of how its organization will perform, and to deny that certainty to an adversary, the offensive is likely to be technically more complex, quantitatively more demanding.

There are many extra contingencies for which an offensive military instrument must be prepared. An attacking army encounters natural obstacles that must be crossed, creating a demand for engineers. Fortifications encountered may demand more and heavier artillery for their reduction. The offensive army may have to go anywhere, requiring special technical capabilities in its equipment. Nothing can be specialized for the environment of the home country. Aircraft need greater range and payload. All of these factors require an extensive logistics capability to uncoil behind the advancing military force. Troops will be required to guard and defend this line of communication. Operations at range will impose greater wear and tear on the equipment—demanding large numbers in reserve, and still more support capability. While various characteristics of geography, politics, and technology might place these same demands on a defensive force, as a general rule offensive doctrines impose them to a greater extent. Deterrent doctrines offer the most minimal material opportunities for military organizations. This is partly because they are more dependent on political will than on military capabilities. Partly it is a result of the clarity of the punishment mission, which allows rather extreme specialization.

5. Military organizations will prefer offensive doctrines because they enhance military autonomy. As noted earlier, civilian intervention in operational matters can be a key source of uncertainty for military organizations. Offensive doctrines tend to be more complicated than defensive or deterrent doctrines, and thus increase the difficulties for civilians who wish to understand military matters. Defense and deterrence are relatively easy for civilians to master. Deterrent warfare with nuclear weapons has consistently proved to be the easiest form of warfare for civilian analysts to understand in the post-war period. Deterrent warfare by means of popular resistance—extended guerrilla action, for example—depends so heavily on the legitimacy of the government and its authority over its people that it may be the highest form of political–military warfare. Defense or denial does not present the complications of the offensive, and again includes such strong cooperation with civilian authorities as to restrict the operational autonomy of the army. The offensive, however, can be waged off national soil, and therefore immediately involves less civilian interference. Offensive operations are elaborate combinations of forces and stratagems—more art than science. Denial is more straightforward, and punishment is simplest of all. From specialists in victory, defense turns soldiers into specialists in attrition, and deterrence makes them specialists in slaughter.

There is little in organization theory or the civil–military relations literature to suggest that modern militaries will prefer anything but offensive doctrines, if such doctrines are in any way feasible.

### Geography

6. Organization theory suggests a somewhat muted geographical influence on military doctrine. (The influence of technology will be discussed below.) Where

geography can plausibly be argued to favor an offensive doctrine, it reinforces the organizational tendencies outlined above. For instance, it has become commonplace to explain the affinity of Prussia-Germany (in the past) and Israel (in the present) for offensive doctrines by their a) being surrounded and outnumbered by powerful enemies and b) enjoying the advantage of interior lines (with the ability to shift forces quickly from one front to another). Thus, the sequential defeat of the members of an enemy coalition with a series of rapid offensives, before they can pull their forces together and coordinate an attack, is deemed to be very attractive. Presumably, any state finding itself in a similar position would agree.

One less often finds the reverse argued—that some particular geographic configuration generally and sensibly leads to a defensive military doctrine. At the level of grand strategy, of course, both Britain and the United States have exploited the defensive advantage bestowed by ocean barriers. Yet, the navies of both powers have periodically argued for offensive military strategies to achieve "command of the sea." They usually have been constrained to operate in a more limited fashion, but the preference for the offensive, even in situations where it seems unreasonable, is striking.

Numerous examples of military organizations that undervalue the defensive utility of geography can be found. British colonial soldiers in India viewed Afghanistan as a potential Russian invasion route, and sought to control it. Yet, one British military expedition after another met with disaster brought on by wild Afghan raiders, treacherous terrain and weather, and long distances. This stark evidence of the area's unsuitability as an invasion route was ignored, as subsequent expeditions were deemed necessary. In World War I the Russians underrated the defensive value of the Masurian Lakes to the Germans. The lakes ultimately split the large Russian force, allowing a smaller German army to defeat it piecemeal. At the outset of World War I the British dispatched a small force to Persia, to guard the Abadan oil facilities. Its commanders opted for an attack on Baghdad, a distant objective for which the force was woefully inadequate. Currently, the U.S. Navy advocates an offensive strategy against Soviet naval forces based in the Barents Sea and Murmansk—a tough and distant target. NATO has geographic choke points off the Norwegian North Cape, and in the Greenland–Iceland–United Kingdom Gap, that provide a powerful defensive advantage against any Soviet naval offensive, and all but obviate the need for an offensive against the north. In short, organization theory suggests that geographic factors that support offensive doctrines will more often be correctly assessed than those that support a defensive doctrine. History seems to confirm this observation.

### Hypotheses—Integration[2]

It was over a century and a half ago that Clausewitz made his now famous remarks on the relationship of war to policy. Most simply, "war is not a mere act of policy but a true political instrument, a continuation of political activity by other means." Political considerations reach into the military means, to influence *"the planning of war, of the campaign, and often even of the battle"* (my emphasis). Clausewitz clearly believed that statesmen could and should ensure that policy infuse military operations. Those in charge of policy require "a certain grasp of military affairs." They need not be soldiers, however. "What is needed in the post is distinguished intellect and character. He [the statesman] can always get the necessary military information somehow or other." Clausewitz was overoptimistic on this score. Few have challenged his judgment that policy must infuse acts of war, but the achievement of this goal has proven more difficult than he imagined. . . .

Functional specialization between soldiers and statesmen, and the tendency of soldiers to seek as much independence from civilian interference as possible, combine to make political–military integration an uncertain prospect. These two fundamental aspects of state structure and organization lead to the following deductions:

1. As a rule, soldiers are not going to go out of their way to reconcile the means they employ with the ends of state policy. This is not necessarily to argue that they deliberately try to disconnect their means from political ends. Often, however, soldiers will elevate the narrow technical requirements of preferred operations above the needs of civilian policy. In the case of the European militaries prior to World War I, the single-minded pursuit of battlefield advantage closed off diplomatic options for statesmen.

2. This cause of disintegration is exacerbated because military organizations are unwilling to provide civilian authorities with information that relates to doctrinal questions, especially those having the most to do with the actual conduct of operations. Thus, civilians are simply unaware of the ways military doctrine may conflict with the ends of state policy. Policymakers may simply not know enough about the operational practices of their military organizations to either alter their political strategy or force changes in military doctrine that would bring it in line with the existing political strategy. Nevertheless, in spite of the limits of information, organization theory would seem to suggest that if political–military integration is to be achieved, civilian intervention into doctrinal matters is essential. The question is, given the obstacles, what is sufficient to cause civilian intervention? This is a question better answered by balance-of-power theory.

3. The setting of priorities among military forces and missions is a key aspect of political–military integration. In multiservice military organizations, civilian intervention is critical to the setting of priorities. This is another way civilian intervention causes integration. . . . [It was argued earlier] that one of the tasks of grand strategy is to set priorities among threats and opportunities in the environment, and to set priorities among forces to match these threats and opportunities. Interpreting the external environment is the specialty of civilians. Building and operating military forces is the task of services. Setting priorities among the services, and

among forces or branches within services, is a central task of grand strategy. Yet, the tendency of individuals within organizations to preserve the task and power of their organization or suborganization suggests that *among* or *within* services the goal of autonomy should be just as strong as it is for the military as a whole. Thus, it is very difficult for a group of services to accomplish the task of setting priorities. The inclination of a group of services or subservices to set priorities among themselves is going to be low.

In the absence of civilian intervention, and the exercise of the legitimate authority that only the civilians possess, militaries will arrange a "negotiated environment." This is likely to take the form of either preserving a customary budgetary split or dividing shares equally. Each service will prepare for its own war. Forces will not cooperate effectively. Neither will they be well balanced. A tendency will emerge for each service to set requirements as if it were fighting the war alone. This can easily result in misallocation of the scarce security resources of the state.

Left to themselves, a group of services cannot make a military doctrine that will be well integrated with the political aspects of the state's grand strategy. They can simply assemble a batch of service doctrines. This is less true within services, where higher authority can make allocation decisions. Even within services, priorities may not be set according to strategic criteria. A service doctrine may be as difficult to produce as an overall grand strategy. . . .

### Hypotheses—Innovation in Military Doctrine

*Obstacles*

1. Because of the process of institutionalization, innovation in military doctrine should be rare. It will only occasionally be sponsored by the military organization itself. As already remarked, according to organization theory organizations try to control the behavior of their members in order to achieve purposes. One way of doing this is by distributing power through the organization so as to ensure that certain tasks will be accomplished. Individuals develop a vested interest in the distribution of power and in the purposes it protects. Generally, it is not in the interests of most of an organization's members to promote or succumb to radical change.

2. Innovations in military doctrine will be rare because they increase operational uncertainty. While innovation is in process, the organization's SOPs and programs will be in turmoil. The ability of commanders to "fight" the organization with confidence will decline. Should a war come during the transition, the organization will find itself between doctrines. Under combat conditions, even a bad doctrine may be better than no doctrine. It is possible to argue that the Prussians at Jena, the French in 1940, and the Russians in 1941 were taken in the midst of doctrinal transition.

3. Because of the obstacles to innovation discussed above, a technology that has not been tested in war can seldom function by itself as the catalyst for doctrinal innovation. Military organizations often graft new pieces of technology on to old doctrines. As Bernard Brodie has noted, "Conservatism of the military, about which we hear so much, seems always to have been confined to their adaptation to new weaponry rather than their acceptance of it."[3] . . . A new technology will normally be assimilated to an old doctrine rather than stimulate change to a new one. . . . This problem stems from the difficulty of proving anything about a new military technology without using it in a major war.

*Causes of Innovation*

In the military sphere, there are two exceptions to the preceding proposition that military organizations generally fail to innovate in response to new technology:

4. Military organizations do seem willing to learn from wars fought by their client states—with the weapons and perhaps the doctrine of the patron. Both the U.S. and Soviet militaries are willing to draw lessons from the 1973 Arab-Israeli war, although many of the "lessons" are not entirely clear.

5. Military organizations are even better able to learn about technology by using it in their own wars. Perhaps the best example of direct experience leading to correct appraisal of technology is found in the evolution of Prussian doctrine from 1850 to 1870. Prussia's attempted railroad mobilization against Austria in 1850 was a fiasco. Learning from the experience, the Prussians turned the railroad into an efficient war instrument by 1866.

There are limits to the power of this proposition. In the American Civil War, frontline soldiers adjusted rapidly to the technological facts of modern firepower. They "dug in" whenever they had the chance. The generals understood the least, ordering frontal assaults against prepared positions throughout the war. The same occurred in World War I, with generals ordering repeated costly offensives. Bernard Brodie notes that the generals "seemed incapable of learning from experience, largely because of the unprecedented separation of the high command from the front lines." This seems a plausible explanation, and again is entirely consistent with organization theory. . . .

The preceding examples also offer insights into the relationship between technology and the offensive, defensive, or deterrent character of military doctrine. Most simply, if a military organization has adopted an offensive doctrine, or is bent on adopting one, technological lessons on the advantage of defense are likely to be ignored, corrupted, or suppressed. This is consistent with the argument advanced earlier concerning the probable offensive preferences of most military organizations.

Organization theory predicts at least two causes of innovation that are much stronger and more reliable in their operation than experience with new technology: (6) military organizations innovate when they have failed—suffered a defeat—and (7) they innovate when civilians intervene from without. These hypotheses can be deduced from the basic survival motive of large organizations. Failure to achieve their organizational purpose, the successful defense of the state, can cause military organizations to reexamine their basic doctrinal preferences. Similarly, soldiers may respond to the civilian intervention that defeat often precipitates in order to defend the organization's autonomy, which is under attack.

Failure and civilian intervention often go hand in hand. Soldiers fail; civilians get angry and scared; pressure is put on the military. Sometimes the pressure is indirect. Civilian leaders become disenchanted with the performance of one service and shift resources to another. These resources may provide the "slack" for the newly favored service to attempt some innovations. The loser strives to win back his lost position. Interservice rivalry in postwar America may have produced some benefits—a menu of innovations for policymakers. Arguably, interservice rivalry has been a major factor in the growth of the "Triad," which has on the whole increased U.S. security. Similarly, aggrandizement at the expense of another service may be a motive for innovation.

Although civilian intervention into military doctrine would seem to be a key determinant of innovation, it involves special problems. The division of labor between civilians and soldiers is intense. Civilians are not likely to have the capability to dream up whole new doctrines. Thus, civil intervention is dependent on finding sources of military knowledge. Civil intervention should take the form of choosing from the thin innovation menu thrown up by the services. In multiservice defense establishments, civilians have the possibility, depending on the strategic position of the state, of choosing among competing services. Within services, hierarchy and the chain of command should tend to suppress the emergence of new doctrinal alternatives at levels where the civilians cannot find them. None of this is to say that innovation in military doctrine is impossible. These are merely tendencies. . . .

### Summary: Organization Theory Hypotheses

*Offense, Defense, and Deterrence*

1. The need for standard scenarios to reduce operational uncertainty encourages military organizations to prefer offensive doctrines.
2. The incentive, arising from the highly competitive nature of warfare, to deny an adversary his "standard scenario" encourages offensive doctrines.
3. The inability of military organizations to calculate comparative national will causes them to dislike deterrent doctrines.
4. Offensive doctrines will be preferred by military organizations because they increase organizational size and wealth.

5. Offensive doctrines will be preferred by military organizations because they enhance organizational independence from civilian authority.

6. Because the organizational incentives to pursue offensive doctrines are strong, military organizations will generally fix on geographic and technological factors that favor the offensive, but underrate or overlook such factors that favor defense or deterrence.

*Integration*

1. Because military organizations seek independence from civilian authority in order to reduce the uncertainties of combat, military doctrines tend to be poorly integrated with the political aspects of grand strategy. Soldiers will avoid including political criteria in their military doctrine if such criteria interfere with strictly instrumental military logic.

2. Because of functional specialization, civilians and soldiers tend to know too little about each other's affairs. Soldiers, again in the quest for autonomy, will exacerbate this problem by withholding important military information from civilians. Inadequate civilian understanding of military matters creates obstacles to political–military integration.

3. Technical specialization within military organizations works against a strategically rational setting of priorities among different services, further contributing to disintegration.

   In spite of the obstacles, civilian intervention into military doctrine is likely to be the primary cause of political–military integration of grand strategy, simply because civilians alone have the interest and the authority to reconcile political ends with military means and set priorities among military services according to some rational calculus.

*Innovation*

Most propositions about military innovation are negative.

1. Because of the process of institutionalization, which gives most members of an organization a stake in the way things are, doctrinal innovation will only rarely be sponsored by the organization itself.

2. Because doctrinal innovation increases operational uncertainty, it will rarely be sponsored by the organization itself.

3. New technology, when it has not been tried in combat, is seldom by itself a catalyst of doctrinal innovation.

4. A client state's combat experience with a new technology can cause innovation.

5. Direct combat experience with a new technology can cause innovation.

6. Failure on the battlefield can cause doctrinal innovation.

7. Civilian intervention can cause military innovation.

## BALANCE-OF-POWER THEORY AND MILITARY DOCTRINE

Organization theory suggests a tendency toward offensive, stagnant military doctrines, poorly integrated with the political elements of a state's grand strategy.
Balance-of-power theory predicts greater heterogeneity in military doctrine,
dependent on reasonable appraisals by each state of its political, technological,
economic, and geographical problems and possibilities in the international political system. The three case studies will show that although organization theory
does accurately predict certain tendencies in military doctrine, overall outcomes
are more consistent with balance-of-power theory predictions.

From balance-of-power theory specific propositions about the variables
offense–defense–deterrence, innovation–stagnation, and integration–disintegration can be deduced. Balance-of-power theory also describes the circumstances
under which these propositions are most likely to hold true. In times of relative
international calm, when statesmen and soldiers perceive the probability of war
as remote, the organizational dynamics outlined above tend to operate. When
threats appear greater, or war appears more probable, balancing behavior occurs.
A key element of that behavior is greater civilian attention to matters military.

Such attention puts the more ossified, organizationally self-serving, and politically unacceptable aspects of military doctrine under a harsher light. Fear of disaster or defeat prompts statesmen to question long-standing beliefs, to challenge
service preferences, to alter budget shares, and to find new sources of military
advice and leadership. Civilians intervene to change details, including posture
and doctrine, not merely general principles. Organization theory would view
civilian influence at such a level as unlikely. Moreover, soldiers, fearful that policies long preferred for their peacetime utility may be found wanting in war, are
(according to balance of power theory) somewhat more amenable to outside criticism than in times of international calm. Soldiers themselves are more likely to
examine their traditional premises. They will not abandon them, but they may
hedge against their failure. These military tendencies are insufficiently strong in
their own right to produce military doctrines consistent with balance-of-power
theory predictions. It is the combination of civilian intervention and increased
military open-mindedness that produces the results predicted. . . .

### Hypotheses—Offense, Deterrence, and Defense

Discussion of individual hypotheses on the causes of offensive, defensive,
and deterrent doctrines must be prefaced with a defense of the overarching
hypothesis that balance-of-power theory implies heterogeneity rather than homo-

geneity on this dimension. I have argued that organization theory suggests that most militaries will prefer the offensive. If balance-of-power theory also suggested homogeneity on this dimension—the predominance among doctrines of *one* of the three categories—that could make the task of competitive theory testing either simpler or more difficult. The task would be simple if balance-of-power theory implied that states would prefer defensive doctrines, since we could easily examine a large number of military doctrines and discover if they were usually offensive or usually defensive. On the other hand, if balance-of-power theory predicted offensive doctrines, then both theories would be predicting the same outcome, and one could hardly test them against each other. In cases where we found offensive doctrines, we would have an "overdetermination" problem—explanation of over 100 percent of the outcome. Of course, in cases where defensive or deterrent doctrines were found, both theories would be discredited. Balance of power theory does not predict homogeneous outcomes, however, although a misreading of the theory might suggest this.

Several students of state behavior whose analyses reflect the balance-of-power perspective have predicted state policies that would seem to demand offensive doctrines. Hans Morgenthau, John Herz, and to a lesser extent Robert Gilpin predict that states will generally try to expand their power. States will seek not simply equality, but superiority. States are likely to behave this way because power is the key to survival in an anarchical system; since relative power is difficult to measure, the state never knows when it has enough, and it should therefore logically strive for a fairly wide margin of superiority. Basically, these theorists argue, as I have argued, that the security dilemma is always present. Effectively, they also argue, as I have *not*, that the security dilemma is usually quite intense. If this view of the system and its effects on actors were complete, then it would seem logical to deduce that all states will prefer offensive doctrines in order to be ready to expand their power. Because an offensive doctrine may allow the conquest of one's neighbors and the seizure of power assets that lie beyond one's borders, it might appear to be the military option that provides the most security.

This view, however, is not complete. It is *ahistorical* in the most fundamental sense, assuming that states are effectively newborn children, thrust into the jungle of international politics with nothing more than an orientation briefing on the "law of tooth and claw" to guide their actions. Under such conditions the security dilemma might indeed operate with extraordinary intensity. Robert Gilpin, however, admits that states make cost-benefit calculations when deliberating about whether or not to attempt expansion, and that perceptions of cost are affected by the state's historical experience. Of particular importance are the consequences of its own or others' attempts at expansion, and the lessons learned from those episodes. While states, or those who act for them, frequently misread the lessons of history, balance-of-power theory itself suggests that expanding hegemons will be opposed and stopped. *We have ample historical evidence that this is the case.* This is a lesson that is easy to learn. Indeed, such learning is consistent with Kenneth Waltz's prediction that states will become socialized to the norms of the system that they inhabit. Not all states learn the lesson—not well enough to sustain perpetual peace—but enough learning takes place to make violent, unlimited, expansionist policies the exception rather than the rule. Status-quo policies are the rule rather than the exception. France under Louis XIV and Napoleon, Germany under the Kaiser and Hitler, are already too many would-be European hegemons for those who have had to oppose them, but surprisingly few for a three-century game that has often involved as many as six major players.

A status-quo policy, of course, need not lead to a defensive military doctrine, but it certainly need not lead to an offensive one either. Instead, status-quo powers will assess their political, geographical, and technological positions and possibilities, and devise a military doctrine that preserves their interests at the lowest costs and risks. Thus, an inference from balance-of-power theory is that military doctrines will be heterogeneous along the dimension of offense–defense deterrence.

*Offense*

1. States bent on conquest will prefer offensive military doctrines. This proposition is not deduced from balance-of-power theory, but rather is a matter of common sense. Louis XIV, Napoleon Bonaparte, and Adolph Hitler all had expansionist foreign policies, and required offensive instruments to pursue those policies.

2. States will try to pass on the costs of war to others. Offensive operations are one way to accomplish this. If war seems to involve high collateral damage, states will try to arrange that the war will be fought on the territory of the enemy, of neutrals, or even of allies. Nicholas Spykman once admonished, "Only in periods of weakness and decline have states fought at home. In periods of vitality and strength, they fight on other people's territory."[4] Of course, not all states have the option of fighting abroad, but those that do tend to avail themselves of it. . . .

3. States will support offensive doctrines when power appears to be shifting against them. Offensive doctrines are necessary to fight "preventive" wars. It also seems probable that in environments where power might rapidly shift, statesmen will want to keep an offensive capability "in the hole." A particularly intense arms race would seem to promote offensive doctrines. (We have already seen how the reverse can be true.) Preventive war is a peculiar sort of balancing behavior. "Because I cannot keep you from catching up I will cut you down now." Israel's cooperation in the Franco–British attack on Egypt in 1956 is explained in part by the fear that Egypt's new claim on the arsenals of the Eastern bloc would give her a permanent arms-race advantage. Hitler preferred an offensive doctrine partly because he believed that he had rearmed more quickly than his putative adver-

saries, but that they would soon catch up. An offensive doctrine would allow him to prevent this by permitting Germany to strike the Allies before they could remedy their military deficiencies.

4. Similarly, states without allies, *facing multiple threats*, will be attracted to offensive doctrines. An offensive doctrine allows the state to choose the time and place of battle. If the joint capabilities of the adversaries are superior, offensive doctrines will be particularly attractive. In an offensive move, an isolated state can attack and defeat its adversaries sequentially, minimizing the effect of the imbalance of capabilities. This is a variety of preventive war. Instead of waging one dangerous war against a superior coalition, the offender elects to wage what amounts to a separate war against each of the members of the opposing coalition in turn. An offensive doctrine is thus a method of power balancing.

5. The force of the preceding hypothesis is increased if the geographic factor of encirclement is added. The military history of Prussia and later of Germany reveals a constant affinity for offensive doctrines. This is explained in part by the frequent threats of multifront wars. Israel's offensive doctrine allows her to defeat the Arab states sequentially. It may be that the offensiveness of the Soviet military doctrine—both in the rocket forces and in the ground forces—is partially a response to the existence of hostile states on every border.

6. Statesmen will prefer offensive military doctrines if they lack powerful allies, because such doctrines allow them to manipulate the threat of war with credibility. Offensive doctrines are best for making threats. States can use both the threat of alliance and the threat of military force to aid diplomacy in communicating power and will. In the absence of strong allies, the full burden of this task falls on the state's military capabilities. This was the major characteristic of Hitler's early diplomacy. It provided the motivation for former Secretary of Defense James Schlesinger's merchandising of substantial nuclear counterforce capability in the guise of "flexible strategic options." To some extent, this motivation appears to have been behind the offensive aspects of Strategic Air Command doctrine in the 1950s. Military demonstrations and an offensive doctrine are also important elements of Israeli grand strategy.

7. A state need not be politically isolated or geographically encircled to find defensive doctrines unattractive. States with far-flung security dependencies may find it advisable to defend such allies by concentrating offensive, disarming military power, or deterrent, punitive military power, against its adversary (or adversaries) rather than dispersing its scarce military capabilities in futile denial efforts in many places. Such dependencies, like NATO Europe in the 1950s, may be far from the guarantor, close to a major power adversary, and too weak to contribute much to their own defense. The security of such states is difficult to guarantee by defensive/denial means alone. If the United States had had to secure postwar Europe with conventional denial means, there would probably have been a great many more American troops in Europe than there were. The Soviet adversary had to be dissuaded from going to war against U.S. dependencies. The same was true

if French allies in eastern Europe were going to be protected during the inter-war period.

How is dissuasion to be accomplished if defensive/denial means are ruled out? Only deterrence and offense remain. While the United States has relied mainly on deterrence in the Cold War, offense has also played an important role. Many have argued against reliance on deterrence alone, since the adversary could punish the United States in return for any strike we might deliver. Extended deterrence is difficult because, whereas a state's readiness to inflict punishment on an adversary that aggresses directly against it might be unquestionable, its willingness to punish the same adversary for offenses against far-removed dependencies, and so to draw fresh fire and suffering on itself, is less likely to be credited. The credibility of the commitment is believed to go up with an ability to limit damage to ourselves by disarming the adversary. . . .

*Deterrence*

8. Far-flung security dependencies and powerful adversaries can lead a great power to either deterrent or offensive doctrines. Offensive doctrines will be preferred, but often the sheer scope of the problem and the capabilities of the adversary (or adversaries) make offensive capabilities hard to get. Technology and geography are frequently the key determinants of the scope of the problem. Before World War II Britain hoped to hold possessions half a globe away. She lacked the raw capability to project much power such a distance—particularly after ensuring the homeland against more immediate adversaries. Even if she could have mustered the capabilities and mastered the distances, Britain lacked a military technology that could disarm Japan and keep her disarmed. When states face such a situation, they will accept, although they may not embrace, deterrent doctrines.

The political organisms that most often find themselves in this situation seem to be the great empires of history. The British found it advantageous in the 1920s and '30s to police Arabian tribesmen not by pitched battle, but by bombing from the air. They could either obey the rules or be punished. A close examination of British defense policy in the 1930s shows a pronounced inclination toward deterrence. The politicians of the period frequently used the term. Due to economic, industrial, and technological constraints, the actual operations envisioned were more of the denial than the punishment variety. However, dissuasion was the goal, and one finds a constant concern with the manipulation of military capability and potential military capability to discourage aggression. Only with the short-lived commitment to the population bombing doctrine of Bomber Command were any punitive operations planned in the 1930s. . . .

9. As noted previously, small states threatened by powerful adversaries often make recourse to deterrent doctrines. The peculiar coincidence of doctrines among the very strong and the very weak is easy to explain. In both cases, insufficient capabilities drive states to such doctrines. When a state's capabilities fall

short of its aims or needs, it may throw its political "will" into the balance. Will is as much a product of a state's political cohesion as it is a product of any material source. Thus, whenever states face security threats and are, by reason of the magnitude of the task or their own poverty, short of resources, we can expect to see deterrent doctrines.

### Defense

I have argued that coalition formation is a common method both of enhancing perceived power for diplomacy and mustering real power for war. Yet, coalition management has its problems. Napoleon once declared that if he had to make war, he would prefer to make it against a coalition. Alfred Vagts observes, "Of all types of war, this is the one in which it is most likely that political aims will crowd out and repress strategic aims. And even if this is not intended, the other partner or partners will still suspect it, will try to spare their own forces and sacrifice those of the ally."

10. Defensive doctrines, or doctrines with strong defensive elements, will be preferred by statesmen with status-quo policies who are preparing to fight in coalitions. Such doctrines give the states in the coalition more time to settle the division of costs and benefits of the war. This phenomenon will be particularly pronounced if the costs of going on the offensive are seen to be high. One paradoxical example is found in Egyptian behavior during the 1973 Arab-Israeli war. Although the Egyptians had mounted a successful offensive to cross the Suez Canal, after crossing they chose a low-risk strategy of staying behind their air and anti-tank defenses. By so doing, they allowed Israel the luxury of concentrating the bulk of her military capability on the dangerous Syrian offensive. Egypt passed on the costs of the war to the Syrians. Egypt only left her defensive positions when frenzied Syrian protests suggested Israel's imminent victory. When Egypt finally attacked, its offensive was shattered. Britain and France were guilty of similar "buck-passing" in the 1930s. In both the Egyptian-Syrian case and the British-French case, the costs of going on the offensive were seen to be high. In the case of the 1914 powers, the cost of the offensive was seen to be low. This explains the less cautious behavior in the earlier period.

11. The preceding hypothesis may be attenuated by another constraint. Although states may seek military doctrines that allow them to pass some of their defense costs onto coalition partners, they must in some measure please these present or potential allies in order to attract them. Thus, alliance suitors may adopt the doctrines of their intended allies. A given military doctrine may fail to achieve both the goal of buck-passing and the goal of alliance-making, and when it does, a state can face difficult choices. In 1973, Egypt appears to have portrayed her military doctrine one way to achieve Syrian cooperation in the initial attack; operated another to spare her own forces early in the war; and finally shifted back to a strategy more accommodating to the Syrians in the abortive offensive against Israeli forces in the Sinai passes. France in the 1930s, on the other hand, could

both attract British support and control her own contribution to any ultimate war effort with a defensive doctrine. Britain did not want any provocation of Germany, and that was fine with France.

12. Status-quo states will generally prefer defensive doctrines if geography or technology makes such doctrines attractive. They are more likely to correctly interpret such factors than are non–status-quo states, and since their goal is to conserve power, they are more likely to exploit them militarily.

13. Status-quo states may prefer defensive doctrines simply because those states know that they are unlikely to strike the first blow. Since they expect to suffer the first blow, it is reasonable for them to expend their military effort learning how to parry it.

### Hypotheses—The Causes of Civilian Intervention and Its Effects on Integration and Innovation

I have discussed some causes of the character of military doctrine. Organization theory identifies external intervention as a key source of integration and innovation, but also predicts that such intervention will be very difficult. Balance-of-power theory predicts that, difficult or not, such intervention will occur if it is necessary to secure the state. If balance-of-power theory successfully predicts not only intervention, but also the circumstances under which it occurs, then the theory gains in credibility relative to organization theory. Thus, it is important to address the causes of civilian intervention into military matters.

1. Political leaders with aggression in mind will often take a look at their military forces to see if they are ready to go. Hitler was most attentive to his military capabilities and, as we shall see, was a prime mover in the development of Blitzkrieg. This is not so much a proposition deduced from balance-of-power theory as a matter of common sense. The anarchy of international politics permits mischief. The military value of the object in view may or may not be a motive for mischief. If political leaders contemplate aggression for the purpose of expanding their resources for security, then their intervention can be loosely explained in terms of structural constraints. Otherwise, we must fall back on avarice and "bloody-mindedness" as an explanation.

For whatever reasons civilian policymakers choose a path of aggression, soldiers must either carry out the orders of their chiefs or resign. The prospect of war can have a catalytic effect on the behavior of soldiers whose lives or careers will inevitably be put into jeopardy. The final steps to the Blitzkrieg doctrine were taken by the commanders of the Germany Army only late in 1939 and early in 1940, when it became clear that Hitler was committed to an offensive against the Allies.

2. If planned aggression for political ends is one general cause of civilian intervention in military matters, the other is fear. This is consistent with balance-of-power theory. It is easy for statesmen to become frightened by events in the

international environment. Many different kinds of events may threaten the state's security. Just as states "balance" materially by arms-racing or coalition formation, they "balance" qualitatively by taking a close look at the doctrine, competence, and readiness of their military organizations. They do not do so all the time, but when they do, fear is most often the driving force.

3. The same fear increases military organizations' receptivity to outside criticism and also sharpens their own self-critical faculties. The force of this proposition is attenuated in multipolar systems, however, if a given state perceives itself to have alliance possibilities. Under conditions of threat, civilians may divide their energies between chasing allies and reviewing their military posture. This may so reduce the pressure on a given military organization as to allow organizational dynamics to triumph. More specific propositions on this matter can be generated.

4. In the face of any sort of security problem, states without allies will tend to pay a good deal of attention to their military organizations. This is true of states that are politically isolated. Israel is a good current example: military leaders retire to become key political leaders, and politicians are generally well versed in military matters. This sort of attention is also characteristic of both poles in a bipolar system. Since the dawn of the Cold War, American leaders have paid more attention to military matters than in any prior period of our history.

Examples of military innovation caused by civilian intervention and stimulated by political isolation are the development of the standing army in France under Louis XIV and the mass army during the French Revolution. Recall the important role played by Cardinal Richelieu and the civilian war minister Michel Le Tellier in the development of France's first all-professional, standing army. What had driven France in this direction? Historian Michael Howard writes, "On the death of Gustavus, . . . Richelieu saw himself faced with the necessity of improvising an army and entering the field himself if Habsburg power, Spanish and Austrian, was not to become dominant in Europe." Le Tellier's son, the marquis de Louvois, completed his father's work, creating the army with which Louis XIV waged war on nearly all of Europe.

The case of Revolutionary France is similar. The Directory had accumulated six major adversaries, and by August 23, 1793, the danger had become so great that the Committee on Public Safety ordered universal conscription for the first time in any modern European state. By the following summer, the French army fielded three-quarters of a million men, the largest armed force in Europe since the barbarian invasions. The Committee did not simply invent the mass army. Lazare Carnot, a former military professional and a man with new ideas about military organizations and tactics, had joined the Revolution. It was his hand that guided French military innovation.

While political isolation provides an added spur to civilian intervention, even states with alliance possibilities show tendencies to civilian intervention in the face of new or growing threats. The best example of this is found in British behavior in

1934–1940. The rising military power of Germany brought not only a return to substantial defense spending, but greater civilian attention to the plans of the military. In spite of a military organization committed to an offensive doctrine, civilians intervened to promote a major defensive innovation—the development of the country's integrated air defense system, the first of its kind in history. . . . While the RAF did not wholeheartedly embrace air defense, and jealously guarded Bomber Command, that organization's support for air defense increased as the possibility of war loomed larger.

5. Disasters fresh in a state's memory are great promoters of civilian intervention, even if no immediate threat appears on the horizon. (This proposition and those that follow have their counterparts at the organizational level.) If a threat is apparent, the tendency will be more pronounced. The most recent example is the apparently very thorough review by Israel's Agranat Commission of all the events leading up to and including the 1973 war. While the Commission included two former chiefs of staff, the chairman and the other two members were civilians. Most of the report remains secret, but it is known to have generated wide-ranging reform in Israel's armed forces.

Another example is found in the case of Prussia. Between October 7 and November 7, 1806, Napoleon Bonaparte completely destroyed the armies of the heirs of Frederick the Great. The "army with a country" was swept aside by the superior numbers and methods of the French. Following this disaster, both civilian and military reformers came to the fore. Before the war, reforms of either bureaucracy or army were practically impossible. After the war, under the leadership of the soldiers Gerhard Scharnhorst and Count August Gneisenau, a commission was set up to reform the army. Opposition was not wanting, and in fact was suppressed only by the direct intervention of the king, who removed the opponents of reform from the commission.

6. Some civilian intervention is produced not by disaster but by the high costs expected of a particular military exercise. A victorious but very costly war can substantially weaken a state. Even in the context of a superiority that provided some damage-limiting capability, U.S. civilian policymakers in the 1950s watched their nuclear forces more closely than they had ever watched military forces before. Though the United States might have "prevailed" in a nuclear conflict, the game was not likely to be worth the candle. . . .

The experience or expectation of military disaster provides a key avenue by which technology can influence military doctrine. Civilians especially are moved to interpret new technology and integrate such interpretations into military doctrine when the technology presents some very clear and unambiguous threat to the state's survival. The threat may be of defeat or the probability of high collateral damage. Civilian intervention is unlikely unless demonstration of the technology, by test or combat-use, is sufficiently stark and frightening to shake civilians' faith in the ability of their own military organizations to handle it. The attitudes of French civilians to any chance of a replay of World War I, British civilians to the spectre of bombs falling on London, and American civilians to nuclear weapons are all good examples. Even here, though, the impact of technology is not determinative. In the French case technology was seen to be largely immutable, a force to be accepted and dealt with. In the British case, technology was seen as something to be changed.

Simple fear of defeat provides another motivation for civilian intervention. If an adversary appears particularly impressive, potentially capable of a decisive victory, civilians will pay considerable attention to their military instrument. The intervention of British civilians into the doctrine of the RAF, for instance, was driven by fear of the German "knock-out-blow-from-the-air."

### Summary: Balance-of-Power Theory Hypotheses

*Offense, Defense, and Deterrence*

In general, the theory predicts heterogeneity along the dimension offense–defense–deterrence.

1. Expansionist powers will prefer offensive doctrines.
2. States will prefer offensive doctrines when war appears to involve very high collateral damage, because offense allows the state to take the war somewhere else.
3. States with a favorable power position that is suffering erosion will prefer offensive doctrines. (Offensive doctrines are a vehicle for preventive war.)
4. States that face several adversaries may prefer offensive doctrines. (Again, offensive doctrines are the vehicle for preventive war.)
5. Similarly, geographically encircled states may prefer offensive doctrines.
6. States without allies will prefer offensive doctrines because they must exploit military power for diplomacy, a purpose best served by offensive capabilities.
7. States with widely distributed security dependencies will prefer offensive doctrines because they allow the concentration of scarce military assets.
8. States with far-flung security dependencies will accept deterrent doctrines when it is not feasible to sustain offensive or defensive doctrines. Deterrent doctrines are a vehicle for throwing political will into the military balance.
9. Similarly, small states may opt for deterrent doctrines because their capabilities are insufficient to support any other kind.
10. The possibility of coalition warfare can lead a state to a defensive doctrine because such doctrines permit a pace of warfare that allows allies to settle the division of the risks, costs, and benefits of war.
11. States preparing to fight in coalitions must also please their prospective coalition partners. This dilutes the power of proposition 10. If, for its own special reasons, a state adopts an offensive doctrine, its suitors may find it necessary

to conform. By the same token, however, conformity to a defensive doctrine is likely if the state being wooed adopts a defensive doctrine.

12. Status-quo states will generally prefer defensive doctrines if geography or technology makes such doctrines attractive.

13. Status-quo states may prefer defensive doctrines simply because they know that they are unlikely to strike first.

*Integration and Innovation*

1. Statesmen contemplating aggression will tend to intervene in their military organizations.

2. Generally, anything that increases the perceived threat to state security is a cause of civilian intervention in military matters and hence a possible cause of integration and innovation.

3. Soldiers themselves tend to be more amenable to external prodding when the threat of war looms larger.

4. In states that are either politically isolated or geographically surrounded, civilians tend to intervene in military matters more frequently, and soldiers tend to approach war more seriously than in states with more favorable security conditions. Thus, both integration and innovation should be more frequent in such states.

5. Recent military disasters can be causes of integration and innovation.

6. Anticipated high costs of warfare can be a cause of civilian intervention. Because new technology (e.g., nuclear weapons) can greatly affect anticipated costs, this is one way technology can exert an influence on integration and innovation.

    All of the preceding possible causes can be weakened in multipolar systems, where allies appear to be easy to come by. States and statesmen may spend too much time chasing allies, and not enough time auditing their war machines.

## SUMMARY

In this chapter I have offered brief surveys of organization theory and balance-of-power theory, and from these theories I have inferred hypotheses about what causes military doctrine to vary along the dimensions offense–defense–deterrence, innovation–stagnation, and integration–disintegration. I have integrated with these hypotheses a small group of propositions that concern the influence of technology and geography upon military doctrine. Most of these propositions are consistent with one or the other of the two theories introduced.

As argued in the opening pages of this chapter, these are structural theories. They are appropriate for the examination of the cases that follow. These theories will be used in combination to explain the military doctrines of France, Britain, and Germany. Because in some of the cases contradictory hypotheses about doctrine are generated by the two theories, a comparison of these military doctrines allows us to examine and weigh the explanatory power of each theory.

In the broadest sense military doctrine should, according to *organization theory*, show a tendency to be offensive, disintegrated, and stagnant. This is suggested both by the character of military organizations and by their functional separation from the political decision makers of the state. *Balance-of-power theory* predicts somewhat different outcomes, depending on the state's situation. In general, anything that makes the civilian leaders of a state more fearful should encourage political–military integration and operational innovation. Civilian preferences for offense, defense, or deterrence will be influenced by the international environment. Finally, if the two theories introduced here have any validity at all, we should find that *technology* and *geography* are rarely determinative in their own right, although they should often have an important effect on doctrine.

Under what conditions will organization theory enjoy its greatest explanatory power? Under what conditions will the international environment have the greatest influence? In times of relative international calm we should expect a high degree of organizational determinism. In times of threat we should see greater accommodation of doctrine to the international system—integration should be more pronounced, innovation more likely. Among states, doctrines should show more heterogeneity. However, even under such circumstances all will not necessarily be well. Multipolar structures, although they exert an important influence on doctrine, may so confuse decision makers as to allow organizational determinants to come to the fore once again. The effects can be disastrous.

## NOTES

1. SOPs are shorthand for "Standard Operating Procedures."
2. By integration (and disintegration), Posen means how well (and how poorly) suited a nation's military forces and doctrine are to its foreign policy goals.
3. Bernard Brodie, "Technological Change, Strategic Doctrine, and Political Outcomes," in *Historical Dimensions,* ed. Knorr, p. 299.
4. Spykman, *America's Strategy in World Politics.* New York: Harcourt, Brace, and World, 1942, p. 29.

# 3

# Offense, Defense, and the Causes of War

## STEPHEN VAN EVERA

Is war more likely when conquest is easy? Could peace be strengthened by making conquest more difficult? What are the causes of offense dominance?[1] How can these causes be controlled? These are the questions this chapter addresses.

I argue that war is far more likely when conquest is easy, and that shifts in the offense–defense balance have a large effect on the risk of war. Ten war-causing effects (summarized in Figure 3.1) arise when the offense dominates. (1) States more often pursue opportunistic expansion, because attempts at expansion succeed more often and also offer greater rewards (explanation A). (2) States more often pursue defensive expansion because they feel less secure. Being more vulnerable to conquest, they are more anxious to extend their borders and to cut strong neighbors down to size (explanation B). (3) Their greater insecurity also drives states to resist others' expansion more fiercely. Power gains by others raise larger threats to national security; hence expansionism prompts a more violent response (explanation C). (4) First-strike advantages are larger, raising dangers of preemptive war (explanation D). (5) Windows of opportunity and vulnerability are larger, raising dangers of preventive war (explanation E). (6) States more often adopt fait accompli diplomatic tactics, and such tactics more often trigger war (explanation F). (7) States negotiate less readily and cooperatively; hence negotiations fail more often, and disputes fester unresolved (explanation G). (8) States enshroud foreign and defense policy in tighter secrecy, raising the risk of miscalculation and diplomatic blunder (explanation H). (9) Arms racing is faster and harder to control, raising the risk of preventive wars and wars of false optimism (explanation I). (10) Offense dominance is self-feeding.[2] As conquest grows easier, states adopt policies (e.g.,

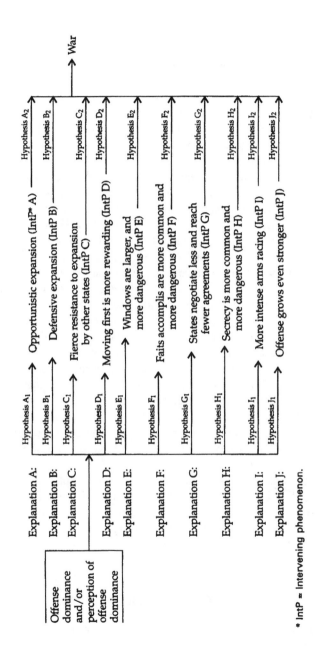

**FIGURE 3.1** Offense–Defense Theory. Prime hypothesis: War is more likely when conquest is easy.

* IntP = Intervening phenomenon.

more offensive military doctrines) that make conquest still easier. This magnifies effects 1–9 (explanation J).

The perception of offense dominance raises these same ten dangers, even without the reality. If states think the offense is strong, they will act as if it were. Thus offense–defense theory has two parallel variants, real and perceptual. These variants are considered together here. . . .

What causes offense and defense dominance? Military technology and doctrine, geography, national social structure, and diplomatic arrangements (specifically, defensive alliances and balancing behavior by offshore powers) all matter. The net offense–defense balance is an aggregate of these military, geographic, social, and diplomatic factors.

How can offense dominance be controlled? Defensive military doctrines and defensive alliance-making offer good solutions, although there is some tension between them: offensive forces can be needed to defend allies. Offense dominance is more often imagined than real, however. Thus the more urgent question is: How can illusions of offense dominance be controlled? Answers are elusive because the roots of these illusions are obscure.

On balance, how does offense-defense theory measure up? It has the attributes of good theory. In addition to having theoretical importance, offense-defense theory has wide explanatory range and prescriptive richness. It explains an array of important war causes (opportunistic expansionism, defensive expansionism, fierce resistance to others' expansion, first-strike advantage, windows of opportunity and vulnerability, faits accomplis, negotiation failure, secrecy, arms races, and offense dominance itself) that were once thought to be independent. In so doing, offense–defense theory explains the dangers that these war causes produce and the wars they cause. This simplifies the problem of power and war: a number of disparate dangers are fed by a single taproot. Moreover, both the reality and the perception of easy conquest can be shaped by human action; hence offense-defense theory offers prescriptions for controlling the dangers it frames.

The next section outlines offense-defense theory's ten explanations for war. The following section identifies causes of offense and defense dominance. The fourth section frames predictions that can be inferred from offense-defense theory, and offers . . . [two] case studies as tests of the theory: Europe since 1789 . . . and the United States since 1789. The final section assesses the general quality of offense–defense theory.

## HYPOTHESES ON THE EFFECTS OF OFFENSE DOMINANCE

A host of dangers arise when conquest is easy. Some are obvious and some more subtle, some are direct and some indirect. Together they make war very likely when the offense dominates.

### A. Opportunistic Expansionism

When conquest is hard, states are dissuaded from aggression by the fear that victory will prove costly or unattainable. When conquest is easy, aggression is more alluring: it costs less to attempt and succeeds more often. Aggressors can also move with less fear of reprisal because they win their wars more decisively, leaving their victims less able to retaliate later. Thus even aggressor states are deterred from attacking if the defense is strong, and even quite benign powers are tempted to attack if the offense is strong.

### B and C. Defensive Expansionism and Fierce Resistance to Expansion

When conquest is hard, states are blessed with secure borders; hence they are less aggressive and more willing to accept the status quo. They have less need for more territory because their current territory is already defensible. They are less anxious to cut neighbors down to size because even strong neighbors cannot conquer them. They have less urge to intervene in other states' internal affairs because hostile governments can do them less harm.

Conversely, when conquest is easy, states are more expansionist because their current borders are less defensible. They seek wider territories to gain resources that would bolster their defenses. They find strong neighbors more frightening; and they are quicker to use force to destroy their neighbors' power. They worry more when hostile regimes arise nearby because such neighbors are harder to defend against; hence they are quicker to intervene in their neighbors' domestic policies. These motives drive states to become aggressors and foreign intervenors.[3] States also resist others' expansion more fiercely when conquest is easy. Adversaries can parlay smaller gains into larger conquests; hence stronger steps to prevent gains by others are more appropriate. This attitude makes disputes more intractable.

The basic problem is that resources are more cumulative when conquest is easy. The ability to conquer others and to defend oneself is more elastic to one's control over strategic areas and resources. As a result, gains are more additive— states can parlay small conquests into larger ones—and losses are less reversible. Hence small losses can spell one's demise, and small gains can open the way to hegemonic dominance. States therefore compete harder to control any assets that confer power, seeking wider spheres for themselves while fiercely resisting others' efforts to expand.

This problem is compounded by its malignant effect on states' expectations about one another's conduct. When conquest is hard, states are blessed with neighbors made benign by their own security and by the high cost of attacking others. Hence states have less reason to expect attack. This leaves states even more secure and better able to pursue pacific policies. Conversely, when the offense dominates, states are cursed with neighbors made aggressive by both temptation and fear. These neighbors see easy gains from aggression and danger in standing pat. Plagued with such aggressive neighbors, all states face greater risk of attack. This drives them to compete still harder to control resources and create conditions that provide security. . . .

### D. Moving First Is More Rewarding

When conquest is easy, the incentive to strike first is larger because a successful surprise attack provides larger rewards and averts greater dangers. Smaller shifts in ratios of forces between states create greater shifts in their relative capacity to conquer and defend territory. . . . Hence a surprise strike that shifts the force ratio in the attacker's favor pays it a greater reward. This expands the danger of preemptive war and makes crises more explosive. States grow more trigger-happy, launching first strikes to exploit the advantage of the initiative, and to deny it to an opponent.

Conversely, if the defense dominates, the first-move dividend is small because little can be done with any material advantage gained by moving first. Most aggressors can be checked even if they gain the initiative, and defenders can succeed even if they lose the initiative. Hence preemptive war has less attraction.

### E. Windows Are Larger and More Dangerous

When conquest is easy, arguments for preventive war carry more weight. Smaller shifts in force ratios have larger effects on relative capacity to conquer or defend territory; hence smaller prospective shifts in force ratios cause greater hope and alarm. Also, stemming decline by using force is more feasible because rising states can be overrun with greater ease. This bolsters arguments for shutting "windows of vulnerability" by war. As a result, all international change is more dangerous. Events that tip the balance of resources in any direction trigger thoughts of war among states that face relative decline.

Conversely, if the defense dominates, arguments for preventive war lose force because declining states can more successfully defend against aggressors even after their decline, making preventive war unnecessary. States are also deterred from preventive war by the likelihood that their attack will fail, defeated by their enemy's strong defenses.

### F. Faits Accomplis Are More Common and More Dangerous

When conquest is easy, states adopt more dangerous diplomatic tactics—specifically, fait accompli tactics—and these tactics are more likely to cause war.

A fait accompli is a halfway step to war. It promises greater chance of political victory than quiet consultation, but it also raises greater risk of violence. The acting side moves without warning, facing others with an accomplished fact. It cannot retreat without losing face, a dilemma that it exploits to compel the others to concede. But if the others stand firm, a collision is hard to avoid. Faits accomplis also pose a second danger: because they are planned in secret, the planning circle is small, raising the risk that flawed policies will escape scrutiny because critics cannot quarrel with mistaken premises.

Faits accomplis are more common when the offense dominates because the rewards they promise are more valuable. When security is scarce, winning disputes grows more important than avoiding war. Leaders care more how spoils are divided than about avoiding violence, because failure to gain their share can spell their doom. This leads to gain-maximizing, war-risking diplomatic strategies— above all, to fait accompli tactics.

Faits accomplis are more dangerous when the offense dominates because a successful fait accompli has a greater effect on the distribution of international power. A sudden resource gain now gives an opponent more capacity to threaten its neighbors' safety. Hence faits accomplis are more alarming and evoke a stronger response from others. States faced with a fait accompli will shoot more quickly because their interests are more badly damaged by it.

### G. States Negotiate Less and Reach Fewer Agreements

When conquest is easy, states have less faith in agreements because others break them more often; states bargain harder and concede more grudgingly, causing more deadlocks; compliance with agreements is harder to verify; and states insist on better verification and compliance. As a result, states negotiate less often and settle fewer disputes; hence more issues remain unsettled and misperceptions survive that dialogue might dispel.

States break agreements more quickly when the offense dominates because cheating pays larger rewards. Bad faith and betrayal become the norm. The secure can afford the luxury of dealing in good faith, but the insecure must worry more about short-term survival. This drives them toward back-alley behavior, including deceits and sudden betrayals of all kinds—diplomatic faits accomplis, military surprise attacks, and breaking of other solemn agreements. Hence compliance with agreements is less expected. . . .

Verification of compliance with agreements is both more necessary and more difficult when the offense dominates. States insist on better verification of the other's compliance because smaller violations can have larger security implications; for example, an opponent might convert a small advantage gained by cheating on an arms control agreement into a larger offensive threat. At the same time, verification of compliance is harder because states are more secretive when security is scarce (see explanation G). As a result, the range of issues that can be negotiated is narrowed to the few where near-certain verification is possible despite tight state secrecy.

As a net result, states let more disputes fester when the offense dominates.

### H. States Are More Secretive

Governments cloak their foreign and defense policies in greater secrecy when conquest is easy. An information advantage confers more rewards, and a disadvantage raises more dangers: lost secrets could risk a state's existence. Thus states compete for information advantage by concealing their foreign policy strategies and military plans and forces.

Secrecy in turn is a hydra-headed cause of war. It can lead opponents to underestimate one another's capabilities and blunder into a war of false optimism. It can ease surprise attack by concealing preparations from the victim. It opens windows of opportunity and vulnerability by delaying states' reactions to others' military buildups, raising the risk of preventive war. It fosters policy blunders by narrowing the circle of experts consulted on policy, increasing the risk that flawed policies will survive unexamined. It prevents arms control agreements by making compliance harder to verify.

### I. States Arms Race Harder and Faster

Offense dominance intensifies arms racing, whereas defense dominance slows it down. Arms racing in turn raises other dangers. It opens windows of opportunity and vulnerability as one side or the other races into the lead. It also fosters false optimism by causing rapid military change that confuses policymakers' estimates of relative power. Thus offense dominance is a remote cause of the dangers that arms racing produces.

States have seven incentives to build larger forces when the offense is strong.

- Resources are more cumulative (see explanations B and C). Wartime gains and losses matter more: gains provide a greater increase in security, and losses are less reversible. Therefore the forces that provide these gains and protect against these losses are also worth more.

- Self-defense is more difficult because others' forces have more inherent offensive capability. Hence states require more forces to offset others' deployments.

- States are more expectant of war. Their neighbors are more aggressive (see explanation B), so they must be better prepared for attack or invasion.

- The early phase of war is more decisive. Lacking time to mobilize their economies and societies in the event of war, states maintain larger standing forces. The possibility of quick victory puts a premium on forces-in-being.

- States transfer military resources from defense to offense because offense is more effective (see explanation J). Others then counterbuild because their neighbors' capabilities are more dangerous and so require a larger response. States also infer aggressive intent from their neighbors' offensive buildups, leading them to fear attack and to build up in anticipation.

- States hold military secrets more tightly when the offense dominates (see explanation H). This causes rational overarming, as states gauge their defense efforts to worst-case estimates of enemy strength, on grounds that underspending is disastrous whereas overspending is merely wasteful. It also allows national militaries to monopolize defense information more tightly. Given that militaries are prone to inflate threats, states will overspend groundlessly when militaries have an information monopoly that lets them alone assess the threat. Thus "action-reaction" becomes "action-overreaction-overreaction."

- States reach fewer arms control agreements when the offense dominates, because agreements of all kinds are fewer (see explanation G). Hence states are less able to limit arms competition through agreement.

If the defense dominates, things are reversed. States build smaller offensive forces because offense is less effective, and because other states have less aggressive aims. States are safe without wider empires; hence offensive forces that could provide empires lose utility. The national military therefore grows defense-heavy. This causes other states to feel safer, which in turn makes them less aggressive, further lowering all states' insecurity—hence their need for empire and for offense—up to a point.

States also reduce defensive forces when the defense dominates because defense is easier and attack seems more remote. Moreover, as their neighbors buy less offense, they need even less defense because their defense faces less challenge.

In short, states buy smaller forces in general, and less offense in particular, when the defense dominates. This leads to still smaller forces and still less offense. If information were perfect, arms racing would slow to a crawl if the defense strongly dominated.

### J. Conquest Grows Still Easier

Offense dominance is self-reinforcing for three main reasons. First, states buy relatively more offensive forces when the offense dominates. They prefer the more successful type of force, so they buy defensive forces when the defense is strong and offensive forces when the offense is strong. This reinforces the initial dominance of the defense or the offense.

Second, alliances assume a more offensive character[4] when the offense dominates because aggressors can more easily drag their allies into their wars of aggression. Insecure states can less afford to see allies destroyed, so they must support even bellicose allies who bring war on themselves. Knowing this, the allies feel freer to get into wars. As a net result, even de jure defensive alliances operate as defensive-and-offensive alliances. Alliances also assume a more offensive character if the allies adopt purely offensive military doctrines. This hamstrings states that would demand that their allies confine themselves to defensive preparations in a crisis, given that all preparations are offensive.

Third, status-quo states are less able to protect their allies from conquest when the offense dominates because attackers can overrun defenders before help can arrive.

Thus offense dominance raises the danger of greater offense dominance. Once entered, an offense-dominant world is hard to escape. . . .

These are the dangers raised by offense dominance. As noted above, these same ten dangers arise when the offense is weak but governments think it dominates. They then act as if it dominates, with comparable effects. . . .

## CAUSES OF OFFENSE AND DEFENSE DOMINANCE

The feasibility of conquest is shaped by military factors, geographic factors, domestic social and political factors, and the nature of diplomacy. Discussions of the offense–defense balance often focus on military technology, but technology is only one part of the picture.

### Military Factors

Military technology, doctrine, and force posture and deployments all affect the military offense-defense balance.[5] Military technology can favor the aggressor or the defender. In past centuries, strong fortification techniques bolstered the defense, and strong methods of siege warfare strengthened the offense. Technologies that favored mass infantry warfare (e.g., cheap iron, allowing mass production of infantry weapons) strengthened the offense because large mass armies could bypass fortifications more easily, and because mass armies fostered more egalitarian polities that could raise loyal popular armies that would not melt away when sent on imperial expeditions. Technologies that favored chariot or cavalry warfare (e.g., the stirrup) strengthened the defense, because cavalry warfare required smaller forces that were more easily stopped by fortifications, and fostered hierarchic societies that could not raise armies that would remain loyal if sent on quests for empire. In modern times, technology that gave defenders more lethal firepower (e.g., the machine gun) or greater mobility (e.g., the railroad) strengthened the defense. When these technologies were neutralized by still newer technologies (motorized armor), the offense grew stronger.

Thus when fortresses and cavalry dominated in the late Middle Ages, the defense held the advantage. Cannons then made fortifications vulnerable and restored the strength of the offense. In the seventeenth and eighteenth centuries new fortification techniques strengthened the defense. The mercenary armies of the age also remained tightly tied to logistical tails that kept them close to home: one historian writes that an eighteenth-century army "was like a diver in the sea, its movements strictly limited and tied by the long, slender communicating tube which gave it life." Then revolutionary France's mass armies strengthened the offense because they had greater mobility. Their size let them sweep past border forts without leaving the bulk of their manpower behind for siege duty, and their more loyal troops could be trusted to forage without deserting, so they needed less logistical support. After the conservative restoration in France, Europe abandoned the mass army because it required, and fostered, popular government. This restored the power of the defense, which then waned somewhat as Europe democratized and large mass armies reappeared in the mid-nineteenth century.[6]

The combined effects of lethal small arms (accurate fast-firing rifles and machine guns), barbed wire, entrenchments, and railroads gave the defense an enormous advantage during World War I. The first three—lethal small arms, barbed wire, and trenches—gave defenders a large advantage at any point of attack. The fourth—railroads—let defenders reinforce points of attack faster than invaders could, because invaders could not use the defenders' railroads (given that railroad gauges differed across states, and defenders destroyed rail lines as they retreated) while the defenders had full use of their own lines. During 1919–45 the power of the offense was restored by motorized armor and an offensive doctrine—blitzkrieg—for its employment; this overrode machine guns, trenches, and barbed wire. Then after 1945 thermonuclear weapons restored the power of the defense—this time giving it an overwhelming advantage. . . .

States shape the military offense-defense balance by their military posture and force deployments. Thus Stalin eased attack for both himself and Hitler during 1939–41 by moving most of the Red Army out of strong defensive positions on the Stalin Line and forward into newly seized territories in Poland, Bessarabia, Finland, and the Baltic states. This left Soviet forces better positioned to attack Germany and far easier for Germany to attack, as the early success of Hitler's 1941 invasion revealed. The United States eased offense for both itself and Japan in 1941 when it deployed its fleet forward to Pearl Harbor and bombers forward to the Philippines. Egypt eased Israel's assault by its chaotic forward deployment of troops into poorly prepared Sinai positions in the crisis before the 1967 war.

States also can change the offense–defense balance through their wartime military operations. Aggressive operations can corrode key enemy defenses, and reckless operations can expose one's own defenses. Thus the dangers of offense dominance can be conjured up by unthinking wartime policymakers. For example, General Douglas MacArthur's reckless rush to the Yalu River in 1950 created an offensive threat to China's core territory and, by exposing badly deployed U.S. forces to attack, eased a Chinese offensive.

### Geography

Conquest is harder when geography insulates states from invasion or strangulation. Hence conquest is hindered when national borders coincide with oceans, lakes, mountains, wide rivers, dense jungles, trackless deserts, or other natural barriers that impede offensive movement or give defenders natural strong points. Human-made obstacles along borders, such as urban sprawl, can also serve as barriers to armored invasion. Conquest is hindered if foes are separated by wide buffer regions (third states or demilitarized zones) that neither side can enter in peacetime. Conquest is hindered when national territories are mountainous or heavily forested, and when populations live mainly in rural settings, easing guerrilla resistance to invaders. Conquest is hindered when states are large and their critical war resources or industries lie far in their interior, where they cannot be quickly overrun. Conquest is hindered when states are invulnerable to economic strangulation. Hence conquest is hindered when states are self-sufficient in supplies of water, energy, food, and critical raw materials, or when their trade routes cannot be severed by land or sea blockade. . . .

## Social and Political Order

Popular regimes are generally better at both conquest and self-defense than are unpopular regimes, but these effects do not cancel out. On net, conquest is probably harder among popular than unpopular regimes today, but in past centuries the reverse was likely true.

Popular governments can better raise larger, more loyal armies that can bypass others' border forts and can operate far from home with less logistical support. This gives popular regimes greater offensive power. Popular regimes can better organize their citizens for guerrilla resistance, making them harder to conquer. Citizen-defense guerrilla strategies are viable for Switzerland or China, but not for Guatemala or ancient Sparta, because these unpopular governments cannot arm their people without risking revolution. The citizens of unpopular oligarchies may actively assist advancing invaders. This gives attackers more penetrating power and makes early losses less reversible. Thus Sparta feared an invading army might grow if it entered Spartan territory, because Spartan slaves and dissident tribes would desert to the enemy.

Unpopular regimes are more vulnerable to subversion or revolution inspired from abroad. Subversion is a form of offense, and it affects international relations in the same way as do offensive military capabilities. Frail regimes are more frightened of unfriendly neighbors, making them more determined to impose congenial regimes on neighboring states. The French revolutionary regime and the oligarchic Austrian regime worried that the other side might subvert them in 1792, causing both sides to become more aggressive. After the Russian Revolution similar fears fueled Soviet–Western conflict, as each side feared subversion by the other.

On balance, is conquest easier in a world of popular or unpopular regimes? Popularity of regimes probably aided offense before roughly 1800 and has aided defense since then. The reversal stems from the appearance of cheap, mass-produced weapons useful for guerrilla war—assault rifles and machine guns, light mortars, and mines. The weapons of early times (sword and shield, pike and harquebus, heavy slow-firing muskets, etc.) were poorly adapted for guerrilla resistance. Guerrilla warfare has burgeoned since 1800 partly because the mass production of cheap small arms has tipped the balance toward guerrillas, allowing the hit-and-run harassment that characterizes guerrilla operations. The defensive power of popular regimes has risen in step with this increase in guerrilla warfare.

**Diplomatic Factors**

Three types of diplomatic arrangements strengthen the defense: collective security systems, defensive alliances, and balancing behavior by neutral states. All three impede conquest by adding allies to the defending side.

States in a collective security system (e.g., the League of Nations) promise mutual aid against aggression by any system member. Such aggressors will face large defending coalitions if the system operates.

States in a defensive alliance promise mutual aid against outside aggressors, leaving such aggressors outnumbered by resisting opponents. Thus during 1879–87 Bismarck wove a network of defensive alliances that discouraged aggression and helped preserve peace throughout central and eastern Europe.

Collective security systems and defensive alliances differ only in the kind of aggressor they target (system members versus outside aggressors). Both kinds of aggressors could be targeted at once, and a hybrid system that did this would offer defenders the most protection.

Neutral states act as balancers when they join the weaker of two competing coalitions to restore balance between them. Aggression is self-limiting when neutrals balance because aggressors generate more opposition as they expand. Britain and the United States traditionally played balancers to Europe, providing a counterweight to potential continental hegemons.

Balancing behavior is more selective than defensive alliance. Balancers balance to avert regional hegemony; hence pure balancers oppose expansion only by potential regional hegemons. Smaller states are left free to aggress. But balancing does contain hegemons and leaves their potential victims more secure. Conversely, if states bandwagon—join the stronger coalition against the weaker one—conquest is easier because aggressors win more allies as they seize more resources.

Diplomatic arrangements have had a large influence on the offense-defense balance in modern Europe, and shifts in diplomatic arrangements have produced large shifts in the overall offense-defense balance. Collective security was never effective, but defensive alliances came and went, erecting barriers to conquest when they appeared. Balancing behavior rose and fell as the power and activism of the two traditional offshore balancers, Britain and the United States, waxed and waned. When the United States and/or Britain were strong and willing to intervene against aspiring continental hegemons, conquest on the continent was difficult. To succeed, a hegemon had to defeat both its continental victims and the offshore power. But when Britain and the United States were weak or isolationist, continental powers could expand against less resistance, leaving all states less secure.

## TESTS OF OFFENSE–DEFENSE THEORY

What predictions can be inferred from offense–defense theory? How much history does offense–defense theory explain?

### Predictions and Tests

Offense–defense theory's predictions can be grouped in two broad types, *prime* predictions and *explanatory* predictions. The theory's prime predictions derive from its prime hypothesis ("War is more likely when conquest is easy"; or, for the theory's perceptual variant, "War is more likely when states think conquest is easy"). Tests of these predictions shed light on whether offense dominance (or perceptions of offense dominance) causes war.

Offense–defense theory's explanatory predictions derive from the hypotheses that comprise its ten explanations. Tests of these predictions shed light on both *whether* and *how* offense dominance (or perceptions of offense dominance) causes war.

*Prime Predictions*

Three prime predictions of offense–defense theory are tested here.

1. War will be more common in periods when conquest is easy or is believed easy, less common when conquest is difficult or is believed difficult.
2. States that have or believe they have large offensive opportunities or defensive vulnerabilities will initiate and fight more wars than other states.
3. A state will initiate and fight more wars in periods when it has, or thinks that it has, larger offensive opportunities and defensive capabilities.

These predictions are tested below in . . . [two] case studies: Europe since 1789 (treated as a single regional case study) . . . and the United States since 1789. I selected these cases because the offense-defense balance (or perceptions of it) varies sharply across time in all three, creating a good setting for "multiple within-case comparisons" tests that contrast different periods in the same case; because the United States is very secure relative to other countries, creating a good setting for a "comparison to typical values" tests that contrasts U.S. conduct with the conduct of average states, and because two of these cases are well recorded (Europe since 1789 and the United States since 1789).

The case of Europe since 1789 allows tests of prime predictions 1 and 2.[7] We can make crude indices of the offense-defense balances (actual and perceived) for Europe over the past two centuries, and match them with the incidence of war (see Table 3.1). Offense–defense theory predicts more war when conquest is easy or is believed easy. We can also estimate the offensive opportunities and defensive vulnerabilities of individual powers—for example, since 1789 Prussia/ Germany has been more vulnerable and has had more offensive opportunity than Spain, Italy, Britain, or the United States—and can match these estimates with states' rates of war involvement and war initiation. Offense-defense theory predicts that states with more defensive vulnerability and offensive opportunity will be more warlike. . . .

The U.S. case allows testing of prime predictions 2 and 3. The United States is less vulnerable to foreign military threats than are other states; hence offense-defense theory predicts that it should start fewer wars and be involved in fewer wars than other states. Americans have also felt more vulnerable to foreign military threats in some eras than in others. The U.S. propensity for war involvement and war initiation should co-vary with this sense of vulnerability.

*Explanatory Predictions*

Offense–defense theory posits that offense dominance leads to war through the war-causing action of its ten intervening phenomena A–J: opportunistic expansionism, defensive expansionism, fierce resistance to others' expansion, first-strike advantages, windows of opportunity and vulnerability, faits accomplis and belligerent reactions to them, reluctance to solve conflicts through negotiation, policies of secrecy, intense arms racing, and policies that ease conquest, such as offensive force postures and offensive alliances. If offense–defense theory is valid, these intervening phenomena should correlate with the real and perceived offense–defense balance. Two explanatory predictions can be inferred.

1. Phenomena A–J will be more abundant in eras of real or perceived offense dominance: the ten phenomena should increase as offense strengthens and diminish as offense weakens.

2. States that have or believe they have large offensive opportunities or defensive vulnerabilities will more strongly embrace policies that embody phenomena A–J.[8]

Two of the case studies presented here shed light on these explanatory predictions. The case of Europe allows a partial test of both. We can code only two of offense–defense theory's ten intervening phenomena (IntPs A and B, opportunistic and defensive expansionism) for the whole period. We have fragmentary data for values on the other eight intervening variables. Hence the case lets us test explanations A and B fairly completely and offers scattered evidence on

# TABLE 3.1
## THE OFFENSE–DEFENSE BALANCE AMONG GREAT POWERS, 1700s–PRESENT

| Era | Military realities favored | Military realities were thought to favor | Diplomatic realities favored | Diplomatic realities were thought to favor | In aggregate military and diplomatic realities favored | In aggregate military and diplomatic realities were thought to favor | Amount of warfare among great powers |
|---|---|---|---|---|---|---|---|
| Pre–1792 | Defs. | Defs. | Med. | Med. | Med. | Med. | Medium |
| 1792–1815 | Aggrs. | Aggrs. | Med. | Aggrs. | Aggrs. | Aggrs.[3] | High |
| 1816–56 | Defs. | Defs. | Defs. | Defs. | Defs. | Defs. | Low |
| 1856–71 | Med. | Med. | Aggrs. | Aggrs. | Aggrs. | Aggrs. | Medium |
| 1871–90 | Defs. | Med. | Defs. | Defs. | Defs. | Defs.[3] | Low |
| 1890–1918 | Defs. | Aggrs. | Aggrs. | Aggrs. | Defs. | Aggrs. | High |
| 1919–45 | Aggrs. | Mixed[1] | Aggrs. | Aggrs.[2] | Aggrs. | Aggrs.[4] | High |
| 1945–1990s | Defs. | Med. | Defs. | Defs. | Defs. | Defs.[3] | Low |

Aggrs.: The factor favors aggressors.
Defs.: The factor favors defenders.
Med.: A medium value: things are somewhere in between, cut both ways.
Mixed: Some national elites saw defense dominance, some saw offense dominance.

The perceptions entries are an average of the perceptions of the great power elites. In some cases, the perceptions of these elites varied sharply across states, for example, perceptions of military realities in the 1930s.

1. Things varied across states. The German elite recognized the military power of the offensive in the late 1930s; the elites of other great powers thought the defense was dominant.

2. Things varied across states. The German elite (above all Hitler) exaggerated the considerable actual diplomatic weakness of the defense; the elites of other great powers recognized this weakness but did not overstate it. These beliefs average to a perception of substantial diplomatic offense dominance.

3. Elites exaggerated the strength of the offense during 1792–1815, 1871–1890, and 1945–1990s, but not by enough to give the realities and perceptions of the offense-defense balance different scores.

4. When we aggregate perceptions of the offense-defense balance, the errors of Germany and the other powers cancel each other out. Germany's exaggeration of the diplomatic power of the offense offsets other powers' exaggeration of the military power of the defense, leaving an aggregate perception fairly close to the offense-dominant reality.

explanations C–J. To test explanations A and B, we ask if expansionism correlates over time with periods of real or perceived offense dominance, and if states that were (or believed they were) less secure and more able to aggress were more expansionist.

The case of the United States since 1789 allows a more complete, if rather weak, test of explanatory prediction 2.

### Test 1: Europe 1789–1990s

A composite measure of the offense-defense balance in Europe since 1789 can be fashioned by blending the histories of Europe's military and diplomatic offense–defense balances, as outlined above.[9] In sum, the offense–defense balance went through six phases comprising three up–down oscillations after 1789. Conquest was never easy in an absolute sense during these two centuries. Conquest was, however, markedly easier during 1792–1815, 1856–71, and 1930s–1945 than it was during 1815–56, 1871–1920s, and 1945–1990s.

Elite perceptions of the offense–defense balance track these oscillations quite closely, but not exactly. Elites chronically exaggerated the power of the offense, but did so far more in some periods than in others. Most important, they greatly exaggerated the power of the offense during 1890–1918: elites then wrongly thought conquest was very easy when in fact it was very hard. Thus the pattern of reality and perception run roughly parallel, with the major exception of 1890–1918.

Tides of war and peace correlate loosely with the offense–defense balance during this period, and tightly with the perceived offense–defense balance. Expansionism and war were more common when conquest was easy than when it was difficult, and were far more common when conquest was believed easy than when it was believed difficult. Moreover, states that believed they faced large offensive opportunities and defensive vulnerabilities (especially Prussia/Germany) were the largest troublemakers. They were more expansionist, they were involved in more wars, and they started more wars than other states.

#### 1792–1815

During 1792–1815 the offense was fairly strong militarily, as a result of France's adoption of the popular mass army (enabled by the popularity of the French revolutionary government). Moreover, European elites widely exaggerated one another's vulnerability to conquest: at the outset of the War of 1792 all three belligerents (France, Austria, and Prussia) thought their opponents were on the verge of collapse and could be quickly crushed. Defense-enhancing diplomacy was sluggish: Britain, Europe's traditional balancer, stood by indifferently during the crisis that produced the War of 1792, issuing a formal declaration of neutrality. Moreover, French leaders underestimated the power of defense-enhancing diplomacy because they widely believed that other states would bandwagon with threats instead of balancing against them. In short, military factors helped the offense, and this help was further exaggerated; political factors did little to help bolster defenders, and this help was underestimated.

*1815–1856*

After 1815 both arms and diplomacy favored defenders, as outlined above. Mass armies disappeared, British economic power grew, and Britain remained active on the continent as a balancer. Continental powers expected Britain to balance and believed British strength could not be overridden.

This defense-dominant arrangement lasted until midcentury. It began weakening before the Crimean War (1853–56). When war in Crimea broke out, military factors still favored defenders, but elites underestimated the power of the defense: Britain and France launched their 1854 Crimean offensive in false expectation of quick and easy victory. In general, diplomatic factors favored the defense (Britain still balanced actively), but during the prewar crisis in 1853, diplomacy favored the offense because Britain and France blundered by giving Turkey unconditional backing that amounted to an offensive alliance. This encouraged the Turkish aggressions that sparked the war.

*1856–1871*

After the Crimean War the offense–defense balance shifted further toward the offense. Changes in the military realm cut both ways. Mass armies were appearing (bolstering the offense), but small arms were growing more lethal and railroads were expanding (bolstering the defense). In the diplomatic realm, however, the power of defenders fell dramatically because defense-enhancing diplomacy largely broke down. Most important, Britain entered an isolationist phase that lasted into the 1870s, and Russia lost interest in maintaining the balance among the western powers. As a result, diplomatic obstacles to continental conquest largely disappeared, giving continental aggressors a fairly open field. This diplomatic change gave France and Sardinia, and then Prussia, a yawning offensive opportunity, which they exploited by launching a series of wars of opportunistic expansion—in 1859, 1864, 1866, and 1870. But defense-enhancing diplomacy had not disappeared completely, and it helped keep these wars short and limited.

In 1859 British and Russian neutrality gave France and Sardinia a free hand, which they used to seize Lombardy from Austria. In 1864 British, Russian, and French neutrality gave Prussia and Austria a free hand, which they used to seize Schleswig-Holstein from Denmark. In 1866 British, French, and Russian neutrality gave Prussia carte blanche against Austria, which Prussia used to smash Austria and consolidate its control of North Germany. Even after war broke out, major fighting proceeded for weeks before any outside state even threatened intervention. . . .

In 1870 Bismarck ensured the neutrality of the other European powers by shifting responsibility for the war to France and convincing Europe that the war stemmed from French expansionism. As a result, Prussia again had a free hand to pursue its expansionist aims. It used this to smash France, seize Alsace-Lorraine, and consolidate control over South Germany.

### 1871–1890

For some twenty years after the Franco-Prussian War, the defense dominated because of Bismarck's new diplomacy and Britain's renewed activism. In the military area the cult of the offensive had not yet taken hold. In diplomacy Bismarck wove a web of defensive alliances that deterred aggressors and calmed status-quo powers after 1879.[10] British power waned slightly, but this was offset by the recovery of Britain's will to play the balancer. The "war-in-sight" crisis of 1875 illustrates the change: Britain and Russia together deterred a renewed German attack on France by warning that they would not allow a repeat of 1870–71.

### 1890–1919

After 1890 military realities increasingly favored the defense, but elites mistakenly believed the opposite. Diplomatic realities swung toward the offense, and elites believed they favored the offense even more than they did.

European militaries were seized by a "cult of the offensive." All the European powers adopted offensive military doctrines, culminating with France's adoption of the highly offensive Plan XVII in 1913 and with Russia's adoption of the highly offensive Plan 20 in 1914. More important, militaries persuaded civilian leaders and publics that the offense dominated and conquest was easy. As a result, elites and publics widely believed the next war would be quickly won by a decisive offensive.

Bismarck's defensive alliances withered or evolved into defensive-and-offensive alliances after he left office in 1890, largely because the cult of the offensive made defensive alliances hard to maintain. Pacts conditioned on defensive conduct became hard to frame because states defended by attacking, and status-quo powers shrank from enforcing defensive conduct on allies they felt less able to lose. For example, Britain and France felt unable to enforce defensive conduct on a Russian ally that defended by attacking and that they could not afford to see defeated. Elites also thought that aggressors could overrun their victims before allies could intervene to save them, making defensive alliances less effective. Thus Britain seemed less able to save France before Germany overran it, leading Germany to discount British power. Lastly, German leaders subscribed to a bandwagon theory of diplomacy, which led them to underestimate others' resistance to German expansion. Overall, the years before 1914 were the all-time high point of perceived offense dominance.

Nine of the ten intervening phenomena predicted by offense–defense theory (all except phenomenon G, nonnegotiation) flourished in this world of assumed offense dominance. Opportunistic and defensive expansionist ideas multiplied and spread, especially in Germany. Russia and France mobilized their armies preemptively in the 1914 July crisis. That crisis arose from a fait accompli that Germany and Austria instigated in part to shut a looming window of vulnerability. This window in turn had emerged from a land arms race that erupted during 1912–14. The powers enshrouded their military and political plans in secrecy—a secrecy that fostered crisis-management blunders during July 1914. These blunders in turn evoked rapid, violent reactions that helped drive the crisis out of control. Belief in the offense fueled offensive military doctrines throughout the continent and impeded efforts to restrain allies. Together these dangers formed a prime cause of the war: they bore the 1914 July crisis and helped make it uncontrollable.

### 1919–1945

The interwar years were a mixed bag, but overall the offense gained the upper hand by 1939, and the German elite believed the offense even stronger than in fact it was.

Military doctrine and technology gave the defense the advantage until the late 1930s, when German blitzkrieg doctrine combined armor and infantry in an effective offensive combination. This offensive innovation was unrecognized outside Germany and doubted by many in Germany, but the man who counted most, Adolf Hitler, firmly believed in it. This reflected his faith in the offense as a general principle, imbibed from international social Darwinist propaganda in his youth.[11]

More important, the workings of interwar diplomacy opened a yawning political opportunity for Nazi expansion. Britain fell into a deep isolationism that left it less willing to commit this declining power to curb continental aggressors. The United States also withdrew into isolation, removing the counterweight that checked Germany in 1918. The breakup of Austria-Hungary in that year created a new diplomatic constellation that further eased German expansion. Austria-Hungary would have balanced against German expansion, but its smaller successor states tended to bandwagon. This let Hitler extend German influence into southeast Europe by intimidation and subversion.

The Soviet Union and the Western powers failed to cooperate against Hitler. Ideological hostility divided them. Britain also feared that a defensive alliance against Hitler would arouse German fears of allied encirclement, spurring German aggressiveness. This chilled British enthusiasm for an Anglo–French–Soviet alliance.

Hitler exaggerated the already-large advantage that diplomacy gave the offense because he thought bandwagoning prevailed over balancing in international affairs. This false faith colored all his political forecasts and led him to vastly underestimate others states' resistance to his aggressions. Before the war he failed to foresee that Britain and France would balance German power by coming to Poland's rescue. Once the war began he believed Germany could intimidate Britain into seeking alliance with Germany after Germany crushed France—or, he later held, after Germany smashed the Soviet Union. He thought the United States could be cowed into staying neutral by the 1940 German–Japanese alliance (the alliance had the opposite effect, spurring U.S. intervention). In short, Hitler's false theories of diplomacy made three of his most dangerous opponents shrink to insignificance in his mind.

These realities and beliefs left Hitler to face temptations like those facing Bismarck in 1866 and 1870. Hitler thought he could conquer his victims seriatim. He also thought his conquests would arouse little countervailing opposition from distant neutral powers.[12] As a result, he believed he faced a yawning opportunity for aggression.

Unlike 1914, the late 1930s were not a pure case of perceived offense dominance. Instead, the 1930s saw status-quo powers' perceptions of defense dominance create real offensive opportunities for an aggressor state. Hitler thought the offense strong and even exaggerated its strength, but other powers (the Soviet Union, Britain, and France) underestimated its strength. Their perceptions of defense dominance relaxed their urge to jump the gun at early signs of threat (as Russia did in 1914); this made things safer. But this perception also relaxed their will to balance Germany, because they found German expansion less frightening. This weakened the coalition against Hitler, leaving him wider running room.

### 1945–1990s

After 1945 two changes swung the offense–defense balance back toward the defense. First, the end of American isolationism transformed European political affairs. The United States replaced Britain as continental balancer, bringing far more power to bear in Europe than Britain ever had. As a result, Europe in the years after 1945 was unusually defense dominant from a diplomatic standpoint.

Second, the nuclear revolution gave defenders a large military advantage—so large that conquest among great powers became virtually impossible. Conquest now required a nuclear first-strike capability (the capacity to launch a nuclear strike that leaves the defender unable to inflict unacceptable damage in retaliation). Defenders could secure themselves merely by maintaining a second-strike capability (the capacity to inflict unacceptable damage on the attacker's society after absorbing an all-out strike). The characteristics of nuclear weapons—their vast power, small size, light weight, and low cost—ensured that a first-strike capability would be very hard to attain, while a second-strike capability could be sustained at little cost. As a result, the great powers became essentially unconquerable, and even lesser powers could now stand against far stronger enemies. Overall, the nuclear revolution gave defenders an even more lopsided advantage than the machine-gun–barbed-wire–entrenchments–railroad complex that emerged before 1914. . . .

In sum, the events of 1789–1990s clearly corroborate offense–defense theory predictions—specifically, prime predictions 1 and 2, as well as both explanatory predictions. These conclusions rest on rather sketchy data—especially regarding the explanatory predictions—but that data confirm offense–defense theory so clearly that other data would have to be very different to reverse the result.

- The incidence of war correlates loosely with the offense–defense balance and very tightly with perceptions of the offense–defense balance (for a summary see Table 3.1).

- Europe's less-secure and more offensively capable continental powers were perennial troublemakers, while more secure and less offensively capable off-shore powers were perennial defenders of the status quo. Prussia/Germany was cursed with the least defensible borders and faced the most offensive temptations. It started the largest number of major wars (1864, 1866, 1914, 1939, and shared responsibility for 1870 with France). France and Russia, with more defensible borders and fewer temptations, started fewer major wars.[13] Britain and the United States, blessed with even more insulating borders, joined a number of European wars but started none.[14] Spain, Sweden, and Switzerland, also insulated from other powers by mountains or oceans, fought very little.

  Thus the timing of war and the identities of the belligerents tightly fit prime predictions 1 and 2.

- Sketchy evidence suggests that opportunistic and defensive expansionism were more prominent during the periods of perceived offense dominance (1792–1815, 1859–71, 1890–1914, 1930s–1945) than at other times. The years 1792–1815 saw a strong surge of French expansionism, nearly matched at the outset by parallel Prussian expansionism. The mid-nineteenth century saw large opportunistic expansionism in Prussia and some French expansionism. The years 1890–1914 saw vast expansionist ambitions develop in Wilhelmine Germany, matched by fierce resistance to this German expansionism in Russia and France, and by lesser French and Russian expansionism. Large German expansionism then reappeared under the Nazis in the 1930s. During other periods European expansionism was more muted: European powers had smaller ambitions and acted on them less often. This supports explanatory prediction 1.

- Opportunistic and defensive expansionism were prominent among those states that saw the clearest defensive vulnerability and offensive opportunity (especially Prussia/Germany, also revolutionary France), while being more muted among states with more secure borders and fewer offensive opportunities (Britain, the United States, the Scandinavian states, and Spain). This corroborates explanatory prediction 2. . . .

. . . in Europe since 1789, the nature of international relations has gyrated sharply with shifts in the perceived offense–defense balance. War is far more common when elites believe that the offense dominates, and states are far more belligerent when they perceive large defensive vulnerabilities and offensive opportunities for themselves. This indicates that perceptions of the offense–defense balance have a large impact on international relations. Offense–defense theory is important as well as valid. . . .

### Test 2: United States 1789–1990s

Since 1815 the United States has been by far the most secure of the world's great powers, blessed with two vast ocean moats, no nearby great powers, and (after 1890) the world's largest economy. In the nineteenth century the United States also had substantial offensive opportunities, embodied in chances for continental and then Pacific expansion against weak defenders. However, America's security endowments were quite extraordinary, while its offensive opportunities were more ordinary. Offense–defense theory predicts that such a state will exhibit perhaps average offensive opportunism but markedly less defensive belligerence than other states. Hence, on net, it will start fewer wars and be involved in fewer wars than others (see prime prediction 2).

This forecast is confirmed, although not dramatically, by the pattern of past U.S. foreign policy. The United States has fought other great powers only three times in its two-hundred–year history—in 1812, 1917, and 1941—a low count for a great power.[15] The 1812 war stemmed mainly from U.S. belligerence, but the wars of 1917 and 1941 resulted mainly from others' belligerence. The United States did start some of its lesser wars (1846 and 1898), but it joined other wars more reactively (Korea and Vietnam).

Offense–defense theory also predicts that while the United States will pursue some opportunistic expansionism (intervening phenomenon A), it will embrace few policies that embody offense–defense theory's other intervening phenomena (B–J) (explanatory prediction 2). Where the record allows judgments, this forecast is borne out. Regarding expansionism, the United States has confined itself largely to opportunistic imperialism against frail opponents. Defensive expansionism has been muted, and overall, expansionist ideas have held less sway in the United States than in other powers. This is reflected in the relatively small size of the U.S. empire. The modern American empire has been limited to a few formal colonies seized from Spain in the 1890s and an informal empire in the Caribbean/Central American area, with only intermittent control exerted more widely—a zone far smaller than the vast empires of the European powers.

The U.S. impulse to engage in preemptive and preventive war has been small. In sharp contrast to Germany and Japan, the United States has launched a stealthy first strike on another major power just once (in 1812) and has jumped through only one window of opportunity (in 1812). Surprise first strikes and window-jumping were considered on other occasions (e.g., preventive war was discussed during 1949–54, and surprise attack on Cuba was considered during the Cuban missile crisis), but seldom seriously.

American diplomacy has been strikingly free of fait accompli tactics. American foreign and security policy has generally been less secretive than those of the European continental powers, especially during the late Cold War, when the United States published military data that most powers would highly classify as state secrets. The U.S. arms-raced with the Soviet Union energetically during the Cold War, but earlier maintained very small standing military forces—far smaller than those of other great powers. Overall, intervening phenomena B–J of offense–defense theory are strikingly absent in the U.S. case.

In sum, the United States has not been a shrinking violet, but it has been less bellicose than the average great power. Compare, for example, U.S. conduct with the far greater imperial aggressions of Athens, Rome, Carthage, Spain, Prussia/ Germany, Japan, Russia, and France.

Offense–defense theory further predicts that levels of American bellicosity should vary inversely with shifts over time in America's sense of security and directly with the scope of perceived external threats (see prime prediction 3)—as in fact they have.

During 1789–1815 the United States saw large foreign threats on its borders and large opportunities to dispel them with force. It responded with a bellicose foreign policy that produced the 1812 war with Britain.

During 1815–1914 the United States was protected from the threat of a Eurasian continental hegemon by Britain's active continental balancing, and protected from extracontinental European expansion into the Western hemisphere by the British fleet, which was the de facto enforcer of the Monroe Doctrine. The United States responded by withdrawing from European affairs and maintaining very small standing military forces, although it did pursue continental expansion before 1898 and limited overseas imperial expansion after 1898.

During 1914–91 Britain could no longer maintain the European balance. This deprived the United States of its shield against continental European aggressors. Then followed the great era of American activism—fitful at first (1917–47), then steady and persistent (1947–91). This era ended when the Soviet threat suddenly vanished during 1989–91. After 1991 the United States maintained its security alliances, but reduced its troops stationed overseas and sharply reduced its defense effort. . . .

## What Prescriptions Follow?

If offense dominance is dangerous, policies that control it should be pursued. Governments should adopt defensive military-force postures and seek arms-control agreements to limit offensive forces. Governments should also maintain defensive alliances. American security guarantees in Europe and Asia have made conquest much harder since 1949 and have played a major role in preserving peace. A U.S. withdrawal from either region would raise the risk of conflict. . . .

## CONCLUSION: OFFENSE–DEFENSE THEORY IN PERSPECTIVE

. . . [O]ffense–defense theory is quite satisfying, although it leaves important questions unanswered. In uncovering the roots of its ten intervening phenomena, offense– defense theory offers a more satisfying (and simpler) explanation than do interpretations pointing directly to these phenomena. However, it also raises another mystery: Why is the strength of the offense so often exaggerated?

History suggests that offense dominance is at the same time dangerous, quite rare, and widely overstated. It further suggests that this exaggeration of insecurity, and the bellicose conduct it fosters, are prime causes of national insecurity and war. States are seldom as insecure as they think they are. Moreover, if they are insecure, this insecurity often grows from their own efforts to escape imagined insecurity.

The rarity of real insecurity is suggested by the low death rate of modern great powers. In ancient times great powers often disappeared, but in modern times (since 1789) no great powers have permanently lost sovereignty, and only twice (France in 1870–71 and in 1940) has any been even temporarily overrun by an unprovoked aggressor. Both times France soon regained its sovereignty through the intervention of outside powers—illustrating the powerful defensive influence of great-power balancing behavior. . . .

Paradoxically, a chief source of insecurity in Europe since medieval times has been this false belief that security was scarce. This belief was a self-fulfilling prophecy, fostering bellicose policies that left all states less secure. Modern great powers have been overrun by unprovoked aggressors only twice, but they have been overrun by provoked aggressors six times—usually by aggressors provoked by the victim's fantasy-driven defensive bellicosity. Wilhelmine and Nazi Germany, Imperial Japan, Napoleonic France, and Austria-Hungary were all destroyed by dangers that they created by their efforts to escape from exaggerated or imaginary threats to their safety.

If so, the prime threat to the security of modern great powers is . . . themselves. Their greatest menace lies in their own tendency to exaggerate the dangers they face, and to respond with counterproductive belligerence. The causes of this syndrome pose a large question for students of international relations.

## NOTES

1. In this chapter "offense dominant" means that conquest is fairly easy; "defense dominant" means that conquest is very difficult. It is almost never easier to conquer than to defend, so I use "offense dominant" broadly, to denote that offense is easier than usual, although perhaps not actually easier than defense. I use "offense–defense balance" to denote the relative ease of aggression and defense against aggression. As noted below, this balance is shaped by both military and diplomatic/political factors. Two measures of the overall offense–defense balance work well: (1) the probability that a determined aggressor could conquer and subjugate a target state with comparable resources; or (2) the resource

advantage that an aggressor requires to gain a given chance of conquering a target state. I use "offense" to refer to strategic offensive action—the taking and holding of territory—as opposed to tactical offensive action, which involves the attack but not the seizure and holding of territory.

2. I use "offense–defense theory" to label the hypothesis that war is more likely when conquest is easy, plus explanatory hypotheses that define how this causation operates. The classic work on the topic is Robert Jervis, "Cooperation under the Security Dilemma," *World Politics*, Vol. 30, No. 2 (January 1978), pp. 167-214 at 169. An overview is Sean M. Lynn-Jones, "Offense–Defense Theory and Its Critics," *Security Studies*, Vol. 4, No. 4 (Summer 1995), pp. 660–691. The theory I frame here subsumes and elaborates on Jervis's theory.

3. It also seems possible that states should be more careful to avoid war when conquest is easy, because war then brings greater risk of total defeat. If so, offense dominance should cause more caution than belligerence among states, and should lower the risk of war. . . .

4. A defensive alliance is conditioned on defensive behavior by the ally; the alliance operates if the ally is attacked but not if it attacks. A defensive-and-offensive alliance operates in the event of war regardless of which side started it. The distinction began with Thucydides, who used "empimachy" to denote defensive alliance, "symmachy" for defensive-and-offensive alliances. G.E.M. de Ste. Croix, *The Origins of the Peloponnesian War* (Ithaca, N.Y.: Cornell University Press, 1972), pp. 60, 72–73, 106–108, 184, 298–302, 328.

5. Several measures of the military offense–defense balance could be adopted, such as: (1) the probability that an offensive force can overcome a defensive force of equal cost; (2) the relative cost that attackers and defenders must pay for forces that offset incremental improvements by the other; or (3) the loss ratio when an offensive force attacks a defensive force of equal cost. All three measures (and more are possible) capture the concept of relative military difficulty of conquest and defense. For a list of possible measures, see Charles L. Glaser and Chaim Kaufmann, "What Is Offense–Defense Balance and How Can We Measure It?" *International Security*, Vol. 22, No. 4 (Spring 1998), pp. 44–82.

6. Large armies aid the offense only up to a point, however. Once armies grow so big that they can cover an entire frontier (as on the western front in World War I), their size aids the defense because offensive outflanking maneuvers against them become impossible.

7. In principle, prime prediction 3 could also be tested with this case. This, however, would require tracing and describing trends in each state's sense of vulnerability over time—a large task that would fill many pages.

8. Explanatory predictions 1 and 2 are inferred from the "left side" of offense–defense theory, that is, from hypotheses $A_1$–$J_1$, which frame the claim that offense dominance causes intervening phenomena A–J (see Figure 3.1). Predictions could also be inferred from hypotheses $A_2$–$J_2$, which comprise the "right side" of the theory, and frame the claim that intervening phenomena A–J cause war. For example, we could infer that (6) warfare will be more common in eras and regions where phenomena A–J are more prevalent, and (7) states that embrace policies that embody phenomena A–J will be involved in more wars and will initiate more wars than other states. I leave "right side" hypotheses untested here because the effects of phenomena A-J are less debated than their causes. Most agree that they cause trouble.

9. My composite index represents my own "author's estimates" based on sources provided throughout this chapter. I measured the actual and perceived Europe-wide

offense–defense balances by asking: (1) Did military technology, force posture, and doctrine favor the offense or the defense? Did elites and publics believe these factors favored the offense or the defense? (2) Did geography and the domestic social and political order of states favor the offense or the defense? Did elites and publics believe they favored the offense or defense? (3) How numerous and powerful were balancer states, and how strongly did they balance? Did elites believe that other states would balance or bandwagon? (4) Did defensive alliances form, and did they operate effectively? Did elites believe that they operated effectively? I gave these factors the same rough relative weight they receive in standard historical accounts.

10. Bismarck formed defensive alliances with Austria, Italy, and Romania, and a more limited defensive accord with Russia—specifically, a reciprocal agreement not to join a war against the other unless the other attacked France (in the German case) or Austria (in the Russian case). . . .

11. Hitler's faith in the offensive differed from that of the pre-1914 cultists of the offensive in three ways. First, he saw offensive capabilities arising from a long search for offensive methods, not from permanent properties of war. In his mind offense could be created, but also had to be; Germany would discover offensive answers only after a long effort. In contrast, the pre-1914 cultists thought offense inherently easier than defense; deep thought need not be given to how to make it superior, because it already was. Second, Hitler's offensive optimism was based on racism and social prejudice, as well as on assessment of military factors. Specifically, his contempt for Slavs and Jews led him to expect that the Soviets would quickly collapse under German attack. Third, Hitler's concerns for German security focused on fear of conquest by economic strangulation, not conquest by French or Soviet blitzkrieg. He thought German security was precarious, but for reasons rooted more in the political economy of war than in the nature of doctrine or weaponry. These differences aside, the logical implications of Hitler's offensive cult were the same as those of the pre-1914 cult. He exaggerated both German insecurity and the feasibility of imperial solutions to redress it.

12. The fine-grained pattern of events during 1938–40—who attacked whom and when—also fits the predictions of offense–defense theory (specifically, prime prediction 3). The Western allies stood without attacking Germany in 1938 and again in 1939–40 because they doubted they could win a decisive victory. Germany stood without attacking westward in the fall of 1939 for the same reason, and finally attacked in May 1940 after German military leaders developed a plausible plan for decisive attack. . . .

13. France can be assigned prime responsibility for 1792 and 1859, and shared responsibility for Crimea and 1870. Russia deserves prime responsibility for the Cold War and shared responsibility for Crimea and the 1904–05 Russo-Japanese War.

14. Britain does share responsibility for the Crimean War with Russia, France, and Turkey.

15. Britain, France, Russia, and Prussia/Germany fought other great powers an average of five times over the same two hundred years, by my count. None fought as few as three times.

# 4

# Coercive Diplomacy

## ALEXANDER L. GEORGE

Coercive diplomacy, or coercive persuasion as some might prefer to call it, is not an esoteric concept. Intimidation of one kind or another in order to get others to comply with one's wishes is an everyday occurrence in human affairs. And what we refer to as coercive diplomacy has often been employed in the long history of international conflict, sometimes successfully and sometimes not. The general idea of coercive diplomacy is to back one's demand on an adversary with a threat of punishment for noncompliance that he will consider credible and potent enough to persuade him to comply with the demand. Hence, it should be noted, the abstract theory of coercive diplomacy assumes pure rationality on the part of the opponent—an ability to receive all relevant information, evaluate it correctly, make proper judgments as to the credibility and potency of the threat, and see that it is in his interest to accede to the demand made on him. The abstract theory of coercive diplomacy, therefore, does not take into account the possibility of mis-perception and miscalculation or that an opponent's "rationality" is affected by psychological variables and by values, culture, and tradition that may differ from those of the coercive state. These possibilities are of critical importance and must receive careful attention whenever policymakers attempt to devise a strategy of coercive diplomacy in a particular situation against a particular opponent.

## THE CONCEPT OF COERCIVE DIPLOMACY

First, we need to clarify how the concept of coercive diplomacy is being used in this study and to differentiate it from other ways threats are used as an instrument of policy.[1] In this study the term coercive diplomacy is restricted to *defen-*

*sive* uses of the strategy—that is, efforts to persuade an opponent to stop and/or undo an action he is already embarked upon. Of course coercive threats can also be employed aggressively to persuade a victim to give up something of value without putting up resistance. Such offensive uses of coercive threats are better designated by the term "blackmail strategy." Coercive diplomacy also needs to be distinguished from deterrence, a strategy that employs threats to dissuade an adversary from undertaking a damaging action in the future. In contrast, coercive diplomacy is a response to an encroachment already undertaken. The term "compellance," which Thomas Schelling introduced into the literature over twenty years ago, is often employed to encompass both coercive diplomacy and blackmail. I prefer not to use that term for two reasons. First, it is useful to distinguish, as compellance does not, between defensive and offensive uses of coercive threats. Second, the concept of compellance implies exclusive or heavy reliance on coercive threats to influence an adversary, whereas I wish to emphasize the possibility of a more flexible diplomacy that can employ noncoercive persuasion and accommodation as well as coercive threats.

Coercive diplomacy does indeed offer an alternative to reliance on military action. It seeks to *persuade* an opponent to cease his aggression rather than bludgeon him into stopping. In contrast to the blunt use of force to repel an adversary, coercive diplomacy emphasizes the use of threats to punish the adversary if he does not comply with what is demanded of him. If force is used in coercive diplomacy, it consists of an exemplary use of quite limited force to persuade the opponent to back down. By "exemplary" I mean the use of just enough force of an appropriate kind to demonstrate resolution to protect one's interests and to establish the credibility of one's determination to use more force if necessary.[2] Even a relatively small exemplary action (for example, President Kennedy's order to U.S. "civilian advisers" in Laos in April 1961 to put on their uniforms) can have a disproportionately large coercive impact if it is coupled with a credible threat of additional action. The strategy of coercive diplomacy, however, does not require use of exemplary actions. The crisis may be satisfactorily resolved without an exemplary use of force; or the strategy of coercive diplomacy may be abandoned in favor of full-scale military operations without a preliminary use of exemplary force.

In employing coercive diplomacy, which may already include nonmilitary sanctions, one gives the adversary an opportunity to stop or back off before one resorts to military operations. Notice that either of two demands can be made on the adversary. He may be asked merely to *stop* what he is doing; or he may be asked to *undo* what he has done—that is, to reverse what he has managed to accomplish. The first type of demand generally asks less of the opponent and may be easier to accomplish in a particular situation than the second type. The use of threats (and of exemplary use of limited force) should be closely coordinated with appropriate communications to the opponent. Therefore, signaling, bargaining, and negotiating are important dimensions of coercive diplomacy, though their roles vary in different crises.

Coercive diplomacy is an attractive strategy insofar as it offers the possibility of achieving one's objective in a crisis economically, with little or no bloodshed, fewer political and psychological costs, and often with less risk of unwanted escalation than does traditional military strategy. But for this very reason coercive diplomacy can be a beguiling strategy. Particularly leaders of militarily powerful countries may be tempted sometimes to believe that they can, with little risk, intimidate weaker opponents to give up their gains and their objectives. But, of course, the militarily weaker side may be strongly motivated by what is at stake and refuse to back down, in effect calling the bluff of the coercing power. The latter must then decide whether to back off, accept a compromise settlement, or escalate to the use of military force to gain its objective. In addition, as the case studies will illustrate, a powerful country may encounter other constraints, risks, and uncertainties in attempting to make effective use of the strategy.

## VARIANTS OF COERCIVE DIPLOMACY STRATEGY

The general concept of coercive diplomacy, I suggest, contains a number of "empty boxes" (i.e., variables) that policymakers must fill in when constructing a particular strategy of coercive diplomacy to apply in a specific situation. Policymakers must decide (1) what to demand of the opponent; (2) whether and how to create a sense of urgency for compliance with the demand; (3) whether and what kind of punishment to threaten for noncompliance; and (4) whether to rely solely on the threat of punishment or also to offer conditional inducements of a positive character to secure acceptance of the demand.

Depending on how policymakers deal with these four components of the general model, significantly different variants of the strategy are possible. Let us identify first those variants of the strategy that stem from differences in how the first three variables are formulated.

The starkest variant of the strategy includes all three ingredients of a full-fledged ultimatum. A classic ultimatum has three components: (1) a demand on the opponent; (2) a time limit or sense of urgency for compliance with the demand; and (3) a threat of punishment for noncompliance that is both credible to the opponent and sufficiently potent to impress upon him that compliance is preferable. An ultimatum, although the starkest variant of coercive diplomacy, is not necessarily the most effective. There are often reasons why an ultimatum may be inappropriate, infeasible, or even highly risky in a particular situation. . . .

When an explicit time limit is not set forth but a sense of real urgency is conveyed by other means, one may refer to this variant of the strategy as a "tacit" ultimatum, which is not, for that reason, necessarily less potent. Similarly, when the threat of punishment is not specifically set forth but nonetheless is credibly conveyed by actions, one may refer to this variant also as a tacit ultimatum. Forgoing the delivery of an explicit ultimatum, a state may prefer to convey the gist of it by some combination of military preparation and stern warning.

Let us turn now to other variants of coercive diplomacy in which one of the three components of an ultimatum is diluted or absent. One variant is the "try-and-see" approach. In this version of the strategy, only the first element of an ultimatum—a clear demand—is conveyed; the coercing power does not announce a time limit or convey a strong sense of urgency for compliance. Instead, it takes one limited coercive threat or action and waits to see whether it will suffice to persuade the opponent before threatening or taking another step. There are several versions of the try-and-see approach, as will be evident in some of the case studies.

Somewhat stronger in coercive impact, although still falling well short of the ultimatum, is the variant that relies on a "gradual turning of the screw." It differs from the try-and-see approach in that a threat to step up pressure gradually is conveyed at the outset and is carried out incrementally. At the same time, the gradual turning of the screw differs from the ultimatum in that it lacks a sense of time urgency for compliance and relies on the threat of a gradual, incremental increase in coercive pressure rather than threatening large escalation to strong, decisive military action if the opponent does not comply. In practice, the analytical distinction between try-and-see and turning of the screw may be blurred if the policymaker wavers or behaves inconsistently.

Several observations about these variants of coercive diplomacy will be made later. When an ultimatum or tacit ultimatum is simply not appropriate or feasible, or may be considered premature or too risky, a try-and-see or turning of the screw approach may be judged to fit better the domestic political-diplomatic-military configuration of the conflict situation. It should be noted that, as happened in some of our historical cases, policymakers may shift from one variant of coercive diplomacy to another.

Thus far we have presented distinctions among four different forms that the strategy of coercive diplomacy may take: the ultimatum, tacit ultimatum, try-and-see, and gradual turning of the screw variants. While such distinctions are useful for some purposes, it would be misleading to assume that the form of the strategy alone determines the likelihood of success. Certainly from a formalistic standpoint the ultimatum is a stronger, or starker, variant than the try-and-see approach. But the coercive impact of any form of the strategy and whether it will be effective depends on other factors.

## TWO LEVELS OF COMMUNICATION IN COERCIVE DIPLOMACY

It is important to recognize that coercive diplomacy often operates on two levels of communication: words and actions. In addition to what is said, significant nonverbal communication or signaling can occur via either military moves or political-diplomatic activities. Nonverbal communication often emerges from the structure and development of the situation. Coercive persuasion depends not merely or exclusively on whether all three components of a classic ultimatum are present in verbal messages to the opponent. The structure of the situation as it develops can enhance or weaken the impact of coercive threats. The actions taken or not taken during the crisis—for example, whether and what kind of military forces are deployed or alerted, whether the coercing power undertakes political and diplomatic preparations of the kind needed to carry out its threats of force— can reinforce verbal threats and make them more credible or can dilute and weaken the impact of even strong verbal threats.

Actions may reinforce strong words, or they may compensate for weak words when it is not possible or prudent to utter strong words. But, contrary to the conventional wisdom, actions do not always speak louder than words. However strong the actions, they may be perceived by the adversary as equivocal or as bluffs. Words, then, may be needed in some situations to clarify the meaning of the actions taken or to convey unalterable commitment and resolution. Similarly, of course, actions may be needed to avoid the possibility that threatening words may be dismissed as bluff.

We conclude, therefore, that the relationship between actions and words—the two levels of communication—is likely to be very important in employing the strategy of coercive diplomacy. But there is no single, simple way of stating what the relationship between words and actions must be to ensure the success of the strategy. Crises in which coercive diplomacy is employed are replete with opportunities for miscommunication and miscalculation. And this is another aspect of coercive diplomacy that can make it an elusive, problematical, and risky strategy.

## THE CARROT-AND-STICK APPROACH

The reader will have noted that the discussion of variants of coercive diplomacy thus far has focused exclusively, and much too narrowly, on the use of threats of punishment. We turn now to the fourth "empty box" or variable-component of the theory of coercive diplomacy—one that requires the policymaker to decide whether to rely solely on the threat of punishment or also to offer positive inducements. As in diplomacy more generally, the strategy of coercive diplomacy can use positive inducements and assurances as well as punitive threats to influence an adversary; when it does so it is often referred to as a strategy of "carrots and sticks." This approach greatly enhances the flexibility and adaptability of the strategy and gives the negotiation and bargaining dimensions of coercive diplomacy even greater prominence.

The policymaker must decide whether to rely exclusively or largely on the threat of punishment (as the United States and the United Nations coalition did in the Persian Gulf crisis) or also offer conditional positive inducements (as Kennedy finally did toward the end of the Cuban missile crisis). The carrot in such a strategy can be any of a variety of things the target of coercion values. And the magnitude and significance of the carrot can range from a seemingly trivial concession of a face-saving character to substantial concessions that bring about a settlement of the crisis through a genuine, balanced quid pro quo.

Whether coercive diplomacy will work in a particular case may depend on whether it relies solely on negative sanctions or combines threats with positive inducements and assurances. This point is of considerable practical as well as theoretical significance. Recognition that coercive diplomacy in principle can use a carrot-and-stick approach leaves open the question whether in practice the policymaker employing the strategy is willing or able to offer a positive inducement and, if so, to decide what conditional offer and concessions to make.

Nonetheless, the essential point remains: what the threatened stick cannot achieve by itself, unless it is a very formidable one, may possibly be achieved by combining it with a carrot. It should be said, too, that just as threats of punishment must be credible to the opponent, so must the positive inducements and reassurances offered be credible.

## THE CENTRAL TASK OF COERCIVE DIPLOMACY

Let us turn now to the central task of a coercive strategy: to create in the opponent the expectation of costs of sufficient magnitude to erode his motivation to continue what he is doing. As already noted, success may depend on whether the initial coercive action or threat stands alone or is part of a broader credible threat to escalate pressure further if necessary.

How much of a threat, or combination of threat with positive inducement, is necessary to persuade an opponent to comply? The abstract, general theory of coercive diplomacy tells us that the answer depends very much on two variables: what one demands of the opponent and how strongly disinclined he is to comply with that demand. Of course, these two variables are not independent of each other, and the relationship between them must receive the careful attention of the side that is employing a strategy of coercive diplomacy. The critical point to remember is that the strength of the opponent's motivation not to comply is highly dependent on what is demanded of him. Thus, asking relatively little of the opponent makes it easier for him to permit himself to be coerced. Conversely, demanding a great deal will strengthen an opponent's resistance and make the task of coercing him more difficult. Demanding a great deal may mean not only requiring an opponent to give up the material gains he has or is about to achieve but also requiring him to pay the often-substantial psychological and political costs of compliance with the demand. Also critical, of course, is the adversary's perception of the costs to him, which may be significantly greater than what the coercing power believes it is demanding.

The general, abstract theory correctly emphasizes that what is demanded of the opponent and his motivation to resist are closely related. As will be seen in the case studies, the outcome of coercive diplomacy is extremely sensitive to the relative motivations of the two sides. Motivation, in turn, reflects the way they perceive the balance of interests engaged by the dispute. Motivation here refers to each side's conception of what is at stake in the dispute, the importance it attaches to the various interests engaged by the crisis, and what costs and risks it is willing to incur on behalf of these interests. The choice of the demand made on the opponent, therefore, is of considerable importance in shaping the relative motivation of the two sides. Not only does the demand influence the level of the other side's motivation, as already noted; the motivation of the coercing power will also vary depending on the nature and magnitude of the demand it makes on the opponent. In other words, there is often an important strategic dimension to the choice of the objective on behalf of which coercive diplomacy is employed. Quite simply, it affects the motivation of both sides and the balance of motivation between them.

According to the logic of the abstract model of coercive diplomacy, it is more likely to be successful if the objective selected—and the demand made—by the coercing power reflects only the most important of its interests. Such a choice is more likely to create an asymmetry of interests, and therefore an asymmetry of motivation, in its favor. Conversely, if the coercing power pursues ambitious objectives that do not reflect its vital or very important interests or makes demands that infringe on vital or very important interests of the adversary, the asymmetry of interests and the balance of motivation is likely to operate in favor of the adversary. (The importance of asymmetry of motivation will be seen in several of the historical cases. For example, in the Cuban missile crisis President Kennedy limited his demand to removal of the missiles, an objective which he then succeeded in persuading Khrushchev was more important to the United States than it was to the Soviet Union. Had Kennedy chosen more ambitious objectives, as some of his advisers urged—the elimination of Castro or the removal of Soviet influence from Cuba—Khrushchev's motivation to resist would have been greater, and quite possibly the variable of relative motivation would have operated in his favor. That is, confronted by such demands, Khrushchev might have been willing to accept greater risks to prevent Kennedy from achieving those objectives than Kennedy would have been willing to accept to achieve them.)

The general theory emphasizes still another dimension of this central task of coercive diplomacy. It is not enough that the policymaker feel confident that he has conveyed a threat of punishment for noncompliance with his demand that is potent and credible enough to convince the opponent to comply. Rather, it is the *target's* estimate of the credibility and potency of the threat that is critical. As in so much of coercive diplomacy, many of the critical variables are psychological ones having to do with the perceptions and judgment of the target. The possibility of misperceptions and miscalculations by the opponent is ever present and can determine the outcome.

# 5

# International Terrorism

## BRIAN M. JENKINS

## INTRODUCTION

Terrorism appears to have increased markedly in the past few years. Political and criminal extremists in various parts of the world have attacked passengers in airline terminals and railway stations; planted bombs in government buildings, the offices of multinational corporations, pubs, and theatres; hijacked airliners and ships, even ferryboats in Singapore; held hundreds of passengers hostage; seized embassies; and kidnapped government officials, diplomats, and business executives. We read of new incidents almost daily. Terrorists may strike citizens of another country while they are living overseas, in transit from one country to another, or at home in their own country. Terrorism has become a new element in international relations.

## DEFINING TERRORISM

When we talk about terrorism, what exactly are we talking about? The word has no precise or widely accepted definition. One noted lawyer has defined terrorism as acts which in themselves may be classic forms of crime—murder, arson, the use of explosives—but which differ from classic criminal acts in that they are executed "with the deliberate intention of causing panic, disorder, and terror within an organized society, in order to destroy social discipline, paralyze the forces of reaction of a society, and increase the misery and suffering of the community." Two scholars in the United States have provided a somewhat broader definition of terrorism:

murder, assassination, sabotage and subversion, the destruction of public records, the spreading of rumor, the closing of churches, the sequestration of property, the breakdown of criminal law enforcement, the prostitution of the courts, the narcosis of the press—all these, as they contribute to a common end, constitute terror.

Without attempting to define terrorism in a way that will satisfy all lawyers and scholars, we may for the moment satisfy ourselves with the following description: the threat of violence, individual acts of violence, or a campaign of violence designed primarily to instill fear—to terrorize—may be called terrorism. Terrorism is violence for effect, not only, and sometimes not at all, for the effect on the actual victims of the terrorists. In fact, the victim may be totally unrelated to the terrorist's cause. Terrorism is violence aimed at the people watching. Fear is the intended effect, not the by-product of terrorism. That, at least, distinguishes terrorist tactics from mugging and other common forms of violent crime that may terrify but are not terrorism.

Those we call terrorists may include revolutionaries and other political extremists, criminals professing political aims, and a few authentic lunatics. Terrorists may operate alone or may be members of a large and well-organized group. Terrorists may even be government agents. Their cause may have extreme goals, such as the destruction of all government—in itself not a new idea—or their cause may be one that is comparatively reasonable and understandable—self-rule for a particular ethnic group. Or their motive may be purely personal—money or revenge. The ambition of terrorists may be limited and local—the overthrow of a particular regime—or they may be global—a simultaneous worldwide revolution. . . .

## THE THEORY OF TERRORISM

Terrorism is often described as *mindless* violence, *senseless* violence, or *irrational* violence. If we put aside the actions of a few authentic lunatics, terrorism is seldom mindless or irrational. There is a theory of terrorism, and it often works. To understand the theory, it must first be understood that terrorism is a means to an end, not an end in itself. In other words, terrorism has objectives, although those who carry out acts of terrorism may be so dedicated to violent action that even they sometimes seem to miss this point.

Unless we try to think like terrorists, we are also liable to miss the point, for the objectives of terrorism are often obscured by the fact that specific terrorist attacks may appear to be random, directed against targets whose death or destruction does not appear directly to benefit the terrorist's cause. . . . But the objectives of terrorism are not those of conventional combat. Terrorists do not try to take and hold ground or physically destroy their opponents' forces. Terrorists usually lack that kind of power, or having it, are constrained from applying it. We must be able to see beyond the apparent meaninglessness, sometimes even the tragic absurdity, of a single terrorist act to determine the objectives and the logic of terrorism.

While terrorists may kill, by our standards sometimes wantonly, and while they may threaten a lot of people, the objective of terrorism is *not* mass murder. *Terrorists want a lot of people watching and a lot of people listening, and not a lot of people dead.* A credible threat, a demonstration of the capacity to strike, may be from the terrorists' point of view often preferable to actually carrying out the threatened deed, which may explain why, apart from the technical difficulties involved, terrorists have not done some of the terribly damaging and terrifying things they could do, such as poisoning a city's water supply, spreading chemical or biological agents, or other things that could produce mass casualties.

## THE PURPOSES OF TERROR

Terrorists attempt to inspire and manipulate fear to achieve a variety of purposes. Terrorism may be aimed simultaneously at several objectives: specific tactical objectives, made explicit by the terrorists, and broader strategic objectives, which may be implicit in the choice of tactics or targets. First, individual acts of terrorism may be aimed at wringing specific concessions, such as the payment of ransom, the release of prisoners, or the publication of a terrorist message, under threat of death or destruction. Terrorists may seek to improve their bargaining power by creating a dramatic hostage situation and thereby coerce a government into fulfilling certain demands.

Secondly, terrorism may also be aimed at gaining publicity. Through terrorism, the terrorists hope to attract attention to their cause and project themselves as a force that merits recognition and that must be reckoned with. The publicity gained by frightening acts of violence and the atmosphere of fear and alarm created cause people to exaggerate the importance and strength of the terrorists and their movement. Since most terrorist groups are actually small and weak, the violence they carry out must be all the more dramatic and deliberately shocking. . . . Terrorism is aimed at the people watching, not at the actual victims. Terrorism is theatre. . . .

Thirdly, terrorism may be aimed at causing widespread disorder, at demoralizing society, and at breaking down the social order. This objective is typical of revolutionary, nihilistic, or anarchistic terrorists. Impatient at the reluctance of the "people"—on whose behalf the revolution is to be carried out—to join them, terrorists may reject society's normal rules and relationships as intolerable complacency. If the benefits of political obedience are destroyed; if the complacency of uninvolvement is not allowed; if the government's ability to protect its citizens (which is after all the origin and most basic reason for the existence of government) is demonstrated to be ineffectual; if the government can be made to strike back brutally but blindly; and if there is no place to hide in the ensuing battle, then, it is presumed, the "people" will join the opponents of that government and a revolution will be carried out. Such a strategy often backfires. With no immunity from random terrorist violence, even sympathizers may turn against the terrorist violence, and the terrorists, and support the government's moves to destroy them.

Fourthly, terrorism may be aimed at deliberately provoking repressions, reprisals, and counterterrorism, which may ultimately lead to the collapse of an unpopular government. In the past, such terrorism has frequently been directed against government security and law-enforcement personnel, but there are also examples of deliberately outrageous acts, the kidnapping of a foreign diplomat for example, or random violence against civilians designed to embarrass a government and compel it to react with a heavy hand. The government may thus be induced by the terrorists into a course leading to self-destruction.

Fifthly, terrorism may also be used to enforce obedience and cooperation. This is the usual purpose of state or official terrorism, or what is frequently called "institutional violence," but terrorists themselves may also employ institutional violence against their own members to ensure their loyalty. The outcome desired by the terrorists in this case is a prescribed pattern of behavior: obedience to the state or to the cause, and full cooperation in identifying and rooting out infiltrators or enemies. The success of such terrorism again depends on the creation of an atmosphere of fear, reinforced by the seeming omnipresence of the internal security apparatus. As in other forms of terrorism, terrorism which is aimed at enforcing obedience contains elements of deliberate drama: defectors are abducted or mysteriously assassinated; dissidents are arrested at midnight; people disappear; and stories (often real) spread of dungeons, concentration camps, and torture. And as in other forms of terrorism, the objective is the effect all this has on the target audience. However, enforcement terrorism seldom chooses victims at random and does not seek widespread publicity, especially at the international level.

Sixthly, terrorism is frequently meant to punish. Terrorists often declare that the victim of their attack, whether person or object, is somehow guilty, or is the symbol of something the terrorists consider guilty. A person may be judged guilty because he has committed some crime himself—actively opposed, disobeyed, or informed upon the terrorists—or because he has tacitly cooperated with a guilty party. "Cooperated" is often interpreted rather broadly to mean that the individual worked for, tacitly supported, accepted a visa from, or travelled on the national carrier of an enemy government. Victims of terrorists also have been chosen because their success in business or their lifestyle represented a system despised by the terrorists. Objects or buildings have been destroyed because they were symbols of a despised government, institution, or system. . . .

Thus, while the leading effect of terrorism is fear and alarm, terrorism may be employed to accomplish a variety of objectives: specific concessions, widespread publicity for the terrorists and their cause, the dissolution of social norms, the provoking of repression, obedience to an organization or its cause, and the punishment of those considered guilty by the terrorists. A single episode may be aimed at accomplishing several of these objectives simultaneously. Terrorism may be an instrument of government as well as a tactic of revolutionary and other antigovernment forces.

## INDISCRIMINATE OR SELECTIVE VIOLENCE

Terrorism may appear to be either indiscriminate or highly selective. Violence that appears totally and deliberately indiscriminate—that is, attacks which appear to be directed at random against civilian bystanders innocent of any involvement on either side of the struggle being carried on by the terrorists—is frequently called *pure terrorism*. The massacre of passengers at the Lod Airport in Israel, whatever the terrorists said later about their being guilty by simply being there, and the bombing of the Tower of London in which a number of tourists were killed or injured, closely approached pure terrorism. Pure terrorism is a cynical but rather effective means of attracting attention and of creating alarm. It is also difficult to protect against.

Very few acts of terrorism, however, are meant by the terrorists to appear indiscriminate. Terrorists normally want to appear selective. They may assassinate particular leaders, perhaps even forewarning their victims or potential victims with the publication of a death list, thus instilling terror among those named but still living. Or terrorists may strike only the members of a selected group, policemen for example, or village chiefs.

While indiscriminate violence may produce greater fear and alarm among the general population, selective but unpredictable attacks may cause greater alarm within the selected group. Sometimes terrorists may be selective in choosing actual physical targets—government buildings or the airliners of a specific national carrier, for example—but they are not particularly concerned about who may be killed during the actual attack or bombing, and thus their violence appears indiscriminate.

## DEFINING INTERNATIONAL TERRORISM

The problem of defining international terrorism is complicated by international politics. Apart from a few categories of incidents that most nations have agreed to call international terrorism—airliner hijacking or the kidnapping of diplomats, for example—few nations agree on what international terrorism is. The most simple definition of international terrorism comprises acts of terrorism that have clear international consequences: incidents in which terrorists go abroad to strike their targets, select victims or targets because of their connections to a foreign state (diplomats, local executives, or officers of foreign corporations), attack airliners in international flights, or force airliners to fly to another country. International terrorism would not include the local activities of dissident groups when carried out against a local government or citizens in their own country if no foreign connection is involved.

International terrorism may also be defined as acts of violence or campaigns of violence waged outside the accepted rules and procedures of international diplomacy and war. Breaking the rules may include attacking diplomats and other internationally protected persons, attacking international travel and commerce, or exporting violence by various means to nations that normally would not, under the traditional rules, be considered participants in the local conflict.

International terrorism in this sense is violence against the "system," waged outside the "system." Therefore, the rules of the "system" do not apply. For example, most other forms of warfare, at least in theory, recognize categories of civilians who are not directly engaged in the struggle—women and children, for example—and who therefore are not targets of violence. Terrorists recognize far fewer immune civilians. Terrorists may regard a person as an enemy, and therefore a target, solely on the basis of nationality, ethnicity, or religion. Or a person can become a target by mere chance—by watching a movie in a theatre when a bomb goes off, or by passing through an airport waiting room when passengers are machine-gunned. This is not to say that people we call terrorists are always indiscriminate killers, or that groups we call armies are always scrupulously discriminating; but exceptions do not invalidate our definition—they simply compel us to recognize that soldiers may sometimes be terrorists. Indeed, a number of bombing campaigns undertaken by both sides during the Second World War and in subsequent wars—for example, the bombing of targets that in themselves had little military value to the enemy but were struck primarily to punish, to shock, to cause alarm, and to create disorder among the population of the enemy state—could qualify as terrorism under our definition of that term.

According to this definition, we could say that international terrorism, as employed recently by revolutionary and other dissident groups, is a new kind of warfare. It is warfare without territory, waged without armies as we know them. It is warfare that is not limited territorially: sporadic "battles" may take place worldwide. It is warfare without neutrals, and with few or no civilian innocent bystanders. . . .

In sum, what is called international terrorism may refer broadly to any terrorist violence that has international repercussions; or to acts of violence which are outside the accepted norms of international diplomacy and rules of war. It may refer to a narrow set of acts which have been specifically identified and outlawed by international agreements; or, finally, it may refer to a collection of different definitions proposed by various national governments. . . .

## NEW TARGETS AND NEW CAPABILITIES

Terrorism is not new, but a number of technical developments have made terrorism a more potent—and to groups that lack other means of applying power, an attractive—means of struggle. Progress has provided terrorists with new targets and new capabilities. Jet air travel furnishes unprecedented mobility and with it the ability to strike anywhere in the world. New weapons, including powerful explosives and sophisticated timing and detonating devices, are increasing terrorists' capacity for violence. The most ominous recent development is the discovery of Soviet hand-held, heat-seeking, ground-to-air missiles in the hands of terrorists near the Rome airport.

Recent developments in news broadcasting—radio, television, communication satellites—are also a boon to publicity-seeking terrorists. The willingness and capability of the news media to report and broadcast dramatic incidents of violence throughout the world enhances and may even encourage terrorism as an effective means of propaganda. Terrorists may now be assured that their actions will receive immediate worldwide coverage on radio, on television, and in the press. The world is now their stage. The whole world is probably watching.

This historical trend is important. The vulnerabilities inherent in a modern society increasingly dependent on its technology afford terrorists opportunities to create greater disruption than in the past. These increasing vulnerabilities in our society plus the increasing capacities for violence afforded by new developments in weaponry mean that smaller and smaller groups have a greater and greater capacity for disruption and destruction. Or, put another way, the small bands of extremists and irreconcilables that have always existed may become an increasingly potent force.

## "SIMULTANEOUS REVOLUTION" OR SURROGATE WARFARE

What direction will terrorism take in the future? While it is incorrect to speak of terrorism in terms of an international conspiracy, as if all terrorists in the world were members of a single organization, it is apparent that links are increasing between terrorists in various parts of the world. . . .

The growing links between terrorist groups are extremely important. They provide small terrorist organizations with the resources to undertake far more serious operations than they would be capable of otherwise. They make identification more difficult, since local citizens can be used to carry out attacks; and they could ultimately produce some kind of worldwide terrorist movement directed against some group of countries for vague ideological, political, or economic reasons, a concept that has been referred to by some terrorists as "simultaneous revolution."

A second possible trend is in the direction of more extravagant and destructive acts made possible by the creation of new vulnerabilities and new weapons, and made necessary as the public and governments become bored with what terrorists do now. There are many new vulnerabilities. One that has received a great deal of public attention lately is nuclear power. The probable proliferation of nuclear-power facilities in the next few decades, and the amount of traffic in fissionable material and radioactive waste that will accompany this, raises a number of new possibilities for political extortion and mass hostage situations on a scale that we have not yet seen.

At the same time, technological advances are creating a new range of small, portable, cheap, relatively easy to operate, highly accurate, and highly destructive weapons which, if produced on a large scale, will undoubtedly find their way into the hands of terrorists. . . .

On the other hand, terrorist violence may be self-limiting in the sense that terrorists depend to a degree on the support of some constituency or the toleration of at least some governments. Too much violence could provoke harsh reactions and greater international cooperation against the terrorists.

A third possible trend is that national governments will recognize the achievements of terrorist groups and begin to employ them or their tactics as a means of surrogate warfare against other nations. . . . Terrorism, though now rejected as a legitimate mode of warfare by most conventional military establishments, could become an accepted form of warfare in the future. Terrorists could be employed to provoke international incidents, create alarm in an adversary's country, compel it to divert valuable resources to protect itself, destroy its morale, and carry out specific acts of sabotage. Governments could employ existing terrorist groups to attack their opponents, or they could create their own terrorists. Terrorism only requires a small investment, certainly far less than what it costs to wage conventional war. It can be debilitating to the enemy. . . .

Where does this take us? The primary purpose of government in whatever form is to provide security for its citizens. If governments cannot protect their citizens, as terrorists seem to be demonstrating, will governments as we know them become obsolete? The historical growth of national governments in the first place depended in part on national leadership, often a monarch, being able to monopolize the means of organized violence. If the military-power relationships are altered drastically in favor of small groups that obey no government, will we enter an era of international warlordism in which the people of the world and their governments are subjected to the extortion demands of many small groups? Or, in the face of growing terrorism and the threat of worldwide anarchy, will governments fall to the temptation of repression and use their still comparatively superior technical resources to become increasingly authoritarian? Or will governments put aside their political differences on this issue and delegate some of their jealously guarded sovereignty to an international force capable of dealing with international terrorists? Or will governments simply accept new concepts of warfare as redefined by terrorists, adopt their tactics to wage war against another nation, and take direct military action against enemy terrorists wherever they are?

# 6

# The Unimpressive Record
# of Atomic Diplomacy

## McGeorge Bundy

In addressing the question of the role of nuclear weapons in diplomacy, it is well to begin with an expression of one's own general position on the nuclear problem. My view of these weapons is that for my own country they are a necessary evil. I do not think it acceptable for the United States to renounce the possession of nuclear capabilities while they are maintained in the Soviet Union. In that most basic sense I accept the need for nuclear deterrence and am unimpressed by arguments that neglect this requirement. . . .

I also believe that not all the consequences of the nuclear arsenals are bad. The very existence of nuclear stockpiles has created and enforced a considerable caution in the relations among nuclear-weapon states, so that where the interests of those states are clear and their political and military engagement manifest, as with the Soviet Union and the United States in Eastern and Western Europe respectively, there is an intrinsic inhibition on adventure which is none the less real for being essentially independent of doctrines—and even of nuclear deployments—on either side. I have elsewhere called this phenomenon "existential deterrence,"[1] and I think it has more to do with the persisting peace—and division—of Europe than all the particular nuclear doctrines and deployments that have so often bedeviled the European scene. . . .

Indeed the acceptance of nuclear deterrence, for me as for the American Catholic bishops, is "strictly conditioned," not only on a constant readiness to move to agreed arms reductions as drastic as the most skillful and dedicated negotiations permit, but also on a reluctance to depend on nuclear weapons for purposes beyond that of preventing nuclear war. On the historical record since

Nagasaki, I think that these weapons have not been of great use to any government for such wider purposes, and I also think a misreading of that record has led to grossly mistaken judgments and to unnecessary, costly, and sometimes dangerous nuclear deployments by both superpowers, and perhaps by others. Let us begin by considering what good these weapons have done the United States, which was their first and for a short four years their only possessor. I am willing to concede, though it cannot be proven, that in the years of American monopoly, and perhaps for a short time thereafter (in my view, not beyond 1955, at the latest) American nuclear superiority had some military and political value in Europe. We must recognize that fear of what the Russians would otherwise do with what was then an enormous advantage in conventional strength was not limited to Winston Churchill. Niels Bohr too believed that the American atomic bomb was a necessary balancing force, and so did many other highly peaceable men. But the time has long since passed when either side could hope to enjoy either monopoly or overwhelming superiority, so from the standpoint of the present and the future it is not necessary to challenge this particular bit of conventional wisdom. We do not really know that the American monopoly saved Europe in the early postwar years, but we do not know it did not, and we need not decide.

What is more interesting is to examine these years of evident American nuclear advantage from another angle, to try to see what usefulness that advantage may have had in supporting American diplomacy or in restraining specific adventures of others outside Western Europe. Aside from this debatable European case, there is very little evidence that American atomic supremacy was helpful in American diplomacy. Broadly speaking, the years from 1945 to 1949 were a time in which Soviet power and the power of such major Soviet allies as the Chinese communists was expanding and consolidating itself at a rate not remotely equaled since then, and there is no evidence whatever that fear of the American bomb had any restraining effect on this enormous process. It is true that for a short time in the autumn of 1945 Secretary of State James Byrnes believed that the silent presence of the bomb might constructively affect Soviet behavior at the negotiating table, but in fact it had no such impact, and before the end of the year Byrnes himself had changed his tactics. The importance of this brief and foolish flirtation with atomic diplomacy has been grossly exaggerated by students misreading a marginal and passing state of mind into a calculated effort in which Hiroshima itself is read largely as an effort to impress the Russians.[2] But this misreading is less important than the deeper point that to whatever degree atomic diplomacy may have tempted this or that American leader at this or that moment in those years, it did not work.

The point becomes still more evident when we look at moments which American presidents themselves, in later years, came to see as evidence of the power of the atomic possibility. The two most notable cases are the Soviet withdrawal from Iran in 1946 and the armistice agreement that ended the Korean War in 1953.

In April 1952 President Harry Truman told an astonished press conference that not long after the end of World War II he had given Joseph Stalin "an ultimatum"—to get his troops out of Iran—and "they got out." Truman was referring to events in March 1946, when the Soviet Union kept troops in northern Iran after the expiration of an agreed date for British and Russian withdrawal that had been honored by the British. The Soviet stance stirred a vigorous international reaction, and after three weeks of increasing tension there came a Soviet announcement of a decision to withdraw that was executed over the following weeks. Truman never doubted that his messages had been decisive. Out of office, in 1957, he described his action still more vividly: "The Soviet Union persisted in its occupation until I personally saw to it that Stalin was informed that I had given orders to our military chiefs to prepare for the movement of our ground, sea and air forces. Stalin then did what I knew he would do. He moved his troops out." If this statement were accurate, it would be an extraordinary confirmation of the effectiveness of American threats in the age of atomic monopoly, because a troop movement of this sort, in 1946, into an area so near the Soviet Union and so far from the United States could only have been ventured, or feared, because of the nuclear monopoly.[3]

The only trouble with this picture is that no such message ever went to Stalin and no such orders to American officers. What actually happened is wholly different. Stalin did indeed attempt to gain a special position in Iran by keeping his troops beyond the deadline, but what made his effort a failure was not an ultimatum from Truman but primarily the resourceful resistance of the Iranian government, supported indeed by American diplomacy (especially at the United Nations) and still more by a wide and general international reaction. Stalin's was a low-stake venture in an area of persistent Soviet hope. He pulled back when he found the Iranian government firm but not belligerent, his Iranian supporters weak, and the rest of the watching world critical. One of the critics was Harry Truman, and we need not doubt the strength of his feelings. But the messages he actually sent (all now published) were careful and genuinely diplomatic. The United States Government "cannot remain indifferent," and "expresses the earnest hope" of immediate Soviet withdrawal, all "in the spirit of friendly association." There is no deadline and no threat. What we have here is no more than an understandable bit of retrospective braggadocio. As George Kennan later remarked—he had been *chargé d'affaires* in Moscow at the time and was the man who would have had to deliver any ultimatum—Truman "had an unfortunate tendency to exaggerate, in later years, certain aspects of the role that he played" in relations with Stalin.[4]

Regrettably, Truman's retrospective version of events was not harmless. Among stouthearted and uncomplicated anticommunists it became a part of the folklore showing that Harry Truman knew how to stop aggression by toughness, when in fact what he and his colleagues knew, in this case, was something much more important: that their task was to help keep up Iranian courage, but precisely *not* to confront Stalin directly. American diplomacy was adroit but not menacing, and Kennan is right again in describing the result: "It was enough for Stalin to learn that a further effort by the Soviet Union to retain its forces in Persia would create serious international complications. He had enough problems at the moment without that." Truman's messages had certainly helped in this learning process, and not least because they had expressly avoided the kind of threat he later came to believe he made. So his faulty memory led others to learn the wrong lesson.

Dwight Eisenhower contributed even more than Harry Truman to the folklore of atomic diplomacy. He believed that it was the threat of atomic war that brought an armistice in Korea in 1953. In his memoirs he cited a number of warnings and signals to make his case, and his Secretary of State, John Foster Dulles, told allied statesmen in private a lurid tale of nuclear deployments made known to the Chinese. But here again the historical record raises questions. The decisive shift in the position of the communists, a shift away from insistence on the forced repatriation of prisoners, occurred before any of these signals was given, shortly after the death of Stalin in March. While Eisenhower certainly intended the whiff of nuclear danger to reach Peking, the records now available make it clear that he in fact held back from any audible threat because of his recognition that it would be as divisive in 1953 as it had been in 1950, when Harry Truman, by a casual press conference response to a question on the possibility of using nuclear weapons, had brought Prime Minister Attlee across the Atlantic to receive assurance that no such step was in prospect. Quite aside from any nuclear threat, there were other and excellent reasons in 1953 for the communist side to want to end the war: their own heavy losses, the absence of any prospect for further gains, and the continuing high cost of unsuccessful probes of United Nations forces on the ground. At the most the springtime signals of a nuclear possibility were a reinforcement to Chinese preferences already established before those signals were conveyed.

Yet Eisenhower clearly did believe that the Korean case showed the value of nuclear threats, and indeed he and Dulles made the threat permanent in the language of a public declaration after the armistice that those who had supported South Korea would respond to any renewed aggression in ways that might not be limited. In two later crises, over the offshore islands of Quemoy and Matsu in 1955 and 1958, Eisenhower used both open references to nuclear weapons and visible deployments of nuclear-armed forces to underline the risks Mao was running. What actually held off the attacking Chinese forces, in both crises, was not these threats but the effective use of local air and naval superiority, but it cannot be denied that the nuclear possibility may have contributed to Chinese unwillingness to raise the stakes. It is also possible that the readiness of the United States to help defend these small and unimportant islands was increased by the fact that against China the United States then held a nuclear monopoly.

In this case too the threat was almost as alarming to friends as to opponents. Fully aware of the fiercely divisive consequences of any actual use of a nuclear weapon, Eisenhower devoted himself in these crises to the energetic and skillful support of the conventional forces and tactics which fended off the Chinese attacks. He was very careful indeed not to lose his control over the nuclear choice, either by any unconditional public threat or by a delegation of authority. The nuclear reply remained a possibility, not a policy. As he told Nixon in 1958, "You should never let the enemy know what you will not do." In the offshore islands affair as in Korea, Eisenhower kept the use of nuclear weapons as something the enemy could not know he would not do, and believed he gained from this stance.[5]

But the President was teaching his Vice President a lesson that was going out of date even as he explained it. The offshore islands crisis of 1958, so far from being a model for the future, turns out to be the last case we have of a crisis between the United States and a nation not the Soviet Union in which nuclear weapons or threats of their use play any role whatever. Consider the war in Vietnam. Here the president whose inaction proves the point conclusively is the same Richard Nixon who had been Eisenhower's eager student. Nixon came to the White House in 1969 determined to apply to Hanoi the same techniques of credible threat that he thought he had seen used successfully in Korea. If he had continued to believe a nuclear threat would be credible, he would surely have conveyed it. But once he considered the matter carefully he was forced to recognize that there was in reality no way of making a credible nuclear threat because the men in Hanoi knew as well as he did that no American president, by 1969, could in fact have used nuclear weapons in Indochina. To do so would plainly outrage allies and split his own country in half. What you cannot conceivably execute, you cannot plausibly threaten.[6]

The evolution from what Eisenhower believed in 1958 to what Nixon was forced to recognize in 1969 is extraordinarily important, and not all the reasons for it are clear. One of them certainly is the spreading awareness of the danger inherent in the thermonuclear age. The end of the 1950s saw the first large-scale popular reactions to nuclear danger, and the searing experience of the Cuban Missile Crisis gave the threat of nuclear warfare new meaning. More broadly, if less consciously, men had come to believe more and more strongly in the value and importance of respecting the "firebreak" between conventional and nuclear weapons. In September 1964, President Lyndon Johnson had stated the case with characteristic passion and force during his campaign against Barry Goldwater:

Make no mistake. There is no such thing as a conventional nuclear weapon. For nineteen peril-filled years no nation has loosed the atom against another. To do so now is a political decision of the highest order. And it would lead us down an uncertain path of blows and counterblows whose outcome none may know.[7]

To all these general considerations one must add that by 1969 the morality of the Vietnam War was a profoundly divisive question in the United States. To resort to nuclear weapons in such a war would be to outrage still further the angry opponents of the war and probably to multiply their numbers.

So what Richard Nixon thought he had learned turned out only ten years later not to be so, and by his own wise refusal to present a nuclear threat to Hanoi he reinforced the very tradition whose strength he had not at first understood. If the United States could not threaten the use of nuclear weapons even in such a long and painful contest as Vietnam, in what case was such a threat possible? The answer, today, on all the evidence, is that the only places where a nuclear threat remains remotely plausible are those where it has been present for decades—in Western Europe and in Korea, because of the special historical connections noted above, and much more diffusely and existentially in the general reality that any prospect of direct confrontation between the United States and the Soviet Union presents nuclear risks which enforce caution.

A stronger proposition may be asserted. International support for the maintenance of the nuclear firebreak now operates not only to make nuclear threats largely ineffective, but also to penalize any government that resorts to them. This rule applies as much to the Soviet Union as to the United States. The Soviet government, in the heyday of Nikita Khrushchev, set international records for nuclear bluster. The favorite target was the United Kingdom, not only in the Suez crisis but more generally. Khrushchev clearly believed that his rockets gave him a politically usable superiority and talked accordingly. Yet in fact Soviet threats were not decisive at Suez; they were not even issued until what really was decisive—American opposition to the adventure—had been clear for several days. By 1957 Soviet reminders of British vulnerability, so logical from the point of view of believers in the political value of atomic superiority, were serving only to strengthen the Macmillan government in its determination to maintain and improve its own deterrent. The Soviet triumph in launching Sputnik did indeed help Soviet prestige, but attempts to capitalize on it by crude threats were unproductive.

Still more striking is the failure of Soviet atomic diplomacy in relation to China. Having first made the enormous mistake of helping the Chinese toward nuclear weapons, the Soviets reversed their field at the end of the 1950s and addressed themselves assiduously, but with no success whatever, to an effort to persuade the Chinese that they would be happier without any nuclear weapons of their own. Neither cajolery nor the withdrawal of assistance was effective. Probably nothing could have changed the Chinese purpose, but Soviet unreliability only intensified it, and at no time before the first Chinese explosion in 1964 was the Kremlin prepared to make the matter one of war or peace. By the time that possibility was actively considered, in 1969, the Chinese bomb was a reality requiring caution. In a limited but crucial way the Chinese themselves now had an existential deterrent.

But of course Khrushchev's greatest adventure in atomic diplomacy was also his worst fiasco: the deployment of missiles to Cuba in 1962. It is not clear yet how he hoped to gain from the adventure, but he must have believed that placing these weapons in Cuba would produce advantages of some sort. Whether they were there to be bargained against concessions in Europe, or to demonstrate Soviet will and American impotence, or to establish a less uneven strategic balance, we cannot know. That they were there merely to be traded for a pledge against a U.S. invasion of Cuba we must doubt. Nor need we linger on the fact of the failure.

What deserves attention is rather that in this most important crisis of all we can see clearly three persistent realities. First, it was not what the weapons could actually do but the political impact of the deployment that counted most to both sides; second, both leaders understood that any nuclear exchange would be a personal, political, and national catastrophe; third, as a consequence the determinant of the crisis must be in the level of will and ability to act by less than nuclear means. While this set of propositions does not of itself justify President Kennedy's course, it does make clear the folly of Khrushchev's: He left himself open to the use of conventional superiority by an opponent for whom the choice of inaction was politically impossible. I recognize that many students have asserted the commanding importance of U.S. nuclear superiority in the Cuban Missile Crisis, but I am deeply convinced that they are wrong. Along with five other senior members of the Kennedy administration, including Dean Rusk and Robert McNamara, I am convinced that the missile crisis illustrates "not the significance but the insignificance of nuclear superiority in the face of survivable thermonuclear retaliatory forces."[8]

The missile crisis had powerful and lasting consequences for the notion of atomic diplomacy. It showed the world that both great governments had a profound lack of enthusiasm for nuclear war, and in so doing it reduced the plausibility of nuclear threats of any kind. It also increased the political costs of such posturing. Even before 1962 Khrushchev had learned to try to couch his threats in relatively civil terms—of course I don't want to crush you, but it's only sensible to note that I can.[9] In October 1962, it was precisely nuclear war that both sides plainly chose to stay clear of, and the world took note. Since that time there has been no open nuclear threat by any government. I think it is not too much to say that this particular type of atomic diplomacy has been permanently discredited.

Even the very occasional use of nuclear signals in a crisis has had low importance in recent decades. The most notable case available is the short alert called in President Nixon's name on October 24, 1973, at the height of Yom Kippur war for the purpose of deterring unilateral Soviet action. This alert, by Henry Kissinger's authoritative account, was intended as a general show of resolution and in no way as a specifically thermonuclear threat. More significantly still, Kissinger's account makes it clear that the alert was unnecessary. The possibility of a unilateral Soviet troop movement to Egypt was effectively blocked by

Sadat's overnight decision, before he ever heard of the U.S. alert, to back away from the Soviet proposals.

In recent years there has been one remarkable revival of the notion of atomic diplomacy, together with an equally remarkable demonstration of its lack of content. The revival occurred among frightened American hawks eager to demonstrate that the Soviet nuclear build-up of the 1970s was conferring on Moscow a level of superiority that would inescapably translate into usable political leverage. In its most dramatic form the argument was that the Russians were getting a superiority in large, accurate ICBMs that would soon allow them to knock out our own ICBMs and defy us to reply for fear of annihilation. This was the famous "window of vulnerability," and the argument was that this kind of strategic superiority, because both sides would be aware of it, would make the Soviet Union's political pressures irresistible around the world. It was all supposed to happen before now—in the early 1980s. The argument was riddled with analytical errors, ranging from the oversimplification of the problems of such an attack through the much too facile assumption that no credible reply could be offered, and on to the quite untested notion that a threat of this kind would have useful results for the threat-maker. It is not at all surprising that history has shown the notion empty. There has been no Soviet action anywhere that can be plausibly attributed to the so-called window of vulnerability, and indeed after riding this wave of fear—and others—into the White House, the Reagan administration eventually managed to discover that the window did not exist. First, in the spring of 1983, the Scowcroft Commission concluded that the existing capabilities of American forces, taken as a whole, made such a scenario implausible, and in early 1984 Ronald Reagan himself concluded that we are all safer now because "America is back—standing tall," though out there in the real world the strategic balance remains almost exactly the one which led to the foolish fears in the first place. The notion of a new vulnerability to nuclear diplomacy was unreal; perhaps we were dealing instead with a little atomic politics. . . .

My general moral is a simple one. The more we learn about living with nuclear arsenals, the less we are able to find any good use for them but one—the deterrence of nuclear aggression by others—and the more we are led to the conclusion that this one valid and necessary role is not nearly as demanding as the theorists of countervailing strategy assert. No sane government wants nuclear war, and the men in the Kremlin, brutal and cynical tyrants to be sure, are eminently sane. . . .

**NOTES**

1. McGeorge Bundy, "The Bishops and the Bomb," *New York Review of Books*, June 16, 1983.

2. The case for the prosecution was presented by Gar Alperowitz in *Atomic Diplomacy: Hiroshima and Potsdam* (New York, 1956). His thesis has not fared well under

analysis by more careful historians, many themselves revisionists—see, e.g., Barton J. Bernstein, ed., *The Atomic Bomb: The Critical Issues* (Boston, 1976), 69–71.

3 Truman's press conference is in the *Public Papers of the Presidents* (1952), at pages 290–96. His 1957 remarks appeared in the *New York Times*, August 25, 1957, and are quoted in Stephen S. Kaplan, *Diplomacy of Power: Soviet Armed Forces as a Political Instrument* (Washington, D.C.: Brookings Institute, 1981), 70–71.

4. Truman's message of March 6 is printed in part in his own *Memoirs, II, Years of Trial and Hope* (Garden City, New York, 1956), 94–95, and is available also now in *Foreign Relations of the United States* (1946), 7: 340–43. The whole episode is covered with great clarity in Bruce R. Kuniholm, *The Origins of the Cold War in the Near East: Great Power Conflict and Diplomacy in Iran, Turkey and Greece* (Princeton, N.J.: Princeton University Press, 1980), 304–37. Kennan's later remark and the one quoted below are in a letter to Kuniholm printed at page 321.

5. Eisenhower to Nixon is in Richard Nixon, *The Real War* (New York, 1980), 255.

6. Nixon's recognition that he could not use nuclear weapons in Vietnam is described in his *Memoirs* at page 347.

7. *Public Papers of the Presidents, 1963–4*, 2: 1051.

8. See "The Lessons of the Cuban Missile Crisis," *Time*, September 27, 1982, 85.

9. For a good example of this sort of thing, see Adam Ulam, *Expansion and Coexistence*, 2nd ed. (New York, 1974), 612.

# 7

# The Utility of
# Nuclear Deterrence

ROBERT JERVIS

Perhaps the most striking characteristic of the postwar world is just that—it can be called "postwar" because the major powers have not fought each other since 1945. Such a lengthy period of peace among the most powerful states is unprecedented. Almost as unusual is the caution with which each superpower has treated the other. Although we often model superpower relations as a game of chicken, in fact the United States and USSR have not behaved like reckless teenagers. Indeed, superpower crises are becoming at least as rare as wars were in the past. Unless one strains and counts 1973, we have gone over a quarter of a century without a severe crisis. Furthermore, in those that have occurred, each side has been willing to make concessions to avoid venturing too near the brink of war. Thus the more we see of the Cuban missile crisis, the more it appears as compromise rather than an American victory. Kennedy was not willing to withhold all inducements and push the Russians as hard as he could if this required using force or even continuing the volatile confrontation.

It has been common to attribute these effects to the existence of nuclear weapons. Because neither side could successfully protect itself in an all-out war, no one could win—or, to use John Mueller's phrase, profit from it. Of course this does not mean that wars will not occur. It is rational to start a war one does not expect to win (to be more technical, whose expected utility is negative), if it is believed that the likely consequences of not fighting are even worse.[1] War could also come through inadvertence, loss of control, or irrationality. But if decision makers are "sensible," peace is the most likely outcome. Furthermore, nuclear weapons can explain superpower caution. When the cost of seeking

**94**

excessive gains is an increased probability of total destruction, moderation makes sense.

Some analysts have argued that these effects either have not occurred or are not likely to be sustained in the future. Thus Fred Iklé is not alone in asking whether nuclear deterrence can last out the century.[2] It is often claimed that the threat of all-out retaliation is credible only as a response to the other side's all-out attack: Thus Robert McNamara agrees with more conservative analysts whose views he usually does not share that the "sole purpose" of strategic nuclear force "is to deter the other side's first use of its strategic forces."[3] At best, then, nuclear weapons will keep the nuclear peace, they will not prevent—and, indeed, may even facilitate—the use of lower levels of violence. It is then not surprising that some observers attribute Soviet adventurism, particularly in Africa, to the Russians' ability to use the nuclear stalemate as a shield behind which they can deploy pressure, military aid, surrogate troops, and even their own forces in areas they had not previously controlled. The moderation mentioned earlier seems, to some, to be only one-sided. Indeed, American defense policy in the past decade has been driven by the felt need to create limited nuclear options to deter Soviet incursions that, while deeply menacing to our values, fall short of threatening immediate destruction of the United States.

Furthermore, while nuclear weapons may have helped keep the peace between the United States and the USSR, ominous possibilities for the future are hinted at by other states' experiences. Allies of nuclear-armed states have been attacked: Vietnam conquered Cambodia and China attacked Vietnam. Two nuclear powers have fought each other, albeit on a very small scale: Russia and China skirmished on their common border. A nonnuclear power has even threatened the heartland of a nuclear power: Syria nearly pushed Israel off the Golan Heights in 1973 and there was no reason for Israel to be confident that Syria was not trying to move into Israel proper. Some of those who do not expect the United States to face such a menace have predicted that continued reliance on the threat of mutual destruction "would lead eventually to the demoralization of the West. It is not possible indefinitely to tell democratic republics that their security depends on the mass extermination of civilians . . . without sooner or later producing pacifism and unilateral disarmament."[4]

John Mueller has posed a different kind of challenge to claims for a "nuclear revolution." He disputes, not the existence of a pattern of peace and stability, but the attributed cause. Nuclear weapons are "essentially irrelevant" to this effect; modernity and highly destructive nonnuclear weapons would have brought us pretty much to the same situation had it not been possible to split the atom. Such intelligent revisionism makes us think about questions whose answers had seemed self-evident. But I think that, on closer inspection, the conventional wisdom turns out to be correct. Nevertheless, there is much force in Mueller's arguments, particularly in the importance of what he calls "general stability" and the reminder that the fact that nuclear war would be so disastrous does not mean that conventional wars would be cheap.

Mueller is certainly right that the atom does not have magical properties. There is nothing crucial about the fact that people, weapons, industry, and agriculture may be destroyed as a result of a particular kind of explosion, although fission and fusion do produce special byproducts like fallout and electromagnetic pulse. What is important are the political effects that nuclear weapons produce, not the physics and chemistry of the explosion. We need to determine what these effects are, how they are produced, and whether modern conventional weapons would replicate them.

## POLITICAL EFFECTS OF NUCLEAR WEAPONS

The existence of large nuclear stockpiles influences superpower politics from three directions. Two perspectives are familiar: First, the devastation of an all-out war would be unimaginably enormous. Second, neither side—nor, indeed, third parties—would be spared this devastation. As Bernard Brodie, Thomas Schelling, and many others have noted, what is significant about nuclear weapons is not "overkill" but "mutual kill."[5] That is, no country could win an all-out nuclear war, not only in the sense of coming out of the war better than it went in, but in the sense of being better off fighting than making the concessions needed to avoid the conflict. It should be noted that although many past wars, such as World War II for all the Allies except the United States (and, perhaps, the USSR), would not pass the first test, they would pass the second. For example: Although Britain and France did not improve their positions by fighting, they were better off than they would have been had the Nazis succeeded. Thus it made sense for them to fight even though, as they feared at the outset, they would not profit from the conflict. Furthermore, had the Allies lost the war, the Germans—or at least the Nazis—would have won in a very meaningful sense, even if the cost had been extremely high. But "a nuclear war," as Reagan and Gorbachev affirmed in their joint statement after the November 1985 summit, "cannot be won and must never be fought."[6]

A third effect of nuclear weapons on superpower politics springs from the fact that the devastation could occur extremely quickly, within a matter of days or even hours. This is not to argue that a severe crisis or the limited use of force—even nuclear force—would inevitably trigger total destruction, but only that this is a possibility that cannot be dismissed. At any point, even in calm times, one side or the other could decide to launch an unprovoked all-out strike. More likely, a crisis could lead to limited uses of force which in turn, through a variety of mechanisms, could produce an all-out war. Even if neither side initially wanted this result, there is a significant, although impossible to quantify, possibility of quick and deadly escalation.

Mueller overstates the extent to which conventional explosives could substitute for nuclear ones in these characteristics of destructiveness, evenhandedness, and speed. One does not have to underestimate the horrors of previous wars to stress that the level of destruction we are now contemplating is much greater. Here, as in other areas, there comes a point at which a quantitative difference becomes a qualitative one. Charles De Gaulle put it eloquently: After a nuclear war, "two sides would have neither powers, nor laws, nor cities, nor cultures, nor cradles, nor tombs."[7] While a total "nuclear winter" and the extermination of human life would not follow a nuclear war, the worldwide effects would be an order of magnitude greater than those of any previous war. Mueller understates the differences in the scale of potential destruction: "World War II did not cause total destruction in the world, but it did utterly annihilate the three national regimes that brought it about. It is probably quite a bit more terrifying to think about a jump from the 50th floor than about a jump from the 5th floor, but anyone who finds life even minimally satisfying is extremely unlikely to do either." The war did indeed destroy these national regimes, but it did not utterly destroy the country itself or even all the values the previous regimes supported. Most people in the Axis countries survived World War II; many went on to prosper. Their children, by and large, have done well. There is an enormous gulf between this outcome—even for the states that lost the war—and a nuclear holocaust. It is far from clear whether societies could ever be reconstituted after a nuclear war or whether economies would ever recover. Furthermore, we should not neglect the impact of the prospect of destruction of culture, art, and national heritage: even a decision maker who was willing to risk the lives of half his population might hesitate at the thought of destroying what has been treasured throughout history.

Mueller's argument just quoted is misleading on a second count as well: The countries that started World War II were destroyed, but the Allies were not. It was more than an accident but less than predetermined that the countries that were destroyed were those that sought to overturn the status quo; what is crucial in this context is that with conventional weapons at least one side can hope, if not expect, to profit from war. Mueller is quite correct to argue that near-absolute levels of punishment are rarely required for deterrence, even when the conflict of interest between the two sides is great—i.e., when states believe that the gross gains (as contrasted with the net gains) from war would be quite high. The United States, after all, could have defeated North Vietnam. Similarly, as Mueller notes, the United States was deterred from trying to liberate East Europe even in the era of American nuclear monopoly.

But, again, one should not lose sight of the change in scale that nuclear explosives produce. In a nuclear war the "winner" might end up distinguishably less worse off than the "loser," but we should not make too much of this difference. Some have. As Harold Brown put it when he was Secretary of the Air Force, "if the Soviets thought they may be able to recover in some period of time while the U.S. would take three or four times as long, or would never recover, then the Soviets might not be deterred."[8] . . . .

But this view is a remarkably apolitical one. It does not relate the costs of the war to the objectives and ask whether the destruction would be so great that the "winner," as well as the loser, would regret having fought it. Mueller avoids this trap, but does not sufficiently consider the possibility that, absent nuclear explosives, the kinds of analyses quoted above would in fact be appropriate. Even very high levels of destruction can rationally be compatible with a focus on who will come out ahead in an armed conflict. A state strongly motivated to change the status quo could believe that the advantages of domination were sufficiently great to justify enormous blood-letting. For example, the Russians may feel that World War II was worth the cost not only when compared with being conquered by Hitler, but also when compared with the enormous increase in Soviet prestige, influence, and relative power.

Furthermore, without nuclear weapons, states almost surely would devote great energies to seeking ways of reducing the costs of victory. The two world wars were enormously destructive because they lasted so long. Modern technology, especially when combined with nationalism and with alliances that can bring others to the rescue of a defeated state, makes it likely that wars will last long: Defense is generally more efficacious than offense. But this is not automatically true; conventional wars are not necessarily wars of attrition, as the successes of Germany in 1939–40 and Israel in 1967 remind us. Blitzkrieg can work under special circumstances, and when these are believed to apply, conventional deterrence will no longer be strong. Over an extended period of time, one side or the other could on occasion come to believe that a quick victory was possible. Indeed, for many years most American officials have believed not only that the Soviets could win a conventional war in Europe or the Persian Gulf, but that they could do so at low cost. Were the United States to be pushed off the continent, the considerations Mueller gives might well lead it to make peace rather than pay the price of refighting World War II. Thus, extended deterrence could be more difficult without nuclear weapons. Of course, in their absence, NATO might build up a larger army and better defenses, but each side would continually explore new weapons and tactics that might permit a successful attack. At worst, such efforts would succeed. At best, they would heighten arms competition, national anxiety, and international tension. If both sides were certain that any new conventional war would last for years, the chances of war would be slight. But we should not be too quick to assume that conventional war with modern societies and weapons is synonymous with wars of attrition.

The length of the war is important in a related way as well. The fact that a war of attrition is slow makes a difference. It is true, as George Quester notes, that for some purposes all that matters is the amount of costs and pain the state has to bear, not the length of time over which it is spread.[9] But a conventional war would have to last a long time to do an enormous amount of damage; and it would not *necessarily* last a long time. Either side can open negotiations or make concessions during the war if the expected costs of continued fighting seem intolerable. Obviously, a timely termination is not guaranteed—the fitful attempts at negotiation during World War II and the stronger attempts during World War I were not fruitful. But the possibility of ending the war before the costs become excessive is never foreclosed. Of course, states can believe that a nuclear war would be prolonged, with relatively little damage being done each day, thus permitting intra-war bargaining. But no one can overlook the possibility that at any point the war could escalate to all-out destruction. Unlike the past, neither side could be certain that there would be a prolonged period for negotiation and intimidation. This blocks another path which statesmen in nonnuclear eras could see as a route to meaningful victory.

Furthermore, the possibility that escalation could occur even though neither side desires this outcome—what Schelling calls "the threat that leaves something to chance"[10]—induces caution in crises as well. The fact that sharp confrontations can get out of control, leading to the eventual destruction of both sides, means that states will trigger them only when the incentives to do so are extremely high. Of course, crises in the conventional era also could escalate, but the possibility of quick and total destruction means that the risk, while struggling near the brink, of falling into the abyss is greater and harder to control than it was in the past. Fears of this type dominated the bargaining during the Cuban missile crisis: Kennedy's worry was "based on fear, not of Khrushchev's intention, but of human error, of something going terribly wrong down the line." Thus when Kennedy was told that a U-2 had made a navigational error and was flying over Russia, he commented: "There is always some so-and-so who doesn't get the word."[11] The knowledge of these dangers—which does not seem lacking on the Soviet side as well—is a powerful force for caution.

Empirical findings on deterrence failure in the nuclear era confirm this argument. George and Smoke show that: "The initiator's belief that the risks of his action are calculable and that the unacceptable risks of it can be controlled and avoided is, with very few exceptions, a necessary (though not sufficient) condition for a decision to challenge deterrence."[12] The possibility of rapid escalation obviously does not make such beliefs impossible, but it does discourage them. The chance of escalation means that local military advantage cannot be confidently and safely employed to drive the defender out of areas in which its interests are deeply involved. Were status-quo states able to threaten only a war of attrition, extended deterrence would be more difficult.

## GENERAL STABILITY

But is very much deterrence needed? Is either superpower strongly driven to try to change the status quo? On these points I agree with much of Mueller's argument—the likely gains from war are now relatively low, thus producing what he calls general stability. The set of transformations that go under the heading of "modernization" have not only increased the costs of war, but have created alternative paths to established goals, and, more profoundly, have altered values in ways that make peace more likely. Our focus on deterrence and, even more narrowly, on matters military has led to a distorted view of international behavior. In a parallel manner, it has adversely affected policy prescriptions. We have not paid sufficient attention to the incentives states feel to change the status quo, or to the need to use inducements and reassurance, as well as threats and deterrence.

States that are strongly motivated to challenge the status quo may try to do so even if the military prospects are bleak and the chances of destruction considerable. Not only can rational calculation lead such states to challenge the status quo, but people who believe that a situation is intolerable feel strong psychological pressures to conclude that it can be changed. Thus nuclear weapons by themselves—and even mutual second-strike capability—might not be sufficient to produce peace. Contrary to Waltz's argument, proliferation among strongly dissatisfied countries would not necessarily recapitulate the Soviet–American pattern of stability.

The crucial questions in this context are the strength of the Soviet motivation to change the status quo and the effect of American policy on Soviet drives and calculations. Indeed, differences of opinion on these matters explain much of the debate over the application of deterrence strategies toward the USSR. Most of this dispute is beyond our scope here. Two points, however, are not. I think Mueller is correct to stress that not only Nazi Germany, but Hitler himself, was exceptional in the willingness to chance an enormously destructive war in order to try to dominate the world. While of course such a leader could recur, we should not let either our theories or our policies be dominated by this possibility.

A second point is one of disagreement: Even if Mueller is correct to believe that the Soviet Union is basically a satisfied power—and I share his conclusion— war is still possible. Wars have broken out in the past between countries whose primary goal was to preserve the status quo. States' conceptions of what is necessary for their security often clash with one another. Because one state may be able to increase its security only by making others less secure, the premise that both sides are basically satisfied with the status quo does not lead to the conclusion that the relations between them will be peaceful and stable. But here too nuclear weapons may help. As long as all-out war means mutual devastation, it cannot be seen as a path to security. The general question of how nuclear weapons make mutual security more feasible than it often was in the past is too large a topic to engage here. But I can at least suggest that they permit the superpowers to adopt military doctrines and bargaining tactics that make it possible for them to take advantage of their shared interest in preserving the status quo. Winston Churchill was right: "Safety [may] be the sturdy child of terror."

## NOTES

1. Alternatively, to be even more technical, a decision maker could expect to lose a war and at the same time could see its expected utility as positive if the slight chance of

victory was justified by the size of the gains that victory would bring. But the analysis here requires only the simpler formulation.

2. Fred Iklé. "Can Nuclear Deterrence Last Out the Century?" *Foreign Affairs* 51, no. 2 (January 1973): 267–85.

3. Robert McNamara, "The Military Role of Nuclear Weapons," *Foreign Affairs* 62, no. 4 (Fall 1983): 68. For his comments on how he came to this view, see his interview in Michael Charlton, *From Deterrence to Defense* (Cambridge: Harvard University Press, 1987), 18.

4. Henry Kissinger, "After Reykjavik: Current East–West Negotiations." *The San Francisco Meeting of the Tri-Lateral Commission, March 1987* (New York: The Trilateral Commission, 1987), 4; see also ibid., 7, and his interview in Charlton, *From Deterrence to Defense*, 34.

5. Bernard Brodie, ed., *The Absolute Weapon: Atomic Power and World Order* (New York: Harcourt Brace, 1946); Thomas Schelling, *Arms and Influence* (New Haven: Yale University Press, 1966).

6. *New York Times*, November 22, 1985, A12.

7. Speech of May 31, 1960, in Charles De Gaulle, *Discours Et Messages*, 3 (Paris: Plon, 1970): 218. I am grateful to McGeorge Bundy for the reference and translation.

8. U.S. Senate, Preparedness Investigating Subcommittee of the Committee on Armed Services, *Hearings on Status of U.S. Strategic Power*, 90th Cong., 2d sess., April 30, 1968 (Washington, D.C.: U.S. Government Printing Office, 1968), 186.

9. George Quester, "Crisis and the Unexpected," *Journal of Interdisciplinary History*, 18, no. 3 (Spring 1988): 701–3.

10. Thomas Schelling, *The Strategy of Conflict* (Cambridge: Harvard University Press, 1960), 187–203; Schelling, *Arms and Influence*, 92–125. . . .

11. Arthur M. Schlesinger, Jr., *Robert Kennedy and His Times* (Boston: Houghton Mifflin, 1978), 529; quoted in Roger Hilsman, *To Move a Nation* (Garden City, N.Y.: Doubleday, 1964), 221.

12. Alexander L. George and Richard Smoke, *Deterrence in American Foreign Policy* (New York: Columbia University Press, 1974), 529.

# 8

# Nuclear Myths
# and Political Realities

## Kenneth N. Waltz

Nuclear weapons have been given a bad name not just by the left, as one might have expected, but by the center and right as well. Throughout the long life of NATO, calls for strengthening conventional forces have been recurrently heard, reflecting and furthering debate about the wisdom of relying on nuclear deterrence. Doubts were spread more widely when McGeorge Bundy, George Kennan, Robert McNamara, and Gerard Smith published their argument for adopting a NATO policy of "no first use" in the spring, 1982, issue of *Foreign Affairs*. From the right came glib talk about the need to be prepared to fight a protracted nuclear war in order to "deter" the Soviet Union and proclaiming the possibility of doing so. Brigadier General Louis Guifridda, when he was Director of the Federal Emergency Management Agency, well described the Reagan administration's intended nuclear stance. "The administration," he said, "categorically rejected the short war. We're trying to inject a long-war mentality." Such statements, having scared people at home and abroad out of their wits, quickly disappeared from public discourse. Preparation to carry the policy through nevertheless proceeded apace. In 1982, Secretary of Defense Caspar Weinberger signed the five-year Defense Guidance Plan, which was to provide the means of sustaining a nuclear war, and in March of that year, an elaborate war game, dubbed Ivy League, "showed" that it could be done. Finally, in March of 1983, President Reagan offered his vision of a world in which defensive systems would render nuclear weapons obsolete.

With their immense destructive power, nuclear weapons are bound to make people uneasy. Decades of fuzzy thinking in high places about what deterrence is, how it works, and what it can and cannot do have deepened the nuclear malaise. Forty-some years after the first atomic bombs fell on Japan, we have yet to come to grips with the strategic implications of nuclear weapons. This essay applies nuclear reasoning to military policy and, in doing so, contrasts the logic of conventional and nuclear weapons.

Uneasiness over nuclear weapons, and the search for alternative means of security, stem in large measure from widespread failure to understand the nature and requirements of deterrence. Not unexpectedly, the language of strategic discourse has deteriorated over the decades. This happens whenever discussion enters the political arena, where words take on the meanings and colorations that reflect the preferences of their users. Early in the nuclear era, "deterrence" carried its dictionary definition—dissuading somebody from doing something by frightening him with the consequences that his action may produce. To deter an adversary from attacking one need have only a force that can survive a first strike and strike back hard enough to outweigh any gain the aggressor had hoped to realize. Deterrence in its pure form entails no ability to defend; a deterrent strategy promises not to fend off an aggressor but to damage or destroy things the aggressor holds dear. Both defense and deterrence are strategies that a status-quo country may follow, hoping to dissuade a state from attacking. They are different strategies designed to accomplish a common end in different ways, using different weapons differently deployed. Wars can be prevented, as they can be caused, in various ways.

Deterrence antedates nuclear weapons, but in a conventional world deterrent threats are problematic. Stanley Baldwin warned in the middle 1930s when he was Prime Minister of England that the bomber would always get through, a thought that helped to demoralize England. It proved seriously misleading in the war that soon followed. Bombers have to make their way past fighter planes and through ground fire before finding their targets and hitting them quite squarely. Nuclear weapons purify deterrent strategies by removing elements of defense and war fighting from them. Nuclear warheads eliminate the necessity of fighting and remove the possibility of defending, because only a small number of warheads need to reach their targets.

Ironically, as multiplication of missiles increased the ease with which destructive blows can be delivered, the distinction between deterrence and defense began to blur. Early in President Kennedy's administration, Secretary McNamara began to promote a strategy of Flexible Response, which was half-heartedly adopted by NATO in 1967. Flexible Response calls for the ability to meet threats at all levels from irregular warfare through the conventional and to the nuclear level. In the 1970s and '80s, more and more emphasis was placed on the need to fight and defend at all levels in order to "deter." The melding of defense, war fighting, and deterrence overlooks a simple truth, proclaimed in the title of a book of essays Bernard Brodie coauthored and edited in 1946: nuclear weapons are absolute. Nuclear weapons can carry out their deterrent task no matter what other countries do. If one nuclear power should gain the ability to destroy almost all of another's strategic warheads with practical certainty, or to defend against all but a few strategic warheads coming in, nuclear weapons would lose their absolute quality. Because so much explosive power comes in such small packages, the invulnerability of a sufficient number of warheads is easy to achieve and the delivery of fairly large numbers of warheads impossible to thwart. These statements will hold as far into the future as one can see. The absolute quality of nuclear weapons sharply sets a nuclear world off from a conventional one.

## WHAT DETERS?

Most discussions of deterrence are based on the belief that deterrence is difficult to achieve. In the Eisenhower years, "massive retaliation" was the phrase popularly used to describe the response we would supposedly make should the Soviet Union attack. Deterrence must be difficult if the threat of massive retaliation is required to achieve it. As the Soviet Union's arsenal grew, MAD (mutual assured destruction) became the acronym of choice, thus preserving the notion that deterrence depends on being willing and able to destroy much if not most of a country.

That one must be able to destroy a country in order to deter it is an odd notion, but one of distinguished lineage. During the 1950s, emphasis was put on the "massive" in massive retaliation. Beginning in the 1960s, the emphasis was put on the "assured destruction" in the doctrine of MAD. Thus viewed, deterrence becomes a monstrous policy, as innumerable critics have charged. One quotation can stand for many others. In a warning to NATO defense ministers that became famous, Henry Kissinger counselled the European allies not to keep "asking us to multiply strategic assurances that we cannot possibly mean or if we do mean, we should not want to execute because if we execute, we risk the destruction of civilization." The notion that the failure of deterrence would lead to national suicide or to mutual annihilation betrays a misunderstanding of both political behavior and nuclear realities.

Introducing the Eisenhower administration's New Look policy in January of 1954, John Foster Dulles gave the impression that aggression anywhere would elicit heavy nuclear retaliation. Just three months later, he sensibly amended the policy. Nuclear deterrence, Dulles and many others quickly came to realize, works not against minor aggression at the periphery but only against major aggression at the center of international politics. Moreover, to deter major aggression, Dulles now said, "the probable hurt" need only "outbalance the probable gain." Like Brodie before him, Dulles based deterrence on the principle of proportionality—let the punishment fit the crime.

What would we expect the United States to do if the Soviet Union should launch a major conventional attack against vital American interests, say, in Western Europe? Military actions have to be related to an objective. Because of the awesome power of nuclear weapons, the pressure to use them in ways that achieve the objective at hand while doing and suffering a minimum of destruction would be immense. It is preposterous to think that if a Soviet attack should break through NATO's defenses, the United States would strike thousands of Soviet military targets or hundreds of Soviet cities. Doing so would serve no purpose. Who would want to make a bad situation worse by launching wantonly destructive attacks on a country that can strike back with comparable force, or, for that matter, on a country that could not do so? We might strike a target or two, military or industrial, chosen to keep casualties low. If the Soviet Union had run the preposterous risk of attacking the center of Europe, believing it could escape retaliation, we would thus show them that they were wrong, while conveying the idea that more will follow if they persist. Among countries having abundant nuclear weapons, none can gain an advantage by striking first. The purpose of demonstration shots is simply to remind everyone—should anyone forget—that catastrophe threatens. Some people purport to believe that if a few warheads go off, many will follow. This would seem to be the least likely of all the unlikely possibilities. That no country gains by destroying another's cities and then seeing a comparable number of its own destroyed in return is obvious to everyone.

Despite widespread beliefs to the contrary, deterrence does not depend on destroying cities. Deterrence depends on what one *can* do, not on what one *will* do. What deters is the fact that we can do as much damage to them as we choose, and they to us. The country suffering the retaliatory attack cannot limit the damage done. Only the retaliator can do that.

With nuclear weapons, countries need threaten to use only a small amount of force. This is so because once the willingness to use a little force is shown, so much more can so easily be added. This is not true with conventional weapons, and therefore it is often useful for a country to threaten to use a lot of force if conflict should lead to war. The stance may be intended as a deterrent one, but the ability to carry the threat through is problematic. With conventional weapons, countries tend to emphasize the first phase of war. Striking hard to achieve a quick victory may decrease the cost of war. With nuclear weapons, political leaders worry not about what may happen in the first phase of fighting but about what may happen in the end. As Clausewitz wrote, if war should ever approach the absolute, it would become "imperative . . . not to take the first step without considering what may be the last."

Since war now approaches the absolute, it is hardly surprising that President Kennedy echoed Clausewitz's words during the Cuban Missile Crisis of 1962. "It isn't the first step that concerns me," he said, "but both sides escalating to the fourth and fifth step—and we don't go to the sixth because there is no one around to do so." In conventional crises, leaders may sensibly seek one advantage or another. They may bluff by threatening escalatory steps they are in fact unwilling to take. They may try one stratagem or another and run considerable risks. Since none of the parties to the struggle can predict what the outcome will be, they may have good reason to prolong crises, even crises entailing the risk of war. A conventional country enjoying military superiority is tempted to use it before other countries right the military balance. A nuclear country enjoying superiority is reluctant to use it because no one can promise the full success of a disarming first strike. As Henry Kissinger retrospectively said of the Cuban missile crisis, the Soviet Union had only "60–70 truly strategic weapons while we had something like 2,000 in missiles and bombs." But, he added, "with some proportion of Soviet delivery vehicles surviving, the Soviet Union could do horrendous damage to the United States." We could not be sure that our 2,000 weapons would destroy almost all of their 60 or 70. Even with numbers immensely disproportionate, a small force strongly inhibits the use of a large one.

The catastrophe promised by nuclear war contrasts sharply with the extreme difficulty of predicting outcomes among conventional competitors. This makes one wonder about the claimed dependence of deterrence on perceptions and the alleged problem of credibility. In conventional competitions, the comparative qualities of troops, weaponry, strategies, and leaders are difficult to gauge. So complex is the fighting of wars with conventional weapons that their outcomes have been extremely difficult to predict. Wars start more easily because the uncertainties of their outcome make it easier for the leaders of states to entertain illusions of victory at supportable cost. In contrast, contemplating war when the use of nuclear weapons is possible focuses one's attention not on the probability of victory but on the possibility of annihilation. Because catastrophic outcomes of nuclear exchanges are easy to imagine, leaders of states will shrink in horror from initiating them. With nuclear weapons, stability and peace rest on easy calculations of what one country can do to another. Anyone—political leader or man in the street—can see that catastrophe lurks if events spiral out of control and nuclear warheads begin to fly. The problem of the credibility of deterrence, a big worry in a conventional world, disappears in a nuclear one.

Yet the credibility of deterrence has been a constant American worry. The worry is a hangover from the 1930s. Concern over credibility, and the related efforts to show resolve in crises or wars where only peripheral interests are at stake, were reinforced because the formative experiences of most of the policymakers of the 1950s and '60s took place in the 1930s. In rearming Germany, in reoccupying the Rhineland, in annexing Austria, in dismantling Czechoslovakia, Hitler went to the brink and won. "We must not let that happen again" was the lesson learned, but in a nuclear world the lesson no longer applies. Despite rhetoric to the contrary, practice accords with nuclear logic because its persuasive force is so strong and the possible consequences of ignoring it so grave. Thus, John Foster Dulles, who proclaimed that maintaining peace requires the courage to go to the brink of war, shrank from the precipice during the Hungarian uprising of 1956. And so it has been every time that events even remotely threatened to get out of hand at the center of international politics.

Still, strategists' and commentators' minds prove to be impressively fertile. The imagined difficulties of deterrence multiply apace. One example will do. Paul Nitze argued in the late 1970s that, given a certain balance of strategic forces, given the Soviet Union's supposed goal of world domination, and given its presumed willingness to run great risks, the Soviet Union might launch a first-strike against our land-based missiles, our bombers on the ground, and our strategic submarines in port. The Soviet Union's strike would tilt the balance of strategic forces sharply against us. Rather than retaliate, our president might decide to acquiesce. That is, we might be "self deterred." Nitze's scenario is based on faulty assumptions, unfounded distinctions, and preposterous notions about how governments behave. Soviet leaders, according to him, may have concluded from the trend in the balance of nuclear forces in the middle 1970s that our relatively small warheads and their civil defense would enable the Soviet Union to limit the casualties resulting from our retaliation to 3 or 4 percent of their population. Their hope for such a "happy" outcome would presumably rest on confidence that their first strike would be well timed and accurate and that their intelligence agencies would have revealed the exact location of almost all of their intended targets. In short, their leaders would have to believe that all would go well in a huge, unrehearsed missile barrage, that the United States would fail to launch on warning, and that if by chance they had failed to "deter our deterrent," they would still be able to limit casualties to only ten million people or so.[1] How could they entertain such a hope when, by Nitze's estimate, their first strike would have left us with 2,000 warheads in our submarine force in addition to warheads carried by surviving bombers?

Nitze's fear rested on the distinction between counterforce and countervalue strikes—between strikes aimed at weapons and strikes aimed at cities. Because the Soviet Union's first strike would be counterforce, any American president would seemingly have good reason to refrain from retaliation, thus avoiding the loss of cities still held hostage by the Soviet Union's remaining strategic forces. But this thought overlooks the fact that, once strategic missiles numbered in the low hundreds are fired, the counterforce/countervalue distinction blurs. One would no longer know what the attackers' intended targets might be. The Soviet Union's counterforce strike would require that thousands, not hundreds, of warheads be fired. Moreover, the extent of their casualties, should we decide to retaliate, would depend on how many of our warheads we chose to fire, on what targets we aimed at, and on whether we used ground bursts to increase fallout. Several hundred warheads can destroy the United States or the Soviet Union as going societies. The assumptions made in the effort to make a Soviet first strike appear possible are ridiculous. How could the Soviet Union, or any country, somehow bring itself to run stupendous risks in the presence of nuclear weapons? What objectives might its leaders seek that could justify the risks entailed? Answering these questions sensibly leads one to conclude that deterrence is deeply stable. Those who favor increasing the strength of our strategic forces, however, shift to a different question. "The crucial question," according to Nitze, "is whether a future U.S. president should be left with only the option of deciding within minutes, or at most within two or three hours, to retaliate after a counterforce attack in a manner certain to result not only in military defeat for the United States but in wholly disproportionate and truly irremediable destruction to the American people." One of the marvels of the nuclear age is how easily those who write about the unreliability of deterrence focus on the retaliator's possible inhibitions and play down the attacker's obvious risks. Doing so makes deterrence seem hard and leads to arguments for increasing our military spending in order "to deny the Soviet Union the possibility of a successful war-fighting capability," a strategic capability that the Soviet Union has never remotely approached.

We do not need ever-larger forces to deter. Smaller forces, so long as they are invulnerable, would be quite sufficient. Yet the vulnerability of fixed, land-based missiles has proved worrisome. Those who do the worrying dwell on the vulnerability of one class of weapons. The militarily important question, however, is not about the vulnerability of one class of weapons but about the vulnerability of a whole strategic-weapons system. Submarine-launched missiles make land-based missiles invulnerable since destroying only the latter would leave thousands of strategic warheads intact. To overlook this again reflects conventional thinking. In the absence of a dominant weapon, the vulnerability of one weapon or another may be a big problem. If the means of protecting sealanes of communications were destroyed, for example, we would be unable to deploy and support troops abroad. The problem disappears in a nuclear world. Destroying a portion of one's strategic force means little if sufficient weapons for deterrence survive.

Thinking about deterrence is often faulted for being abstract and deductive, for not being grounded in experience. The criticism is an odd one since all statements about the military implications of nuclear weapons are inferred from their characteristics. Deterrers from Brodie onward have drawn conclusions from the all but unimaginable increase in easily delivered firepower that nuclear warheads embody. Those who in the nuclear era apply lessons learned in conventional warfare make the more problematic claim that despite profound changes in military technology the classic principles of warfare endure. We all, happily, lack the benefit of experience. Moreover, just as deterrent logic is abstract and deductive, so too are the weaknesses attributed to it. Scenarios showing how deterrence might fail are not only abstract but also farfetched. Deterrence rests on simple propositions and relies on forces obviously sufficient for their purpose.

## DETERRING THE SOVIET UNION

Underlying much of the concern about the reliability of nuclear deterrence is the conviction that the Soviet Union is especially hard to deter. Three main reasons are given for believing this. First, the Soviet Union's ambitions are said to be unlimited. In 1984, Secretary of Defense Caspar Weinberger, when asked why the Soviet Union armed itself so heavily, answered the question bluntly: "World domination, it's that simple." Second, her military doctrine seemed to contemplate the possibility of fighting and winning combined conventional and nuclear wars, while rejecting the doctrine of deterrence. Third, the Soviet Union has appeared to many people in the West to be striving for military superiority.

These three points make a surprisingly weak case, even though it has been widely accepted. Ambitions aside, looking at the Soviet Union's behavior one is impressed with its caution when acting where conflict might lead to the use of major force. Leaders of the Soviet Union may hope that they can one day turn the world to Communism. Although the Soviet Union's intentions may be extraordinary, her behavior has not been. Everyone agrees that, except in the military sector, the Soviet Union is the lagging competitor in a two-party race. The Soviet Union has been opportunistic and disruptive, but one expects the lagging party to score a point or two whenever it can. The Soviet Union has not scored many. Her limited international successes should not obscure the fact that what the Soviet Union has done mostly since 1948 is lose.

The second point rests on basic misunderstandings about deterrence. It has often been argued that we could not rely on deterrence when the Soviet Union was rejecting the doctrine. One of the drawbacks of the "theory" of assured destruction, according to Henry Kissinger, was that "the Soviets did not believe it." The efficacy of nuclear deterrence, however, does not depend on anyone's accepting it. Secretaries of Defense nevertheless continue to worry that Soviet values, perceptions, and calculations may be different from ours. Thus Secretary of Defense Harold Brown, worried by the Soviets' emphasis "on the acquisition of war-winning capabilities," concluded that we must "continue to adapt and update our countervailing capabilities so that the Soviets will clearly understand that we will never allow them to use their nuclear forces to achieve any aggressive aim at an acceptable cost."

The belief that the Soviet Union's having an aggressive military doctrine makes her especially hard to deter is another hangover from conventional days. Germany and Japan in the 1930s were hard to deter, but then the instruments for deterrence were not available. We can fairly say that their leaders were less averse to running risks than most political leaders are. But that is no warrant for believing that had they been confronted with second-strike nuclear forces, they would have been so foolhardy as to risk the sudden destruction of their countries. The decision to challenge the vital interests of a nuclear state, whether by major conventional assault or by nuclear first strike, would be a collective decision involving a number of political and military leaders. One would have to believe that a whole set of leaders might suddenly go mad. Rulers like to continue to rule. Except in the relatively few countries of settled democratic institutions, one is struck by how tenaciously rulers cling to power. We have no reason to expect Russian leaders to be any different. The notion that Russian leaders might risk losing even a small number of cities by questing militarily for uncertain gains is fanciful. Malenkov and Khrushchev lost their positions for lesser failures.

With conventional weapons a status-quo country must ask itself how much power it must harness to its policy in order to dissuade an especially aggressive state from striking. Countries willing to run high risks are hard to dissuade. The varied qualities of governments and the temperaments of leaders have to be carefully weighed. In a nuclear world, any state will be deterred by another state's second-strike forces. One need not become preoccupied with the characteristics of the state that is to be deterred or scrutinize its leaders.

The third worry remains: the Soviet Union's seeming aspiration for military superiority. One might think that the worry should have run the other way through most of the years of the Cold War. In the nuclear business, the United States moved from monopoly to superiority. In the late fifties, Khrushchev deeply cut conventional arms, and the Soviet Union failed to produce strategic warheads and missiles as rapidly as we had expected. Nevertheless, the Kennedy administration undertook the largest peacetime military buildup the world had yet seen, in both nuclear and conventional weaponry. So far did we forge ahead strategically that McNamara thought the Soviet Union would not even try to catch up. "There is," he said, "no indication that the Soviets are seeking to develop a strategic nuclear force as large as ours." To expect that the Soviet Union would give up one had to believe that it would behave in a historically unprecedented manner. Instead, the Soviet Union tried to compete. Yet to catch up with the United States was difficult. In the 1970s, the decade in which we are told the Soviet Union moved toward superiority—or, according to President Reagan, achieved it—the United States in fact added more nuclear warheads to its arsenal than the Soviet Union did.

We have exaggerated the strength of the Soviet Union, and they, no doubt, have exaggerated ours. One may wonder whether the Soviet Union ever thought itself superior, or believed it could become so. Americans easily forget that the Soviet Union has the strategic weapons of four countries pointed at it and sees itself threatened from the East as well as the West. More fundamentally, continued preoccupation with denying "superiority" to the Soviet Union, if not seeking it ourselves, suggests that a basic strategic implication of nuclear weapons is yet to be appreciated. So long as two or more countries have second-strike forces, to compare them is pointless. If no state can launch a disarming attack with high confidence, force comparisons become irrelevant. For deterrence one asks how much is enough, and enough is defined as having a second-strike capability. This does not imply that a deterrent force deters everything, but rather that beyond a certain level of capability, additional forces provide no additional coverage for one party and pose no additional threat to others. The United States and the Soviet Union have long had second-strike forces, with neither able to launch a disarming first strike against the other. Two countries with second-strike forces have the same amount of strategic power, since short of attaining a first-strike capability, adding more weapons does not change the effective military balance.

## WHY NUCLEAR WEAPONS DOMINATE STRATEGY

Deterrence is easier to contrive than most strategists have believed. With conventional weapons, weapons that are relative and not absolute, a number of strategies are available, strategies combining and deploying forces in different ways. Strategies may do more than weapons to determine the outcomes of wars. Nuclear weapons are different; they dominate strategies. As Brodie clearly saw, the effects of nuclear weapons derive not from any particular design for their employment in war, but simply from their presence. Indeed, in an important sense, nuclear weapons eliminate strategy. If one thinks of strategies as being designed for the defense of national objectives or for the gaining of them by military force, and if one thinks of strategies as implying a choice about how major wars will be fought, then nuclear weapons make strategy obsolete. Nevertheless, the conviction that the only reliable deterrent force is one able to win a war, or fight one in a way that leaves us in a better position than the Soviet Union, is widespread. Linton F. Brooks, while a Captain in the United States Navy, wrote that "War is the ultimate test of any strategy; a strategy useless in war cannot deter."

NATO policy well illustrates the futility of trying to transcend deterrence by fashioning war-fighting strategies. The supposed difficulties of extending deterrence to cover major allies has led some to argue that we require nuclear superiority, that we need nuclear war-fighting capabilities, and that we must build up our conventional forces. Once the Soviet Union achieved nuclear parity, confidence in our extended deterrent declined in the West. One wonders whether it did in the East. Denis Healey once said that one chance in a hundred that a country will retaliate is enough to deter an adversary, although not enough to reassure an ally. Many have repeated his statement, but none, I believe, has added that reassuring allies is unnecessary militarily and unwise politically. Politically, allies who are unsure of one another's support have reason to work harder for the sake of their own security. Militarily, deterrence requires only that conventional forces be able to defend long enough to determine that an attack is a major one and not merely a foray. For this a trip-wire force as envisioned in the 1950s, with perhaps 50,000 American troops in Europe, would be sufficient. Beyond that, deterrence requires only that forces be invulnerable and that the area protected be of manifestly vital interest. Western European countries can be counted on to maintain forces of trip-wire capability.

Nuclear weapons strip conventional forces of most of their functions. Bernard Brodie pointed out that in "a total war" the army "might have no function at all." Herman Kahn cited "the claim that in a thermonuclear war it is important to keep the sealanes open" as an example of the "quaint ideas" still held by the military.[2] Conventional forces have only a narrow role in any confrontation between nuclear states over vital interests, since fighting beyond the trip-wire level serves no useful purpose. Enlarging conventional capabilities does nothing to strengthen deterrence. Strategic stalemate does shift military competition to the tactical level. But one must add what is usually omitted: Nuclear stalemate limits the use of conventional forces and reduces the extent of the gains one can seek without risking devastation. For decades American policy has nevertheless aimed at raising the nuclear threshold in Europe. Stronger conventional forces would presumably enable NATO to sustain a longer war in Europe at higher levels of violence. At some moment in a major war, however, one side or the other—or perhaps both—would believe itself to be losing. The temptation to introduce nuclear weapons may then prove irresistible, and they would be fired in the chaos of defeat with little chance of limited and discriminant use. Early use would promise surer control and closer limitation of damage. In a nuclear world, a conventional war-fighting strategy would appear to be the worst possible one, more dangerous than a strategy of relying on deterrence.

Attempts to gain escalation dominance, like efforts to raise the nuclear threshold, betray a failure to appreciate the strategic implications of nuclear weapons. Escalation dominance, so it is said, requires "a seamless web of capabilities" up and down "the escalation ladder." Earlier it had been thought that the credibility of deterrence would be greater if some rungs of the escalation ladder were missing. The inability to fight at some levels would make the threat to use higher levels of force easy to credit. But, again, since credibility is not a problem, this scarcely matters militarily. Filling in the missing rungs neither helps nor hurts. Escalation dominance is useful for countries contending with conventional weapons only. Dominance, however, is difficult to achieve in the absence of a decisive weapon. Among nuclear adversaries the question of dominance is pointless because one second-strike force cannot dominate another. Since strategic nuclear weapons will always prevail, the game of escalation dominance cannot be played. Everyone knows that anyone can quickly move to the top rung of the ladder. Beause anyone can do so, all of the parties in a serious crisis have an overriding incentive to ask themselves one question: How can we get out of this mess without nuclear warheads exploding? Deescalation, not escalation, becomes the problem that the presence of nuclear weapons forces them to solve.

To gain escalation dominance, were it imaginable, would require the ability to fight nuclear wars. War-fighting strategies take nuclear weapons to be relative, with the country having more and better ones able in some unspecified way to prevail. No one, however, has shown how such a war could be fought. Indeed, Desmond Ball has argued that a nuclear war could not be sustained beyond the exchange of strategic warheads numbered not in the hundreds but in the tens. After a small number of exchanges no one would know what was going on or be able to maintain control. Yet, as ever, nuclear weapons save us from our folly. Fanciful strategies are irrelevant because no one will run the appalling risk of testing them.

Deterrence has been faulted for its lack of credibility, its dependence on perceptions, its destructive implications, and its inability to cover interests abroad. The trouble with deterrence, however, lies elsewhere. The trouble with deterrence is that it can be implemented cheaply. The claim that we need a seamless web of capabilities in order to deter does serve one purpose: It keeps military budgets wondrously high. Efforts to fashion a defensive and war-fighting strategy for NATO are pointless because deterrence prevails, and futile because strategy cannot transcend the military conditions that nuclear weapons create.

## NUCLEAR ARMS AND DISARMAMENT

The probability of major war among states having nuclear weapons approaches zero. But the "real war" may, as William James claimed, lie in the preparation for waging it. The logic of deterrence, if followed, circumscribes the causes of "real wars." Nuclear weapons make it possible for a state to limit the size of its strategic forces as long as other states are unable to achieve disarming first-strike capabilities by improving their forces.

Within very wide ranges, a nuclear balance is insensitive to variation in numbers and size of warheads. This has occasionally been seen by responsible officials. Harold Brown said, when he was Secretary of Defense, purely deterrent forces "can be relatively modest, and their size can perhaps be made substantially, though not completely, insensitive to changes in the posture of an opponent." Somehow he nevertheless managed to argue that we need "to design our forces on the basis of essential equivalents." Typically over the past three decades, Secretaries of Defense have sought, albeit vainly, the superiority that would supposedly give us a war-fighting capability. But they have failed to explain what we can do with 12,000 strategic nuclear warheads that we could not do with 2,000, or with a still smaller number. What difference does it make if we have 2,000 strategic weapons and the Soviet Union has 4,000? We thought our deterrent did not deter very much, and did not work with sufficient reliability, just as we were reaching a peak of numerical superiority in the mid-1960s. Flexible response, with emphasis on conventional arms, was a policy produced in our era of nuclear plenty. "Superiority" and "parity" have had the same effect on our policy.

Many who urge us to build ever more strategic weapons in effect admit the military irrelevance of additional forces when, as so often, they give political rather than military reasons for doing so. Spending less, it is said, would signal weakness of will. Yet militarily only one perception counts, and that is the perception that a country has second-strike forces. Nuclear weapons make it possible for states to escape the dynamics of arms racing, yet the United States and the Soviet Union have multiplied their weaponry far beyond the requirements of deterrence. Each has obsessively measured its strategic forces against the other's. The arms competition between them has arisen from failure to appreciate the implications of nuclear weapons for military strategy and, no doubt, from internal military and political pressures in both countries.

Many of the obstacles to arms reduction among conventional powers disappear or dwindle among nuclear nations. For the former, the careful comparison of the quantities and qualities of forces is important. Because this is not so with nuclear weapons, the problem of verifying agreements largely disappears. Provisions for verification may be necessary in order to persuade the Senate to ratify an agreement, but the possibility of noncompliance is not very worrisome. Agreements that reduce one category of conventional weapons may shift competition to other types of weapons and lead to increases in their numbers and capabilities. Because with nuclear weapons sufficiency is easily defined, there is no military reason for reductions in some weapons to result in increases in others. Conventionally, multiparty agreements are hard to arrive at because each party has to consider how shifting alignments may alter the balance of forces if agreements are reached to reduce them. In a world of second-strike nuclear forces, alliances have little effect on the strategic balance. The Soviet Union's failure to insist that British, French, and Chinese forces be counted in strategic arms negotiations may reflect its appreciation of this point. Finally, conventional powers have to compare weapons of uncertain effectiveness. Arms agreements are difficult to reach because their provisions may bear directly on the prospects for victory or defeat. Because in a nuclear world peace is maintained by the presence of deterrent forces, strategic arms agreements have not military but economic and political significance. They can benefit countries economically and help to improve their relations.

A minority of American military analysts have understood the folly of maintaining more nuclear weapons than deterrence requires. In the Soviet Union, Mikhail Gorbachev and some others have put forth the notion of "reasonable sufficiency," defined as having a strategic force roughly equal to ours and able, in retaliation, to inflict unacceptable damage. Edward Warner points out that some civilian analysts have gone further, "suggesting that as long as the USSR had a secure second-strike capability that could inflict unacceptable damage, it would not have to be concerned about maintaining approximate numerical parity with U.S. strategic nuclear forces." If leaders in both countries come to accept the minority view—and also realize that a deterrent force greatly reduces conventional requirements on central fronts—both countries can enjoy security at much lower cost.

## STRATEGIC DEFENSE

Strategic defenses would radically change the propositions advanced in this chapter. The Strategic Defense Initiative, in Reagan's vision, was to provide an area defense that would protect the entire population of the United States. Strategic defenses were to pose an absolute defense against what have been absolute weapons, thus rendering them obsolete. The consequences that would follow from mounting such a defense boggle the mind. That a perfect defense against nuclear weapons could be deployed and sustained is inconceivable. This is so for two reasons. First, nuclear weapons are small and light; they are easy to move, easy to hide, and easy to deliver in a variety of ways. Even an unimaginably perfect defense against ballistic missiles would fail to negate nuclear weapons. Such a defense would instead put a premium on the other side's ability to deliver nuclear weapons in different ways: firing missiles on depressed trajectories, carrying bombs in suitcases, placing nuclear warheads on freighters to be anchored in American harbors. Indeed, someone has suggested that the Soviet Union can always hide warheads in bales of marijuana, knowing we cannot keep them from crossing our borders. To have even modestly effective defenses we would, among other things, have to become a police state. We would have to go to extraordinary lengths to police our borders and exercise control within them. Presumably, the Soviet Union does these things better than we do. It is impossible to imagine that an area defense can be a success because there are so many ways to thwart it. In no way can we prevent the Soviet Union from exploding nuclear warheads on or in the United States if it is determined to do so.

Second, let us imagine for a moment that an airtight defense, however defined, is about to be deployed by one country or the other. The closer one country came to deploying such a defense, the harder the other would work to overcome it. When he was Secretary of Defense, Robert McNamara argued that the appropriate response to a Soviet defensive deployment would be to expand our deterrent force. More recently, Caspar Weinberger and Mikhail Gorbachev have made similar statements. Any country deploying a defense effective for a moment cannot expect it to remain so. The ease of delivering nuclear warheads, and the destructiveness of small numbers of them, make the durability of defenses highly suspect.

The logic of strategic defense is the logic of conventional weaponry. Conventional strategies pit weapons against weapons. That is exactly what a strategic defense would do, thereby recreating the temptations and instabilities that have plagued countries armed only with conventional weapons. If the United States and the Soviet Union deploy defensive systems, each will worry, no doubt excessively, about the balance of offensive and defensive capabilities. Each will fear that the other may score an offensive or defensive breakthrough. If one side should do so, it might be tempted to strike in order to exploit its temporary advantage. The dreaded specter of the hair-trigger would reappear. Under such circumstances, a defensive system would serve as the shield that makes the sword useful. An offensive/defensive race would introduce many uncertainties. A country enjoying a momentary defensive advantage would be tempted to strike in the forlorn hope that its defenses would be able to handle a ragged and reduced response to its first strike. Both countries would prepare to launch on warning, while obsessively weighing the balance between offensive and defensive forces.

Finally, let us imagine what is most unimaginable of all—that both sides deploy defenses that are impregnable and durable. Such defenses would make the world safe for World War III, fought presumably in the manner of World War II but with conventional weapons of much greater destructive power.

Still, some have argued that, even if some American cities remain vulnerable, defenses are very good for the cities they do cover. The claim is spurious. In response to the Soviet Union's deploying antiballistic missiles to protect Moscow, we multiplied the number of missiles aimed at that city. We expect to overcome their defenses and still deliver the "required" number of warheads. The result of defending cities may be that more warheads strike them. This is especially so since we and they, working on worst-case assumptions, are likely to overestimate the number of missiles the other country's system will be able to shoot down. Strategic defenses are likely to increase the damage done.

Most knowledgeable people believe that an almost leak-proof defense cannot be built. Many, however, believe that if improved hard-point defenses result from the SDI program, they will have justified its price. Defense of missiles and of command, control, and communications installations will strengthen deterrence, so the argument goes. That would be a solution all right, but we lack a problem to go with it. Deterrence is vibrantly healthy. If the Soviet Union believes that even one Trident submarine would survive its first strike, surely it will be deterred.[3] Since we do not need hard-point defenses, we should not buy them. The deployment of such defenses by one side would be seen by the other as the first step in deploying an area defense. Strategic considerations should dominate technical ones. In a nuclear world, defensive systems are predictably destabilizing. It would be folly to move from a condition of stable deterrence to one of unstable defense.

## CONCLUSION

Nuclear weapons dissuade states from going to war more surely than conventional weapons do. In a conventional world, states going to war can at once believe that they may win and that, should they lose, the price of defeat will be bearable. World Wars I and II called the latter belief into question before atomic bombs were ever dropped. Were the United States and the Soviet Union now armed only with conventional weapons, the lesson of those wars would be strongly remembered, especially by Russia since she has suffered more in war than we have. Had the atom never been split, the United States and the Soviet Union would still have much to fear from each other. The stark opposition of countries of continental size, armed with ever more destructive conventional weapons, would strongly constrain them. Yet in a conventional world, even strong and sad lessons have proved to be exceedingly difficult for states to learn. Recurrently in modern history, one great power or another has looked as though it might become dangerously strong: Louis XIV's and Napoleon's France, Wilhelm II's and Hitler's Germany. Each time an opposing coalition formed, if belatedly, and turned the expansive state back. The lesson would seem to be clear: In international politics, success leads to failure. The excessive accumulation of power by one state or coalition of states elicits the opposition of others. The leaders of expansionist states have nevertheless been able to persuade themselves that skillful diplomacy and clever strategy would enable them to transcend the normal processes of balance-of-power politics. The Schlieffen Plan, for example, seemed to offer a strategy that would enable Germany to engage enemies on two fronts but to do so serially. Germany would defeat France before Russia could mobilize fully and move westward in force. Later Hitler, while denouncing the "boobs" of Wilhelmine Germany for getting themselves into a war on two fronts, reenacted their errors.

How can we perpetuate peace without solving the problem of war? This is the question that states having nuclear weapons must constantly answer. Nuclear states continue to compete militarily. With each state tending to its security interests as best it can, war is constantly possible. Although the possibility of war remains, nuclear weapons have drastically reduced the probability of its being fought by states having them. Wars that might bring nuclear weapons into play have become extraordinarily hard to start. Over the centuries great powers have fought more wars and lesser states have fought fewer. The frequency of war has correlated less closely with the attributes of states than with their international standing. Yet, because of a profound change in military technology, waging war has more and more become the privilege of poor and weak states. Nuclear weapons have reversed the fates of strong and weak states. Never since the Treaty of Westphalia in 1648, which conventionally marks the beginning of modern history, have great powers enjoyed a longer period of peace than we have known since the Second World War. One can scarcely believe that the presence of nuclear weapons does not greatly help to explain this happy condition.

## NOTES

1. Nitze blandly adds that, if we do launch on warning, "the estimates in the Soviet civil defense manuals are overoptimistic from the Soviet viewpoint."

2. Quaint ideas die hard. In the fall of 1989, NATO resisted discussing naval disarmament with the Soviet Union because of the need for forces to guard the sealanes to Europe.

3. An Ohio-class Trident submarine carries 24 missiles, each having eight warheads.

# PART II

---

# CASE STUDIES IN THE
# USE OF FORCE

---

THE SELECTIONS IN Part II are taken from the past one hundred years and are arranged in chronological order. Their purpose is to illustrate the general principles discussed in Part I. The cases deal with different types of military technologies, ranging from land warfare to nuclear weapons, and treat the use of military power in both peace and war. Each case demonstrates one, and sometimes several, of the following: a specific way of using military power, the motives for the specific use, the factors that restrained a state in its use of force, and the reasons for the state's success or failure.

The readings under the heading "The Great Power Era" deal with the use of force by and among the great powers prior to 1946. Jack Snyder shows why belief in the powers of the offense gripped both military and civilian leaders before World War I. John Mearsheimer shows how Germany's blitzkrieg strategy evolved before World War II and why Hitler's role was central in its evolution. Sir George Sansom explains why the Japanese decided to launch what they considered to be a preventive war against the United States and demonstrates how their strategic calculations were faulty. Finally, Louis Morton discusses the reasons why the United States used the atomic bomb to end the war with Japan.

The selections under the heading "The Superpower Era" examine instances in which the superpowers were involved in using either conventional forces or nuclear threats. Morton Halperin describes the evolution of a system of mutual restraints in the American and Chinese use of force during the Korean War and suggests why they were accepted. David Welch, James Blight, and Bruce Allyn explain the reasons why the Soviet Union put missiles in Cuba in September 1962 and why it took them out in October and November of the same year. John Lewis Gaddis describes the Kennedy administration's strategy of flexible response and demonstrates why it failed in the Vietnam War.

The selections under the heading "The Contemporary Era" examine two significant uses of military power since the end of the Cold War. Steven Burg analyzes America's and NATO's (the North Atlantic Treaty Organization's) use of coercive diplomacy in Bosnia and Kosovo in the 1990s and shows why coercive diplomacy succeeded in the former case and failed in the latter. Michael O'Hanlon analyzes why the United States was able to conduct a successful war against the Taliban regime in 2001 in Afghanistan in order to end that regime's support of al-Qaeda.

# 9

# The Cult of the Offensive in 1914

JACK SNYDER

Military technology should have made the European strategic balance in July 1914 a model of stability, but offensive military strategies defied those technological realities, trapping European statesmen in a war-causing spiral of insecurity and instability. As the Boer and Russo–Japanese Wars had foreshadowed and the Great War itself confirmed, prevailing weaponry and means of transport strongly favored the defender. Tactically, withering firepower gave a huge advantage to entrenched defenders; strategically, defenders operating on their own territory could use railroads to outmaneuver marching invaders. Despite these inexorable constraints, each of the major continental powers began the war with an offensive campaign. These war plans and the offensive doctrines behind them were in themselves an important and perhaps decisive cause of the war. Security, not conquest, was the principal criterion used by the designers of the plans, but their net effect was to reduce everyone's security and to convince at least some states that only preventive aggression could ensure their survival.

Even if the outbreak of war is taken as a given, the offensive plans must still be judged disasters. Each offensive failed to achieve its ambitious goals and, in doing so, created major disadvantages for the state that launched it. Germany's invasion of Belgium and France ensured that Britain would join the opposing coalition and implement a blockade. The miscarriage of France's ill-conceived frontal attack almost provided the margin of help that the Schlieffen Plan needed. Though the worst was averted by a last-minute railway maneuver, the Germans nonetheless occupied a key portion of France's industrial northeast, making a settlement based on the status quo ante impossible to negotiate. Meanwhile, in East

121

Prussia the annihilation of an over-extended Russian invasion force squandered troops that might have been decisive if used to reinforce the undermanned advance into Austria. In each case, a defensive or more limited offensive strategy would have left the state in a more favorable strategic position.

None of these disasters was unpredictable or unpredicted. It was not only seers like [the Russian] Ivan Bloch who anticipated the stalemated positional warfare. General Staff strategists themselves, in their more lucid moments, foresaw these outcomes with astonishing accuracy. Schlieffen directed a war game in which he defeated his own plan with precisely the railway maneuver that Joffre employed to prevail on the Marne. In another German war game, which actually fell into Russian hands, Schlieffen used the advantage of railway mobility to defeat piecemeal the two prongs of a Russian advance around the Masurian Lakes—precisely the maneuver that led to the encirclement of Sazonov's Second Army at Tannenberg in August 1914. This is not to say that European war planners fully appreciated the overwhelming advantages of the defender; partly they underrated those advantages, partly they defied them. The point is that our own 20/20 hindsight is not qualitatively different from the understanding that was achievable by the historical protagonists.

Why then were these self-defeating, war-causing strategies adopted? Although the particulars varied from country to country, in each case strategic policymaking was skewed by a pathological pattern of civil–military relations that allowed or encouraged the military to use wartime operational strategy to solve its institutional problems. When strategy went awry, it was because a penchant for offense helped the military organization to preserve its autonomy, prestige, and traditions, to simplify its institutional routines, or to resolve a dispute within the organization. As further discussion will show, it was not just a quirk of fate that offensive strategies served these functions. On balance, offense tends to suit the needs of military organizations better than defense does, and militaries normally exhibit at least a moderate preference for offensive strategies and doctrines for that reason. What was special about the period before World War I was that the state of civil–military relations in each of the major powers tended to exacerbate that normal offensive bias, either because the lack of civilian control allowed it to grow unchecked or because an abnormal degree of civil–military conflict heightened the need for a self-protective ideology. . . .

As in 1914, today's military technologies favor the defender of the status quo, but the superpowers are adopting offensive counterforce strategies in defiance of these technological constraints. Like machine guns and railroads, survivable nuclear weapons render trivial the marginal advantages to be gained by striking first. In the view of some, this stabilizing effect even neutralizes whatever first-strike advantages may exist at the conventional level, since the fear of uncontrollable escalation will restrain even the first steps in that direction. Since the would-be aggressor has the "last clear chance" to avoid disaster and normally cares less about the outcome than the defender does, mutual assured destruction works strongly for stability and the defense of the status quo. In this way, the absolute power to inflict punishment eases the security dilemma. All states possessing survivable second-strike forces can be simultaneously secure. . . .

As in 1914, the danger today is that war will occur because of an erroneous belief that a disarming, offensive blow is feasible and necessary to ensure the attacker's security. In order to understand the forces that are eroding the stability of the strategic balance in our own era, it may be helpful to reflect on the causes and consequences of the "cult of the offensive" of 1914. . . .

## HOW OFFENSE PROMOTED WAR

. . . [O]ffensive plans not only reflected the belief that states are vulnerable and conquest is easy; they actually caused the states adopting them to *be* vulnerable and consequently fearful. Even the Fischer school, which emphasizes Germany's "grasping for 'World Power'" as the primary cause of the war, admits that Germany's decision to provoke a conflict in 1914 was also due to the huge Russian army increases then in progress, which would have left Germany at Russia's mercy upon their completion in 1917. This impending vulnerability, though real enough, was largely a function of the Schlieffen Plan, which had to strip the eastern front in order to amass the forces needed to deal with the strategic conundrums and additional opponents created by the march through Belgium. If the Germans had used a positional defense on the short Franco–German border to achieve economies of force, they could have handled even the enlarged Russian contingents planned for 1917.

In these ways, offensive strategies helped to cause the war and ensured that, when war occurred, it would be a world war. Prevailing technologies should have made the world of 1914 an arms controllers' dream; instead, military planners created a nightmare of strategic instability.

## GERMANY: UNCONTROLLED MILITARY OR MILITARIZED CIVILIANS?

The offensive character of German war planning in the years before World War I was primarily an expression of the professional interests and outlook of the General Staff. Civilian foreign-policy aims and attitudes about international politics were at most a permissive cause of the Schlieffen Plan. On balance, the General Staff's all-or-nothing war plan was more a hindrance than a help in implementing the diplomats' strategy of brinkmanship. The reason that the military was allowed to indulge its strategic preferences was not so much that the civilians agreed with them; rather, it was because war planning was considered to be within the autonomous purview of the General Staff. Military preferences were never decisive on questions of the use of force, however, since this was not considered their legitimate sphere. But indirectly, war plans trapped the diplomats by handing them a blunt instrument suitable for massive preventive war, but ill-designed for controlled coercion. The military's unchecked preference for an unlimited offensive strategy and the mismatch between German military and diplomatic strategy were important causes of strategic instability rooted in the problem of civil–military relations. . . .

The Schlieffen Plan embodied all of the desiderata commonly found in field manuals and treatises on strategy written by military officers: it was an offensive campaign, designed to seize the initiative, to exploit fleeting opportunities, and to achieve a decisive victory by the rapid annihilation of the opponents' military forces. War was to be an "instrument of politics," not in the sense that political ends would restrain and shape military means, but along lines that the General Staff found more congenial: war would solve the tangle of political problems that the diplomats could not solve for themselves. "The complete defeat of the enemy always serves politics," argued General Colmar von der Goltz in his influential book, *The Nation in Arms*. "Observance of this principle not only grants the greatest measure of freedom in the political sphere but also gives widest scope to the proper use of resources in war."

To do this, Schlieffen sought to capitalize on the relatively slow mobilization of the Russian army, which could not bring its full weight to bear until the second month of the campaign. Schlieffen reasoned that he had to use this "window of opportunity" to decisively alter the balance of forces in Germany's favor. . . . Schlieffen saw that a rapid decision could be achieved only by deploying the bulk of the German army on one front in order to carry out a grandiose encirclement maneuver. France had to be the first victim, because the Russians might spoil the encirclement by retreating into their vast spaces. With Paris at risk, the French would have to stand and fight. By 1897, Schlieffen had concluded that this scheme could not succeed without traversing Belgium, since the Franco–German frontier in Alsace–Lorraine was too narrow and too easily defended to permit a decisive maneuver. In the mature conception of 1905, most of the German army (including some units that did not yet exist) would march for three or four weeks through Belgium and northern France, encircling and destroying the French army, and then board trains for the eastern front to reinforce the few divisions left to cover East Prussia.

Even Schlieffen was aware that his plan was "an enterprise for which we are too weak." He and his successor, the younger Moltke, understood most of the pitfalls of this maneuver quite well: the gratuitous provocation of new enemies, the logistical nightmares, the possibility of a rapid French redeployment to nullify the German flank maneuver, the numerical insufficiency of the German army, the tendency of the attacker's strength to wane with every step forward and the defender's to grow, and the lack of time to finish with France before Russia would attack. . . .

In short, German war planning, especially after 1890, showed a strong bias in favor of offensive schemes for decisive victory and against defensive or more limited offensive schemes, even though the latter had a greater prospect of success. . . . The explanation for the General Staff's bias in favor of offensive strategy is rooted in the organizational interests and parochial outlook of the professional military. The Germans' pursuit of a strategy for a short, offensive, decisive war despite its operational infeasibility is simply an extreme case of an endemic bias of military organizations. . . .

### Explaining the Offensive Bias

Several explanations for this offensive bias have been advanced. A number of them are consistent with the evidence provided by the German case. A particularly important explanation stems from the division of labor and the narrow focus of attention that necessarily follows from it. The professional training and duties of the soldier force him to focus on threats to his state's security and on the conflictual side of international relations. Necessarily preoccupied with the prospect of armed conflict, he sees war as a pervasive aspect of international life. Focusing on the role of military means in ensuring the security of the state, he forgets that other means can also be used towards that end. For these reasons, the military professional tends to hold a simplified, zero-sum view of international politics and the nature of war, in which wars are seen as difficult to avoid and almost impossible to limit. . . .

The assumption of extreme hostility also favors the notion that decisive, offensive operations are always needed to end wars. If the conflict of interest between the parties is seen as limited, then a decisive victory may not be needed to end the fighting on mutually acceptable terms. In fact, denying the opponent his objectives by means of a successful defense may suffice. However, when the opponent is believed to be extremely hostile, disarming him completely may seem to be the only way to induce him to break off his attacks. For this reason, offensive doctrines and plans are needed, even if defense is easier operationally. . . .

A second explanation emphasizes the need of large, complex organizations to operate in a predictable, structured environment. Organizations like to work according to a plan that ties together the standard operating procedures of all the subunits into a prepackaged script. So that they can stick to this script at all costs, organizations try to dominate their environment rather than react to it. Reacting to unpredictable circumstances means throwing out the plan, improvising, and perhaps even deviating from standard operating procedures. As Barry Posen points out, "taking the offensive, exercising the initiative, is a way of structuring the battle." Defense, in contrast, is more reactive, less structured, and harder to plan. Van Evera argues that the military will prefer a task that is easier to plan even if it is more difficult to execute successfully. . . .

[I]t is difficult to ignore the argument ubiquitously advanced by European military writers that defense leads to uncertainty, confusion, passivity, and incoherent action, whereas offense focuses the efforts of the army and the mind of the commander on a single, unwavering goal. Even when they understood the uncertainties and improvisations required by offensive operations, as Groener did, they may still have feared the uncertainties of the defensive more. An offensive plan at least gives the illusion of certainty. . . .

Other explanations for the offensive bias are rooted even more directly in the parochial interests of the military, including the autonomy, prestige, size, and wealth of the organization. The German case shows the function of the offensive strategy as a means towards the goal of operational autonomy. The elder Moltke succinctly stated the universal wish of military commanders: "The politician should fall silent the moment that mobilization begins." This is least likely to happen in the case of limited or defensive wars, where the whole point of fighting is to negotiate a diplomatic solution. Political considerations—and hence politicians—have to figure in operational decisions. The operational autonomy of the military is most likely to be allowed when the operational goal is to disarm the adversary quickly and decisively by offensive means. For this reason, the military will seek to force doctrine and planning into this mold.

The prestige, self-image, and material health of military institutions will prosper if the military can convince civilians and themselves that wars can be short, decisive, and socially beneficial. One of the attractions of decisive, offensive strategies is that they hold out the promise of a demonstrable return on the nation's investment in military capability. Von der Goltz, for example, pushed the view that "modern wars have become the nation's way of doing business"—a perspective that made sense only if wars were short, cheap, and hence offensive. . . . As Posen puts it, offense makes soldiers "specialists in victory," defense makes them "specialists in attrition," and in our own era mutual assured destruction makes them "specialists in slaughter." . . .

### The Mismatch between Military Strategy and Diplomacy

It is sometimes thought that Germany required an unlimited, offensive military strategy because German civilian elites were hell-bent on overturning the continental balance of power as a first step in their drive for "World Power." In this view, the Schlieffen Plan was simply the tool needed to achieve this high-risk, high-payoff goal, around which a national consensus of both military and civilian elites had formed. There are several problems with this view. The first is that the civilians made virtually no input into the strategic planning process. . . . Later, when Reich Chancellor von Bülow learned of Schlieffen's intention to violate Belgian neutrality, his reaction was: "If the Chief of Staff, especially a strategic authority such as Schlieffen, believes such a measure to be necessary, then it is the obligation of diplomacy to adjust to it and prepare for it in every possible way." In 1912 Foreign Secretary von Jagow urged a reevaluation of the need to cross Belgian territory, but a memo from the younger Moltke ended the matter. In short, the civilians knew what Schlieffen was planning to do, but they were relatively passive bystanders in part because military strategy was not in their sphere of competence and legitimate authority, and perhaps also because they were quite happy with the notion that the war could be won quickly and decisively. This optimism alleviated their fear that a long war would mean the destruction of existing social and economic institutions, no matter who won it. . . . Mostly, the civilians passively accepted whatever operational plan the military deemed necessary. . . .

[The] mismatch between military and diplomatic strategy dogged German policy down through 1914. Bethmann Hollweg described his strategy in 1912 as one of controlled coercion, sometimes asserting German demands, sometimes lulling and mollifying opponents to control the risk of war. "On all fronts we must drive forward quietly and patiently," he explained, "without having to risk our existence." Bethmann's personal secretary, Kurt Riezler, explained this strategy of calculated risk in a 1914 volume, *Grundzüge der Weltpolitik*. A kind of cross between Thomas Schelling and Norman Angell, Riezler explained that wars were too costly to actually fight in the modern, interdependent, capitalist world. Nonetheless, states can still use the threat of war to gain unilateral advantages, forcing the opponent to calculate whether costs, benefits, and the probability of success warrant resorting to force. His calculations can be affected in several ways. Arms-racing can be used, *á la* Samuel Huntington, as a substitute for war—that is, a bloodless way to show the opponent that he would surely lose if it came to a fight. Brinkmanship and bluffing can be used to demonstrate resolve; *faits accomplis* and salami tactics can be used to shift the onus for starting the undesired war onto the opponent. But, Riezler warns, this strategy will not work if one is greedy and impatient to overturn the balance of power. Opponents will fight if they sense that their vital interests are at stake. Consequently, "victory belongs to the steady, tenacious, and gradual achievement of small successes . . . without provocation."

Although this may have been a fair approximation of Bethmann's thinking in 1912, the theory of the calculated risk had undergone a major transformation by July 1914. By that time, Bethmann wanted a major diplomatic or military victory and was willing to risk a continental war—perhaps even a world war—to achieve it. *Fait accompli* and onus-shifting were still part of the strategy, but with a goal of keeping Britain out of the war and gaining the support of German socialists, not with a goal of avoiding war altogether.

The Schlieffen Plan played an important role in the transformation of Bethmann's strategy and in its failure to keep Britain neutral in the July crisis. Riezler's diary shows Bethmann's obsession in July 1914 with Germany's need for a dramatic victory to forestall the impending period of vulnerability that the Russian army increases and the possible collapse of Austria-Hungary would bring on. . . . The Schlieffen Plan [however] only increased Germany's vulnerability to the Russian buildup, stripping the eastern front and squandering forces in the vain attempt to knock France out of the war. In this sense, it was the Schlieffen Plan that led Bethmann to transform the calculated-risk theory from a cautious tool of coercive diplomacy into a blind hope of gaining a major victory without incurring an unwanted world war.

Just as the Schlieffen Plan made trouble for Bethmann's diplomacy, so too German brinkmanship made trouble for the Schlieffen Plan. The Russian army increases, provoked by German belligerence in the 1909 Bosnian crisis and Austrian coercion of the Serbs in 1912, made the German war plan untenable. The arms-racing produced by this aggressive diplomacy was not a "substitute for war"; rather, it created a window of vulnerability that helped to cause the war. Thus, Riezler (and Bethmann) failed to consider how easily a diplomatic strategy of calculated brinkmanship could set off a chain of uncontrollable consequences in a world of military instability.

Even the transformed version of the calculated-risk theory, implemented in July 1914, was ill-served by the Schlieffen Plan. If Bethmann had had eastern-oriented or otherwise limited military options, all sorts of possibilities would have been available for defending Austria, bloodying the Russians, driving a wedge between Paris and St. Petersburg, and keeping Britain neutral. In contrast, the Schlieffen Plan cut short any chance for coercive diplomacy and ensured that Britain would fight. . . .

## FRANCE: CIVIL–MILITARY TRUCE AND CONFLICT

France before the Dreyfus Affair exemplifies the healthiest pattern of civil–military relations among the European states, but after Dreyfus, the most destructive. In the former period civilian defense experts who understood and respected the military contained the latent conflict between the professional army and republican politicians by striking a bargain that satisfied the main concerns of both sides. In this setting, the use of operational doctrine as a weapon of institutional defense was minimal, so plans and doctrine were a moderate combination of offense and defense. After the Dreyfus watershed, the truce broke. Politicians set out to "republicanize" the army, and the officer corps responded by developing the doctrine of *offensive à outrance*, which helped to reverse the slide towards a military system based overwhelmingly on reservists and capable only of defensive operations. . . .

The deepening of the Dreyfus crisis in 1898 rekindled old fears on both sides and destroyed the system of mutual respect and reassurance constructed by Freycinet. The military's persistence in a blatant miscarriage of justice against a Jewish General Staff officer accused of espionage confirmed the republicans' view of the army as a state within the state, subject to no law but the reactionary principles of unthinking obedience and blind loyalty. When conservatives and monarchists rallied to the military's side, it made the officer corps appear (undeservedly) to be the spearhead of a movement to overthrow the Republic. Likewise, attacks by the Dreyfusards confirmed the worst fears of the military. Irresponsible Radicals were demanding to meddle in the army's internal affairs, impeaching the integrity of future wartime commanders, and undermining morale. Regardless of Dreyfus's guilt or innocence, the honor of the military had to be defended for the sake of national security.

The upshot of the affair was a leftward realignment of French politics. The new Radical government appointed as War Minister a young reformist general, Louis André, with instructions to "republicanize" the army. André, aided by an intelligence network of Masonic Lodges, politicized promotions and war college admissions, curtailed officers' perquisites and disciplinary powers, and forced Catholic officers to participate in inventorying church property. In 1905, the term of conscription was reduced to two years, with reservists intended to play a more prominent role in war plans, field exercises, and the daily life of the regiment.

In this hostile environment, a number of officers—especially the group of "Young Turks" around Colonel Loyzeaux de Grandmaison—began to reemphasize in extreme form the organizational ideology propounded earlier by Gilbert. Its elements read like a list of the errors of Plan 17: *offensive à outrance*, mystical belief in group *élan* achieved by long service together, denigration of reservists, and disdain for reactive war plans driven by intelligence estimates. Aided by the Agadir Crisis of 1911, General Joffre and other senior figures seeking a reassertion of professional military values used the Young Turks' doctrine to scuttle the reformist plans of the "republican" commander in chief, Victor Michel, and to hound him from office. Michel, correctly anticipating the Germans' use of reserve corps in the opening battles and the consequent extension of their right wing across northern Belgium, had sought to meet this threat by a cordon defense, making intensive use of French reservists. Even middle-of-the-road officers considered ruinous the organizational changes needed to implement this scheme. It was no coincidence that Grandmaison's operational doctrine provided a tool for attacking Michel's ideas point-by-point, without having to admit too blatantly that it was the institutional implications of Michel's reservist-based plan that were its most objectionable aspect. Having served to oust Michel in 1911, the Grandmaison doctrine also played a role (along with the trumped-up scenario of a German standing-start attack) in justifying a return to the three-year term of service in 1913. The problem was that this ideology, so useful as a tool for institutional defense, became internalized by the French General Staff, who based Plan 17 on its profoundly erroneous tenets.

Obviously, there is much that is idiosyncratic in the story of the *offensive à outrance*. The overlapping of social and civil–military cleavages, which produced an unusually intense threat to the "organizational essence" and autonomy of the French army, may have no close analog in the contemporary era. At a higher level of abstraction, however, a broadly applicable hypothesis may nonetheless be gleaned from the French experience. That is, doctrinal bias is likely to become more extreme whenever strategic doctrine can be used as an ideological weapon to protect the military organization from threats to its institutional interests.

Under such circumstances, doctrine becomes unhinged from strategic reality and responds primarily to the more pressing requirements of domestic and intragovernmental politics.

## RUSSIA: INSTITUTIONAL PLURALISM AND STRATEGIC OVERCOMMITMENT

Between 1910 and 1912, Russia changed from an extremely cautious defensive war plan to an overcommitted double offensive against both Germany and Austria. The general direction of this change can be easily explained in terms of rational strategic calculations. Russia's military power had increased relative to Germany's, making an offensive more feasible, and the tightening of alliances made it more obvious that Germany would deploy the bulk of its army against France in the first phase of the fighting, regardless of the political circumstances giving rise to the conflict. Russian war planners consequently had a strong incentive to invade Germany or Austria during the "window of opportunity" provided by the Schlieffen Plan. Attacking East Prussia would put pressure on Germany's rear, thus helping France to survive the onslaught; attacking the Austrian army in Galicia might decisively shift the balance of power by knocking Germany's ally out of the war, while eliminating opposition to Russian imperial aims in Turkey and the Balkans.

What is harder to explain is the decision to invade both Germany and Austria, which ensured that neither effort would have sufficient forces to achieve its objectives. At a superficial level the explanation for this failure to set priorities is simple enough: General Yuri Danilov and the General Staff in St. Petersburg wanted to use the bulk of Russia's forces to attack Germany, while defending against Austria; General Mikhail Alekseev and other regional commanders wanted to attack Austria, leaving a weak defensive screen facing East Prussia. Each faction had powerful political connections and good arguments. No higher arbiter could or would choose between the contradictory schemes, so a *de facto* compromise allowed each to pursue its preferred offensive with insufficient forces. At this level, we have a familiar tale of bureaucratic politics producing an overcommitted, Christmas-tree "resultant." . . .

Nonetheless, the main differences between Danilov and Alekseev were intellectual, not bureaucratic. Danilov was fundamentally pessimistic about Russia's ability to compete with modern, efficient Germany. He considered Russia too weak to indulge in imperial dreams, whether against Austria or Turkey, arguing that national survival required an absolute priority be given to containing the German danger. In 1910, this pessimism was expressed in his ultra-defensive plan, based on the fear that Russia would have to face Germany virtually alone. By 1913–1914, Danilov's pessimism took a different form. The improved military balance, the tighter alliance with France after Agadir, and telling criticism from Alekseev convinced Danilov that a porcupine strategy was infeasible politically and undesirable strategically. Now his nightmare was that France would succumb in a few weeks, once again leaving backward Russia to face Germany virtually alone. To prevent this, he planned a hasty attack into East Prussia, designed to draw German forces away from the decisive battle in France. . . .

Personality differences may explain Danilov's extreme pessimism and Alekseev's relative optimism, but this begs the question of why each man was able to gain support for his view. What evidence exists points to idiosyncratic explanations: Danilov's plan got support from Zhilinskii (it fit the agreements he made with Joffre), the commander-designate of the East Prussian front (it gave him more troops), and the General Staff apparatus (a military elite disdainful of and pessimistic about the rabble who would implement their plans). Alekseev won support from operational commanders and probably from Grand Duke Nikolai Nikolaevitch, the future commander-in-chief and a quintessential optimist about Russian capabilities and ambitions. The War Minister, the Czar, and the political parties seem to have played little role in strategic planning, leaving the intramilitary factions to logroll their own disputes.

Perhaps the most important question is why the outcome of the logrolling was not to scale down the aims of both offensives to fit the diminished forces available to each. In particular, why did Danilov insist on an early-start, two-pincer advance into East Prussia, when the weakness of each pincer made them both vulnerable to piecemeal destruction? Why not wait a few days until each pincer could be reinforced by late-arriving units, or why not advance only on one side of the lakes? The answer seems to lie in Danilov's extreme fears about the viability of the French and his consequent conviction that Russian survival depended on early and substantial pressure on the German rear. This task was a necessity, given his outlook, something that had to be attempted whether available forces were adequate or not. Trapped by his pessimism about Russia's prospects in the long run, Danilov's only way out was through unwarranted optimism about operational prospects in the short run. Like most cornered decision-makers, Danilov saw the "necessary" as possible.

This is an important theme in the German case as well. Schlieffen and the younger Moltke demonstrated an ability to be ruthlessly realistic about the shortcomings of their operational plans, but realism was suppressed when it would call into question their fundamental beliefs and values. Schlieffen's qualms about his war plan's feasibility pervade early drafts, but disappear later on, without analytical justification. He entertained doubts as long as he thought they would lead to improvements, but once he saw that no further tinkering would resolve the plan's remaining contradictions, he swept them under the rug. The younger Moltke did the same thing, resorting to blithe optimism only on make-or-break issues, like the seizure of Liège, where a realistic assessment of the risks would have spotlighted the dubiousness of *any* strategy for rapid, decisive victory. Rather than totally rethink their strategic assumptions, which were all bound up with fundamental interests and even personal characteristics, all of these strategists chose to see the "necessary" as possible.

Two hypotheses emerge from the Russian case. The first points to bureau-cratic logrolling as a factor that is likely to exacerbate the normal offensive bias of military organizations. In the absence of a powerful central authority, two factions or suborganizations will each pursue its own preferred offensive despite a dramatic deficit of available forces. Thus, offensives that are moderately ambitious when considered separately become extremely overcommitted under the pressure of scarce resources and the need to logroll with other factions competing for their allocation. The German case showed how the lack of civilian control can produce doctrinal extremism when the military is united; the Russian case shows how lack of civilian control can also lead to extreme offensives when the military is divided.

The second hypothesis, which is supported by the findings of cognitive theory, is that military decision-makers will tend to overestimate the feasibility of an operational plan if a realistic assessment would require forsaking fundamental beliefs or values. Whenever offensive doctrines are inextricably tied to the auton-omy, "essence," or basic worldview of the military, the cognitive need to see the offensive as possible will be strong.

## EXTERNAL INFLUENCES ON STRATEGY AND CIVIL–MILITARY RELATIONS

The offensive strategies of 1914 were largely domestic in origin, rooted in bureaucratic, sociopolitical, and psychological causes. To some extent, however, external influences exacerbated—and occasionally diminished—these offensive biases. Although these external factors were usually secondary, they are particularly interesting for their lessons about sources of leverage over the destabilizing policies of one's opponents. The most important of these lessons—and the one stressed by Van Evera elsewhere in this issue—is that offense tends to promote offense and defense tends to promote defense in the international system.

One way that offense was exported from one state to another was by means of military writings. The French discovered Clausewitz in the 1880s, reading misinterpretations of him by contemporary German militarists who focused narrowly on his concept of the "decisive battle." At the same time, reading the retrograde Russian tactician Dragomirov reinforced their home-grown overemphasis on the connection between the offensive and morale. Russian writings later reimported these ideas under the label of *offensive à outrance*, while borrowing from Germany the short-war doctrine. Each of Europe's militaries cited the others in parroting the standard lessons drawn from the Russo–Japanese War: offense was becoming tactically more difficult but was still advantageous strategically. None of this shuffling and sharing of rationales for offense was the initial cause of anyone's offensive bias. Everyone was exporting offense to everyone else; no one was just receiving. Its main effect was mutual reinforcement. The military could believe (and argue to others) that offense must be advantageous, since everyone else said so, and that the prevalence of offensive doctrines was somebody else's fault.

The main vehicle for exporting offensive strategies was through aggressive policies, not offensive ideas. The aggressive diplomacy and offensive war plans of one state frequently encouraged offensive strategies in neighboring states both directly, by changing their strategic situation, and indirectly, by changing their pattern of civil–military relations. German belligerence in the Agadir crisis of 1911 led French civilians to conclude that war was likely and that they had better start appeasing their own military by giving them leaders in which they would have confidence. This led directly to Michel's fall and the rise of Joffre, Castelnau, and the proponents of the *offensive à outrance*. German belligerence in the Bosnian crisis of 1908–1909 had a similar, if less direct effect on Russia. It convinced Alekseev that a limited war against Austria alone would be impossible, and it put everyone in a receptive mood when the French urged the tightening of the alliance in 1911. Before Bosnia, people sometimes thought in terms of a strategic modus vivendi with Germany; afterwards, they thought in terms of a breathing spell while gaining strength for the final confrontation. Combined with the Russians' growing realization of the probable character of the German war plan, this led inexorably to the conclusions that war was coming, that it could not be limited, and that an unbridled offensive was required to exploit the window of opportunity provided by the Schlieffen Plan's westward orientation. Caught in this logic, Russian civilians who sought limited options in July 1914 were easily refuted by Danilov and the military. Completing the spiral, the huge Russian arms increases provoked by German belligerence allowed the younger Moltke to argue persuasively that Germany should seek a pretext for preventive war before those increases reached fruition in 1917. This recommendation was persuasive only in the context of the Schlieffen Plan, which made Germany look weaker than it really was by creating needless enemies and wasting troops on an impossible task. Without the Schlieffen Plan, Germany would not have been vulnerable in 1917.

In short, the European militaries cannot be blamed for the belligerent diplomacy that set the ball rolling towards World War I. Once the process began, however, their penchant for offense and their quickness to view war as inevitable created a slide towards war that the diplomats did not foresee. The best place to intervene to stop the destabilizing spiral of exported offense was, of course, at the beginning. If German statesmen had had a theory of civil–military relations and of the security dilemma to help them calculate risks more accurately, their choice of a diplomatic strategy might have been different.

If offense gets exported when states adopt aggressive policies, it also gets exported when states try to defend themselves in ways that are indistinguishable from preparations for aggression. In the 1880s, the Russians improved their railroads in Poland and increased the number of troops there in peacetime, primarily in order to decrease their vulnerability to German attack in the early weeks of a war. The German General Staff saw these measures as a sign that a Russian attack was imminent, so counseled launching a preventive strike before Russian preparations proceeded further. Bismarck thought otherwise, so the incident did not end in the same way as the superficially similar 1914 case. Several factors may account for the difference: Bismarck's greater power over the military, his lack of interest in expansion for its own sake, and the absence of political conditions that would make war seem inevitable to anyone but a General Staff officer. Perhaps the most important difference, however, was that in 1914 the younger Moltke was anticipating a future of extreme vulnerability, whereas in 1887 the elder Moltke was anticipating a future of strategic stalemate. Moltke, planning for a defense in the west in any event, believed that the Germans could in the worst case hold out for thirty years if France and Russia forced war upon them.

Although states can provoke offensive responses by seeming too aggressive, they can also invite offensive predation by seeming too weak. German hopes for a rapid victory, whether expressed in the eastward plan of the 1880s or the westward Schlieffen Plan, always rested on the slowness of Russia's mobilization. Likewise, Germany's weakness on the eastern front, artificially created by the Schlieffen Plan, promoted the development of offensive plans in Russia. Finally, Belgian weakness allowed the Germans to retain their illusions about decisive victory by providing an apparent point of entry into the French keep.

States who want to export defense, then, should try to appear neither weak nor aggressive. The French achieved this in the early 1880s, when a force posture heavy on fortifications made them an unpromising target and an ineffective aggressor. In the short run, this only redirected Moltke's offensive toward a more vulnerable target, Russia. But by 1888–1890, when Russia too had strengthened its fortifications and its defensive posture in Poland generally, Moltke was stymied and became very pessimistic about offensive operations. Schlieffen, however, was harder to discourage. When attacking Russia became unpromising, he simply redirected his attention towards France, pursuing the least unpromising offensive option. For hard-core cases like Schlieffen, one wonders whether any strategy of nonprovocative defense, no matter how effective and nonthreatening, could induce abandoning the offensive.

## SOVIET STRATEGY AND CIVIL–MILITARY RELATIONS

In 1914, flawed civil–military relations exacerbated and liberated the military's endemic bias for offensive strategies, creating strategic instability despite military technologies that aided the defender of the status quo. Some of the factors that produced this outcome may have been peculiar to that historical epoch. The full professionalization of military staffs had been a relatively recent development, for example, and both civilians and military were still groping for a satisfactory *modus vivendi*. After the First World War, military purveyors of the "cult of the offensive" were fairly well chastened except in Japan, where the phenomenon was recapitulated. Our own era has seen nothing this extreme, but more moderate versions of the military's offensive bias are arguably still with us. It will be worthwhile, therefore, to reiterate the kinds of conditions that have intensified this bias in the past in order to assess the likelihood of their recurrence.

First, offensive bias is exacerbated when civilian control is weak. In Germany before 1914, a long period of military autonomy in strategic planning allowed the dogmatization of an offensive doctrine, rooted in the parochial interests and outlook of the General Staff. In Russia, the absence of firm, unified civilian control fostered logrolling between two military factions, compounding the offensive preferences exhibited by each. Second, offensive bias grows more extreme when operational doctrine is used as a weapon in civil–military disputes about domestic politics, institutional arrangements, or other nonstrategic issues. The French *offensive à outrance*, often dismissed as some mystical aberration, is best explained in these terms.

Once it appears, an acute offensive bias tends to be self-replicating and resistant to disconfirming evidence. Offensive doctrinal writings are readily transmitted across international boundaries. More important, offensive strategies tend to spread in a chain reaction, since one state's offensive tends to create impending dangers or fleeting opportunities for other states, who must adopt their own offensives to forestall or exploit them. Finally, hard operational evidence of the infeasibility of an offensive strategy will be rationalized away when the offensive is closely linked to the organization's "essence," autonomy, or fundamental ideology.

I believe that these findings, derived from the World War I cases, resonate strongly with the development of Soviet nuclear strategy and with certain patterns in the U.S.–Soviet strategic relationship. At a time when current events are stimulating considerable interest in the state of civil–military relations in the Soviet Union, the following thoughts are offered not as answers but as questions that researchers may find worth considering.

Soviet military doctrine, as depicted by conventional wisdom, embodies all of the desiderata typically expressed in professional military writings throughout the developed world since Napoleon. Like Schlieffen's doctrine, it stresses offense, the initiative, and decisive results through the annihilation of the opponent's ability to resist. It is suspicious of political limitations on violence based on mutual restraint, especially in nuclear matters. Both in style and substance, Sidorenko reads like a throwback to the military writers of the Second Reich, warning that "a forest which has not been completely cut down grows up again." The similarity is not accidental. Not only does offense serve some of the same institutional functions for the Soviet military as it did for the German General Staff, but Soviet doctrine is to some degree their lineal descendant. "In our military schools," a 1937 *Pravda* editorial averred, "we study Clausewitz, Moltke, Schlieffen, and Ludendorff." Soviet nuclear doctrine also parallels pre-1914 German strategy in that both cut against the grain of the prevailing technology. The Soviets have never been in a position to achieve anything but disaster by seizing the initiative and striving for decisive results; neither was Schlieffen.

There are also parallels in the political and historical circumstances that permitted the development of these doctrines. The Soviet victories in World War II, like the German victories in 1866 and 1870, were nation-building and regime-legitimating enterprises that lent prestige and authority to the military profession, notwithstanding Stalin's attempt to check it. This did not produce a man on horseback in either country, nor did it allow the military to usurp authority on questions of the use of force. But in both cases the military retained a monopoly of military operational expertise and was either never challenged or eventually prevailed in practical doctrinal disputes. In the German case, at least, it was military autonomy on questions of operational plans and doctrine that made war more likely; direct lobbying for preventive strikes caused less trouble because it was clearly illegitimate.

While many accounts of the origins of Soviet nuclear strategy acknowledge the effect of the professional military perspective, they often lay more stress on civilian sources of offensive, warfighting doctrines: for example, Marxism–Leninism, expansionist foreign-policy goals, and historical experiences making Russia a "militarized society." Political leaders, in this view, promote or at least accept the military's warfighting doctrine because it serves their foreign-policy goals and/or reflects a shared view of international politics as a zero-sum struggle. Thus, Lenin is quoted as favoring a preemptive first strike, Frunze as linking offense to the proletarian spirit. The military principle of annihilation of the opposing armed force is equated with the Leninist credo of *kto kogo*.

Although this view may capture part of the truth, it fails to account for recurrent statements by Soviet political leaders implying that nuclear war is unwinnable, that meaningful damage limitation cannot be achieved through superior warfighting capabilities, and that open-ended expenditures on strategic programs are wasteful and perhaps pointless. These themes have been voiced in the context of budgetary disputes (not just for public-relations purposes) by Malenkov, Khrushchev, Brezhnev, and Ustinov. To varying degrees, all of these civilian leaders have chafed at the cost of open-ended warfighting programs and against the redundant offensive capabilities demanded by each of several military suborganizations. McNamara discovered in the United States that the doctrine of mutual assured destruction, with its emphasis on the irrelevance of marginal advantages and the infeasibility of counterforce damage-limitation strategies, had great utility in budgetary debates. Likewise, recent discussions in the Soviet Union on the feasibility of victory seem to be connected with the question of how much is enough. Setting aside certain problems of nuance and interpretation, a case can be made that the civilian leadership, speaking through Defense Minister Ustinov, has been using strategic doctrine to justify slowing down the growth of military spending. In the context of arguments about whether the Reagan strategic buildup will really make the Soviet Union more vulnerable, Ustinov has quite clearly laid out the argument that neither super-power can expect to gain anything by striking first, since both have survivable retaliatory forces and launch-on-warning capabilities. . . .

# 10

# Hitler and the Blitzkrieg Strategy

JOHN J. MEARSHEIMER

## THE ORIGINAL STRATEGY AND THE PRINCIPAL ACTORS

### The Original Strategy

On 27 September [1939,] before the formal conclusion of the Polish campaign, Hitler informed his military leaders that he planned to strike in the West in the immediate future. At the time, no plans existed for such an operation, and in fact, the military was preparing to assume a defensive posture in the West. There was widespread agreement among the top military leaders that the Allies would not move into Belgium and Holland, much less strike against Germany. In the words of Gen. Alfred Jodl, the chief of the Operations Staff at the High Command of the Armed Forces (OKW), "There was, particularly in the Army, a widespread opinion that the war would die a natural death if we only kept quiet in the West."

Hitler's view of the situation was very different and more complex. Basically, there were two motives behind Hitler's insistence that Germany strike against the Allies. First, unlike his generals, he believed that the Allies were preparing to move into the Low Countries, where they would be in an excellent position to attack the Ruhr. Hitler was determined to beat the Allies to the punch and to occupy the Low Countries before they did. But he had a second and ultimately more important reason for taking the offensive. He intended to establish German hegemony on the Continent, and to do this he realized that he had to conquer France and to drive the British from the Continent. Hitler saw no possibility of peace with the Allies. His political goals, however, had to be weighed against the capabilities of the German military. As will become evident, this weighing process led to much controversy. . . .

## THE DECISION-MAKING PROCESS: OCTOBER 1939–MAY 1940

### The Movement to Dissuade Hitler from Attacking in the West

Three days after Hitler announced his plan to strike in the West, [army commander in chief, General] Brauchitsch, and [army chief of staff, General] Halder met with him and submitted a memorandum calling for a defensive posture in the West. On 4 October, General Jodl, the chief of the Operations Staff at OKW, told Halder that Hitler was very upset with his commanders for dragging their feet. Jodl's warning had little impact. On 7 October, Brauchitsch and Halder met with Hitler and again attempted to dissuade him from assuming the offensive in the West. They were not successful. Hitler made it clear at this meeting that he was willing to attack even if he could achieve only limited objectives. He told Brauchitsch and Halder that they must take the offensive, "even if we fall short of the original objectives and attain only a line which would afford better protection for the Ruhr." . . .

On 17 October, Brauchitsch met with Hitler and tried again to persuade him not to strike in the West. Afterward Brauchitsch described the situation as "hopeless." Two days later, on the nineteenth, the army forwarded its first plan of attack to OKW. . . . [See Figure 10.1.] The objective was limited. In fact, the plan did not even address the question of occupying French territory. "The order dealt only with operations against Holland, Belgium, and Luxembourg."

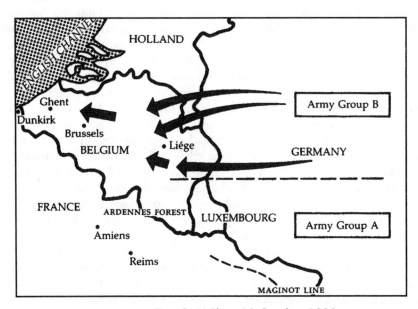

**FIGURE 10.1** First OKH Plan, 19 October 1939.

There was widespread dissatisfaction with the plan from the start. On 25 October, Hitler met with Brauchitsch and Halder to discuss the matter. Hitler told the generals that he wanted to place the main axis of advance south of Liége and to strike toward Amiens and Reims. Hitler's proposal to place the weight of the attack south of Liége and to strike in a southwesterly direction contrasted sharply with the army's plan to locate the weight of the attack north of Liége and to strike in a northwesterly direction. Significantly, Hitler's proposal would force the German army to defeat a larger portion of the Allied forces than would the army plan, as was consistent with his view that the strategy, even if proffered as a limited one, should maximize the chances of achieving a decisive victory. . . .

While this meeting on the twenty-fifth was in progress, General Bock and his subordinates, Generals Reichenau and Kluge, joined the discussion. Bock was the commander of Army Group B, which would make the main attack in the forthcoming offensive. Reichenau was the commander of the forces that composed the powerful northern pincer in the OKH plan, while Kluge commanded the southern pincer. Bock, Kluge, and Reichenau, who realized that Hitler was intent on launching the attack in fall 1939 joined with Brauchitsch and Halder to discourage Hitler from attacking. At this point, Hitler must have realized how widespread the opposition was to his scheme. . . .

Brauchitsch and Halder met again with Hitler two days later, on 27 October, and Hitler told them that the attack would commence on 12 November. Brauchitsch said that the army would not be prepared for action before 26 November. Hitler responded that this date was "much too late." Time was growing short for Halder and Brauchitsch. The two army leaders met again the following day with Hitler, who outlined the changes he wanted made in the first OKH plan. There would still be armies from Army Group B located north and south of Liége , but the main weight of the attack was to shift to the south of Liége, and the envelopment west of Liége was to be abandoned. Instead the Germans would launch an essentially frontal attack with the aim of driving the Allies straight across central and northern Belgium to the Channel coast (see Figure 10.2). Army Group A was to move across the southern part of Belgium and to protect Army Group B's southern flank. Although the new plan was somewhat more ambitious in scope than the original, the two were very similar. Both relied on Army Group B to make the main attack and to capture the northern portion of Belgium. Although the original plan relied on an envelopment west of Liége, it was, like the second version, basically a frontal attack designed to push the Allies back along a broad front. This point was not lost on German military leaders, who recognized that such a strategy would lead to a repeat of World War I.

The mood of Brauchitsch and Halder remained pessimistic. Then, on 31 October, they received another memorandum from Leeb spelling out the grave dangers associated with an attack in the West. The intensity of Leeb's concern is reflected in his concluding sentence: "I am prepared to stand behind you personally to the fullest extent in the days to come and to bear the consequences desirable or

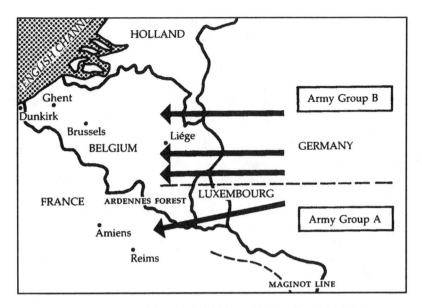

**FIGURE 10.2** Second OKH Plan, 29 October 1939.

necessary." That same day they received a memorandum from Army Group A arguing that the existing plan would lead to catastrophe. . . .

On his return from the front, Halder met with Gen. Georg Thomas, the head of the War Economy and Armaments Office at OKW. Thomas told Halder that significant economic problems would result from an offensive in the West. Previously, in September, Thomas had given Halder and Gen. Walter Warlimont of OKW information about the state of the German economy that provided ammunition for those who opposed Hitler's plan to attack in the West. If the German military could not deliver a rapid knockout blow and was thus forced to fight a protracted war (which Brauchitsch, Halder, and Leeb saw as the logical outcome of a limited aims strategy), then a strong German war economy would be essential. Thomas, who was an active member in the group conspiring to depose Hitler, provided Halder with evidence that the German economy was not prepared to sustain the protracted war that now seemed inevitable.

After returning from the meetings with the commanders at the front, Brauchitsch asked to meet with Hitler. He felt that he should make one more effort to change Hitler's mind. The meeting took place on 5 November, and the results were disastrous. Brauchitsch took a memorandum with him that had been written in direct response to Hitler's 9 October Memorandum; it "attempted to prove that any offensive was ruled out at the moment." After failing to make any headway with the standard litany of arguments, Brauchitsch tried to convince Hitler that the German troops might not be prepared to assume the offensive. He told Hitler that the troops had not been aggressive in Poland and that there had been discipline problems in that first campaign. For Hitler, who was not familiar with these claims, this was the last straw. He launched into a tirade that left Brauchitsch stunned and badly shaken. As a consequence of this key meeting, Brauchitsch's influence with Hitler plummeted. Moreover, after the 5 November meeting, it was manifest that Hitler could not be dissuaded from an offensive against the Allies.

The opposition to an offensive nevertheless continued. In the wake of the 5 November meeting, the three army group commanders (Bock, Leeb, and Rundstedt) held a secret meeting to discuss how to prevent Hitler from striking in the West. The commanders voiced some differences. For example, Leeb was against an offensive altogether, while Rundstedt wanted to adopt a different strategy and then to attack. Such differences were not crucial in fall 1939 because there was an overriding concern: stopping Hitler from opening an offensive in the West. The three army commanders agreed to do everything possible to achieve that end.

While the generals were doing their best to keep Hitler from striking, the blitzkrieg began to emerge as a viable option. It took approximately four months before this strategy was formally adopted, and the decision-making process was complex. Army Group A was the main driving force behind the blitzkrieg, although it is clear that Hitler's influence was of crucial importance. Moreover, a number of events in the early part of 1940, principally an airplane crash and two sand table exercises, facilitated the adoption of the blitzkrieg.

The leaders of Army Group A were particularly dissatisfied with the first two OKH plans. They believed that it would be suicidal to launch an offensive that did not promise a decisive victory. They also believed that a plan of their own would allow the German army to defeat the Allies decisively. On 31 October, Rundstedt, the commander of Army Group A, forwarded a letter and a memorandum outlining Army Group A's views to OKH. During the next three months. Rundstedt and Manstein, Army Group A's chief of staff, sent seven more memorandums to OKH. Furthermore, they talked directly with Halder and Brauchitsch on a number of occasions, trying always to convince the OKH chiefs of the merits of their plan. More often than not, OKH refused to respond to Army Group A's memorandums. When there was a response, Rundstedt and Manstein were told that the existing plan could not be altered. By late January 1940, when the weather had finally forced postponement of the operation until spring, there was no evidence that Army Group A had made any headway in winning acceptance of its proposal. The limited aims strategy was still in place.

Army Group A's initial proposal differed in a number of important respects from the final plan that operationalized the blitzkrieg. Nevertheless, the general outline of the final plan is present in the first proposal that Rundstedt sent to OKH. Most important, he called for shifting the main weight of the attack from

Army Group B in the north to Army Group A in the south. Actually, Rundstedt envisioned Army Group A's forces working closely with the southernmost elements of Army Group B. Their objective was not to push the Allies back along a broad front, as was the case with the existing plan, but instead to pierce the Allies' front somewhere between Liége and Namur and then to drive deep into the Allies' rear. It is clear that Army Group A was concerned to effect a deep strategic penetration, the central element in the blitzkrieg.

As we know, a blitzkrieg provides that large armored units operating independently should conduct the deep attacks. It is evident from Rundstedt's first memorandum that the panzer forces were expected to play an important role in Army Group A's proposed plan. This emphasis is hardly surprising, since panzer forces had contributed significantly to the recent German victory in Poland. . . . Army Group A's failure to provide details on the employment of armor notwithstanding, the plan laid out in the first memorandum was very close to being a blitzkrieg.

During this same period, Hitler began to focus attention on Army Group A. His new interest was a consequence of his general dissatisfaction with the existing plan as well as of his specific desire to broaden its scope so as to maximize the chances of achieving a decisive victory. At the aforementioned 25 October meeting, where Hitler had discussed the first OKH plan with his generals, he actually asked about the possibility of placing the main weight of the attack opposite the Ardennes, the principal topographical feature in southern Belgium. He quickly dismissed his own idea, however, and none of the assembled generals saw fit to defend it. But on 30 October, one day after the second OKH plan was issued, Jodl noted in his diary: "Fuhrer comes with new idea about having an armored and a motorized division attack Sedan via Arlon." In effect, this meant giving Army Group A a *small* armored force that would attack through the Ardennes. There is no evidence that at this point Hitler was aware of Army Group A's idea for shifting the main weight of the offensive. Brauchitsch was made aware of Hitler's "new idea," and on 12 November the Nineteenth Panzer Corps, which was commanded by Guderian, was assigned to Army Group A.

This change was significant for a number of reasons. First, Army Group A had hitherto comprised only infantry divisions. The new assignment also meant, however, that the panzer divisions would not be concentrated with one army group but would instead be spread out across a broad front. Third, and very important, Guderian, the foremost proponent of the blitzkrieg in Germany, was now united with Manstein and Rundstedt, who had by this time already given OKH two memorandums outlining their plan.

Although Hitler was responsible for assigning the Nineteenth Panzer Corps to Army Group A, he was not shifting the main weight of the attack away from Army Group B. . . . Shortly after Nineteenth Panzer Corps joined Army Group A, Guderian and Manstein met to discuss the upcoming offensive. Guderian told

Manstein of his displeasure with the distribution of the panzer divisions across a wide front. Manstein then described his plan to Guderian, who reacted enthusiastically, although he warned Manstein that it was imperative to employ a large number of armored divisions at the main point of attack. Specifically, this caution meant that Army Group A should rely on panzer divisions to make the initial breakthrough and then to effect the deep strategic penetration. Manstein did not disagree. It is clear that, from this point forward, Manstein and Guderian completely agreed on the shape of the proposed offensive.

Their agreement is apparent in the first memorandum that Manstein forwarded to OKH after the Nineteenth Panzer Corps had been assigned to Army Group A:

For the A Gp it is, however, important, after dashing through Luxembourg making maximum use of the element of surprise, to break through the fortified Belgian positions before the French are able to form up their defence forces and to entirely defeat in *Belgium* those French elements initially to be expected for encounter. This is the prerequisite both for the continuation of the operation over the Meuse and for the formation of a defensive front toward the south. Therefore the A Gp has placed the XIX Corps with 3 div in the front line *forward of the front* and has allocated to it alone four trunk roads to try to break through the fortified Belgian positions.

Now, Army Group A's proposal contained all the ingredients of the blitzkrieg, although it was clear that Army Group A would need more armored forces. The Nineteenth Panzer Corps alone was not enough to effect a breakthrough and to conduct a deep strategic penetration. As I noted earlier, OKH placed the Fourteenth Motorized Corps *behind* Army Group A in late November. Shortly thereafter, Manstein and Rundstedt asked OKH to assign the Fourteenth Motorized Corps to Army Group A so that it could be employed with the Nineteenth Panzer Corps in the front of the army group. OKH refused the request.

As 1939 came to a close, OKH remained tied to its own limited plan. Although Army Group A continued sending memorandums to OKH, no more important changes were made in the disposition of forces until the blitzkrieg was adopted in mid-February 1940. On 27 December 1939, OKW announced that the date for the beginning of the offensive would be decided by 9 January. On 10 January, the weather forecast was favorable, and Hitler decided that the attack would start on 17 January. Also on 10 January, a German airplane carrying a copy of the OKH plan crashed in Belgium. Jodl's subsequent entry in his diary sums up the German reaction to this development: "If enemy is in possession of all the files, situation catastrophic." The attack was canceled for the last time on 13 January. In light of the plane crash and the onset of winter, it was decided to postpone the attack until spring 1940.

With this decision, the military leaders, as well as Hitler, had time to consider the options in front of them carefully. Then, too, the divulgence of the existing plan had certainly made it imperative to consider alternatives. Army Group A continued to plead its case. The final two of its eight memorandums were forwarded to OKH after the plane crash. At a key conference on 25 January, Rundstedt and Manstein tried to persuade the OKH chiefs of the merits of their plan. Again they were unsuccessful. As the month ended, the limited plan devised in October and slightly modified in November remained intact.

In February, that plan was finally abandoned, and the blitzkrieg championed by Army Group A was adopted. It appears that the change came about largely because of two very important sand table exercises and the intervention of Hitler. Ironically, Manstein was informed on 27 January that he was being transferred to command a reserve infantry corps, effective on 9 February. Before the transfer took place, Manstein helped run a sand table exercise at Army Group A headquarters in Coblenz (7 February). At this exercise, which was attended by the OKH chiefs, a large-scale simulation of the existing plan was conducted for the first time. Here it became evident that the Nineteenth Panzer Corps would have to be reinforced immediately. Perception of this need was due in part to new intelligence indicating that the French were increasing the strength of their forces opposite the Ardennes. In any case, however, Army Group A had always recognized that one armored corps would not be sufficient to pierce the Allied front and then to effect a deep strategic penetration. It was also apparent that Guderian would reach the Meuse within four days. Guderian and Halder engaged in a heated debate as to whether Army Group A should attack across the Meuse immediately (Guderian) or whether it should wait until the "ninth or tenth day of the offensive" (Halder). In effect, Halder wanted to wait for the infantry to catch up with the armor before he crossed the Meuse. Guderian maintained that the panzer divisions could cross the river alone. Nevertheless, Manstein believed that Halder was finally beginning to see the merits of Army Group A's proposal.

Another sand table exercise was held one week later on 14 February. Again it was clear that the Nineteenth Panzer Corps would reach the Meuse very quickly and that, moreover, if Army Group A had any hope of driving into the depths of the Allied rear, reinforcements would be needed before the attack was launched. Guderian and Halder continued their argument about the proper time to cross the Meuse and the proper kind of formations to use. Halder, who still favored using infantry divisions and armored divisions together, remarked in his diary for that day: "*Guderian and Witersheim* [commander of the Fourteenth Motorized Corps] plainly show lack of confidence in success. Guderian: Has lost confidence—The whole tank operation is planned wrong!" Unfortunately for Guderian, Manstein was not present at this second war game. He had departed for his new assignment five days earlier. Although Halder had not formally acknowledged acceptance of the Army Group A plan and disagreed with Guderian's ideas concerning the Meuse crossing, he did recognize the need to increase the weight of Army Group A.

As this perceptible shift in Halder's view was taking place, Hitler was reviewing the existing plan. On 13 February, he was given the detailed breakdown of the disposition of German forces that he had requested. After examining the report, Hitler remarked to Jodl:

Most of the gun-armed tanks have been expended on places which are not decisive. The armoured divisions with the Fourth Army [which formed part of Army Group B's attacking force] can do little in areas where there are obstructions and fortifications. They will come to a standstill at the Meuse, if not before. . . . They should be concentrated in the direction of Sedan where the enemy does not expect our main thrust. The documents carried by the aircraft which made the landing have still further confirmed their opinion that our only concern is to occupy the Channel coastline of Holland and Belgium.

Jodl warned Hitler that "the thrust against Sedan is a tactical gamble, where one can be surprised by the God of War." Hitler was not impressed. That same afternoon, Colonels Grieffenberg and Heusinger, both from the Operations Staff at OKH, were summoned to Jodl's office. Jodl told them about Hitler's ideas and then directed them to provide a detailed study of the matter. Four days later, on 17 February, Hitler called Manstein aside after a routine meeting of recently appointed corps commanders. He asked Manstein to outline his views on the offensive in the West. When Manstein had finished detailing his plan, Hitler "indicated his agreement with the ideas put forward." The next day (18 February) Halder met with Hitler to present the results of the study that OKH had conducted in response to Jodl's 13 February meeting with Grieffenberg and Heusinger. OKH recommended shifting the main weight of the attack to Army Group A, as Hitler had prescribed. OKH's position was now of course consistent with Army Group A's views on the reshaping of the offensive. Shortly thereafter, the new plan was formally adopted. . . .

The new plan itself undoubtedly held a certain attraction for Hitler. Although it was audacious, it would, if successful, produce the decisive victory that he wanted so badly. Furthermore, Hitler had always been favorably disposed toward upgrading Army Group A's role in the offensive. OKW Directive No. 8, which mandated that the capability be developed to shift the main weight of the attack to Army Group A, highlights this point. Furthermore, as I noted earlier, Hitler at a meeting in October 1939 had actually mentioned the possibility of placing the main axis of advance through Sedan. Not surprisingly, once Hitler was convinced that the idea of attacking through Sedan was sound, he claimed credit for having devised the scheme. . . .

### The New Plan

On 24 February, Halder reviewed the proposed plan with his commanders at OKH headquarters and issued the final operations order. Despite the OKH leadership's hostility to the Manstein proposal before February, they staunchly supported it once they had been won over. In fact, as Telford Taylor notes, OKH's version of the Army Group A plan was actually "far more drastic than anything Manstein had ever proposed." The key assumption was that once the fighting in the West began, the Allies would push forward into northern and central Belgium, placing the majority of the Allied forces opposite Army Group B, which was now the weaker of the two principal German army groups. In southern Belgium in the area of the Ardennes, the Allies would have a relatively weak force matched against the main weight of the German army. While the Allies were engaged with Army Group B in northern and central Belgium, Army Group A would drive through the Ardennes, would cross the Meuse, and would then head straight for the French coast. In effect, this group would pin the bulk of the Allied forces against the North Sea (see Figure 10.3). By moving their main forces forward into Belgium, the Allies would make it much easier for the Germans, once they had penetrated the Allied line opposite the Ardennes, to effect a deep strategic penetration. If the Allies remained along the Franco–Belgian border, they would be in a much better position to retreat and to prevent the Germans from penetrating into their rear. As a result of information gleaned through intelligence channels, the Germans were confident that the Allies would play into their hands by moving into Belgium.

It is noteworthy that the majority of panzer divisions were transferred from Army Group B to Army Group A. To make the breakthrough and effect the deep strategic penetration, the Germans created an "armored wedge" within Army Group A. Two armored corps and a motorized infantry corps were placed under a special command. A third armored corps was also assigned to Army Group A. The armored forces, operating independently of the standard infantry divisions,

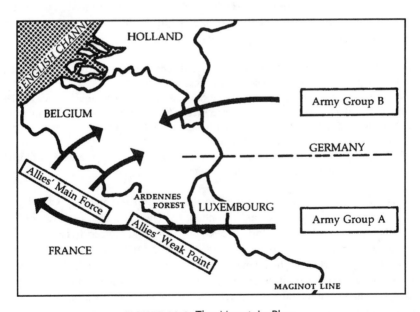

**FIGURE 10.3** The Manstein Plan.

were to be the main striking arm of the German army. This was to be a classic blitzkrieg.

## Opposition to the Blitzkrieg

A small number of senior officers were not pleased with the role assigned to the panzer divisions. Specifically, they questioned whether armored forces *alone* were capable of piercing the Allied front and then effecting a deep strategic penetration. They felt that the infantry divisions should fight the breakthrough battles, with the armored forces held in the rear, waiting to exploit any breakthroughs that might occur. Furthermore, once the panzer divisions were employed, there should be greater emphasis on having them work in tandem with standard infantry divisions. These ideas, of course, threatened the very essence of the blitzkrieg.

The principal proponent of reducing the role of the panzer divisions was Gen. Georg von Sodenstern, who replaced Manstein as chief of staff of Army Group A. The other two officers who were skeptical of the idea of assigning the armored forces an independent role were Rundstedt and Blumentritt, who were also from Army Group A. Ironically, Rundstedt, who played such an important role in the fight to win acceptance of Army Group A's plan, began doubting the capabilities of the armored forces before the first sand table exercise on 7 February. . . .

Manstein's replacement [as chief of staff of Army Group A, Georg von] Sodenstern, was the most forceful opponent of assigning panzer divisions the key role in the forthcoming offensive. He secured Rundstedt's permission to send a memorandum to OKH expressing his own concern. In this memorandum, which Rundstedt significantly did not sign, Sodenstern argued:

I have grave misgivings with regard to the commitment of strong panzer and motorized forces moving ahead of the front line of the attacking armies.

These mobile formations . . . should be held back as an operational reserve to be employed in seeking the decision only *after* a successful breakthrough of the enemy front has been achieved. I fear that they will not be able to fulfill the tasks assigned to them within the scope of the forthcoming offensive.

I am . . . convinced that we cannot force the crossing of the Meuse with motorized forces, but that we must fight our way across with infantry.

Sodenstern's doubts went even further. He also questioned whether it was wise to rely so heavily on armored forces to conduct the deep strategic penetration. He favored closely coordinated efforts between infantry and panzer divisions.

This memorandum, however, had little effect at OKH because Halder, who was the most powerful individual in the German army at this point, had completely broken with his earlier position and had accepted the arguments of Guderian and Manstein. The extent of Halder's conversion is reflected in the new plan, for which he bore full responsibility. Halder, who had consistently rejected Army Group A's proposals and who had challenged Guderian on the issue of how to use panzer divisions at both of the sand table exercises, had now become one of the principal defenders of the blitzkrieg. This transformation is perhaps best reflected in his reply to Sodenstern's memorandum, which is worth quoting at length.

The mission assigned to the German Army is a very difficult one. Given the terrain (Meuse) and the ratio of forces on both sides—especially with regard to artillery—this mission cannot be fulfilled if we employ those means which were relevant in the last war. We will have to use exceptional means and take the resulting risk.

Whether the panzer divisions of the forward wave appear on the Meuse in full combat power is less important to me than the necessity of demonstrating resolute daring in pursuit of the retreating enemy and in making the initial crossing to the western Meuse bank decisive. . . .

I am absolutely aware of the fact that these units, when dashing forward, will have hours of severe crisis on the western Meuse bank. The Luftwaffe will relieve them by fully bringing to bear its superior combat power. Without taking this risk we might never be able to reach the left Meuse bank. But I am convinced that, in this operation, too, our panzer leaders will have an advantage, due to their energy and flexibility, combined with the effect of setting personal examples. Against an enemy proceeding methodically and less trained in commanding panzers, they will be able to exploit the severe psychological burden imposed by the appearance of German panzers on a unit which lacks battle testing. . . .

Halder's reply to Sodenstern ended debate on this issue. Army Group A did not raise the question again. When the principal commanders of Army Group A met with Hitler and Halder to discuss the new strategy on 15 March, they addressed the question of how the Nineteenth Panzer Corps would be employed in the upcoming offensive. Guderian, that staunch advocate of the blitzkrieg, told the assembled leaders that armored units would operate independently of the infantry units. Here was the perfect opportunity for Rundstedt to contest Guderian. Yet he remained silent. Guderian, not Sodenstern, had triumphed.

## DETERRENCE AND THE BLITZKRIEG

With the adoption of the blitzkrieg, deterrence no longer obtained, simply because there was widespread agreement among the key German decision makers that the Allies would be defeated rapidly and decisively. . . . The influential Guderian, who was the most vocal proponent of using armored forces to effect a deep strategic penetration, remained in command of the Nineteenth Panzer Corps. He had a number of key allies within Army Group A. Colonels Blumentritt and Tresckow, two of Manstein's most loyal supporters throughout the battle to win acceptance of his proposal, remained in their influential positions in Army Group A. Furthermore, the various commanders of the armored and motorized units that would deliver the decisive blow were convinced that they would accomplish their goal. . . .

Hitler, who had never been satisfied with the various versions of the original OKH plan, was firmly convinced that the new plan would succeed. Halder remarks in his diary for 17 March, "The Fuehrer now approves the preparations made and is manifestly confident of success." At OKH, which had long been the center of resistance to the Manstein plan, a radical change of heart took place. The most important convert was Halder, whose influence at OKH had grown after Brauchitsch's fall from grace in early November 1939. Halder became the leading proponent of the new plan. Despite Brauchitsch's decreased influence, he too supported the blitzkrieg. Thus we find him telling Hitler in April that it is imperative not to postpone the attack because "long waiting would not improve the situation." Furthermore, two of the principal staff officers at OKH, Colonels Heusinger and Grieffenberg, had been favorably disposed toward Army Group A's plan even before it was formally adopted.

Even Leeb, the commander of Army Group C and a vociferous opponent of the original plan, raised no arguments against the final version. Bock simply could not marshall any support for his position. Even Reichenau, the commander of Bock's main army, was satisfied. The majority of military leaders had accepted the new plan and expected to score a decisive victory. Gen. Walter Warlimont, one of the most respected officers at OKW, aptly characterized the general outlook of the German military in the spring of 1940 when he wrote: "The criticism was often made that senior officers, including Hitler himself, were prisoners of their memories of the first World War and therefore did not reckon on such a resounding success of the offense in the West. This may have been true in the autumn of 1939 but it clearly was not early in 1940."

It should be evident by this point that the evidence contradicts the claim that the Germans were leaping into the dark in May 1940 and that an irrational Hitler was dragging a reluctant military into another world war. Furthermore, A. J. P. Taylor's claim that the Germans merely hoped to occupy the Channel coast in May 1940 and that their overwhelming success caught them by surprise is not accurate. The Germans had abandoned the limited aims strategy by mid-February 1940 and had replaced it with a blitzkrieg. When one side thinks that it has the capability to launch a successful blitzkrieg, deterrence is very likely to fail, as it did in spring 1940. On the other hand, when a potential attacker sees either an attrition strategy or a limited aims strategy as the only possibility, deterrence is much more likely to obtain, as it did in fall 1939.

## CONCLUSION

Although the Germans did not attack in fall 1939, Hitler wanted to do so very badly. He was thwarted in part by the weather but mainly by the determined opposition of his generals, all of whom firmly believed that to attack with the existing plan would lead to disaster. In essence, deterrence obtained. Nevertheless, it is important to emphasize that Hitler was willing to attack with the plan that his generals found so unsatisfactory and about which even he had reservations. He believed that if the offensive was launched while the British forces were still few in number, the Germans stood a good chance of winning a decisive victory. Still, he recognized that this was an extremely risky endeavor. He was willing to take such a gamble, however, because of an overriding political consideration: his desire to establish German hegemony on the European continent. He also believed, of course, that the Allies were preparing to launch an offensive into the Low Countries, and he wanted to strike before they did. His generals, however, did not accept his reasoning, and without their support, Hitler was unable to strike in the West.

In the early months of 1940, the Germans radically altered the existing plan and adopted the blitzkrieg. From that point forward, there was no doubt that the German military would strike as soon as the weather permitted. Some further words about the emergence of the blitzkrieg are in order. It clearly cannot be argued that the Germans developed and adopted the blitzkrieg during the interwar period and then applied it for the first time in Poland. When the German military finally adopted the blitzkrieg in February 1940, it won acceptance outside a small circle of advocates for the first time. Plainly neither Hitler nor the majority of the German generals grasped the potential of the blitzkrieg before February 1940. It is noteworthy, however, that those generals, and especially Hitler, were favorably disposed toward panzer divisions. In this respect, the importance of the Polish campaign cannot be underestimated. Although the Germans did not employ a blitzkrieg in Poland, the operation demonstrated that, regardless of the strategy, panzer divisions were a valuable asset on the battlefield. The Polish campaign was an important first step in erasing the more conservative officers' doubts about the general utility of panzer divisions. The growing respect for the armored forces, coupled with the German military's traditional emphasis on winning quick victories, meant that the senior German generals did not have to alter their views greatly to endorse the blitzkrieg. These German generals were not like their counterparts in France, who were irrevocably tied to an obsolete image of war.

Although Germany's military leaders were more likely to accept Guderian's ideas on the employment of armor than were the French military leaders, it is clear that the blitzkrieg would not have emerged had Hitler not maintained relentless pressure on all of the decision makers, including himself, to devise a plan for defeating the Allies decisively. Hitler, who was determined to make Germany the dominant power on the Continent, drove his military advisers, as well as himself, toward the blitzkrieg. If the German generals had been left to their own devices, the blitzkrieg would not have emerged.

Hitler, of course, did more than simply pressure the military to find an acceptable strategy. He also directly intervened in the planning process—and, as I have noted, he played a key role in the evolution of the various plans. In fact, without his direct interference, it is hard to imagine how Army Group A's strategy would have been adopted. I do not deny the importance of efforts by Rundstedt, Manstein, and Guderian to win acceptance of their scheme, nor do I deny the importance of the proposal itself—which not only influenced Hitler but also formed the basis of OKH's final plan. Army Group A, however, working through the normal chain of command, was unable to persuade the top leaders of the wisdom of its plan. OKH was a formidable roadblock. Hitler's intervention, coupled with three key events in the first months of 1940 (the airplane crash and the two sand table exercises), was needed to break down OKH's resistance.

After the overwhelming victory in spring 1940, Hitler turned to the East and invaded the Soviet Union. The German military, fresh from its victory in the West, enthusiastically supported Hitler's decision, believing that it could employ the blitzkrieg against the Soviets and could gain a quick and decisive victory. The Germans were wrong this time. The Soviets stopped the German offensive, and after 1942, the Germans were on the defensive on all fronts. In the end, World War II, like World War I, was won through attrition. The Allies on both the eastern and western fronts simply wore down the Germans.

# 11

# Japan's Fatal Blunder

SIR GEORGE SANSOM

In the light of what we know today the decision of the leaders of Japan to make war upon the United States appears as an act of folly, by which they committed themselves to a hopeless struggle against a Power with perhaps ten times their own potential industrial and military strength. But was that decision in fact as reckless as it now seems, or can it be regarded as the taking of a justifiable risk in the circumstances in which it was made?

Perhaps it is too soon to expect a complete answer to this question, but there is already available a good deal of useful information upon which a preliminary judgement can be based. There is, for instance, an interesting series of reports published by the United States Strategic Bombing Survey,[1] which was conducted (by civilians) primarily for the purpose of ascertaining the degree to which airpower contributed to the defeat of Japan. During this enquiry there was collected a mass of statistical and other information regarding political and economic conditions in Japan prior to and during the war. These studies, together with two volumes of Interrogations compiled by the United States Navy,[2] include valuable data based upon oral and documentary evidence obtained in Japan in 1945, not long after the surrender, when memories were fresh. It should be understood that the answers elicited by interrogations cannot all be taken at face value. Allowance must be made for certain factors of error. Thus, the "Summaries" of the Bombing Survey, in which general conclusions are drawn, naturally tend to place emphasis on the part played by aircraft in reducing Japan to the point of surrender and, by implication, to underestimate the importance of the general strategic conduct of the war and the particular effectiveness of submarine action on vital Japanese lines of communication by sea. Moreover, the interrogations were not always skillfully conducted and the replies sometimes betray a desire to please

153

the questioners, if not to mislead them. Different and more reliable results might have been obtained from really searching cross-examination by experienced persons. Nevertheless,the documents are extremely interesting and suffice to establish beyond reasonable doubt a number of important facts. The following tentative appraisal draws freely upon information which they contain, though it is supplemented at a few points by knowledge derived by the writer from other sources during a visit to Japan early in 1946.

There is no doubt that Japan was preparing for war at least a decade before 1941, but this does not necessarily mean that she had decided before that year to make war upon the United States or the British Commonwealth. The most that can be safely said is that certain influential army leaders and their civilian supporters contemplated war if the European situation should so develop as to make it feasible and advantageous. There was no concealment of Japan's intention to get ready for war. But during 1940 there was still no agreement in influential circles as to the course which Japan should take in international affairs, or even as to the lines upon which her economy should be further developed and controlled. The full powers which the Government had progressively acquired in preceding years were exercised only partially; a medley of State controls existed side by side with autonomous direction in separate branches of production and trade; and, in general, conflict between the military and the leaders of industry and finance continued unabated and unresolved.

It is sometimes stated by British and American writers that Big Business in Japan—the so-called *Zaibatsu*—co-operated enthusiastically in preparations for war or at least meekly gave way to military pressure. The evidence for this view is poor. On the contrary, during the early part of 1940 the influential Economic Federation of Japan (*Nihon Keizai Remmei*) resisted the Government's plans for industrial expansion, arguing that they were basically unsound. Their opposition was, it is true, based on technical rather than political grounds, but it cannot be said that they co-operated freely with the military leaders in the development of an economy designed for warlike purposes.

In fact, under the Yonai Government, which was in power until July 1940, there were still elements in the Cabinet that favored a cautious if not a pacific foreign policy, and were inclined to take the side of the industrialists in resisting totalitarian trends. It was at this point that the military used their strongest political weapon. By withdrawing the War Minister, they forced the resignation of the Yonai Cabinet, in which the relatively liberal Mr. Arita was Foreign Minister. The second Konoye Cabinet was then formed, with Tojo, a convinced expansionist, as War Minister. Its announced policy was the development of a highly organized National Defense State and the consolidation of an Asiatic "Co-Prosperity Sphere." This was definitely a war Cabinet, and its immediate purpose was to bring the industrialists to heel. Once the Government reached a firm decision the resistance of the industrialists was sooner or later bound to collapse. The close concentration of industrial power in Japan, having historically been achieved largely under official direction or with official support, had never acquired true independence or substantial political strength. It could struggle against this measure or that, but in matters of high policy it could not successfully challenge the authority of the bureaucracy with which it was so organically related.

In September 1940, Tojo let it be known that national mobilization required an intensified control which was inconsistent with the old liberal economic structure. But still the struggle continued and, surprisingly, the resistance of the industrial and financial leaders, represented by the Economic Federation, increased rather than diminished. The planned economy which was the object of Hoshino and Ohashi—two officials who had gained experience in Manchuria—was fought with some success by members of the *Zaibatsu* who, whatever their views as to war and peace, realized the limitations of the Japanese economy. But they were at length forced to execute plans in which they had little faith.

These facts are cited as showing that as late as 1941, despite long preparation, there was yet no effective centralized control of the Japanese industrial structure; and, quite apart from the conflict between Government and private enterprise, there was another defect in the country's war-making capacity, for the administrative machine, seemingly so efficient in normal times, turned out to be rigid and unmanageable. It was even necessary for Tojo, when he became Prime Minister in 1941, to seek legislation which would compel the various ministries to obey his orders. Such a diagnosis of the radical weaknesses in Japan's governmental structure at a juncture when her national existence was about to be staked upon its efficiency may seem too sweeping, but it could be supported by further evidence. It is sufficient to say here that the subsequent course of events, in both the economic and military spheres, shows that part of the failure of the Japanese economy to meet the demands made upon it in time of war can be traced back to faulty arrangements in time of peace. That governments or individuals should contract bad habits is not surprising, but it is surprising that the rulers of Japan should not have realized how inadequate, even by their own standards, was their country's organization for a war of their own choosing against powerful enemies.

The degree of their economic miscalculations is easy to measure by results. More difficult is an assessment of their political judgement. There can be no doubt that the coalition which began to rule Japan in July 1940 was determined to make use of the European war to further an expansionist policy in Asia and, if possible, to settle the conflict with China on favorable terms. When France was defeated and England appeared to the Japanese to be about to follow her in disaster, the Konoye Government began to feel confident enough to probe the weaknesses of possible antagonists by such measures as flouting British and American interests in China, blackmailing the United Kingdom into closing the Burma Road, pressing the Netherland Indies for economic concessions and moving troops into northern Indo-China. In the summer of 1940 it even looked as if an attack upon British possessions in the Far East was imminent. But action was postponed, partly because the progress of the Battle of Britain raised doubts about the expected collapse of the United Kingdom, but also because the Japanese army and navy wished to complete their armament and to collect further stocks of basic materials. They appear to have decided that, tempting as it was, an attack upon British and Dutch territories alone would be strategically unsound, because it would leave on their flank unimpaired American strength which might intervene at a moment chosen by the United States. They were, moreover, not yet satisfied that they had the whole country with them, for despite their vigorous domestic propaganda there were still dissidents in high places and doubtless also among the people. The distribution of political influence within Japan was traditionally such that any decisive move required much bargaining and persuasion. The firmly established system of checks and balances was customary rather than constitutional, but it had the effect of delaying political action. Even within the ruling coalition there were differences of opinion on the timing and the length of each step taken on the road to war, and there were cautious or conservative elements whose hesitations had to be overcome.

This was the condition reached by the summer of 1941. The extremists continued to strengthen their position step by step, by committing Japan to engagements from which it was difficult if not impossible to withdraw. Perhaps this period was the most crucial in Japanese history, since a vital decision on war or peace is not a simple choice of alternatives at a given moment, but is influenced by the cumulative effect of previous commitments, none of which is separately decisive. The extremists had in July 1941, by a series of gradual manoeuvres, gone far towards creating a situation in which their voice would be dominant. They then took a long step by establishing bases in Southern Indo-China. All available evidence goes to show that they did not expect this move to evoke strong reactions from the United States or the United Kingdom. It was represented as nothing but a strategical development in the war against China, but its implications were perfectly clear. It was the first phase of a projected southward movement. It is interesting to note, from the captured German documents published in January 1948 by the United States Government, that the draft secret protocol of November 1940 to the agreement between the U.S.S.R. and the Tripartite Powers states that "Japan declares that her territorial aspirations centre in the area of Eastern Asia to the south of the Island Empire of Japan."[3] The sharp counter-measures of the United States and the United Kingdom came as a surprise to the extremists and threw the moderates into confusion, though they must have had some warning from the Japanese Embassy in Washington. The situation is well described in the Summary Report of the United States Bombing Survey, as follows:

Though the conservative wing of the ruling coalition had endorsed each move of its coalition partners, it hoped at each stage that the current step would not be the breaking-point leading to war. It arranged and concluded the Tripartite Pact (September 1940) and hoped that the Western Powers would be sufficiently impressed with the might and solidarity of the Axis to understand the futility of further resistance. It approved of the Indo-China adventure, assuming that Japan would get away with this act of aggression as easily as with previous ones.

But while the freezing of Japanese assets and the embargo upon the export of strategic materials to Japan imposed by the Western Powers shocked the conservatives and frightened the moderates, they had already gone too far in their acquiescence. They could not now suggest any course but negotiations with the United States, and over the terms of these negotiations they could exercise no control, since the power of final decision had already passed into the hands of the extremists. All they could now hope for was that the extremists would make enough concessions to satisfy the United States, and this was a vain hope, because to make any effective concessions would be to admit that the whole of Japanese policy since 1931 had been a blunder, for which the military party and its civilian allies were responsible. The Army's prestige would never recover from such a blow. War was inevitable. The only question now was what kind of war.

Such in broad outline was the political background of the decision to go to war. It remains to consider on what grounds the military leaders of Japan based their judgement that Japan could successfully challenge the United States and the British Commonwealth. It cannot be assumed that they blindly led their country into war with no prospect of success. Theirs was a considered policy, attended by calculated risks. Examined in retrospect it proves to have been based upon mistaken assumptions, and executed with insufficient skill and foresight; but it was not, as conceived, irrational. It must also be remembered that the economic sanctions imposed upon Japan in 1941 were such as to make war appear a reasonable, if dangerous, alternative.

The planners who decided that the risk of war could be taken were not blind to the frightful disparity between their own strength and that of their enemies. They counted upon certain favorable circumstances to balance their own deficiencies. Late in the summer of 1941 they were convinced that Germany would be victorious and that within a few months, Russia having been defeated, the United States and the United Kingdom would be obliged to accept supremacy of Germany in Europe. This outlook, though it promised them membership of a successful alliance, was in one respect not entirely pleasing to them, since they felt some distrust of their Axis partners, which the Germans in Japan by their arrogant behavior did nothing to diminish. Some Japanese expansionists therefore felt that their plans might be upset by a premature settlement of the European conflict, which would leave them without any spoils of war in the Pacific; and this fear probably, though not certainly, was an additional motive for the rapid seizure of territories in Asia from which they could derive supplies of oil and rubber, and strategic bargaining power. As they saw the position, those objectives—stepping stones to further expansion—could be attained by a short and restricted campaign. They would engage in hostilities in the Pacific for a strictly limited purpose. First they would conquer an area enclosed within a perimeter including Burma, Malaya, Sumatra, Java, Northern New Guinea, the Bismarck Archipelago, the Gilbert and Marshall Islands, Wake and the Kuriles. This, they calculated, could be achieved in a few months if American sea and air power could be weakened by surprise attacks upon Pearl Harbor and the Philippines. The United States, preoccupied with the European situation, would be unable to take the offensive before Japan had accomplished the necessary strengthening of the perimeter and established forward air and sea bases. Once firmly entrenched on that perimeter they could obtain from the occupied areas what they required to sustain and expand their deficient economy—oil, rubber, bauxite, metals, food. Thus supplied, they could wage defensive warfare which, it was supposed, would within a year or two weaken the American purpose and so lead to a compromise peace. Negotiation would leave to Japan a substantial portion of her gains and a dominant position in Eastern Asia.

This was not at that time a strategy which could be condemned out of hand as unrealistic. It could be regarded, and presented to the Japanese people, as a reasonable and honorable alternative to submitting to sanctions. It aroused misgivings in some circles in Japan, and even its proponents knew that it would throw a great strain upon Japan's capacity; but they counted upon the shock of rapid conquests, and upon the fighting qualities of their soldiers and sailors. Certainly in the first few months of the war nothing happened to make them revise their opinions. Their successes were greater and easier than they had foreseen.

So encouraged were they by their achievement that they began to consider an extension of their perimeter. They planned an advance into the Solomons and Port Moresby, to be followed by a further advance into New Caledonia, Samoa, and the Fijis, the capture of Midway and the occupation of the Aleutians. It was here that they made their first cardinal blunder, for . . . "by stretching and overextending her line of advance, Japan was committed to an expensive and exacting supply problem. She delayed the fortification of the perimeter originally decided upon, jeopardized her economic program for exploiting the resources of the area already captured and laid herself open to early counter-attack in far advanced and, as yet, weak positions."[4]

This blunder in execution also laid bare certain weaknesses in the original conceptions of the Japanese planners. Perhaps the most important of these was their misjudgment of the temper of the United States, for the attack on Pearl Harbor had a stimulating psychological effect upon the American people which in military importance far outweighed the losses sustained at Pearl Harbor. The Japanese army had persuaded the Japanese people that the democratic states were materialistic, irresolute, incapable of matching the unique Japanese spirit. They had argued, not without some plausibility, that the United States had for a decade or more shown a strong aversion to protecting its interests in the Far East by warlike measures, despite repeated provocation. They inferred that those interests were not regarded as of vital importance and that consequently in the long run a spirit of compromise would prevail. They seem to have been deceived by their own propaganda, for even after their initial reverses in the first half of 1942 at Midway and towards the end of the year at Guadalcanal, they appear still to have supposed that they could fight the war on their own terms. They did not yet realize that their original plan of restricted warfare, which could be sustained for a limited period by their 1941 economy was no longer feasible.

It was not until 1943 that they had fully grasped the fact that they could no longer dictate the scale or location of hostilities, but were involved in total war in which the initiative had already passed to the American forces. That they made this mistake is indicated by their failure to carry out complete economic mobilization until 1943. An index of the gross national product (computed by the United States Bombing Survey with the assistance of Japanese experts) shows a rise from 100 in 1940 to only 101 in 1941 and 102 in 1942. It was not until 1943 that a substantial increase was gained by a production drive which raised the figure to 113 for 1943 and 124 for 1944. This was the peak of Japanese production, and it was reached by forcing an ever-growing proportion of the total economy into direct war purposes, while straining the civilian population almost to breaking point. It was a remarkable performance, but it was too little and too late. No effort was made to carry out a coherent plan of overall expansion of the Japanese economy, perhaps because a balanced development was impossible in view of its previous distortion. Even if the foregoing explanation of the delay in carrying out full economic mobilization errs in placing too much emphasis upon a tardy appreciation of the strategic position, it is clear that the Japanese tradition of government depending upon slow and cautious compromise was ill-adapted for times of emergency that demanded bold decision and quick performance.

The subsequent course of the Pacific war needs no detailed recital here. It is enough to say that although the Japanese made after 1942 immense military and economic efforts to meet conditions for which they had not originally planned, both were insufficient to stem the tide which began to flow against them. Nearly all their calculations had gone wrong. The British Isles were not invaded, the Soviet Union did not collapse, the United States showed not the least disposition to compromise, but began to plan the outright defeat of Japan. The prospect of a negotiated peace vanished. Plans to draw upon the occupied territories for essential materials could not be executed, because submarine and air attacks upon Japanese shipping prevented not only the carriage of needed supplies to Japan, but also the full support of Japanese forces in the field. Japanese commanders have testified that only 20 percent of the supplies dispatched to Guadalcanal reached their destination, and that of 30,000 troops landed, 10,000 died of starvation or disease and 10,000 were evacuated early in 1943 in a debilitated condition. Though Japanese troops everywhere fought stubbornly and well, inflicting heavy losses upon their opponents, by the opening months of 1943 not only had the Japanese advance been stopped, but their overall strategic plan had been upset. This was the result of an overwhelming superiority of American power, and it revealed a basic error in the initial premises of that plan. It had been sup-posed that the perimeter could be held indefinitely, but American experience showed after the engagements of 1942 that it was not necessary to reduce the whole perimeter. The widely spread Japanese positions were dependent upon sup-ply by sea, and it was necessary to destroy them only at points selected by the American command. So long as attacks upon Japanese shipping were maintained, other points could be by-passed as a general advance was begun towards bases within striking distance of Japan.

It was after the evacuation of Guadalcanal, in February 1943, that thoughtful Japanese began to suspect that their prospects of victory had disappeared, while those who knew all the facts saw that the situation was desperate. It is surprising that, to quote the words of Hoshino, Chief Secretary of the Tojo Cabinet, "the real Japanese war economy only began after Guadalcanal." Perhaps even more sur-prising is the confusion which is revealed in the direction both of the war econ-omy and the national strategy after that date. Full credit must be given to the Japanese people for their efforts to restore and develop their war potential after 1942, but their leaders seem never to have reached a clear and comprehensive view of their country's situation. Some rough estimates of national strength were compiled before the war. They were tentative and incomplete, and perhaps this was in the circumstances unavoidable.

But it is strange that, so far as is known, a full re-appraisal in the light of the new conditions was not attempted until September 1943. This was made not by the Government for its own purposes, but by Takagi, an officer of the Naval Gen-eral Staff, at the request of Admiral Yonai, who had been out of office since his Cabinet fell in 1940. This influential statesman, when asked in 1945 what he con-sidered the turning point of the war replied: "To be very frank, I think the turning point was the start. I felt from the very beginning that there was no chance of suc-cess." Takagi's report strengthened Admiral Yonai's fears that the prosecution of the war by the Tojo Government was unsatisfactory. It confirmed his judgement that Japan should seek a compromise peace before she suffered a crushing defeat. Yonai was not alone in this feeling. It was shared by certain influential persons outside the Government and a number of naval officers. They had indeed good reason for their anxiety. The circumstances beyond Japan's control were grave enough—the growing shortages of materials, losses of aircraft, warships and mer-chant vessels, and the certainty of long-range air attacks upon the centers of pro-duction at home. And, added to these, was growing confusion within Japan.

Nominally, by 1943 the Japanese Government had achieved full control of all national organs and activities, but Japan had evidently not become a solid author-itarian state. Animosity between Army and Navy was such that the submarine service resented the diversion of its vessels from combatant functions to army transport duties, and towards the end of the war the Army began to build sub-marines for its own use and declined naval advice. Army and Navy details, it is said, would fight outside factories for supplies designated for one or the other service. Ginjiro Fujihara, an industrial magnate who at a critical juncture became director of aircraft production, even alleged (no doubt untruthfully) that army and navy rivalry was responsible for keeping down the total output by about 50 per cent. In addition to their inter-service quarrels, the armed forces displayed hostility towards civilian organs. The director of the General Mobilization Bureau testified on interrogation that they would never disclose their stocks or discuss their requirements with him, would not submit demands through the appropriate ministry and thus thwarted all attempts at co-ordination of supply. Control bodies set up by the Government for key materials tried to enforce a system of priorities, but the Army and Navy would help themselves to supplies without troubling to obtain priority-certificates. Civilian manufacturing firms were, it is reported, obliged to resort to black-market transactions in order to secure material or machines. It is of course easy to exaggerate the extent and importance of such abuses, which are common enough in all countries at war; but it is clear that there was a serious lack of harmony between the two fighting services. Admiral Toyoda (Commander-in-Chief Combined Fleet, and later Chief of Naval General Staff) said upon interrogation: "There was not full understanding and agreement between Army and Navy prior to and during the war." This discord he ascribed to the great political power of the Army, which the Navy did not share. It showed itself, he thought, not so much in operational matters as in the division of supplies. But General Yamashita, the Japanese commander in the Philippines, was only apprised of the intended naval strike on Leyte Gulf in a *written* communication from Tokyo which was two weeks on the way and reached him on the day of the operation.

Uneasy relations between Army and Navy were paralleled by quarrels between civilian organs. It is remarkable that, despite their reputed gift for careful and strict organization, the Japanese authorities were not in practice able to exercise their unlimited powers of control. Under a surface appearance of national unity, old divisions of opinions, old patterns of influence, persisted with very little change. It is perhaps comforting to discover that what appears to be a solid monolithic state can hide grave structural weaknesses behind a forbidding exterior.

By July 1944, the invasion of Saipan had succeeded and Tojo's Cabinet had collapsed. The strenuous efforts made to raise production in Japan had led to a considerable increase in capacity, yet by late in the summer output had begun to decline because shipping losses had cut down essential imports. National morale was still high but by the autumn of 1944 Japan was on the verge of economic collapse, and that was before the heavy strategical bombing of the home islands. Tojo was succeeded as Prime Minister by Koiso, a retired general, whose Government set up a Supreme War Direction Council intended ostensibly to strengthen national defense, but in fact obliged to consider ways of terminating the war. The story of the steps by which most of its members at length reached a decision in favor of surrender is a long and complicated one. Not much progress was made at first, but certain members of the Cabinet were cautiously working for peace and carrying on discussions with senior statesmen who, though out of office, retained great personal influence. High naval officers were predominant among the servicemen who favored attempts to secure a negotiated peace, while the Army command still thought in terms of prolonged resistance, hoping that they could inflict such losses upon an invading force that a compromise could be secured, which would leave to Japan something better than the prospect of unconditional surrender. The peace party was growing in confidence, but only slowly, and was hampered by the fear that, since the Japanese people were still ignorant of the true state of affairs, a premature move might bring about internal chaos.

Meanwhile, with the loss of the Philippines and the intensification of bombing, which affected both military targets and urban populations, the situation became more and more desperate in the eyes of the peace party, less and less hopeful in the eyes of the last-ditchers. But it seems that there was little prospect of obtaining the agreement of any substantial portion of the Army leaders so long as Germany continued to resist. It was not until April 8, 1945, that the Koiso Government fell and was succeeded by a Cabinet under Admiral Suzuki, whose mission was to bring the war to an end, though publicly both Government and people were still committed to a continued resistance. Progress towards peace was still slow, for nobody would come out with an open declaration that the war was lost. Early in May, however—shortly after the end of the European war—the balance began to turn in favor of peace. Appraisals of the economic situation showed that the country was utterly incapable of continuing effective resistance, and there were even some signs of a decline in public morale. Still no specific proposals for ending the war were made, though on June 6 the Supreme War Council definitely stated to the Emperor that it was necessary to bring it to an end. On June 20, the Emperor summoned the Council, and showed himself in favor of positive steps, including an approach to the Soviet Union with a request for mediation. Discussions with Russia made no progress, the Soviet Government temporized and the Japanese ambassador in Moscow reported that in his opinion there was no alternative to unconditional surrender.

Time went by, and still no firm decision had been reached when the Potsdam Declaration was issued on July 26, 1945. The Prime Minister, the Foreign Minister and the Navy Minister (Yonai) were in favor of accepting its terms, the War Minister and the Chiefs of Staff were opposed. It is interesting to note, as illustrating the nature of the opposition, that Toyoda had not approved of the War from the beginning, yet was unable to agree to unconditional surrender, which he thought dishonorable. A strong military group still held out for resistance to invasion. Differences of opinion continued until August 9, 1945, by which time an atomic bomb had been dropped on Hiroshima (August 6) and the Soviet Union had declared war upon Japan (August 9). After repeated meetings on August 9, just before midnight the Inner Cabinet appealed to the Emperor for a final expression of his wish and the Emperor declared in favor of peace. There were further cabinet discussions as to the interpretation of the Potsdam terms, but they were finally accepted on August 14. This was more than twelve months after the fall of the Tojo Government, and four months after the formation of the Suzuki Cabinet, which was certainly intended to bring an end to hostilities. It may well be asked why, in the light of Japan's inability, so manifest after the end of 1944, to carry the war to a successful conclusion, the discussion was prolonged well into 1945, while her factories and her houses were being destroyed, her warships sunk and her armies cut off from their homes? The answer is not clear, but it seems as if the delay was something dictated by the nature of Japanese institutions. The slow process by which an apparently unanimous will to war was created before 1941 had to be repeated in reverse before a will to peace could be announced.

The fact that the decision to accept the Potsdam terms was reached soon after the explosion of the atomic bomb and the Russian declaration of war has been interpreted as showing that the bomb and the Russian action were what produced Japan's surrender. This is a view which it is difficult to accept. It might be correct to say that these two menacing events accelerated a decision which was being reached by slow and devious processes characteristic of Japanese political life. But it cannot be truthfully said that any one single cause brought about the surrender; at the same time there is good reason for thinking that, even had no atomic bombing attacks been delivered, the disintegration of Japan's economic life, under sustained blockade and continued aerial and naval bombardment, would within a few months—perhaps weeks—after June 1945 have brought about unconditional surrender, even without the need for invasion. But all this is in the realm of conjecture, and not even the participants themselves can say with certainty what course the debates in the War Council would have taken in hypothetical conditions. Even if we were today certain that it was not the atomic bomb which caused the surrender, it would not follow that the decision to use the bomb was wrong. That decision was necessarily taken in the light of such sure knowledge as was then at the disposal of our Governments; and although intelligence reports on conditions in Japan were remarkably good, that knowledge was not sufficient to justify abstaining from the use of a weapon which might end the war quickly, and save the lives of thousands of allied prisoners, possibly hundreds of thousands of allied soldiers, to say nothing of great numbers of enemy soldiers and civilians. Discussion of the rights and wrongs of the use of the atomic bomb at Hiroshima frequently confuses two separate issues. If the question is whether it was immoral to use such a destructive weapon, then one must bring into consideration incendiary raids, such as that of the night of March 9, 1945, which killed probably 100,000 people and destroyed over 250,000 homes, in circumstances of appalling terror. If the question is whether the use of the atomic bomb was strategically unnecessary or (in the light of subsequent history) politically mistaken, then moral considerations are irrelevant so long as the right of a belligerent to attack civilian targets is admitted. There cannot by any rational standard of morals be a valid distinction between methods of killing civilians in which one is right and the other is wrong because it is quicker and more effective.

**NOTES**

1. United States Strategic Bombing Survey, *Japan's Struggle to End the War* (Washington, D.C.: Government Printing Office, 1946).

2. United States Strategic Bombing Survey, *Interrogations of Japanese Officials*, 2 vols. (Washington, D.C.: Government Printing Office, 1946).

3. J. Sontag and J. S. Beddie, eds., Declaration 3, Draft Secret Protocol No. 1, *Nazi–Soviet Relations*, 1939–40 (U.S.A. Department of State, 1948), p. 257.

4. United States Strategic Bombing Survey, Summary Report, *Pacific War* (Washington, D.C.: United States Government Printing Office, 1946), p. 4.

# 12

## The Decision to Use
## the Atomic Bomb

### LOUIS MORTON

It is now more than ten years since the atomic bomb exploded over Hiroshima and revealed to the world in one blinding flash of light the start of the atomic age. As the meaning of this explosion and the nature of the force unleashed became apparent, a chorus of voices rose in protest against the decision that had opened the Pandora's box of atomic warfare.

The justification for using the atomic bomb was that it had ended the war, or at least ended it sooner and thereby saved countless American—and Japanese—lives. But had it? Had not Japan already been defeated and was she not already on the verge of surrender? What circumstances, it was asked, justified the fateful decision that "blasted the web of history and, like the discovery of fire, severed past from present"?

The first authoritative explanation of how and why it was decided to use the bomb came in February 1947 from Henry L. Stimson, wartime Secretary of War and the man who more than any other was responsible for advising the President. This explanation did not answer all the questions or still the critics. During the years that have followed others have revealed their part in the decision and in the events shaping it. These explanations have not ended the controversy, but they have brought to light additional facts bearing on the decision to use the bomb. With this information and with the perspective of ten years, it may be profitable to look again at the decision that opened the age of atomic warfare.

### THE INTERIM COMMITTEE

The epic story of the development of the atomic bomb is by now well known. It began in 1939 when a small group of eminent scientists in this country called to

165

the attention of the United States Government the vast potentialities of atomic energy for military purposes and warned that the Germans were already carrying on experiments in this field. The program initiated in October of that year with a very modest appropriation and later expanded into the two-billion–dollar Manhattan Project had only one purpose—to harness the energy of the atom in a chain reaction to produce a bomb that could be carried by aircraft if possible, and to produce it before the Germans could.[1] That such a bomb, if produced, would be used, no responsible official even questioned. "At no time from 1941 to 1945," declared Mr. Stimson, "did I ever hear it suggested by the President, or by another responsible member of the Government, that atomic energy should not be used in the war." And Dr. J. Robert Oppenheimer recalled in 1954 that "we always assumed if they [atomic bombs] were needed, they would be used." . . .

After President Roosevelt's death, it fell to [Secretary of State] Stimson to brief the new President about the atomic weapon. At a White House meeting on April 25, he outlined the history and status of the program and predicted that "within four months we shall in all probability have completed the most terrible weapon ever known in human history." This meeting, like Stimson's last meeting with Roosevelt, dealt largely with the political and diplomatic consequences of the use of such a weapon rather than with the timing and manner of employment, the circumstances under which it would be used, or whether it would be used at all. The answers to these questions depended on factors not yet known. But Stimson recommended, and the President approved, the appointment of a special committee to consider them.

This special committee, known as the Interim Committee, played a vital role in the decision to use the bomb. . . . The work of the Interim Committee was completed June 1, 1945, when it submitted its report to the President, recommending unanimously that:

1. The bomb should be used against Japan as soon as possible.

2. It should be used against a military target surrounded by other buildings.

3. It should be used without prior warning of the nature of the weapon. . . .

Thus, by mid-June 1945, there was virtual unanimity among the President's civilian advisers on the use of the bomb. The arguments of the opponents had been considered and rejected. So far as is known the President did not solicit the views of the military or naval staffs, nor were they offered.

## MILITARY CONSIDERATIONS

The military situation on June 1, 1945, when the Interim Committee submitted its recommendations on the use of the atomic bomb, was distinctly favorable to the Allied cause. Germany had surrendered in May and troops from Europe would soon be available for redeployment in the Pacific. Manila had fallen in February;

Iwo Jima was in American hands; and the success of the Okinawa invasion was assured. Air and submarine attacks had virtually cut off Japan from the resources of the Indies, and B-29s from the Marianas were pulverizing Japan's cities and factories. The Pacific Fleet had virtually driven the Imperial Navy from the ocean, and planes of the fast carrier forces were striking Japanese naval bases in the Inland Sea. Clearly, Japan was a defeated nation.

Though defeated in a military sense, Japan showed no disposition to surrender unconditionally. And Japanese troops had demonstrated time and again that they could fight hard and inflict heavy casualties even when the outlook was hopeless. Allied plans in the spring of 1945 took these facts into account and proceeded on the assumption that an invasion of the home islands would be required to achieve at the earliest possible date the unconditional surrender of Japan—the announced objective of the war and the basic assumption of all strategic planning.

Other means of achieving this objective had been considered and, in early June, had not yet been entirely discarded. One of these called for the occupation of a string of bases around Japan in order to increase the intensity of air bombardment. Combined with a tight naval blockade, such a course would, many believed, produce the same results as an invasion and at far less cost of lives. "I was unable to see any justification," Admiral Leahy later wrote, ". . . for an invasion of an already thoroughly defeated Japan. I feared the cost would be enormous in both lives and treasure." Admiral King and other senior naval officers agreed. To them it had always seemed, in King's words, "that the defeat of Japan could be accomplished by sea and air power alone, without the necessity of actual invasion of the Japanese home islands by ground troops."

The main arguments for an invasion of Japan—the plans called for an assault against Kyushu (Olympic) on November 1, 1945, and against Honshu (Coronet) five months later—are perhaps best summarized by General Douglas MacArthur. Writing to the Chief of Staff on April 20, 1945, he declared that this course was the only one that would permit application of the full power of our combined resources—ground, naval and air—on the decisive objective. Japan, he believed, would probably be more difficult to invade the following year. An invasion of Kyushu at an early date would, moreover, place United States forces in the most favorable position for the decisive assault against Honshu in 1946, and would "continue the offensive methods which have proved so successful in Pacific campaigns." Reliance upon bombing alone, MacArthur asserted, was still an unproved formula for success, as was evidenced by the bomber offensive against Germany. The seizure of a ring of bases around Japan would disperse Allied forces even more than they already were, MacArthur pointed out, and (if an attempt was made to seize positions on the China coast) might very well lead to long drawn-out operations on the Asiatic mainland.

Though the Joint Chiefs had accepted the invasion concept as the basis for preparations, and had issued a directive for the Kyushu assault on May 25, it was well understood that the final decision was yet to be made. By mid-June the time had come for such a decision and during that period the Joint Chiefs reviewed the whole problem of Japanese strategy. Finally, on June 18, at a meeting in the White House, they presented the alternatives to President Truman. Also present (according to the minutes) were Secretaries Stimson and Forrestal and Assistant Secretary of War John J. McCloy.[2]

General Marshall presented the case for invasion and carried his colleagues with him, although both Admirals Leahy and King later declared they did not favor the plan. After considerable discussion of casualties and of the difficulties ahead, President Truman made his decision. Kyushu would be invaded as planned and preparations for the landing were to be pushed through to completion. Preparations for the Honshu assault would continue, but no final decision would be made until preparations had reached the point "beyond which there would not be opportunity for a free choice." The program thus approved by Truman called for:

1. Air bombardment and blockade of Japan from bases in Okinawa, Iwo Jima, the Marianas and the Philippines.
2. Assault of Kyushu on November 1, 1945, and intensification of blockade and air bombardment.
3. Invasion of the industrial heart of Japan through the Tokyo Plain in central Honshu, tentative target date March 1, 1946.

During the White House meeting of June 18, there was discussion of the possibility of ending the war by political means. The President displayed a deep interest in the subject and both Stimson and McCloy emphasized the importance of the "large submerged class in Japan who do not favor the present war and whose full opinion and influence had never yet been felt." There was discussion also of the atomic bomb, since everyone present knew about the bomb and the recommendations of the Interim Committee. The suggestion was made that before the bomb was dropped, the Japanese should be warned that the United States had such a weapon. "Not one of the Chiefs nor the Secretary," recalled Mr. McCloy, "thought well of a bomb warning, an effective argument being that no one could be certain, in spite of the assurances of the scientists, that the 'thing would go off.'"

Though the defeat of the enemy's armed forces in the Japanese homeland was considered a prerequisite to Japan's surrender, it did not follow that Japanese forces elsewhere, especially those on the Asiatic mainland, would surrender also. It was to provide for just this contingency, as well as to pin down those forces during the invasion of the home islands, that the Joint Chiefs had recommended Soviet entry into the war against Japan.

Soviet participation was a goal long pursued by the Americans. Both political and military authorities seem to have been convinced from the start that Soviet assistance, conceived in various ways, would shorten the war and lessen the cost.

In October 1943, Marshal Stalin had told Cordell Hull, then in Moscow for a conference, that the Soviet Union would eventually declare war on Japan. At the Tehran Conference in November of that year, Stalin had given the Allies formal notice of this intention and reaffirmed it in October 1944. In February 1945, at the Yalta Conference, Roosevelt and Stalin had agreed on the terms of Soviet participation in the Far Eastern war. Thus, by June 1945, the Americans could look forward to Soviet intervention at a date estimated as three months after the defeat of Germany.

But by the summer of 1945 the Americans had undergone a change of heart. Though the official position of the War Department still held that "Russian entry will have a profound military effect in that almost certainly it will materially shorten the war and thus save American lives," few responsible American officials were eager for Soviet intervention or as willing to make concessions as they had been at an earlier period. What had once appeared extremely desirable appeared less so now that the war in Europe was over and Japan was virtually defeated. President Truman, one official recalled, stated during a meeting devoted to the question of Soviet policy that agreements with Stalin had up to that time been "a one-way street" and that "he intended thereafter to be firm in his dealings with the Russians." And at the June 18 meeting of the Joint Chiefs of Staff with the President, Admiral King had declared that "regardless of the desirability of the Russians entering the war, they were not indispensable and he did not think we should go so far as to beg them to come in." Though the cost would be greater he had no doubt "we could handle it alone."

The failure of the Soviets to abide by agreements at Yalta had also done much to discourage the American desire for further cooperation with them. But after urging Stalin for three years to declare war on Japan, the United States Government could hardly ask him now to remain neutral. Moreover, there was no way of keeping the Russians out even if there had been a will to do so. In Harriman's view, "Russia would come into the war regardless of what we might do."

A further difficulty was that Allied intelligence still indicated that Soviet intervention would be desirable, if not necessary, for the success of the invasion strategy. In Allied intelligence, Japan was portrayed as a defeated nation whose military leaders were blind to defeat. Though her industries had been seriously crippled by air bombardment and naval blockade and her armed forces were critically deficient in many of the resources of war, Japan was still far from surrender. She had ample reserves of weapons and ammunition and an army of 5,000,000 troops, 2,000,000 of them in the home islands. The latter could be expected to put up a strong resistance to invasion. In the opinion of the intelligence experts, neither blockade nor bombing alone would produce unconditional surrender before the date set for invasion. And the invasion itself, they believed, would be costly and possibly prolonged.

According to these intelligence reports, the Japanese leaders were fully aware of their desperate situation but would continue to fight in the hope of avoiding complete defeat by securing a better bargaining position. Allied war-weariness and disunity, or some miracle, they hoped, would offer them a way out. "The Japanese believe," declared an intelligence estimate of June 30, ". . . that unconditional surrender would be the equivalent of national extinction, and there are as yet no indications that they are ready to accept such terms." It appeared also to the intelligence experts that Japan might surrender at any time "depending upon the conditions of surrender" the Allies might offer. Clearly these conditions, to have any chance of acceptance, would have to include retention of the imperial system.

How accurate were these estimates? Judging from postwar accounts of Japan, they were very close to the truth. Since the defeat at Saipan, when Tojo had been forced to resign, the strength of the "peace party" had been increasing. In September 1944 the Swedish Minister in Tokyo had been approached unofficially, presumably in the name of Prince Konoye, to sound out the Allies on terms for peace. This overture came to naught, as did another the following March. But the Swedish Minister did learn that those who advocated peace in Japan regarded the Allied demand for unconditional surrender as their greatest obstacle.

The Suzuki Cabinet that came into power in April 1945 had an unspoken mandate from the Emperor to end the war as quickly as possible. But it was faced immediately with another problem when the Soviet Government announced it would not renew the neutrality pact after April 1946. The German surrender in May produced another crisis in the Japanese Government and led, after considerable discussion, to a decision to seek Soviet mediation. But the first approach, made on June 3 to Jacob Malik, the Soviet Ambassador, produced no results. Malik was noncommittal and merely said the problem needed further study. Another overture to Malik later in the month also came to naught.

At the end of June, the Japanese finally approached the Soviet Government directly through Ambassador Sato in Moscow, asking that it mediate with the Allies to bring the Far Eastern war to an end. In a series of messages between Tokyo and Moscow, which the Americans intercepted and decoded, the Japanese Foreign Office outlined the position of the government and instructed Ambassador Sato to make arrangements for a special envoy from the Emperor who would be empowered to make terms for Soviet mediation. Unconditional surrender, he was told, was completely unacceptable, and time was of the essence. But the Russians, on one pretext and another, delayed their answer until mid-July when Stalin and Molotov left for Potsdam. Thus, the Japanese Government had by then accepted defeat and was seeking desperately for a way out; but it was not willing even at this late date to surrender unconditionally, and would accept no terms that did not include the preservation of the imperial system.

Allied intelligence thus had estimated the situation in Japan correctly. Allied invasion strategy had been reexamined and confirmed in mid-June, and the date for the invasion fixed. The desirability of Soviet assistance had been confirmed also and plans for her entry into the war during August could now be made. No decision had been reached on the use of the atomic bomb, but the President's advisers had recommended it. The decision was the President's and he faced it squarely. But before he could make it he would want to know whether the measures already concerted would produce unconditional surrender at the earliest moment and at the lowest cost. If they could not, then he would have to decide whether circumstances warranted employment of a bomb that Stimson had already labeled as "the most terrible weapon ever known in human history."

## THE DECISION

Though responsibility for the decision to use the atomic bomb was the President's, he exercised it only after careful study of the recommendations of his senior advisers. Chief among these was the Secretary of War, under whose broad supervision the Manhattan Project had been placed. Already deeply concerned over the cost of the projected invasion, the political effects of Soviet intervention and the potential consequences of the use of the atomic bomb, Stimson sought a course that would avoid all these evils. The difficulty, as he saw it, lay in the requirement for unconditional surrender. It was a phrase that might make the Japanese desperate and lead to a long and unnecessary campaign of attrition that would be extremely costly to both sides. But there was no way of getting around the term; it was firmly rooted in Allied war aims and its renunciation was certain to lead to charges of appeasement.

But if this difficulty could be overcome, would the Japanese respond if terms were offered? The intelligence experts thought so, and the radio intercepts from Tokyo to Moscow bore them out. So far as the Army was concerned there was much to be gained by such a course. Not only might it reduce the enormous cost of the war, but it would also make possible a settlement in the Western Pacific "before too many of our allies are committed there and have made substantial contributions towards the defeat of Japan." In the view of the War Department these aims justified "any concessions which might be attractive to the Japanese, so long as our realistic aims for peace in the Pacific are not adversely affected."

The problem was to formulate terms that would meet these conditions. There was considerable discussion of this problem in Washington in the spring of 1945 by officials in the Department of State and in the War and Navy Departments. Joseph C. Grew, Acting Secretary of State, proposed to the President late in May that he issue a proclamation urging the Japanese to surrender and assuring them that they could keep the Emperor. Though Truman did not act on the suggestion, he thought it "a sound idea" and told Grew to discuss it with his cabinet colleagues and the Joint Chiefs. On June 18, Grew was back with the report that these groups favored the idea, but that there were differences on the timing.

Grew's ideas, as well as those of others concerned, were summarized by Stimson in a long and carefully considered memorandum to the President on July 2. Representing the most informed military and political estimate of the situation at this time, this memorandum constitutes a state paper of the first importance. If any one document can be said to provide the basis for the President's warning to Japan and his final decision to use the atomic bomb, this is it.

The gist of Stimson's argument was that the most promising alternative to the long and costly struggle certain to follow invasion was to warn the Japanese "of what is to come" and to give them an opportunity to surrender. There was, he thought, enough of a chance that such a course would work to make the effort worthwhile. Japan no longer had any allies, her navy was virtually destroyed and she was increasingly vulnerable to air attack and naval blockade. Against her were arrayed the increasingly powerful forces of the Allies, with their "inexhaustible and untouched industrial resources." In these circumstances, Stimson believed the Japanese people would be susceptible to reason if properly approached. "Japan," he pointed out, "is not a nation composed of mad fanatics of an entirely different mentality from ours. On the contrary, she has within the past century shown herself to possess extremely intelligent people. . . ." But any attempt, Stimson added, "to exterminate her armies and her population by gunfire or other means will tend to produce a fusion of race solidity and antipathy. . . ."

A warning to Japan, Stimson contended, should be carefully timed. It should come before the actual invasion, before destruction had reduced the Japanese "to fanatical despair" and, if the Soviet Union had already entered the war, before Russian attack had progressed so far.[3] It should also emphasize, Stimson believed, the inevitability and completeness of the destruction ahead and the determination of the Allies to strip Japan of her conquests and to destroy the influence of the military clique. It should be a strong warning and should leave no doubt in Japanese minds that they would have to surrender unconditionally and submit to Allied occupation.

The warning, as Stimson envisaged it, had a double character. While promising destruction and devastation, it was also to hold out hope to the Japanese if they heeded its message. In his memorandum, therefore, Stimson stressed the positive features of the warning and recommended that it include a disavowal of any intention to destroy the Japanese nation or to occupy the country permanently. Once Japan's military clique had been removed from power and her capacity to wage war destroyed, it was Stimson's belief that the Allies should withdraw and resume normal trade relations with the new and peaceful Japanese Government. "I personally think," he declared, "that if in saying this we should add that we do not exclude a constitutional monarchy under her present dynasty, it would substantially add to the chance of acceptance."

Not once in the course of this lengthy memorandum was mention made of the atomic bomb. There was no need to do so. Everyone concerned understood clearly that the bomb was the instrument that would destroy Japan and impress on the Japanese Government the hopelessness of any course but surrender. As Stimson expressed it, the atomic bomb was "the best possible sanction," the single weapon that would convince the Japanese "of our power to destroy the empire."

Though Stimson considered a warning combined with an offer of terms and backed up by the sanction of the atomic bomb as the most promising means of inducing surrender at any early date, there were other courses that some thought might produce the same result. One was the continuation and intensification of air bombardment coupled with surface and underwater blockade. This course had already been considered and rejected as insufficient to produce surrender, though its advocates were by no means convinced that this decision was a wise one. And Stimson himself later justified the use of the bomb on the ground that by November 1 conventional bombardment would have caused greater destruction than the bomb. This apparent contradiction is explained by the fact that the atomic bomb was considered to have a psychological effect entirely apart from the damage wrought.

Nor did Stimson, in his memorandum, consider the effect of the Soviet Union's entry into the war. By itself, this action could not be counted on to force Japan to capitulate, but combined with bombardment and blockade it might do so. At least that was the view of Brigadier-General George A. Lincoln, one of the Army's top planners, who wrote in June that "probably it will take Russian entry into the war, coupled with a landing, or imminent threat of landing, on Japan proper by us, to convince them [the Japanese] of the hopelessness of their position." Why, therefore, was it not possible to issue the warning prior to a Soviet declaration of war against Japan and rely on that event, together with an intensified air bombardment, to produce the desired result? If together they could not secure Japan's surrender, would there not still be time to use the bomb before the scheduled invasion of Kyushu in November?

No final answer to this question is possible with the evidence at hand. But one cannot ignore the fact that some responsible officials feared the political consequences of Soviet intervention and hoped that ultimately it would prove unnecessary. This feeling may unconsciously have made the atom bomb solution more attractive than it might otherwise have been. Some officials may have believed, too, that the bomb could be used as a powerful deterrent to Soviet expansion in Europe, where the Red tide had successfully engulfed Rumania, Bulgaria, Yugoslavia, Czechoslovakia and Hungary. In an interview with three of the top scientists in the Manhattan Project early in June, Mr. Byrnes did not, according to Leo Szilard, argue that the bomb was needed to defeat Japan, but rather that it should be dropped to "make Russia more manageable in Europe."

It has been asserted also that the desire to justify the expenditure of the two billion dollars spent on the Manhattan Project may have disposed some favorably toward the use of the bomb. Already questions had been asked in Congress, and the end of the war would almost certainly bring on a full-scale investigation. What more striking justification of the Manhattan Project than a new weapon that had ended the war in one sudden blow and saved countless American lives? "It was my reaction," wrote Admiral Leahy, "that the scientists and others wanted to make this test because of the vast sums that had been spent on the project. Truman knew that, and so did other people involved."

This explanation hardly does credit to those involved in the Manhattan Project and not even P. M. S. Blackett, one of the severest critics of the decision to use the bomb, accepted it. "The wit of man," he declared, "could hardly devise a theory of the dropping of the bomb, both more insulting to the American people, or more likely to lead to an energetically pursued Soviet defense policy."

But even if the need to justify these huge expenditures is discounted—and certainly by itself it could not have produced the decision—the question still remains whether those who held in their hands a weapon thought capable of ending the war in one stroke could justify withholding that weapon. Would they not be open to criticism for failing to use every means at their disposal to defeat the enemy as quickly as possible, thereby saving many American lives?

And even at that time there were some who believed that the new weapon would ultimately prove the most effective deterrent to war yet produced. How better to outlaw war forever than to demonstrate the tremendous destructive power of this weapon by using it against an actual target?

By early 1945 the stage had been set for the final decision. Stimson's memorandum had been approved in principle and on July 4 the British had given their consent to the use of the bomb against Japan. It remained only to decide on the terms and timing of the warning. This was the situation when the Potsdam Conference opened on July 17, one day after the bomb had been successfully exploded in a spectacular demonstration at Alamogordo, New Mexico. The atomic bomb was a reality and when the news reached Potsdam there was great excitement among those who were let in on the secret. Instead of the prospect of long and bitter months of fighting the Japanese, there was now a vision, "fair and bright indeed it seemed" to Churchill, "of the end of the whole war in one or two violent shocks."

President Truman's first action was to call together his chief advisers— Byrnes, Stimson, Leahy, Marshall, King and Arnold. "I asked for their opinion whether the bomb should be used," he later wrote. The consensus was that it should.[4] Here at last was the miracle to end the war and solve all the perplexing problems posed by the necessity for invasion. But because no one could tell what effect the bomb might have "physically or psychologically," it was decided to proceed with the military plans for the invasion.

No one at this time, or later in the conference, raised the question of whether the Japanese should be informed of the existence of the bomb. That question, it will be recalled, had been discussed by the Scientific Panel on June 16 and at the White House meeting with the JCS, the service Secretaries and Mr. McCloy on June 18. For a variety of reasons, including uncertainty as to whether the bomb would work, it had then been decided that the Japanese should not be warned of the existence of the new weapon. The successful explosion of the first bomb on July 17 did not apparently outweigh the reasons advanced earlier for keeping the bomb a secret, and evidently none of the men involved thought the question needed to be reviewed. The Japanese would learn of the atomic bomb only when it was dropped on them.

The secrecy that had shrouded the development of the atomic bomb was torn aside briefly at Potsdam, but with no visible effect. On July 24, on the advice of his chief advisers, Truman informed Marshal Stalin "casually" that the Americans had "a new weapon of unusual destructive force." "The Russian Premier," he recalled, "showed no special interest. All he said was that he was glad to hear it and hoped we would make 'good use of it against the Japanese.'" One cannot but wonder whether the Marshal was preoccupied at the moment or simulating a lack of interest.

On the military side, the Potsdam Conference developed nothing new. The plans already made were noted and approved. Even at this late stage the question of the bomb was divorced entirely from military plans and the final report of the conference accepted as the main effort the invasion of the Japanese home islands. November 15, 1946, was accepted as the planning date for the end of the war against Japan.

During the conference, Stalin told Truman about the Japanese overtures— information that the Americans already had. The Marshal spoke of the matter also to Churchill, who discussed it with Truman, suggesting cautiously that some offer be made to Japan. "Mr. Stimson, General Marshall, and the President," he later wrote, "were evidently searching their hearts, and we had no need to press them. We knew of course that the Japanese were ready to give up all conquests made in the war." That same night, after dining with Stalin and Truman, the Prime Minister wrote that the Russians intended to attack Japan soon after August 8—perhaps within two weeks after that date. Truman presumably received the same information, confirming Harry Hopkin's report of his conversation with Stalin in Moscow in May.

All that remained now was to warn Japan and give her an opportunity to surrender. In this matter Stimson's and Grew's views, as outlined in the memorandum of July 2, were accepted, but apparently on the advice of the former Secretary of State Cordell Hull it was decided to omit any reference to the Emperor. Hull's view, solicited by Byrnes before his departure for Potsdam, was that the proposal smacked of appeasement and "seemed to guarantee continuance not only of the Emperor but also of the feudal privileges of a ruling caste." And should the Japanese reject the warning, the proposal to retain the imperial system might well encourage resistance and have "terrible political repercussions" in the United States. For these reasons he recommended that no statement about the Emperor be made until "the climax of Allied bombing and Russia's entry into the war." Thus, the final terms offered to the Japanese in the Potsdam Declaration on July 26 made no mention of the Emperor or of the imperial system. Neither did the declaration contain any reference to the atom bomb but simply warned the Japanese of the consequences of continued resistance. Only those already familiar with the weapon could have read the references to inevitable and complete destruction as a warning of atomic warfare.

The receipt of the Potsdam Declaration in Japan led to frantic meetings to decide what should be done. It was finally decided not to reject the note but to await the results of the Soviet overture. At this point, the military insisted that the government make some statement to the people, and on July 28 Premier Suzuki declared to the press that Japan would ignore the declaration, a statement that was interpreted by the Allies as a rejection.

To the Americans the rejection of the Potsdam Declaration confirmed the view that the military was still in control of Japan and that only a decisive act of violence could remove them. The instrument for such action lay at hand in the atomic bomb; events now seemed to justify its use. But in the hope that the Japanese might still change their minds, Truman held off orders on the use of the bomb for a few days. Only silence came from Tokyo, for the Japanese were waiting for a reply from the Soviet Government, which would not come until the return of Stalin and Molotov from Potsdam on August 6. Prophetically, Foreign Minister Tojo wrote Sato on August 2, the day the Potsdam Conference ended, that he could not afford to lose a single day in his efforts to conclude arrangements with the Russians "if we were to end the war before the assault on our mainland." By that time, President Truman had already decided on the use of the bomb.

Preparations for dropping the two atomic bombs produced thus far had been under way for some time. The components of the bombs had been sent by cruiser to Tinian in May and the fissionable material was flown out in mid-July. The B-29s and crews were ready and trained, standing by for orders, which would come through the Commanding General, U.S. Army Strategic Air Forces in the Pacific, General Spaatz. Detailed arrangements and schedules were completed and all that was necessary was to issue orders.

At General Arnold's insistence, the responsibility for selecting the particular target and fixing the exact date and hour of the attack was assigned to the field commander, General Spaatz. In orders issued on July 25 and approved by Stimson and Marshall, Spaatz was ordered to drop the "first special bomb as soon as weather will permit visual bombing after about 3 August 1945 on one of the targets: Hiroshima, Kokura, Niigata, and Nagasaki." He was instructed also to deliver a copy of this order personally to MacArthur and Nimitz. Weather was the critical factor because the bomb had to be dropped by visual means, and Spaatz delegated to his chief of staff, Major-General Curtis E. LeMay, the job of deciding when the weather was right for this most important mission.

From the dating of the order to General Spaatz it has been argued that President Truman was certain the warning would be rejected and had fixed the date for the bombing of Hiroshima even before the issuance of the Potsdam Declaration. But such an argument ignores the military necessities. For operational reasons, the orders had to be issued in sufficient time "to set the military wheels in motion." In a sense, therefore, the decision was made on July 25. It would stand unless the President changed his mind. "I had made the decision," wrote Truman in 1955. "I also instructed Stimson that the order would stand unless I notified him that the Japanese reply to our ultimatum was acceptable." The rejection by the Japanese of the Potsdam Declaration confirmed the orders Spaatz had already received.

## THE JAPANESE SURRENDER

On Tinian and Guam, preparations for dropping the bomb had been completed by August 3. The original plan was to carry out the operation on August 4, but General LeMay deferred the attack because of bad weather over the target. On August 5 the forecasts were favorable and he gave the word to proceed with the mission the following day. At 0245 on August 6, the bomb-carrying plane was airborne. Six and a half hours later the bomb was released over Hiroshima, Japan's eighth largest city, to explode 50 seconds later at a height of about 2,000 feet. The age of atomic warfare had opened.

Aboard the cruiser *Augusta* on his way back to the United States, President Truman received the news by radio. That same day a previously prepared release from Washington announced to the world that an atomic bomb had been dropped on Hiroshima and warned the Japanese that if they did not surrender they could expect "a rain of ruin from the air, the like of which has never been seen on this earth."

On August 7, Ambassador Sato in Moscow received word at last that Molotov would see him the next afternoon. At the appointed hour he arrived at the Kremlin, full of hope that he would receive a favorable reply to the Japanese proposal for Soviet mediation with the Allies to end the war. Instead, he was handed the Soviet declaration of war, effective on August 9. Thus, three months to the day after Germany's surrender, Marshal Stalin had lived up to his promise to the Allies.

Meanwhile, President Truman had authorized the use of the second bomb— the last then available. The objective was Kokura, the date August 9. But the plane carrying the bomb failed to make its run over the primary target and hit the secondary target, Nagasaki, instead. The next day Japan sued for peace.

The close sequence of events between August 6 and 10, combined with the fact that the bomb was dropped almost three months before the scheduled invasion of Kyushu and while the Japanese were trying desperately to get out of the war, has suggested to some that the bombing of Hiroshima had a deeper purpose than the desire to end the war quickly. This purpose, it is claimed, was nothing less than a desire to forestall Soviet intervention into the Far Eastern war. Else why this necessity for speed? Certainly nothing in the military situation seemed to call for such hasty action. But if the purpose was to forestall Soviet intervention, then there was every reason for speed. And even if the Russians could not be kept out of the war, at least they would be prevented from making more than a token contribution to victory over Japan. In this sense it may be argued that the bomb proved a success, for the war ended with the United States in full control of Japan.

This theory leaves several matters unexplained. In the first place, the Americans did not know the exact date on which the Soviet Union would declare war but believed it would be within a week or two of August 8. If they had wished to forestall a Soviet declaration of war, then they could reasonably have been expected to act sooner than they did. Such close timing left little if any margin for error. Secondly, had the United States desired above everything else to keep the Russians out, it could have responded to one of several unofficial Japanese overtures, or made the Potsdam Declaration more attractive to Japan. Certainly the failure to put a time limit on the declaration suggests that speed was not of the essence in American calculations. Finally, the date and time of the bombing were left to Generals Spaatz and LeMay, who certainly had no way of knowing Soviet intentions. Bad weather or any other untoward incident could have delayed the attack a week or more.

There is reason to believe that the Russians at the last moved more quickly than they had intended. In his conversations with Harry Hopkins in May 1945 and at Potsdam, Marshal Stalin had linked Soviet entry with negotiations then in progress with Chinese representatives in Moscow. When these were completed, he had said, he would act. On August 8 these negotiations were still in progress.

Did the atomic bomb accomplish its purpose? Was it, in fact, as Stimson said, "the best possible sanction" after Japan rejected the Potsdam Declaration? The sequence of events argues strongly that it was, for bombs were dropped on the 6th and 9th, and on the 10th Japan surrendered. But in the excitement over the announcement of the first use of an atomic bomb and then of Japan's surrender, many overlooked the significance of the Soviet Union's entry into the war on the 9th. The first bomb had produced consternation and confusion among the leaders of Japan, but no disposition to surrender. The Soviet declaration of war, though not entirely unexpected, was a devastating blow and, by removing all hope of Soviet mediation, gave the advocates of peace their first opportunity to come boldly out into the open. When Premier Suzuki arrived at the palace on the morning of the 9th, he was told that the Emperor believed Japan's only course now was to accept the Potsdam Declaration. The militarists could and did minimize the effects of the bomb, but they could not evade the obvious consequences of Soviet intervention, which ended all hope of dividing their enemies and securing softer peace terms.

In this atmosphere, the leaders of Japan held a series of meetings on August 9, but were unable to come to agreement. In the morning came word of the fate of Nagasaki. This additional disaster failed to resolve the issues between the military and those who advocated surrender. Finally the Emperor took the unprecedented step of calling an Imperial Conference, which lasted until 3 o'clock the next morning. When it, too, failed to produce agreement the Emperor told his ministers that he wished the war brought to an end. The constitutional significance of this action is difficult for Westerners to comprehend, but it resolved the crisis and produced in the cabinet a formal decision to accept the Potsdam Declaration, provided it did not prejudice the position of the Emperor.

What finally forced the Japanese to surrender? Was it air bombardment, naval power, the atomic bomb or Soviet entry? The United States Strategic Bombing Survey concluded that Japan would have surrendered by the end of the year, without invasion and without the atomic bomb. Other equally informed opinion maintained that it was the atomic bomb that forced Japan to surrender. "Without its use," Dr. Karl T. Compton asserted, "the war would have continued for many months." Admiral Nimitz believed firmly that the decisive factor was "the complete impunity with which the Pacific Fleet pounded Japan," and General Arnold claimed it was air bombardment that had brought Japan to the verge of collapse. But Major-General Claire Chennault, wartime air commander in China, maintained that Soviet entry into the Far Eastern war brought about the surrender of Japan and would have done so "even if no atomic bombs had been dropped."

It would be a fruitless task to weigh accurately the relative importance of all the factors leading to the Japanese surrender. There is no doubt that Japan had been defeated by the summer of 1945, if not earlier. But defeat did not mean that the military clique had given up; the Army intended to fight on and had made elaborate preparations for the defense of the homeland. Whether air bombardment and naval blockade or the threat of invasion would have produced an early surrender and averted the heavy losses almost certain to accompany the actual landings in Japan is a moot question. Certainly they had a profound effect on the Japanese position. It is equally impossible to assert categorically that the atomic bomb alone or Soviet intervention alone was the decisive factor in bringing the war to an end. All that can be said on the available evidence is that Japan was defeated in the military sense by August 1945 and that the bombing of Hiroshima, followed by the Soviet Union's declaration of war and then the bombing of Nagasaki and the threat of still further bombing, acted as catalytic agents to produce the Japanese decision to surrender. Together they created so extreme a crisis that the Emperor himself, in an unprecedented move, took matters into his own hands and ordered his ministers to surrender. Whether any other set of circumstances would have resolved the crisis and produced the final decision to surrender is a question history cannot yet answer.

## NOTES

1. The one exception was the Navy's work in the field of atomic energy as a source of power for naval vessels. *Hearings before the Special Committee on Atomic Energy*, Senate, 79th Cong., 1st Sess., S.R. 179, pt. 3, pp. 364–389, testimony of Dr. Ross Gunn.

2. Forrestal says in his *Diaries* that neither he nor Stimson was present, while McCloy's definite recollection is that Stimson was present but Forrestal was not. . . .

3. In his diary, under the date June 19, Stimson wrote: "The last-chance warning . . . must be given before an actual landing of the ground forces in Japan, and fortunately the plans provide for enough time to bring in the sanctions to our warning in the shape of heavy ordinary bombing attack and an attack of S-1 [the atomic bomb]."

4. General Eisenhower was at Potsdam and his advice, Truman says, was asked. The various participants differ in their recollections of this meeting. . . .

# 13

## The Korean War

### MORTON H. HALPERIN

#### FOREIGN-POLICY OBJECTIVES

Prior to the outbreak of the Korean War, the United States believed that a major objective of the Soviet Union was to expand the area under its control. Thus, in responding to the North Korean attack—which had not been anticipated—American objectives were developed in the framework of the belief that the attack was part of a general plan for expansion and perhaps a prelude to general war. The United States sought to prevent the success of this Communist attempt to expand by the use of force in the belief that allowing the Soviets to succeed in Korea would encourage aggression elsewhere. General Omar Bradley expressed this purpose at the MacArthur hearings in describing Korea as "a preventive limited war aimed at avoiding World War III."[1] President Harry Truman later described his objectives in intervening in the Korean War in similar terms:

Communism was acting in Korea just as Hitler, Mussolini, and the Japanese had acted ten, fifteen, and twenty years earlier. I felt certain that if South Korea was allowed to fall Communist leaders would be emboldened to override nations closer to our own shores. If the Communists were permitted to force their way into the Republic of Korea without opposition from the free world, no small nation would have the courage to resist threats and aggression by stronger Communist neighbors. If this was allowed to go unchallenged it would mean a third world war, just as similar incidents had brought on the second world war.[2]

The defense of Korea was partly motivated by the feeling that the action was necessary to convince the West Europeans that the United States would come to their aid. The Administration was wary of committing its military power, thereby leaving itself exposed to Soviet aggression in Europe. During the latter stages of the Korean War, in fact, the major American buildup occurred in Europe and not in the Far East. The Administration was also aware of the danger of splitting the NATO alliance in a dispute over Far Eastern policy. A major objective throughout the war was to prevent adverse repercussions in Europe while using the episode to strengthen NATO and build up its military capability. America's NATO allies, particularly the British, constantly applied pressure on the United States to prevent expansion of the war and to bring it swiftly to a conclusion. Following an almost inadvertent reference by President Truman at a press conference to the possibility of using atomic weapons, British Prime Minister Clement Attlee flew to the United States to confer with Truman and to propose the seeking of a cease fire in Korea to be followed by the admission of Communist China to the United Nations. Partly because the defense effort in Korea was carried on under UN auspices, the United States felt obliged constantly to consult its allies on policy and was influenced by their continuous efforts to halt the expansion of the war and to bring about its conclusion.

Soviet objectives were more closely related to the situation in the Far East. The Soviets were interested in the capture of South Korea for its own sake and probably expected a relatively quick and easy North Korean victory. In addition, the Soviets probably hoped to prevent Japan's alignment with the Western powers. Allen Whiting has suggested the nature of the Soviet Far Eastern objective:

In view of the multiple pressures directed at Japanese foreign policy, the Communist leaders may have conceived the Korean War as serving ends beyond the immediate control of the peninsula. Military victories in Taiwan and Korea could be heralded as ushering in the Communist era in Asia, and as demonstrating the impotence of America's "puppets," Chiang Kai-shek and Syngman Rhee. The resultant effect upon Japan might swing opportunistic groups behind existing neutralist opposition to Yoshida and prevent his supporting American policy.[3]

This interpretation of Soviet strategy in the Korean War was offered by John Foster Dulles right after the North Korean attack. Dulles, who was at the time the State Department planner for the Japanese Peace Treaty, suggested that the Korean attack may have been motivated in part by a desire to block American efforts to make Japan a full member of the free world. He conjectured also that the attack may have been ordered because the Communists could not tolerate the "hopeful, attractive Asiatic experiment in democracy" that was under way in South Korea.

The Chinese objectives in entering the Korean War were also based on general political considerations, but of a defensive nature. According to Whiting the Chinese also hoped to influence the course of United States–Japanese relations. Moreover they were worried about the loss of prestige they would suffer if they allowed the Western "imperialists" to march unhindered to their borders. And they were perhaps most concerned with the beneficial effects of United Nations success in Korea on the many opponents of the Communist regime still active and on Taiwan. Whiting concluded:

In sum, it was not the particular problems of safeguarding electric-power supplies in North Korea or the industrial base in Manchuria that aroused Peking to military action. Instead, the final step seems to have been prompted in part by general concern over the range of opportunities within China that might be exploited by a determined, powerful enemy on China's doorstep. At the least, a military response might deter the enemy from further adventures. At the most, it might succeed in inflicting sufficient damage to force the enemy to compromise his objectives and to accede to some of Peking's demands. Contrary to some belief, the Chinese Communist leadership did not enter the Korean War either full of self-assertive confidence or for primarily expansionist goals.[4]

The Chinese apparently entered the war with the aim of saving at least some of North Korea. Their minimal objective was to preserve the identity of Communist North Korea rather than its total territorial integrity.

In an effort to secure the political effects discussed, American battlefield objectives and war-termination conditions underwent considerable fluctuation during the course of the war. When the United States first intervened, its objective was simply to restore peace and the South Korean border. Very early in the war and after the Chinese intervention, the United States considered a total withdrawal from Korea. Later its battlefield objective expanded to include the unification of Korea. But in the end, the United States accepted a truce line which closely approximated the *status quo ante*. As Richard Neustadt has pointed out, Truman's original decision to seek the unification of Korea failed to take into account the political-effects objectives that the United States was pursuing, and in the end the recognition of this forced the abandonment of the unification effort.

Had the unification of Korea been Truman's dearest object, its announcement as a war aim would have been another matter. But it was among the least of the objectives on his mind. In July and August 1950, in December after Chinese intervention, in his struggles with MacArthur, and thereafter through his last two years of office, his behavior leaves no doubt about the many things he wanted more than that. He wanted to affirm that the UN was not a League of Nations, that aggression would be met with counterforce, that "police actions" were well worth their cost, that the "lesson of the 1930s" had been learned. He wanted to avoid "the wrong war, in the wrong place, at the wrong time," as General Bradley put it— and any "War," if possible. He wanted NATO strengthened fast, both militarily and psychologically. He wanted the United States rearmed without inflation, and prepared, thereafter, to sustain a level of expenditure for military forces and for foreign aid far higher than had seemed achievable before Korea.[5]

Once the Soviets recognized that they could not easily secure their objective of demonstrating American weakness and unwillingness to use force, they seemed to have abandoned the battlefield objective of capturing all of Korea. They may have been willing to accept an end to the war with part or perhaps even all of North Korea in Western hands, and ultimately settled for a virtual restoration of the *status quo ante*.

## RISK OF CENTRAL WAR

The Korean War was fought before the era of intercontinental ballistic missiles and fusion weapons. Thus, while both sides could have expanded the war quickly and decisively, there was not the danger that now exists of a sudden unleashing of nuclear missiles which within an hour could destroy a large part of both the United States and the Soviet Union.

Even without this threat of a mutually devastating strategic exchange, the danger of a world war was nevertheless present, and both sides seem to have been determined to prevent its occurrence. Truman has reported that the major American aim in Korea was to prevent a third world war. The Russian decision to remain out of the war seemed to be partly motivated by a fear of igniting a global war. In this situation where neither side could gain a decisive advantage by going first, both sides seemed to recognize that, no matter who started the global war, both would suffer major losses. Though the United States could have attacked the Soviet Union with its very limited stockpile of atomic weapons, it probably could not have prevented a Soviet ground attack in Western Europe which might have resulted in Communist domination of the European continent. The Soviets had almost no capacity to attack the United States and could not have prevented an American attack on the Soviet Union. Though both sides avoided forcing the other into starting a global war, neither was constantly concerned with the possibility of "preemption" by its adversary.

The United States, however, was concerned that the Korean War should not lead it to expend those military capabilities which were considered an important deterrent to general war. In Korea the United States was employing the troops and the matériel which it felt were necessary to deter general war. At the MacArthur hearings, Air Force General Vandenburg rejected a senator's suggestion that the United States should commit a major part of the American Air Force to the Korean War effort. He argued instead that the United States must get a cease fire

without endangering that one potential that we have which has kept the peace so far, which the United States Air Force; which, if utilized in a manner to do what you are suggesting, would [*sic*], because of attrition and because the size of the Air Force is such and the size of the air force industry is such that we could not still be that deterrent to [general] war which we are today.[6]

Soviet action during the war, including the failure to commit combat forces, suggests that they shared with the United States the desire to avoid a global war.

## IMAGES OF THE ROLE OF FORCE

The North Korean attack on South Korea suggested the willingness of the Communists to seek a limited objective by a limited use of force. The Soviets probably intended to seize South Korea with the use of North Korean forces and then to halt their military operations. When the United States intervened, they recognized their miscalculation of American intentions, but proceeded on the assumption that American intervention need not lead to world war. The attack into South Korea, moreover, seems to have been motivated by the Soviet compulsion to fill power vacuums. In view of the specific United States declaration that South Korea was outside its defense perimeter, the Soviets reasonably could have counted on a quick and easy victory by the North Koreans. But, while Communist conduct during the war reflected a doctrine that included the limited use of military force and limited objectives, neither the Chinese nor the Russians seemed to have any idea of the optimum methods of communicating intentions and capabilities to the other side in the course of such a war.

American images of the role of force, on the other hand, seem to have been much less hospitable to the limitation of warfare. It would appear that the United States had not foreseen the possibility of Soviet military action in South Korea or any other local area unconnected with a general Soviet military offensive. The result was the American decision not to prepare for the defense of South Korea in view of the low estimate of its value in a general war. Thus the decision of June 1950 to defend South Korea was not based on a reestimate of South Korea's military importance, but on recognition that something had occurred for which American military doctrine had not been prepared. In making its policy decisions throughout the war, the United States was operating without any general theoretical notions of the nature of local war in the atomic age, and its decisions were probably affected by the lack of such theory.

Each side's image of the other's intentions influenced its decisions. The Soviets clearly underestimated the likelihood of American intervention. In the Soviet view American action in withdrawing its troops from Korea and the American declarations that it would defend South Korea only as part of its United Nations obligations had meant that the United States would not in fact defend South Korea. The Soviets failed to anticipate the partly moral and partly political American reaction to aggression. They were insensitive to the importance that the United States would attach to repelling "illegal" aggression, as opposed to less clear-cut violations of international law.

The American decision to intervene in Korea and the subsequent decisions were also based on and influenced by estimates of Soviet intentions. In assessing the motives of the North Korean attack, American policy makers gave consideration and, to some extent, credence to five different interpretations, as follows:

1. The "diversionary move" interpretation. In view of the number of other areas, particularly Western Europe, that appeared more militarily significant than South Korea, the North Korean attack was seen as a diversionary move, aimed to draw American resources away from the areas where they were most important. Truman reports that he shared this view in part and was determined not to leave Europe vulnerable to Soviet aggression.

2. The "soft-spot probing" interpretation. By this image of Soviet doctrine, the Soviet compulsion to fill power vacuums had led to the attack on South Korea which had been abandoned by the United States and which was clearly incapable of defending itself.

3. The "testing" interpretation. This was the view that seemed to influence most Truman's image of the North Korean attack. It recalled the progress of Hitler's aggressive moves and asserted that the North Korean attack should be seen as a prelude to attacks in other areas if that aggression were allowed to succeed. This view differed from the "soft-spot probing" interpretation in its assumption that the Communists' success in Korea would encourage them to attempt aggression in the other areas where Western defense capabilities were far stronger. In short the purpose of the Korean attack was to probe the firmness of Western intentions, and not simply to fill a power vacuum.

4. The "demonstration" interpretation. By this interpretation, the Soviets were mainly concerned with demonstrating their own strength and American weakness in order to promote, on a long-term basis, important shifts in political allegiance throughout the world.

5. The "Soviet–Far-East strategy" interpretation. This interpretation put emphasis on the idea, already discussed, that the Soviets hoped to prevent the entrance of Japan into the Western camp and to pave the way for further Communist expansion in the Far East.

. . . The inclination of American policy makers toward the "testing" interpretation of Soviet doctrine—in which the Korean attack was equated with Hitler's early expansionist moves—may have reinforced the likelihood that the United States would intervene in Korea. If the "soft-spot probing" interpretation of Soviet conduct had been accepted instead, the United States might have been more prone to cede South Korea while taking steps to prevent the existence of power vacuums elsewhere. The belief that successful aggression would embolden the Soviets made the defense of South Korea seem crucial.

## DOMESTIC POLITICAL PRESSURES

During the Korean War the Truman administration continued to pursue its domestic political goals. Despite the war there was politics-as-usual on both sides of the political fence. The President was constantly concerned with promoting his Fair Deal program, consolidating the position of the Democratic Party, strengthening his northern and western liberal support in Congress, and calming the political crises raised by such men as Senator Joseph McCarthy. Nor was the Administration immune to criticism from the Republican Party, which felt that it was possible, necessary, and desirable to attack the Administration's conduct as well as to question the basic concept of limiting war.

After the MacArthur hearings, a Republican minority report declared:

We believe that a policy of victory must be announced to the American people in order to restore unity and confidence. It is too much to expect that our people will accept a limited war. Our policy must be to win. Our strategy must be devised to bring about decisive victory.[7]

These few sentences suggest a number of important assumptions about the nature of wartime politics. The first is the notion that the unity of the American people can be achieved only with a declaration that victory is the goal. A further implication is that, after such a declaration, the method of achieving a battlefield victory becomes a "military" problem that is beyond the realm of partisan domestic politics. On the other hand, once the government admits that there are other political considerations that affect and moderate the goal of a strictly military victory, then, according to this Republican statement, it is legitimate to criticize the particular policy adopted. Unity will come only when the country is asked to back an absolute goal. If there is no such goal, then the opposition has a duty to examine and critically appraise the war effort.

Congress, as a whole, also felt itself free to criticize. The hearings into the firing of General Douglas MacArthur were striking in that they required the Administration, *during the war*, to justify its conduct and to explain what it hoped to accomplish in the war and how the war was being conducted, as well as to explicate a host of particulars which must have been of as much interest to the Communists as they were to the senators across the table. Actually the Chinese and the Russians did not have that motivation. However, the senators' questions at the hearings provided a unique and invaluable opportunity for the Administration to communicate what it wanted to communicate to this hearing. Congress forced the Administration to discuss its strategy and objectives during the war without any apparent consideration of the effect this would have on the American war effort.

The quotation from the report of the Republican senators also reflects the then still strong American opposition to fighting a local war. The Senators stated flatly that the American people would not accept a strategy of limiting war, and indicated their rejection of the strategy as well. The implication is that during a local war the American government will be subjected to attacks from the political opposition, from Congress, and from public citizens on two grounds: the legitimacy of fighting such a war and the particular strategy employed in the war.

The general public seems to have shared the Republican senators' dissatisfaction with the course of the Korean War, at least in its later stages. On the other hand, the public apparently approved the decision of the Eisenhower administration to end the war short of victory as it had approved the initial decision to intervene. The public's frustration with the continuing war probably added to the margin of Eisenhower's victory in 1952; his ending the war enhanced the Republican image as the party of peace and increased the Eisenhower plurality in 1956. The

Korean War does not seem to have had a major or lasting impact on popular political attitudes. In this respect, American political leaders seem to have overestimated the effect of the war on the voting public. Korea is taken as demonstrating—as to some extent it did—that extended local wars which cannot be decisively won are not popular with the American public. Leading the United States into a major local war or expanding the war without securing a clear victory is likely to be perceived as a political liability; ending a war on almost any terms may be a political asset.

All these domestic pressures undoubtedly influenced the manner in which the Truman administration conducted its Korean operations, both by hampering its freedom of action and by increasing the costs of various actions.

## ATOMIC WEAPONS

The most dramatic limit on the Korean War was that neither side used its atomic weapons. According to Brodie there were four reasons why these weapons were not used by the United States:[8]

1. The Joint Chiefs of Staff and civilian policy makers continued to feel that the war in Korea was basically a Soviet feint. There was, therefore, a strong case for conserving the then relatively limited stockpile of atomic weapons for the principal war which, they thought, would come in Europe. Their fear was not that the employment of nuclear weapons would lead to an expansion of the war and a Soviet attack on Europe, but rather that Korea was deliberately designed as a decoy to get the United States to exhaust its nuclear stockpile and conventional military resources so that the Soviets could later attack with impunity in Europe. It was the desire, then, to save resources and not the fear of provoking the enemy that was one of the main causes of the American decision not to use nuclear weapons in Korea.

2. American policy was also affected by the reports of local Air Force commanders that there were no suitable targets for atomic weapons in Korea. While the impact of this view was considerable, it apparently reflected an uninformed attitude about the possible uses of atomic weapons. Commanders in the field came to think, for example, that atomic bombs were of little use against bridges, a belief which Brodie explained as follows:

   This odd idea probably resulted from a mis-reading of the results at Hiroshima and Nagasaki. Some bridges were indeed badly damaged at those places and some were not, but for the latter it was generally forgotten that a bridge only 270 feet from ground zero at Hiroshima was actually 2,100 feet from the point of explosion, and also that it received its blast effect from above rather than from the side.[9]

   Nuclear weapons were still relatively new and had not been extensively tested, and it is probable that commanders in the field were too busy to search out potential targets for nuclear weapons.

3. American allies, particularly the British, were strongly and emotionally opposed to the use of atomic weapons in the Korean War. This pressure from allies strengthened America's own anxieties and moral doubts about again using these weapons.

4. A subsidiary reason for the failure to use atomic weapons in the Korean War was the fear of the retaliatory employment by the Soviets of the few atomic weapons in their possession against Pusan or Japan, despite the American near monopoly of these weapons. Brodie doubts, however, whether this fear played a conscious part in the relevant decisions.

The first two motives just discussed will not be important in the future. The American stockpile of tactical nuclear weapons is now so great that military commanders may urge their use precisely because they are a nonscarce military resource, and certainly no argument can be made that they should not be used because they are scarce. Military officers now have a much better understanding of the capabilities of nuclear weapons, which, moreover, now come in much smaller packages. Thus it will be clear to military commanders that there would be suitable targets for their use in any conceivable future major limited war. While we can expect continued pressure from our allies against the use of nuclear weapons, certain allies might advocate their use in some situations. There will, however, be other international political pressures—for example, from the uncommitted or neutral states—against nuclear weapons, and the possibility of a Soviet nuclear response will be a much more important determinant of the decision.

We know much less about the details of the Russian decision not to use atomic weapons in Korea. The Russians seemed determined not to supply any matériel to the forces fighting in Korea which could clearly be labeled as having been supplied by them after the war began. This would certainly be the case with atomic weapons. In addition, the Soviet stockpile of such weapons was so small that its use in a localized military encounter might have seemed wasteful.

The limit observed by both sides seems not to have resulted from an attempt—or even an awareness of the need—to bargain with the enemy. However the Soviets were probably more restrained than the United States by the fear that the initiation of nuclear attacks would be met by a response in kind.

The Chinese Communists seem genuinely to have feared the possibility of the American use of atomic weapons when they intervened in the Korean War. According to Whiting the Chinese felt that a nuclear response was a real possibility; intervention was considered risky and every effort was made to delay it and to minimize its consequences. The extent of this Chinese concern was reflected both in its shelter-building program and in domestic Chinese Communist propaganda. But Peking was reassured by the three-week testing period of relatively small Chinese intervention which revealed that United States aircraft, though authorized to bomb the Korean ends of the Yalu bridges, were forbidden to venture into Chinese territory.

The background of the limit on the use of atomic weapons in the Korean War, then, suggests a failure of both sides to understand what the other side was likely to do and what the other side's fears and goals were. It also suggests that, to a large extent, the determination of limits is based on considerations other than those that result from the battlefield interaction. Some of the other limiting points established in the war reveal the same pattern.

## CHINESE INTERVENTION

One of the major expansions of the Korean War was the decision of the United Nations Command to cross the thirty-eighth parallel. This decision was based partly on the military consideration that one could not stand by and allow the enemy forces to regroup for renewed attack just beyond the border, but also on political grounds—when the battlefield conditions changed in its favor, the United States decided to pursue the unification of Korea by military means. In crossing the parallel the United States was aware of the risk that it might trigger Chinese Communist intervention, and tried by reassuring statements to prevent it. But it apparently underestimated the Chinese reaction and, at the same time, failed to develop a concurrent strategy which, by retaliatory threats or other sanctions, could succeed in preventing Chinese intervention. As Whiting has suggested the threat to use atomic weapons on the Chinese mainland if the Chinese intervened might have been a much more effective deterrent than the attempt to reassure them that a march to the border did not presage an attack on mainland China. The threat to use atomic weapons would have involved major political costs for the United States, and the American government might not have threatened to launch an atomic attack even if it had recognized that the threat might be effective. Had the Administration been aware of the fact that the fear of greater expansion might have deterred Chinese intervention, an alternative course might have been to threaten to expand the war to China with conventional weapons. But even this was not done. In fact, a decision was made before the intervention that Chinese intervention would not lead to conventional bombing beyond the Yalu. MacArthur reportedly believed that this decision had been leaked to the Chinese.

In choosing, instead, to inform the Chinese of its limited objectives, the United States also considered it important to reassure the Chinese that their hydroelectric plants would not be jeopardized by a march up to the Yalu. But, as Whiting has pointed out:

It was widely believed in Western circles that a determining factor in Chinese Communist concern over North Korea was the reliance of Manchurian industry upon power supplies across the border as well as along the Yalu River. This belief prompted explicit reassurances from Western spokesmen, both in Washington and at Lake Success, concerning "China's legitimate interests" near the frontier. Yet we have seen that Peking ignored this issue completely in its domestic as well as its foreign communications. The absence of propaganda about the protection of the hydroelectric installations, despite the need to maximize popular response to mobilization of "volunteers," suggests that this consideration played little if any role in motivating Chinese Communist intervention.[10]

In its advance through North Korea, then, the United Nations Command was attempting to communicate two points to the Chinese Communists: first, that it was prepared to go up to but not beyond the Yalu; and second, that it was prepared to respect China's legitimate interests in the northern regions of North Korea. The United States sought, therefore, to establish its limited objectives: that United Nations forces would take all North Korea, that the North Korean government would cease to exist, but China's legitimate industrial interests would be protected. An effort was made to assure the Chinese that the capture of North Korea would not be used as a springboard for an attack into China. The United States assumed that the limits were ones that the Chinese were interested in, and that these limits would serve to keep the Chinese out of the war. But Chinese interests were different and could only be satisfied by different boundary conditions to the war.

Neustadt argues that the Chinese were not in any way affected by the announcement of the United Nations' aim to destroy the North Korean government.

To judge from what the Chinese said, and later did, Peking's concern was with MacArthur's military progress, never mind its foreign policy objective. Chinese concern was not confined to anything so simple as a buffer zone along the border; an entity called North Korea, not the border, was at stake (perhaps in roughly the same sense that South Korea, under reverse circumstances, was for Washington). Even had the UN promised restoration of an independent North once all resistance ceased—which, naturally, no one proposed— I know of nothing to suggest that Peking would have withheld intervention. The communist world does not take kindly, it appears, to the dismantling of a member state's facilities for governance: the party and the army. MacArthur's military progress threatened both, no matter what came after. In short, the military risks and diplomatic dangers usually associated with MacArthur's march across the parallel existed independent of the words used in the UN resolution. MacArthur's march was authorized before the words were seen, much less approved, at Lake Success.[11]

Washington was apparently convinced even in retrospect that its declarations did not influence the Chinese decision to enter the war and that no other declaratory policy could have altered the Chinese decision. American policy makers concluded that once the decision was made to cross the thirty-eighth parallel, nothing could be done to affect the Chinese decision. In fact, the State Department reportedly argued in December of 1950 that the Chinese decision to intervene was made prior to the crossing of the thirty-eighth parallel. In one sense, at least, this conclusion may be wrong: the Chinese position might have been altered by threats to expand the war with the use of atomic weapons against China. Moreover it is by no means certain that the Chinese were concerned with the preservation of the total territorial integrity of North Korea. As Whiting suggests an American commitment to advance only part way up the peninsula—that is, to permit the maintenance of the North Korean government in some part of its territory—might have been sufficient to deter the Chinese entrance into the war.

Neither before nor during the first three months of war [Whiting wrote] did the degree of interest in Pyongyang evinced by Peking warrant acceptance at face value of its concern for a "just" peace, based upon the *status quo ante bellum*.

This is not to say that the Chinese Communist leadership was prepared to accept with equanimity the total defeat of North Korea. As a minimal goal, intervention must have been attempted to preserve an entity identifiable as the DPRK, and to prevent unification of all Korea under U.N. supervision. The late date of Chinese Communist entry into the war suggests that it was the political importance of the North Korean government, rather than its territorial integrity, that was at stake. Although intervention was officially predicated upon U.N. crossing of the thirty-eighth parallel, no Chinese People's Volunteers and Democratic People's Republic of Korea defense lines were established during the August–October period, not even to protect Pyongyang. To Peking, a "just" Korean peace was not an end in itself but rather a means towards fulfilling other related goals of policy.[12]

Thus, even after the crossing of the thirty-eighth parallel, Chinese intervention might have been prevented had the United States acted differently. Although trying to impose limits on expansion, the United States failed to grasp adequately either the reasons that the Chinese felt intervention was necessary or the threats that might have deterred their intervention. Both sides expanded the war, the United Nations by crossing the thirty-eighth parallel and the Chinese by entering the war. Each side failed to convey to the other the kind of counteraction to be expected which might have deterred expansion. China attempted to prevent the crossing of the thirty-eighth parallel by declaring her intention to intervene, but this intention, relayed by the Indian ambassador, was not taken seriously by the United Nations Command. The United Nations sought to prevent the Chinese entrance, not by threatening a further expansion but by attempting to satisfy the Chinese security interests that, it was assumed, might lead her to enter the war.

## PORTS AND TROOPS

Despite the fact that United States planes, taking off from airfields in South Korea and Japan and from aircraft carriers, consistently bombed targets in North Korea, the Communists engaged in almost no bombing south of the thirty-eighth parallel. This was one of the major asymmetries of the war both from a legalistic point of view and in terms of interfering with the military operations of the enemy. Both sides apparently devoted considerable attention to the question of what targets to attack, and a variety of motives affected the relevant decisions.

The American decision to bomb targets in North Korea was made prior to the commitment of American ground troops in June 1950. A month later permission was given to bomb industrial targets in North Korea, but the use of incendiary bombs was not allowed because of the civil damage that would have resulted.

The Air Force was not authorized to bomb areas close to the Soviet and Chinese borders. Rashin was the single industrial center within the forbidden area and it was the only industrial target in North Korea which was not destroyed by mid-September when an end to strategic bombing was ordered by the Joint Chiefs. Not until June 1952 were attacks on the hydroelectric plants in North Korea authorized; within two weeks almost 90 percent of the North Korea power capacity was destroyed.

American attacks on targets in North Korea steadily expanded. The attacks were aimed at affecting the immediate military situation. The restraints observed had several motives: (1) to avoid extensive civilian destruction considered undesirable on both humanitarian and propaganda grounds; (2) to avoid a spillover of the war into China or the Soviet Union (the spillover into China prior to her entry into the war probably did not have a major impact on Chinese policy, but the incursion did create propaganda and political difficulties); (3) to avoid damaging, in the case of the hydroelectric plants, targets considered vital to the Chinese so as to avoid their entrance into the war, presumably in retaliation.

The Communists exercised far greater restraint on their air forces. Except for a few night "heckling" attacks from small biplanes in the spring of 1951 no air attacks were made on any targets in South Korea. The Communist restraint was not the result of the absence of inviting military targets. The port of Pusan was an extremely inviting target for bombardment and mining. It was the key to the American logistic effort and frequently was lighted up all night. American logistic convoys and troops in the field also could have been hampered by air attacks. A number of factors seem to have influenced the Communist decision not to respond in kind to United Nations air attacks on North Korea:

1. The Communists might have believed that it would have been very difficult, if not impossible, for the United Nations to continue its operations in Korea if Pusan came under heavy attack, and that, once the United Nations committed itself to the defense of South Korea, it was no longer in a position to accept complete withdrawal. Therefore, if attacks on logistic lines made impossible the continued conduct of an effective ground war in Korea, the United States might have been forced to engage in strategic strikes against the Chinese, if not the Russian, homeland.[13] If the Communists found this supposition credible, they may have concluded that, once their initial grab for South Korea failed, they could not afford to do anything that would lead to their complete control over South Korea. They may have recognized that American confinement of the war to the Korean peninsula was dependent on her ability to fight there effectively.

2. In order to avoid attacks on Chinese air bases just north of the Yalu, Red airmen were not allowed to attack United Nations positions from these bases. Although the Communists were permitting the United States the sanctuary of bases in Japan and on aircraft carriers, they apparently were afraid that they

would not be granted a similar sanctuary for bombing operations. United States planes managed to keep the North Korean airfields out of commission almost continuously throughout the war. Thus, given that the Chinese limited the use of their fields to staging operations and to fighter planes, the Communists were incapable of bombing operations.

3. There is some evidence to suggest that Soviet pilots constituted a significant part of the "Chinese" air force during the Korean War. If this is true the explanation for target restraint may have been the desire to avoid the capture of Soviet airmen. This proof of direct Soviet involvement in the war would at the least have been politically damaging and, from a Soviet point of view, might have created an intolerable risk of American retaliation.

By the end of the war the United States was exercising almost no target restraint in North Korea and the Communists were doing no bombing in South Korea. Each side was guided by a complex series of motives and incentives. However, despite the asymmetry of the actions, there is nothing to suggest that either side treated its decisions on targeting as being closely related to, affected by, or likely to affect, the opponent's decisions on these questions.

### EXPANSION AND LIMITATION

Decisions on expanding the United Nations operations resulted from the rejecting or approving of the field commanders' proposals by the Joint Chiefs of Staff or civilian officials. In some cases, particularly on the question of using atomic weapons, the military never made the request, and so, in some sense, no decision was made. On three occasions General MacArthur was refused his requests: to employ Chinese Nationalist troops, to impose a naval blockade on China, and to bomb bases and supply lines in China. But a number of MacArthur's requests for permission to expand the war were approved. These included the commitment of American ground forces, the Inchon offensive, and the crossing of the thirty-eighth parallel.

President Truman states that the National Security Council recommended the consideration of three factors relevant to the decision of whether to go on the offensive: action by the Soviet Union and the Chinese Communists, the views of friendly members of the United Nations, and the risk of general war. These and other decisions were also influenced by American doctrine as well as by domestic political pressures. The balancing of the factors varied from decision to decision, but all played a role in the major decisions to limit or expand the war.

Much less is known about the Communist decision-making process or the factors which influenced their decisions to limit or expand the war. The initial decision to keep the Chinese out of the war seems to have been based largely on domestic conditions in China, particularly the desire of the Chinese to implement their program of economic growth and development, and their desire to avoid military entanglements at a time when they had not yet consolidated their hold over their own country. The reasons for the Russians' abstention from open intervention in the war are less clear. The Soviets were determined not to do anything that directly labeled them as participants; they did not publicize the participation of any Russian "volunteers" in the war, nor provide any atomic capability, although they did supply large amounts of conventional military equipment. One likely explanation is the Russian fear that intervention would lead to general war. The United States had the capability of inflicting great destruction on the Soviet homeland with its stock of atomic weapons, while the Soviets had no capability of directly attacking the United States, although they might have been able to capture a large part of Western Europe with ground forces. Thus the Soviets, aware of their inferior strategic position, were probably determined to keep out of the war and to provide no excuse for a direct American attack on the Soviet Union.

Each side apparently made its decisions to limit the war for different reasons and with minimal attention to the battlefield interaction. In addition the two sides observed very different limits. What the United States did in North Korea was quite different from what the Communists did in South Korea, but the Chinese used a much greater percentage of their gross national product than the United States did. Nevertheless, while the United States used naval vessels and airplanes to bomb troops and airfields within Korea, the Communists did not. The United States engaged in logistical interdiction; the Communists did not. Each side, then, observed its own series of limits and restraints only in some very general way related to, and dependent on, the limits of the other side.

At least a few of the limits were symmetrical. Both sides restricted their military operations almost entirely to Korea, and neither used nuclear weapons. There was lack of symmetry in that all the military targets in North Korea were attacked but most in South Korea were not. The United States attacked the Chinese points of entry—the Yalu bridges; but the Chinese did not attack the United States' points of entry—the ports. Both sides observed a number of what Schelling has called "legalistic" limitations.[14] The United Nations carefully observed both the Chinese and Russian borders and tried to avoid crossing them inadvertently. There was symmetry in the absence of official declaration of war. The United Nations troops participated in the war in a "police action" capacity, and none of the countries involved, including the United States, declared war. The Chinese used "volunteers," and the Russians supplied equipment and presumably technicians, but little manpower for the battle.

In some cases the limits represented a recognition of the battlefield interaction. But the origin of many of the limits observed, and part of the explanation for others, lay not within the dynamics of the war itself, but within the domestic and international context in which the war was fought.

## NOTES

1. Hearings before the Committee on Armed Services and the Committee on Foreign Relations, *Military Situation in the Far East*, U.S. Senate, 82nd Congress, 1st Session, 1951, five parts, p. 154.

2. Harry S. Truman, *Memoirs*, Vol. II: *Years of Trial and Hope* (Garden City, N.Y.: Doubleday & Co., 1956), p. 333.

3. Allen S. Whiting, *China Crosses the Yalu: The Decision to Enter the Korean War.* (New York: Macmillan Co., 1960), p. 37.

4. Whiting, op. cit., p. 159.

5. Richard E. Neustadt, *Presidential Power: The Politics of Leadership* (New York: John Wiley and Sons, 1960), p. 126.

6. *Military Situation in the Far East*, op. cit., p. 1385.

7. *Military Situation in the Far East*, op. cit., p. 3590.

8. Bernard Brodie, *Strategy in the Missile Age* (Princeton, N.J.: Princeton University Press, 1959).

9. Ibid., p. 319n.

10. Whiting, op. cit., pp. 151–52.

11. Neustadt, op. cit., p. 125.

12. Whiting, op. cit., pp. 155–56.

13. The United States had secured British concurrence to bomb bases in China in the event of heavy air attacks from Chinese bases on United Nations troops (*H.C. Debs.*, 5th Series, CDXCVI, 970, Feb. 26, 1952) and this was probably communicated to the Chinese. However, Truman reported that he was convinced that Russia would come in if Manchurian bases were bombed.

14. Thomas C. Schelling, *Nuclear Weapons and Limited War.* RAND P-1620, Feb. 20, 1959, p. 1.

# 14

---

# The Cuban Missile Crisis

## DAVID A. WELCH, JAMES G. BLIGHT, AND BRUCE J. ALLYN

The event referred to as the "Cuban missile crisis" in the United States is called the "Caribbean crisis" in the Soviet Union, and the "October crisis" in Cuba; but in all three countries it is widely acknowledged to have been the single most dangerous episode of the Cold War. Analysis of the crisis has heretofore been one-sided. Although information about the American side of the crisis is relatively plentiful, both Cuba and the Soviet Union have closely guarded the histories of their sides of the event. *Glasnost*, however, has led to a series of unprecedented discussions between East and West on the history and significance of the crisis, culminating in a tripartite conference in Moscow in January 1989. Drawing on the evidence and testimony presented at that conference, at the earlier U.S.–Soviet conference in Cambridge, Massachusetts, in October 1987, and in supplemental interviews, we present here a summary and analysis of the new light that has recently been shed on "all three" crises.

New information and testimony illuminate the longstanding debate about Soviet motives for deploying missiles to Cuba; the meaning, significance, and perceptions of American military activities and covert operations in 1962; the genesis, terms, and conduct of the missile deployment; the operational status of the missiles; decision-making during the early phases of the crisis; the origin of Khrushchev's Turkish missile trade proposal; the U-2 shootdown of October 27; the diplomacy leading to a resolution of the crisis; the sources of Khrushchev's sense of urgency at the climax of the confrontation; and the acute tensions in Soviet-Cuban relations immediately following its resolution. We organize our treatment by topic—and, where possible, in chronological order—

on the assumption that the reader will be familiar with the main events of the crisis itself. We highlight those areas in which recent discussions have most significantly advanced our understanding of the event.

## MOTIVES FOR THE SOVIET DEPLOYMENT

The Soviet decision to deploy medium- and intermediate-range ballistic missiles (MRBMs and IRBMs) in Cuba appears to have been a response to three main concerns: first, the perceived need to deter an American invasion of Cuba and prevent the destruction of the Cuban revolution; second, the perceived need to redress the gross imbalance in deliverable strategic nuclear weapons that favored the United States; and third, the desire, born of national pride and prestige, to counter American deployments of nuclear weapons on the Soviet periphery, by exercise of the Soviet Union's "equal right" to deploy its own nuclear missiles on territory adjacent to the United States. According to recent Soviet testimony, the first and second appear to have been the most important motivations, though there is disagreement on the proper assignments of weight to each. Interestingly, Soviets have continued without exception to deny any direct connection between the Cuban missile crisis and the unstable Berlin situation; in Moscow, Andrei Gromyko added his voice to the chorus.

The desire to deter an American invasion of Cuba emerged shortly after the crisis itself as the official Soviet rationale for the deployment. Most Western commentators have dismissed or discounted this motivation, however, because it seemed calculated to justify the public terms on which the crisis was ultimately resolved—the missiles in Cuba were withdrawn in return for an American pledge not to invade the island. But several well-placed Soviets, including Andrei Gromyko, Aleksandr Alekseev, Sergei Khrushchev, and Sergo Mikoyan, have insisted that fears of an American invasion were in fact uppermost in Khrushchev's mind. These fears were grounded in what appeared to be a consistent and deliberate pattern of American activity designed to subvert and overthrow the regime of Fidel Castro, leading up to and including the use of American military force if necessary.

When asked by Khrushchev, Defense Minister Rodion Ya. Malinovsky reportedly informed the Soviet premier that Cuba could resist a full-scale American invasion for three or four days—hardly long enough to send reinforcements. According to Ambassador Alekseev, Khrushchev maintained at meetings with Presidium members that "there was no other path" to save the Cuban revolution than through the installation of nuclear missiles. Thus, Khrushchev may have believed that a deployment of conventional forces to the island as a trip wire would not have sufficed (possibly because of the marginal credibility of any explicit or implicit strategic nuclear threat undergirding it), and that the Soviet Union could not credibly deter an American invasion by threats of retaliation elsewhere.

However, at the Moscow conference, Cuban participants sharply contradicted Khrushchev's analysis in several ways. Though stopping short of insisting that Cuba could have held off a full-scale American attack, Cuban Politburo member Jorge Risquet contended that Cuba could have resisted far longer than three days, and expressed indignation at the estimate attributed to Malinovsky. Sergio del Valle, chief of staff of the Cuban army in 1962, claimed that Cuba had armed and mobilized 270,000 people—double Secretary of Defense Robert McNamara's 1962 estimate.[1] If this is correct, then the five American divisions slated for the invasion under 316 OPLAN would certainly have faced stiffer resistance than the United States anticipated. Even more striking, the Cuban delegation maintained that Fidel Castro's grounds for approving the deployment differed significantly from Khrushchev's grounds for proposing it. Dismissing the utility of Soviet nuclear missiles in Cuba for deterrence or defense (noting that they served primarily to turn Cuba into a target), Emilio Aragonés, one of the six members of the Cuban Communist Party Secretariat in 1962, claimed that Castro and the Cuban leadership accepted the deployment for two reasons: first, because the missiles would have shifted the global correlation of forces in favor of socialism; and second, because Cuba should accept "its share of the risk," since Cuba owed a debt of gratitude to the Soviet Union for efforts made on its behalf. Although the deployment posed certain risks for Cuba, the Soviet Union had already taken risks in support of the Cuban revolution. Castro himself has made similar statements in the past. It is clear, however, that Cuba's national pride is better preserved by these claims than by the admission that Cuba required assistance from another nation, in the form of a nuclear deterrent, to protect her own sovereignty and independence. In subsequent interviews, both del Valle and Aragonés acknowledged that in 1962, they had been attracted to the idea of the deployment largely because of its potential for deterring an American invasion.

The Cubans' argument at the Moscow conference, however, serves to highlight the link between the deployment of missiles to Cuba and the Soviet desire to redress the strategic nuclear imbalance. General Dimitry Volkogonov, who had reviewed the relevant archival materials, stated at the Moscow conference that in 1962, the Soviet Union had succeeded in deploying only twenty ICBMs capable of reaching the United States, far fewer than the seventy-five hitherto estimated by Western intelligence analysts. Thus the disparity in strategic nuclear weapons appears to have been even greater than was appreciated at the time. A successful Cuban deployment could have more than quadrupled the number of warheads that Soviet missiles could have delivered on the United States.[2] Most Western analysts have assumed that some such calculation was the primary, though not fully articulated, initial motivation for the deployment of missiles. Even if Khrushchev's chief concern had been the political problem of preserving a socialist Cuba, the strategic value of the deployment probably contributed to the attractiveness of the deployment. . . . In short, different individuals within the Soviet decision-making establishment, and different branches of the Soviet state, seem to have understood the deployment in different ways, which may have complicated Khrushchev's task of enlisting support for the terms on which the crisis was ultimately resolved.

There is little doubt that Khrushchev was attracted to the idea of deploying missiles to Cuba at least partly because of its apparent symmetry with the deployment of American Jupiter missiles in Turkey. His speeches in Bulgaria in May 1962—where, he writes in his memoirs, the idea of the deployment first occurred to him—refer repeatedly and vehemently to the presence of American nuclear missiles so close to the Soviet border. Moreover, Fyodor Burlatsky reports that Yuri Andropov gave him a letter to edit from Khrushchev to Castro, in which Khrushchev emphasized the symmetry between the deployment of missiles in Cuba and the deployment of Jupiters in Turkey. But though this seems to have been on Khrushchev's mind, there is no evidence that it rivaled the other motivations in urgency or importance. It is more likely that the perceived symmetry with the Turkish deployment bolstered, rather than led to, the idea in the first place.[3]

In any retrospective discussion, of course, it is appropriate to ask whether the motivations and contingencies were, in the event itself, well-thought-out in advance. Khrushchev's personality was undoubtedly an important factor. Gromyko acknowledged that "Khrushchev was an emotional man. He had enough emotion for ten people—at least." But, not surprisingly, Gromyko argued that the deployment had been decided upon only after a thorough, careful, "cool-headed" evaluation. Jorge Risquet, on the other hand, expressed some doubt, claiming that "Comrade Khrushchev did not think through all the moves in advance." Anatoly Dobrynin agreed to some extent, stating that there was "improvisation as things unfolded; at least, that is what we felt in the embassy."[4] The discussions at the Moscow conference gave little reason for revising the common wisdom that the venture was, in important respects, ill conceived and subject to insufficient critical examination.

## THE AMERICAN THREAT TO CUBA:
## PERCEPTION AND MISPERCEPTION

American intentions toward Cuba in 1962 have long been the subject of debate, and continue to be so. The crucial question is whether or not the Kennedy administration intended, at some point, to use American military force to oust Fidel Castro and establish a regime more congenial to American interests. Soviet and Cuban fears that this was the case seem to have played an important part in the decision to deploy nuclear missiles; disavowals of any such intention by former Kennedy administration officials have long been received with skepticism by Soviets, Cubans, and revisionist historians in the United States. More is at stake in the debate than simply the accuracy of the historical record or the reputation of the Kennedy administration. The issue sheds important light on the role of perceptions and misperceptions in the genesis of a crisis.

Former Secretary of Defense Robert McNamara insisted at the Moscow conference that, "If I was a Cuban and read the evidence of covert American action against their government, I would be quite ready to believe that the U.S. intended to mount an invasion." His frankness on this point was welcomed by both the Soviet and Cuban delegations. McNamara insisted, however, that despite the extent of American covert operations against Castro, and despite the preparation of military contingencies in October 1962, the Kennedy administration did not intend to invade Cuba; that is, no political decision to invade Cuba had been taken, and no serious discussions to consider such an operation had taken place among senior policy-makers. The Cuban and Soviet delegations in Moscow expressed skepticism on this point.

Several publications have called into question the veracity of McNamara's disclaimer. Attention has focused on recently declassified documents that show that the Kennedy administration actively sought to destroy the Castro regime. One memorandum, for example—the "Cuba Project" program review dated February 20, 1962, and signed by Chief of Operations Brigadier General Edward G. Lansdale—specified late October 1962 as the target for Castro's ouster, and suggested that American military force might be required to accomplish that objective. CINCLANT (commander in chief, Atlantic fleet) Admiral Robert L. Dennison's official retrospective history of the crisis records that on October 1, more than two weeks before the missiles were discovered, orders were given to prepare the airstrike option, 312 OPLAN, for "maximum readiness" by October 20.

These documents show clearly that the United States was increasingly harassing the government of Fidel Castro, and that the Kennedy administration was actively laying the military groundwork for possible contingencies, such as a discovery of nuclear weapons in Cuba. This much, both McNamara and McGeorge Bundy concede.[5] However, the stronger claim—that such documents show that the Kennedy administration had actually decided to use American military force against Cuba—is entirely speculative. The evidence suggests otherwise. For example, the tapes of the White House discussions on October 16, immediately following the discovery of the missiles in Cuba, strongly evince a belligerent attitude on the part of the president and his advisers, but nowhere refer to any prior decision to invade Cuba, any established intention to invade Cuba, or even any previous exploration of the desirability of such an invasion. If indeed there had been serious consideration of the possibility, one would expect it to be reflected in those early, formative discussions, because an invasion would have been a comparatively well-formulated option already on the table. Instead, the process of option-formation began from scratch. President Kennedy's reluctance to use more than a display of force during the crisis itself further reinforces doubt that he had harbored an intention to initiate serious military action against Cuba before the discovery of the missiles.

· Despite the fact that there is no evidence of intent on the part of the Kennedy administration to invade Cuba prior to the deployment of the missiles, it seems clear that Cuba and the Soviet Union quite understandably applied worst-case analyses to the various covert activities of CIA operatives in Cuba and to the activities of the American military in 1961 and 1962. The Cuban participants at the Moscow conference reported that Cuba had well-placed informants in the American defense and intelligence communities who kept them abreast of the various contingencies under consideration. Ambassador Alekseev explicitly claimed that the Cubans had "precise data" about American plans to invade the island. Although operational plans and operational contingencies are not conclusive evidence of political intentions, they are nevertheless strong evidence of the worst possible case, and were apparently interpreted by Cuban and Soviet intelligence as reflecting a policy decision of the Kennedy administration to invade Cuba and to overthrow Castro. When McNamara explicitly refers to these interpretations as Soviet and Cuban "misperceptions," he correctly points out that mistaken conclusions were drawn from the available evidence. But the United States had provided virtually *no* evidence suggesting otherwise. As current Deputy Foreign Minister Viktor Komplektov argued at the Moscow conference, "Everything suggested that there *were* intentions." Indeed, it was the avowed policy of the United States to destabilize the Castro regime, and part of that effort involved convincing Cuba of its vulnerability to American attack. The Kennedy administration, therefore, actively promoted the very "misperceptions" that led, in part, to the Soviet decision to deploy nuclear missiles to Cuba.

## THE GENESIS, TERMS, AND CONDUCT OF THE DEPLOYMENT

In his memoirs, Khrushchev claims that the idea to deploy nuclear missiles in Cuba first occurred to him when he was in Bulgaria, between May 14 and 20, 1962. But, according to Sergo Mikoyan, Khrushchev had already discussed the idea with First Deputy Premier Anastas I. Mikoyan at the end of April, during a walk in the Lenin Hills. The aim, Khrushchev told Mikoyan, would be to deploy the missiles very rapidly under a cloak of secrecy, in September or October, and to reveal their presence to the U.S. president after the mid-term congressional elections in November, by means of a letter delivered to Kennedy by the Soviet ambassador in Washington, Anatoly Dobrynin.

Gromyko reports that Khrushchev first discussed the idea with him on the flight home from Bulgaria. Soon after his return, Khrushchev assembled a small group to consider the matter; its members included Mikoyan, Gromyko, Malinovsky, Biryuzov, and Secretary of the Central Committee Frol R. Kozlov. Shortly thereafter, the whole Presidium was included in the deliberations.

According to Gromyko, the discussions during the formative phase were candid and exploratory, though Khrushchev was clearly the "dominant" figure. Sergei Khrushchev reports that Anastas Mikoyan expressed strong reservations, cautioning that this was "a very dangerous step." According to Sergo Mikoyan, his father had two misgivings: first, he did not believe Castro would agree, and second, he did not believe it would be possible to install the missiles secretly. The only other member reported to have expressed doubt in Presidium meetings was Otto Kuusinen.

Gromyko reports that he told Khrushchev in May that a deployment of nuclear missiles in Cuba would trigger a "political explosion" in the United States, but Khrushchev seemed bent on the plan. Though it was not characteristic of Gromyko to object to an idea proposed by Khrushchev, it is quite plausible that he voiced pros and cons of the idea. If his testimony is accurate, then Khrushchev ultimately decided to disregard the cautions of both Mikoyan and Gromyko, two of his advisers who knew American politics best.

Aleksandr Alekseev was at that time a Soviet press representative in Cuba who was on very friendly terms with both Fidel Castro and his brother, Minister of Defense Raúl Castro. On Mikoyan's recommendation, Alekseev was urgently recalled to Moscow at the beginning of May and informed that he would be the new ambassador to Havana, replacing Sergei M. Kudryavtsev, whom Castro strongly disliked. Alekseev was officially appointed ambassador effective May 31, by order of the Presidium of the Supreme Soviet on May 7. When Khrushchev returned from Bulgaria, Alekseev was informed of the plan to deploy nuclear missiles to Cuba and was included in the decision-making circle. When Khrushchev asked him how Castro would react to the proposal, Alekseev reports that he expressed grave doubts that Castro would agree.[6] Khrushchev decided to send a special mission to Cuba to find out, and to determine whether the missiles could be installed secretly.

A ten-day Soviet "agricultural mission" traveled to Havana at the very end of May. The mission included Alekseev, Sharif Rashidov, an alternate member of the Presidium, Biryuzov, traveling under the pseudonym "engineer Petrov," and two other rocket specialists named Ushakov and Ageyev. The group arrived in Havana even before Kudryavtsev had been informed of his imminent departure, which indicates the secrecy and urgency surrounding the operation. Upon arrival, Alekseev informed Raúl Castro that "engineer Petrov" was actually the commander of the Strategic Rocket Forces, and a meeting was arranged with Fidel Castro for that same evening. According to Alekseev, Fidel Castro expressed immediate interest in the proposal, and left to confer with the other five members of the Cuban secretariat. Aragonés reports that all five—Raúl Castro, Che Guevara, President Osvaldo Dorticós, Blas Roca, and himself—were unanimously in favor of the idea.

Much to Mikoyan's surprise, Biryuzov returned to the Soviet Union with Fidel Castro's agreement and with an optimistic assessment of the chances of deploying the missiles secretly. At a meeting of the Presidium on June 10, Biryuzov reported the results of the negotiations. The Presidium officially ordered the Defense Ministry to develop specific plans for the missile deployment, as well as the deployment of associated air and coastal defense forces.

In early July, a Cuban delegation led by Raúl Castro visited Moscow to discuss Soviet arms shipments to Cuba, and to finalize operational details of the missile deployment. Delegations led by Raúl Castro and Marshal Malinovsky met for two weeks, with Khrushchev himself present at meetings on July 3 and 8. The first step would be to install a network of the latest Soviet SA-2 surface-to-air-missiles (SAMs) around the perimeter of the island, and especially near the MRBM and IRBM sites at San Cristobal, Sagua la Grande, Guanajay, and Remedios.[7] The first SAMs and supporting equipment for the MRBMs were shipped at the very end of July.

While in Moscow, Raúl Castro and Malinovsky drafted an agreement covering various details of the deployment, including the rights and obligations of the host country and of the Soviet forces building and manning the missile sites. The agreement was a formal treaty with the following terms: (1) the Soviets would at all times have complete custody and control of the nuclear missiles in Cuba (but the exact number of missiles was not specified); (2) the Soviets would be given temporary use of the sites as rocket bases for a period of five years, though the sites themselves would remain sovereign Cuban territory; (3) after five years, there would be a further decision to annul or continue the arrangement; (4) all costs associated with the deployment were to be borne by the Soviet Union; and (5) some SAMs were to be provided to the Cubans, though the SA-2 SAMs would initially be installed, manned, and operated by the Soviets until Cuban forces could be trained to operate and maintain them. Raúl Castro and Malinovsky signed each paragraph of the agreement, and space was provided at the end of the document for the signatures of Fidel Castro and Nikita Khrushchev. But the two leaders, intending to sign it at a public ceremony in Havana in November, never did so.

When Raúl Castro returned from Moscow with a draft of the document in hand, his brother elaborated and modified the wording of the preamble. His amended version declared that the purpose of the agreement was "to provide mutual military assistance" rather than "to save the Cuban revolution," and it strongly affirmed the legality of the deployment. Che Guevara and Emilio Aragonés traveled to Moscow at the end of the summer (August 27–September 2) to secure Soviet approval for Castro's changes. While there, they proposed that the agreement be made public immediately, prior to the deployment itself, to remove any pretext for a hostile American reaction. The Cubans warned the Soviet leadership that the situation in the United States was becoming increasingly volatile. Concerned by the prospect that rising suspicions in the United States might eventually lead to war hysteria, they sought to draw international attention to the legality of the deployment. Aragonés reported that they told Khrushchev that there might be "a preventive strike with severe consequences for us" if the Americans were not given adequate opportunity to reconcile themselves to the deployment; but Khrushchev assured the Cubans that there would be no problem. Making the deployment public would be a terrible mistake, Khrushchev insisted; it might precipitate the very invasion the missiles were intended to fore-stall. And if the Americans did attack Cuba in the meantime, Khrushchev pro-claimed, then he would promptly send the Baltic Fleet. Though skeptical of Khrushchev's promise of naval support, the Cubans deferred to Khrushchev's assessment of the Americans, because of the Soviets' greater experience in for-eign affairs, and agreed to let the matter drop.[8] At the Moscow conference, the Cuban delegation identified Khrushchev's judgment as a serious mistake.[9]

The Soviet expedition to Cuba was under the overall command of General Issa Pliyev, a former cavalry officer with no experience with nuclear missiles. Why Khrushchev chose Pliyev is unclear, though one plausible explanation is offered by Ambassador Alekseev, who suggests that he did so to throw American intelligence off the scent. As part of the operation, according to General Volko-gonov, over 40,000 Soviet troops were sent to Cuba, under secrecy so tight that only the commanding officers of the units dispatched knew where they were headed.[10] Unaware of their destination, Soviet soldiers reportedly brought with them full winter gear, and were only told where they were going after their ships had passed the Strait of Gibraltar. Some Soviet sources claim that the command-ers of the vessels involved in the operation were instructed to open sealed orders, at a predetermined point in the voyage, that charged them to scuttle their ships if an attempt was made to stop and search them, and that when American recon-naissance planes flew overhead, Soviet personnel would dance on deck in an attempt to look like tourists.

The first SS-4 MRBMs arrived on September 15, eleven days after President Kennedy's first major warning against the deployment of "offensive weapons" to Cuba, two days after his second warning, and just four days after a denial by TASS that any such deployment was in the offing. Once in Cuban ports, the mis-siles and their related equipment were off-loaded under cover of darkness, with elaborate precautions to ensure that the shipments went undetected. As part of the deception, Soviet troops wore civilian sportshirts to disguise their numbers and identities. One of those who came off a Soviet ship was the thirty-nine-year-old commander of a motorized infantry regiment, Lieutenant Colonel Dimitry Yazov, now Soviet Minister of Defense.

Only Soviets were involved in the unloading, transportation, and installation of the missiles; indeed, the Soviets themselves had even chosen the locations of the missile sites. The Cuban armed forces' role in the deployment was limited to guiding the preliminary exploration of the terrain, choosing the routes from the ports to the missile sites, and building roads where necessary.

Camouflage was also a Soviet responsibility; yet the Soviets' failure to cam-ouflage the missile sites permitted American intelligence to discover the deploy-ment prematurely, by means of reconnaissance photographs taken on October 14. It appears that the reason the Soviets failed to camouflage the missiles is that Soviet standard operating procedures for constructing nuclear missile sites did not include the use of camouflage. All previous installations had been on Soviet territory; the installation crews in Cuba simply overlooked the importance of disguising their activities on foreign soil under the watchful eyes of the Americans. Castro is reported later to have expressed his astonishment and dismay that Cubans had not been consulted on camouflage measures; the sites could easily have been disguised as agricultural projects, Castro maintained, had the Soviets only asked for help.

## SOVIET MISSILES IN CUBA: WARHEADS, TARGETS, AND ORDERS

One of the more persistent puzzles of the Cuban missile crisis concerns whether or not nuclear warheads for the Soviet MRBMs ever reached Cuba. American intelligence never detected nuclear warheads in Cuba, and interpreted the fact that the assembly of likely warhead storage bunkers at the missile sites was incomplete (shown by reconnaissance photographs), as evidence that they had not yet arrived. But the Kennedy administration, in the face of uncertainty, operated on the assumption that they had.

According to General Volkogonov, twenty nuclear warheads had arrived in Cuba in late September or early October, and twenty others were in transit aboard the *Poltava* when the quarantine went into effect. Apparently, the Soviets did not keep the Cubans well informed of the warhead shipments. General del Valle, the Cuban chief of staff, was informed on October 23 or 24 by General Pliyev merely that "everything was ready," which del Valle interpreted to mean that warheads had arrived. Only later did he learn the details of the warhead shipments, and discover that they were incomplete.[11]

According to Volkogonov, the warheads that had arrived in Cuba were kept "well away" from the missiles themselves, and at no time were measures taken to mate them, even when alert levels were raised following President Kennedy's speech of October 22. Had the order to prepare the missiles come down, Volkogonov claimed, they could have been targeted in four hours, and would have required a subsequent countdown of fifteen minutes.

Sergei Khrushchev claimed at the Moscow conference that the inaccuracy of the SS-4 missiles restricted their useful targets to large cities and industrial centers such as Washington or New York. Contrary to newspaper accounts of the conference, however, at no time did Khrushchev suggest that either Washington or New York was actually targeted, because at no time were targeting procedures under way. "My father would not have allowed [the warheads] to be mounted," Sergei Khrushchev insisted. "He felt that would have made it easier for a madman to start a war."

General Volkogonov said that the standing orders given to the three SS-4 and two SS-5 regiments deployed to Cuba were extremely clear. He read from Defense Ministry Archives to the Moscow conferees that: "The rocket forces are to be used only in the event of a U.S. attack, unleashing a war, and under the strict condition of receiving a command from Moscow." Both conditions had to be satisfied before the missiles were to be used. While these orders defined the limits of the local commanders' authority to launch nuclear missiles, however, none of the Soviets interviewed for this study believed that physical mechanisms preventing unauthorized use (such as modern permissive action links) were built into the warheads.

## THE EARLY PHASE OF THE CRISIS: OCTOBER 16–26

President Kennedy learned of the Soviet deployment on October 16; he and his advisers spent almost a full week formulating a response before announcing the discovery publicly. During that week, on October 18, Soviet Foreign Minister Gromyko paid a visit to the White House which he described as "the most complex discussion" of his diplomatic career. Kennedy did not ask Gromyko directly about the presence of Soviet missiles in Cuba, nor did Gromyko volunteer any information about them, much to the relief of both. Gromyko has since asserted, however, that he was instructed to be forthcoming if confronted directly. At the Moscow conference, he maintained merely that he would have given a "proper answer" to a direct question from the president; but in a subsequent article, he claimed that he was instructed by Moscow to say that the Soviets were deploying a "small quantity of missiles of a defensive nature" to Cuba, and to encourage quiet diplomacy if Kennedy's reaction were negative.

On October 22, at 7:00 P.M. Eastern time, President Kennedy went on national television to announce the discovery of Soviet missiles in Cuba and his intention to impose a naval quarantine on all shipments of offensive weapons to the island. Just an hour before, Secretary of State Dean Rusk had handed Ambassador Dobrynin an advance copy of the president's speech. Rusk recalls, "I saw him age ten years right in front of my eyes." We now know why: Dobrynin had not been informed by his own government of the deployment.[12]

Khrushchev apparently reacted to Kennedy's speech with anger, ordering work accelerated on construction of the missile sites, and ordering Soviet ships to ignore the naval quarantine, scheduled to take effect at 10:00 A.M. on Wednesday, October 24. The order to ignore the quarantine seems to have been rescinded before the first Soviet vessels reached the quarantine line. But not until October 26 would Khrushchev publicly take a conciliatory, cooperative attitude toward resolving the crisis. The Cuban response to Kennedy's speech was also angry, bellicose, and defiant, but unlike Khrushchev's, it appears not to have mellowed as the days passed.

From Wednesday, October 24, to Friday, October 26, stalemate set in. Neither the United States nor the Soviet Union backed away from its public position, but both sides avoided a confrontation. At 1:00 P.M. on October 26, Aleksandr Fomin, an official at the Soviet embassy in Washington known to be the senior KGB official in Washington, met ABC's State Department correspondent John Scali, at Fomin's request. Fomin asked Scali to determine whether or not the United States would be interested in resolving the crisis by pledging not to invade Cuba in return for the withdrawal of the nuclear missiles. In so doing, Fomin was apparently acting on his own initiative. Scali replied at 7:30 P.M. that the administration was interested in Fomin's suggestion. Dobrynin was uncertain whether this channel reflected the views of the White House, and did not authorize a telegram to Moscow. Fomin may have cabled a report notwithstanding.

The State Department began to receive a private, conciliatory letter from Khrushchev to Kennedy between 6:00 and 9:00 P.M. on Friday, October 26, vaguely proposing to conclude a deal along the same lines as Fomin had suggested to Scali. Most students of the crisis have assumed that the letter merely formalized Fomin's earlier trial balloon; but it appears now that this assumption is incorrect. The American embassy in Moscow had begun to receive the message at 4:43 P.M. Moscow time (early Friday morning in Washington), many hours before Fomin's initiative. The Fomin–Scali communication would have been too late to influence the content of the letter.

Khrushchev's letter clearly evinced exhaustion and anxiety. His tone of somber realism convinced many in the ExComm that Khrushchev was looking for a peaceful way out of the crisis; it convinced many in Cuba that Khrushchev was losing his nerve and that he was about to cave in to American pressure. In his memoirs, Khrushchev acknowledges that his anxiety during this time was "intense." The pressure had led him to look for a relatively quick way out of the confrontation, even on what he himself must surely have recognized as sub-optimal terms. Khrushchev later reported a feeling among some of his military advisers during the crisis that a harder line was in order. But Western suppositions, that Khrushchev at this point faced a divided Presidium and threats to his own authority, have been unequivocally denied by knowledgeable Soviets.

## THE ORIGIN OF THE TURKISH MISSILE TRADE

On Saturday, October 27, before President Kennedy could respond to Khrushchev's letter of the day before, a second letter, taking a harder line, was broadcast by Radio Moscow. Khrushchev now insisted that the United States remove its intermediate-range Jupiter missiles in Turkey in return for the removal of Soviet missiles in Cuba. Khrushchev's quick about-face has always puzzled not only Western students of the crisis, but members of the ExComm as well, who show considerable surprise and confusion in the transcripts of the October 27 meetings.

In 1987, Georgy Shakhnazarov conveyed a message from Anatoly Dobrynin to the participants in the Cambridge conference, indicating that the idea for the missile trade had been hatched in the Soviet embassy in Washington. His rather cryptic remark remained unclear until the Moscow conference, where Dobrynin provided further details previously unknown. He and Robert Kennedy met secretly on the night of Friday, October 26, as part of a series of private, late-night back-channel discussions between the two. Dobrynin remarked to the attorney general that the administration's extreme reaction to the deployment of Soviet missiles in Cuba was puzzling in view of the fact that the United States had deployed similar missiles in Turkey, next door to the Soviet Union. In raising the issue, Dobrynin says, he was acting entirely on his own initiative, not expecting it to be interpreted as part of a negotiating position. He was merely attempting to make the point that the Soviet side had an equal right to provide for its own security. Dobrynin reports:

Robert Kennedy said, "You are interested in the missiles in Turkey?" He thought pensively and said, "One minute, I will go and talk to the President." He went out of the room. . . . [He] came back and said, "The President said that we are ready to consider the question of Turkey, to examine favorably the question of Turkey."[13]

Dobrynin immediately reported this conversation to Moscow. Shortly thereafter, Khrushchev demanded the missile trade. Dobrynin hastened to add that although he believes his cable to have been the source of the missile trade proposal, it is possible that the idea arose simultaneously in Moscow. No one at the Moscow conference, however, offered the latter interpretation, even though some, such as Andrei Gromyko, were presumably in a position to know.

If Dobrynin's story is accurate, then some traditional understandings of the climax of the crisis must give way. The tapes of the ExComm meetings of October 27 clearly indicate that the question of the missile trade dominated the discussion, and that the president himself was its strongest advocate. But at no point in those discussions did the president or his brother discuss Robert Kennedy's meeting with Dobrynin of the previous day; nor did they reveal that they had already communicated to the Soviet Union that the Jupiter missiles in Turkey were negotiable. In conjunction with the recent revelation of the "Cordier maneuver,"[14] and in view of the secrecy surrounding Robert Kennedy's October 27 meeting with Ambassador Dobrynin (several members of the ExComm were unaware even that such a meeting was to take place), the president's reticence in the transcripts of the October 27 meetings strongly suggests that the ExComm had become largely irrelevant to the president's decision-making at the height of the crisis. Crucial decisions were being made by the president and a few close advisers, well away from—and unknown to—the ExComm as a whole. The group that had played a central role in the early option-formation phase of the crisis seems to have been left out of important aspects of decision-making at its climax.

## THE U-2 SHOOT-DOWN OF OCTOBER 27

As the ExComm puzzled over Khrushchev's new demand on October 27, word reached Washington that an American U-2 reconnaissance aircraft had been shot down over Cuba by an SA-2 surface-to-air missile fired from the Los Angeles battery, near the port of Banes. It has generally been supposed in the West that the missile that downed the aircraft was fired by Soviet troops, because the SA-2s were believed to have been under strict Soviet control. But it has always been difficult to imagine why Khrushchev would have risked a serious escalation of the crisis at that point. Some have surmised that the shoot-down was the unauthorized act of a Soviet officer in Cuba. Others have supposed that Cubans had in fact fired the missile, either after seizing control of the SAM site in a firefight with Soviets,[15] or by exercising their discretion in a dual-control arrangement of some kind. Most fantastic is Carlos Franqui's recent report that Castro once claimed that he himself had shot down the aircraft.

At the Moscow conference, the Soviet side released new details confirming that the U-2 shoot-down was indeed an unauthorized act by Soviet air defense forces. According to Alekseev, two generals were involved in the decision-making when the U-2 was detected at approximately 10:00 A.M. on Saturday, October 27. General Volkogonov publicly identified one as Pliyev's deputy for air defense, the late Lieutenant General Stepan N. Grechko. The second general was apparently Leonid S. Garbuz, now retired, then Pliyev's deputy for military training.

Once the U-2 was spotted near Banes, the two generals had twenty minutes to make a decision whether or not to fire. After attempting unsuccessfully to contact General Pliyev, they decided to shoot on their own authority. As recently disclosed by the newspaper of the Cuban armed forces, *Bastión*, the local commander who actually gave the order to fire was General Georgy A. Voronkov, now retired and living in Odessa.

Contrary to previous accounts of the shoot-down, which suggested that Soviet SAM units had standing orders not to fire on American aircraft, Alekseev claims that there was "no direct prohibition" against doing so. Del Valle confirms this, noting that the officer on site was criticized by Khrushchev, but that he defended himself by saying that he had only followed Soviet standing orders "to fire on any aircraft that flies overhead in wartime," an action for which he was later decorated by Fidel Castro personally. From the Cuban point of view, the situation could indeed have been construed as "wartime." Throughout the crisis, Castro had authorized his own anti-aircraft (AA) artillery to fire at groups of two or more low-flying American planes; on October 26, he ordered his AA units to fire on any American aircraft within range. That same day, Voronkov received an order to begin operating the radar stations. Cuban Politburo member Jorge Risquet claimed at the Moscow conference that Soviet air defense forces were willing to fire on American aircraft on October 27 because they had been "inspired by the enthusiasm of the Cubans." Indeed, the downing of the U-2 was a tremendous boost to Cuban morale; news of it spread rapidly throughout the island, and was greeted everywhere with wild celebration. As Risquet put it, "our people felt that we were not defenseless." But many Cuban leaders reportedly felt that the shoot-down was "very dangerous," and worried "that it would inflame the situation."

At the Moscow conference, Volkogonov read from Malinovsky's telegram to Pliyev immediately following the shoot-down, rebuking him for "hastily [shooting] down the U.S. plane" because "an agreement for a peaceful way to deter an invasion of Cuba was already taking shape." This contradicts the English version of Khrushchev's memoirs, which indicate that he believed that it was Cubans who had shot down the American plane. Yet Sergei Khrushchev insists that his father knew at the time that Soviets had shot down the plane, and that in the tape recordings on which Khrushchev's memoirs were based, he clearly stated this. Strobe Talbott, editor and translator of Khrushchev's memoirs, reports the discrepancy in the English edition as a "mistake." The Russian-language version of Khrushchev's memoirs published by Progress Publishers (currently in limited special circulation in the Soviet Union) also states that Cubans shot down the plane, because it is a re-translation of Talbott's English version.

There is some evidence to suggest that there may have been a partial, unsuccessful cover-up attempt by the Soviet military. Ambassador Alekseev reported that he did not find out that Soviets were responsible for the shoot-down until over a decade later, and he has speculated that Malinovsky himself may have tried to prevent details of the event from spreading in order to prevent embarrassment to the Ministry of Defense and the responsible Soviet officers in Cuba.

We now know that the ExComm's reaction to the shoot-down was more measured and restrained than the hysteria suggested in many memoirists' previous accounts. Khrushchev, however, must have been seriously shaken by the event, which made it painfully clear that his control over developments in Cuba had significantly eroded. Kennedy's control over events, as it turned out, was equally tenuous. Later that same day, an American U-2 on a routine air sampling mission in the Arctic strayed into Siberian air space as the result of a navigational error. Khrushchev may have read the incident as a provocation, but also seems to have been sensitive to the possibility that it was accidental. According to several Soviets at the Moscow conference, the risks that unintended actions might lead to an escalation of the confrontation were very much in the forefront of Khrushchev's mind as the crisis reached its crescendo.

## THE RESOLUTION OF THE CRISIS

At 7:15 P.M. on Saturday, October 27, Robert Kennedy telephoned Dobrynin to request another meeting. The two met at 7:45 in the Department of Justice. The reports of important aspects of the meeting in Robert Kennedy's *Thirteen Days* were starkly contradicted by Ambassador Dobrynin in Moscow. First, Robert Kennedy reported telling Dobrynin that "we had to have a commitment by tomorrow that those bases would be removed. I was not giving them an ultimatum but a statement of fact. He should understand that if they did not remove those bases, we would remove them."[16] Though the attorney general explicitly denied that this was an ultimatum, it has generally been interpreted by Western historians as a clear compellent threat.[17] However, Dobrynin denied that Robert Kennedy issued any ultimatum or made any threats. He further denies that Robert Kennedy warned of an imminent coup or loss of civilian control of the military, in contradiction to Soviet accounts of the meeting, including Khrushchev's own.[18] In fact, according to Dobrynin, Robert Kennedy soft-pedaled the danger of imminent American action, and Dobrynin claims that his cable to Moscow reporting the meeting was similarly low-key on that point.

The second respect in which Dobrynin contradicts Robert Kennedy's account of the meeting helps explain the first, and concerns the status of the missile trade. Robert Kennedy wrote:

He asked me what offer the United States was making, and I told him of the letter that President Kennedy had just transmitted to Khrushchev. He raised the question of our removing the missiles from Turkey. I said that there could be no quid pro quo or any arrangement made under this kind of threat or pressure, and that in the last analysis this was a decision that would have to be made by NATO. However, I said, the President had been anxious to remove those missiles from Turkey and Italy for a long period of time. He had ordered their removal some time ago, and it was our judgment that, within a short time after this crisis was over, those missiles would be gone.

Dobrynin insists that it was Robert Kennedy who pursued the idea of an explicit "deal" on the Turkish missiles; that he wished to portray it as a significant concession by the United States; and that he never said that the president had already ordered their removal. Dobrynin's version of the meeting was confirmed in an important respect at the Moscow conference by Theodore Sorensen, who edited *Thirteen Days* prior to its publication. Sorensen confessed that the missile trade had been portrayed as an explicit deal in the diaries on which the book was based, and that he had seen fit to revise that account in view of the fact that the trade was still a secret at the time, known to only six members of the ExComm.

Andrei Gromyko stressed at the Moscow conference that the question of the Turkish missiles was "not trivial," and that the Soviet Union had a solid foundation to consider that their removal was part of the terms on which the crisis was resolved. Indeed, Khrushchev sent the president a letter after the conclusion of the crisis, in which he described the withdrawal of the Jupiter missiles from Turkey as an integral part of the agreement on which the crisis was resolved. In Moscow, Sorensen conceded that this letter had been received, but explained its absence from the collected Kennedy–Khrushchev correspondence by noting that the administration decided against acknowledging the withdrawal of the Jupiters as a quid pro quo, and returned the letter as if it had never been opened.

It appears, therefore, that the withdrawal of the Jupiter missiles from Turkey in the spring of 1963 was indeed part of a private deal that led to the withdrawal of Soviet missiles from Cuba in November 1962. However, both the United States and the Soviet Union have subsequently found it expedient not to insist on this point, the United States because of the complications and ill-will it would cause among its NATO allies (and because of the domestic political consequences to the president had he publicly acknowledged the trade of the missiles), and the Soviet Union because of Castro's objection to being treated like a "bargaining chip" on a par with a "minor" NATO ally such as Turkey.

## KHRUSHCHEV'S SENSE OF URGENCY

Between the time Dobrynin took his leave of Robert Kennedy on October 27 and the time the ExComm met again at 9:00 on Sunday morning, Khrushchev had decided to bring the confrontation to an end. Western students of the crisis have long wondered what caused Khrushchev to do so at that particular time. Dobrynin's claim that he did not interpret Robert Kennedy's message of October 27 as a threat or an ultimatum only adds to the puzzle, since Robert Kennedy's account of the meeting has been widely regarded as the best explanation of Khrushchev's sense of urgency.

That Khrushchev felt a sense of urgency can hardly be questioned. According to Fyodor Burlatsky, the letter of October 28 accepting Kennedy's noninvasion pledge in return for withdrawal of the missiles from Cuba "was prepared at Khrushchev's dacha [at Kuntsevo] thirty kilometers from Moscow. When the letter was finished, a man was dispatched with it to drive very quickly to the radio station. He was told to have it for transmission before three o'clock. They were very nervous." Sergo Mikoyan added, "At Radio Moscow there are six elevators in the building. Someone had telephoned ahead, and they reserved one elevator just for this letter to arrive."

If indeed Khrushchev's urgency was a reaction to any verbal message, it may have been to that of John Scali, rather than to Robert Kennedy's. At the Moscow conference, Aleksandr Fomin reported that in his meeting with Scali on Saturday, October 27, at which Scali attempted to ascertain the reason why Khrushchev's Friday letter had been so quickly superseded by a letter demanding a missile trade, Scali angrily threatened that there would be an American attack within hours if the missiles were not removed. After the resolution of the crisis, Fomin communicated a personal message from Khrushchev to Scali that his outburst had been "very valuable."

It seems probable, however, that Khrushchev was paying greater attention to his own intelligence sources than to Scali's extracurricular theatrics, since Scali was not the only one who appeared to be speaking for the administration. During the night of October 25–26, Soviet intelligence apparently reported persuasive evidence of an imminent American attack, leading Khrushchev to propose conciliatory terms in his Friday letter. Later in the day on October 26, Soviet intelligence reversed its earlier estimate, possibly encouraging Khrushchev to toughen his terms in the second letter. But some time still later on October 26 or October 27, Soviet and Cuban intelligence appear once again to have concluded that an American attack could be expected momentarily. If this indeed was their assessment, it may have weighed heavily in Khrushchev's decision to bring the crisis to an end.

Other factors apparently played a significant role. The U-2 shoot-down and the inadvertent straying of another American U-2 over Soviet air space on October 27 indicated that events were slipping out of control. But perhaps as important, it appears that Khrushchev was influenced by a communication from Castro through Alekseev on October 27. That message came to light at the Moscow conference, and was reported in the press as Castro's attempt to urge Khrushchev to fire the nuclear missiles in Cuba against the United States.

It remains unclear exactly what Castro communicated to Khrushchev. We have reason to believe that in an unpublished passage of his memoirs, Khrushchev reported it thus: "Suddenly, we received through our Ambassador a cable from Castro. The Ambassador reported that Castro had given him the report face-to-face. Castro informed him that he had reliable information that an American invasion would take place within a few hours. Therefore, he was proposing to preempt the invasion and inflict a nuclear strike on the U.S."[19]

But well-placed Soviets and Cubans deny that Castro's message urged a nuclear strike. According to both Ambassador Alekseev (who transmitted the message to Khrushchev) and Emilio Aragonés (who helped draft it, and who had felt on October 26 that Khrushchev's resolve was weakening), the telegram was intended to communicate the Cuban people's willingness to fight to the last man and the last bullet in the event of an American attack, and to urge Khrushchev to show firmness. Both Alekseev and Aragonés believe that Khrushchev misinterpreted the telegram as urging a preemptive strike, an entirely plausible belief given Khrushchev's state of mind at the climax of the confrontation.

Until the cable itself is made public by the Soviets or Cubans, the issue cannot be resolved conclusively. A great deal depends upon the precise wording of the telegram, and whether it accurately reflects Castro's verbal communication to Alekseev.[20] But if Khrushchev did misinterpret the telegram from Castro, then it would stand as one more reminder of the significance of major miscommunications during crises. In this case, a misinterpretation may have facilitated a rapid resolution; in other circumstances, it might have complicated one.

## CUBA AND THE CONCLUSION OF THE CRISIS

Castro's displeasure at Khrushchev's failure to consult him before agreeing to withdraw the missiles from Cuba is a matter of record. Apparently, Cuba first heard of Khrushchev's decision on the radio. Ambassador Alekseev reports that upon hearing the news, "I felt myself the most unhappy man on earth, as I imagined what Fidel's reaction to this would be." Indeed, Castro refused to see him for several days.

Part of Castro's fury at not having been consulted may have stemmed from his conviction that Khrushchev did not get as much as he could have from the Americans. At the Moscow conference, Jorge Risquet insisted that the "five conditions" Castro had publicly proclaimed as the price for his assent to the withdrawal of the missiles had indeed been within reach, including American withdrawal from Guantanamo. If indeed Castro was convinced that this was a concession to which the United States would agree, then it bespeaks an appalling ignorance of American political realities on Castro's part.[21] Aragonés, however, maintains that Castro's five conditions represented merely a statement of principles, not an attempt to stake out a negotiating position, and that they were intended primarily to serve domestic political purposes. Cuba had been badly treated by both superpowers, and its national honor required a public articulation of Cuban dissent.[22]

Raymond Garthoff has reported that Cuban troops surrounded the missile sites on October 28, and only stood down after the arrival in Havana of Soviet First Deputy Premier Anastas Mikoyan, whose task was to persuade Castro to go along with the U.S.–Soviet agreement. The Moscow conference and subsequent discussions have shed light on the issue and have raised interesting new questions in the process. Ambassador Alekseev believes, for example, that the troops that took up positions around the missile sites were in fact Soviet soldiers in Cuban uniforms, and insists that there was no danger of a Soviet-Cuban clash at that time. Both Sergio del Valle and Emilio Aragonés insist that the troops were Cuban antiaircraft units deployed to protect the missile sites from low-level attack.

Anastas Mikoyan's success in persuading Castro to accept the U.S. demand for a November withdrawal of the Il-28 light bombers, in addition to the withdrawal of the missiles, was a remarkable achievement. The American demand that Cuba relinquish weapons intended for the Cuban Air Force, wholly independently of the Soviet missile deployment, only added insult to injury. Mikoyan's success was aided by one of those curious interventions of fate: Castro's initial attitude toward the Soviet representative was softened by the sudden death of Mikoyan's wife at the very moment he arrived in Havana. But according to Cuban testimony, the published American views of the negotiations involving the bombers are mistaken in a variety of ways. First, American intelligence believed in 1962 that forty-two Il-28s had been delivered to Cuba, of which only seven had been assembled; Sergio del Valle, however, maintains that twelve Il-28s had been delivered, of which only three were to be transferred to the Cuban Air Force. None of the three Cuban bombers had been uncrated during the crisis, and the Soviets simply withdrew them at the same time they withdrew their own bombers, an operation facilitated by the fact that the aircraft were all located at the same bases. It may be, therefore, that none of the bombers had yet been formally transferred to Cuba, and that Mikoyan did not have to persuade Castro to relinquish something he had already been given. Second, some American analysts have believed that Mikoyan's task was abetted by President Kennedy's message to the NATO allies of November 19, warning that if the bombers were not promptly withdrawn, air strikes might be necessary to destroy them. The president reportedly intended the message to leak to the Soviets. However, Emilio Aragonés, who was present throughout the negotiations between Castro and Mikoyan, does not recall any discussion of the American threat and does not believe that it was communicated to Castro. Aragonés recalls that Mikoyan represented the withdrawal of the bombers merely as a request from the Soviet and American negotiators in New York, and persuaded him to go along by appealing to the necessity for a quick solution.

The fact that the Il-28 bombers were a subject of debate at all, according to Sergo Mikoyan, was largely the fault of the Soviet Union itself. Khrushchev, by his letter to the president of October 28 stating that he had given an order "to dismantle the arms which you described as offensive," was attempting to deny that the nuclear missiles in Cuba were, in fact, "offensive," and was indeed attempting to avoid using the word "missiles" publicly. But the effect was to give the United States *carte blanche* to specify which weapon systems were to be withdrawn, and the Kennedy administration chose to insist upon the removal of the Il-28s—obsolete, short-range bombers believed to have a nuclear capability, but for which no nuclear weapons had been supplied. The withdrawal of the Il-28s was a blow to Cuba's national pride, and it further strained Soviet-Cuban relations. As Sergo Mikoyan put it, the Soviets fell victim to their own "propagandistic tendencies."

## CONCLUSION

The new testimony from Soviets and Cubans has considerably enriched the story of the Cuban missile crisis, though it has opened as many questions as it has plausibly answered. All of the new evidence assembled here, however, has been testimonial. To date, Western students of the crisis have not seen a single Soviet or Cuban document against which to check the recollections of Soviet and Cuban participants and scholars. Cuba and the Soviet Union have no history of declassifying diplomatic documents for historical uses, and no procedures for doing so; in any case, the relevant diplomatic archives in both Moscow and Havana are probably sparse by American standards. According to Soviet testimony, no written records of Kremlin decision-making were kept prior to October 22, 1962, precisely to avoid breaches of secrecy. The director of the Institute of Cuban History notes that the Cuban government in 1962 was so young and so disorganized that it had not yet established procedures for handling paperwork; most relevant decisions were made in conversations that were not recorded.

The next major step in the historiography of the Cuban missile crisis will have to await the release of those documents that do exist in Moscow and Havana. In the meantime, we must make what we can of verbal testimonies. The weaknesses of oral history are well known: memories are imperfect and selective; current interests and objectives color recollections of historical events. Perhaps most frustrating is the fact that not all key players have survived to give their testimony, and others, because of advancing age, have little time left in which to do so. But until relatively recently, few historians and political scientists believed that they would have the chance to hear the Soviet and Cuban stories at all. We believe that the Soviets and Cubans who have spoken out have treated the opportunity to do so with due seriousness; in our opinion, therefore—bearing in mind the inherent limitations of oral history—their contributions have greatly improved the understanding of the causes, conduct, and implications of the Cuban missile crisis.

## NOTES

1. In a later interview, del Valle claimed that the 270,000 armed and mobilized troops were divided into fifty-six existing divisions, which had been brought up to full strength from reserves. Although they varied considerably in size, each division had on average 4,800 men, considerably smaller than an American division. Twenty-eight divisions deployed on the western side of the island included some of the largest and strongest, since this was where the first wave of an invasion was expected to land. Authors' interview with Sergio del Valle, May 18, 1989, Havana.

2. On October 19, the CIA reported that the Soviet Union was installing twenty-four SS-4 (Soviet designation R-12) MRBM launchers in Cuba—four each at four sites near San Cristóbal, and four at two sites near Sagua la Grande. Each launcher could have been equipped with two missiles, for a possible total of forty-eight MRBMs. Twelve SS-5 (R-14) IRBM launchers were observed under construction, four each at two sites near Guanajay, and four at one site near Remedios, suggesting that twenty-four IRBMs could have been deployed to Cuba (including reloads). With one warhead per missile (25 kt-2 MT yield for the SS-4s, 3-5 MT yield for the SS-5s), seventy-two warheads could have been deployed to Cuba. In such a case, the number of land-based missile warheads capable of reaching the United States would have more than quadrupled, increasing from twenty (the ICBMs in the Soviet Union itself) to ninety-two (twenty on ICBMs, seventy-two on MRBMs and IRBMs in Cuba). See CIA memorandum on the construction of missile sites in Cuba, October 19, 1962, National Security Archive, Washington, D.C. According to General Volkogonov, however, the deployment consisted of three SS-4 regiments (eight launchers each for a total of twenty-four) and two SS-5 regiments (eight launchers each for a total of sixteen); *MCT*. Raymond Garthoff claims that only one warhead was to be provided per launcher even though two missiles were assigned to each (to offset reliability problems). Garthoff, *Reflections on the Cuban Missile Crisis*, 2nd ed. (Washington, D.C.: Brookings, 1989), p. 20. If this is so, the deployment would have tripled the number of warheads that Soviet land-based missiles could have delivered promptly on the United States, from twenty (the ICBMs in the Soviet Union) to sixty (twenty on ICBMs,

forty on MRBMs and IRBMs in Cuba). American intelligence estimated in 1962 that the Soviets had also deployed 155 cruise and ballistic missiles on submarines, and approximately 200 long-range bombers. Although these were severely constrained operationally (because of geographical, logistical, and technical factors), and although they did not represent a serious first-strike threat, they might have succeeded in delivering some number of nuclear warheads on the United States in the event of war. The missiles in Cuba, therefore, probably no more than doubled the number of nuclear weapons of all kinds that the Soviets could have delivered, though an accurate estimate of this increment is impossible to make. See Scott D. Sagan, "SIOP-62: The Nuclear War Plan Briefing of President Kennedy," *International Security* 12, No. 1 (Summer 1987): 27–28; and Raymond L. Garthoff, *Intelligence Assessment and Policymaking: A Decision Point in the Kennedy Administration* (Washington, D.C.: Brookings, 1984), 55.

3. The supposed symmetry between the two deployments was far from obvious to the members of the Kennedy administration, who noted that the Soviet deployment was much larger than the American deployment; it involved no dual-control arrangements; and, perhaps most importantly, it was undertaken in strict secrecy behind the cloak of deception.

4. Bruce J. Allyn, David G. Welch, and James A. Blight, eds. *Proceedings of the Moscow Conference on the Cuban Missile Crisis*, Jan. 27–28, 1989, CSIA Working Paper, Center for Science and International Affairs, Harvard University.

5. Bundy, however, said that he viewed American covert operations against Castro as a "psychological salve," and that he had no expectation that they would succeed in their stated goals. Remarks at a news conference at Harvard University, October 13, 1987.

6. Alekseev claims that the reason he thought Castro would not accept the missiles was that he would jeopardize his support in Latin America if he were to be perceived as too tightly bound to the Soviet Union, and that in that meeting Malinovsky, evidently strongly in favor of the plan, took exception to his doubts. Alekseev says in retrospect that he underestimated Castro's internationalism, and he now believes Castro was sincere when he said he would accept the missiles to bolster socialism on the world scale. Authors' interview with Aleksandr Alekseev, April 27, 1989, Moscow, and Alekseev, "Uroki Karibskogo Krizisa."

7. At the time of the crisis, no IRBMs were present in Cuba, and the first IRBM was not expected to become operational until well into December. Central Intelligence Agency memorandum, "Subject: The Crisis USSR/Cuba," October 27, 1962, National Security Archive, Washington, D.C.

8. Aragonés reports: "He said to Che and me, with Malinovsky in the room, 'You don't have to worry; there will be no big reaction from the U.S. And if there is a problem, we will send the Baltic Fleet.'" Asked, "Did you think he was joking, or did you think he was serious?" Aragonés replied, "He was totally serious. When he said it, Che and I looked at each other with raised eyebrows. But, you know, we were deferential to the Soviets' judgments, because, after all, they had a great deal of experience with the Americans, and they had superior information than we had. We trusted their judgment." James G. Blight and David A. Welch interview with Emilio Aragonés, May 19, 1989, Havana. Khrushchev may have believed from the start that the United States would react to the news of Soviet missiles in Cuba with moderation. Alekseev reports that in May, Khrushchev "said the Americans are a pragmatic people and would not attack if there were missiles in Cuba." Alekseev interview. The Soviet Baltic fleet, however, would have been completely inca-

pable of providing timely or effective naval support, and it is difficult to credit the claim that Khrushchev was serious on this point.

9. When asked at the Moscow conference whether the deployment could have been undertaken openly, Gromyko insisted that a secret deployment was the only viable option. His opinion was widely shared among the Soviet delegation, echoed most forcefully by Viktor Komplektov and Georgy Shakhnazarov, who noted that secrecy was "characteristic of the times." Theodore Sorensen asserted that the president would have found it much more difficult to mobilize world opinion on his side if the deployment had been done openly. McGeorge Bundy strongly agreed.

10. Volkogonov's report is consistent with Sergo Mikoyan's claim at the Cambridge conference that 42,000 Soviet troops were involved in the Cuban deployment. Del Valle claims that the total number of Soviet military involved in the deployment was closer to 44,000, of which approximately 20,000 were armed regulars, the remainder being logistics and construction personnel. Del Valle interview. This figure is much higher than previous American intelligence estimates, which ranged from 4,500 to 16,000 in October and November 1962, and later went to 22,000.

11. Del Valle interview. The details of the deployment in Cuba evince a high degree of Soviet self-reliance, and an equally high degree of Cuban deference. There may have been a dearth of trust on the one side, and an excess of trust on the other.

12. When Dobrynin stated at the Moscow meeting that he did not know about the missiles in Cuba until Dean Rusk told him, Gromyko queried, "What, Anatoly Fyodorovich, you mean I did not tell you, the Ambassador, about the nuclear missiles in Cuba?" Dobrynin responded, "No, you did not tell me." Gromyko wryly replied, "That means it must have been a very big secret." *MCT.*

13. *MCT.* It is worth noting that the idea of a missile trade was not a new one, and that, indeed, the president seems to have been expecting the Soviets to propose it for some time. See David A. Welch and James G. Blight, "The Eleventh Hour of the Cuban Missile Crisis: An Introduction to the ExComm Transcripts," *International Security* 12, No. 3 (Winter 1987/88): 12–13. The missile trade was also proposed by Walter Lippmann in his October 25 column in the *Washington Post*, and had been the subject of considerable public debate.

14. President Kennedy instructed Dean Rusk on the night of October 27 to prepare a contingency plan whereby Columbia University President Andrew Cordier, upon a further signal, would contact U Thant, acting secretary general of the United Nations, to propose a public missile trade.

15. Seymour M. Hersh, "Was Castro Out of Control in 1962?" *Washington Post*, October 11, 1987, pp. H1–H2. Cf. Daniel Ellsberg, "The Day Castro Almost Started World War III," *New York Times*, October 31, 1987, p. 27; see also Adrian G. Montoro, "Moscow Was Caught Between Cuba and U.S.," *New York Times*, November 17, 1987. According to Ellsberg, as told to Hersh, an intercepted radio message from the Soviet naval base at Banes indicated that fire had been exchanged with "non-Russians," and that casualties had been taken. The clash was reported to have taken place at the Los Angeles SAM site on Friday, October 26, the day before that very same site shot down the American U-2. Hersh and Ellsberg speculate that Cubans might have seized control of the site and downed the American plane. At the Moscow conference, Ambassador Alekseev claimed that the incident was a mishandling of ammunition, which resulted in an explosion at the SAM site and

several Soviet casualties. *MCT.* Sergio del Valle, however, claims that the event occurred in 1964 at Guantana, in Pinar del Rio, at the other end of the island. Del Valle interview. Sergo Mikoyan reports that neither he nor, so far as he knows, his father, ever heard of any conflict between Soviet soldiers and Cuban regulars, from either Soviet or Cuban sources. Mikoyan did admit the possibility, however, that there may have been a skirmish at the Los Angeles SAM site between Soviet forces and one of the many bands of anti-Castro "worm squads" known to be operating in the area. Personal communication to DAW. The truth of the matter remains unclear.

16. Robert F. Kennedy, *Thirteen Days: A Memoir of the Cuban Missile Crisis* (New York: Norton, 1969), 108.

17. Daniel Ellsberg interviewed Robert Kennedy in 1964, when Kennedy claimed that he had warned Dobrynin that he had just forty-eight hours to remove the missiles; that if dismantling had not begun by that time, the missiles would be attacked and an invasion would follow; and that any further shoot-downs of American reconnaissance planes would result in an attack on "all the SAM sites immediately and probably the missile sites as well." Hersh, "Was Castro Out of Control in 1962?" p. H2. Ellsberg's conclusion is that, because Khrushchev well understood that he no longer controlled the Cubans, and that he may also have lost control over the SAM batteries, the Soviet leader was compelled to interpret Robert Kennedy's message as an ultimatum, requiring an immediate cessation of the crisis.

18. Personal communication to the authors.

19. This was conveyed to the authors by a knowledgeable source. This passage did not appear in the manuscripts that were delivered to the West in 1970.

20. A confidential source informed the authors that in February 1989, Castro remarked that he believed the missiles should have been fired in the event of a full-scale American invasion, though not preemptively or in the event of an air strike.

21. Dobrynin reported at the Moscow conference that in a confidential letter to President Kennedy on October 29 or 30, the Soviet Union did raise the issue of Guantanamo, but he added that he doubted that any hopes of American concessions on the base were realistic. Andrei Gromyko further remarked that the agreement concluding the crisis included the crucial concession from the United States: a commitment not to invade Cuba. *MCT.* Alekseev reports that he believes Khrushchev deliberately chose not to consult Castro on the removal of the missiles, because he knew he would not agree. Alekseev interview.

22. Aragonés interview. The Cuban delegation to the Moscow conference added that Khrushchev's explanation for his failure to consult Castro—that there was simply insufficient time—was wholly plausible. Indeed, Castro's telegram may have been largely responsible for convincing Khrushchev that time was so short. Nevertheless, the Cuban delegation insisted that Khrushchev should at least have made the October 28 deal contingent upon Cuban agreement. *MCT.*

# 15

# Implementing Flexible Response: Vietnam as a Test Case

## John Lewis Gaddis

In order to discuss the implementation of "flexible response," it is necessary to make a choice. One can examine in overview a series of events in which that strategy manifested itself: the Bay of Pigs, Laos, Berlin, the Cuban missile crisis, the Dominican Republic. Or, one can focus in detail on the event that because of its duration, divisiveness, and cost, overshadowed them all: the war in Vietnam. There are two good reasons for choosing the second approach. First, American policy in Southeast Asia reflected in microcosm virtually all of the elements of "flexible response" as applied in practice. Second, Kennedy, Johnson, and their advisers regarded Vietnam as a fair test of that strategy: it had been Eisenhower's inability to deal with that and comparable problems that had produced the "flexible response" critique in the first place; if the strategy could not be made to work in Vietnam, then there would be serious grounds upon which to question its applicability elsewhere. American leaders took on this test fully aware of the potential difficulties, but at the same time fully confident of their ability to surmount them through a strategy designed to meet just that kind of situation.

To say that their confidence was misplaced is to understate: rarely have accomplishments turned out so totally at variance with intended objectives. The war did not save South Vietnam, it did not deter future aggression, it did not enhance the credibility of United States commitments elsewhere in the world, it did not prevent recriminations at home. It is too easy to blame these disparities on deficiencies in the postwar national security decision-making structure, substantial though those may have been. There has been, as we have seen, no single or consistent approach to containment; to indict all manifestations of that strategy is only to be vague. Nor is it helpful to ascribe the failure in Vietnam to the shift in leadership at the White House after November 22, 1963, however strikingly the personalities of Kennedy and Johnson may have differed. For the fact is that Johnson followed the strategy of "flexible response" faithfully in Vietnam, perhaps more so than Kennedy himself would have done.

The American defeat there rather grew out of assumptions derived quite logically from that strategy: that the defense of Southeast Asia was crucial to the maintenance of world order; that force could be applied in Vietnam with precision and discrimination; that means existed accurately to evaluate performance; and that the effects would be to enhance American power, prestige, and credibility in the world. These assumptions in turn reflected a curiously myopic preoccupation with process—a disproportionate fascination with means at the expense of ends—with the result that a strategy designed to produce a precise correspondence between intentions and accomplishments in fact produced just the opposite.

# I

Officials of the Kennedy and Johnson administrations liked to insist that their policies in Vietnam were consistent with the overall direction of American foreign policy since 1947: that conflict, they maintained, was but another in a long series of steps taken to demonstrate that aggression did not pay. "The challenge that we face today in Southeast Asia," Johnson argued, "is the same challenge that we have faced with courage and that we have met with strength in Greece and Turkey, in Berlin and Korea, in Lebanon and in Cuba." The "great lesson of this generation" was that "wherever we have stood firm, aggression has ultimately been halted." To question the need for a similar commitment to South Vietnam, these statements implied, was to dispute the very assumptions that had sustained the strategy of containment from its beginnings.

In fact, though, a gradual shift had taken place in those assumptions over the years. Kennan, it will be recalled, had stressed distinctions between vital and peripheral interests, between varieties of threats to them, and between levels of feasible response given available means; the Kennedy and Johnson administrations made no such distinctions. Kennan had sought to maintain the global balance of power by applying a combination of political, economic, military, and psychological leverage in carefully selected pivotal areas; Johnson by 1965 was relying almost exclusively on the use of military force in a theater chosen by adversaries. Kennan had hoped to harness forces of nationalism, even where communist, to contain the expanding power and influence of the Soviet Union; Johnson sought to oppose communism, even where nationalist, for the purpose of preserving American credibility in the world. And, in a final ironic twist, Johnson and later Nixon came to rely with plaintive consistency on the assistance of the Soviet Union, the original target of containment, to extricate the United States from the tangle in which its own strategy had ensnared it.

One might explain these remarkable mutations as the result of obtuseness, short-sightedness, or even absent-mindedness, but there is no evidence these qualities played any more prominent role during the Kennedy–Johnson years than is normally the case. What was distinctive about those administrations, though, was their commitment to symmetrical response, and it is here that one must look to account for an evolution of strategic thinking all the more striking for the fact that those carrying it off seemed unaware that it had occurred.

It had been, of course, NSC-68 that had shifted perceptions of threat from the Soviet Union to the international communist movement; that document had also provided a rationale for expanding means and, as a consequence, interests. Eisenhower had rejected the analysis of means set forward in NSC-68, but not its assessment of threats or interests; for this reason he had been willing to extend an ambiguous commitment to the defense of South Vietnam through the SEATO treaty,[1] an initiative consistent with his administration's concern to achieve maximum deterrence at minimum cost. Expense was of less concern to Kennedy who, confronted with an upsurge of Viet Cong insurgency, reverted to NSC-68's concept of expandable means but coupled it with a determination to honor Eisenhower's commitment, even though it had been extended largely as a substitute for means. At the same time, Kennedy was determined to lower the risks of escalation or humiliation that earlier strategy had run; this resolve led, in time, to the deployment of American ground forces, first as "advisers" to the South Vietnamese, then, under Johnson, as full-fledged combatants.

But what, precisely, was the United States' interest in Vietnam? Why was the balance of power at stake there? Walt Rostow had warned in his 1962 "BSNP" draft that "major losses of territory or of resources would make it harder for the U.S. to create the kind of world environment it desires, . . . generate defeatism among governments and peoples in the non-Communist world, or give rise to frustrations at home." But when pressed to explain why the "loss" of such a small and distant country would produce these drastic consequences, Washington officials generally cited the SEATO treaty obligation, which, if not honored, would raise doubts about American commitments elsewhere in the world. "The integrity of the U.S. commitment is the principal pillar of peace throughout the world," Rusk wrote in 1965. "If that commitment becomes unreliable, the communist world would draw conclusions that would lead to our ruin and almost certainly to a catastrophic war."

This was curious reasoning. It required justifying the American commitment to South Vietnam as essential to the maintenance of global stability, but then portraying that stability as endangered by the very vulnerability of Washington's commitment. It involved both deterring aggression and being held hostage to it. The confusion, it would appear, stemmed from the failure of both the Kennedy and Johnson administrations to articulate independently derived conceptions of interest in Southeast Asia; instead, they tended to view the American stake there as determined exclusively by threats and obligations. The security of the United

States, indeed of the entire non-communist world, was thought to be imperiled wherever communist challenges came up against American guarantees. Vietnam might be insignificant in itself, but as a point of intersection between threat and commitment, it was everything.

Nothing in this argument required the threat to be centrally directed, or even coordinated with communist activities elsewhere. There were, to be sure, frequent references early in the war to the Sino–Soviet plan for "world domination," but these became less common as evidence of the Moscow–Peking split became irrefutable. Rationales then shifted to the containment of China, but only briefly; by early 1965 the predominant concern, as Under-Secretary of Defense John McNaughton put it, was simply "to avoid a humiliating U.S. defeat (to our reputation as a guarantor)." Communism need not pose a coordinated threat to the world balance of power, then, but because victories for communism at the expense of the United States, even if uncoordinated, could result in humiliation, the challenge to global stability was no less real. The only difference was that it was now Washington's fear of retreat that linked these threats together, not the internal discipline and control of international communism itself.

Nor did the American commitment in question need to have been prudent. There was a definite sense within the Kennedy administration that Eisenhower had overextended the United States in Southeast Asia: Rostow, as has been seen would have preferred a less formal alliance structure based on offshore strong points; Robert Komer, one of his assistants, privately described SEATO in 1961 as a "millstone" directed against nonexistent dangers of overt aggression. Nonetheless, Rostow wrote Kennedy later that year: "Surely we are hooked in Viet-Nam; surely we shall honor our . . . SEATO commitment." The problem, simply, was that the dangers of disengagement seemed at each stage to outweigh the costs of pressing on. "The reasons why we went into Vietnam . . . are now largely academic," McNaughton wrote in 1966. "At each decision point we have gambled; at each point, to avoid the damage to our effectiveness of defaulting on our commitment, we have upped the ante. We have not defaulted, and the ante (and commitment) is now very high."

There was a distinct self-reinforcing tendency in all of this. The more the administration defended its Vietnam policies in terms of safeguarding credibility, the more American credibility seemed to depend upon the success of those policies. "To leave Viet-Nam to its fate would shake . . . confidence . . . in the value of an American commitment and in the value of America's word," Johnson proclaimed in April 1965. And again, in May: "There are a hundred other little nations . . . watching what happens. . . . If South Viet-Nam can be gobbled up, the same thing can happen to them." And still again, in July: "If we are driven from the field in Viet-Nam, then no nation can ever again have the same confidence in . . . American protection." Perceptions in international relations are only in part the product of what people believe; they arise as well from what nations claim. Given the frequency and intensity of these and other comparable pronouncements, it is hardly surprising that they were taken seriously, both at home and abroad. And yet the irony is that the administration made them to stave off pressures for withdrawal that could lead to humiliation; their effect, though, was to widen the very gap between promise and performance from which humiliation springs.

But why this extreme fear of humiliation in the first place? Partly, one suspects, because it might suggest weakness to adversaries: "lessons" of Munich, after all, were still very much alive. Vietnam had also become something of a matter of personal pride: "we have not lost a single nation to communism since 1959," Johnson liked to boast. But a deeper concern, oddly enough, may have been not so much what the world might think as what the United States might do. There was, within both the Kennedy and Johnson administrations, a strange dread of American irrationality—of the unpredictable and uncontrollable reactions that might ensue if the United States was perceived to have "lost" Vietnam. Rusk and McNamara had warned as early as 1961 that such a development "would stimulate bitter domestic controversies in the United States and would be seized upon by extreme elements to divide the country and harass the Administration." Rostow's "BSNP" draft even raised the possibility that "the U.S. might rashly initiate war" if confronted by a major defeat. Johnson may well have entertained the strongest fears of all: "I knew that if we let Communist aggression succeed in taking over South Vietnam," he later recalled,

there would follow in this country an endless national debate—a mean and destructive debate—that would shatter my Presidency, kill my administration, and damage our democracy. I knew that Harry Truman and Dean Acheson had lost their effectiveness from the day that the Communists took over in China. I believed that the loss of China had played a large role in the rise of Joe McCarthy. And I knew that all these problems, taken together, were chickenshit compared with what might happen if we lost Vietnam.

The ultimate danger, then, was what the United States might do to itself if it failed to meet obligations it itself had established.

Shortly after the Johnson administration left office, William Whitworth, a writer for the *New Yorker*, sought to interview several of the former President's advisers on the underlying geopolitical rationale for the Vietnam War. The only one who would see him was Eugene V. Rostow, Walt Rostow's older brother, who had served as Under-Secretary of State for Political Affairs from 1966 to 1969. The ensuing discussion took on a revealing circularity. Asked why American security depended upon the defense of Southeast Asia, Rostow emphasized the need to maintain a "balance of power" in the world. But when queried as to why it had been necessary to do that, Rostow fell back upon a classic "flexible response" argument: the need to be able to handle, without resort to nuclear weapons, problems such as Vietnam. Whitworth found this puzzling: "We have the balance in order to deal with the problem, and we have to deal with the problem in order to preserve the balance. The theory is eating its own tail." "Well, in a sense, you're right," Rostow replied. "All I can say is that it has always been very dangerous for people when a potentially hostile power establishes hegemony. I can't particularize how that potential hegemony would be exercised, but I would prefer, even at considerable cost, to prevent the risk."

This spectacle of theories eating tails was no rare thing in Vietnam: the expansion of means to honor a commitment made as a substitute for means; the justification of that commitment in terms of a balance of power made shaky by its very existence; the defense, in the interests of credibility, of policies destructive of credibility; the search, ultimately, for domestic consensus by means that destroyed that consensus—all of these reflect the failure of "flexible response" strategy to proceed in an orderly manner through the stages of identifying interests, perceiving threats, and selecting appropriate responses. Instead, both threats and responses became interests in themselves, with the result that the United States either ignored or forgot what it had set out to do in Vietnam at just the moment it was resolving, with unprecedented determination, to do it.

## II

A second prominent feature of "flexible response" as applied in Vietnam was the belief in "calibration," or "fine tuning"—that by being able to move up or down a range of precisely calculated actions, the United States could deter limited aggression without either extreme escalation or humiliation. "Our military forces must be . . . used in a measured, limited, controlled and deliberate way, as an instrument to carry out our foreign policy," one of McNamara's assistants wrote in late 1964. "Never must military operations become an end in themselves." Johnson made the same point some months later: he would not heed, he insisted, "those who urge us to use our great power in a reckless or casual manner. . . . We will do what must be done. And we will do only what must be done." And yet, since this strategy in the end produced *both* escalation *and* humiliation, it would appear to have contained, as did official thinking on the balance of power, certain deficiencies.

Deterrence, ideally, should involve expressing determination without actually having to exhibit it. John Foster Dulles had attempted this delicate maneuver by threatening to use nuclear weapons to discourage aggression at all levels—an approach that at least had the merit of separating the projection of resolve from its actual demonstration, so long as skill, or luck, held out. Lacking the previous administration's self-confidence in such matters, convinced as well of the ineffectiveness of that strategy in limited war situations, Kennedy and his advisers had ruled out nuclear threats in areas like Southeast Asia, but not the need to manifest American firmness there. "We must produce quickly a course of action which convinces the other side we are dead serious," Rostow had warned Kennedy in August 1961. "What the U.S. does or fails to do," Maxwell Taylor added a few months later, "will be decisive to the end result." The difficulty was that, short of embracing Dulles's strategy, all conceivable projections of resolve seemed to require, in one form or another, actual demonstrations of it.

This did not bother the Joint Chiefs of Staff, who, as early as May 1961, had recommended the dispatch of United States troops to South Vietnam "to provide a visible deterrent to potential North Vietnamese and/or Chinese Communist action," and to "indicate the firmness of our intent to all Asian nations." An old Vietnam hand, Brigadier General Edward Lansdale, explained the rationale as follows:

U.S. *combat* forces, even in relatively small units, are the symbol of our national power. If an enemy engages one of our combat units, he is fully aware that he automatically has engaged the entire power of the U.S. This symbol of real national strength, employed wisely in Germany, Greece, and the Formosa Straits in a manner not unlike that contemplated for Thailand and Vietnam, has "kept the peace." When the mission of such U.S. force is properly announced and followed immediately by a firm action, recent history teaches that the effect is just the reverse of "escalation" and that our action obtains world support outside the [Sino–Soviet] Bloc.

"[T]he point of installing token U.S. forces before the event," Robert Komer added, "is to signal our intentions to the other fellow, and thus hopefully avoid having to face up to the commitment of substantial U.S. forces after a fracas has developed." It was true that the United States might "end up with something approaching another Korea, but I think the best way of avoiding this is to move fast now before the war spreads to the extent that a Korean type commitment is required."[2] This theory that immediate small-scale involvement could make massive long-term involvement unnecessary formed the basis of recommendations by Maxwell Taylor and Walt Rostow for the introduction of some 8,000 U.S. combat troops into South Vietnam in November 1961. "In our view," Taylor wrote the President, nothing is more calculated to sober the enemy and to discourage escalation . . . than the knowledge that the United States has prepared itself soundly to deal with aggression at any level."

But Kennedy had long been skeptical about the wisdom of sending American forces to fight in Southeast Asia: he had reminded his advisers the previous July of "the reluctance of the American people and of many distinguished military leaders to see any direct involvement of U.S. troops in that part of the world. . . . [N]othing would be worse than an unsuccessful intervention in this area." State Department assessments reinforced this view:

We do not think the presence of U.S. troops would serve to deter infiltrations short of overt armed intervention. There is not much reason for supposing the Communists would think our troops would be much more successful against guerrilla operations in South Viet-Nam than French troops were in North Viet-Nam. Counter-guerrilla operations require highly selective application of force; selection requires discrimination; and alien troops simply lack the bases for discriminating between friend and foe, except by the direction in which they shoot.

If the South Vietnamese themselves were not willing to make a "serious national effort," Dean Rusk warned in November, then it was "difficult to see how [a] handful [of] American troops can have [a] decisive influence." Persuaded by these arguments, concerned as well about priorities elsewhere (notably Berlin) and the risk of upsetting negotiations then in progress on Laos, Kennedy deferred implementing the Taylor–Rostow recommendation for combat troops. It would have been "like taking a drink," he explained to Arthur Schlesinger. "The effect wears off, and you have to take another."

It is important to note, though, that Kennedy's decision against sending combat troops to Vietnam was not a rejection of "calibration"—just the opposite. The full Taylor–Rostow recommendations, he thought, would have constituted too abrupt an escalation of pressure; he preferred, instead, a more gradual approach, involving an increase of American economic and military aid to Saigon, together with the introduction of U.S. "advisers." Nothing in this procedure precluded the dispatch of ground troops at a later date if that should become necessary. Nor were there illusions as to the impact of these decisions on American credibility: "We are fully cognizant," the State Department cabled Saigon, "of [the] extent to which [these] decisions if implemented . . . will sharply increase the commitment of our prestige struggle to save SVN." Kennedy's actions reflected doubts only about the appropriate level of response necessary to demonstrate American resolve, not about the importance of making that demonstration in the first place.

"Calibration" during the next two years took the form primarily of efforts to transform South Vietnam into a sufficiently self-reliant anticommunist bastion so that no direct commitment of United States forces would be necessary. The goal, according to Roger Hilsman, was to devise "an integrated and systematic military–political–economic strategic counterinsurgency concept," to orient Saigon's military and security forces "increasingly toward counter-guerrilla or unconventional warfare tactics," to "broaden the effective participation of Vietnamese Government officials in the formulation and execution of government policy," and to "identify the populace with the Vietnamese Government's struggle against the Viet Cong." All of this required several delicate balancing acts: moderating President Ngo Dinh Diem's autocratic control enough to win popular support for his government without at the same time weakening it to the point that it could not resist Viet Cong pressures; providing the assistance necessary for Diem to survive without discrediting him as an American puppet; taking care, simultaneously, to see that Washington's interest in Diem's survival did not allow him to make a puppet out of the United States. In the end, the line proved too fine to walk: frustrated by Diem's repression of Buddhist critics, fearful of a secret deal between his government and North Vietnam, Kennedy in August 1963 authorized a carefully orchestrated effort—in itself an example of "calibration"—to overthrow him. As it happened, though, Washington was able to control neither the timing nor the manner of Diem's removal, nor had it given much thought to what would replace him; the effect was that the very instability Kennedy had feared dominated politics in Saigon for the next three years.

The resulting Viet Cong gains led the Johnson administration by the end of 1964 to approve what Kennedy had rejected—a combat role for the United States in Vietnam. Even so, though, the principle of "calibration" would still apply; there would be no sharp, all-out application of force. Rather, the plan, in Johnson's words, was for military pressures against North Vietnam "progressively mounting in scope and intensity for the purpose of convincing the leaders of the DRV that it is to their interest to cease to aid the Viet Cong and to respect the independence and security of South Vietnam." This "slow squeeze" strategy contemplated action strong enough to end the existing deteriorating situation, but not so violent as to knit the North Vietnamese people more closely together, provoke Chinese Communist intervention, arouse world opinion, or preclude opportunities for an eventual negotiated settlement. The objective, Bundy noted on the eve of the first air strikes against the North in February 1965, was "to keep before Hanoi the carrot of our desisting as well as the stick of continued pressure. . . . Once such a policy is put into force, we shall be able to speak in Vietnam on many topics and in many ways, with growing force and effectiveness."3

The bombing campaign against North Vietnam was intended to be the most carefully calibrated military operation in recent history. Great significance was attached to not crossing certain geographic "thresholds" for fear of bringing in the Chinese, as had happened in Korea, to avoiding civilian casualties that might intensify opposition to the war within the United States and elsewhere, and to combining the bombing with various inducements, especially periodic bombing pauses and offers of economic aid, to bring Hanoi to the conference table. Target selection was done in Washington, often in the White House itself, with the President at times personally monitoring the outcome of particular missions. Extraordinary precision was demanded of pilots—one 1966 order specified that piers at Haiphong could be hit only if no tankers were berthed at them, that vessels firing on American planes could be struck only if they were "clearly North Vietnamese," and that no attacks were to be launched on Sunday. Even with such restrictions, though, the scale and intensity of the bombing progressively mounted, from 25,000 sorties and 63,000 tons of bombs dropped in 1965 to 108,000 sorties and 226,000 tons in 1967, from missions directed initially at military bases in the southern "panhandle" of North Vietnam to infiltration routes, transportation facilities, and petroleum storage areas throughout the country, ultimately to factories and power plants in the Hanoi–Haiphong complex itself. And none of it produced discernible progress toward what it was supposed to accomplish: a tapering off of infiltration into South Vietnam, and movement toward negotiations.

Meanwhile, pressures had been building for the introduction of ground troops. Bundy had recommended this option as early as May 1964: the idea, he wrote Johnson, would be one of "marrying Americans to Vietnamese at every level, both civilian and military . . . to provide what [Saigon] has repeatedly asked for: the tall American at every point of stress and strain." "I do not at all think it is a repetition of Korea," he added in August. "It seems to me at least possible that a couple of brigade-size units put in to do specific jobs . . . might be good medicine everywhere." Rostow agreed, pointing out that such troops could usefully serve as bargaining chips in any future negotiations, and by February 1965 Rusk too had endorsed the idea, along with the bombing, as a way to send "a signal to Hanoi and Peiping that they themselves cannot hope to succeed without a substantial escalation on their part, with all the risks they would have to face." The decisive argument in the end, though, proved to be General William Westmoreland's assertion that troops were needed to guard the air base at Da Nang from which some of the strikes against the north were being launched, a claim almost certainly advanced with a view to securing presidential authorization of a combat mission whose scope could then be widened far beyond the limited purposes for which it was made. This "entering wedge" worked, and by early April 1965 Johnson had approved a combat role for United States forces in Vietnam. The pattern of escalation quickly went beyond Bundy's two brigades: from an initial deployment of 3,500 Marines at Da Nang, U.S. troop strength rose to 184,000 by the end of 1965, 385,000 by the end of 1966, and 486,000 by the end of 1967. Nor, as the Tet offensive of early 1968 seemed to show, was there convincing evidence that those troops had come any closer to accomplishing their mission than had the bombing campaign.

What strikes one in retrospect about the strategy of calibrated escalation is the extent to which, as so often happened in Vietnam, the effects produced were precisely opposite from those intended. The objective of applying incremental pressures beginning in 1961 had been to avoid a massive American military involvement: token commitments, it was thought, would demonstrate resolve, thereby obviating the necessity for larger commitments later. The theory was not unlike that of vaccination, in that exposure to minimum risk was expected to provide immunities against more serious dangers. Another analogy, used at the time, was that of a plate-glass window, insufficiently strong in itself to keep out a thief, but capable of producing such conspicuous consequences if shattered as to discourage attempts from being made in the first place. Getting involved, in short, was the best way to avoid getting involved: "I deeply believe," Rostow had written in August of that year, "that the way to save Southeast Asia and to minimize the chance of deep U.S. military involvement there is for the President to make a bold decision very soon."

Bold decisions were made (admittedly not in as bold a manner as Rostow had wanted), but the effect was hardly to minimize American involvement. United States manpower, resources, and prestige were far more deeply committed by 1968 than even "worst-case" scenarios seven years earlier had indicated. McNamara had estimated in November 1961 that in the unlikely event that *both* North Vietnam and Communist China overtly intervened in the war, Washington might have to send six divisions, or 205,000 men. Peking did not intervene, Hanoi kept its own participation below the level of overt acknowledgment, but still the

United States had more than doubled McNamara's prediction as to "the ultimate possible extent of our military commitment." Calibrated pressures as a deterrent obviously had not worked.

One reason for this was a persistent lack of clarity as to who, or what, was being deterred. Impressed by Khrushchev's "wars of national liberation" speech, the Kennedy administration had at first located the roots of Viet Cong insurgency in Moscow: Rostow in 1961 had even advocated an early form of "linkage," making it clear to the Kremlin that no progress toward détente could take place while guerrilla activity continued in Southeast Asia.[4] By 1964, though, Peking, not Moscow, had come to be seen as the culprit: the objective of American policy, National Security Council staff member Michael Forrestal argued late that year, should be to "delay China's swallowing up Southeast Asia until (a) she develops better table manners and (b) the food is somewhat more indigestible." The absence of official relations precluded opportunities for diplomatic "linkage" with Peking, however, and Johnson's advisers, remembering miscalculations during the Korean War, were extremely cautious about applying military pressure in any form. "China is there on the border with 700 million men," Johnson noted; "we could get tied down in a land war in Asia very quickly if we sought to throw our weight around."

The alternative, it would appear, was direct pressure against Hanoi, but things were not quite that simple. John McNaughton in September 1964 identified at least four separate "audiences" aside from Moscow and Peking that the United States would have to influence: "the Communists (who must feel strong pressures), the South Vietnamese (whose morale must be buoyed), our allies (who must trust us as 'underwriters'), and the U.S. public (which must support our risk-taking with U.S. lives and prestige)." The difficulty, of course, was that actions directed at one "audience" might affect others in undesirable ways. Too sharp an escalation aimed at Hanoi risked alienating public opinion in the United States (especially during an election year), and elsewhere in the world, not to mention the danger of Chinese intervention. Moreover, such action would accomplish little as long as instability continued to reign in Saigon, as it had since the overthrow of Diem late in 1963. On the other hand, though, further restraint could only accelerate deterioration of the military situation in the South; it also conveyed the appearance of weakness and indecisiveness, not only in Hanoi and among American allies in Asia, but in Saigon itself, where the resulting low morale produced still more instability. The need, McNaughton argued, was for action taken "with special care—signaling to the DRV that initiatives are being taken, to the GVN that we are behaving energetically . . . and to the U.S. public that we are behaving with good purpose and restraint." But "calibration" implies a single target: where several exist, in a constantly shifting but interrelated pattern, the attainment of a precise correspondence between intentions and consequences becomes no easy matter.[5]

A second problem flowed directly from the first. By eschewing anything other than gradual escalation, matched carefully to the level of enemy provocation, the

Johnson administration was in effect relinquishing the initiative to the other side. This was, of course, a standard military criticism of White House policy: the argument was that if only restraints on air and ground action could be lifted, the war could be ended rapidly.[6] Given the subsequently demonstrated ability of the North Vietnamese and Viet Cong to hold out for years under much heavier pressures, the claim, in retrospect, seems unconvincing. Still, there was one valid element in the military's argument. Theorists of international relations have suggested that deterrence is more likely to work when a potential aggressor is unsure of his ability to control the risks involved in the action he is contemplating. If that confidence exists, deterrence will probably be ineffective. This idea of cultivating uncertainty in the minds of adversaries had been central to Dulles's strategy of "retaliation"—with what effects it is impossible to say, given the difficulty of trying to prove what deterrence deterred. But uncertainty did not carry over into the strategy of "calibration." To proclaim that one intends to do only what is necessary to counter aggression and no more is, after all, to yield control over one's actions to those undertaking the aggression. Washington officials may have had the illusion that they were making decisions on Vietnam force deployments during the Johnson years, but in fact those choices were being made, as a consequence of the administration's own strategy, in Hanoi.

The alternative, of course, was some kind of negotiated settlement with North Vietnam, an option the administration was careful never to rule out. "[We] should strike to hurt but not to destroy," Bundy noted in May 1964, "for the purpose of changing the North Vietnamese decision on intervention in the South." Taylor seconded the point some months later: "it is well to remind ourselves that 'too much' in this matter of coercing Hanoi may be as bad as 'too little.' At some point, we will need a relatively cooperative leadership in Hanoi willing to wind up the VC insurgency on terms satisfactory to us and our SVN allies." But Johnson and his advisers were wary of a "neutralist" solution for South Vietnam along the lines of the shaky 1962 truce in Laos—perhaps with good reason, given the speed with which Hanoi violated the agreements eventually reached at Paris in 1973. The preferred option was to achieve successes on the battlefield, and then approach North Vietnam: "After, *but only after*, we have established [a] clear pattern [of] pressure hurting DRV and leaving no doubts in South Vietnam of our own resolve, we could . . . accept [a] conference broadened to include [the] Vietnam issue," the State Department cabled Saigon in August 1964; such negotiations, if they did occur, would have to bring "Hanoi (and Peiping) eventually [to] accept the idea of getting out." This familiar but elusive position of "negotiation from strength" had two difficulties: it contained no safeguards against attempts by Hanoi to bolster its own negotiating position, or against the progressively deeper American involvement the strategy of "calibration" was supposed to prevent.

Finally, the strategy of "calibration" broke down because it failed to ensure that force, once applied, would be used as a precise and discriminating instrument of policy. It provided no safeguards against the subordination of strategic interests to those of the organizations implementing the strategy. Large bureaucracies all too often develop their own institutional momentum: "standard operating procedures" can make an organization impervious either to instructions from above or feedback from below. One strength of McNamara's reforms in the Pentagon had been the extent to which he had overcome this problem in dealing with the military on nuclear and budgetary matters. No such successes, however, occurred in Vietnam. Instead, once American forces were committed, Washington seemed to lose control, leaving the military with a degree of autonomy surprising in an administration that had prided itself on having reduced military authority over the conduct of national security affairs.

The generalization may seem out of place applied to a war whose soldiers complained regularly about civilian-imposed constraints, but the military's grievances in this regard should be treated with skepticism. It is true that during the early period of American involvement, there were significant restrictions on the nature and scope of U.S. military activity, but as time went on without the desired enemy response, these gradually dropped away. By August of 1967, for example, the White House had authorized for bombing some 95 percent of the North Vietnamese targets requested by the Joint Chiefs of Staff. Moreover, the Air Force's perceived institutional interests were allowed to influence the conduct of the air war in important ways. Despite its obvious (and widely appreciated) inapplicability to guerrilla warfare, the Air Force insisted successfully on a campaign of strategic bombing in North Vietnam, and even on the use of B-52s, designed originally to deliver nuclear weapons against Soviet targets, to hit suspected Viet Cong emplacements in the south. Similarly, it relied heavily on high-performance jet aircraft for other bombing missions in the south, despite studies indicating that slower propeller-driven models would have been three times as accurate, from five to thirteen times less costly, but with roughly the same loss ratio. It was, in retrospect, an adaptation of ends to fit preferred means, rather than the other way around.

The tendency was even more obvious with regard to the ground war. Like most of his army colleagues, General Westmoreland had little sympathy for or understanding of the irregular warfare concepts that had been popular during the early Kennedy administration: the function of infantry, he insisted, was to seek out, pursue, and destroy enemy forces. As a consequence, he never seriously considered the strategy of holding and securing territory recommended by most counterinsurgency theorists, and implemented with considerable success by the Marines in the area around Da Nang in 1965 and 1966. Instead he chose to emphasize large-scale "search and destroy" operations, designed to wear the enemy down through sheer attrition. These not only disrupted efforts at pacification and provided the enemy with sufficient advance warning to escape; they also frequently forced the Americans to destroy villages in order to reach Viet

Cong troops and arms caches located deliberately within those villages. Random "harassment and interdiction" fire against "suspected" but unobserved enemy targets did little to convince inhabitants of the regions affected that their security would be enhanced by supporting Saigon. The Westmoreland strategy even involved, in some instances, the deliberate creation of refugees as a means of securing the countryside, as complete a reversal as can be imagined from the original objectives the American commitment in South Vietnam had been intended to serve.

It was left to the Navy, though, to come up with the most striking example of weapons ill-suited to tasks by retrieving from mothballs the U.S.S. *New Jersey*, the world's last functioning battleship, for the purpose of shelling the jungle in a manner reminiscent of nothing so much as an incident in Joseph Conrad's *Heart of Darkness*:

> Once, I remember, we came upon a man-of-war anchored off the coast. There wasn't even a shed there, and she was shelling the bush. It appears the French had one of their wars going on thereabouts. . . . In the empty immensity of earth, sky, and water, there she was, incomprehensible, firing into a continent. Pop, would go one of the six-inch guns; a small flame would dart and vanish, a little white smoke would disappear, a tiny projectile would give a feeble screech—and nothing happened. Nothing could happen. There was a touch of insanity in the proceeding, a sense of lugubrious drollery in the sight; and it was not dissipated by somebody on board assuring me earnestly there was a camp of natives—he called them enemies—hidden out of sight somewhere.

It was all a remarkable departure from the injunctions to do just enough, but no more than was necessary, with which the United States had entered the conflict in Vietnam.

"[T]he central object of U.S. military policy is to create an environment of stability in a nuclear age," Rostow wrote in 1966; "this requires as never before that military policy be the servant of political purposes and be woven intimately into civil policy." To be sure, this had been the objective all along of the "calibration" strategy: it reflected the immense confidence in the ability to "manage" crises and control bureaucracies that was characteristic of "flexible response," the concern to integrate force and rationality, to find some middle ground between the insanity of nuclear war and the humiliation of appeasement. But it was also a curiously self-centered strategy, vague as to the objects to be deterred, heedless of the extent to which adversaries determined its nature and pace, parochial in its assumption that those adversaries shared its own preoccupations and priorities, blind to the extent to which the indiscriminate use of force had come to replace the measured precision of the original concept. "Despite its violence and difficulties, our commitment to see it through in Vietnam is essentially a stabilizing factor in the world," Rostow had insisted, no doubt with complete sincerity and the best of intentions. But when sincerity and good intentions come to depend upon myopic self-absorption, then the price can be high indeed.

**III**

One of the curious things about the breakdown of "calibration" was official Washington's chronic inability to detect the fact that it had failed. Gaps between objectives sought and results produced widened with only infrequent attempts to call attention to what was happening; those warnings that were advanced produced few discernible responses. This pattern suggests yet another deficiency in "flexible response" theory as applied in Vietnam: a persistent inability to monitor performance, an absence of mechanisms for ensuring that correspondence between the intent of one's actions and their actual consequences that is essential for an effective strategy.

That such lapses should have occurred is puzzling, given the great emphasis both Kennedy and Johnson placed on management techniques designed to achieve precise adaptations of resources to objectives. Exponents of "systems analysis" have explained that their ideas were not applied in Vietnam until it was too late to avoid involvement, but that, once put to use, they quickly revealed the futility of the existing strategy. This view is correct, but narrow. It is true that the Systems Analysis Office in the Pentagon did not begin making independent evaluations of the war until 1966. But, in a larger sense, the Kennedy–Johnson management techniques had been present all along, in the form of both administrations' confidence that they could control bureaucracies with precision, use force with discrimination, weigh costs against benefits, and relate short-term tactics to long-term objectives. The inability to monitor performance, demonstrated so vividly in the failure of "calibration," suggests difficulties in applying these methods, but not their absence.

One reason these methods broke down in Vietnam was their heavy reliance on easily manipulated statistical indices as measurements of "progress" in the war. Here the primary responsibility rests with McNamara, who insisted on applying to that complex situation the same emphasis on quantification that had served him so well in the more familiar worlds of big business and the Pentagon.[7] The difficulty, of course, was that the voluminous calculations McNamara insisted on were no better than the accuracy of the statistics that went into them in the first place: there were few if any safeguards against distortion. *"Ah, les statistiques!"* Roger Hilsman reports one South Vietnamese general as having exclaimed. "Your Secretary of Defense loves statistics. We Vietnamese can give him all he wants. If you want them to go up, they will go up. If you want them to go down, they will go down." Or, in the succinct parlance of a later generation of computer specialists, "garbage in, garbage out."

The problem manifested itself first with regard to South Vietnamese performance following the introduction of United States advisers in 1961. The very presence of the Americans, it had been thought, would make possible more accurate monitoring of the situation, but in fact the opposite occurred. The advisers depended on information furnished them by Diem's officers, many of whom combined a desire to please their powerful ally with a reluctance to risk their own necks in battle. The result was a deliberate inflation of statistical indices, the extent of which became clear only after the fall of Diem in November 1963. Of some 8,600 "strategic hamlets" Diem claimed to have constructed, it turned out that only about 20 percent existed in completed form. A high percentage of military operations initiated by Saigon—possibly as many as one-third—were launched in areas where the Viet Cong were known *not* to be. One district chief had listed all twenty-four hamlets in his district as secure when in fact he controlled only three. "[T]he situation has been deteriorating . . . to a far greater extent than we had realized," McNamara acknowledged ruefully, "because of our undue dependence on distorted Vietnamese reporting."[8]

Not all such misrepresentations came from the South Vietnamese, though. Anxious to meet Washington's expectations of success, General Paul D. Harkins, commander of U.S. advisers in Vietnam, systematically ignored or suppressed reports from his own subordinates questioning Saigon's optimistic assessments of the war. As a result, Taylor and McNamara could report with conviction as late as October 1963 that "the tactics and techniques employed by the Vietnamese under U.S. monitorship are sound and give promise of ultimate victory." Evidence that the situation was not in fact that rosy did occasionally surface, whether from the rare official visitor who managed to evade Harkins's packaged briefings and carefully guided tours, or from the more frequent published reporting of skeptical American correspondents in Saigon, among them Neil Sheehan and David Halberstam. But although Kennedy worried about these discrepancies, he at no point gave up primary reliance on official channels as a means of monitoring progress in the war; Johnson, if anything, depended on them more heavily. It has been suggested that the accuracy of information tends to decline as the level of its classification rises, if for no other reason than that opportunities for independent verification are diminished thereby. The proposition may not be universally applicable, but that the White House would have been better off reading Halberstam than Harkins seems beyond dispute.

These problems did not disappear with the onset of active American military involvement in Vietnam. The most notorious example, of course, was the use of enemy "body counts" as the chief indicator of "progress" in the ground war. The argument has been made that in such a conflict, where conventional indices— territory taken, distances covered, cities occupied—meant little, emphasis on these kinds of macabre statistics was unavoidable.[9] That may be, but what seems odd is the importance accorded them, given their widely acknowledged inaccuracy. Contemporary evaluations identified a margin of error of from 30 to 100 percent in these statistics, partly as the result of double or triple counting, partly because of the difficulty of distinguishing combatants from non-combatants, partly because of pressure from field commanders for higher and higher levels of "performance." A more reliable index of success in the war was available—the number of North Vietnamese–Viet Cong weapons captured—but this was never given the significance of the body counts, probably because the figures were much less impressive. "It is possible that our attrition estimates substantially overstate actual VC/NVA losses," McNamara admitted in 1966. "For example, the VC/NVA apparently lose only about one-sixth as many weapons as people, suggesting the possibility that many of the killed are unarmed porters or bystanders."

Similar statistical inflation occurred in the air war as well. Despite its acknowledged unreliability in an age of high-performance jet aircraft, pilot instead of photographic reconnaissance was generally used to measure the effectiveness of bombing in the North, presumably because damage claims tended to be higher. Photographic confirmation, when requested, was often not for the purpose of verifying pilot reports but to boost "sortie rates." Allocations of fuel and ordnance depended on these rates; they inevitably became an object of competition between the Air Force and the Navy, both of which shared the task of bombing North Vietnam. The results were predictable: a preference for aircraft with small bomb-load capacities which necessitated more frequent missions; the expenditure of bombs on marginal or already destroyed targets; even, during periods of munitions shortages, the flying of sorties without bombs. As one Air Force colonel put it: "bombs or no bombs, you've got to have more Air Force over the target than Navy."

A second reason for the failure to monitor performance was a persistent tendency to disregard discouraging intelligence. It is a myth that the United States stumbled blindly into the Vietnam War. At every stage in the long process of escalation informed estimates were available which accurately (and pessimistically) predicted the outcome.[10] As early as November 1961, for example, the CIA was forecasting that North Vietnam would be able to match, through increased infiltration, any U.S. troop commitment to South Vietnam, and that bombing the North would not significantly impede that process. Two-and-a-half years later, a series of war games in which several key officials of the Johnson administration took part produced precisely the same conclusion. Despite his own enthusiasm for this alternative in 1961 and 1964, Maxwell Taylor by 1965 was strongly opposing the introduction of ground combat forces on the grounds that a "white-faced soldier armed, equipped and trained as he is [is] not [a] suitable guerrilla fighter for Asian forests and jungles." Clark Clifford, Johnson's long-time personal friend and future Defense Secretary, was warning in May 1965 that Vietnam "could be a quagmire. It could turn into an open end commitment on our part that would take more and more ground troops, without a realistic hope of ultimate victory." George Ball, in a series of eloquent dissents from official policy, stressed that "a deep commitment of United States forces in a land war in South Viet-Nam would be a catastrophic error. If there ever was an occasion for a tactical withdrawal, this is it." Even William P. Bundy, one of the original architects of "calibration," had concluded by June of 1965 that any level of commitment beyond 70,000 to 100,000 troops would pass "a point of sharply diminishing returns and adverse consequences."

"There are no signs that we have throttled the inflow of supplies for the VC," McNamara acknowledged after five months of bombing. "Nor have our air attacks on North Vietnam produced tangible evidence of willingness on the part of Hanoi to come to the conference table in a reasonable mood." And even if military successes on the ground could be achieved, there was no guarantee that these would not simply "drive the VC back into the trees" from which they could launch attacks at some future date. "[I]t is not obvious," the Secretary of Defense admitted, "how we will be able to disengage our forces from Vietnam." And yet, despite this gloomy appraisal, McNamara recommended a continuation of the bombing and an increase in troop strength from 75,000 to 175,000–200,000 men. Early in 1966, on the basis of no more encouraging signs of progress in ground or air operations, he endorsed a new troop ceiling of 400,000 men, acknowledging at the same time that the North Vietnamese and Viet Cong could probably match those increases. It might be possible, he thought, eventually to contain the enemy with 600,000 men, but that would risk bringing in the Chinese Communists. "It follows, therefore, that the odds are about even that, even with the recommended deployments, we will be faced in early 1967 with a military standoff at a much higher level, with pacification hardly underway and with the requirement for the deployment of still more U.S. forces."

McNamara's perseverance in the face of pessimism was not atypical—indeed, the Defense Secretary allowed the second sentiment to overwhelm the first sooner than most officials did. Westmoreland, in December 1965, for example, admitted that "notwithstanding the heavy pressures on their transportation system in the past 9 months, they [the North Vietnamese] have demonstrated an ability to deploy forces into South Vietnam at a greater rate than we are deploying U.S. forces." Nevertheless, "our only hope of a major impact on the ability of the DRV to support the war in Vietnam is continuous air attack. . . from the Chinese border to South Vietnam." The CIA, whose assessments of the consequences of escalation had been especially discouraging, acknowledged in March 1966 that the bombing so far had been ineffective, but then recommended more of it, with fewer restraints. Later that year, in a comment characteristic of the resolute optimism of Johnson administration officials, Robert Komer argued that "by themselves, none of our Vietnam programs offer high confidence of a successful outcome. . . . Cumulatively, however, they *can* produce enough of a *bandwagon psychology* among the southerners to lead to such results by end-1967 or sometime in 1968. At any rate, do we have a better alternative?"

The problem, as Komer suggested, was that however unpromising the prospects of continued escalation, the alternatives seemed even worse. Withdrawal would constitute humiliation, with all that implied for the maintenance of world order. Negotiations prior to establishing a "position of strength" could only lead to appeasement. Continuation of the status quo would not work because the status quo was too delicate. Public opinion remained solidly behind escalation until 1968; indeed, Johnson saw himself as applying the brake, not the accelerator. As a result, there developed a curious mixture of gloom and optimism: things were bad, they were likely to get worse before they got better, but since the alternatives to the existing strategy appeared even more forbidding, there seemed to be little choice but to "press on."

What has not been satisfactorily explained, though, is how the Johnson administration came to define its options so narrowly. In retrospect, quite a lot— negotiations on Hanoi's terms, a gradual relinquishment of responsibility for the war to the South Vietnamese, even a phased withdrawal in the anticipation of an eventual North Vietnamese–Viet Cong victory—would have been preferable to the strategy actually followed, which produced those same results but at vastly greater costs than if they had been sought in the mid-1960s. As George Kennan told the Senate Foreign Relations Committee in 1966, "there is more respect to be won in the opinion of this world by a resolute and courageous liquidation of unsound positions than by the most stubborn pursuit of extravagant and unpromising objectives." But Johnson and his advisers could never bring themselves to consider "heretical" options, despite abundant evidence that their strategy was not working. Their hesitancy suggests still another reason for the failure to monitor performance in Vietnam: an absence of mechanisms for forcing the consideration of unpalatable but necessary alternatives.

Several explanations have been advanced to account for this lapse. It has been argued that there was a premium on "toughness" during the Kennedy–Johnson years; that advocates of a compromise settlement bore a far heavier burden of proof than did supporters of escalation. But this view fails to explain Johnson's tenacious search for a negotiated settlement with Hanoi, carried on not just for the purpose of defusing opposition to the war at home but also in the genuine hope of finding a way out consistent with American credibility. It has been pointed out that Johnson's circle of close advisers narrowed as critics of the war proliferated, and that this limited the Chief Executive's exposure to dissenting points of view. But the President did keep on and listen to "house heretics" like George Ball; more significantly, he paid close attention to McNamara's growing doubts about the war in 1966 and 1967, but still refused to change the strategy. It has recently been suggested that the whole national security decision-making system was at fault: the system "worked" in that it produced the results it had been "programmed" to produce, given prevailing assumptions about containment and the balance of power since 1945; the error was in the "programming." But this argument oversimplifies variations in perceptions of interests and threats over the years: while it is true that all postwar administrations have committed themselves to the general objective of containment, they have differed significantly over what was to be contained, and over the means available to do it.

It is this problem of perceived means that best explains the Johnson administration's inability to come up with alternatives in Vietnam. The mechanism that has most often forced the consideration of unpalatable options in the postwar years has been budgetary: when one knows one has only limited resources to work with, then distinctions between what is vital and peripheral, between the feasible and unfeasible, come more easily, if not less painfully. The Eisenhower administration found this out in 1954, when it decided that the "unacceptable" prospect of a communist North Vietnam was in fact preferable to the more costly alternative of direct U.S. military involvement. But, as has been seen, budgetary concerns carried little weight during the Kennedy and Johnson administrations. The theory of "flexible response" implied unlimited means and, hence, little incentive to make hard choices among distasteful alternatives.

Kennedy did from time to time emphasize the existence of limits beyond which Washington could not go in aiding other countries. "[T]he United States is neither omnipotent or omniscient," he pointed out in 1961: "we are only 6 percent of the world's population . . . we cannot right every wrong or reverse each adversary." It has been argued that the abortive 1963 plan for a phased withdrawal of American advisers from South Vietnam reflected Kennedy's sense that the limits of feasible involvement in that country were approaching. But there is no conclusive evidence that Kennedy, on fiscal grounds, was considering a diminished American role there; certainly Johnson did not do so. The new President dutifully stressed the need for economy during his first months in office, but more for the purpose of enhancing his reputation with the business community than from any great concern about the limits of American power in the world scene. And, as the Vietnam crisis intensified, so too did the conviction of Johnson and his advisers that the United States could afford whatever it would take to prevail there.

"[L]et no one doubt for a moment," Johnson proclaimed in August 1964, "that we have the resources and we have the will to follow this course as long as it may take." In a White House meeting the following month, Rusk pointed out that it had cost $50,000 per guerrilla to suppress the insurgency in Greece in the late 1940s; in Vietnam "it would be worth any amount to win." Johnson agreed, emphasizing the need for all to understand "that it was not necessary to spare the horses." "Our assets, as I see them, are sufficient to see this thing through if we enter the exercise with adequate determination to succeed," Rostow wrote in November 1964; "at this stage in history we are the greatest power in the world—if we behave like it." Five months later, as direct American military involvement in Vietnam was beginning, McNamara informed the Joint Chiefs of Staff and the service secretaries that "there is an unlimited appropriation available for the financing of aid to Vietnam. Under no circumstances is a lack of money to stand in the way of aid to that nation." There were always costs in meeting "commitments of honor," Rusk commented in August of that year. "But I would suggest, if we look at the history of the last 30 or 40 years, that the costs of *not* meeting your obligations are far greater than those of meeting your obligations."

"The world's most affluent society can surely afford to spend whatever must be spent for its freedom and security," Johnson told the Congress early in 1965. This assumption of virtually unlimited resources goes far toward explaining the persistence of what was acknowledged to be a costly and inefficient strategy: the idea was that if the United States could simply stay the course, regardless of the expense, it would prevail. "I see no choice," the President added, later that year, "but to continue the course we are on, filled as it is with peril and uncertainty and cost in both money and lives." It might take "months or years or decades," but whatever troops General Westmoreland required would be sent "as requested." "Wastefully, expensively, but nonetheless indisputably, we are winning the war in the South," Robert Komer concluded late in 1966. "Few of our programs—civil or military—are very efficient, but we are grinding the enemy down by sheer weight and mass." Westmoreland agreed. "We'll just go on bleeding them until Hanoi wakes up to the fact that they have bled their country to the point of national disaster for generations. Then they will have to reassess their position."

But McNamara's "systems analysis" specialists had reached the conclusion, by 1966, that it might take generations to bring the North Vietnamese to that point. Their studies showed, for example, that although enemy attacks tended to produce significant enemy casualties, operations launched by U.S. and South Vietnamese forces produced few if any. This suggested that despite the massive American military presence in the south, the North Vietnamese and Viet Cong still retained the initiative, and hence could control their losses. Other studies indicated that while bombing raids against North Vietnam had increased four times between 1965 and 1968, they had not significantly impaired Hanoi's ability to supply its forces in the south: enemy attacks there had increased on the average five times, and in places eight times, during the same period. The bombing was estimated to have done some $600 million worth of damage in the north, but at a cost in lost aircraft alone of $6 billion. Sixty-five percent of the bombs and artillery rounds expended in Vietnam were being used against unobserved targets, at a cost of around $2 billion a year. Such strikes, the analysts concluded, probably killed about 100 North Vietnamese or Viet Cong in 1966, but in the process provided 27,000 tons of dud bombs and shells which the enemy could use to make booby traps, which that same year accounted for 1,000 American deaths. But most devastating of all, the systems analysts demonstrated in 1968 that despite the presence of 500,000 American troops, despite the expenditure of more bomb tonnage than the United States had dropped in all of World War II, despite estimated enemy casualties of up to 140,000 men in 1967, the North Vietnamese could continue to funnel at least 200,000 men a year into South Vietnam indefinitely. As one analyst wrote, "the notion that we can 'win' this war by driving the VC/NVA from the country or by inflicting an unacceptable rate of casualties on them is false."

Only the last of these studies had any noticeable impact outside the Office of the Secretary of Defense, though: persuasive though they were, there was little incentive, in an administration confident that it could sustain the costs of the war indefinitely, to pay any attention to them. It was not until Johnson personally became convinced that the costs of further escalation would outweigh conceivable benefits that the discipline of stringency could begin to take hold. That did not happen until after the Tet offensive of February 1968, when the President received Westmoreland's request for an additional 206,000 troops, a figure that could not have been met without calling up Reserves and without major domestic and international economic dislocations. Johnson had always regarded these as limits beyond which he would not go, not on the basis of rigorous statistical analysis, but rather from the gut political instinct that if he passed those points, public support for the war would quickly deteriorate. In the end, then, the Johnson administration based its ultimate calculation of costs and benefits on criteria no more sophisticated than those employed by Eisenhower prior to 1961, or by Truman prior to 1950. The techniques of systems analysis, which had been designed to avoid the need for such arbitrary judgments, in fact only deferred but did not eliminate them.

Several circumstances discouraged the objective evaluation of performance in Vietnam. The military's relative autonomy gave it a large degree of control over the statistical indices used to measure "progress" in the war; this, combined with the organizationally driven compulsion to demonstrate success and the traditional reluctance of civilians in wartime to challenge military authority, made it difficult to verify charges of ineffectiveness. Such accurate intelligence as did get through tended to be disregarded because the alternative courses of action thereby indicated seemed worse than the option of "pressing on." And the perception of unlimited means made perseverance even in the face of unpromising signals seem feasible: far from widening alternatives, the abundance of means, and the consequent lack of incentives to make hard decisions, actually narrowed them. As a result, the postwar administration most sensitive to the need to monitor its own performance found itself ensnared inextricably in a war it did not understand, could not win, but would not leave.

## IV

But effectiveness in strategy requires not only the ability to identify interests and threats, calibrate responses, and monitor implementation; it also demands a sense of proportion, an awareness of how commitments in one sphere compare with, and can distract attention and resources away from, obligations elsewhere. Johnson and his subordinates thought they had this larger perspective: Vietnam, they repeatedly insisted, was important not just in itself, but as a symbol of American resolve throughout the world.[11] The line between a symbol and a fixation is a fine one, though; once it is crossed, perspectives narrow, often unconsciously, with the result that means employed can become inappropriate to, even destructive of, ends envisaged. This narrowing of perspective, this loss of proportion, this failure to detect the extent to which short-term means can corrupt long-term ends, was the fourth and perhaps most lasting deficiency of "flexible response" as applied in Vietnam.

The tendency appeared vividly in South Vietnam itself, where the administration failed to anticipate the sheer strain several hundred thousand U.S. troops would place on the social and economic structure of that country. Despite American efforts to keep it down, the cost of living in the cities rose by at least 170 percent between 1965 and 1967, just as Westmoreland's "search and destroy" operations were swelling their populations with refugees. Corruption, of course, had always been present in Vietnam, but the proliferation of television sets, motorcycles, watches, refrigerators, and loose cash that accompanied the Americans greatly intensified it. "[T]he vast influx of American dollars," one observer recalls, "had almost as much influence . . . as the bombing had on the countryside":

It turned the society of Saigon inside out. . . . In the new economy a prostitute earned more than a GVN minister, a secretary working for USAID more than a full colonel, a taxi owner who spoke a few words of English more than a university professor. . . . The old rich of Saigon had opposed the Communists as a threat to their position in society; they found that the Americans took away that position in a much quicker and more decisive fashion—and with it, what was left of the underpinning of Vietnamese values.

A similar phenomenon spread to rural areas as well: "Around the American bases from An Khe to Nha Trang, Cu Chi, and Chu Lai, there had grown up entire towns made of packing cases and waste tin . . . entire towns advertising Schlitz, Coca-Cola, or Pepsi Cola . . . towns with exactly three kinds of industry—the taking in of American laundry, the selling of American cold drinks to American soldiers, and prostitution for the benefit of the Americans."

The effect of this overbearing presence was to erode South Vietnam's capacity for self-reliance, the very quality the Americans had sought to strengthen in the first place. To be sure, Washington never succeeded in controlling its clients in all respects: the very profligacy of the U.S. investment in South Vietnam made occasional threats to cut it off less than credible. "The harsh truth is," one report noted early in 1968, "that given a showdown situation or an intolerable divergence between GVN and U.S. methods, the U.S. advisor will lose." But recalcitrance is not the same thing as independence. The same report noted that "[t]he Vietnamese in the street is firmly convinced that the U.S. totally dominates the GVN and dictates exactly what course shall be followed." And Vietnamese at the military or governmental level, while certainly not puppets, while clearly resentful at the extent to which the Americans had come to dominate their culture, were at the same time terrified at the prospect that the Americans might one day leave. The result was an ambiguous but deep dependency, the extent of which became clear only after the United States did at last withdraw from the war, in 1973.

It is hard to say, in retrospect, what the cross-over point would have been between the level of outside aid necessary to sustain South Vietnam against its enemies and the amount beyond which self-reliance would have been impaired.

Perhaps there was no such point; perhaps South Vietnam never had the capacity to stand on its own.What is clear, though, is that Washington made few efforts to find out. The American buildup took place almost totally without regard to the destructive impact it was having on the society it was supposed to defend. "It became necessary to destroy the town, to save it," an Air Force major explained, following the bombing of a Mekong delta village occupied by Viet Cong after the Tet offensive in 1968. The comment could be applied to the whole American experience in Vietnam, and to the dilemma of disproportionate means which the strategy of "flexible response," despite its original emphasis on matching response to offense, never seemed able to resolve.

Securing South Vietnam's independence had not been the only reason for the American presence in that country, though: there had also been a determination to show potential aggressors elsewhere that aggression would not pay. "To withdraw from one battlefield means only to prepare for the next," Johnson argued. "We must say in Southeast Asia—as we did in Europe. . . . 'Hitherto shalt thou come, but no further.'" Interestingly, administration officials did not consider success in South Vietnam as necessarily a requirement in communicating that message. However things turned out there, John McNaughton reflected in 1964, it was "essential . . . that [the] U.S. emerge as a 'good doctor.' We must have kept promises, been tough, taken risks, gotten bloodied, and hurt the enemy very badly." Sustained reprisals against the north might not work, McGeorge Bundy acknowledged early in 1965—the chances of success, he thought, were between 25 and 75 percent. But "even if it fails, the policy will be worth it. At a minimum it will damp down the charge that we did not do all we could. . . . Beyond that, a reprisal policy . . . will set a higher price for the future upon all adventures of guerrilla warfare." The important thing, in projecting resolve, was to make a commitment; failure, while both possible and undesirable, would not be as bad as not having acted in the first place.

And yet, the signal actually communicated was very different. The inability of the steadily growing American commitment to halt North Vietnamese infiltration or Viet Cong attacks—a pattern made painfully evident by the 1968 Tet offensive—seemed only to demonstrate their relevancy of the kind of power the United States could bring to bear in such situations: technology, in this respect, may well have been more of a hindrance than a help in Vietnam. The war also confirmed Mao Tse-tung's theory that relatively primitive forces could prevail against more sophisticated adversaries if they had both patience and will, qualities Ho Chi Minh perceived more accurately than Johnson to be lacking in the American attitude toward Vietnam. Finally, Washington's commitment in that country had grown to the point, by 1968, that the United States would have been hard-pressed to respond anywhere else in the world had a comparable crisis developed. What was demonstrated in Vietnam, then, was not so much the costs of committing aggression as of resisting it. . . .

## NOTES

1. The SEATO treaty, signed September 8, 1954, provided that in case of "armed attack" against any of the signatories or against states or territories which the signatories "by unanimous agreement may hereafter designate," they would "in that event act to meet the common danger in accordance with [their] constitutional processes." In the event of a threat "other than by armed attack" or "by any fact or situation which might endanger the peace of the area," the signatories would "consult immediately in order to agree on the measures which should be taken for the common defense." South Vietnam was not a signatory to the treaty, but a protocol attached to it did extend its provisions to cover "the States of Cambodia and Laos and the free territory under the jurisdiction of the State of Vietnam" (*American Foreign Policy, 1950–1955: Basic Documents* [Washington: 1957], pp. 913–14, 916).

2. "I'm no happier than anyone about getting involved in another squalid, secondary theatre in Asia. But we'll end up doing so sooner or later anyway because we won't be willing to accept another defeat. If so, the real question is not whether but how soon and how much!" (Komer to Bundy, October 31, 1961, Kennedy Papers, NSC Files, Box 231, "Southeast Asia—General.")

3. Eugene Rostow argued that Johnson's "bold but prudent action in Vietnam had posed two things: that we would risk bombs over New York in order to protect Saigon, and that Moscow would not bomb New York to protect Hanoi. This was an event and a demonstration of capital importance, which should greatly fortify our system of alliances, and weaken that of our enemies." (Rostow memorandum, April 10, 1965, enclosed in Bill Moyers to Bundy, April 13, 1965, Johnson Papers, NSF Country Files: Vietnam, Box 16, "Memos—Vol. XXXII.")

4. Rostow wanted Kennedy to warn Khrushchev at Vienna that if the United States were "drawn deeper and more directly on to the Southeast Asian mainland," this would require a major increase in military spending and difficulties in relations with Moscow because "it is difficult for a democracy simultaneously to gear itself for possible military conflict and also to take the steps necessary to ease tensions and to expand the areas of U.S.–Soviet collaboration." (Rostow to Kennedy, May 11, 1961, Kennedy Papers, NSC Files, Box 231, "Southeast Asia—General.") There is no evidence that Kennedy actually raised this point with Khrushchev at Vienna—perhaps he realized that the Soviet leader might welcome rather than regret an American distraction in Southeast Asia.

5. McNamara succinctly summarized the problem of impressing multiple "audiences" in a July 1965 memorandum to Johnson: "Our object in Vietnam is to create conditions for a favorable outcome by demonstrating to the VC/DRV that the odds are against their winning. We want to create these conditions, if possible, without causing the war to expand into one with China or the Soviet Union and in a way which preserves support of the American people and, hopefully, of our allies and friends." (McNamara to Johnson, July 20, 1965, Johnson Papers, NSF Country File: Vietnam, Box 74, "1965 Troop Decision.")

6. Perhaps the most pungent expression of this idea came from General Thomas S. Power, Strategic Air Force Commander, who told a Pentagon audience in 1964 that "the task of the military in war was to kill human beings and destroy man-made objects," and to do it "in the quickest way possible." It had been "the moralists who don't want to kill" that had given "Hitler his start and got us into the mess in Cuba and Viet-Nam." The "com-

puter types who were making defense policy don't know their ass from a hole in the ground." (Summary, Power briefing, April 28, 1964, Johnson Papers, NSF Agency File, Box 11–12, "Defense Dept. Vol. I.")

7. McNamara "has been trying to think of ways of dealing with this problem [Vietnam] for so long that he has gone a little stale," Bundy wrote to Johnson in June 1964. "Also, in a curious way, he has rather mechanized the problem so that he misses some of its real political flavor." (Bundy to Johnson, June 6, 1964, Johnson Papers, NSF—NSC Staff File, Box 2, "Memos for the President, Vol. 5.")

8. The difficulties, of course, did not end in 1963. The number of "Viet Cong" turned in under the Third Party Inducement Program, which provided monetary rewards for identifying "defectors" willing to rally to Saigon's cause, rose from 17,836 in 1968 to 47,088 in 1969, at which point it was discovered that many of the alleged "defectors" were not Viet Cong at all, but South Vietnamese who had made a deal with friends to report them, and then split the reward.

9. The body-count phenomenon even extended, at times, to digging up bodies for counting from freshly dug graves. (Lewy, *America in Vietnam*, p. 80.)

10. "The information I received [on Vietnam] was more complete and balanced than anyone outside the mainstream of official reporting could possibly realize." Lyndon B. Johnson, *The Vantage Point: Perspectives of the Presidency, 1963–1969* (New York: 1971), p. 64.

11. "The idea that we are here simply because the Vietnamese want us to be here . . . ; that we have no national interest in being here ourselves; and that if some of them don't want us to stay, we ought to get out is to me fallacious," Ambassador Henry Cabot Lodge cabled from Saigon in 1966. "In fact, I doubt whether we would have the moral right to make the commitment we have made here solely as a matter of charity towards the Vietnamese and without the existence of a strong United States interest. . . . Some day we may have to decide how much it is worth to us to deny Viet-Nam to Hanoi and Peking—regardless of what the Vietnamese may think." (Lodge to State Department, May 23, 1966, *Pentagon Papers*, IV, 99–100.)

# 16

# Coercive Diplomacy in the Balkans

## STEVEN L. BURG

The use of coercive diplomacy in Bosnia by the United States, in cooperation with its NATO partners and local actors, succeeded in bringing the fighting in that country to an end and in persuading all sides to enter into a negotiated settlement of the war. The attempt by the United States to use coercive diplomacy to end the conflict in Kosovo, in contrast, failed. A prolonged effort during most of 1998 to use the threat of force to encourage the Serbs and Kosovar Albanians to negotiate an end to their conflict was transformed in late 1998 and early 1999 into what Alexander George calls a "blackmail strategy," or simple coercion, directed against Slobodan Milosevic and the Serbs. The success of coercive diplomacy in Bosnia and its failure in Kosovo can be attributed to a number of factors. The most important may be the misreading by some senior U.S. policymakers of the lessons to be learned from the success in Bosnia. But the failure in Kosovo also raises the more fundamental question of whether the application of coercive diplomacy in this case was misconceived from the outset and made the resort to coercion inevitable.

This chapter reviews the characteristics of the coercive diplomacy practiced in Bosnia and the key factors that accounted for its success. I suggest that U.S. policymakers may have misread the Bosnian experience in precisely the manner anticipated by Alexander George, leading to the misapplication of coercive diplomacy in Kosovo. Furthermore, the chapter suggests that Western policymakers may have missed an opportunity to pursue an alternative, peaceful strategy for managing the conflict in Kosovo and identifies the factors that led them instead to rely on force and, ultimately, coercion.

247

## COERCIVE DIPLOMACY IN BOSNIA

The war in Bosnia-Herzegovina was a multidimensional conflict, involving an internal struggle among three national groups (Bosnian Muslims, Bosnian Croats, and Bosnian Serbs), as well as conflicts between the Bosnian state and its neighbors, Croatia and Serbia. The Bosnian war took place in the context of the dissolution of the former Yugoslav federation, of which Bosnia-Herzegovina had been a constituent federal republic. The Bosnian Muslims, who constituted over 40 percent of the population in 1991, sought to follow the lead of Slovenia and Croatia and establish the Bosnian republic as an independent state. The Bosnian Croats and the Bosnian Serbs, however, each sought to separate those parts of Bosnia they claimed as "theirs" and either establish them as independent national states or attach them to their respective neighboring national states, Croatia and Serbia. The nationalist leaders of Croatia and Serbia, Franjo Tudjman and Slobodan Milosevic, supported the efforts of Bosnian Croat and Bosnian Serb nationalists to divide Bosnia. The war in Bosnia-Herzegovina thus involved competing and conflicting claims to national self-determination expressed as demands for independence on the part of the three major national groups in the republic, as well as the conflicting territorial ambitions and competing geostrategic interests of two neighboring states engaged in an ongoing war over the definition of their respective borders. For most of the war, the Bosnian Serbs—backed up by the Yugoslav (Serb) military—enjoyed substantial military superiority, which they employed to seize control of the territory to which they laid claim and ethnically "cleanse" it of Muslims and other non-Serbs. Although the Bosnian Muslims and the Bosnian Croats also engaged in ethnic cleansing in territories under their control, the scope and brutality of the ethnic cleansing carried out by the Serbs—and especially the massacre of thousands of defenseless Bosnian Muslim prisoners at Srebrenica in July 1995—gave rise to charges of war crimes, crimes against humanity, and genocide.

　　European and U.S. policymakers declined to intervene forcefully as the Bosnian tragedy unfolded. They chose instead to try to limit the humanitarian impact of the fighting by deploying a limited UN peacekeeping operation and a UN-led humanitarian relief operation to Bosnia while conducting negotiations to find a political solution to the conflict. The UN Protection Force in Bosnia (UNPROFOR) included troops from Britain, France, and other NATO and non-NATO states, but not the United States. (Some U.S. personnel participated in the headquarters and intelligence operations of UNPROFOR, but there was no significant U.S. troop presence on the ground.) The European states thus had a strong, concrete interest in ending the fighting in Bosnia and took the lead in diplomatic efforts to find a solution. Paul Shoup and I have documented the negotiation efforts in detail elsewhere. Negotiations were carried out under the auspices of the International Conference on the Former Yugoslavia, which was cochaired by representatives of the UN secretary-general (at first, this was former U.S. secretary of state Cyrus Vance) and the European Union (at first, former British foreign secretary Lord David Owen). The Vance-Owen negotiations produced a proposed settlement in April 1993, but this plan failed for lack of enthusiasm on the part of the warring parties and for lack of support from either the Americans or the Europeans, neither of whom was prepared to supply the force that would be necessary to secure the plan's implementation. Vance was succeeded by former Norwegian prime minister Thorvald Stoltenberg in May 1993. The Owen-Stoltenberg peace plan proposed in August 1993 also failed to gain support. Several additional efforts to find a solution, based in large part on de facto partition plans, also failed. The last of these was attempted by the major powers—the United States, Russia, Britain, France, and Germany—acting in concert as the Contact Group. The Contact Group plan for Bosnia was rejected by the Bosnian Serbs in July 1994. Although the Contact Group had characterized its proposal as an ultimatum that the Serbs had to accept, the group was unable to agree on any measures to back up its threat.

The United States had remained at the margins of diplomatic efforts to end the conflict in Bosnia for almost two years. Paul Shoup and I have demonstrated that the United States did not become seriously engaged in a strategy of coercive diplomacy in Bosnia until late 1994; that is, until after the failure of the Contact Group plan made it clear to U.S. policymakers that a credible threat of force was essential to any effort to negotiate an end to the fighting and after policymakers came to perceive the fighting as threatening U.S. national interests. From that point forward, the United States became increasingly determined to bring the fighting to an end.

Over the course of the war, the United States had participated in five attempts to use the threat of force to persuade or compel the Bosnian Serbs to cease certain actions. But these were limited in scope and intent. First, in response to the "strangulation" of Sarajevo by Serb forces that nearly surrounded the city in summer of 1993, NATO issued a vague threat of future action against those who attacked UN forces or obstructed humanitarian aid. Despite signs of differences among the allies, the Bosnian Serbs ended their immediate threat to the city. Second, in February 1994 the United States and its NATO allies responded to a shelling of the Markala marketplace in Sarajevo attributed to the Bosnian Serbs by issuing an ultimatum to the Serbs to withdraw their heavy weapons from around the city or face an air attack by NATO. The NATO threat led the Bosnian Serbs to withdraw, and to the establishment of a heavy weapons exclusion zone around Sarajevo. Third, in April three limited air attacks—derisively characterized in the media as "pinpricks"—were carried out against Serb forces attacking the Muslim-held enclave of Goražde. These were followed by another ultimatum to the Serbs to withdraw and by at least some consideration of a more extensive use of force against them. But any effort to use such force was blocked by the special representative of the UN secretary-general, who exercised joint, or "dual key," control with NATO over the use of force by the West, which was operating in Bosnia under a UN mandate. An exclusion zone was established around

Goražde, but the confrontation was allowed to wind down without a definitive conclusion. Fourth, in November 1994 NATO launched air attacks against a Serb airbase and three Serb SAM missile sites in the Bihać area in response to Serb attacks that threatened to overrun the Muslim-held enclave in western Bosnia. But the allies remained deeply divided over further action, and this crisis, too, ended inconclusively with little net change in the status quo. The fifth and final attempt to use force consisted of the use of airpower against a Bosnian Serb ammunition dump in May 1995, in order to back up an ultimatum to the Bosnian Serbs to withdraw weapons from the exclusion zone around Sarajevo. After the Serbs retaliated by shelling the city of Tuzla and killing seventy-one civilians, NATO launched a second air strike. This attack produced what Alexander George might characterize as an escalatory response on the part of the Bosnian Serbs: they seized UN personnel as hostages, using them as human shields against further attack and compelling NATO to cease its use of force—a response that NATO policymakers should have anticipated on the basis of similar Bosnian Serb reactions to the use of airpower against them at Bihać six months earlier. The May 1995 events contributed to both the collapse of the UN mission in Bosnia and the emergence of a comprehensive U.S. strategy of coercive diplomacy.

The U.S. and NATO threats to use force in connection with the 1993 crisis over the "strangulation" of Sarajevo and in response to the Markala marketplace massacre in February 1994 can be considered successful but limited acts of coercive diplomacy that displayed many of the characteristics identified by Alexander George. George defines coercive diplomacy as an attempt to persuade an adversary to cease an aggression by backing up one's demands with a threat of punishment for noncompliance that the adversary considers credible and potent enough to induce compliance. A strategy of coercive diplomacy, George argues, allows for the possibility of flexible diplomacy, including the use of positive inducements credible and potent enough to achieve compliance. Force need not actually be used. But if it is, it is used in a limited fashion as a means to persuade the adversary to comply. In each of the Sarajevo cases, a threat of air attack was employed to compel the Bosnian Serbs to pull back from the city and reduce, at least temporarily, their attacks. Issuance of an ultimatum was accompanied by crisis negotiations with the party whose actions the coercer was trying to reverse. But in each case, special circumstances secured Serb compliance.

. . . Bosnian Serb agreement was secured in no small part by the fact that in 1993 the Serbs were not required to withdraw so far as to prevent them from renewing artillery fire on the city and that they were able to secure UN occupation of strategic territory, thereby denying it to the Bosnian Muslims. Similarly, in 1994 negotiators agreed to prevent the Muslims from gaining control over territory relinquished by the Serbs by deploying Russian peacekeepers to the territory. In each case the demand advanced by the NATO allies was one to which the Serbs could agree, and agreement itself served Serb interests by keeping alive negotiations for a comprehensive cease-fire that would freeze existing Serb territorial gains. Thus, the Serbs did comply, making these exercises in coercive diplomacy successful, at least in the short run.

However, unlike the situations reviewed by George, the crisis negotiations in both these instances were not carried out by the coercing party (NATO and the United States), but by a third party—the UN commander, who was not under the control of the coercing party and whose interests differed from those of the coercing party. The goals of coercive diplomacy were in each case limited in scope. Speaking of negotiations to end the overall conflict, Madeleine Albright, then U.S. ambassador to the United Nations, argued at the time of the 1994 threat that "[o]ur diplomacy must be backed by a willingness to use force when that is essential in the cause of peace. For it is only force plus diplomacy that can . . . break the stalemate in Geneva."[1] But the threat of force used to secure the pullback of the Serbs from around Sarajevo was not accompanied in either 1993 or 1994 by more comprehensive efforts—at least not on the part of the principal coercer, the United States—to settle the larger conflict.

In some respects, these attempts to use force made matters in Bosnia worse. The apparent increase in U.S. and NATO involvement and the threat of force against the Serbs contributed in each case to a hardening of Bosnian Muslim positions in the negotiations over a political settlement taking place in Geneva under the auspices of the International Conference on the Former Yugoslavia (ICFY). This contradictory outcome suggests one of the difficulties of employing coercive diplomacy against only one party to a conflict involving multiple actors: a threat or inducement aimed at affecting the behavior of one target actor also affects the behaviors of others. Because the interests of the Bosnian actors were most often in opposition, threats or coercion applied against one actor in order to encourage that party to negotiate or comply would make one or more of the others less willing to negotiate or comply. The fact that the threat of force was not actually carried out in connection with either the "strangulation" crisis or the Markala marketplace massacre, and that the Serbs were able to keep their immediate concessions modest and reverse them later, weakened the credibility of subsequent U.S. and NATO threats in the eyes of both the Serbs and the Bosnian Muslims. The later uses of force in Goražde and Bihać represented responses to what were perceived as Serb attempts to alter the military balance decisively in their favor. But the threat and the use of force in Goražde and Bihać were of only limited military value and were not accompanied by a serious effort to extract any larger political concessions from the Serbs. Their net effect, if any, appears to have been to deepen divisions within NATO over the use of force and erode the effectiveness of any future threat to do so.

The divisions within the alliance that followed the limited use of force against the Serbs at Bihać in November 1994 led U.S. policymakers to adopt a more comprehensive approach to ending the conflict in Bosnia. They concluded that the use of force alone was futile, that the Serbs had to be given incentives to accept a settlement, and that if force were to be used it had to support a political settlement.

They entered into direct negotiations with both Milosevic and the Bosnian Serbs and prepared to back up their negotiating positions with a more credible threat of force. The establishment of a credible threat required intensive diplomatic efforts with NATO allies and Russia. These were carried out in the context of the Contact Group. Most important, it also required the continuation of ongoing efforts to shift the military balance on the ground in Bosnia against the Serbs. In order to exercise control over negotiations with the target(s) of coercion, the United States had to shift negotiations over a political settlement away from the ICFY and to the Contact Group. It also had to alter the very nature of those negotiations, replacing mediated exchanges among the warring parties in search of a mutually acceptable solution with exchanges among the Contact Group powers in search of a solution they all could accept and then impose on the warring parties. The United States can thus be said to have laid the basis for a strategy of coercive diplomacy in Bosnia in late 1994. But it was not until July 1995 that policymakers appear self-consciously to have committed themselves to such a strategy.

The resort to coercive diplomacy by the United States in Bosnia in 1995 was driven for the most part by concern on the part of U.S. policymakers that U.S. troops would be drawn into a potentially costly operation to evacuate UN forces, including those of the NATO allies. According to Richard Holbrooke, following the fall of the Muslim-held enclaves of Srebrenica and Zepa in eastern Bosnia to the Serbs in July 1995 and the realization that the UN operation was heading for failure, "the President saw the degree to which involvement was now inevitable, and how much better it would be to have involvement built on success rather than failure."[2] The resort to coercive diplomacy in 1995 was thus driven by a clear sense of national interest in avoiding a potential military catastrophe that might threaten the survival of the NATO alliance. But policymakers in the Clinton administration, including the president, also turned to coercive diplomacy out of a narrower sense of political self-interest; an interest in resolving the Bosnian issue in time to prevent the presumed Republican candidate for president from using it against the administration in the 1996 election. A journalistic account of the policy debates in June and July makes clear the intensity with which policymakers felt these concerns. Thus, domestic political considerations reinforced the inclination of U.S. policymakers to embark on an exercise in coercive diplomacy in Bosnia.

Unlike the earlier uses of force in Bosnia outlined above, the decision to resort to coercive diplomacy in 1995 was directed toward a broader, more comprehensive goal: achieving an agreement that would put an end to the fighting. This was a goal shared by the United States and its allies, who also were concerned about the consequences of a collapse of the UN mission for their troops on the ground. This shared interest in avoiding catastrophe made the management of alliance politics over Bosnia more tractable in the period July–October 1995 than it had been at any point in the previous three years. The actions of the United States combined the "flexible diplomacy" described by Alexander George as including "accommodation" of the interests of the target(s) of coercion, with a "quite limited" use of force. Because coercive diplomacy was being applied to multiple actors in 1995, the threats, inducements, and actual force applied by the coercing party (the United States) varied with respect to each actor over the course of the effort, as well as from actor to actor at any given moment.

The success of coercive diplomacy in Bosnia in 1995 was built first on the foundation of changes in the military situation on the ground in the direction of a stalemate or standoff between the parties. In the literature on conflict resolution, the emergence of such a stalemate is seen as "ripening" and is characterized as "hurting" when each party is assumed to be neither willing or capable of enduring it nor able to overcome it. In Bosnia, . . . contrary to the spontaneous process posited in the literature, the "ripening" process in Bosnia was manufactured or engineered by the coercing power. U.S. support for the development of the regular Croatian army and its war-fighting capacity began more than a year earlier, before coercive diplomacy was adopted as a strategy. Moreover, the stalemate in Bosnia was clearly not "hurting"; it was a stalemate enforced by the United States, which was determined not to allow the strategic balance between Croatia and Serbia that was essential to regional stability to be tipped in favor of Croatia. It should be noted that a major role in establishing the conditions for this stalemate was played by the tragedies in Srebrenica and Zepa, which involved genocidal killing of Muslims by Serbs but which were greeted by some U.S. officials as events that eliminated heretofore thorny "map problems."

The second factor contributing to the success of coercive diplomacy in Bosnia also involved a change in the U.S. political position from one-sided support for the Bosnian Muslims (and Bosnian Croats, to the extent that these two parties could be kept in agreement) to recognition of the need to address the real and often conflicting interests of all sides, including the outside actors, Serbia (Milosevic) and Croatia (Tudjman). A December 1994 NATO declaration calling for "equitable and balanced arrangements" signaled the onset of this transformation. It was completed by the de facto recognition of "Republika Srpska" and partition of Bosnia incorporated in a September 1 agreement negotiated by Holbrooke with Milosevic and the Bosnian Serbs, which provided the general framework for the later Dayton settlement.

The key to securing Milosevic's cooperation from this point on, including his dramatic role at Dayton, appears to have been the combination of a credible threat that the Bosnian Serbs would be defeated on the battlefield, thereby tipping the larger balance of power in the region against Serbia, and the positive inducements of recognition for the Bosnian Serb republic and a promise to lift sanctions against Serbia (formally, the Federal Republic of Yugoslavia, or FRY, which includes the republic of Montenegro). The threat was made credible by the successes of the Croatian army and by the application of limited but significant U.S. and NATO airpower. Milosevic's interest in lifting sanctions had been clear since 1993, and he had been pursuing that interest in intensive negotiations in May and

June 1995 with the U.S. diplomat then responsible for Bosnia, Robert Frasure. Milosevic's cooperation at Dayton, secured in an apparent deal with Holbrooke in exchange for sanctions lifting, is actually the beginning of the overlapping story of intervention in Kosovo, to which we will return later.

The third factor in the successful application of coercive diplomacy to ending the war in Bosnia, of course, was the use of airpower. These words are often followed by the phrase "against the Serbs." But the story in Bosnia, at least, was more subtle; airpower was used not only to pressure the Serbs into specific action on the ground—primarily a withdrawal from around Sarajevo—but also to pressure the Muslims into accepting the emerging partition of Bosnia; and it was the end of bombing that opened the door to a cease-fire agreement and all-party negotiations, not vice versa. The agreement on "basic constitutional principles" for Bosnia, signed by the foreign ministers of Croatia, Serbia, and Bosnia on September 8 in Geneva, was reached while the bombing was still in progress. But the bombing did not, in fact, "bring the Serbs to the negotiating table." Milosevic was already moving in early August toward establishing control over the Bosnian Serbs so as to bring them to the negotiating table, and he had completed his moves before the bombing began. It was the Bosnian Muslims who were brought to the negotiating table by the bombing or, more accurately, by the threat that it would be ended if they did not agree to the U.S. settlement. The initial decision to "suspend" the bombing on September 14 came in exchange for an agreement by the Bosnian Serbs to withdraw their heavy weapons from the exclusion zone around Sarajevo and end the siege of that city.

At the same time, the United States did not allow the combined Croatian-Muslim offensive in western Bosnia that followed the ouster of the Krajina Serbs to inflict too great a defeat on the Bosnian Serbs. To have done so might have drawn Serbia into the conflict directly and threatened the strategic balance in the region. The bombing in Bosnia constituted the "exemplary use of quite limited force to persuade the opponent to back down" consistent with the concept of coercive diplomacy. George defines "exemplary" as "the use of just enough force of an appropriate kind to demonstrate resolution to protect one's interests and to establish the credibility of one's determination to use more force if necessary."[3] A military analyst points out that the total bombing effort in Bosnia "equated to just about a busy day's sorties count for coalition air forces during the Gulf War" and characterizes it as "a strategically limited, tactically intense, high-technology, coalition air campaign, conducted under tight restraints of time and permissible collateral damage . . . aimed at coercing political and military compliance from a regional opponent who had no airpower."[4] The United States and its NATO allies were careful not to use so much force as to lead either side to believe that all was won or lost, thereby creating real incentives to accept the U.S.-brokered settlement.

To a certain extent, the "balancing act" carried out by U.S. diplomats—led by Richard Holbrooke—in their relations with the Serbs, Croats, and Muslims during the bombing was necessitated by the pressures exerted by the British, French, and Russians. The British and the French refused to "wage war on behalf of the Muslim-led government,"[5] while the Russians continued to oppose the bombing. However, "balancing" reflected to a far greater extent the difficulties of applying the techniques of coercive diplomacy to the behaviors of multiple parties with conflicting interests. This is a far more difficult task than attempting to affect the behavior of a single opponent. By facilitating the emergence of a Croatian ground army and using airpower against the Bosnian Serb army, the United States encouraged the political and territorial ambitions of the Croats and the Muslims. The United States, therefore, did not prevent the Bosnian Serbs from using artillery withdrawn from Sarajevo, and Serbian airpower, to stop the Croatian and Muslim advance in western Bosnia. Whereas Holbrooke had blamed the Serbs for the difficulties of negotiations in August and September, for example, by October he was blaming the Muslims for blocking the conclusion of a cease-fire agreement. On October 4 Holbrooke cautioned Bosnian president Alija Izetbegovic that he was "playing craps with the destiny of his country" by refusing to agree to a cease-fire and warned him that "[i]f you want to let the fighting go on, that is your right, but do not expect the United States to be your air force."[6] Despite this threat, the Bosnian Muslims refused to agree to a cease-fire until they had extracted a commitment from the United States to provide them with military assistance. Thus, the coercing power (the United States) was compelled to supply positive inducements to cooperation to all the targets of its coercive actions (the Bosnian Muslims, Serbs, and Croats; and both Croatia/Tudjman and Serbia/Milosevic).

Milosevic's cooperation was the direct result of the coercive diplomacy—the combination of threats, inducements, and actual use of force—exercised by the United States. That cooperation hastened the end of the fighting in Bosnia. Thus, coercive diplomacy in Bosnia in the summer and fall of 1995 achieved its immediate goal and should be considered a success. But the importance of Milosevic's cooperation to secure an end to the fighting, an agreement at Dayton, and its (partial) implementation made it more difficult for the United States and its NATO allies to achieve a similar success with respect to the conflict in Kosovo.

## KOSOVO IN LIGHT OF BOSNIA: DRAWING THE WRONG LESSON

Both U.S. policymakers and the primary target of their attention in Kosovo, Slobodan Milosevic, seem to have learned only some of the lessons of the Bosnian endgame, or to have learned the wrong lessons. One of the most important lessons of Bosnia could be summarized as "the longer a violent conflict is allowed to go on, the more difficult it is to end." Western policymakers simply waited too long to act in Kosovo. Earlier action might have avoided the need for coercive diplomacy.

U.S. and other Western policymakers also seem to have erred in precisely the way Alexander George suggests is likely in "cases in which some version of an ultimatum proved to be effective." George warns that it is "incorrect" to conclude from such cases "that resort to the strong variant of coercive diplomacy was the sole or primary factor contributing to its success." He reiterates that "[c]risis bargaining can use persuasion, coercion, and/or accommodation" and argues that "the policymaker must decide *what combination* of these three elements to employ *and in what sequence*"(George's emphasis).[7] Clearly, finding a viable combination of these elements was even more difficult in Kosovo than in Bosnia; but given timely action, it appears not to have been impossible. The United States was able to turn negotiation of a settlement in Bosnia into a non-zero-sum game. In Kosovo, by the time policymakers turned their attention to the conflict, it had also become three-sided—involving the independence-minded and militant Kosova Liberation Army (KLA); the more moderate nationalist political movement, the Democratic League of Kosova (LDK); and Milosevic—and had turned into a decidedly zero-sum game.

Confronted with the irreconcilable positions of the three parties, U.S. policymakers turned to what Alexander George calls "the starkest variant" of coercive diplomacy: "a full-fledged ultimatum."[8] However, that ultimatum was deficient in two critical respects. The demands finally settled upon by the coercing power (the United States), as defined at Rambouillet, were impossible for the opponent (Milosevic or any other Serbian leadership) to accept in the absence of powerful positive inducements. The threat lacked credibility and, when carried out, proved insufficiently potent to achieve compellence. In attempting to formulate a credible threat to back up their demands, U.S. policymakers neglected the critical role of Croatian ground forces in the Bosnian endgame. The singular emphasis on airpower in Kosovo, and the belief among some senior U.S. policymakers that all it would take would be a few days of bombing, appears to have been based on a faulty interpretation of the events surrounding the endgame in Bosnia. This conviction, as well as concerns about the domestic political costs of committing ground troops, led U.S. policymakers to take even the possibility of deploying ground forces "off the table" and thus to weaken the coercive threat they were attempting to construct.

There is little concrete evidence concerning the policy calculations of the opponent. If the behavior of Milosevic conforms to George's assumption of "pure rationality," then we can infer certain calculations from his actions. On this basis we can say that in constructing his response to the coercive diplomacy being brought to bear against him in fall 1998, Milosevic also seems to have misread the relevant lessons to be drawn from the Bosnian experience. Milosevic clearly failed to understand the singular importance of Srebrenica, the powerful emotive force of the specter of genocide for Western policymakers, and the effect this would have on decisions about the level of force to be used against him. In effect, Milosevic chose to escalate the crisis on the ground in Kosovo—to use George and William Simons's terms, "to initiate war himself rather than accept the demand."[9]

Milosevic's escalatory response appears to have been based on a calculation that failed to take into account the impact of genocidal killing and the flight of massive numbers of refugees on the calculations of U.S. and NATO policymakers. . . .

## FROM COERCIVE DIPLOMACY TO COERCION

The U.S. response to the escalating conflict in Kosovo was formulated in the context of a mounting domestic political crisis. The U.S. House of Representatives was moving in the fall of 1998 toward a vote to impeach President Clinton. That vote was cast in mid-December. The Senate trial of the president took place in early 1999. One consequence of this crisis appears to have been a significant increase in the influence of the secretary of state over U.S. responses to developments in Kosovo. During the Bosnia crisis, then ambassador Albright had been a clear advocate of the use of force even when its use appeared likely to have involved great costs. By the time of Kosovo crisis, some more cautious actors were gone from the administration, as in the case of Chairman of the Joint Chiefs of Staff General Colin Powell, or removed from the foreign policymaking apparatus to bolster the president's effort to defend himself against impeachment, as in the case of Greg Craig, who left as director of the State Department Policy Planning Staff to join the White House legal defense team in mid-September 1998. Thus, as the conflict on the ground in Kosovo grew more violent and efforts to negotiate grew more difficult, the relative influence of the primary advocate of the use of force grew more powerful.

George argues that "both the objective of coercive diplomacy and the means employed on its behalf are likely to be sensitive to the type of relationship the coercing power hopes to have with the opponent after the crisis is over."[10] There is little evidence that U.S. policymakers hoped to have a constructive relationship with Milosevic after the Kosovo crisis. They appear to have been motivated largely by a desire to punish him for his actions in Kosovo, and in no small part by a desire to atone for what some felt to have been their failure to act early enough in Bosnia or even in 1991, when former Yugoslavia collapsed. Animus toward Milosevic had continued to mount in the period since Dayton. For Secretary Albright and others, use of force offered an opportunity to pay Milosevic back for Bosnia, as well as for Kosovo. In March 1998 Secretary Albright had pressed the Contact Group foreign ministers to act by arguing that "history is watching us, and we have an opportunity to make up for the mistakes that had been made four or five years ago."[11] But as one participant in a December 1998 discussion argued, "as long as there were no atrocities committed in Kosovo that might conjure up memories of ethnic cleansing in Bosnia, the West would not intervene."[12]

By perpetrating the brutal massacre of forty-five civilians in the Kosovo village of Račak in January 1999, the Serbs appear to have crossed that perceptual threshold, conjuring up images and memories of Bosnia and diverting attention away from the actions of the KLA. The Račak massacre thus provided the emo-

258 Steven L. Burg

tional impetus for policymakers to abandon what appears to have been a White House strategy of negotiating with Milosevic, as embodied in the Holbrooke missions of May and October, for the strategy of coercion embodied in a plan put forward by Secretary Albright. According to "confidants" of Secretary Albright, quoted in an April 1999 media analysis of the decision to use force, Albright "realized that the galvanizing force of the atrocity would not last long. 'Whatever threat of force you don't get in the next two weeks you're never getting,' one advisor told her, 'at least until the next Racak.'"[13]

According to one participant in the Clinton administration's deliberations, quoted in an April media analysis, the massacre at Račak led U.S. policymakers to adopt a strategy consisting of four elements: a demand that the conflicting parties attend a meeting; presentation at the meeting of demands—including deployment of a NATO implementation force in Kosovo—decided upon in advance by the Contact Group, including Russia; nonnegotiability of these demands; and a credible threat of military force to back up the demands. These elements correspond almost precisely to George's definition of "a full-fledged ultimatum." According to George, "[a] classic ultimatum has three components: (1) a demand on the opponent; (2) a time limit or sense of urgency for compliance with the demand; and (3) a threat of punishment for noncompliance that is both credible to the opponent and sufficiently potent to impress upon him that compliance is preferable."[14]

George's model of coercive diplomacy suggests that whether an ultimatum will succeed depends heavily on the relative interests at stake for each actor. For the United States, the articulated interests were, for the most part, abstract. Secretary Albright defined these in a key public speech before the United States Institute of Peace in early February 1999. They included peace and stability in Southern Europe, strengthening institutions that keep the peace, preserving Bosnia's progress toward peace, and strengthening democratic principles and practices in the region. Secretary Albright also identified three more compelling interests. The first of these, preventing a flood of refugees and creation of havens for international terrorists, drug traffickers, and criminals, was, however, an interest that appeared to be of more immediate concern to the European allies than to the United States. The second and third were interrelated: preventing the spread of conflict to Albania and Macedonia and the involvement of Greece and Turkey, and preserving NATO's credibility as the guarantor of peace and stability in Europe. Unlike the situation in Bosnia in 1995, however, there were as yet no allied troops on the ground and at risk in Kosovo. The threat to alliance cohesion and the survival of NATO was thus not yet as pronounced in Kosovo as it had been in Bosnia in 1995. President Clinton, in a radio talk later in February 1999, underscored the importance of preventing both spillover of the conflict and a massive refugee crisis in the middle of Europe. But these interests represented relatively distant concerns for the United States. For Milosevic, in contrast, it was clear that the territorial integrity of his country was at risk. However, the overriding interest at stake in the conflict for him appears to have been his own personal power.

George warns that "if the coercing power pursues ambitious objectives that go beyond its own vital or important interests, and if its demands infringe on vital or important interests of the adversary, then the asymmetry of interests and balance of motivation will favor the adversary and make successful application of coercive diplomacy much more difficult."[15] In the case of Kosovo the interests at stake appear, at least at the outset, to have been relatively greater for Milosevic than for U.S. policymakers. Thus, using George's terms, the asymmetry of interests and motivations seem to have favored the adversary. This asymmetry appears to have been reinforced in Kosovo by the fact that the demands placed on Milosevic proved unacceptable, and the threat behind the ultimatum lacked, from Milosevic's perspective, sufficient credibility or potency (or both) to require compliance.

## DEMANDS AND THREATS

By late January 1999 the United States and its NATO allies had agreed on a combination of demands and threats. The substantive demands were advanced through the Contact Group, which included the Russians. But because the Russians were not willing to endorse the use of force, the threat of force was advanced through NATO, which excluded the Russians. On January 29 the Contact Group, after acknowledging that "both Belgrade's security forces and the Kosovo Liberation Army (KLA) are responsible" for "the escalation in violence," demanded that Yugoslavia stop all offensive actions/repression in Kosovo; comply fully with the October agreements; cooperate with the Verification Mission and the International Tribunal, including full investigation of the Račak massacre; and promote the safe return of refugees and displaced persons and the delivery of humanitarian aid to the people of Kosovo. These, for the most part, reiterated already-articulated demands. The Contact Group also called upon the Kosovo Albanians to comply with all relevant Security Council resolutions and condemned KLA "provocations." The Contact Group called on "both sides . . . to commit themselves to a process of negotiation leading to a political settlement." It "insisted" on acceptance of the principles set out by the Contact Group and "summoned" representatives of the Kosovo Albanians and Yugoslavia/Serbia to negotiations at Rambouillet, with "the direct involvement of the Contact Group," to be based on a revised version of the draft developed by negotiators but rejected by both sides in late 1998. It set a deadline of seven days for conclusion of an agreement but allowed for the possibility of an extension of "less than one week," if justified.

The Contact Group demands and call for talks on January 29 were backed up by an explicit NATO threat, adopted by the North Atlantic Council on January 30, to "take whatever measures are necessary in the light of both parties' compliance with international commitments and requirements, including in particular assessment by the Contact Group of the response to its demands, to avert a humanitarian catastrophe, by compelling compliance with the demands of the international community and the achievement of a political settlement." The council empowered the NATO secretary-general to "authorize air strikes against targets on FRY territory." But, cognizant of the fact that the conflict in Kosovo had become (at least) three-sided, the council noted that the NATO secretary-general "will take full account of the position and actions of the Kosovar leadership and all Kosovar armed elements in and around Kosovo in reaching his decision on military action. NATO will take all appropriate measures in case of a failure by the Kosovar Albanian side to comply with the demands of the international community."[16] Although no UN Security Council resolution authorized NATO's use of force, UN secretary-general Kofi Annan, speaking at NATO headquarters in Brussels on January 28, emphasized "combination of force and diplomacy" as "the key to peace in the Balkans" and observed that "[t]he bloody wars of the last decade have left us with no illusions about the difficulty of halting internal conflicts—by reason or by force—particularly against the wishes of the government of a sovereign state. But nor have they left us with any illusions about the need to use force, when all other means have failed." He then declared, "We may be reaching that limit, once again, in the former Yugoslavia."[17] This represented a clear, and unprecedented, endorsement of the NATO threat to use force. Thus, the strategy adopted by the United States and its allies in January 1999 had all the characteristics of an ultimatum, directed against Milosevic and the Serbs, but contingent on cooperation by the Kosovar Albanians, including the KLA.

The Contact Group then promulgated a list of "non-negotiable principles/basic elements for a settlement."[18] Prominent among these was the requirement to establish "a mechanism for final settlement after an interim period of three years." Marc Weller reports that Western negotiators presented a draft agreement to the parties at the outset of the conference on February 6. Unlike the Dayton conference that ended the Bosnian war, there is little evidence that either side had agreed to the basic principles or concepts of an agreement. Indeed, . . . there is abundant evidence that both sides had already in late 1998 rejected the approach adopted by negotiators. Nonetheless, the Albanian delegation at Rambouillet, which included a cross section of Kosovar Albanian political leaders including representatives of the KLA, responded constructively to the proposal. The Yugoslav/Serbian delegation remained unresponsive. The British press reported at the time that some European diplomats "close to the Kosovo talks" had warned the United States to "stop treating Serbia like Iraq" and told the KLA that it must drop its demands for independence. Nonetheless, a controversial trip to Belgrade by the chief U.S. negotiator, Ambassador Christopher Hill, to deal directly with Milosevic in an effort to overcome Serb resistance to the proposed settlement produced instead a Serbian response that consisted of an almost complete rejection of the proposal. According to Weller, negotiators then attempted to meet Serbian objections by altering the proposed draft without at the same time consulting the Albanian delegation. When it became apparent that neither the Serbs nor the Albanians could or would agree to the revised draft, . . . more intensive negotiations in the form of "genuine proximity talks" got under way. The Albanian delegation, unhappy with the effort of negotiators to accommodate the Serbs, was persuaded to accept the proposed agreement only under intense pressure from the United States.

Secretary Albright traveled to Rambouillet to lobby the Kosovar Albanian delegation or, in the words of her press spokesman, James Rubin, "help to push the Kosovar Albanians across the finish line so that they can agree to the combined political and military package."[19] At a press conference in Rambouillet Secretary Albright made her argument public. She explained that

[i]f we have a yes from both sides, we will have an implementation force. If the talks crater because the Serbs do not say yes, we will have bombing. If the talks crater because the Albanians have not said yes, we will not be able to support them, and in fact we will have to cut off whatever help they are getting from the outside. If it fails because both parties say no, there will not be bombing of Serbia and we will try to figure out ways to continue trying to deal with both sides.[20]

NATO air strikes against the Serbs were thus explicitly contingent on Kosovar Albanian acquiescence to the Rambouillet accord in much the same way that air strikes against the Serbs in Bosnia had been made contingent on Bosnian Muslim acquiescence to the agreements that later were incorporated in the Dayton Peace Accords. This represented both a positive and a negative inducement to cooperation. The Kosovar Albanians were also offered a more clearly positive inducement to cooperate in the form of incorporation of "the will of the people" into the mechanism for determining a final settlement—manifest in a referendum of the people of Kosovo. For the Albanians, this provision established what appeared to be a road map to independence. For the Serbs, however, there appear to have been few, if any, positive inducements to cooperate. This made it impossible for U.S. negotiators to find a formula that could accommodate both the Kosovar Albanians and the Serbs and ended the Rambouillet process. There is little support in the publicly available documents, however, for the contention of a senior U.S. official, reported in the press after two weeks of bombing, that the proposed agreement "walked right up to the edge of appeasement" of Milosevic.[21]

The proposed settlement put on the table by the United States at the meeting at Rambouillet may be viewed as a valid peace plan, a flawed peace plan that nonetheless represented a genuine effort to reach a settlement, or a "turn-down" proposal. From the latter perspective, the events at Rambouillet are seen not as an effort actually to negotiate a settlement as had been the case at Dayton, but as an effort to gain support for and legitimate the use of force by presenting an ultimatum known in advance to be unacceptable to the Serbs so as to frame the Kosovo conflict as one in which the Serbs "rejected peace." U.S. policymakers understood at the outset that there was, in the words of Ambassador Hill, "zero point zero" chance of the Serbs accepting the proposed settlement. Secretary Albright, as we have seen, publicly linked the use of force to Kosovar Albanian acceptance and Serb rejection of the proposal. She also acknowledged in a later interview with the *New York Times* that Rambouillet was crucial for "getting [the Europeans] to agree to the use of force."[22] But there is insufficient evidence to support this view, and the fact that the last phase of the Rambouillet process involved an effort by U.S. negotiators to meet Serb objections argues against it.

Secretary Albright's apparent eagerness to turn to force was matched, nonetheless, by Milosevic's willingness to accept bombing by NATO rather than sign the agreement. Developments following the October 1998 agreements had made it clear that the withdrawal of Yugoslav forces called for in the implementation provisions would quickly be exploited by the KLA. In Kosovo the coercing power could not control or even influence the KLA as effectively as it had been able to do with respect to the warring parties in Bosnia. The Bosnian Serb and Bosnian Croat forces had been under the effective control of Serbia and Croatia, each of which had broader interests that were better served by peace in Bosnia than by further war, and to which U.S. negotiators could appeal. The KLA was not under the control and was subject to only limited influence by any outside actor. Its medium- and long-term interests were not served by peace and certainly not by any arrangements that preserved a Serbian presence in and sovereignty over Kosovo. Although represented at Rambouillet, the KLA was not a party to the negotiations over the draft proposal leading up to the meeting and remained a competitor or even adversary to the coercing power's main negotiating partner in Kosovo, the LDK. There was little reason to believe that the KLA would comply with the disarmament provisions of the Rambouillet proposal. Acceptance of Rambouillet therefore raised the specter, from Milosevic's perspective, of the occupation of Kosovo by foreign troops and the takeover of power in Kosovo by the KLA.

George cautions that, in formulating a strategy of coercive diplomacy, "the coercing power . . . must leave the opponent with a way out of the crisis that enables him at least to save face and avoid humiliation."[23] George's description of the impact of the U.S. oil embargo on Japan seems to apply equally well to the consequences of the Rambouillet proposal for Milosevic and the Serbs:

Backed into a corner and given no acceptable diplomatic way out, and confronted by the humiliating demand that they give up their imperialistic achievements and aspirations, Japan's desperate leaders felt they were left with no acceptable alternative but to initiate what they knew to be a highly risky war against a militarily and economically stronger opponent.[24]

For Milosevic, initiating war in Kosovo entailed enduring a threatened air attack by NATO while carrying out plans to eliminate the KLA and expel a large proportion of the ethnically Albanian population from Kosovo by force.

The NATO threat failed to compel Milosevic to comply with the Contact Group demands or to deter Milosevic from initiating war. George cautions that with respect to the effectiveness of a threat, it is not the coercing party's commitments and beliefs that are crucial; "[r]ather, it is the target's estimate of the credibility and potency of the threat that is critical."[25] A NATO threat of air strikes against Yugoslavia had been an important element in the successful exercise of coercive diplomacy in October 1998. At that time, General Klaus Naumann explained later to a U.S. Senate committee, "we were sent to Belgrade with a clear stick in our hip pocket, the ultimatum." By January 1999, he argued, "this stick had been transformed into a rubber baton since our threat was not as credible as it used to be in October. We had threatened too often and hadn't done anything."[26]

The credibility of the coercive threat mounted by the United States and its NATO allies also was weakened by Russian and Chinese diplomatic opposition to Security Council authorization of the use of force, which heretofore had been an essential step in the establishment of credibility. On several occasions in September and October 1998 Russian and Chinese officials warned publicly against any use of force against Yugoslavia. Both Russia and China abstained from voting even for UN Security Council Resolution 1203 (October 24, 1998), which endorsed the October agreements, despite the fact that the resolution did not provide authorization for any military action by NATO. While there can be no doubt that a humanitarian disaster was developing in Kosovo at the time, it appears that Western diplomatic and political rhetoric shifted to "humanitarian disaster" as justification for the threat and, later, use of force because Russian and Chinese opposition to the use of force made it unlikely NATO could secure Security Council authorization.

Milosevic's estimate of the probable potency of the NATO threat was likely to have taken into account the relatively limited air campaign conducted in Bosnia in 1995 and the similarly limited action taken by the United States and Britain against Iraq in December 1997. Ivo Daalder and Michael O'Hanlon argue that that action "demonstrated that air strikes designed to 'degrade' an opponent's military capability—even that of an opponent as feared and loathed as Saddam Hussein, ruling a country in a region of critical interest to the United States, and possessing the capacity to produce weapons of mass destruction—would likely last only a few days."[27] Knowledge that some senior U.S. policymakers were, in fact, operating on the assumption that "Milosevic would probably back down after a few visible targets were hit"[28] may also have contributed to lowering his estimate of the NATO threat. Secretary Albright stated publicly at the outset of the bombing that "I don't see this as a long-term operation. . . . I think this is something . . . achievable within a relatively short period of time."[29] Senior British and French defense officials reported in interviews conducted by Robert Art in June and July 2000 that this view was widely shared among the allies.

It is almost certainly the case that the absence of any threat of a ground assault also lowered Milosevic's estimate of the potency of the NATO threat. The central lesson of the endgame in Bosnia for U.S. policymakers should have been that the creation and deployment of a credible ground force—in the case of Bosnia, the army of Croatia and its operations to expel the Serbs from the Krajina region and take control of much of western Bosnia—was critical to the success of coercive diplomacy. Nonetheless, resistance to the use of ground forces on the part of some U.S. policymakers was a matter of public record. This resistance can be attributed to continuing opposition from within the U.S. military, the absence of a viable military plan of action, concern about divisions with Congress and among NATO allies, and opinion polls indicating that the U.S. public believed no U.S. interests were at stake and no U.S. troops should be involved.

Given the reasonable expectation that NATO air strikes would be limited in duration and scope as in Bosnia . . . and [in] the absence of any immediate threat of a ground invasion, the potency of the NATO threat of force was insufficient either to compel or deter Milosevic. However, any expectation on Milosevic's part that the United States and NATO would not be able to sustain the bombing and that, as in Bosnia, the United States would negotiate with him while the bombing unfolded and accommodate at least some of his real interests proved misplaced. Unlike the case in Bosnia, the motivations of U.S. policymakers were quite different now. Within ten days of the start of the bombing, U.S. and European policymakers were considering adding the removal of Milosevic from power to the list of NATO objectives, making it "a condition for stopping the war," and Secretary of State Albright was asking publicly whether it was "going to be possible to deal with somebody that [*sic*] is behind all this?"[30] When the motivation for the use of force is punishment, there are likely to be few constraints on its use, and few incentives to be flexible in diplomacy or to accommodate the interests of one's opponent—key factors contributing to the success of coercive diplomacy in Bosnia. When the motivation for the use of force is, in fact, to oust the opponent from power, the coercing actor may have every incentive to put forward unacceptable demands so as to compel the target to resist, thereby legitimating the use of force against him. . . .

## CONCLUSION

The success of coercive diplomacy in Bosnia, and its contrasting failure and displacement by a strategy of ultimatum in Kosovo, highlight some of the limitations of coercive diplomacy and underscore the importance of certain propositions for its conduct advanced by Alexander George. Both the Bosnian and Kosovo cases suggest the difficulty of employing coercive diplomacy in a conflict involving multiple actors: a threat or inducement aimed at affecting the behavior of one target actor also affects the behaviors of others. Threats or coercion applied against one in order to encourage that party to negotiate or comply may make another less willing to negotiate or comply, or may even be exploited to another's advantage, thereby potentially worsening the situation rather than moving it toward a solution. In Bosnia the United States and its allies faced multiple actors with conflicting interests. But the United States also enjoyed direct or, in the case of the Bosnian Serbs, indirect leverage over all the parties. In Kosovo, in contrast, the coercing party exercised no leverage over the KLA and rapidly declining leverage over the LDK and Milosevic. This absence of leverage over the conflicting parties undermined the October 1998 agreement, which initially had all the makings of a successful exercise in coercive diplomacy. The October 1998 Belgrade agreement looked very much like the coercive diplomacy exercised by NATO in summer 1993 and February 1994 in Bosnia that led to pullbacks of the Bosnian Serbs around Sarajevo. But it is important to recall that one key to securing Bosnian Serb compliance with the NATO ultimatums was preventing the Serbs' adversary—the Bosnian Muslims—from taking advantage of their withdrawals. Similarly, compliance with the October 1998 Belgrade agreement was acceptable to Milosevic and the Serbs only as long as it did not result in gains for the KLA. The resurgence of the KLA in the wake of the October agreement posed a direct threat to Milosevic's leadership in Belgrade and demonstrated the inability of the United States and its allies to contain the KLA threat in the way they had earlier contained the Bosnian Muslims.

The Bosnian and Kosovo cases involve repeated efforts by the United States and its allies to persuade, induce, and even compel compliance in ending an armed conflict. In both cases these efforts remained inadequate—that is, they did not include all the elements of coercive diplomacy or an ultimatum strategy—until the United States and its European allies finally achieved a clear unity of purpose. This did not occur until both U.S. and European policymakers shared the perception of a real threat to their national and common interests. The resort to coercive diplomacy by the United States in Bosnia in 1995 was driven for the most part by a clear sense of national interest in avoiding a potential military catastrophe that could prove costly to the United States and threaten the survival of the NATO alliance. This national interest was reinforced by a sense of political self-interest on the part of the Clinton administration in resolving the Bosnian issue well before the 1996 presidential election campaign. The Europeans were concerned about the consequences of a collapse of the UN mission for their troops on the ground, as well as the implications of unrestrained warfare on their southern flank. This shared interest in avoiding catastrophe made the management of alliance politics over Bosnia more tractable in the period July–October 1995 than it had been at any point in the previous three years. Similarly, in the case of Kosovo it was clear by the April 1999 NATO summit that European and U.S. policymakers perceived the challenge posed by Milosevic as a potential threat to the coherence, if not the survival of the alliance. As in the case of Bosnia, preservation of the NATO alliance was a powerful motivation for the use of force to ensure success and reinforced the commitment of U.S. and European policymakers to a strategy of coercion.

In the Bosnian case the balance of interests and motivations . . . favored Milosevic and the Bosnian Serbs until late 1994/early 1995. At that point, the balance shifted quickly in favor of the United States and its European allies, for the reasons suggested earlier and because Milosevic's interests began to diverge sharply from those of the Bosnian Serbs. That divergence can be attributed to the positive inducement of U.S. promises to lift sanctions on Serbia (Yugoslavia) in exchange for cooperation in ending the Bosnian war. At the same time, concessions to the Bosnian Serbs in the form of de facto partition of Bosnia and establishment of the Bosnian Serb Republic as a constituent part of the Bosnian state acted as strong positive inducements to Bosnian Serb cooperation. The Bosnian Muslims, too, were offered a significant positive inducement to cooperate: the promise of military assistance from the United States. They were also subjected to a threat: abandonment. The Bosnian case thus provides clear evidence of the importance of positive inducements to a successful strategy of coercive diplomacy.

In the Kosovo case the interests at stake appear, at least at the outset, to have been relatively greater for Milosevic than for U.S. policymakers. Those interests all favored resisting the NATO ultimatum. George warns that "if the coercing power pursues ambitious objectives that go beyond its own vital or important interests, and if its demands infringe on vital or important interests of the adversary, then the asymmetry of interests and balance of motivation will favor the adversary and make successful application of coercive diplomacy much more difficult."[31] Thus, in George's terms, the asymmetry of interests and motivations seem to have favored Milosevic at the outset of the NATO bombing campaign. This asymmetry was reinforced by the fact that there were few positive inducements for Milosevic to cooperate once the KLA reemerged after the October 1998 agreements and that the threat behind the NATO ultimatum lacked, from Milosevic's perspective, sufficient credibility or potency (or both) to command compliance. This asymmetry appears to have been an important factor leading Milosevic to adopt an asymmetrical response to the NATO ultimatum—escalation in the form of ethnic cleansing and mass expulsions of the Kosovar Albanians. In terms of George's analytical framework, however, Milosevic's escalatory response shifted the asymmetry of motivations in favor of the United States and its allies, making it easier for them to sustain the ultimatum strategy and engage in an escalation of their own.

George argues that "both the objective of coercive diplomacy and the means employed on its behalf are likely to be sensitive to the type of relationship the coercing power hopes to have with the opponent after the crisis is over."[32] In Bosnia it was clear that the West would have to continue to deal with Milosevic in order to secure the settlement in Bosnia and resolve other outstanding issues, including Kosovo. But in the case of Kosovo, in contrast, there is little evidence that U.S. policymakers hoped to have a constructive relationship with Milosevic after the crisis. As we have seen, U.S. policymakers appear to have been motivated largely by a desire to punish Milosevic for his actions in Kosovo and in Bosnia. When the motivation for the use of force is punishment, there are likely to be few constraints on its use against the target, and few incentives to be flexible in diplomacy or to accommodate the interests of the adversary. The actions of the United States and its allies in Bosnia thus combined the "flexible diplomacy" described by Alexander George as including "accommodation" of the interests of the target(s) of coercion, with a "quite limited" use of force. These were key factors contributing to the success of coercive diplomacy in Bosnia, and their absence in Kosovo led inevitably to adoption of the ultimatum strategy by U.S. policymakers. As we have seen, within ten days of the start of the bombing, U.S. and European policymakers were considering adding the removal of Milosevic from power to the list of NATO objectives. In late May Milosevic was indicted for war crimes by The Hague Tribunal, with substantial support from the United States. When the motivation for the use of force is, in fact, to oust the opponent from power, the constraints on the use of force and the incentives to be flexible for the coercing actor are even weaker, thereby legitimating the escalation of force against him.

Escalation of the air campaign against Milosevic and Yugoslavia was consistent with the full-fledged ultimatum strategy on which the United States and the European allies embarked in January 1999. In the absence of negotiation, however, escalation can end only with the military defeat of the adversary. This was an outcome that far exceeded the goals of NATO in Kosovo, raised even greater problems for the alliance than the conflict in Kosovo, and contradicted the allies' own interests. According to then U.S. deputy national security adviser James Steinberg, speaking in May 1999, "A ground war in Kosovo . . . could lead to a split in the NATO alliance or a rupture with Russia that would threaten U.S. interests and European stability in ways reaching far beyond the Balkans."[33] In order to end the war in a manner consistent with their own interest in avoiding a ground war and the inevitable need to defeat and occupy Serbia, the coercing power(s) were required to move from the pure strategy of coercion, or ultimatum, upon which the bombing was initiated, to a strategy involving at least limited, mediated negotiations with the target of their actions. . . . Russian participation was crucial to the success of this effort. As a result, Western and particularly U.S. actions moved somewhat closer to the model of coercive diplomacy outlined by Alexander George, in which "signaling, bargaining, and negotiating are important dimensions . . . though their roles vary in different crises."[34] In the Kosovo case we can say that the role of bargaining was far more limited than it was in Bosnia, but its reintroduction reflected the inherent limits of the full-fledged ultimatum strategy.

## NOTES

1. Madeleine Albright, quoted in Steven L. Burg and Paul S. Shoup, *The War in Bosnia-Herzegovina: Ethnic Conflict and International Intervention* (Armonk, N.Y.: M. E. Sharpe, 1999), 291.

2. Richard Holbrooke, quoted in Burg and Shoup, *The War in Bosnia-Herzegovina,* 325.

3. Alexander L. George, *Forceful Persuasion: Coercive Diplomacy as an Alternative to War* (Washington, D.C.: United States Institute of Peace Press, 991), 5.

4. Robert C. Owen, "The Balkans Air Campaign Study," part 1 and part 2, *Airpower Journal* 11, nos. 2 and 3 (summer 1997 and fall 1997): part 2, 8, 20.

5. Bob Woodward, *The Choice* (New York: Simon & Schuster, 1996), 357.

6. Richard Holbrooke, quoted in Woodward, *The Choice,* 359.

7. George, *Forceful Persuasion,* 73.

8. Ibid., 7.

9. Alexander L. George and William Simons, "Findings and Conclusions," in *The Limits of Coercive Diplomacy,* ed. Alexander L. George and William E. Simons, 2d ed. (Boulder, Colo.: Westview Press, 1994), 277.

10. George, *Forceful Persuasion,* 71.

11. *Washington Post,* April 18, 1999, www.washingtonpost.com.

12. Steven L. Burg, "The Failure of Early Warning in Kosovo," in *The Application of Prevention,* Report of the Center for Preventive Action's Fifth Annual Conference (New York: Council on Foreign Relations, December 11, 1998), 8.

13. *Washington Post,* April 18, 1999, A1, www.washingtonpost.com; and *New York Times,* April 18, 1999, 13.

14. George, *Forceful Persuasion,* 7.

15. Alexander L. George, "Theory and Practice," in *The Limits of Coercive Diplomacy,* 15.

16. North Atlantic Council, *Statement by the North Atlantic Council on Kosovo* (Brussels: North Atlantic Council, January 30, 1999).

17. United Nations, *Secretary-General Calls for Unconditional Respect for Human Rights of Kosovo Citizens, in Statement to North Atlantic Treaty Organization,* United Nations Press Release SG/SM/6878 (January 28, 1999). The subtitle of the press release (*Kofi Annan Stresses Peaceful Negotiation Only Way to Resolve Kosovo Conflict*) contradicts the substance of Annan's remarks and may represent an attempt by UN staff to distance the organization from the NATO threat.

18. These are reproduced in Marc Weller, "The Rambouillet Conference on Kosovo," *International Affairs* 75, no. 2 (1999): 225–256.

19. James P. Rubin, *Press Briefing on the Kosovo Peace Talks,* Rambouillet, France, February 21, 1999, released by the Office of the Spokesman (Paris), U.S. Department of State, secretary.state.gov/www/statements/1999.

20. Secretary of State Madeleine K. Albright, *Press Availability on the Kosovo Peace Talks,* Rambouillet, France, February 21, 1999, released by the Office of the Spokesman (Paris), U.S. Department of State, secretary.state.gov/www/statements/1999.

21. *Washington Post,* April 7, 1999, A1, www.washingtonpost.com.

22. *New York Times,* April 18, 1999, 13.

23. Alexander George, "The Role of Force in Diplomacy: A Continuing Dilemma for U.S. Foreign Policy" (paper prepared for the Dedication Conference of the George Bush School of Government and Public Service, Texas A&M University, College Station, September 9–10, 1997), 42.

24. Alexander L. George and William Simons, "Findings and Conclusions," in *The Limits of Coercive Diplomacy,* 275.

25. George, *Forceful Persuasion,* 14.

26.  U.S. Senate Committee on Armed Services, *Hearing on Operation Allied Force and Relief Operations in Kosovo*, November 3, 1999, as published by Federal Document Clearing House on CIS Congressional Universe (Lexis-Nexis).

27.  Daalder and O'Hanlon, *Winning Ugly*, 95.

28.  *Washington Post*, April 7, 1999, A1, www.washingtonpost.com.

29.  *Washington Post*, April 8, 1999, A26, www.washingtonpost.com.

30.  *Washington Post*, April 5, 1999, A12, www.washingtonpost.com.

31.  George, "Theory and Practice," 15.

32.  George, *Forceful Persuasion*, 71.

33.  *Washington Post*, May 16, 1999, A1, www.washingtonpost.com.

34.  George, *Forceful Persuasion*, 6.

# 17

## The Afghani War:
## A Flawed Masterpiece

### MICHAEL E. O'HANLON

Throughout most of the twentieth century, the U.S. armed forces were seen as an overmuscled giant, able to win wars through brute strength but often lacking in daring and cleverness. This basic strategy worked during the two world wars, making the United States relatively tough to challenge. But it failed in Vietnam, produced mediocre results in Korea, and worked in the Persian Gulf War largely because the terrain was ideally suited to American strengths.

What a difference a new century makes. Operation Enduring Freedom has been, for the most part, a masterpiece of military creativity and finesse. Secretary of Defense Donald Rumsfeld, U.S. Central Command (CENTCOM) head General Tommy Franks, and Director of Central Intelligence George Tenet devised a plan for using limited but well-chosen types of American power in conjunction with the Afghan opposition to defeat the Taliban and al Qaeda. Secretary of State Colin Powell helped persuade Pakistan to sever its ties with the Taliban, work with Afghanistan's Northern Alliance, provide the bases and overflight rights needed by U.S. forces, and contribute to the general war effort. Besides pushing his national security team to develop an innovative and decisive war-fighting strategy, President George W. Bush rallied the American people behind the war effort and established a close relationship with Russian President Vladimir Putin, making it far easier for the United States to work militarily in Central Asia. The U.S. effort to overthrow the Taliban deprived al Qaeda of its sanctuary within Afghanistan and left its surviving leaders running for their lives.

At their peak, the U.S. forces involved in the war effort numbered no more than 60,000 (about half of which were in the Persian Gulf), and Western allies added no more than 15,000. But the U.S.-led military campaign has hardly been small in scale. By the end of January, the United States had flown about 25,000 sorties in the air campaign and dropped 18,000 bombs, including 10,000 precision munitions. The number of U.S. sorties exceeded the number of U.S. sorties flown in the 1999 Kosovo war, and the United States dropped more smart bombs on Afghanistan than NATO dropped on Serbia in 1999. In fact, the total number of precision munitions expended in Afghanistan amounted to more than half the number used in Operation Desert Storm. (In addition, more than 3,000 U.S. and French bombs were dropped on surviving enemy forces in March during Operation Anaconda, in which some 1,500 Western forces and 2,000 Afghans launched a major offensive against about 1,000 enemy troops in the mountainous region of eastern Afghanistan.)

If the U.S. strategy has had many virtues, however, it has also had flaws. Most important, it has apparently failed to achieve a key war goal: capturing or killing Osama bin Laden and other top enemy leaders. Such hunts are inherently difficult, but the prospects for success in this case were reduced considerably by U.S. reliance on Pakistani forces and Afghan militias for sealing off enemy escape routes and conducting cave-to-cave searches during critical periods. If most al Qaeda leaders stay at large, the United States and other countries will remain more vulnerable to terrorism than they would be otherwise—perhaps significantly so.

But on balance, Operation Enduring Freedom has been very impressive. It may wind up being more notable in the annals of American military history than anything since Douglas MacArthur's invasion at Inchon in Korea half a century ago. Even Norman Schwarzkopf's famous "left hook" around Iraqi forces in Operation Desert Storm was less bold; had it been detected, U.S. airpower still could have protected coalition flanks, and American forces could have outrun Iraqi troops toward most objectives on the ground. By contrast, Operation Enduring Freedom's impressive outcome was far from preordained. Too much American force (e.g., a protracted and punishing strategic air campaign or an outright ground invasion) risked uniting Afghan tribes and militias to fight the outside power, angering the Arab world, destabilizing Pakistan, and spawning more terrorists. Too little force, or the wrong kind of force, risked outright military failure and a worsening of Afghanistan's humanitarian crisis—especially given the limited capabilities of the small militias that made up the anti-Taliban coalition.

## ZEROING IN

Beginning on October 7, Afghans, Americans, and coalition partners cooperated to produce a remarkable military victory in Afghanistan. The winning elements included 15,000 Northern Alliance Fighters (primarily from the Tajik and Uzbek ethnic groups), 100 combat sorties a day by U.S. planes, 300–500 Western special operations forces and intelligence operatives, a few thousand Western ground forces, and thousands of Pashtun soldiers in southern Afghanistan who came over to the winning side in November. Together they defeated the Taliban forces, estimated at 50,000 to 60,000 strong, as well as a few thousand al Qaeda fighters.

Various Western countries, particularly several NATO allies and Australia, played important roles as well. A formal NATO role in the war was neither necessary nor desirable, given the location of the conflict and the need for a supple and secretive military strategy. Still, NATO allies stood squarely by America's side, invoking the alliance's Article V mutual-defense clause after September 11, and demonstrated that commitment by sending five AWACS aircraft to help patrol U.S. airspace. Forces from the United Kingdom, Australia, France, and Canada appear to have frequently contributed to the effort in Afghanistan; forces from Denmark, Norway, and Germany also participated in Operation Anaconda in March. Allied aircraft flew a total of some 3,000 sorties on relief, reconnaissance, and other missions. As noted, France dropped bombs during Operation Anaconda, and the United Kingdom fired several cruise missiles on the first day of battle as well. Numerous countries, including the Netherlands, Italy, and Japan, deployed ships to the Arabian Sea. . . .

The short war has had several phases. The first began on October 7 and lasted a month; the second ran through November and saw the Taliban lose control of the country; the third was characterized by intensive bombing of suspected al Qaeda strongholds in the Tora Bora mountain and cave complex in December; the fourth began with the inauguration of Hamid Karzai as interim prime minister and continues. . . .

During the first part of the war, Taliban forces lost their large physical assets such as radar, aircraft, and command-and-control systems, but they hung on to power in most regions. Most al Qaeda training camps and headquarters were also destroyed. Although Taliban forces did not quickly collapse, they were increasingly isolated in pockets near the major cities. Cut off from each other physically, they were unable to resupply or reinforce very well and had problems communicating effectively.

In the first week of the war, U.S. aircraft averaged only 25 combat sorties a day, but they soon upped that total to around 100. (Some 70 Tomahawk cruise missiles were fired in the early going; a total of about 100 had been used by December.) The United States comparably increased the number of airlift, refueling, and other support missions. U.S. air strikes by B-52 and B-1 bombers operating out of Diego Garcia typically involved six sorties a day; other land-based aircraft, primarily F-15ES and AC-130 gunships from Oman, flew about as much. Planes from the three U.S. aircraft carriers based in the Arabian Sea provided the rest of the combat punch. Reconnaissance and refueling flights originated from the Persian Gulf region and Diego Garcia. Some air support and relief missions also came from, or flew over, Central Asia, where U.S. Army soldiers from the Tenth Mountain Division helped protect airfields.

Most air attacks occurred around Afghanistan's perimeter, because the rugged central highlands were not a major operating area for the Taliban or al Qaeda. By the middle of October, most fixed assets worth striking had already been hit, so combat sorties turned to targeting Taliban and al Qaeda forces in the field. Aircraft continued to fly at an altitude of at least 10,000 feet, because the Pentagon was fearful of antiaircraft artillery, Soviet SA-7 and SA-13 portable antiaircraft missiles, and some 200–300 Stinger antiaircraft missiles presumed to be in Taliban or al Qaeda possession. But most precision-guided weapons are equally effective regardless of their altitude of origin, provided that good targeting information is available—as it was in this case, thanks to U.S. troops on the ground.

The first month of the war produced only limited results and had many defense and strategic analysts worried about the basic course of the campaign. Some of those critics began, rather intemperately and unrealistically, to call for a ground invasion; others opposed an invasion but thought that a substantial intensification of efforts would prove necessary.

In phase two, beginning in early November, that intensification occurred. But it was due not so much to an increased number of airplanes as to an increase in their effectiveness. By then, 80 percent of U.S. combat sorties could be devoted to directly supporting opposition forces in the field; by late November, the tally was 90 percent. In addition, the deployment of more unmanned aerial vehicles and Joint Surveillance and Target Attack Radar System (JSTARS) aircraft to the region helped the United States maintain continuous reconnaissance of enemy forces in many places. Most important, the number of U.S. special operations forces and CIA teams working with various opposition elements increased greatly. In mid-October, only three special operations "A teams," each consisting of a dozen personnel, were in Afghanistan; in mid-November, the tally was 10; by December 8, it was 17. This change meant the United States could increasingly call in supplies for the opposition, help it with tactics, and designate Taliban and al Qaeda targets for U.S. air strikes using global positioning system (GPS) technology and laser range finders. The Marine Corps also began to provide logistical support for these teams as the war advanced.

As a result, enemy forces collapsed in northern cities such as Mazar-i-Sharif and Taloqan over the weekend of November 9–11. Taliban fighters ran for their lives, provoking their leader, Mullah Muhammad Omar, to broadcast a demand that his troops stop "behaving like chickens." Kabul fell soon afterward. By November 16, Pentagon officials were estimating that the Taliban controlled less than one-third of the country, in contrast to 85 percent just a week before. Reports also suggested that Muhammad Atef, a key al Qaeda operative, was killed by U.S. bombs in mid-November. Kunduz, the last northern stronghold of enemy forces where several thousand Taliban and al Qaeda troops apparently remained, fell on November 24–25.

In late November, more than 1,000 U.S. marines of the 15th and 26th Marine Expeditionary Units established a base about 60 miles southwest of Kandahar, which the Taliban continued to hold. They deployed there directly from ships in the Arabian Sea, leapfrogging over Pakistani territory at night (to minimize political difficulties for the government of President Pervez Musharraf) and flying 400 miles inland to what became known as Camp Rhino. Their subsequent resupply needs were largely met using Pakistani bases. Once deployed, they began to interdict some road traffic and carry out support missions for special operations forces.

Meanwhile, Pashtun tribes had begun to oppose the Taliban openly. By November, they were accepting the help of U.S. special forces, who had previously been active principally in the north of the country. Two groups in particular—one led by Hamid Karzai, the other by another tribal leader, Gul Agha Shirzai—closed in on Kandahar. Mullah Omar offered to surrender in early December but in the end fled with most of his fighters, leaving the city open by December 8–9. Pockets of Taliban and al Qaeda resistance, each with hundreds of fighters or more, remained in areas near Mazar-i-Sharif, Kabul, Kandahar, and possibly elsewhere, but the Taliban no longer held cities or major transportation routes.

Why this part of the campaign achieved such a rapid and radical victory remains unclear. Taliban forces presumably could have held out longer if they had hunkered down in the cities and put weapons near mosques, hospitals, and homes, making their arsenal hard to attack from the air. Opposition fighters were too few to defeat them in street-to-street fighting in most places, and starving out the Taliban would have required the unthinkable tactic of starving local civilian populations as well.

Most likely, the Taliban got caught in positions outside major cities that they could neither easily escape nor defend. Once the Afghan opposition began to engage the enemy seriously in November and Taliban forces returned fire, they revealed their positions to American special operations personnel who could call in devastating air strikes. Sometimes they were tricked into revealing their locations over the radio. Even trench lines were poor defenses against 2-ton bombs delivered within 10 to 15 meters of their targets. Just what Taliban fighters could have done differently, once stranded in that open terrain, is unclear. They might have been better advised either to go on the offensive or to try to escape back into urban settings under cover of night or poor weather, although many U.S. reconnaissance assets work well under such conditions. But both approaches would have been difficult and dangerous, especially for a relatively unsophisticated military force such as the Taliban.

The third main phase of the war began in early December. By this time, U.S. intelligence had finally pinpointed much of al Qaeda's strength near Jalalabad, in eastern Afghanistan. In particular, al Qaeda forces, including Osama bin Laden, were supposedly holed up in the mountain redoubts of Tora Bora. Traveling with perhaps 1,000 to 2,000 foreign fighters, most of them fellow Arabs, bin Laden could not easily evade detection from curious eyes even if he might elude U.S. overhead reconnaissance. Thus, once Afghan opposition fighters, together with CIA and special operations forces, were deployed in the vicinity, U.S. air strikes against the caves could become quite effective. By mid-December, the fight for Tora Bora was over. Most significant cave openings were destroyed and virtually all signs of live al Qaeda fighters disappeared. Sporadic bombing continued in the area, and it was not until mid-January that a major al Qaeda training base, Zawar Kili, was destroyed. But most bombing ended by late 2001.

So why did bin Laden and other top al Qaeda leaders apparently get away? The United States relied too much on Pakistan and its Afghan allies to close off possible escape routes from the Tora Bora region. It is not clear that these allies had the same incentives as the United States to conduct the effort with dogged persistence. Moreover, the mission was inherently difficult. By mid-December, the Pentagon felt considerably less sure than it had been of the likely whereabouts of bin Laden, even though it suspected that he and most of his top lieutenants were still alive.

Although estimates remain rough, Taliban losses in the war were considerable. According to New York Times correspondent Nicholas Kristof, as many as 8,000 to 12,000 were killed—roughly 20 percent of the Taliban's initial fighting capability. Assuming conservatively at least two wounded for every person killed, Taliban losses could have represented half their initial fighting strength, a point at which most armies have traditionally started to crumble. Another 7,000 or more were taken prisoner. Kristof's tally also suggests that Afghan civilian casualties totaled only about 1,000, a mercifully low number despite several wrongly targeted U.S. bombings and raids during the war. Although a couple of those U.S. mistakes probably should have been prevented, they do not change the basic conclusion that the war caused relatively modest harm to innocents.

U.S. forces had lost about 30 personnel by the middle of March: about a dozen on the battlefield (8 during Operation Anaconda) and the rest in and around Afghanistan through accidents. Most were Marine Corps and Army troops, but other personnel were lost as well, including a CIA operative. The casualty total was 50 percent greater than those of the invasions of Grenada and Haiti in the 1980s but less than the number of troops killed in Somalia in 1992–93.

## FOLLOW THE LEADER

On the whole, Operation Enduring Freedom has been masterful in both design and execution. Using specially equipped CIA teams and special operations forces in tandem with precision-strike aircraft allowed for accurate and effective bombing of Taliban and al Qaeda positions. U.S. personnel also contributed immensely to helping the Northern Alliance tactically and logistically. By early November, the strategy had produced mass Taliban retreats in the north of the country; it had probably caused many Taliban casualties as well.

More notably, the U.S. effort helped quickly galvanize Pashtun forces to organize and fight effectively against the Taliban in the south, which many analysts had considered a highly risky proposition and CENTCOM had itself considered far from certain. Had these Pashtun forces decided that they feared the Northern Alliance and the United States more than the Taliban, Afghanistan might have become effectively partitioned, with al Qaeda taking refuge exclusively in the south and the war effort rendered largely futile. Convincing these Pashtun to change sides and fight against the Taliban required just the right mix of diplomacy, military momentum and finesse, and battlefield assistance from CIA and special operations teams.

Yet despite the overall accomplishments, mistakes were made. The big U.S. mistake . . . , concerned the hunt for top al Qaeda leaders. If Osama bin Laden, Ayman al-Zawahiri, Abu Zubaydah, and other top al Qaeda officials are found to have survived, the war will have failed to achieve a top objective. Rather than relying on Afghan and Pakistani forces to do the job in December near Tora Bora, Rumsfeld and Franks should have tried to prevent al Qaeda fighters from fleeing into Pakistan by deploying American forces on or near the border. U.S. troops should also have been used in pursuit of Mullah Omar and remnants of the Taliban, even though this mission was less important than the one against al Qaeda leaders.

Admittedly, there were good reasons not to put many Americans in Afghanistan. First, Washington feared a possible anti-American backlash, as Rumsfeld made clear in public comments. Complicating matters, the United States would have had a hard time getting many tens of thousands of troops into Afghanistan, since no neighboring country except Pakistan would have been a viable staging base—and Pakistan was not willing to play that role.

But even though Rumsfeld's reasoning was correct in general, it was wrong for Tora Bora. Putting several thousand U.S. forces in that mountainous, inland region would have been difficult and dangerous. Yet given the enormity of the stakes in this war, it would have been appropriate. Indeed, CENTCOM made preparations for doing so. But in the end, partly because of logistical challenges but perhaps partly because of the Pentagon's aversion to casualties, the idea was dropped. It is supremely ironic that a tough-on-defense Republican administration fighting for vital national security interests appeared almost as reluctant to risk American lives in combat as the Clinton administration had been in humanitarian missions—at least until Operation Anaconda, when it may have been largely too late.

Furthermore, local U.S. allies were just not up to the job in Tora Bora. Pakistan deployed about 4,000 regular army forces along the border itself. But they were not always fully committed to the mission, and there were too few well-equipped troops to prevent al Qaeda and Taliban fighters from outflanking them, as many hundreds of enemy personnel appear to have done. Afghan opposition forces were also less than fully committed, and they were not very proficient in fighting at night.

What would have been needed for the United States to perform this mission? To close off the 100 to 150 escape routes along the 25-mile stretch of the Afghan-Pakistani border closest to Tora Bora would have required perhaps 1,000 to 3,000 American troops. Deploying such a force from the United States would have required several hundred airlift flights, followed by ferrying the troops and supplies to frontline positions via helicopter. According to CENTCOM, a new airfield might have had to be created, largely for delivering fuel. Such an operation would have taken a week or more. But two Marine Corps units with more than 1,000 personnel were already in the country in December and were somewhat idle at that time. If redeployed to Tora Bora, they could have helped prevent al Qaeda's escape themselves. They also could have been reinforced over subsequent days and weeks by Army light forces or more marines, who could have closed off possible escape routes into the interior of Afghanistan. Such an effort would not have assured success, but the odds would have favored the United States.

How much does it matter if bin Laden, al-Zawahiri, and their cohorts go free? Even with its top leaders presumably alive, al Qaeda is weaker without its Afghan sanctuary. It has lost training bases, secure meeting sites, weapons production and storage facilities, and protection from the host-country government. But as terrorism expert Paul Pillar has pointed out, the history of violent organizations with charismatic leaders, such as the Shining Path in Peru and the Kurdistan Workers' Party (PKK) in Turkey, suggests that they are far stronger with their leaders than without them. The imprisonment of Abimael Guzman in 1992 and Abdullah Ocalan in 1999 did much to hurt those organizations, just as the 1995 assassination of Fathi Shikaki of the Palestinian Islamic Jihad weakened that group significantly. Some groups may survive the loss of an important leader or become more violent as a result—for example, Hamas flourished after the Israelis killed "the Engineer" Yahya Ayyash in 1996. But even they may have a hard time coming up with new tactics and concepts of operations after such a loss.

If bin Laden, al-Zawahiri, and other top al Qaeda leaders continue to evade capture, they may have to spend the rest of their lives on the run. And their access to finances may be sharply curtailed. But they could still inspire followers and design future terrorist attacks. If successful, their escape would be a major setback.

## EVOLUTION IN MILITARY AFFAIRS

Even though advocates of the famous "revolution in military affairs" have generally felt frustrated over the past decade, a number of important military innovations appeared in Operation Enduring Freedom. They may not be as revolutionary as blitzkrieg, aircraft-carrier war, and nuclear weapons, but they are impressive nonetheless. Advocates of radical change have tended to underestimate the degree to which the U.S. military can and does innovate even without dramatic transformation.

Several developments were particularly notable. First, there was the widespread deployment of special operations forces with laser rangefinders and GPS devices to call in extremely precise air strikes. Ground spotters have appeared in the annals of warfare for as long as airplanes themselves, but this was the first time they were frequently able to provide targeting information accurate to within several meters and do so quickly.

Second, U.S. reconnaissance capabilities showed real improvement. Unmanned aerial vehicles (UAVS), together with imaging satellites and JSTARS, maintained frequent surveillance of much of the battlefield and continuous coverage of certain specific sites—providing a capability that General Myers described as "persistence."

Also notable were advances in battlefield communications. The networks established between UAVS, satellites, combat aircraft, and command centers were faster than in any previous war, making "persistence" even more valuable. The networks were not always fast enough, especially when the political leadership needed to intercede in specific targeting decisions. Nor were they available for all combat aircraft in the theater; for example, the Air Force's "Link 16" data links are not yet installed on many strike aircraft. But they did often reduce the time between detecting a target and destroying it to less than 20 minutes.

Perhaps most historic was the use of CIA-owned Predator UAVS to drop weapons on ground targets. Aside from cruise missiles, this was the first time in warfare that an unmanned aircraft had dropped bombs in combat, in the form of "Hellfire" air-to-ground missiles. There were also further milestones in the realm of precision weapons, which for the first time in major warfare constituted the majority of bombs dropped. They were dropped from a wide range of aircraft, including carrier-based jets, ground-based attack aircraft, and B-52 as well as B-1 bombers. The bombers were used effectively as close-air support platforms, loitering over the battlefield for hours until targets could be identified. They delivered about 70 percent of the war's total ordnance.

In addition to the laser-guided bomb, the weapon of choice for the United States quickly became the joint direct attack munition (JDAM). First used in Kosovo, it is a one-ton iron bomb furnished with a $20,000 kit that helps steer it to within 10 to 15 meters of its target using GPS and inertial guidance. It is not quite as accurate as a laser-guided bomb but is much more resistant to the effects of weather. In the Kosovo war, only the B-2 could deliver it, but now the JDAM can be dropped by most U.S. attack aircraft. By the end of January, the United States had dropped more than 4,000 laser-guided bombs and more than 4,000 JDAMS as well.

Other ordnance was also important. Up to 1,000 cluster bombs were used, with accuracy of about 30 meters once outfitted with a wind-correcting mechanism. Although controversial because of their dud rate, cluster bombs were devastating against Taliban and al Qaeda troops unlucky enough to be caught in the open. A number of special-purpose munitions were used in smaller numbers, including cave-busting munitions equipped with nickel-cobalt steel-alloy tips and special software; these could penetrate up to 10 feet of rock or 100 feet of soil.

The ability to deliver most U.S. combat punch from the air kept the costs of war relatively modest. Through January 8, the total had reached $3.8 billion, while the military costs of homeland security efforts in the United States had reached $2.6 billion. The bills in Afghanistan included $1.9 billion for deploying troops, $400 million for munitions, $400 million for replacing damaged or destroyed equipment, and about $1 billion for fuel and other operating costs.

## LESSONS FOR THE FUTURE

What broad lessons emerge from this conflict? First, military progress does not always depend on highly expensive weapons platforms. Many important contemporary trends in military technology and tactics concern information networks and munitions more than aircraft, ships, and ground vehicles. To take an extreme example, B-52 bombers with JDAM were more useful in Operation Enduring Freedom than were the stealthy B-2s. Second, human skills remain important in war, as demonstrated best by the performance of special operations forces and CIA personnel. The basic infantry skills, foreign language abilities, competence and care in using and maintaining equipment, and physical and mental toughness of U.S. troops contributed to victory every bit as much as did high-tech weaponry.

Third, military mobility and deployability should continue to be improved. The Marine Corps did execute an impressive ship-to-objective maneuver, forgoing the usual ship-to-shore operation and moving 400 miles inland directly. But most parts of the Army still cannot move so quickly and smoothly. Part of the solution may be the Army's long-term plans for new and lighter combat equipment. (The Marine Corps' V-22 Osprey tilt-rotor aircraft may be useful, too, at least in modest numbers and once proven safe.) But the Army could also emulate the Marine Corps' organization, training, and logistics where possible—and soon. The task is hardly hopeless; Army forces were tactically quite mobile and impressive in Operation Anaconda.

Finally, the war showed that more joint-service experimentation and innovation are highly desirable, given that the synergies between special operations forces on the ground and Air Force and Navy aircraft in the skies were perhaps the most important keys to victory. . . .

A final assessment of Operation Enduring Freedom depends on whether bin Laden and his top lieutenants have escaped Afghanistan. It could be a while before anyone knows; indeed, Rumsfeld has speculated that U.S. troops could remain in Afghanistan into 2003. A verdict will also have to await a better sense of where Afghanistan is headed. Whatever the stability of the post-Taliban government, it is doubtful that the Taliban and al Qaeda will ever control large swaths of the country again. But if pockets of terrorists remain in the country, or if Afghanistan again descends into civil war, the victory will be incomplete. In the former case, Afghanistan could still be an important if diminished asset for al Qaeda; in the latter, the U.S. image throughout the Islamic world may take another blow as critics find more fuel for their claims that Americans care little about the fate of Muslim peoples.

To prevent such outcomes, Washington needs to work hard with other donors to make reconstruction and aid programs succeed in Afghanistan. The Bush administration also needs to rethink its policy on peacekeeping. Its current unwillingness to contribute to a stability force for Afghanistan is a major mistake that U.S. allies may not be able to redress entirely on their own. A force of 20,000 to 30,000 troops is clearly needed for the country as a whole; several thousand troops in Kabul will probably not suffice.

That said, the situation in Afghanistan has improved enormously since October 7—and so has U.S. security. The Afghan resistance, the Bush administration, its international coalition partners, the U.S. armed forces, and the CIA have accomplished what will likely be remembered as one of the greater military successes of the twenty-first century.

# PART III

# CURRENT MILITARY ISSUES

THE CURRENT ERA raises four key questions about the role of military power. First, should the United States, the world's premier military power, continue to use its might for its own interests and for those of other states as well, and if so, how should its military might be employed? Second, how much of a danger is the spread of nuclear weapons, and how can the danger be dealt with? Third, can outside powers intervene effectively in the internal conflicts of other states, and if they do intervene, what tactics will be most effective? Fourth, how has terrorism changed over the past thirty years, and what can be done to counter it?

In the first section, Christopher Layne argues that the United States should switch from the Cold War strategy of stationing forces abroad to the post-Cold War strategy of offshore balancing and then bring its troops home. Robert J. Art argues the contrary: for its own interests the United States should continue to forward deploy its troops in Europe, East Asia, and the Persian Gulf. John Ikenberry argues that the United States should avoid the preemptive and unilateral use of force and, instead, should exercise its formidable military power as multilaterally as possible.

In the second section, Victor Utgoff argues that American missile defenses will enable the United States to intervene to stop aggressors, even if the aggressors have missiles armed with nuclear warheads, and that the missile defenses will work strongly against the further spread of nuclear weapons. Kenneth Waltz argues the opposite: American missile defenses will cause additional states to want to have their own nuclear weapons. Barry Posen asks what the United States would have done in 1990-1991 if Iraq had possessed nuclear weapons and answers that it would have used military force anyway, lest small nuclear-

281

weapons states believe that they can commit aggression with impunity because of U.S. fear of their weapons. Scott Sagan and Kenneth Waltz argue, respectively, that India's and Pakistan's nuclear weapons make the subcontinent a more dangerous and a less dangerous area.

In the third section, Chaim Kaufmann, Barry Posen, and Barbara Walter analyze how the international community can intervene militarily in civil wars. Kaufmann shows why military intervention is a losing proposition in ideological civil wars and how it can be effective in ethnic conflicts. Posen shows in what ways states can successfully use force to protect refugees from the ravages of civil wars. Walter shows that unless neutral third parties are willing to step in and give credible security guarantees to the warring parties, armistices and negotiated ends to civil wars are likely to fail.

In the fourth section, Walter Laqueur places terrorism in its historical context. Brahma Chellaney shows how terrorism has geographically concentrated in South Asia and draws some lessons from the experience there. Richard Falkenrath, Robert Newman, and Bradley Thayer ask how the United States can affect the inclination of terrorists to use weapons of mass destruction and suggest how we can strengthen international norms against the use of nuclear, biological, and chemical weapons. Paul Pillar argues that, although terrorism cannot be defeated, it can be reduced and controlled, and he suggests how to set about doing so.

# 18

# From Preponderance to Offshore Balancing

## CHRISTOPHER LAYNE

The Soviet Union's collapse transformed the international system dramatically, but there has been no corresponding change in U.S. grand strategy. In terms of ambitions, interests, and alliances, the United States is following the same grand strategy it pursued from 1945 until 1991: that of preponderance. Whether this strategy will serve U.S. interests in the early twenty-first century is problematic. Hence, in this article my purpose is to stimulate a more searching debate about future U.S. grand strategic options. To accomplish this, I compare the strategy of preponderance to a proposed alternative grand strategy: offshore balancing.

My argument for adopting an alternative grand strategy is prospective: although sustainable for perhaps another decade, the strategy of preponderance cannot be maintained much beyond that period. The changing distribution of power in the international system—specifically, the relative decline of U.S. power and the corresponding rise of new great powers—will render the strategy untenable. The strategy also is being undermined because the robustness of America's extended deterrence strategy is eroding rapidly. Over time, the costs and risks of the strategy of preponderance will rise to unacceptably high levels. The time to think about alternative grand strategies is now—before the United States is overtaken by events.

An offshore balancing strategy would have two crucial objectives: minimizing the risk of U.S. involvement in a future great power (possibly nuclear) war, and enhancing America's relative power in the international system. Capitalizing on its geopolitically insular position, the United States would disengage from its current alliance commitments in East Asia and Europe. By sharply circumscribing its overseas engagement, the United States would be more secure and more powerful as an offshore balancer in the early twenty-first century than it would be if it continues to follow the strategy of preponderance. In advocating this strategy, I do not deprecate those who believe that bad things (e.g., increased geopolitical instability) could happen if the United States abandons its strategy of preponderance. Indeed, they may; however, that is only half of the argument. The other half, seldom acknowledged by champions of preponderance, is that bad things—perhaps far worse things—could happen if the United States stays on its present grand strategic course. Grand strategies must be judged by the amount of security they provide; whether, given international systemic constraints, they are sustainable; their cost; the degree of risk they entail; and their tangible and intangible domestic effects. Any serious debate about U.S. grand strategy must use these criteria to assess the comparative merits of both the current grand strategy and its competitors. I hope to foster an awareness that fairly soon the strategy of preponderance will be unable to pass these tests.

This chapter is structured as follows. First, I analyze the strategy of preponderance, paying particular attention to its theoretical underpinnings, causal logic, and policy components. Second, I demonstrate the strategy's weaknesses. Third, I outline the elements of an alternative grand strategy, offshore balancing, and show why it would be a better strategy for the United States to follow in the twenty-first century.

## THEORY AND GRAND STRATEGY: THE STRATEGY OF PREPONDERANCE

Grand strategy is a three-step process: determining a state's vital security interests; identifying the threats to those interests; and deciding how best to employ the state's political, military, and economic resources to protect those interests. The outcome of the process, however, is indeterminate: the specific grand strategy that emerges will reflect policymakers' views of how the world works. Hence debates about grand strategy also are debates about international relations theory. Because theories are not monolithic, competing grand strategies can emanate not only from rival theories but also from the same theoretical approach. Thus both competing strategies I consider in this article—preponderance and offshore balancing—are rooted in the realist tradition notwithstanding their sharply different policy implications. . . .

The United States has pursued the same grand strategy, preponderance, since the late 1940s. The key elements of this strategy are creation and maintenance of a U.S.-led world order based on preeminent U.S. political, military, and economic power, and on American values; maximization of U.S. control over the international system by preventing the emergence of rival great powers in Europe and East Asia; and maintenance of economic interdependence as a vital U.S. security interest. The logic of the strategy is that interdependence is the paramount interest the strategy promotes; instability is the threat to interdependence; and extended deterrence is the means by which the strategy deals with this threat. . . .

The strategy of preponderance assumes that the United States has a vital "milieu" interest in maintaining stability in the international system. Underlying the strategy is fear of what *might* happen in a world no longer shaped by predominant U.S. power. Continued American hegemony is important because it is seen as the prerequisite for systemic stability (primacy *is* world order). Instability is dangerous because it threatens the link that connects U.S. security to the strategic and economic interests furthered by interdependence. Interdependence is an overriding U.S. interest for economic reasons and, more important, for politico–military reasons: it is viewed as both a cause and a consequence of peace and stability in the international system. Indeed, the role of interdependence in the strategy of preponderance is tautological: Interdependence is a vital interest because it leads to peace and stability (and prosperity); however, peace and stability must preexist in the international system order for interdependence to take root.

Geographically, the strategy of preponderance identifies Europe, East Asia, and the Persian Gulf as regions in which the United States has vital security interests. Europe and East Asia (the zone of peace and prosperity) are important because they are the regions from which new great powers could emerge and where future great-power war could occur; central to the functioning of an interdependent international economic system; and vital to U.S. prosperity. The Persian Gulf is important because of oil. Geographically, these three regions constitute America's vital interests; however, its security interests are not confined to these regions. The United States must also be concerned with the peripheries because turmoil there could affect the core.

The strategy of preponderance identifies the rise of new great powers and the spillover of instability from strategically peripheral areas to regions of core strategic interest as the two main threats to U.S. interests in stability and interdependence. The emergence of new great powers would have two deleterious consequences for the United States. First, new great powers could become aspiring hegemons and, if successful, would seriously threaten U.S. security. Offensive and defensive realists concur that China is the state most likely to emerge as a hegemonic challenger in the early twenty-first century. Offensive realists believe that the United States should respond to the prospect of emerging Chinese power by moving now to contain Beijing. While holding the containment option in reserve, defensive realists prefer to engage China now in the hope that democratization and interdependence will have meliorating effects on Beijing's foreign policy.

Second, the emergence of new great powers is always a destabilizing geopolitical phenomenon. Although the United States may have to acquiesce in China's rise to great-power status, the strategy of preponderance clearly aims to prevent the great-power emergence of Germany and Japan. U.S. policymakers fear that a "renationalized" Japan or Germany could trigger an adverse geopolitical chain reaction. For their neighbors, resurgent German and Japanese power would revive the security dilemma (dormant during the Cold War). At best, the ensuing security competitions that could occur in Europe and East Asia would make cooperation more difficult. At worst, renationalization could fuel a cycle of rising tensions and arms racing (possibly including nuclear proliferation) that would undermine regional stability and perhaps lead to war. Either way, however, U.S. strategic and economic interests in interdependence would be imperiled.

The strategy's aversion to the emergence of new great powers reflects the belief that multipolar international systems are unstable and war prone. . . . Advocates of preponderance regard multipolarity with trepidation because they embrace the realist assumptions that in multipolar systems balancing may fail (leading to war) because of coordination and collective action problems, and difficulties in calculating relative power relationships accurately.

Instability in the peripheries (caused by failed states or by internal conflict triggered by ethnic, religious, or national strife) can also jeopardize America's interest in international stability. Turmoil in the periphery could prompt America's allies to act independently to maintain order (again raising the specter of renationalization), or could ripple back into the core and undercut prosperity by disrupting the economic links that bind the United States to Europe and East Asia.

U.S. security guarantees to Europe and East Asia—implemented by extended deterrence—are the means by which the strategy of preponderance maintains a benign international political order conducive to interdependence. Through extended deterrence, the United States retains the primary responsibility for defending German and Japanese security interests both in the core and in the periphery. The United States thereby negates German and Japanese incentives to renationalize their foreign and security policies. . . .

## PREPONDERANCE IN THE POST–COLD WAR WORLD: A CRITIQUE

In this section I critique the strategy of preponderance, focusing on interdependence's central geopolitical role in American grand strategy. Interdependence leads to strategic overextension, encourages threat inflation, and forces the United States to rely on an increasingly problematic extended deterrence strategy.

The strategy's fixation with international stability stems from its concern with ensuring that conditions exist in which interdependence can survive and flourish. The causal logic of commercial liberalism holds that economic interdependence leads to peace. The causal logic of preponderance, however, reflects a different view of the relationship between peace and interdependence: it is peace—specifically the international security framework the United States has maintained from 1945 to the present—that makes economic interdependence possible. . . .

## INTERDEPENDENCE AND SECURITY:
## AN OVERLOOKED CONNECTION

There is a tight linkage—too often neglected by many international relations theorists—between security and economic interdependence. I call this the "security/interdependence nexus." To preserve an international environment conducive to economic interdependence, the United States must engage in an extended deterrence strategy that undertakes to defend its allies' vital interests by protecting them from hostile powers, threats emanating in the periphery, and each other. The need to rely on extended deterrence to maintain the conditions in which interdependence can take root leads inexorably to strategic overextension: the United States must extend deterrence to secure interdependence against threats emanating in both the core and the periphery, and the synergy between credibility concerns and threat inflation causes the United States to expand the scope of its security commitments. Economic interdependence therefore brings with it an increased risk of war and a decrease in America's relative power. . . .

The strategy of preponderance assumes that the international system will be relatively orderly and stable if the United States defends others' vital interests, but would become disorderly and unstable if others acquired the means to defend their own vital interests. Thus, to ensure a post–Cold War geopolitical setting conductive to interdependence, the United States "will retain the preeminent responsibility for selectively addressing those wrongs which threaten *not only our interests but those of our allies or friends*, which could seriously unsettle international relations." The corollary is that the United States must defend its allies' interests in both the core *and* in the periphery. . . . [A] case illustrate[s] how the security/interdependence nexus invariably leads to U.S. strategic overextension: . . . [for example,] its current intervention in Bosnia. . . .

Although a few commentators have contended that U.S. intervention in Bosnia was animated by humanitarian concerns, this is not the case. U.S. policymakers, including President Bill Clinton, made clear that their overriding concerns were to ensure European stability by preventing the Balkan conflict from spreading, and to reestablish NATO's credibility. Indeed, some of preponderance's proponents believe that U.S. intervention in Bosnia alone is insufficient to prevent peripheral instability from spreading to Western Europe. To forestall a geopolitical snowball, they contend, it is necessary to enlarge NATO by incorporating the states of East Central Europe.

These expressed fears about the spillover of instability from Bosnia (or East Central Europe) into Europe are, without explication, vague. A number of U.S. policymakers and analysts have detailed their concerns, however: they fear that spreading instability could affect the United States economically given its interdependence with Europe. . . .

With respect to U.S. commitments, the strategy of preponderance is open-ended. Even the strategy's proponents who acknowledge that there are limits to

U.S. security interests are hard-pressed to practice restraint in actual cases. Robert Art's writings are illustrative. In 1991 he argued the only U.S. security concern in Europe and the Far East is to ensure that great power war does not occur because only conflicts of that magnitude could negatively affect economic interdependence. "In contrast," he wrote, "wars among the lesser powers in either region (for example, a war between Hungary and Romania over Transylvania) would not require American involvement." Yet in 1996 Art suggested that U.S. intervention in Bosnia (by any standard, a "war among lesser powers") was necessary because the Balkan war had implicated NATO's cohesion and viability and raised doubts about America's leadership and its willingness to remain engaged in Europe. Absent continued U.S. involvement in European security matters, he argued, NATO would be unable to perform its post–Cold War tasks of maintaining a benign security order conducive to Western Europe's continuing politico–economic integration, containing resurgent German power, and preventing the West European states from renationalizing their security policies. . . .

Bosnia demonstrate[s] how the strategy of preponderance expands America's frontiers of insecurity. The security/interdependence nexus requires the United States to impose order on, and control over, the international system. To do so, it must continually enlarge the geographic scope of its strategic responsibilities to maintain the security of its established interests. . . . [T]his process becomes self-sustaining because each time the United States pushes its security interests outward, threats to the new security frontier will be apprehended. . . . Core and periphery are interdependent strategically; however, while the core remains constant, the turbulent frontier in the periphery is constantly expanding. . . . The need to defend America's perceived interest in maintaining a security framework in which economic interdependence can flourish has become the primary rationale for expanding its security commitments in East Asia and in Europe. To preserve a security framework favorable to interdependence, the United States does not, in fact, intervene everywhere; however, the logic underlying the strategy of preponderance can be used to justify U.S. intervention anywhere.

## THREAT INFLATION, CREDIBILITY, AND INTERDEPENDENCE

The security/interdependence nexus results in the exaggeration of threats to American strategic interests because it requires the United States to defend its core interests by intervening in the peripheries. There are three reasons for this. First . . . order-maintenance strategies are biased inherently toward threat exaggeration. Threats to order generate an anxiety "that has at its center the fear of the unknown. It is not just security, but the pattern of order upon which the sense of security depends that is threatened." Second, because the strategy of preponderance requires U.S. intervention in places that concededly have no intrinsic strategic value, U.S. policymakers are compelled to overstate the dangers to American interests to mobilize domestic support for their policies. Third, the tendency to exaggerate threats is tightly linked to the strategy of preponderance's concern with maintaining U.S. credibility. . . .

Preponderance's concern with credibility leads to the belief that U.S. commitments are interdependent. . . . If others perceive that the United States has acted irresolutely in a specific crisis, they will conclude that it will not honor its commitments in future crises. Hence, as happened repeatedly in the Cold War, the United States has taken military action in peripheral areas to demonstrate—both to allies and potential adversaries—that it will uphold its security obligations in core areas.

## INTERDEPENDENCE AND EXTENDED DETERRENCE IN THE TWENTY-FIRST CENTURY

Views about U.S. grand strategy are linked inextricably to attitudes about nuclear proliferation and deterrence. . . . The strategy of preponderance reflects "proliferation pessimism," the belief that the spread of nuclear weapons will have negative consequences: specifically, renationalization and an increased risk of nuclear conflict. The strategy rests on the assumption that the United States can prevent these consequences by bringing potential proliferators within the shelter of its security umbrella. Thus the strategy is based not only on proliferation pessimism but on *extended* deterrence optimism: a belief (or faith) in the continuing robustness of the U.S. security umbrella.

Extended deterrence optimism is quite problematic, however. . . . [S]tates that obtain nuclear weapons are driven to do so by security imperatives. Proliferation is a demand-driven problem. . . . The strategy of preponderance attempts to solve this demand-driven cause of proliferation by assuaging the protected states' security fears. Whether the strategy can work is a function of two interrelated factors. First, is extended deterrence credible? That is, will it actually dissuade an adversary from attacking the target state? Second, will U.S. guarantees reassure the protected state? . . .

Despite its perceived complexities, it appears that extended deterrence "worked" in Europe during the Cold War and was easier to execute successfully than generally was thought. One should not assume, however, that extended deterrence will work similarly well in the early twenty-first century, because the unique coincidence of contextual variables is unlikely to be replicated in the future; they include: bipolarity; a clearly defined, and accepted, geopolitical status quo; the intrinsic value to the defender of the protected region; and the permanent forward deployment by the defender of sizeable military forces in the protected region.

The international system's polarity affects extended deterrence's efficacy. During the Cold War, the bipolar nature of the U.S.–Soviet rivalry in Europe stabilized the superpower relationship by demarcating the continent into U.S. and Soviet spheres of influence that delineated the vital interests of both superpowers. Each knew it courted disaster if it challenged the other's sphere. Also, the superpowers were able to exercise control over their major allies to minimize the risk of being chain-ganged into a conflict. In the early twenty-first century, however, the international system will be multipolar and, arguably, less stable and more conflict prone than a bipolar international system. Spheres of influence will not be delineated clearly. In addition, because other states will have more latitude to pursue their own foreign and security policy agendas than they did during the Cold War, the risk will be much greater that the United States could be chain-ganged into a conflict because of a protected state's irresponsible behavior. . . .

A crucial factor in weighing the credibility of a defender's extended deterrence commitments is the extent of its interest in the protected area. Had the Soviets contemplated seriously an attack on Western Europe, the risk calculus probably would have dissuaded them. In a bipolar setting Western Europe's security was a matter of supreme importance to the United States for both strategic and reputational reasons. In the early twenty-first century, however, the intrinsic value of many of the regions where the United States may wish to extend deterrence will be doubtful. . . . It thus will be difficult to convince a potential attacker that U.S. deterrence commitments are credible. Moreover, the attenuated nature of U.S. interests will result in motivational asymmetries favoring potential challengers. That is, the "balance of resolve" will lie with the challenger, not with the United States, because the challenger will have more at stake. . . .

Deterrence theory holds that extended deterrence is strengthened when the guarantor deploys its own military forces on the protected state's territory. Thus during the Cold War, the presence of large numbers of U.S. combat forces and tactical nuclear weapons in Europe underscored its importance to the United States and bolstered extended deterrence's credibility. The defender's deployment of forces is one of the most powerful factors in ensuring extended deterrence success, because it is a visible signal that the defender "means business." In contrast, in the early twenty-first century in many places where the United States may seek to implement extended deterrence, the strategy's effectiveness will be undercut because the United States will not have a permanent, sizeable military presence in the target state (Korea is a notable exception). . . .

The United States of course could attempt to enhance the robustness of extended deterrence by increasing the size of its conventional deployments in key regions; however, it is doubtful that this would be either feasible or effective. Significantly increasing the number of U.S. forward-deployed forces in Europe and East Asia would be expensive. And even then, the effect on the credibility of U.S. extended deterrence guarantees would be uncertain. After all, during the Cold War even the presence of over 300,000 U.S. troops in Europe was insufficient to reassure policymakers in the United States and Western Europe that extended deterrence was robust.

## ECONOMIC INTERDEPENDENCE AND DECLINING RELATIVE POWER

The strategy of preponderance incorporates contradictory assumptions about the importance of relative power. On the one hand, the strategy seeks to maximize America's military power by perpetuating its role as the predominant great power in the international system. Yet the strategy's economic dimension is curiously indifferent to the security implications of the redistribution of relative power in the international political system resulting from economic interdependence. Nor does it resolve the following conundrum: given that economic power is the foundation of military strength, how will the United States be able to retain its hegemonic position in the international political system if its relative economic power continues to decline?

Contrary to the strategy of preponderance, the security/interdependence nexus posits that economic openness has adverse strategic consequences: it contributes to, and accelerates, a redistribution of relative power among states in the international system (allowing rising competitors to catch up to the United States more quickly than they otherwise would). This leads to the emergence of new great powers. The resulting power transition, which occurs as a formerly dominant power declines and new challengers arise, usually climaxes in great-power war. Because great-power emergence is driven by uneven growth rates, there is little-short of preventive war—that the United States can do to prevent the rise of new great powers. But, to some extent, U.S. grand strategy can affect both the pace and the magnitude of America's relative power decline.

A crucial relationship exists between America's relative power and its strategic commitments. . . . Ultimately, the decline in its relative power leaves a waning hegemon less well placed to fend off challenges to its systemwide strategic interests. Preponderance's key strategic commitments were undertaken in the late 1940s, when the United States was near the zenith of its relative power. Yet, during the 1980s and 1990s, although its relative economic power has declined, U.S. commitments have continued to expand. It is not inappropriate to infer that the attempt to sustain expanding commitments on a shrinking relative power base is harmful to America's economic performance. . . .

It is difficult to quantify the strategy of preponderance's economic costs; Jim Hanson's 1993 analysis suggests, however, that the strategy's costs include: loss of domestic savings, trade deficits, overseas investment and loan losses, employment loss and welfare costs (attributable to the export of jobs), a swelling federal budget deficit, ballooning interest on the federal debt, foreign economic and military aid, and one-half of U.S. defense spending (attributable to "imperial" security responsibilities).[1] According to Hanson's study, as of 1990 the cost of maintaining the American empire was $970 trillion, nearly 20 percent of GNP. Although the specifics of the study's accounting methodology can be questioned, the basic point remains: There is a strong prima facie case that for the United

States the strategy of preponderance is expensive, and over the long term the strategy will retard its economic performance; decrease its relative economic power; and weaken its geopolitical standing in the emerging twenty-first century multipolar system.

## OFFSHORE BALANCING: AN ALTERNATIVE GRAND STRATEGY

An alternative to the strategy of preponderance is offshore balancing. In this section I describe a U.S. grand strategy of offshore balancing, delineate the realist premises on which the strategy rests, and demonstrate how the strategy is deduced from these premises.

Offshore balancing is a strategy for the multipolar world that already is emerging. Its underlying premise is that it will become increasingly more difficult, dangerous, and costly for the United States to maintain order in, and control over, the international political system as called for by the strategy of preponderance. Offshore balancing would define U.S. interests narrowly in terms of defending the United States's territorial integrity and preventing the rise of a Eurasian hegemon. As an offshore balancer, the United States would disengage from its military commitments in Europe, Japan, and South Korea. The overriding objectives of an offshore balancing strategy would be to insulate the United States from future great-power wars and maximize its relative power position in the international system. Offshore balancing would reject the strategy of preponderance's commitment to economic interdependence because interdependence has negative strategic consequences. Offshore balancing also would eschew any ambition of perpetuating U.S. hegemony and would abandon the ideological pretensions embedded in the strategy of preponderance. As an offshore balancer, the United States would not assertively export democracy, engage directly in peace-enforcement operations, attempt to save "failed states" (like Somalia and Haiti), or use military power for the purpose of humanitarian intervention.

An offshore balancing strategy would be considerably less expensive than the strategy of preponderance. It would require defense budgets in the range of 2–2.5 percent of GNP. American military strategy for possible interventions would be based on the principle of limited liability. In contrast to the force structure currently underpinning the strategy of preponderance, offshore balancing would sharply reduce the size and role of U.S. ground forces. The strategy's backbone would be robust nuclear deterrence, air power, and—most important—overwhelming naval power. In the latter respect, an offshore balancing strategy would stress sea-based ballistic missile defense (crucial in the event the United States has to wage coalitional warfare in the early twenty-first century) and sea-based precision, standoff weapons systems (enabling the United States to bring its military power to bear without committing ground forces to combat). The United States also could use naval power as a lever against others' economic interests to achieve its political objectives. As an offshore balancer, the United States would seek simultaneously to maximize its comparative military-technological advantages and its strategic flexibility.

## THEORETICAL ASSUMPTIONS

Offshore balancing is a grand strategy deduced from realist international-relations theory. Specifically, the strategy is based on the following assumptions: balance-of-power strategies are superior to hegemonic ones; for a great power like the United States, interdependence is an illusion, not a reality; the robustness of U.S. extended deterrence commitments will be significantly degraded in coming years; U.S. strategy need not be burdened by excessive concern with credibility, resolve, and reputation; geography has important grand strategic implications; the risk of a rival Eurasian hegemon emerging is small; U.S. grand strategy can confidently assume that other states would balance against a potential hegemon; the dynamics of alliance relationships favor an offshore balancing strategy; and relative power concerns remain the bedrock of a prudent grand strategy.

Offshore balancing is a balance-of-power strategy, not a hegemonic one. It assumes that the United States would be more secure in a multipolar system than it would be attempting to perpetuate its current preeminence. It is, up to a point, an offensive realist strategy. Unlike the offensive realist variant of the strategy of preponderance, however, this strategy would be predicated on the assumption that attempting to maintain U.S. hegemony is self-defeating because it will provoke other states to balance against the United States, and result in the depletion of America's relative power—thereby leaving it worse off than it would have been by accommodating multipolarity. An offshore balancing strategy also would reject the balance-of-threat argument advanced by preponderance's defensive realist proponents: it is the very fact of the hegemon's unbalanced power that threatens others (and spurs the emergence of new great powers). An offshore balancing strategy would accept that the United States cannot prevent the rise of new great powers either within or outside its sphere of influence.

It is logically inconsistent for preponderance's proponents to claim simultaneously that the United States is preeminent and that it is interdependent. In fact, unlike states with smaller economies, very large and powerful states have relatively little interaction with the international economy. Offshore balancing would recognize that the United States, in fact, is not economically interdependent with the international economy. The United States is well placed to adopt an insular grand strategy because it can diversify its export markets; it can minimize its reliance on overseas raw materials (including petroleum) by stockpiling, diversification, and substitution; and external trade is a relatively small component of its gross domestic product (GDP). Merchandise exports account for only about 6 percent of U.S. GDP (the average for industrialized states is about 24 percent). To be sure, such aggregate figures may fail to capture the true extent of economic interdependence (because a large part of international trade now is attributable to cross-national trade within individual firms). Hence it could be claimed that turmoil in the international system would have a greater impact on U.S. prosperity than the above figure suggests. This argument should not be dismissed; however, if the United States adopts an offshore balancing strategy, markets would adjust to a changing political and strategic context, and over time investment and trade flows would be altered. More geopolitically secure regions—especially the United States—would be the beneficiaries of these alterations.

An offshore balancing strategy would recognize explicitly that the credibility of U.S. extended deterrence guarantees will be vitiated in coming years. The United States would be more secure if it withdraws its deterrent umbrella and allows other states to defend themselves. As an offshore balancer, the United States would accept that some (preferably managed) nuclear proliferation is inevitable. Extended deterrence's eroding credibility is an important reason why U.S. hegemony will be unsustainable in the twenty-first century. As potential great powers come to doubt the reliability of the U.S. security umbrella (which will occur even if the United States sticks with the strategy of preponderance), they inevitably will seek strategic self-sufficiency (including nuclear weapons). It is unlikely, however, that an offshore balancing strategy would touch off a proliferation chain reaction. Middle and small powers, given their limited resources, might well decide that they would be more secure by enhancing their conventional forces than by acquiring nuclear weapons.

Offshore balancing is not an extended deterrence strategy. Hence if it adopts this strategy, the United States would not need to be overly preoccupied with reputational concerns. Indeed, in this respect, the strategy of preponderance is based on incorrect premises about reputation. Jonathan Mercer has shown, for example, that whether a state stands firm in a crisis seldom affects its reputation for resoluteness with others (either adversaries or rivals) because others rarely predict the state's future behavior from that crisis's outcome. That is, others' perceptions of a defender's resolve are context specific: resolve is a function of the magnitude of the defender's interests in a particular situation, not by its behavior in previous crises. Using recent empirical research, offshore balancing proponents reject the notion that America must fight in the peripheries to establish its commitment to defend its core interests. The strategy would be based on the belief that concrete vital interests should determine U.S. commitments (rather than credibility determining commitments and commitments, in turn, determining interests). When America's intrinsic stakes in a specific crisis are high (and its capabilities robust), neither adversaries nor others will question its resolve. Conversely, when the United States fails to intervene in peripheral areas, others will not draw adverse inferences about its willingness to defend vital, core interests.

The strategy of preponderance assumes that multipolar systems are unstable. As a generalization this may be true, but instability does not affect all states equally. Preponderance's advocates fail to consider geography's differential effects. An offshore balancing strategy, however, would account explicitly for geography's impact on grand strategy. Insular great powers are substantially less likely to be affected by instability than are states that face geographically proximate rivals. Hence the United States could effectively insulate itself from the future great-power wars likely to be caused by power transition effects. Because of the interlocking effects of geography, nuclear weapons (which enhance insularity's strategic advantages), and formidable military and economic capabilities, the United States is virtually impregnable against direct attack. The risk of conflict, and the possible exposure of the American homeland to attack, derive directly from the overseas commitments mandated by preponderance's expansive definition of U.S. interests.

In multipolar systems, insular great powers have a much broader range of strategic choices than less fortunately placed powers. Because their strategic interdependence with others is low, they can avoid being entrapped by alliance commitments and need worry little about being abandoned by actual or potential allies. Offshore great powers also have the choice of staying out of great-power wars altogether or of limiting their involvement—a choice unavailable to states that live in dangerous neighborhoods in which rivals lurk nearby. As an insular great power in a multipolar world, the United States would retain a free hand strategically: although it might need to enter into temporary coalitions, the United States would disengage from permanent alliance relationships. Because of its insularity and capabilities, the United States would seldom need to engage in external balancing. Internal balancing is always preferable to external balancing because alliance commitments are constraining strategically. An insular great power like the United States seldom needs to subject itself to strategic constraints of this kind.

In the early-twenty-first–century multipolar system the risk that a Eurasian hegemon will emerge is slight. Even if a Eurasian hegemon were to appear, America's core security probably would be unthreatened. The fear that a future Eurasian hegemon would command sufficient resources to imperil the United States is a strategic artifact of the prenuclear era. A good strategy, however, hedges against unknown (and unknowable) future contingencies. Hence an offshore balancing strategy would not rule out the possibility that, as the balancer of last resort, the United States might need to intervene to thwart the emergence of a hegemonic challenger. Three reasons explain why the possibility of intervention cannot be foreclosed completely. First, the military-technological backdrop to international politics may change in the future because of the Revolution in Military Affairs (RMA). Some analysts predict that the RMA will result in greatly enhanced conventional war-fighting capabilities. If so, deterrence could be weakened and the nuclear revolution (which bolsters insularity) could be  partially offset. In that case, traditional concerns about the military effects of capability and resource distributions among states again could become salient. Second, a Eurasian hegemon might be able to use its power diplomatically to coerce the United States. Third, it might be too uncomfortable psychologically for the United States to live in a world dominated by another power.

The strategy of preponderance is based in part on the assumption that the United States must prevent the rise of a hegemonic challenger because other states either will not or will not do so effectively. In contrast, an offshore balancing strategy would be based on the assumptions that in a multipolar world other states will balance against potential hegemons, and it is to America's advantage to shift this responsibility to others. In a multipolar world the United States could be confident that effective balancing ultimately would occur because to ensure their survival, other states have the incentive to balance against geographically proximate rivals, and great powers do not bandwagon. Because of its insularity, the United States can stand aloof from others' security competitions and engage in "bystanding" and "buck-passing" behavior, thereby forcing others to assume the risks and costs of antihegemonic balancing. When an offshore balancer shifts to others the dangers entailed by "going first," it can reasonably hope that it may never have to become involved.

The strategy of preponderance commits the United States to alliance relationships that run counter to geostrategic logic: it imposes the greatest burden (in terms of danger and cost) on the alliance partner (the United States) whose security is least at risk. An offshore balancing strategy would reverse this pattern of alliance relations. There is no inherent reason that the United States should be compelled to bear the high costs of providing security for other states. Japan and Western Europe, for example, long have possessed the economic and technological capabilities to defend themselves. The strategy of preponderance, however (notwithstanding U.S. complaints about burden-sharing inequities), has actively discouraged them from doing so because American policymakers fear any diminution of U.S. control over the international system—including control over U.S. allies—would have adverse geopolitical consequences. Washington has decided that it is preferable strategically for the United States to defend Germany and Japan rather than for Germany and Japan to defend themselves. In contrast, offshore balancing would rest on the assumption that America's overall strategic position would be enhanced by devolving to others the responsibility for their own defense.

An offshore balancing strategy would be grounded on the assumption that relative economic power matters. Domestic economic revitalization and a neomercantilist international economic policy would be integral components of the strategy. The strategy, however, also would seek to maximize U.S. relative power by capitalizing on its geostrategically privileged position. If the United States adopted an offshore balancing strategy, security competitions almost certainly would occur in East Asia and Europe. The United States would be the primary beneficiary of these rivalries between (among) the other great powers in the emerging multipolar system. Noninsular states' constant worry about possible threats from nearby neighbors is a factor that historically has increased the relative power position of insular states. Offshore balancing thus would be a more sophisticated power-maximizing strategy than preponderance: the United States would be able to enhance its relative power without having to confront rivals directly. Great powers that stand on the sidelines while their peers engage in security competitions and conflict invariably gain in relative power.

Multipolarity challenges strategists because a state can be threatened by more than a single adversary. It is often unclear which of potential multiple rivals poses the most salient threat, whether measured in terms of capabilities, intentions, or time. In East Asia, where China and Japan are emerging great powers, the United States confronts this dilemma of multiple rivals. Offshore balancing is the classic grand strategic response of an insular great power facing two (or more) potential peer competitors in the same region. As an offshore balancer, the United States would increase its relative power against both China and Japan by letting them compete and balance against, and contain, each other.

## OFFSHORE BALANCING VERSUS PREPONDERANCE: DEFINING THE DEBATE

Two critical objections could be lodged against an offshore balancing grand strategy: an offshore balancing strategy would increase—not lower—the risk of U.S. involvement in a major war, and the strategy of preponderance should not be abandoned because its benefits exceed its costs. Advocates of preponderance believe it is illusory to think that the United States can disengage from international commitments, because it inevitably would be drawn into major wars even if initially it tried to remain aloof. The example of Europe is frequently invoked: whenever a major European war breaks out, it is said, the United States invariably is compelled to intervene. Preponderance's advocates also claim that U.S. security commitments in Europe and East Asia are a form of insurance: it is cheaper and safer for the United States to retain its security commitments and thereby deter wars from happening than to stand on the sidelines only to be compelled to intervene later under what presumably would be more dangerous conditions. Yet this argument is unsupported by the historical record, and it is not evident that the strategy of preponderance will in fact minimize the risk of U.S. involvement in future wars. . . .

The insurance argument advanced by the strategy of preponderance's advocates is also problematic. Great-power war is rare because it is always an uncertain undertaking: war is to some extent its own deterrent. It is, however, an imperfect deterrent: great-power wars do happen, and they will happen in the future. In a world where nuclear weapons exist the consequences of U.S. involvement could be enormous. The strategy of preponderance purports to insure the United States against the risk of war. If extended deterrence fails, however, the strategy actually ensures that America will be involved in war at its onset. As Californians know, there are some risks (earthquakes, for example) for which insurance is either prohibitively expensive or not available at any price because, although the probability of the event may be small, if it occurred the cost to the insurer would be catastrophic. Offshore balancing has the considerable advantage of giving the United States a high degree of strategic choice and, unlike the strategy of preponderance, a substantial measure of control over its fate. . . .

## CONCLUSION: STRATEGIES, INTERESTS, AND VALUES

It is unsurprising that having fulfilled their hegemonic ambitions following the Soviet Union's collapse, preponderance's advocates want to keep the world the way it is. U.S. grand strategists view the prospect of change in international politics in much the same way that British Prime Minister Lord Salisbury did toward the end of the nineteenth century. "What ever happens will be for the worse," Salisbury said, "and therefore it is in our interest that as little should happen as possible." International politics, however, is dynamic, not static. U.S. hegemony cannot last indefinitely. As Paul Kennedy has observed, "it simply has not been given to any one society to remain *permanently* ahead of all the others." . . . Thus the strategy of preponderance must be reassessed. I have attempted to demonstrate that, in fact, the United States can pursue an alternative grand strategy without sacrificing its security. The debate between advocates of preponderance and offshore balancing, however, is about more than strategy; it is also about values. The United States is secure enough from external threat that, should it wish to do so, it could choose restraint over intervention, nation over empire, and an emphasis on domestic needs over external ambitions. And it *should* do so. In this sense, offshore balancing—an *innenpolitik* grand strategy that posits the primacy of domestic over foreign policy—is ethically driven: America's mission lies at home, not abroad. As George F. Kennan says, there is nothing wrong with taking advantage of the Cold War's end to focus on economic and social challenges at home: "What we should want, in these circumstances, is the minimum, not the maximum, of external involvement."[2] No doubt, some would maintain that offshore balancing is both selfish and immoral. In fact, such a policy is indeed self-interested and most assuredly moral. America First is an imperative, not a pejorative: Offshore balancing is a twenty-first–century grand strategy consistent with America's interests *and* its values.

## NOTES

1  Jim Hanson, *The Decline of the American Empire* (Westport, Conn.: Praeger, 1993).
2.  George F. Kennan, *Around the Cragged Hill: A Personal and Political Philosophy* (New York: W. W. Norton, 1993), 183.

# 19

# The Strategy of
# Selective Engagement

## ROBERT J. ART

In the current era, what grand strategy best serves the United States? There are seven to choose from: dominion, global collective security, regional collective security, cooperative security, containment, isolationism, and selective engagement. I argue that selective engagement is the best strategy, and the purpose of this chapter is to show why.

Formulating an American grand strategy requires making two big choices: selecting basic goals (what are America's national interests?) and choosing appropriate means (how can America's military power best protect these interests?). Selective engagement is the superior strategy because it correctly understands America's interests and because it most effectively uses the nation's military power to protect them. It is also the most balanced of all the grand strategies because it is a hybrid, taking the good elements from its six competitors but avoiding their pitfalls. To make the case for selective engagement, I proceed as follows: First, I lay out the essential features of the strategy. Second, I explain the importance of the six national interests that selective engagement prescribes for the United States. Third, I compare selective engagement to its competitors and show why it is superior to them. . . .

## THE STRATEGY OF SELECTIVE ENGAGEMENT

As I conceive it, selective engagement has eight main features. The first three deal with the nature of America's national interests; the next five, with how to use America's military power to protect them.

## Basic Goals

Selective engagement prescribes six national interests (described more fully in the next section). They are: (1) preventing an attack on the American homeland, primarily by keeping out of the wrong hands nuclear, biological, and chemical (NBC) weapons, which are also referred to as weapons of mass destruction (WMD); (2) preventing great-power wars and destructive security competitions among the Eurasian great powers; (3) maintaining secure oil supplies at stable prices, in large part by keeping Persian Gulf reserves divided among the oil-rich Gulf states; (4) preserving an open international economic order; (5) fostering the spread of democracy and respect for human rights, and preventing mass murder and genocide; and (6) protecting the global environment from the adverse effects of global warming and ozone depletion.

### Selective Action

Selective engagement is, by definition, selective. It steers the middle course between an isolationist, unilateralist course, on the one hand, and a world-policeman, highly interventionist role, on the other. It avoids both an overly restrictive and an overly expansive definition of America's interests, and it strikes a balance between doing too much and too little militarily to support them. It allocates political attention and material resources to the vital interests first, but holds out hope that the desirable interests can be partially realized. Selective engagement continues, but with important modifications, the internationalist path the United States has followed since 1945.

### Realism Cum Liberalism

Selective engagement seeks both realist and liberal goals and can therefore be termed a "realpolitik plus" strategy. It aims to keep the United States secure and prosperous, but goes beyond those classical realist goals to attain liberal goals as well: to nudge the world toward the values the nation holds dear—democracy, free markets, human rights, and international openness. Selective engagement aims to do well not only for the United States, but for others too, in the belief that if others benefit in the ways just described, so too does the United States.

### Utility of Force

Selective engagement holds that military power remains a useful and fungible instrument of statecraft. This means that military power is useful for producing not only military but also nonmilitary results, and therefore that the United States can use its military forces to help shape the international environment so as to make it more congenial to America's political and economic interests.

## Early Action

Selective engagement is a precautionary strategy. Where possible, it seeks to prevent circumstances adverse to the United States from arising, rather than simply reacting to them once they have occurred. It argues that forestalling bad things is more effective and ultimately cheaper than having to pick up the pieces after they have happened.

## Forward Defense

Selective engagement is a forward-defense strategy. It therefore prescribes retention of America's core alliances—the North Atlantic Treaty Organization (NATO), the U.S.–Japan alliance, the U.S.–South Korea alliance, and those with Saudi Arabia and Kuwait—and the basing of American troops overseas in eastern and western Eurasia and the Persian Gulf to keep these alliances strong.

Selective engagement contends that America's core alliances and forward-deployed troops serve several useful functions. First, they help keep the peace and dampen security competitions among the great powers in western and eastern Eurasia and to a lesser degree among the states in the Persian Gulf by providing both military deterrence and political reassurance. Second, to the extent that they help maintain peace and dampen security competitions, these alliances and troops help retard NBC spread, preserve openness, and foster the spread of democracy. Third, these alliances facilitate war waging, peacekeeping, and peacemaking when the United States decides to undertake any of those tasks, because standing alliances permit more rapid and more effective action than assembling ad hoc coalitions. Fourth, America's alliances serve as institutional forums where important political–military issues can be managed by maintaining close political–military links with four of the world's six other great powers—Britain, France, Germany, and Japan. (To the extent that the Founding Act between Russia and NATO establishes a useful institutional link with Russia, a fifth great power may also come into America's political–military institutional orbit.) For these reasons, America's core alliances remain valuable instruments of its statecraft.

## Primacy of States

Selective engagement assumes that states continue to be the primary actors in world politics, that differences in national interests provide ever-present sources of conflict among states, and therefore that nationalism and national self-interest remain the most potent forces in international affairs today, overriding ethnic, religious, and cultural cleavages. Consequently, selective engagement takes account of national differences and rivalries and uses them to serve American interests.

### Necessity for American Leadership

Selective engagement holds that America's leadership is both essential and advantaged. It is essential because effective coalitions of the willing to handle key international issues will not materialize unless the world's most powerful state throws its weight behind them. It is advantaged because none of the other great powers possesses America's military–economic might or its political acceptability. Other great powers often resent America's leadership, but their preference is for the United States to lead because they trust the United States more than they trust each other. In sum, America's indispensable role is based on both its power and its purpose, and no other state is yet able to compete with it on either ground, much less both at once.

## AMERICA'S NATIONAL INTERESTS

Determining a nation's interests is the central task of grand strategy. How a nation defines its interests both sets its fundamental course in world affairs and significantly shapes the means chosen to get there. Selective engagement posits six American national interests. The first three—preventing NBC weapons from falling into the wrong hands, maintaining a deep Eurasian great-power peace, and keeping Persian Gulf oil reserves divided—are vital and generally accord with what are termed realist goals. The last three—preserving an open international economy, fostering the spread of democracy and the observance of human rights, and averting severe climate change and ozone depletion—are desirable and generally accord with what are termed liberal goals.

Vital interests are those whose costs to the nation are somewhere between severe to catastrophic if not protected and whose benefits are large when protected. Homeland defense is the most important: upon it everything else depends, and failure here could bring catastrophe. Eurasian peace and access to oil bring large benefits to the United States, respectively, by keeping it out of great-power wars and by helping fuel its economy. By the same token, embroilment in a major Eurasian war would threaten U.S. security, while a serious disruption in oil supplies risks either severe inflation or a steep economic decline. Thus vital interests are the ones most central to America's physical security and economic well-being.

Desirable interests are those whose realization contributes an additional amount to America's prosperity or makes its external environment more congenial to the values it espouses, and whose nonrealization imposes a cost, but not a severe one, to its well-being or to a congenial international environment. Participation in an open international economy, for example, benefits the United States, but 90 percent of America's gross domestic product (GDP) is produced at home. A retreat from openness would not cause a cessation of all imports, only more expensive ones. This would result in some decline in America's standard of living through higher prices, but not a catastrophic one. Similarly, the spread of democracy and the widespread protection of human rights would make the international environment more congenial to America's interests, but if neither materialized the results would not be catastrophic. Thus desirable interests do not carry the same magnitude of potential costs and benefits to the nation as the vital ones.

### Vital Interests

Most analysts would agree that retarding NBC spread, maintaining Eurasian great-power peace, and preserving access to secure and stable oil supplies are important interests for the United States. Not all would agree, however, that they are vital interests. I explain why they are.

*Homeland Security*

Homeland security is the prevention of attack, invasion, conquest, or destruction of a state's territory, and it is the prime directive of any grand strategy. For selective engagers, the threat to worry about today is rogue states or fanatical terrorists (or both) armed with NBC weapons, not conventional attacks from strong states or nuclear threats from "normal" states.[1]

Conventional attacks and "normal" nuclear threats pose little risk to the American homeland. First, the only realistic attack that could cause great destruction conventionally would have to come either by air- or sea-launched cruise missiles in the thousands or by massive bomber attacks. No state today, except the United States, can mount such attacks across the Atlantic and Pacific Oceans. Should either threat ever materialize, the United States could take effective countermeasures. Second, the United States need not worry much about nuclear attacks from "normal" nuclear-armed states, because they are governed by leaders committed to the traditional rules of great-power politics—the prime one being the survival of the state. Such leaders do not attempt the deliberate destruction of other states that they know can swiftly destroy them in return. Deterrence—the threat of retaliation in kind against a nuclear attack—is the means by which the United States will protect itself against future nuclear threats from states that calculate according to the traditional rules. Deterrence worked during the Cold War; it will work after the Cold War.

It is the third type of threat—fanatical terrorists or rogue states armed with NBC weapons—that the United States should worry about most. Such groups and states possess three attributes that could make them harder to deter than normal actors[2]: First, they are highly motivated to gain their aims, making them more prepared than normal actors to use force to achieve their objectives. Second, they are indifferent to the suffering of their citizens or supporters, making them more willing to take greater losses. Third, they are poor calculators, making them more likely to misperceive a defender's threats or to ignore such threats. If governments or terrorist groups possess such traits, they will be hard to deter and more willing to use NBC weapons if they have them to achieve their political objectives.

Has this third threat fully materialized? "No, not yet." Will it definitely materialize? "No." Is it certain that rogues and terrorists are harder to deter and more likely to attack the United States if and when they become NBC-armed? "No." Is this threat therefore something we should ignore? "Only at our potential peril."

Some analysts downplay the threat. Brian Jenkins has long argued that "terrorists want a lot of people watching, not a lot of people dead." Following Jenkins's logic, Kenneth Waltz asserts that terrorists are rational political actors with long-term goals, and as a consequence they would not use nuclear weapons (or anything else that would achieve the same mass-killing results), because terrorists cannot hope to achieve their aims "by issuing unsustainable threats to wreck great destruction, threats they would not want to execute anyway." In this view NBC terrorism is counterproductive: either it undermines the political support terrorists hope to obtain, or it makes the targeted state more determined than ever not to give in. Moreover, Waltz argues: "Nobody but an idiot can fail to comprehend their [nuclear weapons'] destructive force. How can leaders miscalculate? For a country to strike first without certainty of success, most of those who control a nation's nuclear weapons would have to go mad at the same time."[3] By this logic, normal nuclear-armed states have nothing to fear from rogue nuclear-armed states. According to the Jenkins–Waltz logic, then, neither rogues nor terrorists that are NBC-armed should worry the United States. Finally, the evidence favors their case because it shows that: (1) NBC terrorism has been practically nonexistent; (2) state use of NBC weapons has been rare; and (3) only non-NBC-armed states should worry about NBC attacks.[4]

In light of the Jenkins–Waltz logic and the supporting evidence, should we not accept the view that the United States has little or nothing to fear from NBC-armed rogues and terrorists? I believe not. It is folly to calculate that the past is prologue. This has never been the case in national security affairs; why should it be so now?

Three reasons should make us take the NBC-armed rogue-terrorist threat seriously: First, sadly, NBC weapons are coming increasingly within the reach of nonstate terrorist groups, largely as a consequence of more education about, and greater availability of, the basic scientific and engineering knowledge to produce these weapons, as well as the greater ease of acquiring the means to produce them.

Second, terrorist motivations are changing. For starters, there is a disturbing tendency among some terrorist groups toward pure revenge, not political gain. For example, the ad hoc group of terrorists that bombed the New York World Trade Center in 1993 simply wanted to kill 250,000 Americans. They were not trying to influence policy, only to exact retribution. Deterring terrorists becomes nearly impossible if they are hell-bent only on revenge. In that case they have no need to identify themselves, and if there is no return address, there is no chance for retaliation. Deterrence, after all, is the threat to retaliate. Another disturbing trend is the growth of groups that are motivated by religious and millenarian imperatives. Their terrorist acts have become more lethal than those inflicted by the more "traditional" ideological groups. (Aum Shinrikiyo is one such group.) These groups believe in martyrdom and the hereafter, or they believe themselves the agents of change for a new global order. They do not share the same rational objectives of the traditional politically motivated terrorist. Their motives are more ones of retribution and destruction, and they often view their adversaries as sub-human. As a consequence of such beliefs, these groups have become less restrained in their use of force.

Third, although overt and covert rogue-state NBC attacks against the United States appear unlikely, we cannot wholly discount them. Hitler-like leaders who are willing to take their countries down with them when their plans do not succeed may be exceedingly rare, but they cannot be forever ruled out. It happened once in this century (Hitler); it could happen again in the next. We do not want such a leader to be NBC-armed, should one come to power.

None of this means that NBC attacks by rogues or terrorists are a foregone conclusion, but neither does it mean they are impossible. We have here a class of events whose probability of occurrence is low, but whose consequences if they occur are high, even catastrophic. In such cases, it is prudent to make expected-value calculations: a small number (low likelihood of occurrence) multiplied by a very large number (adverse consequences of the event) still yields an unacceptably large number. This is, after all, how the United States treated the chance of nuclear war with the Soviet Union throughout most of the Cold War—as a low-probability but high-cost event—and took the necessary steps to make certain it would not happen. Similarly, selective engagers make expected-value calculations about what would happen if rogues and terrorists were to become NBC-armed, and they treat the threat as real, not fanciful.

Selective engagers also posit that the best way to forestall the threat is to take a strong stance against NBC spread in general. The logic for this stance rests on three propositions. None can be empirically validated, but none can be ruled out either: First, as more states acquire NBC weapons, the likelihood increases that rogue states and fanatical terrorists could obtain them. Wider ownership increases the chances of undesirable ownership, through theft, sale, or outright transfer. Second, weapons that can destroy cities or states in one fell swoop, or that can kill huge numbers of civilians easily and swiftly, should not be readily available to whoever wants them. Deterrence may not hold forever, and we should not tempt fate by allowing NBC weapons to spread widely. Third, rogue-state leaders will markedly increase their power to do evil and harm American interests through conventional means if they acquire NBC weapons. They may well become more emboldened to undertake aggression against their neighbors and in areas where the United States has important interests, seemingly secure in the belief that possession of NBC weapons makes them immune to U.S. retribution.

What, then, is the best way to prevent rogue states, fanatical groups, and other undesirables from acquiring NBC weapons? The first answer is to maintain a vigorous global political commitment against NBC spread. As the world's leader of this effort, the United States has little choice but to take a clear-cut, no-exceptions policy. It cannot publicly make exceptions because that would undermine the norm—and hence the cooperation of other states—against spread. Of necessity, however, if or when spread occurs, a no-exceptions public stance will have to be combined with a graded punishment regime that distinguishes between normal states, on the one hand, and rogue states and terrorists, on the other. None should get off scot-free, but because normal states are less dangerous than rogues and terrorists, the sanctions imposed on them should be less severe. The second way to retard or stop NBC spread is a grab bag of measures: strengthen institutions like the International Atomic Energy Agency, invest more in intelligence to discover covert nuclear and biological weapons programs, develop effective covert capabilities to sabotage terrorist and rogue-state NBC programs, sign treaties that publicly commit states to forgo acquisition, offer enticing carrots to states that abandon nuclear and biological weapons, and threaten adverse political–economic results for states that become NBC-armed. The third way is to use American military power in a fashion that supports the anti–NBC-spread regime.

To selective engagers, this means using American military power in three ways: First, it means the continued provision of reassurance—the maintenance of America's nuclear umbrella over Japan and Germany. These are America's two key allies in Eurasia today. Were they to go nuclear, it would signify the end of their confidence in the American nuclear umbrella. That might risk the end of America's major alliances and its stabilizing military presence in Eurasia, and might bring greater NBC spread to other Eurasian states and the consequent weakening of the global norm against NBC spread. Second, supporting the anti–NBC-spread regime may require the preventive use of force to disrupt or destroy a nascent rogue or terrorist NBC force if all other means, including covert sabotage attempts, have failed to prevent rogues or fanatics in their drive to acquire these weapons. Such use, either before an NBC force is operational or when it remains quite small, is by no means easy, but should not be ruled out in all circumstances. Third, American military power should be used to support a strong declaratory posture against NBC use for aggression. Any state or group that actually uses NBC weapons for aggression against unarmed NBC states or U.S. troops should fear beforehand severe military punishment. (If such use is not punishable, then the penalties against use go down, and the incentives to acquire these weapons go up.) The declaratory posture here is akin to what the United States said to the Soviet Union during the Cold War: "Attack us with nuclear weapons and we will devastate you in return." Whether the United States would have executed its threat, or whether it would have instead pulled its punches to avoid the inevitable Soviet retaliation, was left unclear. The stance should be the same for rogue or terrorist NBC use: an unqualified U.S. declaratory posture of punishment but a tacit understanding that the particular circumstances will determine what military action, if any, shall be taken.

In sum, a world with fewer NBC weapons, and with fewer states possessing them, is better for America's security than its opposite. An American military presence at both ends of Eurasia and in the Persian Gulf is a bulwark—not the only one but an important one—against their spread. Eurasia without an American military presence is likely to be a more heavily armed and dangerous place than with it.

*Eurasian Great-Power Peace*

America's second vital interest is to maintain a deep peace among the Eurasian great powers. This requires that there be neither major wars (ones that involve at least two great powers) nor intense, sustained security competitions (severe political conflicts that manifest themselves in the form of competitive military efforts short of war and that increase the chances of intense crises and war). The United States has three reasons to prevent these from happening.[5]

First, major wars or intense security competitions will reduce America's ability to hold the line against NBC spread. Like previous great-power wars, a future one would not come out of the blue, but would be preceded by a series of intense crises, a prolonged period of arms racing, and arms buildups. These are bound to spur the acquisition and perhaps even the threatened use of NBC weapons, thereby making NBC limitation harder, not easier.

Second, great-power wars or intense security competitions carry great risk of dragging in the United States. There are two possible scenarios: one where the United States has retained its Eurasian alliances; the other, where it has not. In the first, if a war or an intense security competition involved one of America's key Eurasian allies, the United States would be sucked in, certainly diplomatically and likely even militarily in order to meet its alliance commitments. In the second, unless it were strictly a Russian–Chinese affair, the United States would find it hard to stand aside. The reason: the lessons of the past. In the four major Eurasian great-power wars since 1789, the United States was dragged in, in each case to defend its future security and in addition for at least one of the following reasons: to protect its trade, to support historical and cultural bonds, to oppose aggression, or to resist the imposition of odious forms of government on nations with which it identified. No great power has ever lived solely by the dictates of balance of power; the United States is no exception to this rule. We cannot predict the exact paths by which the United States would become entangled in a major Eurasian war, but the probability is better than even that it would.

Third, major wars and intense security competitions are not good for trade, and would be disruptive to America's considerable economic stakes in western and eastern Eurasia, as well as in the Gulf. Over the long term, trade and especially investment do better under stable, not unstable, political conditions. Peace is more stability-producing than intense security competitions and war; it is therefore more conducive to long-term trade and investment.[6] The protection of U.S. economic interests in Eurasia is not a vital interest, but certainly an important one, especially for a nation whose stake in international economic activity has doubled from its historic levels in the last twenty-five years. (Exports plus imports as a percentage of America's GDP held at the 6–10 percent range throughout most of America's history; beginning in the middle 1970s, it increased dramatically, reaching the 18–22 percent range by 1980 and remaining there ever since.)

The Eurasian great powers are presently at peace because of at least two factors: great-power democracies and nuclear deterrence. First is the fact that four of the great powers (Germany, France, Britain, and Japan) are solid democracies. The fifth (Russia) has begun a rocky road to democratization, and the sixth (China) remains poised between the incompatible worlds of command politics and free markets. War is less likely among democracies than it is among nondemocracies or between democracies and nondemocracies. Second is the fact that four of the great powers (Britain, France, Russia, and China) are nuclear-armed, and the other two (Germany and Japan) are protected by the United States. It is hard to get a large war going between nuclear-armed or nuclear-protected states.

We should not be complacent, however, about the pacifying effects of either factor. The peace-among-democracies effect may be a strong force, but it is not an ironclad law of history. It has not overpowered, nor will it invariably overpower, all the other forces at work in world politics. Moreover, although hard, it is not impossible to have a war between nuclear powers. Recall that the Soviet Union and China, both nuclear-armed at the time, did fight a minor border war in 1969. It has also been relatively easy to have intense crises among nuclear-armed states, and they always carry great risk of war. Recall the intense crises between the United States and the Soviet Union during the first half of the Cold War.

To these two factors, therefore, we should add extra insurance: America's military presence at either end of Eurasia. In Western Europe that presence assures Germany's neighbors that it will not return to its ugly past; in East Asia it reassures Japan's neighbors about Japan, and China's neighbors about China. At both ends of Eurasia, therefore, America's military presence makes interstate relations more stable and peacelike than they would otherwise be. In sum, many elements contribute to peace among the Eurasian great powers today. American policy should be to keep it that way.

*Division of Gulf Reserves*

America's third vital national interest is to have a secure supply of oil at stable prices.[7] Security in supply and stability in price are important in order to avoid severe disruptions to the U.S. and the world economies. Interruptions in oil supplies that result in severe cutbacks can wreak havoc by lowering economic activity; so, too, can wild and severe swings in the price of oil, because they disrupt economic calculations, subject economies to the price manipulations of oil suppliers, and make it difficult for oil-consuming states to begin weaning themselves from their heavy dependence on oil. One of the most important ways to keep oil supplies available at stable and reasonable prices is secure access to Persian Gulf oil. This, in turn, is facilitated by preventing a regional hegemon from controlling the Persian Gulf's oil reserves, either directly by military conquest or indirectly by the threat of conquest. Hence America's third vital national interest is well served by keeping the Gulf's oil reserves divided among several, preferably at least four, of the regional states.

The logic for this position rests on five propositions: First, the United States and most of the other industrialized and industrializing states remain heavily reliant on oil and oil imports to fuel their economies for at least the next several decades. America's dependence on imported oil was 25 percent of daily consumption in 1973, is about 53 percent now, and is projected to rise to 70 percent early in the twenty-first century. At some point in the future, America's heavy dependence on oil will diminish as it continues the switch from oil to natural gas for electricity generation and as it gets serious about limiting fossil-fuel burning in order to reduce global warming (see below). Until that day arrives, the United States remains vulnerable either to sustained disruptions in oil supplies, or to swift and steep swings in oil prices.

Second, in spite of discoveries elsewhere, the Gulf still contains the lion's share of the world's proven oil reserves and a significant percentage of its natural gas reserves. In 1949 Saudi Arabia, Iraq, the United Arab Emirates, Kuwait, Iran, Oman, and Qatar had 44 percent of the world's proven oil reserves; in 1975, 54 percent; and in 1993, 65 percent of the world's oil reserves and one-third of the world's proven natural-gas reserves. Recent finds, mostly in the Caspian Sea, have changed the picture somewhat, dropping Gulf reserves as a percentage of proven world oil reserves in 1996 to somewhere between 46 percent and 63 percent, depending on whether the high end (200 billion barrels) or low end (70 billion barrels) estimates are used for Caspian Sea reserves. Even if Caspian reserves prove to be at the higher end of the estimated range, Gulf reserves will remain central to global oil usage because the most current forecasts of the Energy Information Agency show world oil demand rising from 73.4 million barrels a day (mbd) in 1997 to 104.6 mbd in 2015, with the Gulf's share of world oil-production capacity rising from its 1995 level of 28.6 percent to somewhere between 38 percent and 47 percent, depending on whether oil prices are high or low, respectively. Therefore, whatever the exact figure, the Gulf's oil and natural-gas reserves will continue to constitute a large percentage of the world's proven hydrocarbon reserves for the next several decades. Finally, possession of large reserves brings market power, because states with large reserves, such as Saudi Arabia, have the capacity and the interest to act as swing producers, thereby affecting supply and prices.

Third, even though the United States imports little of its oil supplies from the Gulf, it is still dependent on what happens there. The United States today imports more petroleum products (crude oil and refined products) from Venezuela (1,657 mbd) and Canada (1,415 mbd) than it does from Saudi Arabia (1,363 mbd). Mexico ranks fourth at 1,240 mbd. The fact that a huge percentage of America's crude oil and petroleum product imports comes from the Western Hemisphere does not lessen the importance of the Gulf. The world oil market is highly competitive and integrated. What happens in the Gulf will affect the world price and supply should a major disruption occur there. It is therefore fallacious to argue that Gulf production and reserves are of little concern to the United States because it imports little from the region.

Fourth, access to Gulf oil is made safer if proven reserves are divided among a larger rather than a smaller number of states—at least four or more rather than one or two. Consolidation of Gulf reserves among one or two states facilitates collusion; division of its reserves among four states or more makes collusion more difficult. To allow one or two states to control Gulf oil reserves is to put one or both in a powerful position to hold up the world. Oil is the one natural resource for which the demand is highly inelastic in the short to medium term. Oil prices, moreover, have never been determined solely by market factors, but have also been heavily influenced by political and military considerations. The Gulf's oil reserves are too important to be left to the market alone and too valuable to allow one or two regional hegemons to control.

Fifth, an American military presence in the Gulf helps secure access to a stable oil supply by ensuring that neither Iraq nor Iran consolidates control over the Persian Gulf sheikdoms' considerable reserves. Since the late 1970s, the United States has followed a balance-of-power strategy in the Gulf, first leaning toward Iran when Iraq looked stronger, then tilting toward Iraq when Iran looked stronger, all the while acting to protect the Kuwaiti and Saudi oil fields from dominion by either one. This has been and remains a sensible policy, and under current circumstances requires an American military presence in the Gulf. "Divide but not conquer" must be America's dictum toward the Gulf.

### Desirable Interests

America's next three interests are its desirable ones: preserve an open international economic order, foster the spread of democracy and respect for human rights, and protect the global environment. The fact that they are desirable does not make them unimportant, but only of lesser importance when trade-offs between them and the vital ones must be made. Moreover, unlike the vital interests, the desirable ones are served less directly and tangibly by America's military power. That does not make military power useless to attain them, but only that it is better used in a more indirect fashion.

*International Economic Openness*

Openness means low or nonexistent barriers to the exchange of goods and services among states. Openness per se does not create wealth, but it does facilitate the most efficient allocation of the world's factors of production if markets are operating efficiently. This benefits the United States in three ways.[8]

First, international openness makes the United States richer than it would otherwise be because of the gains it reaps from trade. These gains are of two types: static gains—the onetime increase in productivity that occurs with the shift of resources from less to more efficient uses when a state switches from protectionism to freer trade; and dynamic gains—the continuing increases in productivity that more open and larger markets, fiercer competition, and economies of scale produce. Static gains, measured in terms of the costs of protection, are smaller for the United States than for most other states because the United States is the world's most open economy. These gains run at about 0.75 percent of America's gross national product, or $56 billion, a small sum for any given year, but a nontrivial loss in forgone output and wealth when cumulated over many years.[9] Dynamic gains are notoriously difficult to quantify, but most economists deem them to be considerable because they are the ones that lead to the continual increases in productivity, and hence real income, that global competition produces.

Second, openness makes other states richer than they would otherwise be, and this is good for the United States. All states can gain from trade and economic openness, although they will gain unequally because their national efficiencies differ. Each, however, will grow richer and more efficient if market, not political, considerations determine the allocation of resources. If states grow richer, they become better customers for American exports, because rich customers buy more than poor ones.

Third, as other states grow richer, their pacific tendencies should strengthen and so should their prospects for becoming democratic, or more solidly democratic. The strengthening of a state's pacific and democratic proclivities is to America's benefit. Although we cannot assume that the economic interdependence that results from sustained openness by itself produces peace, surely it is a contributing factor. Rich states are likely to be more contented and therefore less aggressive than poor states when they believe that they can become rich through industrialization and trade. In addition, high levels of economic interdependence are peace-conducing because states have a strong self-interest in others doing well economically (they do better with trade if others are prospering). Similarly, the single most important factor historically in the creation of stable democracies has been the creation of large stable middle classes. In turn, since 1945 economic growth has been the single most important factor in the creation of large and stable middle classes. Economic

growth, aided in part by an open international economic order, is therefore a democ-
racy-producing engine.

### Democratic Spread and Human Rights Protection

The spread of democracy, the protection of human rights, and the prevention
of mass murder are values Americans hold dear. All three are morally desirable
in themselves and have greater global appeal than many analysts care to admit.
They also tangibly benefit the United States in at least three ways.

First, the spread of democracy is likely to make states more pacific in their
foreign policies when democracies confront other democracies. Therefore, if
democracy spreads within regions, it will increase the number of peaceful zones,
and this benefits the United States for the simple reason that a more pacific world
is a less dangerous world.

Second, democratic spread is also the best insurance that human rights will be
protected and mass murders avoided. By definition, stable democracies rarely
incarcerate their citizens at will or slaughter huge numbers of them indiscrimi-
nately. If the spread of democracy protects human lives and human rights, then
the need for the international community to intervene in the internal affairs of
states will be lessened. This will reduce the pressures and burdens on the United
States, which is the state usually looked to by the world community to organize
and lead such efforts.

Third, the spread of democracy is good for global economic growth. Command economies do poorly over the long term; market economies do much better. Command political systems are not entirely incompatible with market
economies (witness Chile under Augusto Pinochet or China under Deng Xiao-
ping), but they are not sustainable over the long term, if the change of regime in
Chile and the present tensions in China are reliable guides. Thus more peace
zones, lessened need for intervention, and greater prosperity—these are the likely
benefits of the global spread of democracy.

### The Global Environment

The last desirable interest is to prevent depletion of the earth's ozone layer
and to avert a huge rise in the earth's average global temperature. Both present
serious problems—the former, because of the destructive effects on all forms of
life wrought by the increase in ultraviolet radiation reaching the earth; the latter,
because of the climate change induced by global warming. Neither respects
national boundaries, and both therefore threaten the quality of American life.

The threat of ozone depletion has been "solved," but not in the sense that
the depletion has stopped. It has not; furthermore, it will continue for several
decades, and it will take the ozone layer another fifty years to fully recover
once the chemicals that destroy it are no longer released into the atmosphere.
Instead, ozone depletion has been "solved" in the sense that an international
treaty has been negotiated and signed to severely restrict and then phase out

these dangerous chemicals. The task for international action now is to see that the treaty is fully implemented.

Global warming presents the United States with its greatest environmental threat. Although the country is better placed than most others to deal with its myriad adverse effects because of America's wealth and technology, nonetheless, the United States will not be exempt from them. These include more extreme weather, crop and species loss, coastal erosion caused by thermal expansion, stress on water supplies, increase in urban pollution, loss of up to 40 percent of America's forests, and so on. Reliable and precise estimates of the damage to the United States are hard to come by, but William Cline provides one of the best, estimating that annual damage to the United States from global warming will run between $61.6 and $335.7 billion (in 1990 dollars), or between 1.1 percent and 6 percent of GDP, respectively. These costs could be sustained indefinitely, if abatement costs (the costs to the United States of measures to avert global warming) are larger than damage costs. If abatement costs run well below damage costs, however, then averting climate change represents a good bargain and a desirable interest for the United States.

There is, however, a catch. If global warming continues unabated, it could induce (trigger) a highly adverse, changed state in the earth's climate, with potentially catastrophic consequences. This possibility cannot be discounted, even though its likelihood cannot be estimated. What climatologists do know is this: the magnitude of predicted warming (2–9 degrees centigrade), unless countersteps are quickly taken, will by the end of the twenty-first century approach the range of temperature changes (5–10 degrees centigrade) that accompanied Ice Age transitions; and those transitions occurred in a matter of decades, not centuries. If global warming threatens discontinuous climate change, then averting it becomes a vital, not a desirable, interest for the United States. It therefore makes sense to avert catastrophic climate change by making the investments necessary to retard and ultimately stop human-induced global warming.

### Why Indirect?

Finally, America's military power is best used indirectly to support the achievement of its three desirable interests. The commitment of American military power to Eurasia and the Gulf plays a clear and direct role in retarding the spread of weapons of mass destruction, helping to maintain a deep peace among the great powers, and keeping Persian Gulf oil reserves divided. The link between America's military power and its desirable interests is more diffuse.

In general, the United States should not wage war to make states democratic, nor intervene militarily in their internal affairs to protect human rights. Military intervention for either purpose is a risky and costly proposition: one that usually requires a long-term presence to create the basis for success, as America's experiences with Germany and Japan have illustrated. A better path to democratization and, consequently, to the protection of human rights, is to increase the size of a state's middle class by increasing the state's wealth, which is best achieved through creating a market economy and then having it participate in the global economy. This is the path that South Korea and Taiwan followed, for example. It is a longer lasting and certainly cheaper path than the imposition of democracy by military conquest and long occupation.

There are two clear exceptions to the injunction that the United States should refrain from forceful intervention to create democracy or to protect human rights. The first is the rare occasion when a military intervention by the United States can make the difference in restoring or creating democracy. Such occasions will generally involve small states with weak militaries, an ongoing political crisis, a suitable political base upon which to build democratic institutions, and a willingness on the part of a large segment of the population to welcome an American military presence. There is a further requirement to justify intervention: it must also serve other important American interests. The second exception is to prevent genocidal-like mass murders in those states where outside military intervention is feasible and can be effective. Humanity requires that the international community intervene to prevent or to stop them. Again, such instances are more likely to involve small states with weak militaries, not medium-sized or large states with strong militaries. Even in this instance, however, the United States must eschew going it alone and instead organize international coalitions of the willing, which should also include important actors in the region concerned if possible. Neither type of intervention will be short-term, in-and-out affairs, but will require both a long-term military presence and considerable economic assistance.

Finally, the United States cannot profitably coerce states to engage in free trade at the point of a gun, nor order them under threat of attack to cut back their generation of greenhouse gases. The coercive use of American military power for both these purposes is a losing proposition and beyond America's military might. Instead, a more indirect approach is called for.

America's best hope for achieving its desirable interests is to protect its vital interests. If the line against the spread of weapons of mass destruction can be held, if the world's access to Gulf oil is assured, and if the deep peace among the great powers can be maintained, then what results is an international system that is more peaceful, more prosperous, and more benign than would otherwise be the case. A more peacelike world is an important means for preserving international openness, and openness, in turn, helps generate the wealth that facilitates democratic transitions and that will be necessary to deal with what is likely to prove to be humankind's biggest challenge yet: averting global climatic disaster. A more warlike world, to the contrary, is likely to be less prosperous, more contentious, and less cooperative, and none of these things benefits the United States. In sum, by advancing its vital interests through its military power, the United States can indirectly contribute to realizing its desirable interests and in the process do some good for others.

## THE ALTERNATIVES TO SELECTIVE ENGAGEMENT

Showing that selective engagement has virtues is not equivalent to demonstrating that it is the best grand strategy. That requires a comparison with the six alternatives to it—dominion, global collective security, regional collective security, cooperative security, containment, and isolationism. I argue that the first four are not feasible; the fifth is feasible, but can be readily folded into selective engagement; the sixth is feasible but not desirable.

### The Alternatives

Dominion is a strategy by which the United States literally rules the world. It represents the "Roman option": the United States uses its military power to impose order among all states and to make all of them conform internally to its values. Under the American dominion, world peace and 190-odd American look-alikes would be the results. Dominion is the world policeman role, and for that reason is financially and militarily beyond America's resources. Thus dominion is infeasible.

Next to dominion, collective security is the most demanding grand strategy. Its goal is to stop interstate war, and hence bring interstate peace to all areas where it is imposed. Whether implemented globally or regionally, all states that join a collective security organization take the collective security pledge: all agree to protect one another from aggression—from any and all aggressors. If this system is to work, however, it requires about a 100 percent success rate. Collective security cannot be a sometimes affair: sometimes it works, sometimes it does not. No state will entrust its protection to an organization that purports to protect it from all aggression, but that chooses to do so only selectively.

In the past, moreover, states have not been willing to yield national control over the use of force and give to an international organization a blank check upon which to draw in order to resist or punish aggression. Nor will they do so in the future. Rather, states have retained national control, reserving for themselves the right to decide whether to empower the international organizations they have constructed to punish aggressors. Consequently, the world's two best institutional attempts to prevent aggression on a global scale—the League of Nations and the United Nations—were never genuine collective security organizations, but rather informal concerts of the great powers clothed in collective security rhetoric. For that reason, their combined, punish-the-aggressor record is weak.[10]

Finally, there have been no instances in recorded history of an effective regional collective security organization. The closest approximations in modern times occurred during the Cold War: the Rio Treaty for the Western Hemisphere and the NATO alliance for Western Europe. Neither, however, was a regional collective security organization; rather, both were regional imperiums run and operated by the United States. For all these reasons, then, collective security, too, is politically infeasible and therefore a bad grand strategy for the United States.

The last of the infeasible strategies is cooperative security, the 1990s update of collective security. It consists of two elements: first, a rigorous arms-control approach that aims to make aggression difficult by banning possession of NBC weapons, reducing armaments, emphasizing transparency in military matters, and most important, constructing only defensive weapons; and second, a residual collective security system to protect the victims of aggression in case the arms-control measures fail to prevent it. With these two measures, cooperative security seeks to reduce significantly, if not wholly eliminate, aggressive wars.

This strategy has three problems. First, because cooperative security incorporates a residual collective security system, it depends on a fail-safe procedure that has proven impossible to implement. Second, defensive military systems are incompatible with the requirement for punishing aggressors, because punishment demands that some entity have the offensive military power to punish. Third, cooperative security lodges the punishment power in an entity—the United States and some of its great-power allies—that is politically unacceptable. Cooperative security is in fact a guise for the lesser states of the world to accept a great-power military condominium to impose peace on them. The overwhelming majority of the world's states, however, are not going to accept this and will not practically disarm themselves while the great powers do not. For these reasons, cooperative security is infeasible.

The last two strategies—containment and isolationism—are feasible. Containment is a strategy that seeks to cut down hostile candidate states that aspire to regional or global hegemony before they emerge, or if they do, that prevents them from either expanding territorially or exerting overweening influence over the political and economic affairs of states that come within the aspiring hegemon's orbit. Containment requires military power to prevent territorial expansion, and oftentimes economic and political aid to states on the front line to sustain them in maintaining their independence. For now, there is no state placed to strive for global hegemony; therefore, if the United States applies containment, it will be done regionally. For that reason, it can be easily folded into the strategy of selective engagement in those areas deemed of importance to the United States.

Thus, by a process of elimination, the only serious competitor to selective engagement is isolationism. A grand strategy of isolationism does not call for economic autarky, political noninvolvement with the rest of the world, or abstention from the use of force to protect American interests. Indeed, isolationism is compatible with extensive economic interaction with other nations, vigorous political interactions, and the occasional use of force, often in conjunction with other states, to defend American interests. Rather, the defining characteristics of strategic isolationism are: (1) insistence that the United States make no binding commitments in peacetime to use American military power to aid another state or states, and (2) the most minimal use of force and military involvement abroad. Understood in this sense, isolationism is a unilateralist strategy that retains complete freedom for the United States to determine when, where, how, for what purpose, against whom, and with whom it will use its military power, combined with a determination to do as little militarily as possible abroad. Isolationism, in short, is the policy of the "free hand" and the lightest military touch.

### Selective Engagement Versus Isolationism

An America gone isolationist would cancel all its military alliances because they are peacetime pledges to use American military power to protect other states; would bring all its military forces home, save for its powerful navy periodically sailing the seas and making occasional port stops; and last, would eschew most military involvement overseas. Is this a better option than selective engagement for the United States?

I believe not and think selective engagement preferable to isolationism on four grounds: First, today's isolationists do not embrace all six national interests prescribed above, whereas selective engagers embrace them all.[11] For example, isolationists maintain relative indifference to nuclear spread, and some of them even believe that it may be beneficial because it reduces the probability of war. They assert that America's overseas economic interests no longer require the projection of American military power, and see no great stake in keeping Persian Gulf reserves divided among several powers. To the extent that they believe a deep peace among the Eurasian great powers is important to the United States, they hold that offshore balancing (keeping all American troops in the United States) is as effective as onshore balancing (keeping American forces deployed forward in Eurasia at selected points) and safer. Indeed, most isolationists are prepared to use American military power to defend only two vital American interests: repelling an attack on the American homeland and preventing a great-power hegemon from dominating Eurasia. As a consequence, they can justifiably be called the most selective of selective engagers.

Second, isolationism forgoes the opportunity to exploit the full peacetime political utility of America's alliances and forward-deployed forces to shape events to its advantage. Isolationism's general approach is to cope with events after they have turned adverse rather than to prevent matters from turning adverse in the first place. Thus, even though it does not eschew the use of force, isolationism remains at heart a watching and reactive strategy, not, like selective engagement, a precautionary and proactive one.

Third, isolationism makes more difficult the warlike use of America's military power, when that is required, because it forgoes peacetime forward deployment. This provides the United States with valuable bases, staging areas, intelligence-gathering facilities, in-theater training facilities, and most important, close allies with whom it continuously trains and exercises. These are militarily significant advantages and constitute valuable assets if war needs to be waged. Should the United States have to go to war with an isolationist strategy in force, however, these assets would need to be put together under conditions ranging from less than auspicious to emergency-like. Isolationism thus makes war waging more difficult than it need be.

Fourth, isolationism is not as balanced and diversified a strategy as is selective engagement and not as good a hedge against risk and uncertainty. Selective engagement achieves balance and diversity from its hybrid nature: it borrows the good features from its six competitors but endeavors to avoid their pitfalls and excesses. Like isolationism, selective engagement is wary of the risks of military entanglement overseas, but unlike isolationism, it believes that some entanglements either lower the chances of war or are necessary to protect important American interests even at the risk of war. Unlike collective security, selective engagement does not assume that peace is indivisible, but like collective security, it believes in operating multilaterally in military operations wherever possible to spread the burdens and risks, and asserts that standing alliances make such operations easier to organize and more successful when undertaken. Unlike global containment, selective engagement does not believe current conditions require a full-court press against any great power, but like regional containment, it knows that balancing against an aspiring regional hegemon requires the sustained cooperation of the other powers in the area and that such cooperation is not sustainable without a visible American military presence. Unlike dominion, selective engagement does not seek to dominate others, but like dominion, it understands the power and influence that America's military primacy brings. Finally, like cooperative security, selective engagement seeks transparency in military relations, reductions in armaments, and the control of NBC spread, but unlike cooperative security, it does not put full faith in the reliability of collective security or defensive defense should these laudable aims fail.

Compared to selective engagement, isolationism is less balanced because it is less diversified. It allows standing military coalitions to crumble, forsakes forward deployment, and generally eschews attempts to control the armaments of the other great and not-so-great powers. Isolationism's outstanding virtue is that it achieves complete freedom for the United States to act or not to act whenever it sees fit, but the freedom comes at a cost: the loss of a diversified approach. Most isolationists, of course, are prepared to trade balance and diversity for complete freedom of action, because they see little worth fighting for (save for the two interests enumerated above), because they judge that prior military commitments are not necessary to protect them, and because they calculate that alliances will only put the United States in harm's way.

In sum, selective engagement is a hedging strategy; isolationism is not. To hedge is to make counterbalancing investments in order to avoid or lessen loss. Selective engagement makes hedging bets (primarily through alliances and overseas basing), because it does not believe that the international environment, absent America's precommitted stance and forward presence, will remain benign to America's interests, as apparently does isolationism. An isolationist America in the sense defined above would help produce a more dangerous and less prosperous world; an internationalist America, a more peaceful and prosperous one. As a consequence, engagement rejects the free hand for the selectively committed hand. Thus, for these four reasons—the goals it posits, its proactive stance, its warfighting advantages, and its hedging approach—selective engagement beats isolationism. . . .

## NOTES

1. The differences between rogue and normal states are as follows: Rogue states are usually dictatorships of one sort or another that share three attributes. First, they are opposed to the territorial status quo, committed to expanding their borders at the expense of another state or states. Second, they are prepared to use force, or already have a track record of having used force, to do so. Third, they sponsor terrorists to expand their territory or to achieve other foreign-policy objectives. By these criteria, rogue states are committed expansionists, and Iran, Iraq, Libya, Syria, and North Korea fulfill the criteria. But China, for example, does not. It has not resorted to terrorism. The territories it now claims are either accepted as part of China (Taiwan) or are the subject of contestation and are claimed by many states (the Spratlys in the South China Sea, for example). Finally, China has agreed to settle the Spratly issue diplomatically. By contrast, normal states harbor little or no expansionist designs, are committed to the peaceful resolution of their border and other disputes, and eschew resorting to terrorism for political gain. For a useful survey of America's policy toward the present-day rogues, see Raymond Tanter, *Rogue Regimes: Terrorism and Proliferation* (New York: St. Martin's Press, 1998).

2. I have borrowed these traits from Stephen Van Evera, *The Causes of War: Power and the Roots of War* (Ithaca, N.Y.: Cornell University Press, 1999), chap. 8.

3. The first Waltz quotation is from Kenneth N. Waltz and Scott D. Sagan, *The Spread of Nuclear Weapons: A Debate* (New York: W. W. Norton, 1995), p. 96; the second, from Waltz, "Peace, Stability, and Nuclear Weapons," unpublished ms., January 1997, p. 19.

4. First, there appear to be only two recorded instances of a terrorist group resorting to NBC weapons: the June 1995 sarin (nerve gas) attack on the Japanese city of Matsumoto, which killed 7 people and wounded more than 150; and the March 1995 sarin attack on the Tokyo subway, which killed 12 people and injured thousands of others; both of which were carried out by the Japanese cult group Aum Shinrikiyo. Second, apart from the unrestrained use of chemical weapons during World War I, there have been only twelve other known instances of NBC use by states—only one of which was nuclear (the United States against Japan in 1945); only one biological (Japan against China and the Soviet Union from 1937 to 1945); and the rest chemical, with only three since 1945 that count as rogue-state attacks, two of which involved Iraq. Third, in every one of these twelve cases, the NBC attacks were made on a state or group that could not retaliate in kind. See William J. Broad, "How Japan Germ Terror Alerted World," *New York Times*, May 26, 1998, p. A1, on the first point; and Richard A. Falkenrath, Robert D. Newman, and Bradley A. Thayer, *America's Achilles' Heel: Nuclear, Biological, and Chemical Terrorism and Covert Attack* (Cambridge, Mass.: MIT Press, 1998), p. 91, on the second. For in-depth analyses of the Tokyo sarin attack, see Jessica Stern, "Terrorist Motivations and WMD," unpublished ms., pp. 5–13; and Falkenrath, Newman, and Thayer, *America's Achilles' Heel*, Box 1, pp. 19–26.

5. Notice I have not argued that the United States has an interest in preventing all wars in Eurasia. Non–great-power wars—those between a great and a smaller power or

among smaller powers—affect American interests only to the extent that they dramatically enhance the risk of a great power war, stimulate WMD spread, lead to mass murder, or threaten U.S. alliances.

6. The dampening effects of security competitions on trade is not an ironclad law because the former do not invariably reduce the latter. Peter Liberman has done the best published research to date on the relation between security competitions and trade and concludes that it had little effect in the cases he looked at. I have done research on some of his cases as well as on others, and found that security competitions did significantly reduce trade. See Liberman, "Trading with the Enemy: Security and Relative Economic Gains," *International Security* 21, No. 1 (Summer 1996): pp. 147–76; and Robert J. Art, "Security Competitions and Trade in Historical Perspective," unpublished ms., Brandeis University, July 1998.

7. I favor oil prices that are high enough to encourage conservation and that make alternative sources of energy competitive. For the United States, this requires a higher tax on oil and especially on gasoline because almost two-thirds of America's daily oil consumption goes for transportation.

8. There are those who argue that openness hurts the United States because the United States cannot compete with states that pay lower wages. Openness, these critics assert, is the primary cause of America's loss of manufacturing capacity and lower wages for its unskilled labor. The evidence does not support either proposition. The United States remains the world's most competitive economy (because it maintains greater openness to international competition), and trade plays only a small role (about 20 percent) in the decline in wages for unskilled labor. . . .

9. The static gains estimate comes from Paul Krugman, *The Age of Diminished Expectations: U.S. Economic Policy in the 1990s* (Cambridge, Mass.: MIT Press, 1990), p. 104. It represents Krugman's estimate of the cost to the United States of its protectionist measures in force around 1990. It should also be noted that large economies like the United States reap smaller static gains from free trade because they have already reaped considerable economies of scale from their large internal markets. See Krugman and Maurice Obstfeld, *International Economics: Theory and Practice*, 3d ed. (New York: Harper-Collins, 1994), pp. 228–29, for a discussion of static and dynamic gains from trade.

10. There were thirty-two interstate wars between 1922 and 1991. The League and the United Nations attempted collective security enforcement (punishment of interstate aggression) only three times. The first (League action against Italy in 1936) was a fiasco and effectively destroyed the League. The second (assistance to South Korea to repel a North Korean attack in 1950) was a United Nations operation in name, but in fact an American affair, and took place only because the Soviet Union happened to boycott the Security Council meeting on the day that the action was voted. The third (the 1991 Gulf War to evict Iraq from Kuwait) was another American-run affair and was blessed by the UN. The thirty-two interstate wars for these seventy years can be found in "Correlates of War Project: International and Civil War Data, 1816–1992" (ICPR 9905), Inter-University Consortium for Political and Social Research, Ann Arbor, Michigan, April 1994.

11. I realize that not every one of today's isolationists holds to every one of the propositions portrayed by the sketch in this paragraph. All of today's isolationists, however, do adhere to most of them. Therefore, although this picture distorts to a degree, as all composites do, still it is a rough approximation of the outlook of today's isolationists.

# 20

# America's Imperial Ambition

## G. JOHN IKENBERRY

**THE LURES OF PREEMPTION**

In the shadows of the Bush administration's war on terrorism, sweeping new ideas are circulating about U.S. grand strategy and the restructuring of today's unipolar world. They call for American unilateral and preemptive, even preventive, use of force, facilitated if possible by coalitions of the willing—but ultimately unconstrained by the rules and norms of the international community. And the extreme, these notions form a neoimperial vision in which the United States arrogates to itself the global role of setting standards, determining threats, using force, and meting out justice. It is a vision in which sovereignty becomes more absolute for America even as it becomes more conditional for countries that challenge Washington's standards of internal and external behavior. It is a vision made necessary—at least in the eyes of its advocates—by the new and apocalyptic character of contemporary terrorist threats and by America's unprecedented global dominance. These radical strategic ideas and impulses could transform today's world order in a way that the end of the Cold War, strangely enough, did not. . . .

America's nascent neoimperial grand strategy threatens to rend the fabric of the international community and political partnerships precisely at a time when that community and those partnerships are urgently needed. It is an approach fraught with peril and likely to fail. It is not only politically unsustainable but diplomatically harmful. And if history is a guide, it will trigger antagonism and resistance that will leave America in a more hostile and divided world.

321

## PROVEN LEGACIES

The mainstream of American foreign policy has been defined since the 1940s by two grand strategies that have built the modern international order. One is realist in orientation, organized around containment, deterrence, and the maintenance of the global balance of power. Facing a dangerous and expansive Soviet Union after 1945, the United States stepped forward to fill the vacuum left by a waning British Empire and a collapsing European order to provide a counterweight to Stalin and his Red Army.

The touchstone of this strategy was containment, which sought to deny the Soviet Union the ability to expand its sphere of influence. Order was maintained by managing the bipolar balance between the American and Soviet camps. Stability was achieved through nuclear deterrence. For the first time, nuclear weapons and the doctrine of mutual assured destruction made war between the great powers irrational. But containment and global power-balancing ended with the collapse of the Soviet Union in 1991. Nuclear deterrence is no longer the defining logic of the existing order, although it remains a recessed feature that continues to impart stability in relations among China, Russia, and the West.

This strategy has yielded a bounty of institutions and partnerships for America. The most important have been the NATO and U.S.-Japan alliances, American-led security partnerships that have survived the end of the Cold War by providing a bulwark for stability through commitment and reassurance. The United States maintains a forward presence in Europe and East Asia; its alliance partners gain security protection as well as a measure of regularity in their relationship with the world's leading military power. But Cold War balancing has yielded more than a utilitarian alliance structure; it has generated a political order that has value in itself.

This grand strategy presupposes a loose framework of consultations and agreements to resolve differences: the great powers extend to each other the respect of equals, and they accommodate each other until vital interests come into play. The domestic affairs of these states remain precisely that—domestic. The great powers compete with each other, and although war is not unthinkable, sober statecraft and the balance of power offer the best hope for stability and peace. . . .

The other grand strategy, forged during World War II as the United States planned the reconstruction of the world economy, is liberal in orientation. It seeks to build order around institutionalized political relations among integrated market democracies, supported by an opening of economies. This agenda was not simply an inspiration of American businessmen and economists, however. There have always been geopolitical goals as well. Whereas America's realist grand strategy was aimed at countering Soviet power, its liberal grand strategy was aimed at avoiding a return to the 1930s, an era of regional blocs, trade conflict, and strategic rivalry. Open trade, democracy, and multilateral institutional relations went together. Underlying this strategy was the view that a rule-based international order, especially one in which the United States uses its political weight to derive congenial rules, will most fully protect American interests, conserve its power, and extend its influence.

This grand strategy has been pursued through an array of postwar initiatives that look disarmingly like "low politics": the Bretton Woods institutions, the World Trade Organization (WTO), and the Organization for Economic Cooperation and Development are just a few examples. Together, they form a complex layer cake of integrative initiatives that bind the democratic industrialized world together. During the 1990s, the United States continued to pursue this liberal grand strategy. Both the first Bush and the Clinton administrations attempted to articulate a vision of world order that was not dependent on an external threat or an explicit policy of balance of power. Bush the elder talked about the importance of the transatlantic community and articulated ideas about a more fully integrated Asia-Pacific region. In both cases, the strategy offered a positive vision of alliance and partnership built around common values, tradition, mutual self-interest, and the preservation of stability. The Clinton administration likewise attempted to describe the post–Cold War order in terms of the expansion of democracy and open markets. In this vision, democracy provided the foundation for global and regional community, and trade and capital flows were forces for political reform and integration. . . .

## AMERICA'S HISTORIC BARGAINS

These two grand strategies are rooted in divergent, even antagonistic, intellectual traditions. But over the last 50 years they have worked remarkably well together. The realist grand strategy created a political rationale for establishing major security commitments around the world. The liberal strategy created a positive agenda for American leadership. The United States could exercise its power and achieve its national interests, but it did so in a way that helped deepen the fabric of international community. American power did not destabilize world order; it helped create it. The development of rule-based agreements and political-security partnerships was good both for the United States and for much of the world. By the end of the 1990s, the result was an international political order of unprecedented size and success: a global coalition of democratic states tied together through markets, institutions, and security partnerships.

This international order was built on two historic bargains. One was the U.S. commitment to provide its European and Asian partners with security protection and access to American markets, technology, and supplies within an open world economy. In return, these countries agreed to be reliable partners providing diplomatic, economic, and logistical support for the United States as it led the wider Western postwar order. The other is the liberal bargain that addressed the uncertainties of American power. East Asian and European states agreed to accept American leadership and operate within an agreed-upon political-economic system. The United States, in response, opened itself up and bound itself to its partners. In effect, the United States built an institutionalized coalition of partners and reinforced the stability of these mutually beneficial relations by making itself more "user-friendly"—that is, by playing by the rules and creating ongoing political processes that facilitated consultation and joint decision-making. The United States made its power safe for the world, and in return the world agreed to live within the U.S. system. These bargains date from the 1940s, but they continue to shore up the post–Cold War order. The result has been the most stable and prosperous international system in world history. But new ideas within the Bush administration—crystallized by September 11 and U.S. dominance—are unsettling this order and the political bargains behind it.

## A NEW GRAND STRATEGY

For the first time since the dawn of the Cold War, a new grand strategy is taking shape in Washington. It is advanced most directly as a response to terrorism, but it also constitutes a broader view about how the United States should wield power and organize world order. According to this new paradigm, America is to be less bound to its partners and to global rules and institutions while it steps forward to play a more unilateral and anticipatory role in attacking terrorist threats and confronting rogue states seeking WMD. The United States will use its unrivaled military power to manage the global order.

This new grand strategy has seven elements. It begins with a fundamental commitment to maintaining a unipolar world in which the United States has no peer competitor. No coalition of great powers without the United States will be allowed to achieve hegemony. Bush made this point the centerpiece of American security policy in his West Point commencement address in June: "America has, and intends to keep, military strengths beyond challenges—thereby making the destabilizing arms races of other eras pointless, and limiting rivalries to trade and other pursuits of peace." The United States will not seek security through the more modest realist strategy of operating within a global system of power balancing, nor will it pursue a liberal strategy in which institutions, democracy, and integrated markets reduce the importance of power politics altogether. America will be so much more powerful than other major states that strategic rivalries and security competition among the great powers will disappear, leaving everyone—not just the United States—better off.

This goal made an unsettling early appearance at the end of the first Bush administration in a leaked Pentagon memorandum written by then Assistant Secretary of Defense Paul Wolfowitz. With the collapse of the Soviet Union, he wrote, the United States must act to prevent the rise of peer competitors in Europe and Asia. But the 1990s made this strategic aim moot. The United States grew faster than the other major states during the decade, it reduced military spending more slowly, and it dominated investment in the technological advancement of its forces. Today, however, the new goal is to make these advantages permanent—a fait accompli that will prompt other states to not even try to catch up. Some thinkers have described the strategy as "breakout," in which the United States moves so quickly to develop technological advantages (in robotics, lasers, satellites, precision munitions, etc.) that no state or coalition could ever challenge it as global leader, protector, and enforcer.

The second element is a dramatic new analysis of global threats and how they must be attacked. The grim new reality is that small groups of terrorists—perhaps aided by outlaw states—may soon acquire highly destructive nuclear, chemical, and biological weapons that can inflict catastrophic destruction. These terrorist groups cannot be appeased or deterred, the administration believes, so they must be eliminated. Secretary of Defense Donald Rumsfeld has articulated this frightening view with elegance: regarding the threats that confront the United States, he said, "There are things we know that we know. There are known unknowns. That is to say, there are things that we know we don't know. But there are also unknown unknowns. There are things we don't know we don't know. . . . Each year, we discover a few more of those unknown unknowns." In other words, there could exist groups of terrorists that no one knows about. They may have nuclear, chemical, or biological weapons that the United States did not know they could get, and they might be willing and able to attack without warning. In the age of terror, there is less room for error. Small networks of angry people can inflict unimaginable harm on the rest of the world. They are not nation-states, and they do not play by the accepted rules of the game.

The third element of the new strategy maintains that the Cold War concept of deterrence is outdated. Deterrence, sovereignty, and the balance of power work together. When deterrence is no longer viable, the larger realist edifice starts to crumble. The threat today is not other great powers that must be managed through second-strike nuclear capacity but the transnational terrorist networks that have no home address. They cannot be deterred because they are either willing to die for their cause or able to escape retaliation. The old defensive strategy of building missiles and other weapons that can survive a first strike and be used in a retaliatory strike to punish the attacker will no longer ensure security. The only option, then, is offense.

The use of force, this camp argues, will therefore need to be preemptive and perhaps even preventive—taking on potential threats before they can present a major problem. But this premise plays havoc with the old international rules of self-defense and United Nations norms about the proper use of force. Rumsfeld has articulated the justification for preemptive action by stating that the "absence of evidence is not evidence of absence of weapons of mass destruction." But such an approach renders international norms of self-defense—enshrined by Article 51 of the UN Charter—almost meaningless. The administration should remember that when Israeli jets bombed the Iraqi nuclear reactor at Osirak in 1981 in what Israel described as an act of self-defense, the world condemned it as an act of aggression. Even British Prime Minister Margaret Thatcher and the American ambassador to the UN, Jeane Kirkpatrick, criticized the action, and the United States joined in passing a UN resolution condemning it.

The Bush administration's security doctrine takes this country down the same slippery slope. Even without a clear threat, the United States now claims a right to use preemptive or preventive military force. At West Point, Bush put it succinctly when he stated that "the military must be ready to strike at a moment's notice in any dark corner of the world. All nations that decide for aggression and terror will pay a price." The administration defends this new doctrine as a necessary adjustment to a more uncertain and shifting threat environment. This policy of no regrets errs on the side of action—but it can also easily become national security by hunch or inference, leaving the world without clear-cut norms for justifying force.

As a result, the fourth element of this emerging grand strategy involves a recasting of the terms of sovereignty. Because these terrorist groups cannot be deterred, the United States must be prepared to intervene anywhere, anytime to preemptively destroy the threat. Terrorists do not respect borders, so neither can the United States. Moreover, countries that harbor terrorists, either by consent or because they are unable to enforce their laws within their territory, effectively forfeit their rights of sovereignty. . . .

Here the war on terrorism and the problem of the proliferation of WMD get entangled. The worry is that a few despotic states—Iraq in particular, but also Iran and North Korea—will develop capabilities to produce weapons of mass destruction and put these weapons in the hands of terrorists. The regimes themselves may be deterred from using such capabilities, but they might pass along these weapons to terrorist networks that are not deterred. Thus another emerging principle within the Bush administration: the possession of WMD by unaccountable, unfriendly, despotic governments is itself a threat that must be countered. In the old era, despotic regimes were to be lamented but ultimately tolerated. With the rise of terrorism and weapons of mass destruction, they are now unacceptable threats. Thus states that are not technically in violation of any existing international laws could nevertheless be targets of American force—if Washington determines that they have a prospective capacity to do harm.

The recasting of sovereignty is paradoxical. On the one hand, the new grand strategy reaffirms the importance of the territorial nation-state. After all, if all governments were accountable and capable of enforcing the rule of law within their sovereign territory, terrorists would find it very difficult to operate. The emerging Bush doctrine enshrines this idea: governments will be held responsible for what goes on inside their borders. On the other hand, sovereignty has been made newly conditional: governments that fail to act like respectable, law-abiding states will lose their sovereignty. . . .

The fifth element of this new grand strategy is a general depreciation of international rules, treaties, and security partnerships. This point relates to the new threats themselves: if the stakes are rising and the margins of error are shrinking in the war on terrorism, multilateral norms and agreements that sanction and limit the use of force are just annoying distractions. The critical task is to eliminate the threat. But the emerging unilateral strategy is also informed by a deeper suspicion about the value of international agreements themselves. Part of this view arises from a deeply felt and authentically American belief that the United States should not get entangled in the corrupting and constraining world of multilateral rules and institutions. For some Americans, the belief that American sovereignty is politically sacred leads to a preference for isolationism. But the more influential view—particularly after September 11—is not that the United States should withdraw from the world but that it should operate in the world on its own terms. The Bush administration's repudiation of a remarkable array of treaties and institutions—from the Kyoto Protocol on global warming to the International Criminal Court to the Biological Weapons Convention—reflects this new bias. Likewise, the United States signed a formal agreement with Russia on the reduction of deployed nuclear warheads only after Moscow's insistence; the Bush administration wanted only a "gentlemen's agreement." In other words, the United States has decided it is big enough, powerful enough, and remote enough to go it alone.

Sixth, the new grand strategy argues that the United States will need to play a direct and unconstrained role in responding to threats. This conviction is partially based on a judgment that no other country or coalition—even the European Union—has the force-projection capabilities to respond to terrorist and rogue states around the world. A decade of U.S. defense spending and modernization has left allies of the United States far behind. In combat operations, alliance partners are increasingly finding it difficult to mesh with U.S. forces. This view is also based on the judgment that joint operations and the use of force through coalitions tend to hinder effective operations. To some observers, this lesson became clear in the allied bombing campaign over Kosovo. The sentiment was also expressed during the U.S. and allied military actions in Afghanistan, Rumsfeld explained this point earlier this year, when he said, "The mission must determine the coalition; the coalition must not determine the mission. If it does, the mission will be dumbed down to the lowest common denominator, and we can't afford that."

No one in the Bush administration argues that NATO or the U.S.-Japan alliance should be dismantled. Rather, these alliances are now seen as less useful to the United States as it confronts today's threats. Some officials argue that it is not that the United States chooses to depreciate alliance partnerships, but that the Europeans are unwilling to keep up. Whether that is true, the upgrading of the American military, along with its sheer size relative to the forces of the rest of the world, leaves the United States in a class by itself. In these circumstances, it is increasingly difficult to maintain the illusion of true alliance partnership. America's allies become merely strategic assets that are useful depending on the circumstance. The United States still finds attractive the logistical reach that its global alliance system provides, but the pacts with countries in Asia and Europe become more contingent and less premised on a vision of a common security community.

Finally, the new grand strategy attaches little value to international stability. There is an unsentimental view in the unilateralist camp that the traditions of the past must be shed. Whether it is withdrawal from the Anti-Ballistic Missile Treaty or the resistance to signing other formal arms-control treaties, policymakers are convinced that the United States needs to move beyond outmoded Cold War thinking. Administration officials have noted with some satisfaction that America's withdrawal from the ABM Treaty did not lead to a global arms race but actually paved the way for a historic arms-reduction agreement between the United States and Russia. This move is seen as a validation that moving beyond the old paradigm of great-power relations will not bring the international house down. The world can withstand radically new security approaches, and it will accommodate American unilateralism as well. But stability is not an end in itself. The administration's new hawkish policy toward North Korea, for example, might be destabilizing to the region, but such instability might be the necessary price for dislodging a dangerous and evil regime in Pyongyang.

In this brave new world, neoimperial thinkers contend that the older realist and liberal grand strategies are not very helpful. American security will not be ensured, as realist grand strategy assumes, by the preservation of deterrence and stable relations among the major powers. In a world of asymmetrical threats, the global balance of power is not the linchpin of war and peace. Likewise, liberal strategies of building order around open trade and democratic institutions might have some long-term impact on terrorism, but they do not address the immediacy of the threats. Apocalyptic violence is at our doorstep, so efforts at strengthening the rules and institutions of the international community are of little practical value. If we accept the worst-case imagining of "we don't know what we don't know," everything else is secondary: international rules, traditions of partnership, and standards of legitimacy. It is a war. And as Clausewitz famously remarked, "War is such a dangerous business that the mistakes which come from kindness are the very worst."

## IMPERIAL DANGERS

Pitfalls accompany this neoimperial grand strategy, however. Unchecked U.S. power, shorn of legitimacy and disentangled from the postwar norms and institutions of the international order, will usher in a more hostile international system, making it far harder to achieve American interests. The secret of the United States' long brilliant run as the world's leading state was its ability and willingness to exercise power within alliance and multinational frameworks, which made its power and agenda more acceptable to allies and other key states around the world. This achievement has now been put at risk by the administration's new thinking.

The most immediate problem is that the neoimperialist approach is unsustainable. Going it alone might well succeed in removing Saddam Hussein from power, but it is far less certain that a strategy of counterproliferation, based on American willingness to use unilateral force to confront dangerous dictators, can work over the long term. An American policy that leaves the United States alone to decide which states are threats and how best to deny them weapons of mass destruction will lead to a diminishment of multilateral mechanisms—most important of which is the nonproliferation regime. . . .

The specific doctrine of preemptive action poses a related problem: once the United States feels it can take such a course, nothing will stop other countries from doing the same. Does the United States want this doctrine in the hands of Pakistan, or even China or Russia? After all, it would not require the intervening state to first provide evidence for its actions. The United States argues that to wait until all the evidence is in, or until authoritative international bodies support action, is to wait too long. Yet that approach is the only basis that the United States can use if it needs to appeal for restraint in the actions of others. Moreover, and quite paradoxically, overwhelming American conventional military might, combined with a policy of preemptive strikes, could lead hostile states to accelerate programs to acquire their only possible deterrent to the United States: WMD. This is another version of the security dilemma, but one made worse by a neoimperial grand strategy.

Another problem follows. The use of force to eliminate WMD capabilities or overturn dangerous regimes is never simple, whether it is pursued unilaterally or by a concert of major states. After the military intervention is over, the target country has to be put back together. Peacekeeping and state building are inevitably required, as are long-term strategies that bring the UN, the World Bank, and the major powers together to orchestrate aid and other forms of assistance. This is not heroic work, but it is utterly necessary. Peacekeeping troops may be required for many years, even after a new regime is built. Regional conflicts inflamed by outside military intervention must also be calmed. This is the "long tail" of burdens and commitments that comes with every major military action.

When these costs and obligations are added to America's imperial military role, it becomes even more doubtful that the neoimperial strategy can be sustained at home over the long haul—the classic problem of imperial overstretch. The United States could keep its military predominance for decades if it is supported by a growing and increasingly productive economy. But the indirect burdens of cleaning up the political mess in terrorist-prone failed states levy a hidden cost. Peacekeeping and state building will require coalitions of states and multilateral agencies that can be brought into the process only if the initial decisions about military intervention are hammered out in consultation with other major states. America's older realist and liberal grand strategies suddenly become relevant again.

A third problem with an imperial grand strategy is that it cannot generate the cooperation needed to solve practical problems at the heart of the U.S. foreign policy agenda. In the fight on terrorism, the United States needs cooperation from European and Asian countries in intelligence, law enforcement, and logistics. Outside the security sphere, realizing U.S. objectives depends even more on a continuous stream of amicable working relations with major states around the world. It needs partners for trade liberalization, global financial stabilization, environmental protection, deterring transnational organized crime, managing the rise of China, and a host of other thorny challenges. But it is impossible to expect would-be partners to acquiesce to America's self-appointed global security protectorate and then pursue business as usual in all other domains.

The key policy tool for states confronting a unipolar and unilateral America is to withhold cooperation in day-to-day relations with the United States. One obvious means is trade policy; the European response to the recent American decision to impose tariffs on imported steel is explicable in these terms. This particular struggle concerns specific trade issues, but it is also a struggle over how Washington exercises power. The United States may be a unipolar military power, but economic and political power is more evenly distributed across the globe. The major states may not have much leverage in directly restraining American military policy, but they can make the United States pay a price in other areas.

Finally, the neoimperial grand strategy poses a wider problem for the maintenance of American unipolar power. It steps into the oldest trap of powerful imperial states: self-encirclement. When the most powerful state in the world throws its weight around, unconstrained by rules or norms of legitimacy, it risks a backlash. Other countries will bridle at an international order in which the United States plays only by its own rules. The proponents of the new grand strategy have assumed that the United States can single-handedly deploy military power abroad and not suffer untoward consequences; relations will be coarser with friends and allies, they believe, but such are the costs of leadership. But history shows that powerful states tend to trigger self-encirclement by their own overestimation of their power. Charles V, Louis XIV, Napoleon, and the leaders of post-Bismarck Germany sought to expand their imperial domains and impose a coercive order on others. Their imperial orders were all brought down when other countries decided they were not prepared to live in a world dominated by an overweening coercive state. America's imperial goals and modus operandi are much more limited and benign than were those of age-old emperors. But a hard-line imperial grand strategy runs the risk that history will repeat itself.

## BRING IN THE OLD

Wars change world politics, and so too will America's war on terrorism. How great states fight wars, how they define the stakes, how they make the peace in its aftermath—all give lasting shape to the international system that emerges after the guns fall silent. In mobilizing their societies for battle, wartime leaders have tended to describe the military struggle as more than simply the defeat of an enemy. Woodrow Wilson sent U.S. troops to Europe not only to stop the kaiser's army but to destroy militarism and usher in a worldwide democratic revolution. Franklin Roosevelt saw the war with Germany and Japan as a struggle to secure the "four great freedoms." The Atlantic Charter was a statement of war aims that called not just for the defeat of fascism but for a new dedication to social welfare and human rights within an open and stable world system. To advance these visions, Wilson and Roosevelt proposed new international rules and mechanisms of cooperation. Their message was clear: If you bear the burdens of war, we, your leaders, will use this dreadful conflict to usher in a more peaceful and decent order among states. Fighting the war had as much to do with building global relations as it did with vanquishing an enemy.

Bush has not fully articulated a vision of postwar international order, aside from defining the struggle as one between freedom and evil. The world has seen Washington take determined steps to fight terrorism, but it does not yet have a sense of Bush's larger, positive agenda for a strengthened and more decent international order.

This failure explains why the sympathy and goodwill generated around the world for the United States after September 11 quickly disappeared. Newspapers that once proclaimed, "We are all Americans," now express distrust toward America. The prevailing view is that the United States seems prepared to use its power to go after terrorists and evil regimes, but not to use it to help build a more stable and peaceful world order. The United States appears to be degrading the rules and institutions of international community, not enhancing them. To the rest of the world, neoimperial thinking has more to do with exercising power than with exercising leadership.

In contrast, America's older strategic orientations—balance-of-power realism and liberal multilateralism—suggest a mature world power that seeks stability and pursues its interests in ways that do not fundamentally threaten the positions of other states. They are strategies of co-option and reassurance. The new imperial grand strategy presents the United States very differently: a revisionist state seeking to parlay its momentary power advantages into a world order in which it runs the show. Unlike the hegemonic states of the past, the United States does not seek territory or outright political domination in Europe or Asia; "America has no empire to extend or utopia to establish," Bush noted in his West Point address. But the sheer power advantages that the United States possesses and the doctrines of preemption and counterterrorism that it is articulating do unsettle governments and people around the world. The costs could be high. The last thing the United States wants is for foreign diplomats and government leaders to ask, How can we work around, undermine, contain, and retaliate against U.S. power?

Rather than invent a new grand strategy, the United States should reinvigorate its older strategies, those based on the view that America's security partnerships are not simply instrumental tools but critical components of an American-led world political order that should be preserved. U.S. power is both leveraged and made more legitimate and user-friendly by these partnerships. The neoimperial thinkers are haunted by the specter of catastrophic terrorism and seek a radical reordering of America's role in the world. America's commanding unipolar power and the advent of frightening new terrorist threats feed this imperial temptation. But it is a grand strategic vision that, taken to the extreme, will leave the world more dangerous and divided—and the United States less secure.

# 21

# Missile Defence and American Ambitions

## Victor A. Utgoff

The long campaign to halt and reverse proliferation of nuclear weapons has had both setbacks and victories. There is little doubt that the campaign has been a major factor in keeping the number of nuclear states far below what was projected in the early years of the nuclear age. Still, the campaign has not prevented the number of nuclear states from expanding from five to at least eight since the Non-Proliferation Treaty went into force in 1970. Moreover, at least two states with a history of aggression are currently pursuing nuclear weapons.

Ballistic missiles and the technology to build them have also been proliferating. While this proliferation has been suppressed to some extent by the creation of the Missile Technology and Control Regime in 1987 and other export-control efforts, some states are still exporting technology applicable to long-range missiles, and even selling complete missiles. At least 15 states already have ballistic missiles with a range of 1,000 kilometres or greater, and nine have intercontinental-range ballistic missiles or space-launch capabilities. Further, at least two states with a history of aggression are seeking to upgrade their ballistic missiles to allow delivery of nuclear weapons to intercontinental ranges.

Exactly how far along these various programmes are at this point is uncertain. But no one can be confident that much-improved ballistic missiles armed with nuclear or other weapons of mass destruction will not come into the hands of aggressive states within a few years. It is even possible that some unrevealed capabilities already exist to deliver a few nuclear-armed missile attacks to targets at intercontinental ranges.

These commonplace observations directly support the American pursuit of missile defences. But the utility of effective missile defences goes far beyond the simple fact that they would counter potential nuclear threats or largely reduce the damage caused if aggressive states were to use such weapons. First, if these threats are not countered, potential non-nuclear victims of aggression by nuclear-armed states could doubt that strong and reliable protection would be available. Second, the presumed absence of strong and reliable protection can be expected, before long, to lead to a highly proliferated nuclear world. And third, such a world will prove intolerable for reasons including the very plausible expectation that it will suffer the occasional nuclear war. The first of these points seems clear enough. The second two deserve some discussion.

## ACCELERATING PROLIFERATION

As proliferation continues, it generates increased pressures for further proliferation. For example, some states may be discouraged by each failure of international efforts to limit proliferation and come to see runaway proliferation as inevitable. Accordingly, such states may feel it prudent to make contingency preparations to become nuclear powers themselves, in turn causing other states to do the same. In addition, states may feel encouraged to develop WMD by the extra attention and other types of political and economic gains won by states that have previously done so. Indeed some states will feel that they must have their own nuclear deterrent forces simply because their spread ultimately makes them a key symbol of a modern state.

The strongest increases in pressures to proliferate are felt by states that see themselves as potential targets of aggression by those who have gone nuclear or are about to. Prospective victims cannot expect to counter an opponent's nuclear weapons solely by increases in their own conventional forces. Conventional forces alone cannot destroy an invader nearly as well as the invader could likely paralyse most victims with small numbers of nuclear strikes. Nor can prospective victims solve their problems solely by building defences against attacks with nuclear weapons. Defences are inevitably less than perfect and an opponent who did not fear retaliation in kind would feel little reluctance to test them. Thus, states that feel they have been placed in jeopardy by an aggressor's proliferation will likely conclude they must also have nuclear weapons—either directly, or indirectly through alliance with a strong and reliable state that already has them.

Pressures to develop nuclear weapons can also be driven by increases in the conventional military power of an aggressive state that prospective victims cannot match. And proliferation can be motivated by an aggressor's hope that its nuclear weapons would deter other states from coming to a prospective victim's aid. In all these cases, the most powerful way to minimise pressures for nuclear proliferation is to ensure the availability of reliable protectors strong enough to defeat aggression and capable of retaliation in kind.

This logical argument for the anti-proliferation efficacy of powerful protectors seems reasonably well demonstrated by the history of nuclear proliferation. Even the original development of nuclear weapons by the United States was driven by the fear that Nazi Germany was trying to develop such weapons and the knowledge that only the US could counter this threat if it were to emerge. While a variety of different factors drove proliferation by each successive state that built nuclear weapons, each of the current nuclear states saw great danger from some prospective enemy that already had such weapons, combined with doubts that, lacking such weapons itself, it could get sufficiently strong and reliable protection from others.

Further, the large number of states that became capable of building nuclear weapons over the years, but chose not to, can be reasonably well explained by the fact that most were formally allied with either the United States or the Soviet Union. Both these superpowers had strong nuclear forces and put great pressure on their allies not to build nuclear weapons. Since the Cold War, the US has retained all its allies. In addition, NATO has extended its protection to some of the previous allies of the Soviet Union and plans on taking in more. Nuclear proliferation by India and Pakistan, and proliferation programmes by North Korea, Iran and Iraq, all involve states in the opposite situation: all judged that they faced serious military opposition and had little prospect of establishing a reliable supporting alliance with a suitably strong, nuclear-armed state.

What would await the world if strong protectors, especially the United States, were no longer seen as willing to protect states from nuclear-backed aggression? At least a few additional states would begin to build their own nuclear weapons and the means to deliver them to distant targets, and these initiatives would spur increasing numbers of the world's capable states to follow suit. Restraint would seem ever less necessary and ever more dangerous. Meanwhile, more states are becoming capable of building nuclear weapons and long-range missiles. Many, perhaps most, of the world's states are becoming sufficiently wealthy, and the technology for building nuclear forces continues to improve and spread.

Finally, it seems highly likely that at some point, halting proliferation will come to be seen as a lost cause and the restraints on it will disappear. Once that happens, the transition to a highly proliferated world would probably be very rapid. While some regions might be able to hold the line for a time, the threats posed by wildfire proliferation in most other areas could create pressures that would finally overcome all restraint.

## HAZARDS OF A HIGHLY PROLIFERATED WORLD

Many readers are probably willing to accept that nuclear proliferation is such a grave threat to world peace that every effort should be made to avoid it. However, every effort has not been made in the past, and we are talking about much more substantial efforts now. For new and substantially more burdensome efforts to be made to slow or stop nuclear proliferation, it needs to be established that the highly proliferated nuclear world that would sooner or later evolve without such efforts is not going to be acceptable. And, for many reasons, it is not.

First, the dynamics of getting to a highly proliferated world could be very dangerous. Proliferating states will feel great pressures to obtain nuclear weapons and delivery systems before any potential opponent does. Those who succeed in outracing an opponent may consider preemptive nuclear war before the opponent becomes capable of nuclear retaliation. Those who lag behind might try to pre-empt their opponent's nuclear programme or defeat the opponent using conventional forces. And those who feel threatened but are incapable of building nuclear weapons may still be able to join in this arms race by building other types of weapons of mass destruction, such as biological weapons.

Second, as the world approaches complete proliferation, the hazards posed by nuclear weapons today will be magnified many times over. Fifty or more nations capable of launching nuclear weapons means that the risk of nuclear accidents that could cause serious damage not only to their own populations and environments, but those of others, is hugely increased. The chances of such weapons falling into the hands of renegade military units or terrorists is far greater, as is the number of nations carrying out hazardous manufacturing and storage activities.

## INCREASED PROSPECTS FOR THE OCCASIONAL
## NUCLEAR SHOOTOUT

Worse still, in a highly proliferated world there would be more frequent opportunities for the use of nuclear weapons. And more frequent opportunities means shorter expected times between conflicts in which nuclear weapons get used, unless the probability of use at any opportunity is actually zero. To be sure, some theorists on nuclear deterrence appear to think that in any confrontation between two states known to have reliable nuclear capabilities, the probability of nuclear weapons being used is zero. These theorists think that such states will be so fearful of escalation to nuclear war that they would always avoid or terminate confrontations between them, short of even conventional war. They believe this to be true even if the two states have different cultures or leaders with very eccentric personalities. History and human nature, however, suggest that they are almost surely wrong.

History includes instances in which states known to possess nuclear weapons did engage in direct conventional conflict. China and Russia fought battles along their common border even after both had nuclear weapons. Moreover, logic suggests that if states with nuclear weapons always avoided conflict with one another, surely states without nuclear weapons would avoid conflict with states that had them. Again, history provides counter-examples. Egypt attacked Israel in 1973 even though it saw Israel as a nuclear power at the time. Argentina invaded the Falkland Islands and fought Britain's efforts to take them back, even though Britain had nuclear weapons.

Those who claim that two states with reliable nuclear capabilities to devastate each other will not engage in conventional conflict risking nuclear war also assume that any leader from any culture would not choose suicide for his nation. But his-

tory provides unhappy examples of states whose leaders were ready to choose suicide for themselves and their fellow citizens. Hitler tried to impose a 'victory or
destruction' policy on his people as Nazi Germany was going down to defeat. And
Japan's war minister, during debates on how to respond to the American atomic
bombing, suggested 'Would it not be wondrous for the whole nation to be destroyed
like a beautiful flower?'

If leaders are willing to engage in conflict with nuclear-armed nations, use of
nuclear weapons in any particular instance may not be likely, but its probability
would still be dangerously significant. In particular, human nature suggests that the
threat of retaliation with nuclear weapons is not a reliable guarantee against a disastrous first use of these weapons. While national leaders and their advisors everywhere are usually talented and experienced people, even their most important decisions cannot be counted on to be the product of well-informed and thorough
assessments of all options from all relevant points of view. This is especially so
when the stakes are so large as to defy assessment and there are substantial pressures to act quickly, as could be expected in intense and fast-moving crises between
nuclear-armed states.

Instead, like other human beings, national leaders can be seduced by wishful
thinking. They can misinterpret the words or actions of opposing leaders. Their
advisors may produce answers that they think the leader wants to hear, or coa-
lesce around what they know is an inferior decision because the group urgently
needs the confidence or the sharing of responsibility that results from settling on
something. Moreover, leaders may not recognise clearly where their personal or
party interests diverge from those of their citizens.

Under great stress, human beings can lose their ability to think carefully. They
can refuse to believe that the worst could really happen, oversimplify the problem
at hand, think in terms of simplistic analogies and play hunches. The intuitive rules
for how individuals should respond to insults or signs of weakness in an opponent
may too readily suggest a rash course of action. Anger, fear, greed, ambition and
pride can all lead to bad decisions. The desire for a decisive solution to the problem at hand may lead to an unnecessarily extreme course of action.

We can almost hear the kinds of words that could flow from discussions in
nuclear crises or war. 'These people are not willing to die for this interest'. 'No
sane person would actually use such weapons'. 'Perhaps the opponent will back
down if we show him we mean business by demonstrating a willingness to use
nuclear weapons'. 'If I don't hit them back really hard, I am going to be driven
from office, if not killed'. Whether right or wrong, in the stressful atmosphere of
a nuclear crisis or war, such words from others, or silently from within, might
resonate too readily with a harried leader. Thus, both history and human nature
suggest that nuclear deterrence can be expected to fail from time to time, and we
are fortunate it has not happened yet. But the threat of nuclear war is not just a
matter of a few weapons being used. It could get much worse. Once a conflict
reaches the point where nuclear weapons are employed, the stresses felt by the

leaderships would rise enormously. These stresses can be expected to further degrade their decision-making. The pressures to force the enemy to stop fighting or to surrender could argue for more forceful and decisive military action, which might be the right thing to do in the circumstances, but maybe not. And the horrors of the carnage already suffered may be seen as justification for visiting the most devastating punishment possible on the enemy.

Again, history demonstrates how intense conflict can lead the combatants to escalate violence to the maximum possible levels. In the Second World War, early promises not to bomb cities soon gave way to essentially indiscriminate bombing of civilians. The war between Iran and Iraq during the 1980s led to the use of chemical weapons on both sides and exchanges of missiles against each other's cities. And more recently, violence in the Middle East escalated in a few months from rocks and small arms to heavy weapons on one side, and from police actions to air strikes and armoured attacks on the other.

Escalation of violence is also basic human nature. Once the violence starts, retaliatory exchanges of violent acts can escalate to levels unimagined by the participants beforehand. Intense and blinding anger is a common response to fear or humiliation or abuse. And such anger can lead us to impose on our opponents whatever levels of violence are readily accessible.

In sum, widespread proliferation is likely to lead to an occasional shoot-out with nuclear weapons, and that such shoot-outs will have a substantial probability of escalating to the maximum destruction possible with the weapons at hand. Unless nuclear proliferation is stopped, we are headed toward a world that will mirror the American Wild West of the late 1800s. With most, if not all, nations wearing nuclear 'six-shooters' on their hips, the world may even be a more polite place than it is today, but every once in a while we will all gather on a hill to bury the bodies of dead cities or even whole nations.

This kind of world is in no nation's interest. The means for preventing it must be pursued vigorously. And, as argued above, a most powerful way to prevent it or slow its emergence is to encourage the more capable states to provide reliable protection to others against aggression, even when that aggression could be backed with nuclear weapons. In other words, the world needs at least one state, preferably several, willing and able to play the role of sheriff, or to be members of a sheriff's posse, even in the face of nuclear threats.

## THE MISSILE-DEFENCE ALTERNATIVE

States that intend to confront aggressors armed with nuclear weapons should not be asked to depend on deterrence through devastating retaliation as their only protection against nuclear attack. The chances that nuclear deterrence might fail are too great, given the substantial differences between the security-related perspectives of nuclear-armed regional aggressors and those of the US. These differences are greater than those that came to exist between the US and the Soviet

Union, once both sides had learned the sobering lessons of the Cuban missile crisis. Lowering the prospects that nuclear deterrence will fail is a direct purpose of missile defences.

Differences in perspectives between the US and regional aggressors are worth some discussion. First, in deciding to engage in aggression, the nuclear-armed regional challenger would have made the judgments that his stakes and risks strongly favour aggression, while those of potential protectors from outside the region strongly favour staying on the sidelines. The challenger would likely characterise his issues with the prospective victim as bilateral, perhaps with some significance for the region, but not of substantial importance for outsiders. The challenger would expect prospective protectors to see his commitment to wining as sufficient to make his escalation to the use of nuclear weapons a serious possibility. In contrast, he would expect that the prospective protectors would not value the stakes highly enough to run the risk of nuclear war. But the US and other protectors could see far broader implications. At a minimum, they would see the aggression as a fundamental challenge to international law and order that would likely lead to more such challenges in the same or other regions if not defeated.

Second, and equally important, the challenger and prospective protectors could have very different perceptions of the political and military usefulness of owning nuclear weapons. The challenger could see his hard-won nuclear deterrent as the key to military freedom of action within his region. Again, protectors can be expected to take a broader view. For them, it would be a disaster to ignore aggression that would likely be opposed if the challenger did not have nuclear weapons. Tolerating nuclear-backed aggression would teach a dangerous lesson to everyone, that nuclear weapons could be effective offensive weapons rather than the strictly defensive weapons they have been since the end of the Second World War. This could help spur nuclear proliferation both by states with aggressive ambitions and by those who fear becoming victims.

Third, the challenger and potential protectors might also have very different attitudes toward gambling with the lives of their citizens. For example, an aggressive leader might see the status quo as trapping his state in an intolerable economic and political position. Thus, he might view a challenge that could dramatically improve his nation's long-term prospects as worth a substantial risk that a large fraction of his citizens might be killed or that his regime might be totally defeated. As a less charitable example, an aggressive leader might have a psychological disposition toward taking highly risky initiatives. The leader might also think that the US and other potential protectors were too rich, too soft, or too politically vulnerable to be willing to run any significant risk of being struck with a nuclear weapon.

Fourth, stress levels could also be very different for the challenger and the protectors. In particular, in standing up to aggression by regional states armed with a small number of nuclear weapons, the US would know that its own existence would not be at risk, but the challenger would not. In fact, the challenger might have expected the US to ignore its actions and thus be surprised and shocked to be confronted by a military giant.

Finally, the more likely challengers tend to have very different forms of government with less trustful civil-military relations and cultures that are very different from those of the US and its allies. And they often have leaders with eccentric views. These differences can also refract clear thinking and interpretations of the meanings of other nations' actions and add to the potential that nuclear weapons might get used.

Such differences in perspectives collectively make the probability of a regional war involving the use of nuclear weapons all too high. Accordingly, reducing the destruction that could result if deterrence of nuclear use by a regional aggressor were to fail is a second direct purpose for creating effective missile defences.

## INDIRECT PURPOSES OF MISSILE DEFENCES

Missile defences for the states that may have to protect others from aggression backed with nuclear weapons are also important for other indirect purposes. First, by largely suppressing the effectiveness of a prospective aggressor's nuclear-armed missiles, defences could ruin his confidence that potential protectors would see intervention as too risky and allow his aggression to succeed. Thus, defences would largely restore the degree of effective deterrence of aggression that had existed before the prospective aggressor had acquired its missiles and nuclear weapons.

Second, missile defences are also important for drawing together and maintaining coalitions to confront nuclear-armed aggressors. Unless reasonably strong defences can be provided, states other than the US and those immediately and directly threatened by the aggressor might not be willing to join. But the legitimacy provided by broad coalitions for the kinds of actions that might prove necessary in confronting nuclear-armed aggressors could be especially important. In particular, if nuclear retaliation were to prove necessary, the US should not be seen as having acted unilaterally.

Third, if a nuclear-armed state did launch a nuclear attack, US and allied missile defences could save significantly more lives than one might at first think. While reducing losses suffered by the US and its allies is the most important and direct purpose of the defences, these reductions could also justify a less destructive retaliation. More specifically, every US or allied citizen saved by the defence could mean that one of the aggressor's citizens is saved as well.

Fourth, missile defences could substantially alleviate the pressures for quick action by the US and its allies. For example, by sharply reducing the potential damage an opponent's missiles might cause, defences could allow protectors to take a 'wait and see' approach to any initial aggression, rather than risk starting a war by a preemptive attack against the opponent's weapons. Avoiding unnecessary preemptive attacks would be especially important if destruction of the opponent's weapons were to impose high risks on people in surrounding areas.

Similarly, by reducing the damage wreaked by an aggressor's initial attack, effective missile defences could give decision-makers more scope to delay retaliation. Delay would allow more careful consideration of how to respond, including closer consultation with allies and others involved. This would be important in obtaining a broad legitimisation of US actions. Of course, the US might not want to exploit this possibility in any given case, perhaps seeing very prompt retaliation as most likely to suppress the further use of nuclear weapons in the situation at hand.

Effective defences could also largely suppress any final lashing-out by the attacker if he were faced with total defeat. This, of course, would make it easier for the US and its coalition partners to pursue the attacker's total defeat. Better yet, if the prospective protectors had missile defences, a nuclear-armed state could no longer assume that its opponents could not afford to drive it to the point where it had nothing left to lose. With total defeat a more credible prospect, such aggression should be better deterred.

Note that in all but the first of the foregoing arguments, the effect of missile defences is to increase the freedom of action of the US and its allies. Defences would permit less destructive or less immediate retaliation, make it less risky to forgo or, alternatively, to carry out preemptive attacks, and would reduce the risks and potential costs of imposing total defeat on an aggressor. In some circumstances, the US and its allies might see no advantage in such increased freedom of action. But the enhancements to this freedom come bundled together, and on balance, seem well worth having. In general, increased freedom of action for the protectors should translate into less promising options for aggression.

Defences are also important for the morale of the states that would be expected to defend against aggression backed by nuclear weapons. If the need to confront such aggression arises, the US and its coalition partners would feel entitled to the added assurance that such defences would provide. Facing aggression without such defences, in the knowledge that they could have been provided, could create a certain resentment at having to run unnecessary risks.

Correspondingly, if such defences had been built, especially with the acquiescence of states seriously inconvenienced by their creation, the US would then feel more obligated to perform the duties of protector. Indeed, it would likely be the state best prepared to do so.

## WHAT TO EXPECT FROM AMERICA

The arguments made thus far can be combined as follows. Continued nuclear proliferation will eventually accelerate, leading to a world where many and perhaps most states will have nuclear weapons, which occasionally will be used. Ensuring reliable, strong protection against nuclear-armed aggression is a most powerful way to delay, if not avoid, that dangerous world. Moreover, states that are expected to perform the protector's role, together with their coalition partners, should have the best possible defences against nuclear attack. And, as the aggressive states seeking nuclear weapons have so far chosen ballistic missiles to deliver weapons to distant targets, effective defences against nuclear attacks must include missile defences.

Nonetheless, even if equipped with such defences, the protectors and their coalition partners would still risk substantial damage from the relatively few nuclear attacks that might leak through. If, as a result, they could not be counted on to provide the needed protection, other states should have little reason to accept the inconveniences and concerns that the missile defence initiative could cause them. So how much commitment to protecting non-nuclear states can be expected from the US and its allies? Two arguments seem relevant here.

## MISSILE DEFENCES AND US COMMITMENT

The first argument uses realist assumptions to explain the need for missile defences. It suggests that the commitment of a state to defending any specific interest is largely determined by how the perceived value of the interest compares with the projected risks and other costs of protecting it. This point of view suggests that some less-than-vital interests might be sacrificed if the risk of defending them were to rise sharply, as would happen if a state that sought to challenge such an interest were to obtain nuclear-armed ballistic missiles.

To capitalise on its new capabilities, the newly armed regional challenger would have to identify which interests the US and other prospective protectors no longer saw as worth the risk of defending. We should expect the challenger to think that important gains were possible, given the dramatic increase in risks that it could impose on possible defenders. Nor should we be surprised if the challenger demonstrates considerable confidence and skill in picking interests to test whose values are not the highest in the eyes of their prospective defenders, or at least not clearly appreciated.

The function of effective defences in this case should be obvious. If the defences can largely suppress the threat posed by the challenger's nuclear weapons, the original relationship between the interests in dispute and the risks involved in defending them would be largely restored. Thus, defences would have largely restored the original credibility of the protector's willingness to stand up to aggression against such interests. In other words, defences would have restored something approaching the original level of deterrence of challenges to such interests.

Two examples illustrate this point. First, it is sometimes claimed that the US would not have rolled back Iraq's 1990 invasion of Kuwait if Iraq had had nuclear-armed missiles at the time. This claim may or may not be true, but if the US and its allies had also possessed highly effective missile defences, the situation would have been largely the same as that presented in 1990, and it is reasonable to suppose that the US would have gone ahead. Similarly, Chinese officials have argued that the US would not defend Taiwan at the risk of nuclear strikes against the US homeland. The claim is also disputable, but even if true, highly effective defences against Chinese ICBMs clearly would make defence of Taiwan by the US more credible.

This realist argument, in essence, is that reasonably effective missile defences could largely offset the perceived unwillingness of the US and its partners to defend less-than-vital interests that are threatened by nuclear-armed aggressors. The argument is quite convincing, at least where the strength of the underlying US commitment is strong enough to offset the residual threat of damage posed by leakage through the defences.

## THE US IS COMMITTED ALREADY

The second argument for missile defences originates from the international security role that the US sees itself fulfilling. The long-standing and generally successful US campaign to shape a world much in its own image implies a strong and enduring commitment to protect that world and the US role in it. This commitment seems likely to draw the US into protecting non-nuclear states from aggressors with nuclear-armed missiles, even if the US does not have missile defences and thus depends for its protection on the threat of nuclear retaliation. But if the US is coming to the rescue in any event, its moral claim to such defences is overwhelming. Who could reasonably expect the US to forgo such defences, given their potential to save lives and perhaps even deter the use of nuclear weapons, or even to dissuade the challenges that might lead to such use?

This argument does not rest upon missile defences reducing potential damage to some low level at which the US would become willing to come to the rescue. Rather, missile defences are to reduce *as much as possible* the potential damage if an aggressor were not deterred from using nuclear weapons, and to provide the other useful indirect values discussed earlier.

A realist viewpoint suggests that the US should be motivated to stand up to regional aggression, because failure to do so risks not just an avalanche of proliferation but also, as a result, a radical transformation of the distribution of global military power. As argued above, if the US and the other influential states were to allow aggression backed by nuclear weapons to succeed, these weapons would be transformed from purely defensive weapons, which they have been since the end of the Second World War, into weapons that could enable successful aggression. Aggressive states already owning nuclear weapons could be expected to attempt to capitalise on the offensive potential of their weapons that had thus been revealed. Other states would soon seek nuclear weapons for offensive or defensive purposes.

The resulting political realignments among states could be very dynamic, and the new global political map that ultimately emerged would look significantly different from the one we have today. The distribution of national power would derive less from historical fundamentals such as geographical size, natural resources, population, culture and productivity. Power would be distributed more equally among all states with nuclear weapons. And, whether for good or evil in the eyes of others, the current military predominance and influence of the US would be reduced.

All things considered, it seems likely that most states would be more comfortable with global power arrangements based on the historical fundamentals than with a power distribution based on nuclear weapons. But no matter how other states might answer this question, this prospective change in the distribution of power is easily foreseen and would be very painful for the US. Thus, its prospect can be expected to be a strong motivation for the US to confront such aggression.

Considerations of bureaucratic politics also suggest a substantial US motivation to stand up to regional aggression. The role of US military forces for the last half a century or more has been to intervene overseas in defence of US interests. If US forces came to be judged as unusable or unnecessary for confronting or protecting a growing number of regional states that obtained nuclear weapons, they could seem less worth maintaining. The US military would not disappear, but its character would change dramatically. It would surely be smaller and spend far more time at home than today's US forces with their world-wide roles.

An even stronger set of US motivations to confront regional aggression, even when backed with nuclear weapons, is that failure to do so would risk the United States' deeply held visions of what it is as a nation and the international role that it plays. It seems clear that most Americans believe that the international role that the US has played so successfully and for so long remains the right role for America. In addition, the US would see consequences of failing to confront nuclear-armed aggression not just in terms of the real values of the interests lost and put at risk, but more generally as a threat to the most basic of America's international 'good works', its long-term campaign to support the growth of democracy.

Further, US pride would be at stake. The spectacle of the world's strongest nation averting its eyes while a far weaker state with a small number of nuclear weapons rolled over an even weaker non-nuclear opponent would be devastating to the US image and reputation, at home and abroad. US allies and friends would be shaken to the core and would show it. Unless the US found a way to reverse the damage resulting from a failure to confront nuclear-backed regional aggression, the movement towards a peaceful and cooperative democratic international community aspired to by most states would be thrown roughly into reverse. The US, which perceives itself as the guardian of this world order, would thus feel strongly obliged to confront such aggression.

In summary, for a variety of mutually reinforcing realist, bureaucratic, political and historical–psychological reasons, the US would likely stand up to aggression against other states, even when that aggression was backed by nuclear weapons. And while missile defences can make US and other states more credible protectors, perhaps the stronger claim to such defences is that it is immoral to ask the US and others to run the risks of performing this essential role without them. Finally, states concerned by the US pursuit of missile defences should recognise that by fitting itself so well to continue to play the role of protector, the US is strengthening its obligation to fulfill that role.

## CONCLUSION

Ballistic missile defences appear to be a necessary part of the all-important effort to stop nuclear proliferation. They are needed to assure non-nuclear states that the United States and other supporting nations would be willing to protect them from aggression, even when backed by nuclear-armed ballistic missiles. If the world came to doubt the availability of such protection, widespread nuclear proliferation seems inevitable both by would-be aggressors and by those who would fear becoming their victims. And for reasons elaborated above, a highly proliferated nuclear world will almost surely be marked by occasional bursts of spectacularly devastating nuclear warfare, not the universal peace that some have projected.

On the other hand, seeing the US move towards protecting itself from ballistic missile attacks can disturb not just the rogue states, but others who fear a US with both overwhelming offensive military power and effective defences. Again, for reasons elaborated above, it seems most unlikely that the US could develop a military capability to dominate with impunity an unwilling world, or even that it could bring itself to try to establish such a degree of hegemony.

Nonetheless, US development and deployment of effective defences against ballistic missile attack seems likely to have substantial effects on how nuclear forces around the world evolve, on how the threat posed by nuclear proliferation is perceived, and more generally on how the world at large arranges for its security. Given the potential magnitude and uncertainties of these effects, and the many years that it will take to resolve them, the movement toward missile defences will be a leap of faith for all concerned.

How then can the US and the larger international community make each other more comfortable with this endeavour? Improved understanding of each other's purposes and concerns would help. The US can further clarify the role it expects to play in underwriting international security in the future and especially the general limits it will respect. Operating consistently within reasonable limits would go a long way to curb fears that the US might abuse the great military power needed to underwrite adequate global stability.

At the same time, the international community could do a lot more to clarify its views on practical political–military means for maintaining global peace in a world where weapons of mass destruction could become possible for nearly any state or outlaw group. If there is a better and more feasible solution to this problem than that which the US is moving toward, it is important to find it soon. And pending the appearance of a better solution, cooperation in making defences work to the best advantage of global security and stability seems essential.

## NOTE

1. 'Chairman Stump To Lead Congressional Delegation To Commemorate V-J Day', Press release of the House Committee on Veterans' Affairs, 30 August 1995.

# 22

# Missile Defenses and the Multiplication of Nuclear Weapons

## KENNETH N. WALTZ

The value of missile defenses was debated from the late 1950s onward. Earlier, as now, it was claimed that a fanatical, lightly armed nuclear state might try to blackmail its neighbors, or even attack the United States. In 1967, for example, Secretary of Defense McNamara argued for erecting defenses against China's nascent nuclear capability. He found it "conceivable" that, even though a Chinese nuclear attack on the United States or its allies would be "insane and suicidal," China might "miscalculate."[1] Obviously, it was conceivable—McNamara had just conceived of it. But for China then and for North Korea now, or for Iraq or whomever, the conception is preposterous. Mao Zedong did not reign from 1949 to 1976 by pursuing insane foreign and military policies, nor do Kim Jong Il, Saddam Hussein, or other rulers of so-called rogue states.

Secretary Rumsfeld has noticed that "the genie is out of the bottle. . . . People are going to have very powerful weapons. And they don't care about safety, they don't care about reliability, they don't care about making big volumes of these things. If they get them, they have power and they can alter behavior."[2] They surely are altering ours, and we have made much "bigger volumes of these things" than they ever will. Although rogues do some terrible things, if they behaved as Rumsfeld imagines, they would have awfully short careers. A secretary of defense ought to pay some attention to how other states, including bad states, behave militarily.

National missile defenses pose greater dangers to us and to others than the slow spread of nuclear weapons. The best thing about such defenses is that they won't work. The worst thing about them is that merely setting development and deployment in motion has damaging effects on us and on others.

The many reasons why defenses against nuclear weapons won't work have been rehearsed often enough. According to Rumsfeld, it does not matter if defenses do not work well. Deploying them will make would-be attackers uncertain about how many of their weapons will "slip past the shield," and uncertainty will deter them. Our deterrent forces already make them tremble with fear at the thought of the destruction that might await the perpetrator of a nuclear attack. In Rumsfeld's view, that is not enough to deter, but the prospect of our shooting some things down would be. Presumably they are smart enough to calculate the problematic effects of our future defenses, but too dumb to understand the risks of launching attacks that risk their own destruction. In October of 1964, Khrushchev boasted that the Soviet Union had a new missile that could "hit a fly in the sky." That, of course, is not the problem. One would have to hit many flies in the sky after separating the flies from the fleas. Some warheads may get through, and the attacker and the attacked will both believe that.

Missile defenses would be the most complicated systems ever deployed, and they would have to work with near perfection in meeting their first realistic test—the test of enemy fire. No president will rely on such systems but will instead avoid actions that might provoke an attack. With or without defenses, the constraints on American actions are the same. The would-be attacker who doubts that some of its warheads will get through has three simple recourses. One is to multiply warheads. Since offensive nuclear weapons are much cheaper than defensive measures, that is easily done. To play nuclear defense is to play the mug's game, a game that cannot be won. McNamara, Khrushchev, Brezhnev, Caspar Weinberger, Putin, Sha Zukang, and many others have said that if "they" deploy defenses, "we" will increase the numbers of our warheads.[3] The second way to defeat defenses is by mounting decoys on missiles and spreading chaff to confuse the defense. The third way to thwart missile defenses is to avoid them. ICBMs are the least likely way a rogue state would choose to deliver warheads. Since they can easily be delivered in many other ways, why would rogues not choose the easier ones? An Indian commentator has even suggested delivery by oxcart. One can multiply the ways of placing warheads on targets. An especially bothersome way is delivery by cruise missiles. The international commercial fleet has thousands of container ships, and American ports handle more than thirteen million containers yearly. Even bulky cruise missiles, such as Chinese Silkworms, fit into standard containers and can be fired at any port city in the world. Defending against cruise missiles is even more difficult than shooting ballistic missiles down.

The threat of ballistic missile attacks by North Korea serves as an excuse, albeit a flimsy one, to build defenses that the administration hopes will be useful against China. When Secretary of State Colin Powell was briefed on the deal made by the Clinton administration to supply aid to North Korea in return for its easily verified promise not to develop and test medium- and long-range missiles, he called it "a splendid bargain."[4] His reaction less colorfully echoed George Schultz's earlier remark that trading Star Wars for reductions in the

Soviet Union's nuclear arsenal would be like "giving them the sleeves off our vest."[5] The new Bush administration nevertheless drew back from the arrangement that the Clinton administration had made.

If it is possible to be extremely moderate, Chinese nuclear programs have been that. A light American defense with about one hundred interceptors is expected to knock twenty-five warheads down. Impartial observers may not believe that the defenses will do that well, but China will assume that they may do even better, and it will arm itself accordingly. Where China leads, India and Pakistan will follow. The result, President Putin fears, may be "a hectic uncontrolled arms race on the borders of our country."[6] The only effective response to a nuclear threat, or to a conventional threat that one cannot meet, lies in the ability to retaliate. In the nuclear world, defense looks like offense; SDI, strategic defense initiative, should have been labeled SOI, strategic offense initiative. The shield makes the sword usable. Reagan understood the offensive implications of nuclear defenses, but played them down. With a lack of political sensibility that would be astonishing in other administrations, the present Bush administration plays them up. As Bush has said, "They seek weapons of mass destruction . . . to keep the United States and other responsible nations from helping allies and friends in strategic parts of the world."[7] In short, we want to be able to intervene militarily whenever and wherever we choose. Our nuclear defenses would presumably make that possible even against countries lightly armed with nuclear weapons.

The first effect of developing defenses is to cause other states to multiply the number of their nuclear weapons and to think of sneaky ways of delivering them. The cheapest way for Russia to overcome fears that American defenses will diminish their deterrent, however, is to place more warheads on their land-based missiles, one of the most dangerous forms of nuclear weaponry. The new Bush administration surpasses Clinton's in foolishness. An official of Clinton's administration told Russian officials that if our potential defenses should make Russia uneasy, it could simply keep a thousand missiles on full alert. To implement Bush's and Rumsfeld's dreams of defense is more dangerous for us and the world than a small number of nuclear weapons in the hands of India and Pakistan, or North Korea or Iraq for that matter. Nuclear defenses destroy arms-control agreements. Agreements to control and reduce nuclear weapons are more useful than attempts to defend against them.

Some countries want us to be able to intervene militarily on their behalf; others do not. Given American nuclear and conventional dominance, what are the latter countries to do? Our dominance presses them to find ways of blocking our interventionist moves. As ever, dominance, coupled with immoderate behavior by one country, causes others to look for ways to protect their interests. China wants to incorporate Taiwan if only in loose form. Even if China has no intention of using force, and clearly it prefers not to, it believes that the prospect of American military protection of Taiwan removes the threat of force from China's set of diplomatic tools. Taiwan will have less reason to compromise. China reacts as one would expect it to. Acquiring Russian Oscar II class submarines, capable of disabling our aircraft carriers, is one response. Another is maintaining a minimal nuclear deterrent against the United States.

American intelligence reports that our defenses may prompt China to multiply its nuclear arsenal by ten and to place multiple warheads on its missiles. The mere prospect of American missile defense promotes the vertical proliferation of nuclear weapons. It also encourages the horizontal spread of nuclear weapons from one country to another. Japan, already made uneasy by China's increasing economic and military capabilities, will become uneasier still as China acts to counter America's prospective defenses. Since the new Bush administration has rent the fabric of agreements that brought nuclear weapons under a modicum of control, and since we offer nothing to replace it, other countries try harder to take care of themselves. North Korea, Iraq, Iran, and others believe that America can be held at bay only by deterrence. Weapons of mass destruction are the only means by which they can hope to deter the United States. They cannot hope to do so by relying on conventional weapons. During the cold war we used nuclear weapons to offset the Soviet Union's conventional strength. Other countries may now use nuclear weapons to offset ours. Les Aspin, when he was chairman of the house Armed Services Committee, put this thought in the following words: "A world without nuclear weapons would not be disadvantageous to the United States. In fact, a world without nuclear weapons would actually be better. Nuclear weapons are still the big equalizer, but now the United States is not the equalizer but the equalizee."[8]

Our conventional dominance spurs other countries to resort to unconventional means. To understand others' reactions we have to look to our own behavior. Bush emphasizes our readiness to consult other countries. In his lexicon, "consult" means that we explain our policies and then implement them whether other countries like them or not. "One reads about the world's desire for American leadership only in the United States," a British diplomat has observed. "Everywhere else one reads about American arrogance and unilateralism."[9] When we add to dominance and arrogance the unwillingness to ratify treaties made and the intention to renounce treaties ratified, we have a recipe for encouraging other states to go nuclear. The United States led the way in negotiating the Comprehensive Test Ban Treaty. One hundred and sixty-one countries had signed the treaty as of July 6, 2001, and seventy-seven had ratified it. Yet administration officials now look for ways of escaping from the treaty's restrictions. Moreover, in recent years we have pursued ways of improving the design of warheads and enhancing their power by using such methods as computer simulations, methods in which our abilities far exceed those of others. Why should we not welcome a treaty that so clearly serves our interests? Bush hopes that other countries will reduce the number of their nuclear weapons while we build defenses and improve our weapons. If his fantasy were to become reality, America would be able to act on its whims whenever and wherever it chose to. Because other countries know this, our policies promote the spread of nuclear weapons both upwards and sideways.

Over a span of six decades, relations among nuclear countries have been peaceful beyond historical precedent. Nuclear pessimists have a simple explanation for this: We have been lucky. Kanti Bajpai believes that deterrence is "fragile and fraught" and in the long run unstable. Apparently, fifty-some years is not a long enough run to confirm the stability of nuclear deterrence. General George Lee Butler, commander of STRATCOM before his retirement in 1994, believes that "we escaped disaster by the grace of God."[10] God may, as Otto von Bismarck said, watch out for "fools, drunkards, and the United States." Yet one wonders why He should favor the United States and just those other nations with nuclear weapons while showing little mercy for many others. If indeed the world has skirted nuclear disaster by sustained good luck or by God's grace, then it would be high time to take matters in our own hands. Those who credit the good-luck explanation sometimes propose remedies. Butler's is the abolition of nuclear weapons. Michael Mandelbaum's and Eliot Cohen's is preventive strikes at the nuclear facilities of would-be nuclear states. Reagan's was, and Bush's is, nuclear defense.

Fortunately, all such remedies are fanciful. They would deny the peaceful benefits of nuclear weapons to those who need them. It is far more sensible to face the fact that nuclear weapons are here to stay, and that once in a long while they will spread to another country or two. We should ask how we can continue to reap the benefits of nuclear weapons while reducing the dangers inherent in them. Two obvious ways are by reducing the numbers in the absurdly large arsenals of the United States and Russia and by taking weapons off hair-trigger alert. Dropping defensive measures is a third way.

Even though in the nuclear business deterrence is cheap and easy while defense is costly and difficult, our thought seems to be that we can mount effective defenses because we have the money and the technology that others lack. When one side mounts defenses, however, others seek ways to defeat or outflank them. With conventional weapons, this may be difficult. With nuclear weapons, it is easy. Nuclear defenses attempt to pose an absolute defense against an absolute weapon. The logic of nuclear defense is the logic of conventional warfare. Conventional war pits weapons against weapons. That is exactly what nuclear defenses would do, thereby recreating the instabilities that plague countries armed only with conventional weapons. We know the dangers of offensive/defensive races from centuries of experience with conventional weapons. The major mischief of American defensive efforts is not only that they may sharpen the efforts of a few countries to make their own nuclear weapons but also that they may recreate the contest between offense and defense with all its unfortunate consequences. Why should anyone want to replace stable deterrence with unstable defense?

How can we perpetuate peace without solving the problem of war? This is the question that states with nuclear weapons must constantly answer. Nuclear states continue to compete militarily. With each state tending to its interests as best it can, war is constantly possible. Although the possibility of war remains, nuclear weapons have drastically reduced the probability of its being fought by states having them. Wars that might bring nuclear weapons into play have become extraordinarily hard to start. Over the centuries, great powers have fought more wars and lesser states have fought fewer. The frequency of war has correlated less closely with the attributes of states than with their international standing. Yet, because of a profound change in military technology, waging war has more and more become the privilege of poor and weak states. Nuclear weapons have reversed the fates of strong and weak states. Never in modern history have great powers enjoyed a longer period of peace than we have known since the Second World War. One can scarcely believe that the presence of nuclear weapons does not greatly help to explain this happy condition.

## NOTES

1. Robert S. McNamara, Speech delivered before the editors of the United Press International, San Francisco, September 18, 1967. Excerpted in Robert J. Art and Kenneth N. Waltz, *The Use of Force* (Boston: Little, Brown, 1971), pp. 503ff.

2. James Dao, "Rumsfeld Calls on Europe to Rethink Arms Control," *New York Times,* June 11, 2001, p. A8.

3. Sha is director of arms control and disarmament in China's Foreign Ministry.

4. Powell, cited in Richard Cohen, "Political Science," *Washington Post,* May 3, 2001, p. A21.

5. Schultz, quoted in Frances FitzGerald, "The Poseurs of Missile Defense," *New York Times,* June 4, 2000, sec. 4, p. 19.

6. Patrick E. Tyler, "Putin Says Russia Would Add Arms to Counter Shield," *New York Times,* June 19, 2001, p. A1.

7. Excerpts from President Bush's Speech, *New York Times,* May 2, 2001, p. A10.

8. "Three Propositions for a New Era Nuclear Policy," Commencement Address, Massachusetts Institute of Technology, June 1, 1992. Published in *Tech Talk* by the MIT News Office, Cambridge, Mass., June 3, 1992, p. 2. Available on-line at web.mit.edu/news office/tt/1992/jun03/26094/html.

9. Quoted in Samuel P. Huntington, "The Lonely Superpower," *Foreign Affairs* 78, no 2 (March/April 1999), p. 42.

10. Kanti Bajpai, "The Fallacy of an Indian Deterrent," pp. 179, 150; Butler quoted in James Carroll, "War Inside the Pentagon," *The New Yorker,* August 18, 1997, p. 59.

# 23

---

# What If Iraq Had Had
# Nuclear Weapons?

BARRY R. POSEN

The problem of preventing nuclear proliferation has become one of the highest priority issues on the U.S. national security policy agenda. . . . It is, nevertheless, quite possible that the U.S. will one day confront a situation in which a nuclear-armed regional power threatens to trespass upon, or actually has trespassed upon, a very important U.S. national interest. The U.S. military research and engineering establishment will not have produced an array of offensive and defensive weaponry which permits a senior military commander to assure the president of the United States that the adversary cannot successfully explode a nuclear weapon on the territory of a U.S. ally, or over a U.S. military force, or even on the United States itself. As far as one can tell, the consideration of how the United States would handle this situation has not proceeded very far. The national security policy community, in and out of government, is beguiled by the possibility of a happy ending. It is hoped that nonproliferation policy will prevent most proliferation and that a combination of weapons and tactics will negate the capabilities of those who slip through the policy net.

This essay assesses why the United States might act forcefully in a confrontation with an expansionist state in possession of a modest nuclear retaliatory capability, and how it may proceed. The vehicle for this assessment is a counterfactual historical analysis of the U.S. reaction to Iraq's invasion of Kuwait in 1990. For heuristic purposes, I introduce a small nuclear force into the Iraqi arsenal—a half-dozen weapons and the means to deliver them regionally. These weapons cannot reliably be located for conventional or nuclear preemption, and their delivery systems are sufficiently capable that extant defensive weaponry cannot intercept them

353

reliably. I postulate that Saudi leaders invite the United States to send forces to help deter an Iraqi attack on the kingdom immediately following the invasion of Kuwait. I then ask two questions. Should the United States consider the military liberation of Kuwait? If so, what strategy should it employ to do so? In the sections below entitled "The view from 1990–91," I insert myself, with my premises and analytic tools, into this situation and offer the policy advice that I think I would have given. These premises are broadly consistent with the international relations theoretical tradition known as realism. The tools are offense-defense theory, deterrence theory, and limited war theory. . . . I speculate, in the sections entitled "The view from 1996," on the answers to two additional questions. To what extent would my advice *to act* have found a sympathetic hearing among some of the actual participants in the crisis? To what extent would my advice on *how to act* have found a sympathetic ear? I use evidence from the actual crisis to support my answers to these questions. . . .

Below I develop the following recommendations for the U.S. government about the hypothesized scenario.

1. The United States should have tried to liberate Kuwait because of the general strategic consequences of inaction, not because of the intrinsic strategic value of Kuwait. Indeed, the whole definition of the crisis should have changed to "the first post–cold war nuclear crisis." The likely consequences of inaction are developed at length, and provide the core of the argument for action.

2. To support a liberation campaign, the United States ought to have pursued a strategy of "intrawar deterrence." It needed to make explicit and ferocious threats that nuclear retaliation would occur if Saddam Hussein used nuclear weapons on any member of the Coalition. It had to explain to Saddam Hussein through a very sympathetic diplomatic campaign why the United States was compelled to liberate Kuwait, and would be forced to retaliate with nuclear weapons if Iraq employed them.

3. The Coalition should, however, have pursued a military strategy of "limited war" in this operation: both ends and means ought to have been restrained. This would have been the best way to control the risks. Therefore, to ensure the limitation of U.S. military operations an intensive discussion on the nature and scope of these military operations among and between civilians and soldiers would have been essential.

4. Finally I show that the participants in the crisis did in fact confront issues quite analogous to those I raise. I reason that actual behavior suggests that the three recommendations above would have found a sympathetic hearing.

## THE RISKS OF INACTION

### The View from 1990–91

U.S. decisionmakers must immediately face one very important fact. This is the first post–cold war nuclear crisis. It is a defining moment. The actual stakes—

Kuwait's oil and Iraq's power—are probably secondary to the more fundamental question. What will nuclear weapons mean? The "consensus" at the end of the cold war is that nuclear weapons deter nuclear attacks on oneself or one's allies, and arguably deter conventional invasion of one's own territory, and to a lesser and more debatable extent, the territory of one's allies.

Will the United States and its allies, through inaction, allow Nth country nuclear forces to become potent instruments of aggression against non-nuclear powers? If the Iraqi conquest of Kuwait is permitted to stand, nuclear weapons will come to be viewed as a shield that protects conventional conquests from *any* challenger, including a great power heavily armed with its own nuclear weapons. Conventional forces take; nuclear forces hold! The context will matter as well. Very important interests of the world's sole surviving superpower will have been successfully trampled by a state of modest conventional and tiny nuclear capabilities.

The United States has explicitly asserted a vital interest in the independence of the various Gulf oil states, and in the free flow of oil out of the region, since the fall of the Shah of Iran. The United States has programmed and deployed military forces and assets for the explicit purpose of protecting this interest. The United States has employed military force in operation Earnest Will to defend the free flow of oil. Since 1973, the United States has devoted considerable diplomatic effort and financial resources to the achievement of a settlement of the Arab-Israeli conflict. It is fair to say that there is no place else in the world where the United States has been so active diplomatically and militarily without formal treaty relationships. Capitulation to Saddam Hussein's coup de main will therefore enhance the image of nuclear weapons as great equalizers. Indeed, their successful exploitation to deter a conventional *counterattack* to liberate ill-gotten gains makes them seem even more valuable.

. . . It is important to note that nuclear weapons have not been used by any state in this way since the dawn of the nuclear age. No state has engaged in large-scale conventional aggression, and then explicitly or implicitly tried to protect its gains from a conventional counterattack through nuclear deterrent threats. This gambit is so alien to the ways both theorists and statesmen have understood nuclear weapons that there is almost nothing written about it even from a theoretical perspective. The situation would be analogous to a half-successful Warsaw Pack invasion of West Germany, which stalled after a 100 km gain, going uncounter-attacked by the conventional forces of NATO because of a Soviet claim that its nuclear deterrent umbrella now covered its new real estate. . . .

The closest one can come in the nuclear deterrence literature to an explicit treatment of the question of how conventional aggression could occur between nuclear armed adversaries is the "stability-instability" paradox. This predicts that two states armed with mutual assured destruction capabilities may resort to conventional warfare with each other because they do not fear escalation. The strategic balance is so stable, and the consequences of nuclear war so obvious, that neither side would find it reasonable to employ nuclear weapons, and both would know it. The paradox, however, logically cannot predict conventional attacks without also predicting conventional counterattacks.

Even states that achieved large-scale territorial gains through what were essentially conventional *counterattacks,* did not try to secure their gains with nuclear deterrence; nor did the mere possession of nuclear weapons in fact deter challenges. The United States took North Korea in a counteroffensive, but did not make nuclear threats to dissuade a Chinese challenge to that offensive, even after the appearance of Chinese troops in October 1950. The Chinese were obviously not deterred from entering the war by the known U.S. nuclear capability. The Israelis never formally invoked nuclear weapons to secure their gains of 1967, and obviously their rumored possession of nuclear weapons was not enough to deter an Egyptian and Syrian challenge.

Effectively, the toleration of an Iraqi success in Kuwait would change nuclear weapons from "defenders of the status quo" to instruments of aggression. The consequences for world politics are likely to approximate those that theorists have associated with "offense dominant worlds," at least until most states can acquire secure second strike capabilities. International politics will suddenly turn very competitive.

Ambitious states will be the quickest to take lessons from the episode. Aggressors will strive harder to get these weapons because their utility as "conquest protectors" will have been demonstrated starkly. States that get or already have nuclear weapons, and have claims against their non-nuclear neighbors, would feel substantially freer to enforce those claims. Because their neighbors understand this, and will surely try to get their own nuclear weapons to insure themselves, the ambitious will jump through the "window" of opportunity.

The failure to act to reverse Iraqi aggression would thus also increase the desire of status quo powers for their own nuclear weapons. Status quo states would have to assume that non-nuclear states with claims against them would soon embark on nuclear weapons programs. Whatever "existential deterrence" the nuclear superpowers or middle powers have provided will also have been eroded once a few nuclear weapons deter their action to secure a critical interest. Threatened status quo states will thus find it prudent to try to acquire quickly an independent nuclear capability. The utility of "over the horizon" allies in a conventional war will have been reduced if not eliminated. It will have been demonstrated that the nuclear aggressor can deter the intervention of allies to take back lost territory. If a status quo power is inferior conventionally to a nuclear armed challenger, it would have to act quickly to try to redress the conventional balance on its own. It might also seek the permanent presence of substantial allied conventional forces on its soil. Even if a status quo power can compete conventionally, however, it will never be certain that its conventional defenses will hold in war. Thus, it will want its own nuclear weapons to ensure that, in the event the nuclear adversary achieves military gains, that adversary will not be able to deter a conventional counterattack. Against a nuclear armed aggressor, only the county whose sovereignty or real estate is at risk, has the necessary will to risk a nuclear confrontation.

Ambitious states will see many incentives for preventive war. In particular, evidence of nascent nuclear weapons programs in their prospective victims could spark a conventional attack, because this would be the last opportunity for aggrandizement. Aside from the inclination to take long-coveted land in the event of a window of opportunity, a temporary military advantage, one can also imagine a wave of Osirak-type attacks, in which both status quo and aggressor states attempted to wipe out one another's nascent nuclear capabilities conventionally. To evade preventive attacks, both conventional and nuclear, even status quo states would have powerful incentives to pursue secret nuclear weapons programs, and to try to acquire black market bombs. (Other weapons of mass destruction that might be secretly developed, such as biological, would also become attractive.) This would in turn create new opportunities for those with small nuclear weapons programs in one region to sell weapons to threatened states in other regions. It would also create incentives for theft. Rumors of secret nuclear weapons programs would be rife, causing still more countries to contemplate nuclear acquisition. The Non-Proliferation Treaty would simply be swamped by violations and suspected violations.

This singular failure to act could thus usher in a dynamic pattern of international security competition in which even the "good guys" would have to play a rough game. It would certainly make for regional nuclear and conventional arms races. The incentives for preventive war would intensify. Nuclear weapons states would perceive aggression against non-nuclear states to be relatively easy, whenever their conventional capabilities appeared sufficient to achieve success. After years of trouble, the world might settle down to many stable relationships of mutual deterrence, a series of "micro-cold wars." This process could, however, take a long time, and be very exciting.

A number of plausible real world problems consistent with these general predictions can be identified. Taiwan and South Korea will face the starkest choices. These non-nuclear states face nuclear or near nuclear rivals with strong claims against them. Both are competitive conventionally with their adversaries, but hardly dominant. The South Koreans have a direct U.S. military presence but they will likely clamor for even more U.S. troops—sufficient to block confidently any North Korean attack virtually at its initiation. Seoul's proximity to the border is too tempting a target for the large North Korean standing army, against the record of a United States too intimidated by a few nuclear weapons to even try to take back lost territory. Taiwan is not even as well placed as South Korea, since U.S. forces are not present, and U.S. diplomacy has to some extent conceded the legitimacy of the Chinese claim to Taiwan. Both states have the scientific and industrial capability, and the wealth, to build nuclear weapons, and both once had nascent nuclear weapons programs that U.S. policies managed to stop.

It is implausible that Japan can hold fast to its non-nuclear status. Though free of claims by any state against most of its territory, can it ride out a sudden surge of proliferation on its periphery? It seems unlikely that such a capable state would want to remain dependent on U.S. deterrent promises in such a competitive world. The United States will also likely find itself facing a new round of doubts in the Federal Republic of Germany about the credibility of the U.S. nuclear commitment.

The course of world politics can be changed dramatically for the worse, if the United States fails to act to reverse Iraqi aggression. Effectively, the relative U.S. power position will be undermined. The perceived utility of nuclear weapons will be enhanced. Thus, the incidence of war in general will probably increase, at least in the near term. The probability of nuclear accidents and ecological disasters associated with crash, low-budget nuclear weapons programs will also increase. Most seriously, there will be a greater risk of regional nuclear war. Can the United States find a plausible strategy to live comfortably in such a world? If not, then these dangers seem sufficiently compelling to warrant U.S. action against Iraq.

*Could the United States "Live" in Such a World?*

Three alternative U.S. strategies suggest themselves if these events are set in motion by a failure to act against Iraq: an intensified "counterproliferation" policy; a conventional buildup to provide an ability to defend U.S. allies confidently against conventional aggression; a "fortress America" policy.

Failure to act against Iraqi aggression would prove to U.S. decisionmakers that a few nuclear weapons in the hands of a prospective enemy can utterly paralyze U.S. policy. If the United States is to maintain any freedom of action in the world, then nuclear proliferation must be stopped *before it happens*. The political aftermath of the conquest of Kuwait would make it difficult to place a new emphasis on the nonproliferation treaty. Too many states would have incentives to get nuclear weapons to be placated with great power promises. Instead, the United States would have to concentrate much more on active measures. States bent on getting nuclear weapons, with policies inimical to U.S. interests, have to be denied the completion of their programs. Any means, fair or foul, would be employed to this end. U.S. intelligence agencies would be turned loose to sabotage nascent programs. If these measures failed, then preventive conventional war would be undertaken. These measures would only be acceptable before aspiring nuclear weapons states completed a working bomb. States with a working weapon would have to be left alone.

A second policy effectively calls for the creation of "little NATOs"—forward deployed U.S. capabilities sufficient for a tenacious local defense, plus institutionalized nuclear guarantees—wherever the United States has important interests that might be threatened by a nuclear state. To convince prospective victims not to get nuclear weapons the United States or another superpower would have to guarantee their security with sufficient force to actually stop a conventional aggressor in its tracks. Programs of nuclear cooperation, similar to those arranged between the United States and its NATO allies, might also have to be considered. Desert Shield may last for decades. U.S. forces in Korea will have to be beefed up. The planned drawdown of U.S. troops stationed in Europe may need to be canceled. The fundamental decision about whether or not to fight for Taiwan can no longer be postponed.

The United States would now be called upon to offer nuclear hostages to any ally threatened by a nuclear aggressor—one important function that U.S. troops served in Germany during the cold war. If Germany had been subjected to nuclear attack, U.S. troops (and their dependents) would also have suffered. This increased the probability that the United States would retaliate. The likely indignation of U.S. leaders alone raised the risk of a nuclear response. Failure to respond might also have eroded the credibility of the U.S. nuclear deterrent to discourage nuclear attacks on north America. If U.S. soldiers and citizens could be attacked with nuclear weapons with impunity abroad, U.S. decisionmakers would have had reason to fear that the next step might be that an ambitious aggressor would misperceive his freedom to threaten Americans at home. This fear would have provided an additional incentive for a strong response.

"Extended nuclear deterrence" is unlikely to go even as smoothly as it did during the cold war. The failure to act to counter aggression by a small nuclear weapons state like Iraq would surely raise new doubts about the value of these U.S. hostages. Even during the height of the cold war, the question was frequently asked whether the United States would trade "Boston for Bonn" in the event it was called upon to retaliate for a Soviet nuclear attack. Greater doubts would arise under these new conditions.

Though the previous two policies could be executed separately, they would probably be combined. Perhaps, after considerable "assertive counterproliferation" and a substantial U.S. military build-up the proliferation incentives that would arise from a failure in Kuwait could be dampened. Aggressors would find it dangerous to initiate nuclear programs; status quo powers would find the United States ready to offer the coin of real, in-place conventional military power to forestall invasions, and incidentally provide hostages against coercive nuclear threats.

The human and material costs of this strategy are substantial. One cannot be sure that even these measures would prove adequate against future proliferators; forcible occupation of their countries could prove necessary. This seems probable in the cases of North Korea and Iran, for example. These countries have large populations, baby booms, and conscript armies. They will thus be difficult to conquer and even more difficult to police.

The little NATOs aspect of the strategy could require a force structure equal or greater than that sustained by the United States during the last years of the cold war. U.S. forces in the center region of NATO might shrink somewhat, but greater standing forces would be necessary in the southern region—particularly in Turkey. Forces stationed in South Korea may have to grow. A new permanent force in the Persian Gulf region will prove necessary. Ready forces for new commitments would prove useful to create a general expectation among states that the United States would come to their assistance in the event that their neighbors turned nasty. If coupled with the "preventive war option," an additional "strategic reserve" offensive force would prove necessary.

"Fortress America" is a distinct, third alternative national strategy. The task of U.S. policy would be to divert nuclear competition, and the risks of nuclear war away from its own territory. The United States would simply accept that a hellishly competitive world will emerge. The first step would be a change in U.S. foreign policy in the direction of disengagement. By staying out of overseas political competitions the United States would reduce the incentives for new nuclear powers to threaten the United States or its forces. U.S. theater forces would not be jeopardized by Nth country nuclear forces because there would not be any U.S. theater forces.

The United States would rely more forthrightly on its own nuclear deterrent power; policymakers would stress their intention to respond to any direct attack on the United States with a devastating retaliation. Renewed efforts in the realm of strategic defense would be justified. Just in case others doubt U.S. will, they will also face formidable obstacles to a successful attack. Moreover, in a world of many, not fully competent nuclear powers, one cannot rule out the possibility of an errant weapon coming the way of the United States. U.S. intelligence services would focus intensively on reducing the possibility that nuclear weapons might be smuggled into the United States. More importantly, intelligence agencies would act to backstop U.S. deterrent threats by creating the strong expectation that the United States will determine the return address of any weapon smuggled into the country and find some group or place against which a retaliation can be directed.

This policy would require a major change in the way the United States has conducted its foreign policy since the Second World War, but disengagement from world politics is not unprecedented for this country. Disengagement would, however, require enormous self control to stay out of political disputes abroad that may arouse our passions or idealism. It would also require steady nerves.

### The View From 1996

The actual thinking and behavior of U.S. decisionmakers during the crisis suggests that the foregoing analysis, or something similar, would have been conducted and would have found a ready audience. Though the nuclear issue apparently did not arise in early discussions, there is considerable evidence that broad strategic considerations influenced the thinking of several players, that key decisionmakers worried about the consequences of letting the Iraqi success stand—both globally and regionally. It was feared that Iraqi power would grow, and that the credibility of U.S. threats to deter future Iraqi action would weaken. More broadly, U.S. credibility would suffer, perhaps enough to set off a wave of challenges.

Brent Scowcroft, the president's national security advisor, favored strong action against Iraq's seizure of Kuwait. In one of the earliest National Security Council meetings on the Iraqi invasion of Kuwait, on 3 August 1990, Scowcroft reportedly opened the meeting with this statement, "We have got to examine what the long-term interests are for this country and for the Middle East if the invasion and taking of Kuwait become an accomplished fact. We have to begin our deliberations with the fact that this is unacceptable. Yes, it's hard to do much. There are lots of reasons why we can't do things but it's our job." The conversation in this meeting reportedly moved in the direction of a consensus that Iraq had created a major strategic problem for the United States.

Secretary of Defense Richard Cheney reportedly had ambitious objectives from the outset of the crisis. He was apparently concerned about the future political and military threat Saddam Hussein could pose if he controlled Gulf oil. This must be interpreted as fear of what Iraq could and would do if it became even more powerful. Already, on 2 August, he saw the question as whether the U.S. goal should be just the liberation of Kuwait, or also the overthrow of Saddam Hussein. Dennis Ross, the State Department's director of policy planning, and a key aid to Secretary of State James Baker, saw Saddam Hussein's aggression as an indicator that Iraq had become a threat to the entire Middle East. He apparently concluded that Saddam Hussein's regime would need to be eliminated. UN ambassador Thomas Pickering believed that U.S. credibility in the Middle East would suffer if nothing was done about the invasion of Kuwait.

Deputy Secretary of State Lawrence Eagleburger was also a strong early proponent of rollback. He worried about the precedent that successful Iraqi aggression would set for all the "Quaddafis and Kim Il Sungs of the world, indicating to them that the end of the cold war had created exploitable power vacuums. At the 4 August Camp David meeting one unnamed participant made a mirror image augment. ". . . I think if we succeed this time, the next such crisis might not take all this much agony. In other words, if potential aggressors believe in advance that the civilized world is going to behave in a certain way, they will tend to tailor their actions."[2]

President George Bush seems to have had a "1930s" perspective on Iraqi aggression. He was concerned that if he practiced "appeasement," it would have the same consequences it had in the 1930s. One unnamed presidential adviser observed, "George Bush is deathly afraid of appeasement. His generation had to fight a war over it, and he feels that if he blinks today, he will be leaving a real mess for the next generation to clean up."[3] Bush characterized his views this way in subsequent communications with the staff of U.S. News. ". . . the bottom line was that aggression could not stand. If he was permitted to get away with that, heaven knows where the world would have gone and what forces would have been unleashed."[4] This was clearly a perspective expressed by Prime Minister Margaret Thatcher in a meeting with Bush in Aspen, Colorado, on 2 August. She made an analogy explicitly to Nazi aggression in the 1930s, an analogy which Bush employed repeatedly. Later in the crisis, in a 24 December meeting, Bush indicated that he would no longer settle for an unconditional Iraqi withdrawal; he wanted a military campaign and victory. Chairman of the Joint Chiefs of Staff Colin Powell reports Bush's reasoning: "If the Iraqis withdrew now, it would be with impunity for their crimes. A pullback would also mean that Saddam would leave Kuwait intact with his huge army intact, ready to fight another day."[5] The president appears to have been concerned that a lesson needed to be taught; the aggressor must be punished, and deprived of capabilities for future mischief.

Had the United States confronted a nuclear armed Iraq, the choices would have been difficult. A decision to launch a military operation to liberate Kuwait would have involved immediate and obvious nuclear risks. The consequences of inaction outlined above, and the relatively unpleasant range of possible U.S. alternative policies in the new world thus created, would surely have been enumerated by someone. The costs and risks of inaction, however, would have seemed theoretical and distant. The risks of confrontation with a nuclear Iraq would have seemed clear and imminent. One cannot say with confidence how the consensus among the key decisionmakers would have actually evolved. This analysis, however, does suggest that the often implied proposition that the United States would easily have been deterred by Iraq should be subjected to much closer scrutiny. There were strong reasons for the United States to act. There is also much circumstantial evidence from the way the crisis was actually handled to suggest that these reasons would have resonated with the decisionmakers. Even if the kind of analysis I conducted above did produce a rough consensus in favor of action, a final decision to act would not have been taken without a credible plan for success. Someone would have had to propose a strategy that promised political and military success, with low risks of escalation. Below, I try to develop such a strategy.

## THE REVERSAL OF IRAQI AGGRESSION

### The View from 1990–91

Though the economic embargo on Iraq is taking hold, and ought to be given a fair chance to pressure Saddam Hussein into withdrawal from Kuwait, we cannot count on the success of this strategy. It may fail altogether, or simply "succeed" at such a slow pace that Iraq will have plenty of time to devise diplomatic strategies to erode the integrity of the U.S.-led Coalition. . . .

Sooner or later, the United States and its allies will have to consider military action to eject Iraq from Kuwait. There is no way to devise a reliable algorithm that will tell the United States exactly when it should switch from embargo to war. It is unreasonable to wait until the Coalition begins to suffer erosion. . . . For planning purposes, if Iraq is not out of Kuwait by autumn 1991, the United States and its partners should place themselves in a military position to initiate offensive operations at that time.

*Intrawar deterrence.* Perhaps the most important issue that the Coalition faces is how to neutralize any attempt by the Iraqis to exploit their nuclear weapons to deter a Coalition attack of any kind, or to thwart a Coalition victory. Two methods suggest themselves, a "splendid first strike," or intrawar deterrence. It is clear that we would prefer to knock out Iraqi nuclear weapons in a "splendid first strike" with conventional ordnance. It seems improbable that the military can provide a high-confidence option to do this. Thus, our strategy must be to wage a conventional war with Iraq while deterring its resort to nuclear weapons. Deterrence depends on capability and will. There is no doubt that the United States and its allies command massive conventional and nuclear capability. It ought not to be impossible to explain to Iraq what the United States can do in response to an Iraqi use of nuclear weapons. The problem is convincing Saddam Hussein that the United States *will* retaliate in particularly horrible ways if he employs nuclear weapons. Only diplomacy can convince Saddam Hussein that U.S. will is stronger than his.

The United States must persuade Iraq that it cares more about the liberation of Kuwait than Iraq cares about holding it. Deterrent diplomacy is exactly that; the explanation aspects matter as much as or more than the military ones. The problem is difficult. Iraq is the local power, has developed an "historical" (albeit trumped up) claim to the land, has tried to seize the country once before, can claim (with some legitimacy) a number of injuries inflicted by Kuwait, and has just seized the country. Iraq probably perceives that its bargaining position is very strong relative to ours. Heretofore, we have cared about Kuwait largely for economic reasons. Kuwait has a lot of oil, but there is plenty more in Saudi Arabia and in the Gulf states, and those are now (or soon will be) well protected by the forces entering the region for Desert Shield. Why should Saddam not believe that nuclear treats will stop a Coalition offensive, and, if need be, that a single nuclear explosion will not cause us to reconsider our entire position? The United States, and its many allies, must disabuse Iraqi leaders on this belief.

The United States and its friends must explain to Iraq just how terrible the political world appears to us if Iraq is allowed to enjoy its conquest. The method for accomplishing this is to tell and retell the "story" outlined above, which spells out our expectations about the grave security situation that will result if Iraq is allowed to deter the Coalition from liberating Kuwait. This story is somewhat analogous to the "we don't deal with terrorists and hostage takers" position that many Western countries, including the United States, have taken. (Of course, the United States did, to its great discredit, deviate from this position.) We say we will not deal with terrorists because it leaves one open to future exploitation. Failure to counter Iraqi aggression would effectively do the same, and much more. . . .

Given the cold war experience with coercive diplomacy, it may be reasonable to move some nuclear weapons toward the theater to enhance the credibility of the threat of ferocious retaliation in the event of an Iraqi nuclear attack. There is no particular *technical* utility to such action. It would be purely a diplomatic sig-nal. Some joint Coalition planning for the retaliatory use of such weapons prob-ably ought to occur. Rumors of such consultations would have an additional diplomatic effect. At the same time, such consultations would lend credibility to the message that this is a contingent threat. If Iraq does not use nuclear weapons, neither would we.

### The View from 1996

The issue of intrawar deterrence did, in fact, arise in a muted way during the planning for Desert Storm. Secretary of State Baker, in his 9 January 1991 meet-ing with Tariq Aziz, carried a letter from Bush that threatened somewhat under-specified, but nevertheless horrible consequences in the event that Iraq used chemical or biological weapons. Indeed Aziz thought that these were nuclear threats. Though Iraq had plenty of chemical weapons, it did not use them. Against a nuclear threat, it seems plausible that even more explicit retaliatory threats would have been leveled. It would have been argued that Iraq had to be threat-ened with nuclear retaliation. . . .

Dealing with a nuclear armed Iraq would have demanded a political military strategy of intrawar deterrence. Such a strategy depends both on will and capa-bility. Will, in particular, must be systematically communicated to the adversary. Evidence from the actual crisis on the matter of Iraqi chemical weapons' use shows that such a strategy was followed. Numerous public and private, formal and informal, messages were quite deliberately sent to Iraq. These messages threatened a massive response in the event that Iraq employed chemical weapons. The threats were sufficiently frequent and ferocious that Iraqi officials claim after the fact that they were taken as nuclear threats. Circumstantial evidence suggests that even some of our own allies may have been concerned that the United States was contemplating a nuclear response. The only thing missing from the actual experience is evidence that a particularly comprehensive "explanation" accom-panied the threat to Saddam. The closest thing we see to an explanation is the pas-sage in Bush's 9 January letter to Saddam, "The American people would demand the strongest possible response," a proposition reiterated verbally to Tariq Aziz by Baker. For purposes of my argument, one would have liked to see a statement to the effect that ". . . we will have no choice but to retaliate massively, because we must expect to encounter adversaries in the future who are armed with these weapons, and who must be made to understand the grave consequences of using them against the United States." Nevertheless, we may conclude that the concept of intrawar deterrence, and the mechanics of deterrent diplomacy were well understood by the Bush administration, and were indeed employed. This lends credibility to the proposition that the kind of strategy I outlined above would have met a receptive audience of high-level policymakers.

## THE STRATEGY OF THE WAR

### The View from 1990–91

Intrawar deterrence is one key means to control the risks of a large scale conventional war with a nuclear-armed Iraq. A second potential means is the limitation of Coalition war aims, and constraints on Coalition military operations consistent with these aims. In stark terms, intrawar deterrence aims to discourage Iraq from employing nuclear weapons out of calculation. We must also consider how to avoid provoking the Iraqis into using their nuclear weapons out of desperation.

What should Coalition war aims be? It is the Coalition's irreducible requirement to eject Iraqi forces from Kuwait. Moreover, if this needs to be done by force, it is reasonable to strive for the maximum destruction of Iraqi military capabilities in Kuwait and proximate to it. The Iraqis must be taught a lesson that aggression does not pay. Also, it is a good idea to take this opportunity to whittle down Iraqi military power as a means to help stabilize the region.

There are other plausible objectives beyond these, however. They are tempting, but it may be imprudent to pursue them. It would be wonderful if we could be rid of Saddam entirely. If Saddam's regime cannot be eliminated, it would be beneficial not only for the region, but for the future of U.S. nonproliferation policies, to eliminate Iraq's weapons of mass destruction. Unhappily, for the sake of avoiding Iraqi resort to nuclear weapons out of desperation, the Coalition probably must forgo these objectives. The goals of the war need to be "depersonalized." The Coalition should not even hint that Saddam Hussein is the target of the war; indeed it should explicitly say that neither he, nor the sovereignty of Iraq within its prior boundaries, is at issue. Only Kuwait is at issue. A cornered rat with a nuclear weapon is a pretty dangerous animal. Leave the rat a bolt-hole.

Can Iraq's nuclear weapons program safely be included as a military objective of Coalition conventional military attack? Given that Iraq already has a bomb, this project seems too dangerous. It runs the risk of putting Iraq in a "use or lose" situation. During the cold war, it was generally believed that United States and Soviet nuclear forces were the "family jewels." Though each side targeted the other's nuclear forces, neither side's leadership was under any illusions about the grave risks associated with the initiation of a counterforce campaign. Though Iraq is new to the nuclear club, and possesses only a few weapons, it is reasonable to assume that they place a high value on these weapons. Although it is Iraqi aggression that will have precipitated the Coalition attack, it is nevertheless possible that conventional attacks on Iraqi weapons would be perceived as a prelude to something much worse—if they prove successful. The Coalition ought not to count on Saddam Hussein accepting his gradual nuclear disarmament. It is plausible that he would fear that once the nuclear weapons were gone, the Coalition would feel free to do anything it wanted—perhaps even use a nuclear weapon on him. Though the last possibility might seem slight, an attempt to top-ple the regime would seem quite plausible. Saddam might calculate that the use of a single nuclear weapon, perhaps only as a demonstration, would be enough to cause the Coalition to cease its military campaign to disarm him. . . .

To ensure that Saddam does not overestimate the hostile intent of the Coali-tion, considerable restraint in military operations seems in order. Most notably, the Coalition will have to forgo the bulk of the "strategic" bombing campaign now under consideration. Coalition political leadership will need to draw some notional lines to constrain our own military operations. The boundaries of what we are now calling the "Kuwait Theater of Operations," Kuwait and Southern Iraq, suggest themselves. Intense military operations will be permitted inside the KTO; only limited operations would be permitted in the rest of Iraq.

Because Saddam will not want to be forced to pay a cost for his aggression in terms of damage to his country, the full cost would be extracted from Iraqi field forces. Annihilation to Iraqi combat forces in the theater should be an explicit military goal. The troops can go home, but the equipment stays. The message to Saddam, and to those who might follow, is that the forces one employs for aggres-sive war simply do not see home again. What you invest, you lose.

### The View from 1996

What is the likelihood that these notions of limited war would have found their way into actual Coalition behavior? In the aftermath of Vietnam, and the generally negative appraisal of constraints placed both on military means and political ends in that war, "limited war" has become a very problematical concept in security pol-icy circles, civilian and military. U.S. planning for conventional war with the Soviet Union did not demonstrate any great sensitivity to the question of whether conventional threats against nuclear forces might be escalatory. Yet, both the objectives and conduct of Desert Storm were wrapped in political constraints. Pos-itive and negative civilian intervention into military operational planning on both diplomatic and domestic political grounds occurred. Indeed, Cheney went to con-siderable lengths to educate himself to facilitate such intervention.

A limited war aim is the principal form of restraint practiced during the war, though the precise political reasons for this limitation are murky. Specifically, it was understood from the beginning that the Coalition would not invade and occupy Iraq with an eye toward changing its government. Former secretary of state Baker states that a "march to Baghdad" was never on the table, because everyone understood it was costly and unnecessary. General Powell suggested that the "Hitler rhetoric" be toned down because it could imply that Saddam would in fact be ousted, which was not a primary war aim. At the 27 February 1991 Oval Office meeting where the decision to end the war was made, Baker argued, "We have achieved our aims. We have gotten them out of Kuwait."[6] Pow-ell believed that the war had a specific, limited, objective, and in the controversial endgame supported a rapid termination of the ground war since this limited objective, the liberation of Kuwait, had been achieved. The decision to end the war was made against the backdrop of the fact that Saddam Hussein was still in power. Moreover, though the key decisionmakers were more optimistic about the damage to Iraqi weapons of mass destruction than ultimately proved warranted, they knew then that Iraq still possessed chemical weapons stocks.

Initial accounts of the war suggested that the United States was somehow restrained from intervention inside Iraq by its regional Coalition partners. Two of the more thorough scholars of the war argue the opposite; both Saudi Arabia and Turkey supported intervention during the Iraqi civil war that followed Desert Storm. Therefore, in spite of the ambitious rhetoric that provided the public rationale for the war, and local support for direct intervention in Iraq, it seems reasonable to conclude that the United States was not willing to pay very much to overthrow Saddam Hussein. U.S. war aims were limited because of sensitivity to costs.

If aims were limited, so were means. Cheney went to great lengths to develop his personal ability to assess professional military advice. He asked for, and received, what was essentially a fifteen-briefing short course in military operational planning. He apparently told Paul Wolfowitz that though he did not intend to micromanage the preparation of the war plan, he did ". . . intend to own it when it's finished." He also did not prove to be shy about making his own suggestions. The initial briefings by the CENTCOM planners for a possible counteroffensive into Kuwait disturbed him. "Colin, I have been thinking about this all night. I can't let Norm do this high diddle diddle up-the-middle plan, I just can't let him do it."[7] Cheney proceeded to make his own inquiries and became an advocate of a large-scale, two-division, raid into western Iraq. Though this suggestion was ultimately parried by Schwarzkopf and Powell, it did contribute to the development of the ultimate left-hook plan.

Limitations were also suggested on the air war. Bush was particularly concerned that targets of special historical or cultural significance not be struck. He raised his concerns at two different briefings, one in October, and one in January. A different kind of discussion arose over the issue of direct attacks on presumed Iraqi biological weapons storage facilities. Out of fear of the collateral damage that could have been produced had the agents been inadvertently released, Cheney wanted to be quite sure that there was a very high probability of complete destruction. . . .

## WAR OUTCOME

How would the war have gone had these restraints been observed? Would Iraq have used nuclear weapons? Would the conventional victory have been as splendid? What kind of message would have been sent to other aggressors? What kind of message to those contemplating a nuclear weapons program?

I doubt that Iraq would have used nuclear weapons under these conditions. There would have been no political or military incentive, and many disincentives. Saddam did not use chemical or biological weapons under conditions of conventional disaster; why would he have used nuclear weapons? The more important question, however, is whether Western leaders would have believed that they could deter nuclear escalation by Iraq. It is difficult to judge. My argument is that once they had taken reasonable steps to control the risks, the costs and risks of inaction would have seemed greater than the costs of action. . . .

Important lessons about what nuclear weapons are *not* good for would have been taught. They are not shields for conventional conquests. Where important great power interests are engaged, they are not the great equalizer. Moreover, the (often expensive) conventional forces that one must bet to try to grab these gains face a great risk of annihilation. This lesson might affect those who are meant to take orders, not merely those who give them.

Nevertheless, a lesson will have been taught about what nuclear weapons *are* good for. They are great instruments to deter threats against one's homeland, even conventional threats, even by great powers, even when you are in the wrong. Moreover, by invoking nuclear deterrence, the Coalition would itself have demonstrated in the broadest sense the continued utility of nuclear weapons in international politics. Thus, any hopes of "delegitimizing" these weapons, or sustaining a confidence game regarding their supposed inutility, will be dashed. Some damage will have been done to the cause of non-proliferation; but not nearly as much as would have been done by a failure to act.

**THE FUTURE**

The United States is indeed working energetically to limit the number of nuclear powers in the world. Policymakers struggled to ensure that only one nuclear power emerged from the wreckage of the Soviet Union, and success seems within their grasp. They have worked with considerable effectiveness to dismantle Iraq's nuclear industry and have at least limited North Korea's nuclear materials production capability.

Some U.S. policy analysts call for the abolition of nuclear weaponry, in part to strengthen the legitimacy of the Non-Proliferation Treaty (NPT). The problem of fulfilling the Article VI treaty pledges of the nuclear weapons states to seek complete nuclear disarmament was a key issue of the NPT review conference. It is hoped that there will be further accessions to the treaty, especially by countries widely suspected to have nuclear weapons such as Israel, India, and Pakistan.

The Pentagon has a counterproliferation initiative which includes, among other projects, research and development on various offensive and defensive measures to neutralize Nth country nuclear weapons with conventional means in the event of crisis. These means must be conventional rather than nuclear in order to protect the "devaluation" of nuclear weaponry now presumed to be necessary to support nonproliferation diplomacy. Some hint that these capabilities could be employed preventively, to ensure that nascent nuclear weapons states never complete their programs. Operational and tactical adaptations that might reduce the vulnerability of U.S. military forces to weapons of mass destruction are also under study. The Coalition diplomacy of such confrontations has also received some attention.

Although a combination of international legal instruments and unilateral military means may do much to reduce the proliferation problem, it is unlikely that the success will be total. North Korea's future cooperation simply cannot be counted upon. New nuclear hopefuls will surely arise, with Iran as perhaps the most likely candidate. . . .

It is more likely than not that the United States will someday face a crisis caused by aggression of an Nth nuclear power against an important U.S. interest. It is unlikely that should this occur the United States will have a splendid conventional counter force capability, a combination of offensive and defensive capabilities that could eliminate an adversary's nuclear forces. Thus, the United States will face a defining moment of the kind I have outlined. If so, we will have to assess the very factors discussed here. It seems plausible that the highly competitive political world that could follow U.S. inaction will be perceived as uninviting. Nevertheless, more thinking needs to be done about how the United States might live in that world. Are any of the three alternative strategies outlined above—preventive war; little NATOs, or isolationism, acceptable alternatives for U.S. foreign and security policy? Perhaps I have overlooked other diplomatic and military strategies that would be preferable to the risks of a nuclear confrontation. If the United States chooses to act, however, it is difficult to see any other foundation upon which to rest our action but intrawar nuclear deterrence, and limited war.

## NOTES

1. Bob Woodward, *The Commanders* (New York: Simon & Schuster, 1991), 217–18.

2. U.S. News and World Report, *Triumph Without Victory, The Unreported History of the Persian Gulf War* (New York: Random House, 1992), 72.

3. Steven J. Wayne, "President Bush Goes to War," in *The Political Psychology of the Gulf War: Leaders, Publics, and the Process of Conflict,* ed. Stanley Renshon (Pittsburgh: University of Pittsburgh Press, 1993), 39.

4. *Triumph Without Victory,* 48.

5. Colin Powell, with Joseph Persico, *My American Journey* (New York: Random House, 1995), 499.

6. Michael Gordon and Bernard Trainor, *The General's War: The Inside Story of the Conflict in the Gulf* (Boston: Little, Brown, 1995), 416.

7. Gordon and Trainor, *The General's War,* 141.

# 24

# Nuclear Instability in
# South Asia

## Scott D. Sagan

The emerging nuclear history of India and Pakistan strongly supports the pessimistic predictions of organizational theorists. Military organizational behavior has led to serious problems in meeting all three requirements for stable nuclear deterrence—prevention of preventive war during periods of transition when one side has a temporary advantage, the development of survivable second-strike forces, and avoidance of accidental nuclear war. . . . These problems have now appeared in India and Pakistan.

It should be acknowledged from the start that there are important differences between the nuclear relationship emerging between India and Pakistan and the cold war system that developed over time between the United States and the Soviet Union. While the differences are clear, however, the significance of these differences is not. For example, the nuclear arsenals in South Asia are, and are likely to remain, much smaller and less sophisticated than were the U.S. and Soviet arsenals. This should make each arsenal both more vulnerable to a counterforce attack (an attack on the adversary's own nuclear forces) and less capable of mounting counterforce attacks, and thus the net effect is uncertain. There are also important differences in civil-military relations in the two cases, but these differences, too, are both stabilizing and potentially destabilizing. The Soviets and the Americans both eventually developed an "assertive" command system with tight high-level civilian control over their nuclear weapons. Also India has an extreme system of assertive civilian control of the military, with (at least until recently) very little direct military influence on any aspect of nuclear weapons policy. Pakistan, however, is at the other end of the spectrum, with the military in

370

complete control of the nuclear arsenal, and with only marginal influence from civilian political leaders, even during the periods when there was a civilian-led government in Islamabad. There are, finally, important differences in mutual understanding, proximity, and hostility. India and Pakistan share a common colonial and pre-colonial history, have some common cultural roots, and share a common border; they also have engaged in four wars against each other, and are involved in a violent fifty-year dispute about the status of Kashmir. In contrast, the Americans and Soviets were on opposite sides of the globe and viewed each other as mysterious, often unpredictable adversaries. The cold war superpowers were involved in a deep-seated ideological rivalry, but held no disputed territory between them and had no enduring history of armed violence against each other.

There is also, however, a crucially important similarity between the nuclear conditions that existed in cold war and those that exist in South Asia today. In both cases, the parochial interests and routine behaviors of the organizations that manage nuclear weapons limit the stability of nuclear deterrence. The newest nuclear weapons will not make exactly the same mistakes with nuclear weapons as did their superpower predecessors. They are, however, also unlikely to meet with complete success in the difficult effort to control these weapons and maintain nuclear peace.

## THE PROBLEM OF PREVENTIVE WAR

Pakistan has been under direct military rule for almost half of its existence, and some analysts have argued that the organizational biases of its military leaders had strong effects on strategic decisions concerning the initiation and conduct of the 1965 and 1971 wars with India. In contrast, India has a sustained tradition of strict civilian control over the military since its independence. These patterns of civil-military relations influence nuclear weapons doctrine and operations. In India, the military has traditionally not been involved in decisions concerning nuclear testing, design, or even command and control. In Pakistan, the military largely runs the nuclear weapons program; even during the periods in which civilian prime ministers have held the reins of government, they have neither been told the full details of the nuclear weapons program nor been given direct control over the operational arsenal.

An organizational theory lens suggests that it is very fortunate that it was India, not Pakistan, that was the first to develop nuclear weapons in South Asia. Military rule in Islamabad (and military influence during periods of civilian rule) certainly has played an important role in Pakistani decision making concerning the use of force (see the discussion of the Kargil conflict below). But the Pakistani military did not possess nuclear weapons before India tested in 1974, and thus was not in a position to argue that preventive war now was better than war later after India developed a rudimentary arsenal.

The preventive war problem in South Asia is a complex one, however, and new evidence suggests that military influence in India produced serious risks of preventive war in the 1980s, despite strong institutionalized civilian control. The government of Prime Minister Indira Gandhi considered, but then rejected, plans to attack Pakistan's Kahuta nuclear facility in the early 1980s, a preventive attack plan that was recommended by senior Indian military leaders. Yet, as occurred in the United States, the preferences of senior officers did not suddenly change when civilian leaders ruled against preventive war. Instead, the beliefs went underground, only to resurface later in a potentially more dangerous form.

These beliefs emerged from the shadows during the 1986–87 "Brasstacks" crisis. This serious crisis began in late 1986 when the Indian military initiated a massive military exercise in Rajasthan, involving an estimated 250,000 troops and 1,500 tanks, including the issuance of live ammunition to troops and concluding with a simulated "counter-offensive" attack, including Indian Air Force strikes, into Pakistan. The Pakistani military, fearing that the exercise might turn into a large-scale attack, alerted military forces and conducted exercises along the border, which led to Indian military counter-movements closer to the border and an operational Indian Air Force alert. The resulting crisis produced a flurry of diplomatic activity and was resolved only after direct intervention by the highest political authorities.

The traditional explanation for the Brasstacks crisis has been that it was an accidental crisis, caused by Pakistan's misinterpretation of an inadvertently provocative Indian Army exercise. For example, Devin Hagerty's detailed examination of "New Delhi's intentions in conducting Brasstacks" concludes that "India's conduct of 'normal' exercises rang alarm bells in Pakistan; subsequently, the logic of the security dilemma structured both sides' behavior, with each interpreting the other's defensive moves as preparations for offensive action.[1] A stronger explanation, however, unpacks "New Delhi's intentions" to look at what different Indian decision makers in the capital wanted to do before and during the crisis.

The key is to understand the preventive-war thinking of the then-Indian chief of the Army Staff, General Krishnaswami Sundarji. Sundarji apparently believed that India's security would be greatly eroded by Pakistani development of a usable nuclear arsenal and thus deliberately designed the Brasstacks exercise in hopes of provoking a Pakistani military response. He hoped that this would then provide India with an excuse to implement existing contingency plans to go on the offensive against Pakistan and to take out its nuclear program in a preventive strike. According to the memoirs of Lieutenant General P. N. Hoon, the commander in chief of the Western Army during Brasstacks:

Brasstacks was no military exercise. It was a plan to build up a situation for a fourth war with Pakistan. And what is even more shocking is that the Prime Minister, Mr. Rajiv Gandhi, was not aware of these plans for war.

The preventive war motivation behind Sundarji's plans helps to explain why the Indian military did not provide full notification of the exercise to the Pakistanis and then failed to use the special hotline to explain their operations when information was requested by Pakistan during the crisis. A final piece of evidence confirms that Sundarji advocated a preventive strike against Pakistan during the crisis. Considerations of an attack on Pakistani nuclear facilities went all the way up to the most senior decision makers in New Delhi in January 1987:

[Prime Minister] Rajiv [Gandhi] now considered the possibility that Pakistan might initiate war with India. In a meeting with a handful of senior bureaucrats and General Sundarji, he contemplated beating Pakistan to the draw by launching a preemptive attack on the Army Reserve South. This would have included automatically an attack on Pakistan's nuclear facilities to remove the potential for a Pakistani nuclear riposte to India's attack. Relevant government agencies were not asked to contribute analysis or views to the discussion. Sundarji argued that India's cities could be protected from a Pakistani counterattack (perhaps a nuclear one), but, upon being probed, could not say how. One important advisor from the Ministry of Defense argued eloquently that 'India and Pakistan have already fought their last war, and there is too much to lose in contemplating another one.' This view ultimately prevailed.

## THE KARGIL CONFLICT AND FUTURE PROBLEMS

Optimists cannot accept that the Brasstacks crisis may have been a deliberate attempt to spark a preventive attack, but they might be reassured by the final outcome, as senior political leaders stepped in to stop further escalation. The power of nuclear deterrence to prevent war in South Asia, optimists insist, has been demonstrated in repeated crises: the Indian preventive attack discussions in 1984; the Brasstacks crisis; and the 1990 Kashmir crisis. "There is no more ironclad law in international relations theory than this," Devin Hagerty's detailed study concludes, "nuclear states do not fight wars with each other."[2]

In the spring and summer of 1999, however, one year after the exchange of nuclear tests, India and Pakistan did fight a war in the mountains along the line of control separating the portions of Kashmir controlled by each country, near the Indian town of Kargil. The conflict began in May, when the Indian intelligence services discovered what appeared to be Pakistani regular forces lodged in mountain redoubts on the Indian side of the line of control. For almost two months, Indian Army units attacked the Pakistani forces and Indian Air Force jets bombed their bases high in the Himalayan peaks. Although the Indian forces carefully stayed on their side of the line of control in Kashmir, Indian prime minister Atal Bihari Vajpayee informed the U.S. government that he might have to order attacks into Pakistan. U.S. spy satellites revealed that Indian tanks and heavy artillery were being prepared for a counter-offensive in Rajasthan. The fighting ended in July, when Pakistani prime minister Nawaz Sharif flew to Washington and, after receiving "political cover" in the form of statement that President Bill Clinton would "take a personal interest" in resolving the Kashmir problem, pledged to withdraw forces to the Pakistani side of the line of control. Over one thousand Indian and Pakistani soldiers died in the conflict, and Sharif's decision to pull out was one of the major causes of the coup that overthrew his regime in October 1999.

The 1999 Kargil conflict is disturbing not only because it demonstrates that nuclear-armed states can fight wars, but also because the organizational biases of the Pakistani military were a major cause of the conflict. Moreover, such biases continue to exist and could play a role in starting crises in the future. This increases the dangers of both a preventive and preemptive strike if war is considered inevitable, as well as the risk of a deliberate, but limited, use of nuclear weapons on the battlefield.

Three puzzling aspects of the Kargil conflict are understandable from an organizational perspective. First, in late 1998, the Pakistani military planned the Kargil operation, paying much more attention, as organization theory would predict, to the tactical effects of the surprise military maneuver than to the broader strategic consequences. Ignoring the likely international reaction and the predictable domestic consequences of the military incursion in India, however, proved to be a significant factor in the ultimate failure of the Kargil operation.

Second, the Pakistani Army also started the operation with the apparent belief—following the logic of what has been called the "stability/instability paradox"—that a "stable nuclear balance" between India and Pakistan permitted more offensive actions to take place with impunity in Kashmir. It is important to note that this belief was more strongly held by senior military officers than by civilian leaders. For example, at the height of the fighting near Kargil, Pakistani Army leaders stated that "there is almost a red alert situation," but they nevertheless insisted "there is no chance of the Kargil conflict leading to a full-fledged war between the two sides."[3] Although Prime Minister Nawaz Sharif apparently approved the plan to move forces across the line of control, it is not clear that he was fully briefed on the nature, scope, or potential consequences of the operation. The prime minister's statement that he was "trying to avoid nuclear war" and his suggestion that he feared "that India was getting ready to launch a full-scale military operation against Pakistan" provide a clear contrast to the confident military assessment that there was virtually no risk of an Indian counterattack or escalation to nuclear war.

Third, the current Pakistani military government's interpretation of the Kargil crisis, at least in public, is that Nawaz Sharif lost courage and backed down unnecessarily. This view is not widely shared by Pakistani scholars and journalists, but such a "stab in the back" thesis does serve the parochial self-interests of the Pakistani army, which does not want to acknowledge its errors or those of the current Musharraf regime. The New Delhi government's interpretation, however, is that the Indian threats that military escalation—a counterattack across the international border—would be ordered, if necessary, forced Pakistan to retreat. These different "lessons learned" could produce ominous outcomes in future crises: each side believes that the Kargil conflict proved that if its government displays resolve and threatens to escalate to new levels of violence, the other side will exhibit restraint and back away from the brink.

Future military crises between India and Pakistan are likely to be nuclear crises. Proliferation optimists are not concerned about this likelihood, however, since they argue that the danger of preventive war, if it ever existed at all, has been eliminated by the development of deliverable nuclear weapons in both countries after May 1998. The problem of preventive war during periods of transition in South Asia is only of historical interest now, optimists would insist.

I am not convinced by this argument for two basic reasons. First, there is an arms race looming on the horizon in South Asia. The Indian government has given strong support to the Bush administration's plans to develop missile defense technology and has expressed interest in eventually procuring or developing its own missile defense capability. I believe that the Indian nuclear program is strongly influenced by the fact that hawkish nuclear policies are popular among Indian voters and thus serve the domestic political interests of Indian politicians. China is likely to respond to the U.S. decision to build national missile defenses by increasing the size and readiness of its own missile force. This will in turn encourage the Indian government to increase its own missile deployments and develop defense technology.

These deployments in India, however, will threaten the smaller nuclear deterrent forces in Pakistan, and this would inevitably reopen the window of opportunity for preventive war considerations. Military biases, under the preventive war logic of "better now than later," could encourage precipitous action in either country if the government had even a fleeting moment of superiority in this new kind of arms race.

The second reason to be pessimistic is that, in serious crises, attacks might be initiated based on the belief that an enemy's use of nuclear weapons is imminent and unavoidable. While it is clear that the existence of nuclear weapons in South Asia made both governments cautious in their use of conventional military force in 1999, it is also clear that Indian leaders were prepared to escalate the conflict if necessary. Pakistani political authorities, however, made nuclear threats during the crisis, suggesting that nuclear weapons would be used precisely under such conditions. Moreover, according to U.S. officials the Pakistani military, apparently without the Prime Minister's knowledge took initial steps to alert its nuclear forces during the Kargil conflict.

This dangerous alerting pattern was repeated in the South Asian crises that occurred after the September 11, 2001, terrorist attacks in the United States and the December 13, 2001, terrorist attack on the Parliament in New Delhi. In both cases, the Pakistani government feared that its nuclear forces would be attacked and therefore took alert measures to disperse the nuclear weapons and missiles to new locations away from their storage sites. Pakistani fears that attacks on their nuclear arsenal were being planned may not have been entirely fanciful.

After the September 11 Pentagon and World Trade Center attacks, President

Bush warned Islamabad that Pakistan would either side with the United States in the new war against terrorism or else be treated as a terrorist state. The development of military plans for U.S. commando raids against the Pakistani nuclear weapons sites was soon widely reported. President Musharraf defused the crisis by deciding to abandon support for the Taliban regime in Afghanistan and to provide logistical and intelligence support for the U.S. war there.

After the December 13 terrorist attack against the Indian Parliament, the Indian government sent massive military forces to the Pakistani border and threatened to attack unless Musharraf cracked down on the radical Islamic groups that supported terrorist operations in Kashmir and New Delhi. Before Musharraf could respond, General S. Padmanabhan, the Indian Army chief, issued a bellicose statement announcing that the military buildup "was not an exercise": "A lot of viable options (beginning from a strike on the camps to a full conventional war) are available. We can do it. . . . If we go to war, jolly good."[4] Senior Indian political authorities criticized the Army chief for making the statement, and diplomats in New Delhi speculated that General Padmanabhan had deliberately made it more difficult for the Pakistanis to back down in this crisis, thus increasing the likelihood of war. Again, President Musharraf defused the crisis, at least temporarily, by initiating a crackdown on Islamic Jihadi groups promoting terrorism in Kashmir and the rest of India.

What lessons should be drawn from these dangerous crises? Optimists will look at only the final result and assume that it was inevitable: Deterrence and coercion worked, as serious threats were issued, the Pakistani president compromised, and no war occurred. At a deeper level, however, two more ominous lessons should be learned. First, President Musharraf's decision to back down was by no means inevitable, and he was subject to significant criticism from Islamic parties and some military circles for his conciliatory stance. Other Pakistani leaders could have gone the other way, and, indeed, Musharraf may be less prone to compromise in the future precisely because he was forced to change policies under the threat of attack in these crises. Second, the Pakistani fear that a preventive or preemptive strike against its nuclear arsenal was imminent forced it to take very dangerous military alerting steps in both crises. Taking nuclear weapons and missiles out of their more secure storage locations and deploying them into the field may make the forces less vulnerable to an enemy attack, but it makes the weapons more vulnerable to theft or internal attacks by terrorist organizations. Given the number of al Qaeda members and supporters in Pakistan, this hidden terrorist problem may well have been the most serious nuclear danger of the crises. In short, the crises of 2001 and 2002 demonstrate that nuclear weapons in South Asia may well produce a modicum of restraint, but also momentous dangers.

In future crises in South Asia, the likelihood of either a preventive or preemptive attack will be strongly influenced by a complex mixture of perceptions of the adversary's intent, estimates about its future offensive and defensive capabilities, and estimates of the vulnerability of its current nuclear arsenal. Organizational biases could encourage worst-case assumptions about the adversary's intent and pessimistic beliefs about the prospects for successful strategic deterrence over the long term. Unfortunately, as will be seen below, inherent organizational character- istics can also produce vulnerabilities to an enemy strike.

## SURVIVABILITY OF NUCLEAR FORCES IN SOUTH ASIA

The fear of retaliation is central to successful deterrence, and the second require- ment for stability with nuclear weapons is therefore the development of secure, sec- ond-strike forces. Unfortunately, there are strong reasons to be concerned about the ability of the Indian and Pakistani military to maintain survivable forces. Two prob- lems can already be seen to have reduced (at least temporarily) the survivability of nuclear forces in Pakistan. First, there is evidence that the Pakistani military, as was the case in the cold war examples cited earlier, deployed its missile forces, follow- ing standard operating procedures, in ways that produce signatures giving away their deployment locations. Indian intelligence officers, for example, identified the locations of planned Pakistani deployments of M-11 missiles by spotting the placement of "secret" defense communication terminals nearby. A second, and even more dramatic, example follows a cold war precedent quite closely. Just as the road engineers in the Soviet Union inadvertently gave away the location of their ICBMs because construction crews built roads with wide-radius turns next to the missile silos, Pakistani road construction crews have inadvertently signaled the location of the "secret" M-11 missiles by placing wide-radius roads and roundabouts outside newly constructed garages at the Sargodha military base.

Finally, analysts should also not ignore the possibility that Indian or Pakistani intelligence agencies could intercept messages revealing the "secret" locations of otherwise survivable military forces, an absolutely critical issue with small or opaque nuclear arsenals. The history of the 1971 war, for example, demonstrates that both states' intelligence agencies were able to intercept critical classified messages sent by and to the other side. . . .

Perhaps most dramatically, on December 12, 1971, the Indians intercepted a radio message scheduling a meeting of high-level Pakistani officials at Govern- ment House in Dacca, which led to an air attack on the building in the middle of the meeting. . . .

## NORMAL ACCIDENTS AND UNAUTHORIZED USE IN NUCLEAR SOUTH ASIA

Will the Indian and Pakistani nuclear arsenals be more safe and secure than were the U.S. and Soviet arsenals during the cold war? It is clear that the emerging South Asian nuclear deterrence system is both smaller and less complex today than was the case in the United States or Soviet Union at the height of the cold war. It is also clear, however, that the South Asian nuclear relationship is inherently more tightly coupled, because of geographical proximity. With inadequate warning systems in place and with weapons with short flight times emerging in the region, the time-lines for decision making are highly compressed and the danger that one accident could lead to another and then lead to a catastrophic accidental war is high and growing. The proximity of New Delhi and Islamabad to their potential adversary's border poses particular concerns about rapid "decapitation" attacks on national capitals. Moreover, there are legitimate concerns about social stability and support for terrorists inside Pakistan, problems that could compromise nuclear weapons safety and security.

Proliferation optimists will cite the small sizes of India and Pakistan's nuclear arsenals as a reason to be less worried about these problems. Yet the key from a normal accidents perspective is not the numbers, but rather the structure of the arsenal. Here there is both good and bad news. The good news is that under normal peacetime conditions, neither the Indians, nor the Pakistanis regularly deploy nuclear forces mated with delivery systems in the field. The bad news, however, is two-fold. First, Pakistani nuclear weapons do not have PALs (Permissive Action Links, the advanced electronic locks on U.S. nuclear weapons that require a special code for the weapons' activation) on them. Second, Pakistan has started to alert its nuclear weapons in crises; it did so in 1999 during the Kargil crisis and then again in September and December of 2001, in response to fears of Indian (and maybe U.S.) military action after the terrorist attacks in New York, Washington, and New Delhi.

From an organizational perspective, it is not surprising to find evidence of serious accidents emerging in the Indian nuclear and missile programs. . . . The false warning incident that occurred just prior to the Pakistani nuclear tests in May 1998 . . . demonstrat[es] the dangers of accidental war in South Asia. During the crucial days just prior to Prime Minister Sharif's decision to order the tests of Pakistani nuclear weapons, senior military intelligence officers informed him that the Indian and Israeli air forces were about to launch a preventive strike on the test site. The incident is shrouded in mystery, and the cause of this warning message is not clear. Although it is certainly possible that Pakistani intelligence officers simply misidentified aircraft in the region, a more likely explanation is that Inter-Service Intelligence (ISI) officials did not believe there was any threat of an imminent Indian-Israeli attack in 1998, but deliberately concocted (or exaggerated) the warning of a preventive strike to force the prime minister, who was wavering under U.S. pressure, to test the weapons immediately. It is not clear which of these is the more worrisome interpretation of the incident: false warnings could be catastrophic in a crisis whether they are deliberate provocations by rogue intelligence officers, or genuinely believed, but inaccurate, reports of imminent or actual attack.

It is important to note that the possibility of a false warning producing an accidental nuclear war in South Asia is reduced, but is by no means eliminated, by India's adoption of a nuclear no-first-use policy. Not only might the Pakistani government, following its stated first-use doctrine, respond to intelligence (in this case false) that India was about to attack successfully a large portion of Pakistani nuclear forces, but either government could misidentify an accidental nuclear detonation occurring during transport and alert activities at one of their own military bases as the start of a counterforce attack by the other state. Pakistani officials should be particularly sensitive to this possibility because of the 1988 Ojheri incident, in which a massive conventional munitions explosion at a secret ammunition dump near Rawalpindi caused fears among some decision makers that an Indian attack had begun. The possibility of this kind of accident producing a false warning of an attack cannot, however, be ruled out in India, either, as long as the government plans to alert forces or mate nuclear weapons to delivery vehicles during crises.

In addition, there should be serious concern about whether both countries can maintain centralized control over their nuclear weapons. Although government policy in this regard is, for obvious reasons, kept classified, it is known that Pakistan has no personnel reliability program (PRP) for the officers who control the arsenal or the guards who protect the weapons storage sites. In the United States, the program is a set of psychological tests and organizational checks; each year, between 2.5 percent and 5.0 percent of previously PRP certified individuals have been decertified, that is, deemed unsuitable for nuclear weapons related duties. Presumably, similarly low, but still significant, percentages of officers, soldiers, and civilians in other countries would be of questionable reliability as guardians of the arsenal. This personnel reliability problem is serious in India, where civilian custodians maintain custody of the nuclear weapons; it is particularly worrisome in Pakistan, where the weapons are controlled by a professional military organization facing the difficult challenge of maintaining discipline while dealing with a failing economy, serious social problems, and growing religious fundamentalism. This situation increases the risk of accidents and of unauthorized use, such as theft or use by terrorists groups.

Finally, there is evidence that neither the Indian nor the Pakistani military has focused sufficiently on the danger that a missile test launch during a crisis could be misperceived as the start of a nuclear attack. There was an agreement, as part of the Lahore accords in January 1999, to provide advance notification of missile tests, but even such an agreement is not a fool-proof solution, as the Russians discovered in January 1995 when a bureaucratic snafu in Moscow led to a failure to pass on advance notification of a Norwegian weather rocket launch, that resulted in serious false warning of a missile attack. Moreover, both the Pakistanis and the Indians appear to be planing to use their missile test facilities for actual nuclear weapons launches in war. In India, Wheeler Island is reportedly being used like Vandenberg air force base, a test site in peacetime and crises, and a launch site in war. During Kargil, according to the Indian Army chief of staff, nuclear alert activities were also detected at "some of Pakistan's launch areas—some of the areas where they carried out tests earlier of one of their missiles."[5]

## BEYOND DENIAL

Nuclear South Asia will be a dangerous place, not because of ill will or irrationality among government leaders, nor because of any unique cultural inhibitions against strategic thinking in both countries. India and Pakistan face a dangerous nuclear future because they have become like other nuclear powers. Their leaders seek security through nuclear deterrence, but imperfect humans inside imperfect organizations control their nuclear weapons. If my theories are right, these organizations will someday fail to produce secure nuclear deterrence. Unfortunately, the evidence from these first years of South Asia's nuclear history suggests that the pessimistic predictions of organization theory are likely to come true, even though I cannot predict the precise pathway by which deterrence will break down.

The organizational perspective suggests that there are more similarities than differences between nuclear powers in the way they manage, or at least try to manage, nuclear weapons operations. There is, however, one important structural difference between the new nuclear powers and their cold war predecessors. Just as each new child is born into a different family, each new nuclear power is born into a different nuclear system in which nuclear states influence each other's behavior. Some observers believe that the possibility that other nuclear powers—such as the United States or China—can intervene in future crises in South Asia may be a major constraint on undesired escalation. I fear the opposite: the possibility of intervention may encourage the governments of India and Pakistan to engage in risky behavior, initiating crises or making limited uses of force, precisely because they anticipate (correctly or incorrectly) that other nuclear powers may bail them out diplomatically if the going gets rough.

The possibility that other nuclear states might be able to influence nuclear behavior in South Asia does, however, lead to one final optimistic note. There are many potential unilateral steps and bilateral agreements that could be instituted to reduce the risk of nuclear war between India and Pakistan, and the U.S. government can play a useful role in helping to facilitate such agreements. Many, though not all, of the problems identified in this article can be reduced if nuclear weapons in both countries are maintained in a de-alerted state, with warheads removed from delivery vehicles. U.S. assistance could be helpful in providing the arms verification technology that could permit such de-alerting (or non-alerting in this case) to take place within a cooperative framework. The United States could also be helpful in providing intelligence and warning information, on a case-by-case basis, in peacetime or in crises to reduce the danger of false alarms. Finally, increased security of storage sites and safer management of nuclear weapons operations can be encouraged by sharing better security devices for storage sites and discussing organizational "best practices."

There will be no progress on any of these issues, however, unless Indians, Pakistanis, and Americans stop denying that serious problems exist. A basic awareness of nuclear command and control problems exists in New Delhi and Islamabad, but unfortunately Indian and Pakistani leaders too often trivialize them. The United States, in turn, refused to assist the Indians and Pakistanis in developing improved safety and security for their nuclear weapons until after the terrorist attacks on September 11, 2001. Washington officials argued before the September 11 attacks that any assistance in this area would "reward' Islamabad and New Delhi for testing, and signal to other potential nuclear weapons states that the United States was not serious about its nonproliferation goals. The September 11 attacks led the U.S. government to switch its position, and Pakistani officials accepted, at least in principle, that some assistance with their nuclear weapons security could be useful. It is crucial that such efforts to improve Pakistani nuclear security measures be fully implemented and eventually be extended to India.

Nuclear weapons will remain in Pakistan and India for the foreseeable future, and the conflict over Kashmir will continue to smolder, threatening to erupt into a wider and more dangerous war. The deep political problems between the two South Asian nuclear states may someday be resolved, and the U.S. government should encourage progress toward that end. In the meantime, the U.S. government should do whatever it can to reduce the risk that India and Pakistan will use nuclear weapons against each other.

## NOTES

1. Devin T. Hagerty, *The Consequences of Nuclear Proliferation* (Cambridge, Mass., MIT Press, 1998), p. 92, 106.

2. Hagerty, *The Consequences of Nuclear Proliferation*, p. 184.

3. Ihtashamul Haque, "Peace Linked to Kashmir Solution," *Dawn Wire Service,* June 26, 1999.

4. "Army Ready for War, Says Chief," *The Statesman* (India), January 12, 2002.

5. Raj Chenagappa, "Pakistan Tried Nuclear Blackmail," *The Newspaper Today,* January 12, 2000, www.thenewspapertoday.com/interview/index.phtml?INTERVIEW-INT_PADCOUNT.

# 25

# Nuclear Stability in South Asia

## KENNETH N. WALTZ

The American government and most American journalists look on the blossoming of nuclear forces in South Asia as an ominous event, different in implication and effect from all the similar events that we worried about throughout the cold war. A 1998 *New York Times* headline, for example, proclaimed that "India's Arms Race Isn't Safe Like the Cold War." Few thought the American-Soviet arms race safe at the time, and for good reasons few Indians and Pakistanis expect an arms race now. Most of the alarmist predictions about the fate of the subcontinent display forgetfulness about the past and confusion over the effects of nuclear weapons. In the same *New York Times* article, Joseph Cirincione, director of the Non-Proliferation Project at the Carnegie Endowment, reports that Pentagon war games between Pakistan and India always end with a nuclear exchange. Has everyone in that building forgotten that deterrence works precisely because nuclear states fear that conventional military engagements may escalate to the nuclear level, and therefore they draw back from the brink? Admiral David E. Jeremiah, once vice-chairman of the Joint Chiefs of Staff, laments the cultural mindset that leads Americans to believe that "everybody thinks like us," and a longtime president of the Henry L. Stimson Center, Michael Krepon, worries that because of the Pressler Amendment, which cut off aid to nations developing nuclear weapons, Pakistani officers have not had the benefit of attending our military schools. One's reaction to both statements may well be "thank goodness."

The Brookings Institution totaled up the cost of American nuclear weapons over the decades and arrived at the figure of 5.5 trillion dollars. Strobe Talbott, when he was deputy secretary of state, implied that military competition between

Pakistan and India will cause them to spend on a proportionate scale. When asked why we should not provide India and Pakistan with advice about, and equipment for, safe deterrence, he retorted that "if they locked themselves into the mentality of MAD (Mutual Assured Destruction), they will then be tempted into—like us— a considerable escalation of the arms race."[1] Yet nuclear states need race only to the second-strike level, which is easy to achieve and maintain. Indian and Pakistani leaders have learned from our folly. A minimal deterrent deters as well as a maximal one. Homi Jehangar Bhabha, father of the Indian bomb, called this "absolute deterrence." K. Subrahmanyam, a foremost strategist, emphasizes that Indians have learned that to build large forces is wasteful and foolish. An arsenal of about sixty weapons, he believes, will deter either Pakistan or China; and Pakistan might need, say, twenty to deter India. Some have claimed that no nuclear country has been satisfied with having only a minimum deterrent. Yet China, with even today only about twenty ICBMs, has been content with small numbers; and India and Pakistan would follow its example were it not for the disruptive effects of American missile defenses on the strategic arms balance in Asia. Political as well as economic constraints on both countries ensure this. Talbott has discerned "a global trend away from reliance on nuclear weapons."[2] The United States does rely less on nuclear weapons now because it is the world's dominant conventional power, spending as much on its armed forces in the year 2000 as the next eight big spenders combined. Partly for that reason, some other countries rely more on their nuclear weapons—Russia, for example, with its conventional forces in shambles. Countries that once counted on one of the two great powers for military assistance are now concerned to provide security for themselves: Pakistan, India, Iraq, Japan, and North Korea are all examples.

India tested its "peaceful bomb" in 1974. Its next tests came twenty-four years later. The United States complained loudly both times. Yet the United States tested nuclear weapons many times yearly for many years on end—more than a thousand above and below ground, which is more than the tests of all other countries combined. America's excuse was, at first, that it anticipated a mortal threat from the Soviet Union and, later, that it actually faced such a threat. America's nonproliferation policy denies that such reasoning can legitimate other countries' entering the tight circle of nuclear powers. Nevertheless, the reasoning the United States applied to itself applies to India and to Pakistan as well. Does anyone believe that testing nuclear warheads is something that, in their place, we would not have done?

The question raised by India's and Pakistan's nuclear tests is not whether they should have been conducted, but whether their security requires their becoming nuclear powers. Some countries need nuclear weapons; some do not. Brazil and Argentina set themselves on course to become nuclear states. Both decided to abandon the effort. Neither posed a threat to the other. South Africa became a nuclear state and then, finding no commensurate threat, reversed its policy.

Pakistan obviously needs nuclear weapons. When asked why nuclear weapons are so popular in Pakistan, former prime minister Benazir Bhutto answered, "It's our history. A history of three wars with a larger neighbor. India is five times larger than we are. Their military strength is five times larger. In 1971, our country was disintegrated. So the security issue for Pakistan is an issue of survival." From the other side, Shankar Bajpai, former Indian ambassador to Pakistan, China, and the United States, has said that "Pakistan's quest for a nuclear capability stems from its fear of its larger neighbor, removing that fear should open up immense possibilities"—possibilities for a less worried and more relaxed life. Shamshad Ahmad, Pakistan's foreign secretary, has echoed their thoughts: "In South Asia nuclear deterrence may . . . usher in an era of durable peace between Pakistan and India, providing the requisite incentives for resolving all outstanding issues, especially Jammu and Kashmir."[3] In recent years, some Indians and Pakistanis have begun to talk about a peaceful accommodation, and according to a *New York Times* reporter, "just about everybody" in Kashmir "cites the two countries' possession of nuclear weapons as a factor pushing towards peace."[4]

In the 1980s, after the Soviet occupation of Afghanistan, the United States, knowing of Pakistan's nuclear progress, nevertheless continued to supply Pakistan with sophisticated conventional weapons. The United States did not care much about Pakistan's nuclear progress as long as Soviet worries dominated American policy. Once the Soviet Union went into steep decline and then disappeared, America dropped Pakistan, with a speed that surprised not only Pakistan but India as well. For Pakistan to compete conventionally with India was economically impossible. Nuclear weapons linked to a sensible strategy are a low cost way of leveling the playing field. Understandably Pakistan felt itself pressed to follow the nuclear course.

Can India be seen in a similar light? With its superior conventional forces, it needed no nuclear weapons to protect itself against a Pakistan that lacked them, but what about China? Americans think of India as the dominant power in South Asia. India feels differently. India is part of a hostile world. With a Muslim minority of about 150 million, it adjoins Muslim Pakistan, and beyond lies a Muslim world becoming more fundamentalist and more hostile. To the north is an increasingly nationalist, steadily more powerful, and potentially unstable China. The United States has reinforced India's worries about a Chinese-Pakistani-American axis, notably when America "tilted" toward Pakistan in the 1971 war with India. In the middle of the war, Henry Kissinger told Mao Zedong, "We want to keep the pressure on India both militarily and politically," adding that if China "took measures to protect its security, the US would oppose efforts of others to interfere."[5] In a show of support for Pakistan, the American navy moved the aircraft carrier *Enterprise* into the Indian Ocean. To this day, Indians consider this an attempt to hold them in nuclear awe. They call it blackmail. India continues to believe that America favors China over India. A professor at Jawaharlal Nehru University found nuclear cooperation between Beijing and Islamabad "unprecedented in the history of international relations."[6] And an Indian minister of defense wondered, as many Indians do, "why India and Pakistan should be seen as blowing each other up when nuclear weapons in the hands of the United States and China are seen as stabilizing factors."[7] That the United States seems to trust China as an old nuclear power, and not India as a new one, is a cause of bitter resentment.

The decision to make nuclear weapons was a momentous one for India. The tests of May 1998 were overwhelmingly popular with the public at large, but the decision emerged over decades, with much opposition along the way. Even today, Indians who view nuclear deterrence as a difficult and demanding task believe that India will be unable to develop and deploy a nuclear force sufficient for the deterrence of China. In their view, the main effect of India's developing nuclear capabilities was to cause Pakistan to develop its own. India is therefore worse off with nuclear weapons than it would have been without them. The Indian view that carried the day rests on the contrary argument: namely, that it does not take much to deter.

Is it farfetched for India to worry about a Chinese threat to its security? Any country has trouble seeing the world as others do. Let's try. If the United States shared a two-thousand-mile border with a country that was more populous, more prosperous, more heavily armed, and in possession of nuclear weapons, we would react militarily and, judging from our response to the Soviet Union, more vigorously than India has done. What *is* farfetched is for the United States to worry about a Chinese threat to its security and then wonder why India does too.

Kanti Bajpai, a professor at Nehru University, strongly opposes India's nuclear armament. He doubts that India's nuclear deterrent would dissuade China from seizing Arunachal Pradesh in the northeast or Pakistan from seizing Kashmir in the northwest. This is comparable to the worry, dreamt up in the 1960s, about a "Hamburg grab." Some American military commentators worried that the Soviet Union might suddenly seize Hamburg, which jutted into East Germany, and then in effect ask, "Is NATO's fighting to regain Hamburg worth risking a nuclear conflagration?" Similarly, Kanti Bajpai imagines "a quick grabbing thrust into the two states, backed by nuclear weapons, in the hope of presenting India with a fait accompli."[8] Such worries are as fanciful as American worries were in the cold war. The invader would have to assemble troops near the border. India would then alert its forces, including nuclear ones. With the potential crisis easily foreseeable, why would China or Pakistan run such risks?

One answer to the question is that Pakistan did move troops across the line of control into Kashmir and fight for a time at a fairly high level in the engagement known as Kargil. Joseph Cirincione voices widespread fears when, with the Kashmir conflict in mind, he says, "Just assemble all the risk factors and multiply it out. . . . This is the most dangerous and unstable military situation in the world."[9] His pronouncement repeats the tired old error of inferring from the conventional past what the nuclear future holds, a mistake made almost every time another country gets nuclear weapons. With nuclear weapons added, conventionally dangerous and unstable situations become safer and stabler ones. Nuclear weapons produce what

Joseph Nye calls the "crystal ball" effect. Everyone knows that if force gets out of hand all the parties to a conflict face catastrophe. With conventional weapons, the crystal ball is clouded. With nuclear weapons, it is perfectly clear.

What reasons do we have to believe that India's and Pakistan's crystal balls are clouded? Well, again, Kargil. Some observers worry that Pakistan may believe that it can safely raise the level of conventional violence since nuclear weapons limit the extent of India's response. But, of course, they also limit the size and scope of Pakistan's attack, since Pakistan knows it could face nuclear retaliation. And the same reasoning applies to India. It's the same old story: In the presence of nuclear weapons, a country can achieve a significant victory only by risking devastating retaliation.

Sagan calls Kargil the fourth Indian-Pakistani war because it fits the social science definition holding that a military encounter is a war if it produces more than one thousand battle-related deaths. If Kargil is called a war, then the definition of war requires revision; and now that both countries have nuclear weapons the fifth "war" will be no worse than the so-called fourth one. The late Pakistani chief of the army staff, General Mirza Aslam Beg, remarked that India and Pakistan can no longer fight even a conventional war over Kashmir, and his counterpart, the chief of the Indian army staff, General Krishnaswami Sundarji, concurred. Kargil showed once again that deterrence does not firmly protect disputed areas but does limit the extent of the violence. Indian rear admiral Raja Menon put the larger point simply: "The Kargil crisis demonstrated that the subcontinental nuclear threshold probably lies territorially in the heartland of both countries, and not on the Kashmir cease-fire line."[10]

The obvious conclusion to draw from Kargil is that the presence of nuclear weapons prevented escalation from major skirmish to full-scale war. This contrasts starkly with the bloody 1965 war, in which both parties were armed only with conventional weapons.

Another question is whether India and Pakistan can firmly control and safely deploy nuclear forces sufficient to deter. Because I said enough about the ease of deterrence in chapter 8, I shall concentrate on questions of safety and control. Sagan claims that "the emerging history of nuclear India and nuclear Pakistan strongly supports the pessimistic predictions of organizational theorists." Yet the evidence, accumulated over five decades, shows that nuclear states fight with nuclear states only at low levels, that accidents seldom occur, and that when they do they never have bad effects. If nuclear pessimists were right, nuclear deterrence would have failed again and again. Nuclear pessimists deal with the potential causes of catastrophe; optimists, with the effects the causes do *not* produce. Since the evidence fails to support the predictions of pessimists, one wonders why the spread of nuclear weapons to South Asia should have bad rather than good effects. What differences in the situation of India and Pakistan may cause their fates to depart from the nuclear norm? If they and their situations are different, then the happy history of the nuclear past does not forecast their futures. American commentators dwell on the differences between the United States and the Soviet Union earlier and India and Pakistan today. Among the seeming differences, these are given prominence: differences in the states involved, differences in their histories of conflict, and differences in the distance between the competing parties. I consider them in turn.

## DOES DETERRENCE DEPEND ON WHO IS DETERRING WHOM?

For decades we believed that we were trying to deter two monstrous countries—one an "evil empire" and the other a totalitarian country ruled by a megalomaniac. Now we learn that deterrence worked in the past because the United States, the Soviet Union, and China were settled and sensible societies. Karl Kaiser, of the Research Institute of the German Society for Foreign Affairs, and Arthur G. Rubinoff, of the University of Toronto, for example, argue that the success of deterrence depends on its context, that is, on who the countries are and on how they relate to each other. In Kaiser's view, "the stability of nuclear deterrence between East and West rest[ed] on a multitude of military and political factors which in other regions are either totally missing or are only partially present." In Rubinoff's view, it is foolish to compare the American-Soviet conflict with South Asia, where the dynamics are "reminiscent of the outbreak of the First World War." Reminiscence flickers, however, since no one then had nuclear weapons. With a Hindu chauvinist in power in New Delhi and an Islamic party governing India, Rubinoff finds "no resemblance to the deterrent situation that characterized the U.S.-Soviet conflict."[11] That statement may once have applied to India and Pakistan, but only until they armed themselves with nuclear weapons. The history of the cold war shows that what matters is not the character of the countries that have nuclear weapons but the fact that they have them. Differences among nuclear countries abound, but for keeping the peace what difference have they made?

Whatever the identity of rulers, and whatever the characteristics of their states, the national behaviors they produce are strongly conditioned by the world outside. With conventional weapons, a defensive country has to ask itself how much power it must harness to its policy in order to dissuade an aggressive state from striking. Countries willing to run high risks are hard to dissuade. The characteristics of governments and the temperaments of leaders have to be carefully weighed. With nuclear weapons, any state will be deterred by another state's second-strike forces; one need not be preoccupied with the qualities of the state that is to be deterred or scrutinize its leaders. In a nuclear world, any state—whether ruled by a Stalin, a Mao Zedong, a Saddam Hussein, or a Kim Jong Il—will be deterred by the knowledge that aggressive actions may lead to its own destruction.

## DOES DETERRENCE DEPEND ON THE DETERRERS' RECENT HISTORY?

India and Pakistan have fought three wars in little more than fifty years, and Kashmir is a bone in the throat of Pakistan. In contrast, America and Russia have never fought a war against each other. Yet some other nuclear countries look more like India and Pakistan, and nuclear weapons have kept the peace between them. Russia and China have suffered numerous military invasions by one another over the centuries. In the 1960s, when both had nuclear weapons, skirmishes broke out from time to time along the Siberian frontier, and the fighting was on a fairly large scale. The bitterness of the antagonists rivalled that between India and Pakistan, fueled by ethnic resentments and ideological differences.

Clashes between nuclear countries over peripheral areas are hardly the exception. Of today's eight nuclear countries, five have fought their neighbors in the past half century: Russia, China, Israel, Pakistan, and India. Those who believe that the South Asian situation is without parallel often ignore the Middle East. The parallel is not exact, but it is instructive. The Middle East is unrivalled for long-standing conflict, irreconcilable disputes, feelings of distrust and hatred, and recurrent wars. In 1973, two nonnuclear Arab countries, Egypt and Syria, attacked Israel and fought what by anyone's definition was a war. Limited in extent by one side's nuclear weapons, it nonetheless did not spiral out of control.

## DOES DETERRENCE DEPEND ON DISTANCE?

Proximity is a constantly emphasized difference between the relations of India and Pakistan and that of the United States and the Soviet Union. America and Russia are separated by vast distances; Pakistan and India live cheek by jowl. They continually rub against each other in irritating and dangerous ways. George Perkovich had this in mind when he expressed his fear that "Somebody blows up something big and India says, 'That's it, and takes out targets. Then you're on your way. Who's going to back down?'"[12] Much the same fears in much the same words were expressed during the cold war. The two antagonists might "go to the brink"; one would slip over the edge, and once the exchange of warheads began neither side would be willing to stop it by giving in to the other. In actuality, however, backing down in times of crisis proved not to be such a big problem. Never do two countries share a common interest more completely than when they are locked in death's embrace. Each may want something else as well, but both want most of all to get out of the dire situation they are in. During the Kargil fighting, India went to "Readiness State 3," which means that warheads were prepared for placement on delivery vehicles, and Pakistan apparently took similar steps. These were seen as rash and dangerous moves, but what does one expect? The United States and the Soviet Union alerted their forces a number of times. Doing so is a way of saying, "This is getting serious, and we both had better calm down." Despite the pessimism engendered by the history of South Asia, Indian-Pakistani wars have been, as wars go, quite restrained. As Admiral Menon has written, "Any analysis of the three wars fought often refers to the rather gentlemanly manner in which they were fought with care taken to avoid civilian casualties."[13] Pakistan's 1999 thrust into Kashmir may have been rash, yet as Menon has rightly said, "Subsequent Pakistani attempts to signal an unwillingness to escalate were mature and sober."[14] And in the Kargil campaign, India never sent its troops across the line of control.

History tells us only what we want to know. A pair of *New York Times* journalists contrasts then with now by claiming that, except in Cuba, "the Americans and Soviets took care not to place their troops in direct military confrontation."[15] What, then, were NATO and Warsaw Treaty Organization troops doing in the middle of Europe, where confrontation was a constant and serious business?

Proximity does make warning time short. Missiles can fly between Islamabad and New Delhi in less than five minutes. Yet nuclear countries in the past have often been close militarily if not geographically. Cuba is only ninety miles from American shores, and that is proximity enough. The United States flew planes at the Soviet Union's borders and across them, believing its radars would not spot them. American bravado continues. In April 2001, an American surveillance plane was struck by a Chinese plane over waters near China. Close surveillance is provocative even if international legalities are nicely observed. As President Dwight D. Eisenhower said when an American plane went down thirty-two miles from the Chinese coast in August 1956, "If planes were flying 20 to 50 miles from our shores, we would be very likely to shoot them down if they came in closer, whether through error or not."[16]

Operation Brasstacks was an all-service Indian operation staged in 1987. As Sagan says, it is widely believed that General Sundarji intended it to be a prelude to a war in which India would destroy Pakistan's nuclear facilities. Sundarji may have thought that even if Pakistan had a few bombs, India would be able to destroy them on the ground. In retrospect, Brasstacks looks more like a typical instance of Indian failure to coordinate policies among the Prime Minister's Office, the External Affairs Ministry, the Defense Ministry, and the military services.

Brasstacks is not something new in the nuclear annals. It pales in comparison to provocative acts by the United States and the Soviet Union. In 1983, for example, Able Archer—a recurrent NATO military exercise—was more extensive than ever before. It was held at a time of extraordinary tension. The Soviets believed that surprise was the key to American war plans. During the exercise, the simulated alert of NATO nuclear forces was thought by the Soviets to be a real one. American Pershing II missiles were to be deployed in Europe soon. The Soviets believed that some of them, with their fifty-kiloton payload, fifty-meter accuracy, and ten-minute delivery time to Moscow, had already arrived. Early in the Reagan administration, Defense Secretary Caspar Weinberger and other officials proclaimed that it was our aim to be able to fight, sustain, and win a nuclear war. With some reason, Soviet leaders believed it was about to begin.

Vast distances lie between the United States and Russia. What difference do these distances make when American troops and missiles are stationed in Europe and Northeast Asia? Those who believe that the Indian-Pakistani confrontation is without precedent have either little knowledge of cold war history or oddly defective memories.

Proximity shortens the time between launch and landing. With little warning time, quick decisions would seem to be required. Acting on early warnings of incoming missiles that may turn out to be false could be fatal to both sides. The notion that deterrence demands the threat of swift retaliation was ingrained in American and Russian thinking, and it remains so today, with both forces still on hair-trigger alert. Yet deterrence of a would-be attacker does not depend on the belief that retaliation will be prompt, but only on the belief that the attacked may in due course retaliate. As K. Subrahmanyam has put it, "The strike back need not be highly time-critical."[17] A small force may be a vulnerable force, but smaller is worse than bigger only if the attacker believes he can destroy *all* of the force before *any* of it can be launched.

Students of organizations rightly worry about complex and tightly-coupled systems because they are susceptible to damaging accidents. They wrongly believe that conflicting nuclear states should be thought of as a tightly-coupled system. Fortunately, nuclear weapons loosen the coupling of states by lessening the effects of proximity and by cutting through the complexities of conventional confrontations. Organizational theorists fail to distinguish between the technical complexities of nuclear-weapons systems and the simplicity of the situations they create.

Sagan points out that the survival of Indian and Pakistani forces cannot be guaranteed. But neither can their complete destruction, and that is what matters. Oddly, many pessimists believe that countries with small and technologically limited nuclear forces may be able to accomplish the difficult feat of making a successful first strike but not the easy one of making their own nuclear force appear to be invulnerable. They overlook a basic nuclear truth: If some part of a force is invulnerable, all of the force is invulnerable. Destroying even a major portion of a nuclear force does no good because of the damage a small number of surviving warheads can do. Conventional weapons put a premium on striking first to gain the initial advantage and set the course of the war. Nuclear weapons eliminate this premium. The initial advantage is insignificant if the cost of gaining it is half a dozen cities.

More important than the size of arsenals, the sophistication of command and control, the proximity of competitors, and the history of the relations, are the sensibilities of leaders. Fortunately, nuclear weapons make leaders behave sensibly even though under other circumstances they might be brash and reckless.

The South Asian situation, said so often to be without precedent, finds precedents galore. Rather than assuming that the present differs significantly from the past, we should emphasize the similarities and learn from them. Fortunately, India and Pakistan have learned from their nuclear predecessors. . . .

Sagan believes that future Indian-Pakistani crises may be nuclear. Once countries have nuclear weapons any confrontation that merits the term "crisis" is a nuclear one. With conventional weapons, crises tend toward instability. Because of the perceived, or misperceived, advantage of striking first, war may be the outcome. Nuclear weapons make crises stable, which is an important reason for believing that India and Pakistan are better off with than without them.

Yet because nuclear weapons limit escalation, they may tempt countries to fight small wars. Glenn Snyder long ago identified the strategic stability/tactical instability paradox. Benefits carry costs in the nuclear business just as they do in other endeavors. The possibility of fighting at low levels is not a bad price to pay for the impossibility of fighting at high levels. This impossibility becomes obvious, since in the presence of nuclear weapons no one can score major gains, and all can lose catastrophically.

Sagan carries Snyder's logic a step farther by arguing that Pakistan and India may nevertheless fight to a higher level of violence, believing that if one side or the other begins to lose control, a third party will step in to prevent the use of nuclear weapons. The idea is a hangover from cold war days when the United States and the Soviet Union thought they had compelling reasons to intervene in other countries' conflicts. The end of the cold war reduced the incentives for such intervention. As K. Subrahmanyam has said, "In a world dominated by the Cold War, there was a certain predictability that any Chinese nuclear threat to India would be countervailed by one or the other super power or both. In the aftermath of the Cold War that predictability has disappeared."[18] Intervention by a third party during low-level fighting would still be possible, but neither side could count on it.

Kanti Bajpai spotted another consequence of nuclear weapons that may be harmful: They may drive the antagonists apart by removing the need to agree. Since deterrence works, Bajpai wonders why countries would try to settle their differences. India and Pakistan, however, did not reach agreement on Kashmir or on other issues when neither had nuclear weapons; now both sides have at least an incentive to discuss their problems.

Crises on the subcontinent recur, and when they do, voices of despair predict a conventional clash ending in nuclear blasts. On December 13, 2001, five gunmen attacked the Indian Parliament. Fourteen people died, including the gunmen. India, blaming Pakistani terrorists, mounted its largest mobilization in the past thirty years and massed troops and equipment along the India-Pakistan border. As in the crisis of 1990, the United States deployed its diplomats, this time dispatching Secretary of State Colin Powell to calm the contestants. Tempers on both sides flared, bombast filled the air, and an American commentator pointed out once again that all of the American military's war games show that a conventional Indian-Pakistani war will end in a nuclear conflagration. Both India and Pakistan claimed that they could fight conventionally in the face of nuclear weapons. What reason do we have to believe that military and civilian leaders on either side fail to understand the dangers of fighting a conventional war against a nuclear neighbor? The statements of Pakistan's leader, General Musharraf, were mainly conciliatory. Indian military leaders emphasized that any military engagements would have to be limited to such targets as guerrilla training camps and military facilities used by extremists. As an astute analyst put it, "India's way of looking at this is that we're not threatening Pakistan's core interests, so they would have no incentive to launch their weapons."[19] Indian leaders made it clear that they intended to pressure Pakistan to control military intrusions by irregular forces. Pakistan made it clear that its pressure for a Kashmiri settlement would be unremitting. Except to alarmist observers, mainly American, neither side looked as though it would cross or even approach the nuclear threshold. The proposition that nuclear weapons limit the extent of fighting and ultimately preserve peace again found vindication.

Are India and Pakistan worse or better off now that they have nuclear weapons? Are their futures dimmer or brighter? I will surprise no one by saying "brighter." I have looked in vain for important differences between the plight of India and Pakistan and that of other nuclear countries. Nuclear weapons put all countries that possess them in the same boat. South Asia is said to be the "acid test" for deterrence optimists. So far, nuclear deterrence has passed all of the many tests it has faced.

## NOTES

1. Quoted in Steven Erlanger, "India's Arms Race Isn't Safe Like the Cold War," *New York Times,* July 12, 1998, section 4, p. 18.

2. Strobe Talbott, "Dealing with the Bomb in South Asia," *Foreign Affairs* 78, no. 2 (March/April 1999), p. 117.

3. Claudia Dreifus, "Benazir Bhutto," *New York Times Magazine,* May 15, 1994, p. 39; K. Shankar Bajpai, "Nuclear Exchange," *Far Eastern Economic Review,* June 24, 1993, p. 24; Shamshad Ahmad, "The Nuclear Subcontinent: Bringing Stability to South Asia," *Foreign Affairs* 78, no. 4 (July/August 1999), p. 125.

4. John F. Burns, "War-Weary Kashmiris Contemplate the Price of Peace," *New York Times,* July 11, 2001, p. A3.

5. Quoted in Jonathan Spence, "Kissinger and the Emperor," *New York Review of Books,* March 4, 1999, p. 21.

6. Amitabh Maltoo, "India's Nuclear Policy in an Anarchic World," in Mattoo, ed., *India's Nuclear Deterrent: Pokhran II and Beyond* (New Delhi: Har-Anand, 1999), p. 22.

7. George Fernandes, quoted in John F. Burns, "Indian Defense Chief Calls U.S. Hypocritical," *New York Times,* June 18, 1998, p. A6.

8. Kanti Bajpai, "The Fallacy of an Indian Deterrent," in Amitabh Mattoo, ed., *India's Nuclear Deterrent,* p. 183. China does not recognize Arunachal Pradesh or Sikkim as parts of India.

9. Quoted in Erlanger, "India's Arms Race Isn't Safe Like the Cold War."

10. Raja Menon, *A Nuclear Strategy for India* (New Delhi: Sage, 2000), p. 116.

11. Karl Kaiser, "Nonproliferation and Nuclear Deterrence, *Survival* 31, no. 2 (March/April, 1989), p. 125; Arthur G. Rubinoff, "The Failure of Nuclear Deterrence in South Asia," *Toronto Globe and Mail,* June 1, 1998, p. A17.

12. Quoted in Celia W. Dugger and Barry Bearak, "You've Got the Bomb. So Do I. Now I Dare You to Fight," *New York Times,* January 16, 2000. sec. 4, p. 1.

13. Menon, *A Nuclear Strategy for India,* p. 293.

14. *Ibid.,* p. 197.

15. Celia W. Dugger and Barry Bearak, "You've Got the Bomb. So Do I. Now I Dare You to Fight," *New York Times,* January 16, 2000, section 4, p. 1.

16. James Bamford, "The Dangers of Spy Planes," *New York Times,* April 5, 2001, p. A21.

17. K. Subrahmanyan, "Nuclear Force Design and Minimum Deterrence Strategy," in Bharat Kamad, ed., *Future Imperiled: India's Security in the 1990s and Beyond* (New Delhi: Viking, 1994).

18. *Ibid.,* p. 186.

19. The analyst is Commodore Uday Bhaskar, deputy directory of the Institute for Defense Studies and Analysis, quoted in Rajiv Chandrasekaran "For India, Deterrence May Not Prevent War," *Washington Post Foreign Service,* January 17, 2002, p. A1.

# 26

# Intervention in Ethnic and Ideological Civil Wars

## Chaim Kaufmann

From Somalia to Bosnia to Rwanda, American debates on humanitarian inter-vention in ethnic conflicts have taken virtually identical form. Proponents of intervention argue that war-caused starvation, ethnic "cleansing," and genocide are crimes against humanity so terrible that the international community has an obligation to act to stop them. Opponents argue that any military intervention in a foreign civil war must inevitably become an unwinnable quagmire whose esca-lating cost would ultimately cause the do-gooders to retreat, badly damaging both the international credibility and the domestic cohesion of the intervening powers, while leaving the local victims at least as badly off as before.

In these debates, opponents have painted each prospective intervention as another Vietnam. This understanding has gone largely unchallenged, because pro-ponents of humanitarian interventions have generally conceded that any commit-ment of U.S. ground troops to a foreign civil war would be disastrous, restricting their proposals to strategies based on air power or military aid or to peacekeep-ing missions which are not supposed to involve any ground fighting.

The widespread acceptance of the quagmire image is not surprising, because it reflects a scholarly consensus which is based on America's Cold War experi-ence of counterinsurgency in Vietnam and elsewhere. The conventional wisdom is that outside intervention in civil wars can have only limited leverage on their outcomes. These outcomes are determined mainly by the political strength and competence of the local factions, which outsiders can do little to affect. Massive outside aid risks delegitimating the client, and, especially if ground troops are inserted, the possibility of an open-ended commitment.

The Vietnam analogy, however, is a poor guide to understanding current ethnic conflicts, because it is based on learning from ideological civil wars, which are fundamentally different from ethnic ones. The central difference between the two types is the importance of loyalty competition. Ideological civil wars center around the competition between the government and the insurgents for the loyalties of the people; territorial control is relatively unimportant. By contrast, in ethnic wars neither side can recruit members of the other group because ethnic identities are fixed by birth. Ethnic wars are not political competitions for individual loyalties, but contests over control of territory whose outcomes are determined mainly by the balance of military force.

As a result, both the prospects for foreign intervention and the appropriate methods are very different. Ethnic civil wars are not guerrilla quagmires. Foreign aid or foreign troops can make a tremendous difference to the local balance of forces and, unlike in ideological counterinsurgencies, outsiders can reliably tell friend from foe. Provided that interventions aim at saving lives and establishing defensible territorial settlements, not at reassembling shattered multiethnic states, outside powers can resolve ethnic wars with finite effort in finite time. The United States and other powers motivated to stop ethnic wars and prevent genocide are not helpless. . . .

## TYPES OF CIVIL WARS

Internal conflicts can be divided into two major categories: intracommunity conflicts and intercommunity conflicts. Intracommunity conflicts are primarily about ideology, while intercommunity conflicts are driven primarily by ethnic divisions.

Intracommunity conflicts are disputes within a single national or religious community. All sides agree on the identity and unity of the community. They share a common definition of community membership, a common preference for political organization of the community as a single state, and a common sense of the legitimate physical boundaries of that state. The sides disagree over which personalities, principles, or policies should rule the community-state. Central issues may include class conflicts or other secular ideological issues or interpretation of the shared religion. The opposing sides seek control of the state, not its division or destruction. Examples include the Greek, Vietnamese, and Nicaraguan civil wars.

By contrast, intercommunity conflicts are disputes between groups which see themselves as distinct ethnic, clan, or religious communities. Although contained within the same polity, the opposing communities have irreconcilable visions of the identity, purpose, and legitimate borders of the state. Disputes do not center on the ideologies of alternative parties or on the class impact of government policy, but on the relation between political rights and membership in a particular community. One community may see the state as an expression of its particular identity to the exclusion of others, while others may demand special rights or a degree of autonomy from the state, or even seek to secede to form their own state. Examples include the Nigerian, Yugoslav, Sri Lankan, Rwandan, and Chechnyan civil wars.

### Differences Between Ideological and Ethnic Wars

Ideological and ethnic civil wars have very different dynamics, which in turn imply profound differences in the determinants of victory, the instruments and strategies of conflict, and the prospects for foreign intervention.

The key difference is the flexibility of individual loyalties, which are relatively fluid in ideological conflicts, but almost completely rigid in ethnic wars. Ideological loyalties are changeable, whether voluntarily or under coercion, but ethnic identities are determined by language, culture, religion, and, especially, parentage, and are further hardened by the hypernationalist mobilization that accompanies ethnic war. As a result, the central dynamic in ideological conflicts is the competition between the government and the rebels for the loyalties of the people. Victory depends on building political support while undermining support for the other side. In ethnic conflicts, by contrast, there is no loyalty competition. While not everyone may be mobilized as an active fighter for their own group, hardly anyone ever becomes a supporter of the opposing ethnic group. Almost everything else about both types of conflicts flows from this one fact.

Gathering intelligence on individual loyalties, which in ideological conflicts is critical for both sides but very difficult, is unimportant in ethnic wars because loyalties can be gauged by ethnicity. While in ideological civil wars the entire population serves as the shared mobilization base of both sides, in ethnic wars each side can mobilize only members of its own group, and only in friendly controlled territory. Accordingly, in ideological wars territorial control is often not critical, since military control of a place does not guarantee the loyalties of the residents, while success in the "hearts and minds" battle will eventually lead to control of the entire country. In ethnic wars, however, neither side can afford to surrender any settlement because the enemy is likely to "cleanse" it by massacre, expulsion, or colonization, thus reducing or eliminating its value even if recaptured later.

Finally, while both types of civil war pose security dilemmas, their nature is different. In ideological conflicts, most people's survival does not depend on victory, since either side will accept their allegiance, even if coerced. The only people who face an inescapable security dilemma are faction leaders whose commitments are too famous (or infamous) for their opponents to forgive. Further, this security dilemma normally has no territorial solution, because the victors in an ideological civil war usually insist on control of the whole country; losers can rarely defend a rump territory.

Ethnic wars, by contrast, pose a security dilemma for nearly all members of both sides. Each group's mobilization represents a genuine security threat to the other. Individuals cannot change their ethnic identities and, in an environment saturated by both sides with hypernationalist rhetoric and atrocity tales, are extremely unlikely to trust their security to the mercy of the ethnic enemy. The severity of the security dilemma, however, depends on the geography of group-settlement patterns. Intermixed settlements pose extreme defensive risks as well as offensive opportunities for both sides, thus both causing escalation and preventing demobilization. Conversely, if the groups are largely separated, or become separated by refugee movements during the war, the security dilemma is considerably reduced.

Since ideological wars generally cannot be settled by territorial division, they most often end with decisive victory by one side. Power-sharing outcomes are possible if the balance of forces is nearly equal, as in the Colombian National Front agreement in 1958, or if there is agreement to submit the dispute to new elections, as in Nicaragua in 1989.

Ethnic wars end differently. Decisive victory by one side is possible, but is rarely stable, because the losing side will usually rebel again at any opportunity. Power-sharing agreements or attempts to replace ethnic hostility with inclusive "civic nationalism" usually fail because they cannot solve the security dilemma caused by intermixed demography. The only stable solution to an ethnic civil war is separation of the warring communities into distinct, defensible regions, because only this can eliminate the security dilemma faced by both sides.

Since the discussion to this point has described ideal types, it begs the question of how mixed cases behave. Part of the answer is that there seem to be relatively few civil wars in which both ideology and ethnicity play major roles. There are two keys to classification: First, the basis of mobilization appeals, specifically the relative weight of appeals based on race or confession (ethnic) to those based on political, economic, or social ideals (ideological). Second, the degree to which ethnic divides do or do not match the actual sources of recruits of each side.

Some apparently mixed cases are not. In many ethnic conflicts, one side or the other takes on an ideological identification as a tactical maneuver to gain outside support. This was especially common during the Cold War, when U.S. or Soviet aid was often available. In Angola the faction centered around the Mbundu tribe and urban mestizos (MPLA) accepted aid from the Soviet Union and Cuba, the Bakongo (FNLA) from the United States and Zaire, and the Ovimbundu, Chokwe, and Ngangela (UNITA) first from China and later from the United States and South Africa. Similar phenomena occurred in several different insurgencies in Burma/Myanmar, in Laos, and in Thailand.

There is also at least some tendency, once civil conflicts become highly mobilized, for ethnic divisions to overwhelm and suppress potentially cross-cutting ideological cleavages. The ethnic war in Ethiopia among the Eritrean People's Liberation Front, Tigrean People's Liberation Front, Oromo Liberation Front, and the Mengistu government was in no way ameliorated by the fact that all four were nominally Marxist. In Lebanon's wars, the rightist Phalange never had any non-Christian support, while nearly all leftist parties have also been ethnically or sectarian based. Sinhalese and Tamil leftists have been driven apart by war, not together. The leftist ideological orientations of the Kurdish Worker's Party (PKK) in Turkey and the Kurdish Democratic Party (KDP) have not enabled either to build useful alliances with non-Kurdish leftists.

A few, fairly evenly mixed cases can be found, in which at least one side persisted in pursuing cross-ethnic ideological as well as military recruitment appeals, despite the fact that the movement's membership was initially heavily dominated by one group. The most important are the Yugoslav Partisans in the Second World War and both sides in the Malayan Emergency of 1948–60. Partisan leaders were recruited mainly from prewar Army officers, and throughout most of 1942 the Partisans fielded mainly Montenegrin and Serbian troops, leavened with just a few fighters of other nationalities. Many Partisan commanders pursued specifically Serb rather than pan–Yugoslav objectives, while Croats began to join in numbers only after the war was clearly lost, in 1944. In Malaya, although the communists drew 90 percent of their support from ethnic Chinese, both the British and the communists, for their own reasons, emphasized ideology over ethnicity in their rhetoric and, as much as possible, in their operational methods and recruitment efforts. The military dynamics of these cases do in fact fall between the ideal extremes, and both ended without separation, although both have since seen a resurgence of ethnic violence.

**Dynamics of Ideological Civil Wars**

The basic dynamics of ideological insurgencies are fairly well understood. Although both sides use force, the contest is primarily a political one. To win, the insurgents must gain the political support of population while undermining political support for the regime. For its part, the government must isolate the rebels politically while shoring up it own political base—that is, it must make itself more attractive to most people than the rebels. In principle, the sides in a civil war can employ three main types of strategic instruments: (1) political, economic, and social reform programs; (2) population control; and (3) military action. Political, economic, and social-reform programs are the most important, because they are the key to winning political support, while population control can help "tilt the playing field" by allowing one side to carry out its own programs and to block execution of the other's. Military action matters least, because population control is as much a matter of loyalty intelligence as of territorial control.

*Political and Economic Programs*

Political, social, and economic reform is the most important strategy for both the government and the insurgents. The most important issues are usually local grievances such as poverty, inequality, corruption, and physical insecurity. The rebels typically promise redistribution, such as land reform to break the hold of corrupt and oppressive landlords, political enfranchisement for the excluded, and honest, responsive government. For its part, the popular appeal of the government depends on providing essentially the same things: land reform, real democracy, and uncorrupt "good government." The side which is better able to provide, or credibly promise, such reforms and benefits usually wins.

*Population Control*

Controlling access to the population matters because political and economic programs can only win support if actually implemented, and because the population is the shared mobilization base for both sides. The insurgents especially depend on popular support for food, shelter, money, and recruits; as Mao said, "guerrillas are like fish and the people are the water they swim in."

Territorial control does not guarantee population control, because individual loyalties are both difficult to assess and changeable. Rather, population control requires controlling individual freedom of association and action. Tactics include selective terror, hostage taking, collective punishment, and efforts to control food supplies. Each side will also seek to undermine the other's local leadership by co-optation, intimidation, or assassination. Accuracy and restraint are crucial, however, because innocent victims generate anger, mobilizing survivors, relatives, and neighbors for the enemy. The government may relocate people from settlements seen as vulnerable to penetration to more defensible towns, although this also can be politically damaging if it is seen as arbitrary and disruptive.

*Military Action*

Direct military action is much less important because both sides are constrained in their use of force. A classical insurgency follows the three-stage plan developed by Mao Zedong and modified by General Vo-Nguyen Giap. First, the insurgents form a party to agitate and recruit among the population. Second, beginning in remote and relatively inaccessible areas, the rebels use guerrilla operations to frustrate government forces, create liberated base areas, and build up their forces. Eventually, once rebel forces are strong and government forces have been gutted by defections and morale collapse, the insurgents go on the offensive and conquer the country. Conventionalizing the conflict too soon forfeits the guerrillas' mobility and stealth advantages, allowing the stronger government forces to engage and destroy the insurgents.

The government generally begins with vastly greater military resources, but has difficulty getting to grips with evasive guerrilla bands. Intensive military operations ("sweeps" or "search and destroy" missions) may actually strengthen the rebels, because heavy firepower often kills civilians as "collateral damage." Even worse, troops frustrated by their inability to catch elusive guerrillas often resort to attacking whatever civilians may be at hand. In addition, simply inflicting attrition on the guerrilla forces often does little good; if their base of political support is undamaged, losses will be replaced by new recruits. The government does need a considerable level of force to protect population and administrative centers, but offensive operations should be limited, designed primarily to "clear and hold" more and more of the country, not to pursue and destroy all guerrillas wherever they may be. If the government can protect the population and implement reform, the guerrillas will eventually wither away.

Conversely, as long as the government still commands the loyalty of a large part of the population and can continue to recruit forces willing to fight, the insurgents can never approach military parity, but if the rebels can decisively win the political struggle, the government will collapse like a house of cards.[2]

### Dynamics of Ethnic Wars

In principle, the sides in an ethnic civil war can employ the same three strategies as in ideological insurgency, but their relative importance is reversed: military action is most important, population control second, and political and economic programs least. Military action determines control of territory, which in turn determines population control; political programs matter almost not at all, making at most a marginal difference in mobilizing one's own community or in retarding mobilization by the enemy. To win, each side must gain physical control over the territory in dispute.

*Political and Economic Programs*

Unlike in ideological conflicts, in ethnic civil wars political and economic programs designed to win people's loyalties are beside the point, because there is no contest for loyalty. Offers of institutional reform, political or cultural autonomy, or economic benefits which may be relevant at milder stages of conflict become irrelevant once war starts. Extending such offers will not attract members of the other community, while failure to do so will not cause defection of members of one's own community.

Unlike ideological identities, which, as matters of individual belief or behavior, are relatively soft, ethnic identities are very hard, since they depend on language, culture, and religion, which are hard to change, as well as parentage, which no one can change. Ethnic identities are hardened further by intense conflict, both because of elite efforts to whip up hypernationalist hysteria for mobilization purposes and because of increasing real threats.

Thus, loyalties in ethnic wars are to all intents and purposes fixed, with the result that cross-ethnic appeals, whatever their content, can have little effect on the outcome. First, cross-ethnic recruitment is nearly impossible. In the Second World War, Croats began to join the Yugoslav Partisans only once it was clear that independent Croatia could not survive. In Laos in the 1960s, both communists and anticommunists offered political reform and economic development, but the real conflict was between the hill people (Hmong) and the lowland people (Lao).

Cross-ethnic recruitment efforts bore little fruit, and the war continued until the Hmong were militarily defeated by the Pathet Lao. In the early 1990s, although the mainly Tutsi Rwandan Patriotic Front tried to present a democratic, nonracist program and an ethnically mixed leadership, the Hutu democratic opposition parties in Rwanda would not cooperate with it, nor was it ever able to gain more than a tiny number of Hutu recruits. Although the Bosnian government promised to preserve a democratic, multiethnic state when it tried in early 1992 to organize a national defense force based on the existing police, most Serb members promptly deserted, taking their arms with them.

Second, attempts to dampen enemy mobilization by reassuring members of the other group of benign intent are generally ineffective. Even if one side is less violent toward opposing ethnics than the other, few of the other side are likely to trust the ethnic enemy. Israeli appeals in 1948 to the Arabs of Haifa and certain other cities to remain in place failed to prevent flight. Similarly, despite Tutsi appeals to displaced Hutus to return home, more than 1.7 million of the original 2 million refugees were still outside the country in early 1996. Despite the safety assurances of the Bosnian government and their rights under the Dayton agreement, nearly all Serb residents of towns due to be surrendered to the Muslims fled. Part of the problem is that moderates cannot guarantee the good behavior of all members of their own side. The Bosnian Muslims, Rwandan Tutsis, and Israelis all committed atrocities, even if fewer than their enemies.

Third, extremists within each group are likely to prevent moderates from even attempting cross-ethnic appeals. The most extreme hypernationalists on each side always have an incentive to escalate the conflict in order to gain power for themselves at the expense of relative moderates. Once large-scale violence has taken place, atrocity tales—whether true or invented—provide hardliners with an especially powerful argument. In these circumstances, conciliation is easy to denounce as likely to reduce community security or as actually traitorous. In 1992 Georgian Parliament chairman Eduard Shevardnadze's pursuit of peace talks with Ossetian rebels and agreement to joint Russian–Georgian– Ossetian peacekeeping earned him denunciation as a tool of Russia, and forced him to take a much harder line against Abkhazian secessionism in 1992 and 1993. In Sri Lanka, relatively moderate Tamil parties have been attacked by more extreme nationalists, and the same has occurred on the Sinhalese side. Prime Minister Çiller of Turkey has apparently felt constrained from softening the country's "military solution" approach to the Kurds.

Individual identity choice also largely disappears. Even those who put little value on their ethnic identity are pressed toward ethnic mobilization for two reasons: First, even individuals whose behavior is neutral or cooperative toward the other group are likely to be treated as enemies by fanatical members of that group.[3] Further, extremists within one's own community are likely to impose sanctions on those who do not contribute to the cause. Both the Kurdish guerrillas in Turkey and the Tamil Tigers in Sri Lanka have used terror to keep members of their own community in line. In 1992 Bosnian Serbs who objected to ethnic cleansing of Muslims were threatened or killed. In 1994 insufficiently "patriotic" Hutus were massacred on a large scale. Unlike in ideological conflicts, such terror against one's own group runs little risk of driving the victims into the enemy camp, because the nationalists are likely to enjoy majority support and political legitimacy, and to control the community's government apparatus.

Even moderately high levels of intermarriage do not blur group boundaries enough to matter in an ethnic war. In many ethnically divided societies, ethnic identity rules explicitly account for such cases. Hutu or Tutsi identity, for instance, is inherited from the father. The most important reason why intermarriage doesn't matter, however, is that identity rules are ultimately set by the killers. In Rwanda, in 1994, some Hutus with Tutsi relatives were allowed to buy their relatives' lives, some saw their Tutsi relations killed, and in some cases the *interahamwe* murdered the entire mixed family. Even if a few people change sides to fight for families which they have married into, as in South Ossetia in 1990–91, this does not create an uncommitted population to which both sides can appeal.

*Population Control*

Unlike ideological conflicts, in ethnic wars population control is determined by control of territory, specifically control of population centers. Expensive, careful efforts to assess individual loyalties are not required, because ethnicity can be used as a simple decision rule. Even if some members of both groups remain unmobilized, as long as virtually none actively support the other group, treating all members of one's own ethnic group as friends runs no risk of admitting an enemy agent into one's midst; treating all of the other group as enemies will not result in killing potential recruits.

Each side can almost always identify members of its own and the other group in any territory it has access to. Ethnicity can be identified by public records, private records, local social knowledge, and, often, outward appearance. The ethnicity of Yugoslav men was recorded on their People's Army identification cards. The 1991 Yugoslav census reported the percentage of each nationality in each of the 106 municipalities of Bosnia, ethnicity of partners in mixed marriages, as well as ethnic identity of children of such marriages. In 1994 Rwandan death squads relied on both neighborhood target lists prepared in advance and roadblocks which checked identity cards. Croatian Defence Forces which attacked a mixed town in central Bosnia in 1993 destroyed nearly all Muslim homes without damaging any Croatian homes. While ethnic cleansing efforts do not always catch all their intended targets, perhaps the strongest evidence of intelligence reliability in ethnic conflicts is that—in dramatic contrast to frequent errors in ideological insurgencies—history records almost no instances of mistaken "cleansing" of co-ethnics.

The result is that population control depends wholly on territorial control. Each side's mobilization base is limited to members of its community in friendly controlled territory. Control of individual movement also matters much less, because infiltrators cannot seize political control of a locality unless their side can conquer it militarily.

Population control tactics in ethnic conflicts are different than in ideological conflicts. Whereas in ideological conflicts, selective terror can influence loyalties but indiscriminate terror is usually counterproductive, in ethnic conflicts terror is used less to affect loyalties than to frighten enemy civilians into flight. This includes both "cleansing" of friendly controlled areas as well as terrorization of enemy-held towns in order to make their conquest easier. Bosnian Serb tactics in 1992 and 1993 included both massacres and sporadic murders, rape, beatings, expulsion, dispossession, and deprivation of basic necessities. According to the Serb "Director for Refugees" in Banja Luka in 1993, Muslims were "begging" to leave: "Here what awaits them is a winter without heat, food, and, for many, no place to live." Leadership attacks, unlike in ideological conflicts, are not a means of competing to govern uncommitted people, but simply another means of terrorizing the enemy. In Kozarac in northwest Bosnia in 1993, Serb forces working from prepared lists executed prominent or educated Muslims, including religious, political, and business leaders.

Counter-civilian violence can also be a direct measure to reduce the enemy's mobilization base—that is, genocide. The problem, as the Romans used to put it, is that sword arms will find swords. Ideological combatants do not need to kill everyone because if they win, they expect to educate the children of their enemies; ethnic combatants normally have no such hope. Thus the *interahamwe* were urged to kill the children too, while a June 1987 directive to Iraqi forces fighting Kurdish insurgents ordered that: "All persons captured in those villages shall be detained and interrogated . . . and those between the ages of 15 and 70 shall be executed."

Forcible relocation, unlike in ideological conflicts, is not done to gain an access advantage in the competition for loyalties, but simply to prevent enemy ethnic populations from mobilizing. It is used in place of expulsion or massacre when one side is so strong that it hopes to control the entire territory at issue. In effect, large fractions of the enemy population are imprisoned in de facto concentration camps. Beginning in 1985, the Iraqi government destroyed all rural villages in Kurdistan, as well as animals and orchards, concentrating the Kurdish population in "victory cities" where they could be watched as well as kept dependent on the government for food. The Turkish government is currently doing the same thing in southeastern Turkey. The Burmese government has pursued this strategy against ethnic minority rebels at least since 1968.

*Military Action*

In contrast to ideological conflicts, in ethnic civil wars military operations are decisive, for three reasons: First, attrition matters, because each community's mobilization base is limited by their population size and can be used up, unlike in ideological conflicts where the mobilization base is shared and recruitment potential is limited mainly by the strength of each side's political support.

Second, since each side can recruit only from its own community and only in friendly controlled territory, conquering enemy population centers directly reduces their mobilization base, while any territorial loss reduces one's own mobilization potential. Military control of the entire territory at issue is tantamount to total victory.

Third, the political restraints on the use of firepower in ideological disputes are much weaker. Accidentally inflicting collateral damage on enemy civilians will do little harm since there was never any chance of pacifying them anyway. Even accidentally hitting friendly civilians, while painful, will not cause them to defect. If the military need is great enough, heavy firepower can be used even against mixed settlements. Examples include the Serb bombardments of Sarajevo and Tuzla from 1992 to 1994 and the Russian assault on Grozny in December 1994.

The decisiveness of territorial control in turn influences operational behavior. Guerrilla operations are never preferred; each side will seek to build the strongest conventional forces that its resources allow. Unlike ideological insurgents who will abandon a village rather than risk battle, or a counterinsurgent government which might forbear to attack rather than bombard civilians, the sides in an ethnic war must fight hard for every settlement. Even force conservation may have to be sacrificed to the territorial imperative. For combatants in an ethnic war, even temporary retreat from a friendly settlement is not merely painful—because of economic resources abandoned and the risk of occupation abuses—but potentially catastrophic, because of the fear that the enemy will permanently change the demographics of any surrendered area by massacre, expulsion, destruction of homes, and possibly colonization. By the time the territory can be retaken, its value may have been lost.

Further, a large fraction of the fighters in ethnic wars are motivated primarily to defend their own homes and families, making it difficult for group leaders to organize mobile forces which can be deployed where needed. In the first phase of the Israeli War of Independence in 1947–48, both sides' forces consisted almost wholly of regional and village defense units. The Israelis were successful in part because they were able to generate a small mobile force for flexible national service, while Palestinian village militias remained almost completely independent and inflexible. Similarly, in Bosnia in early 1992, none of the three communities had much more than a network of local militias, but the Serbs and Croats were assisted by Yugoslav Army and Croatian Defense Forces units, respectively. Thus the Muslims were not only outgunned but also lacked flexible forces which could respond to enemy offensives.

## DETERMINANTS OF VICTORY IN CIVIL WARS AND IMPLICATIONS FOR INTERVENTION

The critical question for any state or international organization contemplating intervention in a foreign civil war is the extent to which their intervention can determine the outcome. The answer depends on whether the conflict is fundamentally ideological or fundamentally ethnic. The outcomes of ideological civil wars are determined primarily by the relative political competence of the local factions, which outsiders can rarely do much to change. Outcomes of ethnic civil wars, however, are determined by the balance of force, which outside powers can alter radically.

### Ideological Conflicts

Because ideological conflicts are primarily contests for the allegiance of the population, the most important determinant of victory is the relative political competence of the competing factions. Outside support, whether in the form of economic or military aid or direct military intervention, is not often decisive. Further, more massive involvement does not necessarily produce better results than a lesser involvement, and may actually reduce the chances of the local client.

*Political Competence*

Political competence means the degree to which each side's leadership is committed, uncorrupt, and disciplined, as well as whether it commands sufficient loyalty and obedience from subordinate institutions and agents that its strategy can actually be carried out. The issue is not central control versus local initiative, but cohesion and integrity. A competent movement is one whose local agents act in the interest of the movement rather than using their authority to pursue their own personal, family, factional, or institutional interests.

Competence determines the success of political programs, population control, and military action. For the rebels, this means that programs must offer solutions to local grievances; global ideologies often have to be modified to fit local conditions.[4] The insurgents must also be united, not lapse into factional fighting or regional warlordism. They must have effective central direction and discipline, both to prevent corruption and banditry and to allow calibration of the level of terror or violence used for population control, neither too little nor too much.

For the government, attaining political competence almost always requires major reform, because insurgencies usually do not begin unless exploitation, repression, or corruption have already alienated a great part of the population. The main barrier to reform is usually the resistance of economically and politically powerful groups which resist surrendering their privileges. Even if the top leadership has the political will to separate itself from antireform constituencies, it may still face opposition from entrenched interests in government institutions, including the military and police, as well as regional forces which can gut government-ordered political reforms or economic redistribution. Thus attaining competence depends on recruiting a corps of proreform officials and officers who will not be corrupted by the same exploiters they are supposed to police. . . .

Political competence is more important than initial popularity or legitimacy. A competent side can carry out programs which will improve its legitimacy, while an incompetent one will inevitably lose what legitimacy it initially possessed. Most important, competence is not fungible. No amount of outside aid can substitute for local incompetence and corruption, nor can outside pressure for reform usually overcome local barriers.

*Foreign Aid*

Foreign economic or military aid can be helpful in ideological conflicts, but its potential is limited. Any foreign aid makes the side which receives it vulnerable to accusations of being a tool of foreign interests, and the greater the aid, the more plausible the charge. . . .

*Direct Intervention*

Foreign direct military intervention is even more problematic than aid. Like aid, it delegitimates the supported government. Worse, the intervention forces face an insuperable intelligence problem. As outsiders, the intervention forces generally cannot distinguish friend from foe and, given the inherent elusiveness of ideological identity within a single culture, local guides may not be accurate either, even if the guides are not corrupt or even enemy agents. As a result the intervention forces tend to rely on sheer firepower, resulting in tremendous collateral damage and great numbers of refugees, destroying the legitimacy of the client.[5] . . .

## Determinants of Victory in Ethnic Conflicts

Unlike ideological conflicts, the main determinant of victory in ethnic disputes is relative military strength, which determines the territorial outcome. Political competence is important, primarily for efficient use of resources, but does not determine the size of the resource base itself. Outside economic or military aid can be decisive, because it can dramatically shift the resource balance. Finally, direct military intervention can substitute for local competence if this is lacking.

*Political Competence*

Most of the reasons why political competence is vital in ideological wars have much less weight in ethnic ones. The ability to make credible promises cannot overcome the barriers to cross-ethnic appeals, while ethnic combatants rarely have difficulty telling friend from foe. Corruption, repression, or incompetence may undermine leaders' popularity within their own community, or even lead to their replacement, but will not cause members of the community to defect to the enemy. . . . Unity and obedience to authority are also less important than in ideological cases because even deep rivalries will not cause most leaders or rank and file to prefer defeat at the hands of the main enemy to leadership of their own group by a rival. . . .

Political competence is not irrelevant, since a minimum level of cohesion, integrity, and discipline is indispensable for military mobilization and operations. First, a militarily and politically disorganized ethnic group can be defeated piecemeal by a weaker but better organized enemy. . . . Second, debilitating leadership struggles which permanently injure the ethnic cause can occur, but are rare in wartime because more often one faction gains control or the co-ethnic factions agree to settle scores after dealing with the main enemy. Finally, extreme ill-discipline, such as in the Hutu-dominated Rwandan Army, which routinely looted, raped, and killed the population it was supposed to defend, can weaken both army and popular will to resist. Foreign military intervention can overcome the first of these failures; humanitarian interveners, however, presumably would not want to try to rescue cases of the second or third.

*Foreign Aid*

In ethnic conflicts, outside aid can be decisive. First, foreign aid does not undermine the legitimacy of the local leadership as it does in ideological conflicts. The enemy is already defined to be the opposing ethnic group, and any assistance against that enemy will be welcomed by the whole community.

Unlike in ideological conflicts, economic aid is not important for support of reform programs. It is more important for refugee support, resettlement aid, and postwar economic reconstruction.

Military aid, which has limited potential in ideological conflicts, is far more valuable in ethnic wars. Arms transfers and training can greatly increase the recipient community's military strength. Unlike ideological insurgents, who cannot absorb very much weaponry without conventionalizing the conflict too soon, aid in an ethnic conflict is limited only by the recipient group's manpower pool and organizational capabilities. Foreign military purchases and advisers dramatically reversed the military balance between Croatia and Serb rebels between 1991 and 1995, allowing Croatia to reconquer western Slavonia and the Krajina, and to conquer much of Northwest Bosnia. Similarly, lesser acquisitions by the Bosnian Muslims from 1992 to 1995 gradually increased their ability to defend their population centers and eventually to mount limited offensives.

*Direct Intervention*

There is one way to turn an outside intervention in an ethnic civil war into a hopeless quagmire akin to ideological counterinsurgencies: namely, to attempt to act as even-handed peacekeepers or to try to rebuild a functioning multiethnic society. Direct intervention is viable, but only when the interveners choose a side and concentrate their efforts on gaining the best, safest territorial settlement for the client group. Since the war is in essence a conventional war over territory, outsiders can simply "take over" the war for one side in whole or part.

The main pitfalls which constrain the effectiveness of foreign military intervention in ideological conflicts are either weaker or absent in ethnic civil wars. Most important, loyalty intelligence is both less important and easier. Instead of operating always among a population whose individual loyalties are mixed and uncertain, an intervention force in an ethnic conflict may conduct three types of operations, only one of which even involves an issue of loyalty intelligence. Defense of friendly group settlements is a purely conventional military operation, as would be any offensives to seize territory from the opposing group. Only the control of ethnically mixed areas involves an identification task, and in this situation the outside force can use the same rule that the combatants themselves do: members of the allied community are friends and those of the other are enemies. Even if outsiders can't tell them apart, the locals can, and— unlike in an ideological insurgency—the reliability of guides provided by the local ally can be counted on. Thus the main intelligence task is not assessing individual loyalties but locating enemy forces, a task at which major-power militaries are very good.

Next, the restraints which the "hearts and minds" competition imposes on the use of heavy firepower in ideological conflicts do not apply. If the enemy chooses to defend population centers, collateral damage on enemy civilians may dismay public opinion in the intervening country, but it will not affect the loyalties of anyone in either warring group.

Finally, the interveners can enforce conventionalization of the war. Unlike counterinsurgency campaigns, the enemy's territorial losses will be irreversible. The opposing side cannot simply refuse combat and take up guerrilla warfare; to lose control of its population centers is to lose the war. While relocation or restriction of civilians' movements can cost loyalties in an ideological conflict, in an ethnic war military occupation of the whole enemy population is both necessary and practical. In the Boer War, after defeating the main Boer forces, the British successfully stopped further commando operations by temporarily imprisoning essentially the whole populations of the Orange Free State and Transvaal. The usual guerrilla means of dealing with advancing heavy forces will not avail; any who stay behind among friendly civilians will be arrested along with their co-ethnics, while those who fall back in front of the attack will both be cut off from support and eventually squeezed out of the contested territory altogether as the intervention force continues its advance. . . .

*Conclusion: Wide Scope for Foreign Intervention*

The scope for foreign influence on ethnic civil wars is often great, because everything depends on the balance of military power. A few thousand foreign troops can be decisive if the local sides are weak and evenly matched, although much more may be required to rescue a disorganized and overmatched ethnic group. . . .

## THE STRATEGY OF HUMANITARIAN INTERVENTION

Western diplomats considering intervention in ethnic civil wars must unlearn the lessons of Vietnam. They must recognize that societies torn apart by intense ethnic violence cannot be reconstituted and so winning the hearts and minds of the competing groups is irrelevant. Rather, successful intervention requires a decision to ally formally with one side in order to separate the warring groups into defensible regions, a policy almost certain to require substantial population transfers. The military must abandon the counterinsurgency model, and plan instead for a conventional war of limited conquest. Western leaders, if they hope to raise the necessary domestic support, must also explain to their publics that interventions in ethnic conflicts are not quagmires. They can save lives, establish lasting stability, and have clear intermediate procedures as well as final goals.

Successful intervention to resolve an ethnic war requires five steps. First, the intervening powers must choose the local side they will support. Second, the interveners must decide on the geographic borders to be occupied by the client group. Third, the intervention force must militarily control and physically occupy the designated territory. Fourth, populations must be exchanged across the new border in order to create ethnically homogeneous, integral regions. Finally, the intervention forces should withdraw after guaranteeing the separation lines, by international agreement if possible, or by ongoing military assistance if necessary.

This strategy is not pretty. It requires the interveners to relocate people permanently, which critics may denounce as "ethnic cleansing," albeit with buses rather than snipers, starvation, and rape. It may also involve significant ground combat. As a result, it will not and should not be applied to mild ethnic conflicts, those unlikely to lead to large numbers of civilian deaths. For the worst ethnic wars, however, this solution is the only solution. Where humanitarian interveners are not prepared to do these things, they should not intervene.

### Choose a Side

A common instinct of many who advocate humanitarian intervention is that the intervention should be even-handed and should seek to preserve the integrity of the original state; they see no moral basis for taking on the cause of one side in a civil war, and no legal basis for undermining another state's sovereignty. Goals, however, must be kept in line with actual capabilities. No outside force, no matter how great its advantage in combat power, can pacify ethnic hostilities inflamed by war. Nor can it resolve the intergroup security dilemma except by creating separate, defensible regions for each group.

Second, impartiality is not militarily viable. The intelligence simplicity of ethnic wars depends on partiality. An intervention force which tried to maintain neutrality could rely on neither side, and would soon find itself in the same situation of outside forces in ideological conflicts, surrounded by a population that contains hostile fighters whom it cannot identify. Even-handedness often becomes still more problematic over time, as all sides come to see the outsiders as an obstacle to achieving their legitimate rights. Eventually an even-handed intervention force is likely to find itself under attack from all sides at once, or forced into uneasy cooperation with a group which distrusts it only marginally less than the others do.

Finally, in many cases impartiality is morally and politically untenable. Since the purpose of humanitarian intervention in ethnic wars is to stop ongoing atrocities, it should only be undertaken when the major actors of the international community can agree on the rights and wrongs of the case. This is essential for domestic support; if both sides have behaved so badly that there is little to choose between them, intervention shouldn't and probably won't be undertaken. For the same reason, humanitarian interventions will usually be on behalf of the weaker side. The stronger side needs no defense. If both sides are equally strong, it will be unclear that strengthening one will reduce overall violence and suffering.

The interveners must also isolate the opposing ethnic group from outside sources of economic and military assistance. Since the costs and risks that interveners will accept in pursuit of humanitarian goals will always be limited, intervention will be politically feasible only against a small power without major allies.

**Draw the Separation Line**

The territorial division should be decided in advance, for three reasons. First, the division must seem to the interveners to be fair, be militarily feasible, manageable in terms of population transfers, and ultimately defensible. Second, it must be acceptable to the prospective client. Third and most important, setting a fixed line guarantees specific territory to each side, lessening the security dilemma in the conflict since neither need fear political or physical elimination.

There is likely to be a temptation simply to freeze the status quo because this requires fewer difficult choices and no offensive military operations. In many cases, however, this approach will fail several of the above tests. First, the status quo is likely to seem unfair because the motives for intervention are likely to include territorial and population losses already inflicted on the client by the other side. Second, for the same reason, the status quo is almost certain to be unacceptable to the client. If the interveners pursue a settlement unacceptable to the client, they risk eventually finding themselves in conflict with their erstwhile ally; thus the proposed division must seem to the client much better than it could possibly achieve without help. If agreement on this cannot be reached in advance, intervention should not be undertaken. Finally, if the client has been losing the war, freezing the status quo will not provide a viable state. The line should be drawn so as to be militarily defensible by the client after the intervention force leaves. Borders should be as short as possible, and should make use of natural geographic barriers, even though this may conflict somewhat with manageability of resettlement. Since populations are going to be resettled, it would also be desirable to draw borders so as to minimize the number displaced. Since the intervention will be a response to violence on such a scale that enforced separation seems a lesser evil, however, this criterion should not take precedence over defensibility.

### Occupy the Territory Inside the Separation Line

Occupation must be accomplished by a mixture of military coercion and conventional military conquest. The intervention force and the local ally must occupy all territory inside the separation line. It is *not* necessary to conquer the entire country; there is no reason why friendly ground forces should ever cross the line. Attempts to "pacify" areas which will not belong to the client after the intervention serve little purpose, and involve unnecessary dangers for the intervention force. Friendly forces begin at one end of the target territory (or on already-controlled territory) and advance to capture the entire target region.

As usual in ethnic wars, most members of the opposing ethnic group can be expected to retreat in front of greatly superior force, and should not be hindered from doing so. Those who do not, however, must be interned, pending population exchange after the war. This progressively removes the enemy's local base of support, severely limiting their potential to mount guerrilla operations behind the lines. . . .

Provided that the intervention force enjoys a great superiority of force, the war is likely to be shortened by successful coercion, although how much will be difficult to predict in advance. Once convinced that the intervention force cannot be stopped and will not be deterred, the opposing side has no incentive to lose additional lives, both soldiers and civilians, fighting for territory that will be lost anyway. Combatants in this situation often surrender. This is not to say that the opposition can be expected to give up easily or early; the intervention force might have to fight most of the way to a final victory, but it likely will not have to fight all the way to the bitter end. . . .

### Exchange Populations

Once the conquest is complete, all enemy ethnics in custody must be moved across the separation line. At the same time, all friendly ethnics who wish to immigrate from beyond the line—or, more likely, are expelled by the opposing side—must be resettled.

The client may require substantial resettlement and economic reconstruction aid, which should also be offered to the opposing side as an inducement to accept the territorial outcome. Both sides will certainly make use of abandoned property to settle incoming refugees. Ideally, if the opposing sides agree, an international "refugee property settlements bank" could manage this process. No approach will avoid hardship, but the international community can minimize it by efficient management.

### Guarantee Client Security and Withdraw Troops

Humanitarian intervention would lack purpose unless the client remains secure after the war. Ideally, this would be achieved through an international agreement recognizing the borders of all sides. At the conclusion of the war, however, neither side may accept the other's commitments as credible. Thus, the interveners must be prepared to unilaterally guarantee the security of the client.

The principal task is to give the client the capability to defend itself in a manner least provocative to the ethnic opponent. Since the client will probably have been much weaker to the opponent prior to the intervention, the client group's military forces will need to be strengthened. The goal should be to organize, train, and equip the client with a defensively oriented military doctrine and force posture. The client should not be given types or numbers of arms which would enable it to go on the offensive on its own after the intervention force departs. The continuation of the defense guarantee and military and economic aid should also be contingent on continued acceptance of the border.

The amount of time that foreign troops must spend in the target country will depend on the length of the military phase of the operation, which will depend on terrain, infrastructure, weather, enemy strength, and other conditions. It will, however, generally be much shorter than a counterinsurgency campaign, since territorial gains will be permanent, not ephemeral. Once offensive ground operations are complete, most of the heavy combat forces can be withdrawn, although considerable logistic troops for refugee transportation and relief will still be needed. After the population exchange is substantially complete, nearly all the remaining forces can be withdrawn, leaving just a small cadre of advisers for training. Unless the client is very weak, no permanent garrison should be required. The combination of defensible borders, economic reconstruction, military aid and training, and a guarantee of additional aid in case of attack should be sufficient.[6] Since any future enemy attempt to revise the borders by force would have to take the form of a major conventional assault, and since the rearmed client will possess substantial ground forces, arms aid, and access to logistic and air support, it should be able to deter or, if necessary, smash any attack. . . .

### THE WORST ALTERNATIVE EXCEPT FOR ALL THE OTHERS

Clausewitz said that political ends determine the appropriate military means. The reverse is also true: the available military means limit the feasible political goals.

The strategy of demographic separation is neither pretty nor cheap, but it can provide security for endangered peoples. It can require fighting a war, although the extent and cost of the fighting will depend on how promptly humanitarian interveners can make up their minds to act. The earlier the intervention, the more of the client population and territory can be protected by defensive operations rather than having to be recovered by offensive ones. Thus the least expensive time to intervene will also save the most civilian lives. In Bosnia, this would have been March or April 1992. General Romeo Dallaire, the UN Commander in Rwanda in April 1994, later claimed that if he had had "a 5,000 man mechanized bridge group there would have been hundreds of thousands of lives spared today."

Of course, this strategy violates the international legal norm of state sovereignty. In recent years, the conflict between this norm and the imperative to save lives threatened by ethnic violence has become clear. International law will have to evolve to cope with today's moral problems.

### TABLE 26.1
### IDEOLOGICAL AND ETHNIC WARS

| | Ideological Wars | Ethnic Wars |
|---|---|---|
| **Critical Features** | | |
| Determinants of Individual Loyalties | Loyalty based on persuasion, either expectations of reform or coercion; changeable | Loyalty based on language, culture, religion, parentage; not changeable |
| Loyalty Intelligence | Loyalties hard to assess; many double agents | Loyalties easy to assess; no double agents |
| Mobilization Base | Shared; everyone is a potential recruit for either side; military power ultimately depends on popular loyalty | Mutually exclusive; recruitment limited to members of own community in friendly controlled territory, who can be counted on |
| Value of Territory | Limited; does not guarantee loyalty of population | Critical; cannot abandon any land because enemy will "cleanse" it of members of friendly group |
| Security Dilemma | Affects faction leaders only; no territorial solution | Affects everyone; can be reduced by separation of groups |
| Possible Outcomes | Decisive victory for one side or negotiated powersharing; territory rarely divided | Decisive victory for one side, territorial division via regional autonomy, or secession; powersharing rarely viable |

*(continued)*

## TABLE 26.1 *(continued)*

|  | Ideological Wars | Ethnic Wars |
|---|---|---|
| **Importance of Strategies** | | |
| Political and Economic Programs | Most important; reform corrupt/repressive institutions to win hearts and minds | Unimportant; hypernationalist polarization undermines cross-ethnic appeals |
| Population Control | Important, but risky; relocation to isolate enemies, terror to deter enemy recruits; backlash hard to avoid | Important; terror, expulsion, or massacre to remove/eliminate enemies; little risk of alienating supporters |
| Military Action | Not decisive because territory not critical; excessive firepower causes collateral damage, alienates population | Decisive because territory critical; political restraints on firepower weak |
| **Determinants of Victory** | | |
| Local Competence | Critical; corruption or indiscipline prevents execution of reforms, alienates population | Less important; corruption may reduce effectiveness but will not cause defections |
| Economic and Military Aid | Problematic; risks delegitimating local ally; excessive aid also risks corruption, over-reliance on firepower | Unproblematic; does not threaten legitimacy; no limit on amount |
| Direct Military Intervention | Indecisive; can't tell friend from foe; heavy firepower delegitimates client; military successes may not gain loyalties | Decisive; no intelligence problem; does not undermine client legitimacy; can determine territorial outcome |

# 27

# Military Responses to Refugee Disasters

## BARRY R. POSEN

The problem of refugees, both those who have crossed recognized international borders, and those "internally displaced" who have not, has recently achieved greater policy prominence in the developed world. This new concern has also prompted a greater inclination to consider and apply military remedies to specific refugee problems. Policy makers, analysts, pundits, and activists now perceive vastly diminished constraints on the exercise of military power in the service of "good," compared to their views during the Cold War. The great preponderance of global power now enjoyed by the West due to the collapse of the Soviet Union, and the greatly increased capability of air power demonstrated in Operation Desert Storm, have both contributed to this tendency. This optimism is misplaced; I argue below that the application of military power to this set of problems will often prove politically and militarily difficult. . . .

### THE CAUSES OF MASS DISPLACEMENT

I identify five general political–military causes of mass displacement: genocide/politicide; ethnic cleansing; occupation; collateral damage; and primitive military logistics.

*Genocide* is employed here in the conventional sense of the word: a human community based on ethnic, national, or religious ties is singled out for extermination. In modern times the Armenians and the Jews are the best-known victims. More recently the killings of the Tutsi people in Rwanda appear to be genocide. *Politicide* means the attempt to destroy a political idea, usually by destroying many if not all of those who hold that idea, or at least enough of them to terrorize others into abandoning it. The Khmer Rouge murdered hundreds of thousands to wipe out any positive attitudes towards a Western style economy or society.

What starts as politicide often evolves into genocide. Saddam Hussein and the Iraqi Ba'ath party have attempted to wipe out the idea of Kurdish independence among Iraqi Kurds. In doing so they have tried to find and kill anybody who believes in this idea. Though it does not seem true that there was a policy to kill or eject all Iraqi Kurds, the task of "politicide" has been interpreted expansively by Iraqi security forces, producing consequences for the Kurdish population indistinguishable from deliberate genocide. This seems to be a common outcome where ethnic, national, or religious groups seek political autonomy or secession from governments determined to resist.

*Ethnic cleansing* is a term that has been propelled into political discourse by the wars of Yugoslavia's disintegration. I employ it for deliberate actions to induce populations to leave their homes. Several methods may be employed. Organized military or para-military forces or even mobs terrorize the target population, threatening it with harm or death, to induce out-migration. Considerable killing will occur, though the scale required to terrify people into departure may not be great. Forcible deportation may be organized, in which people are escorted out of an area at gun point. Finally, deliberate starvation can be a tool of deportation. Food can be expropriated from a population, and farms burned, while the import of relief supplies is blocked. People leave in search of food. This has apparently been practiced in Africa. . . .

Under some circumstances, warfare may involve competitive ethnic cleansing, which may deteriorate into competitive terrorism, murder, and even genocide. The parties to a war may be victims one day, and assailants the next; or victims in one place and assailants in another. In the wars of Yugoslavia's disintegration, Croats were victims of Serb cleansing and murder; they were assailants against and killers of Muslims; and they were finally assailants against Serbs. In the 1949 partition of India, Muslims and Hindus were both victims and agents of ethnic cleansing and of murder.

*Fear of occupation* is a third reason why populations leave their place of residence in large numbers. At worst, people may fear that the occupier will launch a genocide; why wait? Or people may fear that the occupier will try to drive them out, and that this will prove violent. Again, why wait? Even if genocide/politicide or violent expulsion are not the assailant's war aims, occupations are never pleasant. The native population has good reason to fear casual brutality, the arbitrariness of martial law, immediate expropriation of property, and systematic long-term economic exploitation. Presumably, the Hutu who recently fled Rwanda feared a "counter-genocide," and still do. Many of the Iraqi Kurds who fled to the Turkish border may simply have feared the likely brutality of Iraqi authorities.

Many Afghan refugees who fled to Pakistan following the Soviet invasion departed due to such fears. . . .

A *dangerous environment* is the fourth reason why populations leave their homes. People often simply flee the area of fighting, because the firepower employed does not easily discriminate between combatants and noncombatants. People seem to have moved back and forth in Lebanon depending on the location of the fighting. Documentary films from World War II and a host of subsequent wars illustrate the phenomenon. Most of the Chechen population that did not intend to fight left the city of Grozny before the Russians turned up. Whether or not these populations return depends upon a host of factors. If the territory is lost to an enemy, they are unlikely to go back. It is also unlikely that the former inhabitants will return to an area where the front has stabilized. . . .

The final cause of mass displacement might be termed *primitive logistics*. In many parts of the world, armed forces have little or no regular supply system. The acquisition of arms and munitions is the first priority for primitive armies. Food, medicine, and even vehicles may be expropriated by the troops in the field. As Machiavelli said, "iron will always find bread." During the Thirty Years War, Germany was devastated by logistics systems of this kind. It was said that one had to become a soldier to avoid starvation.

Primitive armies may steal so much food and livestock from an agricultural or pastoral population that these people cannot survive to plant and harvest a new crop, or they have no animals to manage. Alternatively, expropriation may so reduce the margin of subsistence that the arrival of a drought, on top of war, tips the entire population into an irremediable disaster. These people then move in search of food. . . .

## MILITARY REMEDIES

Five distinct potential military remedies to the causes of displacement are suggested by limited practical experience or deduction. All remedies are not appropriate for all causes, and some only have a chance of working under a very narrow range of circumstances.

*Punishment* of the assailant is very popular among those looking for cheap solutions. Rescuers seeking to help the victimized population should bomb the assailant's homeland to destroy what it values, such as its own population, its economic infrastructure, or its leaders. This punishment would continue until the refugee-producing behavior ceased.

The creation of a *"safe zone"* that protects the victim population where it normally lives is a second option. This is essentially the "Provide Comfort" model, employed with considerable success to protect Iraq's Kurds from the revenge of Saddam Hussein and the Ba'ath Party. The area where the prospective victims live is cordoned off from the assailant, who is denied access. In Iraq this was achieved through the threat to unleash coalition air power against any Iraqi forces, air or ground, that trespassed onto the declared safe zone.

A third option is the creation of circumscribed *"safe havens"* where the displaced can seek protection and sustenance close to their homes, but not in them. Their normal life is essentially destroyed by the assailant. This was attempted most explicitly in Bosnia, where six towns were so designated. Informally this expedient was employed to some extent in the UN Congo operation (ONUC), UN operations in Lebanon (UNIFIL), and in the Restore Hope operation in Somalia. . . .

A fourth option is the imposition of some kind of *"enforced truce"* in the zone of conflict. Outsiders effectively seize some or all of the attributes of sovereignty. Minimally, they act as sheriff. The victimized population is protected from the assailant, but assailants are also protected from counter-attack by victims. The assailant/victim distinction may not be relevant as where, for example, there is mutually genocidal warfare. The enforced truce option was, to some extent, attempted in Somalia. Arguably, it was also what the UN really did in the Congo.

The final military option is an *offensive war* to destroy the military power of the assailant, perhaps even to change the regime. Cold War politics made it inexpedient for observers to acknowledge that it was the Vietnamese invasion of Cambodia that ended the "killing fields." Vietnam undoubtedly invaded for its own reasons, but this was a decisive way to stop the killing. Similarly, the defeat and expulsion of the Hutu-dominated Rwandan Army by the Rwandan Patriotic Front (RPF) decisively ended the killing of Tutsi. The Pakistani repression in East Pakistan (Bengal), which produced the flight of some ten million refugees to India, was ended by the December 1971 Indo–Pakistani War. Indeed, India's firm stand against Pakistan arose in part from its unwillingness to provide permanent homes for these ten million refugees, or to accept even more. The bizarre record of Nazi Germany's energetic pursuit of the genocide against the Jews and the Gypsies, in the face of military defeats on every front and military problems that would have benefited at least somewhat from the resources diverted to the horror, suggests that only complete conquest could have ended the Nazi crime. Because this remedy is fairly straightforward, it will *not* be subjected to systematic analysis below. The examples noted above suggest the circumstances under which invasion will prove the only feasible solution.

## THE STRATEGIC CONTEXT

Those contemplating the use of military force for humanitarian purposes should think of themselves as planning a major foreign-policy initiative that will likely end in war. The threat or use of force for humanitarian purposes is as much an act of strategy as is the threat or use of force to achieve geostrategic goals. We should apply the same analytic tools. Advocates should be interested in estimating the political and military difficulties of the project they are about to undertake. . . .

## Deterrence or Compellence

The most important question about any humanitarian intervention is whether it is fundamentally an act of deterrence or compellence. Each of the military options discussed above has a passive and an active face. Clearly, rescuers would prefer to dissuade assailants from initiating actions that produce refugees. Most cases, however, involve an assailant that has already initiated its depredations; outsiders demand that the actions cease, and indeed that they be reversed. The first case corresponds roughly to the strategist's concept of deterrence, the second to compellence. Compellence is generally considered to be more difficult than deterrence. Humanitarian operations will more often partake of compellence than deterrence. However, advocates of these operations often seem to imagine they are engaged in deterrence, and thus under-estimate the difficulties. A second problem is that much of the thinking about deterrence and compellence arose from the problem of employing nuclear threats. The risk of nuclear escalation gives nuclear deterrence a special claim to effectiveness likely to be missing even from relatively unambiguous nonnuclear stand-offs between unitary nation- states. Conventional "deterrence" among unitary nation-states has often failed. Refugee-producing crises are likely to be even more problematical than these classical conflicts.

Deterrence is judged less difficult than compellence for four main reasons: First, a dissuasive threat is usually leveled to protect an extant status quo. The willingness of the dissuader to suffer, fight, and die to protect that to which it has a long-standing claim should be clear to the challenger. The challenger should expect that the defender of the status quo cares more about the item in dispute than does the challenger. Second, the challenger has to turn a situation of peace into a situation of war, with all the risks and costs that entails. Given the presumption of a defender with a willingness to fight, the challenger must exchange the certainties of peace for the uncertainties of war. It is a big step. Even if the attacker doubts the "will" of the defender, the very act of starting the fighting often has the quality of triggering the deterrent actor's military threat. In the world of nuclear deterrence this is a very powerful force making for challenger inertia. This works to a lesser extent with conventional strategic relationships. Third, the defender of the status quo has massive credibility stakes; if it does not resist the challenge, this is an invitation to future predation, not only from the original challenger, but from others. Thus the challenger has reason to expect that while its own interest is only in the area in dispute, the defender has many other interests attached to the interest in question. Finally, it is easy to agree on the "stopping point," which is the starting point.

Compellence (or coercion) is considered to be more difficult than deterrence (or dissuasion) for reasons that are the mirror image of those above. First, compellence generally tries to get the adversary to change some ongoing behavior in which it has developed some stake. Even the case of trying to get an aggressor to cease its aggression is often viewed by theorists as compellence, since once deterrence has failed, and the attacker has made the painful choice for war, launched an offensive, and had some success, it is now invested in the war. The balance of wills does not clearly favor the "coercer," even in a situation where the coercer is in fact trying to coerce an aggressor into ceasing its aggression. Second, the "peace–war" transition has already been made; fighting is underway. Third, the distribution of "credibility" stakes is more equal. In the case of deterrence, the side defending the status quo has a great deal more to lose than the side challenging it because to concede invites further challenges by the original aggressor *and* by others. The challenger loses its credibility as a bully by failing to carry through with the challenge, but does not necessarily invite predation, since its withdrawal says nothing about its inclination to protect its own core interests. Once war is underway, however, and some territory has changed hands, the object of compellence has its own interest in showing that the application of force, or the threat of escalation, cannot thwart its military power once it has decided to engage. Fourth, no obvious "stopping point" suggests itself. It is a matter for negotiation. The coercer says "stop"; the object asks "where?" The coercer says "here"; the object asks "why not there?"

Rescuers will more often find themselves in the active compellent mode than the deterrent mode, with all the difficulties that entails. The "causes" of mass population displacement, and the actual displacement, will likely be underway before rescuers decide to act. The propensity of any given political conflict to produce refugees is not well understood, because the conflicts themselves are not well understood, either generally, or specifically. . . . Because these crises seem to occur outside of the traditional arenas of great-power conflict, the elements of great- and middle-power intelligence services and foreign offices that follow the areas in question are unlikely to enjoy high priority within their own bureaucracies, and their communications channels to higher authority are likely to be attenuated. Killing of the kind that occurred in Cambodia or Rwanda would not necessarily produce the kind of "signature" that high-technology intelligence means would detect. It may take some time for disparate information to assemble into a recognizable pattern for outside observers. (In Rwanda, photos of streams and rivers full of corpses appeared only after many thousands had been killed. In totalitarian Cambodia, information on the politicide did not quickly reach the outside world.) The combination of inadequate understanding and attenuated internal communications channels is exacerbated by the unpredictable pace of these conflicts, and the refugee flows they produce. . . . These factors all contribute to the likelihood that rescuers will arrive late and find themselves undertaking compellence rather than deterrence.

It is quite likely that the will of the local party, the assailant, is stronger than that of the outside rescuers, because the stakes for the local party are so much greater. Indeed, outsiders are unlikely to have many classical "vital" interests at stake in these conflicts. Assailants often begin their depredations because of some deeply held beliefs about the necessity of their actions. These often reflect extreme interpretations of old disputes among communities. Even when the helpless are being executed, the murderers have often convinced themselves that the helpless are a threat. In short, whether the refugees are fleeing because of deliberate murder, deliberate cleansing, or the unintended consequences of more traditional military action, the assailant is likely to care quite a lot about the outcome. It is extremely difficult for the rescuer to convince the assailant that it cares more, particularly when the source of the concern seems to be an erratic and capricious humanitarian impulse, which varies with the extent of international media coverage; the availability of other dramas in the global village; the skin color, culture, or religion of the victims; the question of whether the assailant happens to be a great nuclear power (Russia vs. Chechnya) or a weak local actor (Serbs vs. Bosnian Muslims).

The will of the assailant may vary with its political nature. A useful distinction is between a gangster regime and a mass-mobilization polity. Some states are controlled by small bands of thugs who rule largely by terror. They may frighten large numbers of people into leaving the country. Their interest in power is mainly pecuniary, however. If challenged militarily from abroad, they will get no help from their own citizens. Having specialized in internal repression, they have little hope of standing against foreign militaries trained for war. The former governments of Haiti and Panama are good examples of such gangster regimes. Interestingly, even these governments were not easy to coerce, but they were easy to beat militarily.

Much tougher customers would be governments (or political movements) that preside over populations mobilized by religion, ideology, or national, ethnic, or tribal identity. These are also not easy to coerce, and neither are they likely to prove easy to fight. The Bosnian Serbs, the Iraqi Ba'ath (at least the Sunni Arabs), and the Somali clan warlords were not easy to push around. The Bosnian Serbs were only pushed to sign the Dayton accords by the combined military power of Croatia, the Bosnian Croats, the militarily rejuvenated Bosnian Muslims, large-scale NATO airstrikes, and a *diktat* by their patron, Slobodan Milosević. The Somali clans fought both U.S. and other UN troops ferociously, suffering hundreds if not thousands of casualties in the process. U.S. planners did not want to find out how well Iraqi Sunnis would fight for the Ba'ath regime if the coalition actually invaded Iraq. Iraqi Republican Guard units that had suffered intense aerial and ground attack by coalition units nevertheless fought ferociously to defend the regime against the Shi'a and Kurdish revolts.

The political organization of the rescuers is also an important factor in a compellence strategy. A coalition is likely to be less effective than a single interested nation-state. But because many of these events fall outside traditional geostrategic concerns, no single state will take responsibility for finding a solution, so a coalition will be required to undertake the mission. Unlike traditional military coalitions, which are usually held together by shared fear of a particular enemy, this one will need to be held together by altruism. Collective responses even to traditional threats are difficult to organize. This is why Napoleon Bonaparte averred that if he had to make war, he preferred to do so against coalitions. While coalitions may have access to more aggregate military power by virtue of their cooperation, they also need elaborate procedures for deciding on goals, strategies, and the allocation of contributions. The members of any coalition will vary in the extent of their commitment, and this is especially true of coalitions based on altruism. Assailants may retard the performance of the coalition by diplomatic approaches to, or military attacks on, its weakest link, which might simply be the least-committed member.

The assailant has greater credibility stakes in the fight than does the "rescuer." The rescuer's national security is usually not at risk in the event of failure. The fact that the United States quickly departed Somalia after a few dozen casualties says little about how it might behave in the event of a challenge to a more traditional security interest. U.S. pusillanimity in Somalia may invite challenges from other bandit leaders to U.S. meddling in their affairs, but it says little about how the United States might act if Iran attacked Saudi Arabia. The local assailant is in a far different situation. If it bows to threats by rescuers, this would invite challenges by local adversaries. This would also provide incentives to its local adversaries to go find an external patron to back up these challenges. Serbs have to worry that backing down in Bosnia will produce challenges by Albanians in Kosovo.

Will is only one part of the coercer's strategy. Capabilities are the other critical factor. The first essential truth is that without the capability to conduct these military operations, the threat to conduct them will have little weight with assailants. The second essential but less obvious truth is that it is not necessarily easy to convince the assailant that the rescuer will bring to bear all the necessary capabilities even if the rescuer possesses them. The precise capabilities that the rescuer will actually muster may turn out to be rather different than what it owns. . . . Assailants can gather information about the real extent of the capabilities they face through a series of probing actions. They can find out what the rescuers are willing to bring to the field; they can find out how good these capabilities are in the local tactical situation; and they can find out what kind of risks the rescuers are willing to take in the application of force. They can run all these experiments in comparative safety because they do not fear nuclear escalation. When the rescuers are altruistically motivated liberal democracies, assailants do not even have good reason to fear a sudden spasm of large-scale counter-value conventional bombing, because in most cases it would be politically complicated to explain to the public that the killing of civilians is necessary to prevent the killing of civilians.

Finally, even active and successful demonstration of these capabilities by rescuers does not produce permanent results: repeated probing operations, low-level tests of will and capability, and local attack followed by tactical retreat are to be expected. Again, the missing threat of spasmodic escalation, the possibility of "more pressing business elsewhere" for the rescuer, and the ability of the assailant to innovate tactically during quiet periods, using the data about the rescuers' military capabilities gathered during the last flare-up of fighting, all create incentives for the assailant to try its luck later, particularly if the assailant remains unpersuaded of the rescuer's genuine will to protect the victims over the long haul.

Supporters of military intervention to eliminate the sources of refugee flows need to have some way of gauging the practicability of the projects they have in mind. In general, rescuers will find themselves practicing coercive diplomacy, that is, compellence. Coercive diplomacy is more difficult than deterrent diplomacy. Rescuers will first try to affect the behavior of the assailant with threats of military action. They hope to induce assailant compliance by the threat to punish, or the threat to establish and successfully defend a safe zone, or the threat to successfully defend a safe haven, or the threat to put in enough good troops with sufficient authority to actually keep order, or the threat to destroy the assailant's armed forces. These threats are unlikely to work.

It is difficult to think of a case where coercive diplomacy accompanied by mere threats strongly affected the behavior of a producer of refugees. Invasion was necessary in the cases of East Pakistan (Bangladesh), Cambodia, and Rwanda. The intervention of substantial military forces and their engagement in some combat was required in Somalia and Bosnia-Herzegovina. Haiti was occupied without initial resistance, but the Cedras regime's capitulation was only assured when the assault force was literally warming its engines, and some combat did prove necessary after the occupation began. The only reason serious combat was not required in Operation Provide Comfort in Kurdish Iraq is that coercive diplomacy traded on the previous military action in Desert Storm, and on the threat mounted by strong residual forces close by.

Thus, intervention advocates should be under no illusions. Those who wish to help threatened peoples avoid becoming refugees will have to do much more than posture. They will need to muster the forces necessary to conduct the operations that have been identified as plausible solutions to the plight of the refugees. These forces will probably have to engage in actual combat, perhaps quite serious combat. Where decisive conquest of the assailant is impractical, it is likely that force will have to be used repeatedly, over a long time. For this reason, great care must be taken in the selection of military remedies, and in mustering sufficient military resources to execute these remedies.

## REMEDIES AND REALITIES

In this section, I discuss in detail the kinds of issues that arise in the selection of military remedies. Because the situation is more often one of compellence than deterrence, thorough military analysis is particularly essential.

### Punishment by Strategic Bombing

When trouble arises anywhere in the world, the first instinct of many is to bomb the miscreants, and through the infliction of pain, convince them to change their behavior. In the course of the war in Bosnia, some commentators argued that Serbia proper should have been bombed. But punitive conventional bombing—essentially strategic bombing—is a very problematical tool. Indeed, it has seldom, if ever, accomplished the purpose of changing the target's behavior. Punishment bombing can be directed against any or all of four distinct classes of targets: the civilian population; the industrial infrastructure; the transportation, communications, and electricity-generating capacity that knits a modern society together; or the political leadership. Each target set has a slightly different casual chain associated with it that is meant to lead to coercive success, but none of them have proven particularly effective. Many practical problems intervene.

*Target Sets*

Western political leaders and their air forces now abjure attacks on civilians. Desert Storm air operations explicitly, and for the most part successfully, avoided civilians. Given that the military operations discussed in this chapter have a humanitarian objective, it seems unlikely that rescuers would choose this target set. Moreover, the bombing of populations did not produce capitulation during the Second World War. Bombing makes the targeted population angry and convinces them that the enemy actually is as terrible as their leaders' propaganda says. It also increases people's dependence on the state, and makes coordinated action to overthrow the regime very difficult, because individuals are simply worried about their personal survival.

Attacks on the economic infrastructure of a country are meant to destroy the sources of its war-making power. The concomitant erosion of the capability of its fielded military forces is meant to induce a realization that defeat is inevitable, and therefore surrender is warranted. This was the basic rationale for the bombing of Japan and Germany during the Second World War. Debate continues on many aspects of these campaigns, but it cannot be argued that conventional bombing produced surrender in either case. Since the Second World War, outside suppliers have provided most of the weaponry in regional conflicts, so industrial bombing could not easily affect the combat power of fielded forces.

A second rationale has thus emerged: the industrial base is a nation's wealth, an important value. The sacrifice of this value should usually seem disproportionate to the state's war aims, whatever they are. This variant of the theory has proven weak, however, because the industrial base of a given country does *not* necessarily matter more to its leaders or its people than its war aims. And this variant may not be useful for humanitarian intervention, simply because many countries do not have much of an industrial base to bomb.

The concept of bombing "critical nodes" or "centers of gravity" assumes that modern societies depend on a small number of potential targets to knit them together socially, politically, and economically. These would include power generation, telephone communications, radio and television, major bridges, perhaps the water supply to the cities. If these are destroyed, the control of the central government wanes; the good people of the society throw out the leaders whose policies engendered this chaos. Or, fearing this outcome, leaders desist from the offenses that precipitated the bombing. But urban industrial societies are probably not as fragile as the theory suggests. When the bombing is successful, it may make conspiracy to overthrow the regime more difficult, since conspirators lose their ability to travel and communicate, and thus to concert action; it may also increase the dependence of the citizenry on the state for their survival.

This strategy has only been tried once, against Iraq in Operation Desert Storm. Much damage was done to Iraq's infrastructure but there is no evidence that Saddam's core Sunni Arab constituency was ever on the verge of rebellion. Iraqi technicians speedily repaired much of the damage after the war. On the other hand, this pattern of bombing, plus the more general destruction of Iraq's field forces, surely helped create the conditions that permitted rebellion in northern and southern Iraq by Kurdish and Shi'ite communities already predisposed to action. But the sequence of events suggests that neither rebellion would have occurred had it not been for the tactical defeat of the bulk of Iraq's ground forces. So, even with an already fissured society, air attacks on critical nodes could not themselves precipitate a rebellion. This is thus, very nearly, a critical test of the "critical nodes" theory. If it did not work in Iraq, it is unlikely to work anywhere.

The United States as a matter of policy does not use political assassination as a tool of foreign policy. But the United States does not abjure military attacks on enemy leadership. U.S. war planes came very close to killing Libyan leader Moammar Khadafi; they certainly targeted every political and military command center in Iraq that they could find in the hopes of killing Ba'ath political and military leaders, particularly Saddam Hussein. The main problem with leadership attacks is that the elimination of a few individuals, or threats to their lives, may not produce decisions to change an important policy. Sometimes they will, but this ought not to be assumed. The near miss on Khadafi seems to have persuaded him to give up his dabbling in the support of overseas terrorism. Had Saddam been killed, it is quite plausible that a successor would have withdrawn from Kuwait. But it seems unlikely that the death of Radovan Karadzić would have much affected the policies of the Bosnian Serbs, or that the death of Pol Pot would have ended the killing fields of Cambodia. Finally, even when one or a few leaders are responsible for a given policy, they can prove surprisingly adept at hiding themselves.

*Practical Problems with Punitive Bombing*

There are many practical problems that must be overcome for a punitive bombing campaign to be a plausible remedy. First, are there appropriate targets for any of the four strategic bombing theories outlined above? In neither Rwanda nor Cambodia can one imagine a target set for punitive bombing strikes. Assailant and victim populations are often dispersed and intermingled. Moreover, in some civil wars the distinction between assailant and victim simply breaks down. War matériel is usually imported from abroad, and often consists of light weaponry that is cheap and easy to move, so industrial-base bombing would be pointless even if the targets existed. Many of the countries and regions that have produced large numbers of refugees do not have much of an industrial base to lose. The states or groups in conflict probably do not depend on "critical nodes" in any important way. Leaders are difficult to find and eliminate, and trouble may be caused by mass movements, in any case.

Second, even if there are appropriate targets, the rescuer may not be politically able to attack them. If the rescuers are operating under UN auspices, will the deliberate bombing of the assailant's civilian population be acceptable? Can liberal democracies acting independently of the UN simply start killing one group of people to convince them to stop oppressing, terrorizing, or killing another? Perhaps they can if the assailant's general population can be reliably identified with the crimes. But this seems the most likely situation for bombing to strengthen rather than weaken resistance, since such general ferocity is usually associated with an ideology that identifies the assailant population as the "defender." . . .

To summarize, some political entities do not offer suitable target sets for strategic bombing. Some strategic-bombing target sets will not be acceptable to some rescuers. Some situations will mix the victims in with the assailants at the possible bombing targets, placing rescuers in a powerful ethical dilemma.

The third question is one of capabilities. Very few countries possess the capabilities to attack the full range of targets identified in the four strategic-bombing theories. In particular, successful attacks on "critical nodes" or leadership require very sophisticated air forces. Attacks on industrial infrastructure require somewhat sophisticated air forces. Only attacks on population are "easy." While there are many combat aircraft in the world, few countries command the special capabilities demonstrated in Operation Desert Storm. In 1990, the U.S. Air Force had a total of slightly over 100 combat aircraft capable of accurately delivering laser-guided bombs at night.[1] Almost all were used in the war, and they did the bulk of the precision-guided munitions (PGM) delivery for the entire coalition. Since the Iraq war, more countries have acquired this capability, but it is still concentrated in liberal industrialized countries, and a few of their close allies. Similar problems arise in the intelligence field; very few countries have the ability to gather the intelligence necessary to permit discriminate targeting. Thus, without the participation of the United States, it is not clear that particularly potent threats against "critical nodes" or leadership can be mounted.

"Access" to the theater of operations is also a crucial question. Fighter aircraft need bases from which to operate. Sustained operations at ranges greater than 600–700 km require substantial support from aerial tankers. The only country that owns tankers in large numbers is the United States. Beyond roughly 1,500 km, sustained tactical air operations become difficult even with tankers, because it is just too hard for pilots and weapons operators to spend that much time in the cockpit. Long-range operations also require complicated planning.

If reasonably close air bases cannot be obtained, the option does exist to employ long-range "strategic" bombers, such as the B-52, B-1b, or B-2. For the foreseeable future, these aircraft have at least one major limitation: There are few precision-guided munitions available for them, and those that do exist have rather limited capabilities. These "dumb bombers" are, for now, mainly area-attack weapons. Except for the stealthy B-2, of which only 20 are currently planned, existing strategic bombers probably ought not to be dispatched over defended air space without fighter escort in any case, which re-surfaces the proximate basing issue.

In sum, there will be many political and military causes of mass population displacement for which strategic bombing is not even a practical answer. If practical, the record suggests that such bombing seldom independently produces positive political results. How many of the causes of population displacement could punitive bombing conceivably address?

*Matching Punitive Bombing to Causes*

If genocide/politicide were the act of an organized government in a developed country, one or another variant of strategic bombing is at least a plausible remedy. In the rare cases where a developed society has launched an explicit genocide against a discrete population, it may be that some combination of attacks on vital centers and leadership is the only option open to potential rescuers, short of invasion. Given the heinousness of the situation, the mere possibility of success would justify an attempt at strategic bombing, though history gives us little reason for confidence in the outcome. One of the most important questions about strategic bombing will therefore be whether or not the situation is so horrible that it merits re-running an experiment that has so seldom worked. The genocide convention defines so many behaviors as genocide that it will be relatively easy for partisans of action to define the situation in this way. But given the low probability of success, and the possibility of making all but the most terrible policies of an assailant a great deal worse, it is my view that a narrow definition should be employed. For it to be "genocide" (or politicide), it would have to look a lot like the Nazi or Khmer Rouge crimes before this remedy should be considered seriously.

If ethnic cleansing were the source of displacement, and if the assailant state were developed and organized, punitive bombing might also be a plausible answer, though the rescuer runs a very real risk of so enraging the assailant that it turns from displacing the victims to murdering them. The problem of refugees who flee because they fear occupation is more difficult. Here the "rescuer" is trying to force two sides fighting a traditional war to stop; more specifically, the successful side is being told to stop. The rescuer is effectively entering an ongoing war on the side of the loser. What if the loser was the one who started it? The same problem may arise if refugees are merely fleeing the sound of the guns. In some cases they flee an internal war among approximate equals, so rescuers would have to bomb all the parties to the war. And of course, these wars often occur in places where there is not anything worth bombing. If occupation has already occurred, and refugees are fleeing its generalized brutality, the assailant has many hostages. The assailant can argue that if you bomb, it will kill them. Where refugees are simply fleeing the misery caused by primitive logistics systems, the nature of the problem suggests that the assailants do not have anything interesting to bomb.

### Safe Zones

True "safe zones" have rarely been attempted. A threatened population remains settled in a distinct area that is effectively placed under the military protection of outsiders, who commit themselves to defend the zone, and to permit the inhabitants to live something like a normal life. There is little political or military precedent for operations of this kind. The protection of the Kurds in Northern Iraq following their unsuccessful rebellion catalyzed by Operation Desert Storm is the model and sole example.

A safe zone is a defensive or "denial" strategy. This is one of its attractions because at the most abstract level defense is easier than offense. If one accepts the argument advanced above, that humanitarian intervention is basically an exercise in coercive diplomacy and hence the rescuer may actually be forced to fight, then rescuers should be interested in finding ways to lower the military cost of action. If defense is the stronger form of war, then setting up a situation where the assailant must attack is favorable to the rescuers and to the victims. A safe zone aims to provide physical protection to the threatened population. It convinces the assailant to stay away by developing a convincing ability to bar entry. Safe zones depend on real military power to defend them, and the willingness of rescuers to use it. Both the type and quantity of military power necessary to establish a safe zone are dependent on the specific situation. Some safe zones may be defended by high-quality air power; others might require ground power as well. Sometimes the threatened population might be able to supply the ground power if outsiders provide them with weaponry; sometimes outsiders must deploy ground forces. Demographic variables and more traditional military variables, such as distance, weather, topography, and vegetation, will influence the size and quality of the necessary military force. Presuming that these variables are generally favorable to a safe zone, then the kinds of questions discussed earlier with regard to strategic bombing come into play. Are there bases nearby? Are there ports, roads, airstrips? Which countries are willing to act as rescuers? Can they bring the right kind of military power to bear?

Safe zones produce a *"de facto"* secession, which may be one of the strongest political obstacles to their employment. While there is currently a lively debate in the international law community on weakening the norm of nonintervention in the internal affairs of sovereign states, that norm still seems quite strong. In situations where the United Nations is involved, the relatively strong commitment of the smaller countries to the old norm will prove an obstacle to the organization of a safe zone. In actual practice, deviation from the sovereignty norm has followed a double standard: when the bad guys are weak, such as Iraq in Kurdistan, intervention pops to the top of the agenda; when they are strong, such as Russia in Chechnya, little is said. . . .

### Safe Havens

Sometimes rescuers will want to provide a sheltered refuge within an area of conflict where the displaced can go, but will not wish to cordon off large areas of a country to do it. In effect, rescuers are trying to arrange things so that victims can flee their homes without fleeing their country. The purpose may be as brutally pragmatic as forestalling a wholesale departure that would produce legitimate claims for refugee status in the interested countries. Or the purpose may be to help the refugees stay close to their original homes as part of a larger diplomatic strategy that aims to settle a conflict and permit them to return to their previous lives.

There are many reasons why a "safe haven" policy could prove expedient. Conflicts that produce refugees will often arise in places where groups—defined by religion, ethnicity, or nationality—are intermixed. A large safe zone of the type discussed above cannot be created unless the rescuers are themselves willing to engage in ethnic cleansing, throwing out the assailant group. Alternatively, the rescuers may not wish to be implicated in a strategy that looks like *de facto* secession. The rescuers may lack the military capability to pursue a safe-zone policy due to their limited capabilities, or to the size of the theater of operations. . . .

A safe-haven policy is a reasonable antidote to several of the causes of refugee flight I have identified, but as usual the specific situation exerts a strong influence. A refuge for those fleeing genocide or politicide would certainly be one potential contribution. It is plausible, however, that the safe-haven instrument is inherently too difficult to defend militarily against assailants whose political passions support genocide or politicide. Assailants will claw away at the safe havens even if they are defended; under some conditions, they will attempt siege warfare, particularly the interdiction of food supplies, water, and energy rather than direct attack. Because assailants are not leaving, they may settle on an attrition policy, and simply wait for the rescuers to tire of a difficult and dangerous mission.

Safe havens may work better against "ethnic cleansing." On the one hand, havens may help assailants by providing an inviting refuge for people trying to decide whether to tough out the terrorist policies of the assailant, or to wait in a safe place in the hopes that this wave of trouble will pass. Thus, assailants may actually see some benefits to the havens. On the other hand, if the havens are close to the areas from which the refugees have been expelled, they leave open the possibility that the assailant's gains will be reversed at a later date. Assailants would clearly prefer the refugees to leave the area or country altogether. Hence, even in this case, the assailants will want to make life in the havens as unpleasant as possible, in the hopes that refugees will move on. They have other means to accomplish this, however. If they move their own people into the homes of those expelled, expropriating homes, land, and businesses, hopelessness about return may gradually spread in the refugee population, and they will try to exit the safe havens and go abroad. The defender of the safe haven, the rescuer, is gradually turned into a jailer, an uncomfortable position. . . .

Safe havens are an excellent solution for the problem of starvation caused by primitive logistics. Here the rescuers are on a more traditional humanitarian mission. Armed protection is necessary precisely because the economy has broken down, and those with weapons are taking food from those without weapons. The rescuers simply provide military protection to traditional humanitarian-assistance efforts. A delimited safe haven is chosen because it is militarily and administratively efficient. The local military actors are probably not especially strong relative to rescuer armies, otherwise they would not have resorted to pre-modern methods of requisition to feed themselves. They may, of course, find themselves in a difficult logistical situation once they no longer have a population to prey upon. But rescuers may also offer some inducements for their good behavior in the form of a share of the humanitarian aid.

The recent and perhaps historically singular effort to attempt a "safe haven" policy has been in Bosnia. Six towns and cities were designated as safe havens: Srebenica, Žepa, Tuzla, Goražde, Bihać, and Sarajevo. The hope was that the residents could remain in relative safety. Displaced persons from the surrounding countryside who had previously taken refuge, or who were still looking for refuge, would find succor and protection there. These areas were provided with varying amounts of food and other resources, overland, by air lift, or by air drop. All had some UN military presence on the ground. The UN warned that if these areas were attacked, NATO air power might be called to defend them. Minor air attacks were in fact mounted around Sarajevo and Goražde. When Bihać was threatened in November of 1994, however, the UN declined to request NATO air strikes to defend the town, although some air attacks were mounted elsewhere. In the end the town held. Srebenica and Žepa fell to the Serbs in 1995 with only limited NATO air action under the auspices of the UN to defend them. When Goražde seemed threatened for the second time, NATO made its first explicit threat to employ air power on a substantial scale against the Bosnian Serb field army. The Bosnian Serbs did not then take the town.

Other than the Bosnia experience, there are no clear real-world examples of an effort to establish safe havens against a competent, determined attacker. . . . The complex record in Bosnia suggests that the overall resources of military capability and political will committed to the safe-haven enterprise were somewhat inadequate, though a dispassionate analysis must acknowledge the success achieved. The civilian inhabitants of Sarajevo, Tuzla, Bihać, and Goražde suffered casualties from shelling and sniping. Interdiction of ground and air lines of communication meant short rations and a mean standard of living. These four largest safe havens did not fall to the Serbs, however. Goražde is a particularly important example of success, because it is close to Serbia, and seems an objective that the Bosnian Serbs clearly wanted, and nearly took. However, the combination of UN threats, peacekeeping troops, and Bosnian infantry was unable to prevent the fall of Srebenica and Žepa, or to prevent several intense combined-arms attacks on Bihać and Goražde. Thus, we have a crude measure of adequacy: some portion of the air combat and airlift resources of NATO, plus several thousand NATO troops acting as UN peacekeepers in the role of "alarm bell ringers," plus thousands of not-well-armed indigenous Bosnian Muslim infantry did successfully compel the Serbs to restrain their assaults on three–four of six safe havens. Even Srebenica and Žepa, which fell to Serb attacks in the summer of 1995, remained untaken for a remarkably long time given their inherent military weakness. At the same time, however, repeated and sometimes successful challenges to this formidable (if rather poorly organized) aggregation of capabilities did occur. . . .

### The "Enforced Truce"

Certain patterns of violence that produce refugees may only be affected by outside intervention that attempts to establish a new source of "law and order." This model, however, is based on the assumption that rescuers can muster sufficient political or economic leverage, or are so intimidating militarily, that they may not need to shoot their way into the country. The target area is not so much invaded as occupied. So-called "failed states," where many armed factions vie for control, could conform to this model. Somalia is the best recent example; one could also argue that the UN operation in the Congo took this form. Because the local factions are too weak to keep rescuers from coming into the country, rescuers can calculate that it is theoretically possible to impose a peace, at least for a time. The purpose is to place enough military force into the area where fighting and killing are underway that little violence can occur out of sight of the rescuers. The rescuers bring enough military power that they can quickly do serious harm to any group breaking the peace. Indeed it is preferable to have sufficient presence that any incident that would break the peace is nipped in the bud.

The implementation of the "enforced truce" will depend on several practical constraints. The size and shape of the country, the number and size of the groups that need protection, and their arrangement will all bear on the size of force necessary to make the "peace" work. So will the scale of armament and military competence of the local fighters. Military analysts typically analogize from "similar" situations that have already occurred. Thus the "soldier+police-to-population" ratios in places like Northern Ireland or the West Bank are taken as good indicators of the minimum size of force that could be necessary. In Northern Ireland this ratio was roughly 20:1,000 in a situation where there were probably never more than 1,500 hardened shooters and bombers on all sides. Where local military forces are stronger and more capable than those in Northern Ireland, the 20:1,000 ratio would probably be insufficient. "Soldier-to-terrorist" (20:1 in Northern Ireland) and "soldier-to-space" ratios are also relevant. Nevertheless, the Northern Ireland ratio of 20:1,000 would suggest a minimum peacekeeping force of 90,000 to police the Vance-Owen plan in Bosnia. It also suggests that NATO forces in Bosnia today are too weak to enforce the political provisions of the Dayton accords, particularly the return of refugees to their former homes, if the warring parties do not implement them voluntarily.

If a rescuer actually wants to protect all from all, the requirements can be very great. If, on the other hand, a rescuer only wishes to suppress local fighting and distribute food, then some economies may be possible. A small local presence backed up by highly mobile combat power may cow the local combatants into relative inactivity, though it will not provide a long-term solution, nor prevent all violence. This expedient will prove more effective if the locals are badly armed. These kinds of tricks worked well in the initial humanitarian intervention in Somalia, permitting a "soldier+police-to-population" ratio of 5–10 per thousand. If a long-term solution is sought, and particularly if locals are to be induced to surrender their arms, then a very high level of local military presence may prove necessary to convince most people that they are safe from one another. And if the local armed forces are competent and committed, the price will be even higher. . . .

Outside intervention to impose a permanent political solution to end an internal conflict is more difficult than intervention to elicit a pause in the fighting in order to ease the plight of refugees. The people to be protected are often the military and political objective of the assailants; indeed, in these situations each faction's noncombatants may be the targets of the other's combatants. However perverse this may seem from outside, the groups are committed to the killing. The rescuer is thus engaged in a war that resembles that most complicated political–military enterprise, counter-insurgency. Moreover, it is difficult to see how the mere enforcement of a pause in the killing is particularly constructive in situations of intense factional or intergroup violence. If political passions have produced an outbreak of mass killing, it is going to be difficult to stop. If the killing is stopped due to the intimidating local power deployed by the rescuers, and not due to the destruction of the multiple assailants' "combat capability" (whatever that means in this context), the rescuers will have to stay for a very long time. It may be difficult for the rescuers to convince the assailants that they care more about the safety of noncombatant victims than the assailants care about their destruction. Assailants might try to attack rescuers in order to raise the costs of humanitarian intervention. Alternatively, they may just wait until the rescuers depart. . . .

## CONCLUSION: SPECIFIC REMEDIES FOR SPECIFIC CAUSES

The most heinous of problems—genocide/politicide—may be the toughest to address with military power. In rare cases, a coercive bombing strategy may have some hope of working. Safe zones and safe havens may be employed when the pattern of settlement of the victims either concentrates them in a specific region, or makes it easy for them to concentrate themselves. Rescuers must consider, however, that the political passions that produce large-scale murder may prove very difficult to influence. Assailants may be strongly motivated to challenge rescuer safe zones and havens. In many cases, only complete invasion and occupation is likely to stop the crime; much killing of innocents can occur during such a campaign.

Where ethnic cleansing is an assailant's objective, it will often be the case that people are settled in particular regions, and thus safe zones or safe havens will prove pragmatic approaches. Safe zones and safe havens may also be reasonable remedies for people fleeing the sound of the guns, or the impoverishment caused by primitive logistics. When demographic, ecological, and geopolitical factors are favorable, the safe zone in particular is inherently an appealing remedy. Alone among the mechanisms described, it aims to permit large numbers of people to live nearly normal lives. A clear demarcation line between assailants and their putative victims tells the assailant when to stop. If the safe zone is large, rescuer air power may be able to prevent large assailant units from getting deep enough into the safe zone to do serious harm. The threatened population may be organized into lightly armed ground forces that can force the assailant into attack postures that facilitate air attack. If rescuers are both lucky and skillful, they may be able to transform the local situation into one of deterrence.

The one drawback to safe zones is their special political problem: the still-powerful respect for sovereignty in international politics. Safe zones will often amount to *de facto* secession implemented by outside powers. This creates short-term obstacles to implementation, in that many smaller countries may not wish to legitimate such intervention. A longer-term problem is also created: what circumstances would encourage outside powers to withdraw their protection and permit the reintegration of the zone in question into the assailant-state's system of government? This problem remains to be faced in Kurdistan.

Safe havens should be viewed as analytically distinct from safe zones. They are primarily refuges, not places of normal existence. They are an expedient to be adopted only in the most dire circumstances. They are very demanding of every aspect of military power, ground and air, and logistics. It is as if the Berlin Airlift and the Siege of Khe Sanh were combined into one operation.

Primitive wars of all against all cause refugees to flee the dangerous environment of combat and the depredations of uncontrolled requisitions. The enforced truce is the obvious response, perhaps combined with the safe zone and safe haven, but it is also particularly demanding of military power. A rough local peace among warring parties may not require a lot of firepower, nor incur many casualties, but substantial numbers of high-quality motorized, mechanized, and helicopter-borne infantry, and a great deal of patience and local knowledge, will be necessary. They may buy time for negotiators to try to effect a local political solution. Failing a local accord, rescuers will find themselves in a dilemma. They can attempt to impose a political solution by force, in effect joining the local war, or they can leave, with the risk that the situation will quickly deteriorate to the conditions that prompted the original intervention. The former will mean casualties, the latter, human tragedy and political embarrassment.

### The Future

When trouble of any kind arises, interested parties look to the United States for help because of its great power and influence. To cite only one example, the United States possesses by far the most capable and diverse air combat and airlift capabilities in the world. Air power, though not a decisive all-purpose tool, is an extremely useful one. The more exercises of this kind the United States does, the more the awareness of its array of special capabilities will spread, and the more frequently other countries, nongovernmental organizations, and international organizations will look to the United States for help. Citizens of the United States should accustom themselves to these appeals, and learn how to analyze the odds of success.

While the problem of politically induced refugee flows is not new, the magnitude of the problem seems to be growing. More importantly, as a result of the diffusion of liberal values in the polities of the most powerful states, the intensification of global communications precipitated by technological and economic change, the weakening of the intensity of great-power rivalries, and the consciousness of the developed-world's remarkable reservoir of Cold War–generated military power, arguments are now frequently offered that "we" should do something, even though traditional geopolitical interests may be absent. These altruistic impulses, and enabling conditions, ought not to obscure one important fact: in most of these cases, what good-hearted people are proposing is war. And war remains the realm of strategy, operations, and tactics; of forces and logistics; of destruction and death. "Humanitarian intervention" will often prove less gentle than it sounds.

**NOTE**

1. Since Desert Storm, the USAF figure has grown to roughly 450 such aircraft.

# 28

# The Critical Barrier to
# Civil War Settlement

## BARBARA F. WALTER

Unlike interstate wars, civil wars rarely end in negotiated settlements. Between 1940 and 1990, 55 percent of interstate wars were resolved at the bargaining table, whereas only 20 percent of civil wars reached similar solutions. Instead, most internal wars ended with the extermination, expulsion, or capitulation of the losing side. In fact, groups fighting civil wars almost always chose to fight to the finish unless an outside power stepped in to guarantee a peace agreement. If a third party agreed to enforce the terms of a peace treaty, negotiations always succeeded regardless of the initial goals, ideology, or ethnicity of the participants. If a third part did not intervene, these talks usually failed.

The fact that civil wars tend to end on the battlefield poses a startling empirical puzzle for political scientists and an increasingly onerous problem for policymakers. Why are domestic enemies unable to negotiate successfully? And what can the international community do to help end these conflicts?

I argue that civil war negotiations rarely end in successful peace settlements because credible guarantees on the terms of the settlement are almost impossible to arrange by the combatants themselves. Negotiations do not fail because indivisible stakes, irreconcilable differences, or high cost tolerances make compromise impossible, as many people argue. They do not fail because bargains cannot be struck. Adversaries often compromise on the basic issues underlying their conflict, and they frequently find mutually acceptable solutions to their problems. Negotiations fail because civil war opponents are asked to do what they consider unthinkable. At a time when no legitimate government and no legal institutions exist to enforce a contract, they are asked to demobilize, disarm, and disengage their military forces and prepare for peace. But once they lay down their weapons and begin to integrate their separate assets into a new united state, it becomes almost impossible to either enforce future cooperation or survive attack. In the end, negotiations fail because civil war adversaries cannot credibly promise to abide by such dangerous terms. Only when an outside enforcer steps in to guarantee the terms do commitments to disarm and share political power become believable. Only then does cooperation become possible.

In this article I have two aims. First, I propose a theory of civil war resolution that rests on reciprocal problems of enforcement and vulnerability rather than on innate differences, goals, or greed. My purpose is to dispel currently popular notions that civil wars are either beyond compromise or only amenable to compromise when accompanied by a military stalemate and exceptionally skilled mediation. Second, I systematically test current theories against forty-one civil war cases. I conclude by presenting the conditions under which negotiated solutions, once reached, can be implemented and maintained and the crucial role that outside intervention can play in resolving these conflicts.

The first section of this article presents a theory of civil war termination: domestic adversaries rarely settle off the battlefield because any attempt to end a civil war will also eliminate any self-enforcing strategies to maintain the peace. The second section explores four alternative theories that focus on high costs, indivisible stakes, bargaining problems, and group identity as the key variables affecting resolution. The third section explains how cases were selected and coded and outlines the steps taken to test the competing hypotheses. The fourth section interprets the findings and discusses what they suggest about foreign involvement in internal wars.

## THE PUZZLE

Ending a war is usually difficult. Organizational inertia, tunnel vision, wishful thinking, and miscommunication all work against early reconciliation and make cooperation difficult. Once fighting begins, plans are set in motion and attitudes toward the enemy become fixed in ways that are not easily reversible. Even if opponents agree to negotiate, they still face the risks and uncertainties of cooperation. Will an opponent fulfill its side of the agreement? Or will the compromise itself turn out to be an inherently bad deal?

Despite these obstacles, international wars usually end with some type of explicit settlement. Civil wars do not. Current explanations claim that power asymmetries, indivisible stakes, bargaining difficulties, or opposing identities make settlement in civil wars nearly impossible. But this seems unlikely. Military stalemates often emerge in civil wars without prompting negotiations; governments can be shared by more than one party; and groups that appear ethnically or religiously incompatible do meet to discuss alternative solutions to war.

Others argue that groups are stuck in what could be called a game or deadlock;

cooperation is impossible because competing domestic groups will always have opposing preferences and interests. But this also seems unlikely. Civil war adversaries do not always continue to fight because they cannot arrange compromise settlements. Between 1940 and 1990, 42 percent of civil wars (seventeen out of forty-one) experienced some form of formal peace negotiation, and 94 percent of these cases drafted at least a cease-fire accord. In other words, adversaries often attempted very serious peace talks that then broke down. In short, none of the current explanations identifies a compelling reason why domestic enemies would forgo negotiations in favor of potentially lengthy battlefield contests. What follows is an attempt to identify additional factors that might inhibit successful civil war resolution and cause even promising negotiations to cycle back into war.

## THE THEORY

### What Is Different About Civil Wars?

The key difference between interstate and civil wars negotiations is that adversaries in a civil war cannot retain separate, independent armed forces if they agree to settle their differences. This difference fundamentally alters incentives to abide by any peace treaty and makes it almost impossible for groups to cooperate. In the following section, I argue that groups fighting civil wars avoid negotiated settlements because they understand that this would require them to relinquish important fall-back defenses at a time when no neutral police force and no legitimate government exist to help them enforce the peace. Knowing they will enter a period of intense vulnerability, neither side can convince the other that they will nobly resist a treaty's temptations or naively fulfill its terms. And so, unable to enforce the agreement or survive exploitation, they avoid cooperation and continue to fight.

#### Interstate Cooperation Under Anarchy

Encouraging and then maintaining cooperation under anarchy is not easy. It is especially difficult in "prisoners' dilemma" situations where both states would benefit from cooperating but would also be far worse off if they naively cooperated while their opponent exploited their trust.

States in the international system have devised a number of military and economic strategies to encourage cooperation even when incentives favor cheating. They can create early warning systems and sophisticated monitoring and verification procedures to check each other's behavior. They can build military defenses, forge external alliances, and set up buffer zones to make aggression more costly. They can also use symbiotic trade relationships, side-payments, and economic coercion to enhance the rewards from cooperation. They can also withhold key resources or use reciprocal punishment strategies to ensure that violations are punished. Each of these strategies helps to create binding agreements.

Nonetheless, even the most sophisticated strategies for ensuring compliance are not foolproof, and states know this. States will, however, often cooperate despite this risk if they can limit the damage caused by cheating. A surprise attack might renew the war, but states with strong defenses and active forces would be no worse off than before the settlement. In fact, states could use this time to refurbish forces and restock supplies and thus increase their security. Under these conditions, the risks of exploitation are manageable and well worth the potential benefits of long-term peace.

### Domestic Cooperation Under Anarchy

None of these strategies is available to groups fighting civil wars. Although the same anarchic conditions exist during times of civil war as those that exist permanently in the international system—no central government exists to insure order, no police or judicial system remains to enforce contracts, and groups have divided into independent armed camps—the pernicious effects of anarchy are actually far more severe. Whereas interstate opponents can augment the benefits of cooperation and sharpen punishments for cheating, civil war adversaries have little ability to do so. If they wish to cooperate, these groups must disband their forces and, in so doing, relinquish their only remaining means for protection. Even states that surrender unconditionally are rarely required to go so far.[1]

Thus the single most detrimental condition operating against cooperation is that civil war adversaries cannot maintain independent armed forces if they decide to reconcile. Once they sign a peace treaty they cannot retreat to their own borders and defensively reinforce their militaries, they do not become trading partners or important allies, and they cannot hide behind buffer zones. Only if they are willing to relinquish control over occupied regions, vital industries, and independent military organizations is a cooperative peace agreement possible.

This situation forces governments and rebels into a paradoxical and unfortunate dilemma. Any attempt to end a civil war and unify the country also eliminates any ability to enforce and ensure the peace. Thus, the only way enemies in a civil war can prematurely end the bloodshed is to force themselves through a transition period during which they can neither encourage cooperation nor survive attack. They must weather a period of extreme vulnerability. Civil war rivals, therefore, are damned if they do and damned if they don't. As soon as they comply with a peace treaty they become powerless to enforce the terms over which they had bargained so hard.

The fact that settlement can leave a group far worse off than it would have been had it simply continued to fight has two devastating effects on cooperation. First, it discredits any promise to abide by the terms of an agreement even if offered in good faith, and, second, it increases groups' anxiety about future security and makes them hypersensitive to even the smallest treaty violation.

The result? In most cases the government and the rebels will recognize the overwhelming risks involved with compliance, and they will refuse to sign any treaty even if all the underlying issues have been resolved and even if both sides sincerely want peace. If they do sign, this fear and insecurity will become so overwhelming that even satisfactory settlements will slowly unravel. In his 1949 report on China, Dean Acheson keenly observed that "[t]he distrust of the leaders of both the Nationalist and Communist Parties for each other proved too deep-seated to permit final agreement, notwithstanding temporary truces and apparently promising negotiations.[2] Since each side understands the profits to be gained by exploiting a peace treaty (and both sides know that their opponent also recognizes this opportunity), their promises to honor and respect the terms of the agreement cannot be trusted. Under these conditions, fighting suddenly appears far more appealing than settlement.

In the end, negotiated settlements in civil wars perish under their own unique demands. Incumbent governments and rebels cannot structure the agreement so that it will, at worst, allow each side to return as close as possible to the status quo should one party decide to cheat. And as long as both factions understand that cooperation will leave them vulnerable and they have no means to avoid this condition, they will prefer to continue fighting rather than risk possible attack.

But could more stable, less risky transitions be designed by the participants themselves? For example, if the government and the rebels fear a one-step advantage, could military integration occur in a step-by-step or reciprocal fashion? Or if one side enjoys a preponderance of military power and its opponent enjoys a preponderance of political support (like the Kuomintang and the Communists in China), could these opposing strengths deter the breakdown of a settlement? And finally, could groups agree to remain armed until all obtained some real control over new government institutions and national security forces? This would impart some protection until more appropriate institutional checks and balances could be established.

Stable, less risky transitions cannot be designed by the participants themselves for three reasons that are tied to problems of credible commitment. First, groups will have great difficulty convincing each other to fully execute any plan that eventually requires them to disarm. Although numerous implementation plans can be designed to reduce vulnerability, in the end even the most incremental and impartial one will require the full demobilization of partisan groups. In civil wars, disarmament can be postponed, and it can be done gradually and in a reciprocal manner, but it can never be avoided. And as long as a threshold exists beyond which unilateral defense is impossible, and both groups realize that an opponent need only wait for this time to attack, they will either avoid compliance altogether or simply renege on further fulfillment at the first sign of default. Second, groups will also have great difficulty convincing each other to accept any plan that offers even the slightest chance of annihilation. A 95 percent risk-free disarmament plan might appear perfectly acceptable on paper, but to the groups involved, even a slight chance of an attack is often too high. In situations of extreme vulnerability, the beliefs groups have about their own safety and their perception of threat matter as much if not more than the actual invulnerability of the treaty design. Finally, groups will also have a difficult time using new institutions to project a credible promise of either effective protection or neutral enforcement during the transition. These institutions are new and untested. They are often designed by "democratic novices"—people inexperienced with multi-party political systems, opposition groups, and peaceful transfers of power. Moreover, these institutions will initially be staffed by former government and rebel officials with lingering partisan loyalties. These institutions might eventually serve to reassure groups that their rights and liberties will be protected, but when new, they could just as well be used as instruments for further repression. Reassuring they are not.

*The Importance of Third-Party Guarantees*

Third-party guarantors can change the level of fear and insecurity that accompanies treaty implementation and thus facilitate settlement. An important and frequent reason why opponents fail to reach successful settlements is because they cannot credibly commit to an agreement that will become far less attractive once implemented. Third parties, however, can guarantee that groups will be protected, terms will be fulfilled, and promises will be kept (or at least they can ensure that groups will survive until a new government and a new national military is formed). In short, they can ensure that the payoffs from cheating on a civil war agreement no longer exceed the payoffs from faithfully executing its terms. Once cheating becomes difficult and costly, promises to cooperate gain credibility and cooperation becomes more likely.

But how does one ensure that promises made by a third party at the negotiating table are themselves credible? To be credible, a guarantee must fulfill at least three basic conditions. First, the outside state must have a self-interest in upholding its promise. Old colonial ties, strategic interests, economic investments, or alliance loyalties will enhance any commitment to intervene and will indicate the political will to persevere. Second, the guarantor must be willing to use force if necessary, and its military capabilities must be sufficient to punish whichever side violates the treaty. Syria could occupy Lebanon, Britain overshadowed Zimbabwe, Ethiopia dwarfed Sudan, and the United States could restrain the Dominican Republic. Equal or greater force is necessary for any threat to effectively deter cheating. Third, the intervening state should be able to signal resolve. The outside power can either station sufficient forces to deter aggression without having to send for additional forces if conflict breaks out, as Syria did in Lebanon. Or it can create some type of military trip wire, as Britain did in Zimbabwe. Outside forces can also be placed at strategically important locations, such as troop assembly areas, borders, or munitions sites, and guarantors can have pre-approval from home governments for further action. These costly signals should allow states to reveal their true preferences and enhance the credibility of their promises.

The credible-commitment theory of civil war resolution, therefore, offers us our first hypothesis for testing. Given the reciprocal problems of enforcement and

*Barbara F. Walter*

vulnerability, hypothesis 1 predicts that the more willing an outside power is to guarantee the safety of the adversaries during the critical implementation phase, the more likely domestic opponents are to reach and execute a final deal.[3] If no such guarantee exists, civil wars should either fail to reach a settlement or such settlements should quickly break down. . . .

### Findings

I created [a] dataset to answer two questions: Why do civil wars rarely end in lasting negotiated settlements, and what conditions ultimately lead to negotiated solutions to these wars? My goal was to see which of the proposed hypotheses could best predict whether a civil war would end through a negotiated settlement or whether fighting would continue until one side or another won a decisive victory. To do this, a simple Pearson correlation coefficient or cross-tab analysis was used to determine which variables were most strongly related to settlement and which had little or no effect.[4]

Overall, the single most successful explanation for why civil war negotiations failed was the credible-commitment argument.[5] Once adversaries agreed to negotiate, every case where a third-party stepped in to guarantee a treaty resulted in a successful settlement (Table 28.1 summarizes the methods of resolution for civil wars with outside security guarantees). Outside powers guaranteed Lebanon's agreement in 1958, the Dominican Republic's "Act of Dominican Reconciliation," the Riyadh Agreement in Lebanon (1976), the Addis Ababa Agreement in Sudan (1972), the Lancaster House Agreement in Zimbabwe (1979), and the Tela Agreement in Nicaragua (1989), and all brought peace. Only two civil wars reached a successful settlement without an outside guarantee (Colombia in 1958 and Yemen in 1970), and the details of these two exceptions tend to confirm the rule.

### TABLE 28.1

**CIVIL WARS WITH OUTSIDE SECURITY GUARANTEES AND THEIR METHOD OF RESOLUTION**

| Type of guarantee | Decisive victory | Successful settlement | Row total |
|---|---|---|---|
| No guarantee | 33 (94%) | 2 (6%) | 35 (100%) |
| Weak guarantee | 0 | 1 (100%) | 1 (100%) |
| Moderate guarantee | 0 | 3 (100%) | 3 (100%) |
| Strong guarantee | 0 | 2 (100%) | 2 (100%) |
| Column total | 33 (80%) | 8 (20%) | 41 (100%) |

Chi-square=10.43; ($p$=.015).

Although Colombia and Yemen did reach settlements without outside guarantees, they were also the only two wars where the opposing parties could not launch surprise attacks against each other. Both wars were fought by relatively uncommitted armies whose loyalties could be procured by the highest bidder; the warring parties themselves did not have organized partisan forces at their command. In Colombia the national army remained relatively uninvolved in the fighting and allowed the war to be fought by small bands of armed peasants. In Yemen, the Royalist rebels had no regular army. In order to fight, "tribal forces had to be assembled by negotiation with the shaikhs for each contemplated operation of any size." Thus, once the Conservatives and Liberals in Colombia and the Royalists and Republicans in Yemen agreed to compromise, they did not have to demobilize and integrate separate, partisan military corps. They simply bought the loyalty of either the powerful Colombian generals or the Yemeni tribes and in this way obtained fairly neutral forces. In short, these adversaries could successfully cooperate because they did not need to pass through a vulnerable demobilization and reintegration period.[6]

Close scrutiny of the other cases confirmed the strong effect that security fears had on settlement. In almost every civil war negotiation, final deliberations were filled with skeptical pronouncements about future security. Nigeria's Ibo population refused to sign a cease-fire agreement because they feared the government would massacre them, and the government refused to sign because they believed "that Ojukwu and his foreign backers will certainly use the cease-fire pause to re-arm and prepare for a bloodier conflict in which more innocent lives will be lost." Neither side trusted that the other would honestly abide by the terms.

In case after case belligerents eventually walked away from the bargaining table if an outside power did not step forward to monitor and enforce a peace treaty. When asked by a reporter if his demand for white control over the police and army during the transition was a make-or-break issue, Ian Smith replied: "Yes, it is, because if the African side goes back on this agreement, then we won't be seeing an interim government any time soon." And when asked if the British had made "a crucial concession" by stationing British and Commonwealth forces in the assembly areas with the Patriotic Front troops, Robert Mugabe, head of the African rebels, echoed:

Yes. We welcomed that because it was the really vital element and it prevented the Rhodesian forces, you see, supported by the South African forces—who were in the country, don't forget—from attacking our assembly points. There were nasty incidents here and there. Yes, that was really vital.

In his words, "it would be ridiculous for the settlers who are murdering the Zimbabweans to be intrusted with [our] security during the crucial transitional period." He made it clear that the Patriotic Front "would rather prefer Ian Smith having 100 percent representation in Parliament and we having the army controlling, than having majority in Parliament with Ian Smith having the army, you see. That's not transference of power at all."[7]

Even if an acceptable military settlement was reached (as it was between the Chinese Communists and the National government in 1945), neither side agreed to sign without some type of outside guarantee. If, however, peacekeeping forces were already in place but were withdrawn after a settlement was reached, as they were in Laos after the 1973 cease-fire and in Vietnam after the 1975 Paris peace talks, fighting always resumed shortly thereafter. Since the outside state had no intention of maintaining any commitment beyond a certain, often declared, date, its military presence had no positive effect on the success of negotiations. In the end, the ultimate success of a peace treaty seemed to rest on a third-party's desire to become involved and remain involved after a treaty was signed.

The relationship between security guarantees and settlement was clear. It was more difficult, however, to determine if the strength of a guarantee affected the likelihood of success since settlements always succeeded when outside guarantees were offered. Closer inspection, however, revealed an interesting pattern. Weak guarantees were generally offered in wars with very high costs and were usually offset by extensive internal power-sharing arrangements. Peace agreements that allowed the individual adversaries to retain as much independent strength as possible—in the form of political representation, veto powers, and a military balance in the national forces—required only weak external security guarantees in order to succeed. Conversely, outside guarantees tended to be strongest in less bloody wars with low costs, and treaties with vague or undeveloped political arrangements. Peace agreements that included few political guarantees for future political participation (or only the promise of elections) and unequal representation of groups in the national army required the strongest external guarantees in order to succeed. In these cases, the belligerents seemed far less certain of their own abilities to deter renewed war.

This inverse relationship between the strength of security guarantees and the extent of postwar internal political and military arrangements becomes clear when the actual treaties are compared. The settlement to end the Sudanese civil war was underwritten by the weakest guarantee of this study. Yet, in this case, Ethiopian Emperor Haile Selassie's fairly thin promise to the Sudanese rebels that "his government was committed to their security" and his personal guarantee that Anya Nya returnees would not suffer reprisal or repression were supplemented by some of the most detailed federal provisions of any settlement. Unlike many of the other peace accords, the Addis Ababa agreement to end the Sudanese war maintained very clear political and military distinctions between the fighting factions of the North and South. The new constitution guaranteed the continued existence of a southern regional government and gave the South enough tax revenue to survive without help from the wealthier North. More importantly, the accord was able to fashion a national army that preserved the armed strength of both factions. Under the terms of the peace accord, the southern command of the new national army would be equally divided between officers and soldiers from both the North and the South.

These detailed and fairly balanced terms can be compared with the very weak political and military arrangements included in the 1958 and 1976 agreements to end the two civil wars in Lebanon. The 1958 agreement only arranged for the creation of a coalition cabinet consisting of two government and two opposition leaders; two members of the new cabinet would be Muslim and two members would be Christian. This treaty was backed by fourteen thousand U.S. troops who were stationed on the ground to ensure that fighting stopped. The 1976 Lebanese agreement was similarly weak; it only dealt with "the military and security aspects of the civil war and made no reference to the political and religious differences between the opposing Lebanese factions." This "weak" treaty was underwritten by an exceptionally strong Arab "deterrent" force.

The three remaining cases with outside guarantees fall somewhere in between these two extremes. Nicaragua (1989), Zimbabwe (1979), and the Dominican Republic (1965) all had extensive political and military power-sharing arrangements, and all were underwritten by moderate guarantees. Nicaragua's August 1989 Election Agreement called for free and open democratic elections and promised to create twenty-three self-governing development zones that the Contras could occupy and police on their own. These zones comprised 20 percent of the country. Numerous arrangements were also made to ensure the safest possible demobilization. Demobilization was asserted to be voluntary, and Contras who did not wish to participate would allegedly not be disturbed. Those who did decide to demobilize could gather at five security zones that would be controlled by ONUCA (United Nations Group in Central America); all Sandinista security forces would be withdrawn from within twenty kilometers of these areas. In return, the Sandinistas were offered an important military concession. After losing the election to Violeta Chamorro, leader of the opposition, Daniel Ortega was allowed to retain his position as commander-in-chief of a re-formed army. This promised to safeguard the Sandinistas against renewed Contra attack. These fairly extensive internal security arrangements were then supplemented by 260 unarmed UN peacekeepers and 800 armed Venezuelan paratroopers.

Zimbabwe had a similar mix of internal and external security arrangements. Black Zimbabweans were offered one-man, one-vote elections in a country where they represented 97 percent of the population. In addition, Rhodesian civilians would be required to surrender their vast private armory of weapons, certain Rhodesian military and paramilitary units would be disbanded, a new civil police would be formed, and white South African forces currently stationed in Rhodesia would not be allowed to interfere in the transition. Finally, assembly points for demobilizing Patriotic Front soldiers would be located near their operation areas and far away from the Rhodesian army bases. This meant that many assembly areas would be located near Mozambique and Zambian borders and thus offer a quick escape should the assembled soldiers be attacked. In return, white Rhodesians were guaranteed 20 percent of the seats in the lower house of Parliament, they were allowed to retain control over the Rhodesian air force, and South

African forces were allowed to remain on Zimbabwean soil. Most importantly, however, these white settlers were permitted to retain dual citizenship with Britain, which offered them their own quick escape should they themselves be threatened. Despite these assurances, the Patriotic Front still only signed the Lancaster House Agreement after Britain agreed to send twelve hundred Commonwealth forces to Zimbabwe and agreed to station them there until the new government was established.

In short, a durable settlement, one that will last even after outside forces withdraw, requires more than temporary police protection. Outside forces are necessary to get the opponents through the tricky transition period, but an effective long-term equilibrium must also be established. Governments and rebels were very concerned with specific power-sharing arrangements during negotiations, although these were not the decisive issues over which negotiations hung. Adversaries were able to enhance their own sense of security through a number of explicit treaty provisions (such as constitutional guarantees, legal protections, and well-balanced security designs). It is important to remember, however, that even the most extensive internal arrangements were not enough to completely alleviate the otherwise intense security dilemma. The Nigerian government promised the Ibos general amnesty, offered them a fair share of employment in federal public services, and promised that police units in Ibo areas would consist mostly of persons of Ibo origin, but this did little to reduce Ibo fear of postwar persecution. Without an external guarantor, this offer had little impact on negotiations, and it eventually failed to produce a settlement. No matter how brutal the war or how generous the terms, the two sides could not succeed on their own. . . .

## IMPLICATIONS

Although even the best quantitative research is never sufficient to make decisions in complex, real-world situations, the findings presented in this article could offer important guidelines to policymakers searching for effective ways to help end civil wars.

First, and most importantly, the only type of peacekeeping that appears to help end a war is that which is backed by a promise to use force. Observers or unarmed peacekeepers with no military backup will have little positive effect on either negotiations or treaty implementation. In fact, these "traditional" peacekeepers will most likely be placed in unstable situations prone to spiral back into violence. Even in the most promising situation—for example, when belligerents have signed a detailed peace agreement—the war will most likely resume, and unarmed peacekeepers will suffer.

Second, if a state wishes to limit its involvement or share responsibility by working through a multilateral organization, it will be much more difficult to make a credible commitment to enforce the settlement, and this type of involvement will more likely fail to foster an agreement. A guarantee will only be as effective as the political will of its backers. Thus, any hesitation or wavering by member states will signal irresolution to the already anxious adversaries and ultimately undermine enforcement operations.

Third, the historical record also indicates that successful guarantors should be willing to stay through the establishment of the new government and a new national army. Intervention will have little effect on facilitating a long-term settlement if a state remains involved only through the signing of a peace treaty. If a state ends its involvement prematurely, it cannot perform the necessary function of enforcing the treaty, and the settlement will fall apart. Negotiations should be viewed as the beginning of the peace process, not the end.

Fourth, strict neutrality by the third party also does not appear necessary. The outside guarantor in most cases was not a wholly unbiased participant, yet this did not seem to reduce their effectiveness. In fact, the Zimbabwe case suggests that when an enormous power disparity exists between the adversaries, a somewhat biased third party in favor of the minority group can actually enhance feelings of security. The fact that Britain was viewed as prejudiced in favor of the white Rhodesians seems to have increased white confidence in their own survival.

Another surprising finding was the negative effect disarmament had on adversaries' sense of security. Rather than reassure former adversaries that they would not be attacked during the transition period, the demand to disarm actually increased their fear of attack. In most cases, adversaries had no illusions about their former enemy's ability to hide or procure weapons if they so chose. Allowing each side to retain observable weapons enhanced their feelings of security and made them more likely to follow through with treaty promises.

Sixth, a striking implication of this study is that alternatives do exist to prolonged and extensive intervention; under certain conditions, outside states can avoid committing large numbers of forces to a foreign country and still facilitate cooperation. Fewer enforcement troops will be needed if extensive internal power-sharing arrangements have been designed and all parties are guaranteed an effective voice in the new government. If, however, one side can easily be shut out of power (as might happen in winner-take-all elections or peace treaties that leave future political arrangements vague or undefined), a stronger force will be required for such settlements to succeed. In short, limited security guarantees can be offset by more detailed internal arrangements, but even the most detailed political plans will require at least some type of outside guarantee.

Finally, two additional points should be emphasized. First, security guarantees are a necessary, not a sufficient condition for settlement. Guarantees in the face of an ongoing war where the combatants have no desire to negotiate are unlikely to succeed. States wishing to facilitate early solutions to civil wars must wait until the groups themselves desire peace before their promises of enforcement will have any positive effect. Second, one should keep in mind that negotiated settlements are not always the least costly solutions to civil wars since the rapid victory of one side over another can bring fewer casualties and longer peace over the long run. Nonetheless, some battles are clearly worth fighting for, as Lincoln's struggle against the U.S. South attests. In short, settlements do have the potential to put an end to enormous suffering, and negotiation sends an important message to the Milosevics of the world that internal aggression will not always be ignored by the international community. Moreover, compromise settlements offer a chance to institute multiparty democratic states in situations that might otherwise result in one-party authoritarian regimes. Negotiations during times of civil war, therefore, could be viewed as moments of great opportunity rather than as futile attempts to create collaborative regimes.

History, therefore, offers good and bad news to the international community. The good news is that outside intervention can end potentially bloody civil wars provided the intervening state is committed to guaranteeing the peace treaty and the two warring parties are in favor of a settlement. The bad news is that nonmilitary intervention, although politically more acceptable and financially less costly, is unlikely to accomplish much. It may provide a temporary solution, but it does not address the more fundamental issue of insecurity. It may stay the bloodshed temporarily, but, by definition, such intervention cannot enforce a peace, since maintaining any settlement and rebuilding a stable community occur only after a war is over. Outside powers can play a critical role in the resolution of civil wars, but only if they are willing to make a solid commitment and bear the necessary costs.

## NOTES

1. Even mandatory force reductions usually included international peace treaties do not leave the adversaries defenseless.

2. "Dean Acheson's July 30, 1949, Letter of Transmittal to President Truman, *The China White Paper,* Department of State Publications 3573," Far Eastern Series 30 (Stanford: Stanford University Press, 1949), xv.

3. This is not to say that outside guarantees can end a war that the combatants have no desire to end. If continued fighting is more favorable than the terms of any possible peace settlement, an outside guarantee will not alter the cost and benefits enough to convince the opponents to cooperate. Outside guarantees will only be effective in cases where the adversaries are themselves seeking an alternative to continued war.

4. It should be emphasized that this analysis is based on the universe of *all* cases of civil wars between 1940 and 1990 and that, because of this, tests of statistical significance might be deemed inappropriate. In other words, one could ask why—if we are looking at the entire universe of nontrivial civil wars and not a sample of them—we should use a statistical test of significance to arbitrarily separate valid hypotheses from the rest? I have chosen to include statistical significance criteria because the inexact nature of the coding process and the limited time period suggest that not all inferences from the data will be wholly accurate. Since there is no way of estimating any possible errors in the data, I include conventional tests of statistical significance as a reasonable measure of the validity of each of the hypotheses.

5. These tests were also repeated using a multivariate logit regression. This analysis generally supported the conclusions of this article, however, the small number of cases caused problems with the logit estimating procedure. Specifically, the strong correlation between guarantees and successful settlement created a null set (there were no cases where security guarantees were offered and the settlement failed), which the logit estimating procedure had difficulty incorporating. Details of this analysis, therefore, were excluded from this article.

6. Colombia's Conservative and Liberal parties also settled their differences using a very rigid and unique power-sharing arrangement. Their agreement called for a 50-50 division of political positions and an alternating presidency. Each party knew exactly how much political power they would receive. This also enhanced their sense of future security.

7. Interview with Mugabe ca. 11–14 May 1977, in Goswin Baumhoegger 1984, *The Struggle for Independence: Documents on the Recent Development of Zimbabwe (1975–1980)*. Vol. 3, 328. (Hamburg: Institute of African Studies).

# 29

---

# The Changing Face of Terror

## WALTER LAQUEUR

Over the centuries, terrorism has appeared in many guises. It is not an ideology or a political doctrine, but rather a method—the substate application of violence or the threat of violence to sow panic and bring about political change. Although it has rarely been absent from history, it has been more common in some ages and some civilizations than in others.

Those who try to understand terrorism in terms of the causes particular terrorists happen to support are bound to be baffled by the frequent and often extreme changes that have taken place in terrorists' political orientation over the years. Throughout the nineteenth and early twentieth centuries, terrorism came predominantly from the left, from anarchists and social revolutionaries, as well from nationalist separatists (as in Ireland). But during the interwar years, the main perpetrators of terrorism were on the extreme right and frequently had fascist sympathies.

Little or no terrorism erupted during World War II or its immediate aftermath, although there was a great deal of guerrilla warfare, which is something quite different. Then, in the late 1960s and 1970s, came a sudden upsurge of left-wing terrorism in Europe, Latin America, and elsewhere. This sudden resurgence had an unfortunate impact on terrorism studies, a field that emerged at about the same time. The news media, along with some in the academy, tended to take the slogans of contemporary terrorists at face value while ignoring terrorism's lengthy history. This led them to see terrorism as a new and unprecedented phenomenon, something that was essentially a response to injustice. If political, social, and economic justice could be achieved, the argument ran, there would be no terrorism, and so the way to deal with it was to address its "root causes": the grievances, stresses, and frustrations that lay behind the violence. Seen in this light, terrorists were fanatical believers driven to despair by intolerable conditions. They were poor and oppressed, or at least on the side of the poor and oppressed, and their inspiration was deeply ideological.

Left-wing terrorism also had a certain influence at this time on nationalist terrorism. The doctrine and the slogans of organizations such as the Basque separatist group ETA, sections of the Irish Republican Army, and the various Popular Fronts for the Liberation of Palestine clearly showed the impact of Marxism-Leninism. Subsequent events, however, would reveal that this ideological patina was merely a reflection of the zeitgeist, did not go very deep or last long, and hardly affected the staunch nationalism at these movements' cores.

Left-wing terrorism lasted for about a decade and then petered out or was suppressed, in Germany and Italy, Uruguay and Argentina—and in the United States. It was followed by a wave of terrorism that came from the extreme right, including attacks on refugees in various European countries and the rise of neofascist groups in Italy and elsewhere. Left-wing terrorist cells did not totally disappear, but they were no longer in the front rank.

Those who had sympathized with what they thought were the justified grievances behind terrorism found themselves in a quandary. The most devastating act of terrorism in American history before the attacks of September 11, for example, was carried out in 1995 in Oklahoma City. No one could deny that Timothy McVeigh had deeply felt grievances, but they were hardly the type with which people on the left wanted to sympathize. They were the grievances of *The Turner Diaries,* of America taken over by foreigners and degenerates, of the holy duty of all patriots to cleanse the country in a river of blood—in short, the worldview of a virulent form of fascism.

McVeigh was not unique, moreover. Similar descriptions could apply to the murderers of Anwar al-Sadat, Yitzhak Rabin, and Mohandas Gandhi. Their assassins belonged to fanatical nationalist and right-wing undergrounds firmly convinced that they were doing their patriotic duty by liquidating traitors. These terrorists could hardly be said to be engaging in "revolutionary violence," nor could poverty, oppression, or free-floating rage help to explain the torching of asylum-seekers' homes in Germany or the unspeakable atrocities perpetrated by Islamist terrorists in Algeria, where they were fighting not colonial rulers but their own compatriots.

## THE NEW VULNERABILITY

Over the last two decades, changes in targets, weapons, and motives combined to make terrorists more dangerous than ever before. As the result of technical progress, developed societies became more vulnerable to attack. (So have the megacities of the developing world, for that matter, but the political repercussions of that vulnerability may take longer to unfold.) Traditional terrorist weapons such as explosives, meanwhile, became more lethal and efficient, and the technology and skills needed to make weapons of mass destruction diffused throughout the world. At the same time, there was also an upsurge of religious fundamentalism in many parts of the globe, and at the margins of this movement radical groups appeared that were prepared to engage in terrorist attacks.

This trend toward increased vulnerability was occurring even before the Internet sped it along. Until the middle of the nineteenth century, a group of people who wanted to kill their enemies had to go quite literally from house to house in order to locate and assassinate their victims. Whole cities could not be paralyzed until after the introduction of power plants, centralized water supplies, and other technical developments resulting in the centralization of services. It is true that even in the 1840s some philosophers of the bomb had already foreseen weapons of mass destruction. Karl Heinzen, a fiery if somewhat unbalanced German revolutionary, envisaged the use of poison gas, not to mention ballistic missiles. But at the time this was no more than terrorist science fiction. He and his followers did not pursue this course of action, and Heinzen went on to a more peaceable career as an editor of German-language newspapers in Louisville, Kentucky, and then Boston.

Many considered the invention of dynamite by Alfred Nobel several decades later to be a turning point in the history of terrorism. But the early bombs were still heavy, bulky, and dangerous to construct, and only with the miniaturization of explosives in the twentieth century did it become possible to launch terrorist bomb attacks on a large scale. Similarly, with the invention of the airplane, another dimension of terrorist attacks materialized, and even before World War I Russian revolutionaries were considering airplanes' terrorist potential, while Irish radicals were contemplating the submarine in similar terms. Both ideas were premature, however, and it would take decades for these fantasies to become realistic possibilities.

Traditional terrorists, whether left-wing, right-wing, or nationalist-separatist, were not greatly drawn to these opportunities for greater destruction. One reason was scruples. A hundred years ago, terrorists often would desist from an attack if their victim happened to be accompanied by family members or if there was a danger that innocents would be killed. Terrorism has become far more brutal and indiscriminate since then, and the terrorists of the second half of the twentieth century managed to persuade themselves that there were no innocents and that indiscriminate murder was permissible if it served the political aim. But even they tended to hesitate before carrying out true mass murder, partly because of the risk of a backlash against their cause, and partly because such actions were alien to their traditions and would repel their own supporters. They hated their enemies, but they had not been totally blinded by their hate. For the radical religious practitioners of the new terrorism, however, murder and destruction of an unprecedented scale did not pose much of a problem.

## THE NEW TERRORISTS

Recent years have witnessed a growth of radical groups on the fringe of several religions. No one has yet fully determined why such processes should take place. In the Muslim world this development may have been connected with the declining attraction of other radical ideologies such as fascism and communism. But the trend was not limited to Islam. It could be found, for example, among certain millenarian Christian sects. As the century drew to a close, these latter groups caused security officers in various places to worry about attacks in conjunction with the turn of the new millennium. Much to the officers' relief, such attacks did not materialize. But the fear had not been unjustified, for it is only one step from believing that the world is deeply corrupt and sinful, and that only massive destruction in a final battle between good and evil will bring about redemption, to deciding to take an active hand in catalyzing the process. Among small extremist Jewish groups in Israel, in fact, could be found the same belief in a final battle between the forces of good and evil (Gog and Magog), and some even thought that acts such as the destruction of the Muslim shrines on the Temple Mount would give history a little push.

Radical religious groups have been particularly strong and particularly prone to turn violent in the Muslim world. Scanning the present world map of terrorism shows that Muslim states or Muslim minorities are involved in almost 90 percent of all substate terrorist conflicts, from the Philippines to the Middle East, from Nigeria to the Balkans. This has not always been the case, nor is there reason to believe that it will always remain so, but about the present state of affairs there can be no two opinions. Other, non-Muslim terrorist groups are continuing the struggles in which they have been engaged, such as those in Ireland, in the Basque country, in Greece, and in Sri Lanka. But these terrorists are relatively small, localized, and unimportant in comparison with the terrorism of radical Islamist groups.

How to explain this upsurge of terrorist violence? It has been argued that wherever Muslims live they have been the subject of oppression and persecution and that terrorism is the natural response to such conditions. This might have been a persuasive explanation prior to World War I, or even World War II, when only a handful of independent Islamic states existed. There are still a few Muslim minorities in the world that have not yet achieved autonomy or independence, but this is true for many non-Muslim minorities as well. Since 1948, many dozens of Muslim states have come into being and the great majority of Muslims now live in states of their own; if there is oppression, it is mainly by their own kind.

Can the frequency of violence be explained as the result of a "clash of civilization"? No, because the bloodiest conflicts have occurred not between Muslim groupos or states and the West but within the Muslim world itself. This holds true for both interstate conflicts (such as the Iran-Iraq War and the Iraqi invasion of Kuwait) as well as intrastate conflict (such as the terrorism of the Algerian Islamists against their fellow citizens, as a result of which some 70,000 people are believed to have been killed). It applies also to the persecution of the Kurds, as well as to the civil war in Afghanistan. It applies to the many assassination attempts, successful and unsuccessful, against Arab and Muslim leaders.

This pattern of events has led to speculation about the possibility of some particularly aggressive element in Islam that inspires terrorism, and it is not difficult to point to various historical examples, such as the notorious sect of the Assassins. Yet although there was Muslim terrorism in the age of imperialism in both India and Egypt, these instances were rare, terrorism was never in the mainstream, and the inspiration was probably more nationalistic than religious.

The recent rise of Islamist radicalism can more usefully be explained as the result of the decline of other political doctrines and the emergence of an intellectual and spiritual vacuum waiting to be filled. Here the adoption of Islamist doctrine by once-Marxist Arab intellectuals is most illuminating. During the 1990s, Horst Mahler, a former leading member and ideologist of the Baader-Meinhof Gang, Germany's left-wing terrorist group, became a spokesperson for extreme right-wing views. There were many Mahlers in the Middle East. This change in the zeitgeist led to a rejection of the Western way of life and Western values, a revolt against modernity in general, and, in extreme cases, a call for *jihad,* or holy war.

Similar trends were by no means wholly unknown to Western civilization. The concept of a crusade, after all, is not Islamic: Christianity has also carried out holy wars. European fascism was also a revolt against the West, the Enlightenment, and humanism, and illuminating parallels can be discovered by comparing certain European fascist movements (for instance, those in Romania and the early Falange in Spain) with the radical Islamists. The Romanian and Spanish fascist movements were mystical and religious in inspiration, in contrast to Nazi Germany and fascist Italy, and their attitudes toward martyrdom and death were similar to that of the radical Islamists. But in Europe the idea of crusades went out of fashion many centuries ago and the clerical-fascist cult has also disappeared, whereas in the Muslim world the concept of *jihad* has had a revival. In other places the general trend has been toward multiculturalism and the coexistence of religions, but this has not been the case in the contemporary Muslim world.

## IDEAS AND POLITICS

Still, the connection between this radical fundamentalist revival and terrorism is not as straightforward as it might appear. Islamist fundamentalism comes in a variety of forms and is often quietist. Saudi Arabia finances Islamist activities in scores of countries, benefiting mosques and cultural institutions that serve as recruiting ground for the terrorists, but the Saudis do not allow any such activities within their own country. One of the guiding lights of modern Islamist radicalism, the Egyptian dissident Sayyid Qutb, argued that existing Arab regimes should be overthrown first because only then would a *jihad* be successful. Some of Qutb's disciples continued the struggle in the spirit of their master, but other militants established a different order of priorities, directing their attacks at the unbelievers of the West instead.

Furthermore, it is unclear whether the upsurge of terrorism can be explained mainly, let alone exclusively, by the history of ideas. In all probability it has as much to do with Muslims' feelings of frustration with their own countries' recent track records, compared to both West and East. These non-Muslim regions have made considerable economic progress, whereas the countries of the Middle East have generally stagnated or shown negative growth. This stagnation has resulted in growing poverty and unemployment, increased numbers of educated young people who have not found jobs in their professions, and growing resentment against those who have been more successful. It has also produced a wish to blame foreigners for the misery—self-criticism being too painful and too dangerous.

The frustration also stems from the lack of progress in much of the Muslim world toward anything resembling democratic institutions. The demand for political democracy may not be overwhelming: according to public-opinion polls only about 10 percent of respondents favor a political system of this kind. But little freedom exists even on the local level, and even Arab critics have conceded the lamentable state of affairs on the cultural and intellectual scene. More important yet, militarily these societies have not been able to assert themselves (witness the repeated defeat of Pakistan by India, the victories of Israel over its Arab neighbors). All these frustrations have created a climate that acts as a breeding ground for terrorist activities. To what extent the prevailing ideology that developed in response to this unhappy state of affairs is radical Islamist, nationalist, or a mixture of the two may be difficult to establish, and generalizations are impossible because the situation varies from place to place and from time to time. But what is common is the feeling that the misery must have been caused by an outside enemy, and hence a resentment and a hate not felt in countries that have made progress.

## KNOW THINE ENEMY

The new terrorism is a fanaticism that expresses itself in, among other things, suicide bombing and the willingness to cause indiscriminate slaughter. In contrast to widespread belief, however, suicide bombing is not a recent phenomenon. On the contrary, until fairly recently terrorism was more or less synonymous with a suicide mission. The main weapon of the attack was the dagger, and unless the victim could be found alone and defenseless, the *sicarii* of Jewish history and the Assassins of Muslim history were unlikely to return from their missions. This was true even for much of the nineteenth century, as the makeshift bombs of the anarchists and the Russian revolutionaries were so unstable that they had to be thrown from a short distance (that is, if they did not explode first in the hands of the attacker). Those who went on an attack of this kind were fully aware of the risk, and many of them wrote farewell letters to their friends and families. Only with the advent of more sophisticated weapons in the twentieth century and the growing conviction among terrorists that it was permissible to kill the innocent did terrorism become less risky.

Even in our age, suicide bombing has by no means been limited to terrorists in Islamic countries. It has been a favorite form of attack by the Liberation Tigers of Tamil Eelam in Sri Lanka, members of which have carried out some 180 such attacks over the years in their country and in India. (The former Indian prime minister Rajiv Gandhi was one of their victims.) In Sri Lanka, the total number of Tamils—who are not Muslim and are not religiously motivated—is only a few million, and their per capita rate of suicide terrorists is thus far higher than that among either Muslims or Arabs. And suicide bombing has occurred, albeit on a smaller scale, in many terrorist movements during the last decade.

Muslim suicide bombers have tended to be young and deeply indoctrinated, led to believe that it is their duty to make the ultimate sacrifice for their group, country, or religion and that a far more enjoyable form of existence awaits them in the hereafter. But the world has also experienced many secular terrorist bombers who had no paradise awaiting them, such as the 4,000 young Japanese who volunteered for kamikaze actions at the end of World War II and the members of elite German SS units asked to undertake suicide missions when the Nazi war effort was approaching final defeat.

It is easier to trace the psychological and cultural sources of terrorist suicide missions than to trace the phenomenon of fanaticism that plays such a central role in the new terrorism. Fanaticism has existed in every civilization and at almost all times, but it has not necessarily expressed itself in terrorist action. At present, fanaticism can be found far more often in certain societies and cultures than in others, and psychiatry has not been of much help in explaining this phenomenon. Psychiatrists have shied away from confronting this subject, doubting whether it was part of their discipline; criminologists have been reluctant to discuss evil, for even if it is real it is a theological concept rather than a social science one. Madness, especially paranoia, plays a role in contemporary terrorism. Not all paranoiacs are terrorists, but all terrorists believe in conspiracies by powerful, hostile forces and suffer from some form of delusion and persecution mania.

Although a disturbed childhood and other forms of deprivation can explain the mind-set of some violent criminals, this profile by no means fits most serial murderers. Similarly, it is a hopeless exercise to try to explain terrorists, individually or collectively, wholly in social categories such as national or social oppression, messianic belief, or protest against injustice. In the bloodiest terrorist campaigns the element of crime and madness plays an important role, even if many are reluctant to acknowledge it.

## WHAT COMES NEXT

Some terrorist campaigns have lasted longer than others, but all have come sooner or later to an end, and the present one will be no exception. Radical Islamist groups are in the forefront of terrorism today, but this is unlikely to remain the case forever. . . .

Are weapons of mass destruction likely to be used soon, and if so by whom? This depends, in part, on the success of the present operations against those responsible for the attacks of September 11 and those responsible for the anthrax mailings. If the operations succeed, terrorist movements—although not all individuals or small groups, whose behavior is unpredictable—will think twice before using nuclear, biological, or chemical weapons in a major way. The recent attacks, moreover, have shown that even conventional weapons can have devastating results if used creatively. Still, we know that the use of weapons of mass destruction has been contemplated by certain radical terrorist groups, and that the barrier to using biological weapons has been broken, and so preparations for such eventualities are imperative. . . .

No society can protect all its members from terrorist attack, but all societies can reduce the risk by taking the offensive, by keeping terrorists on the run rather than concentrating on defense alone. Terrorism in previous periods of history was little more than a nuisance, but as a result of the technological and other trends mentioned above, the danger is now much greater. In past ages, state and society could face terrorists with some equanimity. If one plane was hijacked, all others continued to fly; if one bank was robbed, all others continued to function; if one politician was killed, others were only too willing to take his place. But in an age of weapons of mass destruction this is no longer the case; even one attack can be overwhelmingly devastating.

It is difficult to imagine a world without terrorism in the foreseeable future, for it would imply a world without conflict and tension. . . . Even if the political and religious orientation of terrorists changes, the capacity to inflict unacceptable damage will not. For this reason, one must conclude that the world is now entering a new phase in its history, more dangerous than any before.

# 30

---

# Lessons from Fighting
# Terrorism in Southern Asia

BRAHMA CHELLANEY

## TERRORISM IN SOUTHERN ASIA

Facing mounting terrorist violence, Asia already accounts for 75 percent of all terrorism casualties worldwide. With the world's fastest-growing markets, fastest-rising military expenditures, and most serious hot spots . . . , Asia holds the key to the future global order. Much of Asia's terrorist violence is concentrated in its southern belt, which in the past decade emerged as the international hub of terrorism. This southern part of Asia, encompassing Afghanistan, Pakistan, Uzbekistan, Tajikistan, Chinese-ruled Xinjiang and Tibet, India, Nepal, Sri Lanka, Bangladesh, and Burma, is wracked by terrorist, insurgent, and separatist violence in a manner unmatched elsewhere in the world. The number of annual fatalities in terrorist-related violence in southern Asia far exceeds the death toll in the Middle East, the traditional cradle of terrorism. To be sure, the entire expanse from the Middle East to Southeast Asia is home to militant groups and troubled by terrorist violence, posing a serious challenge to international and regional security. The radicalization of Muslims in Southeast Asia, where Islamist groups are becoming increasingly entrenched, is, however, a more recent phenomenon.

The spread of militancy and terrorism in southern Asia is linked to the Afghan war of the 1980s and the U.S. and Saudi funneling of arms to the anti-Soviet guerrillas through Pakistan's Inter-Services Intelligence (ISI) agency. The Afghan war veterans have come to haunt the security of India, the United States, and several Muslim states. Many returned to their homelands to wage terror campaigns against governments they viewed as tainted by Western influence. Egyptian President Anwar Sadat's assassination, for example, was linked to such terror. Large portions of the multibillion-dollar military aid given to the anti-Soviet Afghan rebels by the U.S. Central Intelligence Agency (CIA) was siphoned off by the conduit—the ISI—to ignite a bloody insurgency in Indian Kashmir after the ISI failed to trigger an uprising in India's Punjab state despite arming Sikh dissidents beginning in the early 1980s.

Substantial quantities of U.S.-supplied weapons, in what was the largest covert operation in the CIA's history, also found their way into the Pakistani black market, promoting a *jihad* culture within Pakistan and spreading illicit arms and militancy from Egypt to the Philippines. Afghan war veterans, or elements associated with them, were held responsible for terrorist attacks on several U.S. targets in the 1990s, including the 1998 bombings outside the American embassies in Nairobi and Dar al-Salam; the 1996 truck bombing of the Khobar Towers, a high-rise compound that housed the 2,000 U.S. military personnel assigned to the King Abdul Aziz Air Base in Saudi Arabia; the 1995 bombing of a U.S.-run military compound in Riyadh; the first World Trade Center bombing in 1993; and the ambush killing of two CIA officials outside the agency's headquarters in Langley, Virginia, also in 1993.

But the greatest impact of the cross-border movement of Afghan war veterans and illegal arms was felt in southern Asia, with India bearing the brunt of the unintended consequences of the foreign interventions in Afghanistan from 1979 to 1989. Terrorism has become a way of life in some areas of southern Asia. The only thriving democracy in this vast region is India, wedged in an arc of authoritarian or totalitarian regimes engaged in covert actions in breach of international law. These regimes either export narcotics and terrorism (Afghanistan, Pakistan, and Burma) or make illicit transfers of nuclear and missile technologies (China). Pakistan indeed has been "waging a war by proxy in Indian-held Kashmir through Islamic militants." The future of the international campaign against terrorism hinges on success in this region to root out terrorist networks and deter regimes from encouraging or harboring armed extremists.

India, in fact, is a sort of laboratory where major acts of terror are first tried out before being replicated in democracies in the West. The logic is that if India, the world's largest democracy, can be shaken, so can other democracies. For example, the 1988 Pan Am 103 bombing over Lockerbie, Scotland, replicated the midair bombing over the Atlantic of an Air-India commercial flight from Canada in 1985. Similarly, the 1993 World Trade Center attack was modeled on the bombings weeks earlier that killed hundreds of people inside high-rise buildings in Bombay in a terror campaign designed to disrupt India's financial market. Parallels also have emerged between the 1999 hijacking to Kandahar of Indian Airlines flight IC-814 and the September 11, 2001, suicide hijackings, including the similar use of box-cutters and the terrorists' knowledge of cockpit systems. . . .

## STEMMING TRANSNATIONAL TERRORISM

. . . Success demands that the United States heed the lessons of the past. The first of these lessions is the need to keep the focus on longer-term goals and not be carried away by political expediency and narrow military objectives. By focusing on immediate goals, U.S. policymakers in the past ended up creating monsters that they now have to fight. The Reagan Doctrine of arming anticommunist "freedom fighters" in places such as Afghanistan, Angola, Cambodia, and Nicaragua put an ideological stamp on a strategic-policy shift that "defined Third World insurgencies and revolutionary governments as the source of the most serious 'future security threats' to the United States."[2] . . .

By funneling billions of dollars worth of arms—including sophisticated surface-to-air missiles, tanks, and howitzer guns—through conduit states and their agencies, the United States allowed the latter to bring into play their own interests, biases, and rivalries. Pakistan, for example, used its participation in the largest-ever U.S. covert operation not so much to rout the Soviet forces in Afghanistan as to strengthen its military position against India and to favor Afghan guerrilla groups based on Peshawar (such as Gulbuddin Hekmatyar's Hezb-e-Islami) rather than assist groups engaged in combat inside Afghanistan. Pakistan could push its own agenda because the United States accepted its condition that the ISI agency control the weapons flow and pinpoint the arms recipients. However, the "ISI appropriated for its own purposes an estimated 50% to 70% of the military resources intended for the *mujahideen*. . . . The diversions were known at the time within the region and within the United States but were accepted as an unpleasant but necessary element of the aid program without an alternative conduit for aid."[3]

. . . This large-scale flow of arms . . . destablized the affected regions (including southern Asia but particularly Pakistan) and created the Frankensteins that have come to haunt Western security. Hekmatyar, fattened by the ISI at the expense of U.S. taxpayers, was responsible more than anyone else in blocking a peaceful transition to post-Soviet rule in Afghanistan. Another Frankenstein, Osama bin Laden, was unsuspectingly endorsed by the CIA during the 1980s' Afghan war. And in response to his subsequent terrorist exploits of the 1990s, Washington has done precisely what bin Laden himself did—it "mythologized him," turning him into a hero for Muslim radicals across the globe. It was at a White House ceremony attended by some "holy warriors" from Afghanistan in the mid-1980s that President Ronald Reagan proclaimed *mujahideen* such as bin Laden as the "moral equivalent of the Founding Fathers" of the United States. One such moral equivalent, Mullah Mohammed Omar, the Taliban chief, gave vent to his destructive genius in the spring of 2001 by demolishing Afghanistan's most famous antiquities, including two towering, 1,500-year-old Buddhas carved into a sandstone cliff at Bamiyan—the priceless legacy of Indian Buddhist pilgrims who settled in the region before the advent of Islam. . . .

A second lesson is that the problem of and solution to terrorism are linked. Terrorism not only threatens the free, secular world but also springs from the rejection of democracy and secularism. The terrorism-breeding swamps can never be fully drained as long as the societies that rear or tolerate them are not de-radicalized and democratized. It has become fashionable to state that because war runs on expediency, with strange bedfellows involved as partners, it makes sense for the United States to line up in the antiterror campaign even unsavory allies—regimes that bankroll militant Islamic fundamentalism overseas, such as those of Saudi Arabia and the United Arab Emirates; the tyrannical Central Asian autocracies run by Soviet holdovers; and military-ruled, terrorism-exporting Pakistan. After all, to get rid of Nazism, the allies needed Stalin. But Stalin did not create Hitler or foster Nazism; nor was Stalin's removal necessary to eradicate Nazism. The antiterror war can succeed only through the reform of states that directly or indirectly contribute to the rise of virulent Islamic fundamentalism extolling violence as a sanctified religious tool.

Saudi Arabia, with its one-century-old political tradition of Wahhabi Islam, practices the "fringe form of Islamic extremism" that President Bush says he is targeting. Pakistan, too, is heavily under the influence of the Wahhabi religious movement, "the source of modern Islamic fundamentalism."[4] So critical has Saudi Arabia been to U.S. energy and regional interests that at no time did Washington seek to restrain its cloistered rulers from funding the establishment of Muslim extremist groups and *madrasas*. From Africa to Southeast Asia, Saudi petrodollars have played a key role in fomenting militant Islamic fundamentalism that regards the West, Israel, and India as its enemies. Only after the role of Saudi suicide hijackers came to light has realization dawned about the thin line separating philanthropy and advocacy of militant fundamentalism.

In many Islamic nations, the United States has worked with the rulers and forgotten the ruled. This top-level focus, from the Gulf to Pakistan, breeds its own problems. Not only does it add to the already wide gap between the rulers and the ruled, but it encourages "street" sentiment to motivate those seeking to wreak vengeance on the United States for propping up the totalitarian rulers as part of an alleged scheme to make the Muslim world subservient to the Christian West.

A third lesson to heed is not to turn the war against terrorism into an ideological battle to serve one's strategic interests. The dangers of adding religious overtones to the fight have been understood well, but not the perils of putting an ideological gloss to it. The first war of the twenty-first century is already being likened to the last war of the twentieth century—the fight against communism—with some commentators suggesting that it will take a new Cold War to defeat terrorism.

From spearheading the fight against communism to leading the war on terrorism, the United States has come full circle. About five decades after President Harry Truman declared that the United States was in a war to protect freedom from communism, Bush proclaimed that it is in war to defend freedom from terrorism. The Cold War emphasis on the containment of communism finds its echo in the new stress on the containment of terrorism. And just as human rights and democracy became secondary to the Cold War imperative of roping in allies, however dictatorial their political setup, there is similar indifference to the record of the new-war partners. It should not be forgotten, however, that terrorism springs from religious extremism, which in turn flows from the rejection of secularism and abrogation of human rights. Democratic societies in general do not breed and shelter international terrorists.

Terrorism can be stemmed only through concerted, sustained international effort, not by employing Cold War–style methods. In any case, the Cold War was won by the West not so much by military means as by spreading market capitalism to other regions that "helped suck the lifeblood out of communism's global appeal," making it incapable of meeting the widespread yearning for a better life. Not only does a new Cold War not fit well with the interests of the only superpower on the world stage with no peer competitor in sight, but it could also prolong the fight against terrorism by deepening the problem. Rather than make the fight divisive, the international consensus on battling terrorism should be preserved and strengthened. This is especially so because critics charge that the United States, having been born in war and having waged war ever since, was uncomfortable without a foe after the end of the Cold War—that is, it was in search of an enemy. Now that the United States has a resilient foe to battle—another "ism"—it should behave as the leader of the world, not of one camp or as a self-absorbed bully. The outcome of this war will determine the security of all free societies. But in the interim the world, disturbingly, seems to be becoming harder, fiercer, and less tolerant.

## NOTES

1. Olivier Roy, "Why War Is Going on in Afghanistan: The Afghan Crisis in Perspective," *Journal of International Affairs,* Vol. 5, No. 4 (December 2000–February 2001), p. 11.
2. Lucy J. Mathiak, "American Jihad: The Reagan Doctrine as Policy and Practice," Ph.D. dissertation, University of Wisconsin–Madison, May 2000, p. 8.
3. Lucy J. Mathiak and Lora Lumpe, "Government Gun-Running to Guerrillas," in Lumpe, ed., *Running Guns: The Global Black Market in Small Arms* (Oslo: Zed Books/ International Peace Research Institute, 2000), p. 61.
4. William Pfaff, "A Strange Alliance with Saudi and Pakistani Foes of Modernity," *International Herald Tribune,* October 1, 2001, p. 8.

# 31

---

# America's Achilles' Heel: Nuclear, Biological, and Chemical Terrorism and Covert Attack

RICHARD A. FALKENRATH, ROBERT D. NEWMAN,

AND BRADLEY A. THAYER

The infrequency of NBC (Nuclear, Biological, Chemical) violence in the past cannot be explained solely, or even principally, by the technical difficulty of obtaining or using weapons of mass destruction. Many states, some non-state actors, and perhaps even a few individuals have had NBC weapons within their reach. Only a handful, however, have taken the fateful steps of acquisition and use. The reasons for this are primarily pragmatic. Potential aggressors undertake some sort of risk calculation when they consider using weapons of mass destruction. They may weigh the value of the objective they wish to achieve, the extent to which the use of NBC weapons will contribute to this goal, and the likely responses of their adversaries—in particular, the expected damage from retaliatory action. The rarity of NBC violence in the past is best explained in reference to these calculations. Simply put, aggressors capable of NBC weapons use have not often judged the benefits of use to outweigh the costs. The risk of retaliation in kind—that is, of a reciprocal or escalatory exchange of NBC weapons—has weighed heavily, perhaps decisively, in many decisions against NBC use.

The United States has some capacity to affect the calculations of its potential adversaries, including those that may conduct covert NBC attacks. Historically, much of this effort has fallen under the rubric of deterrence. During the Cold War, the United States sought to deter Soviet aggression (both strategic nuclear attack and, more dubiously, conventional aggression in distant regions) by threatening nuclear escalation or retaliation. To make this threat credible, and hence to enhance

463

the quality of deterrence, the United States invested heavily in its strategic nuclear capabilities, and American leaders, in their actions and statements, constantly sought to maintain the Soviet perception that the United States was prepared to initiate the use of nuclear weapons if necessary, and certainly to carry out retaliatory strikes. This was essentially a strategy of deterrence by the threat of punishment. It is, however, also possible to deter an adversary by denial—that is, by undertaking defensive preparations designed to lower the adversary's confidence in its ability to achieve its objectives by force. This distinction is quite important in considering how the United States can deter covert NBC attacks.

Any state or non-state actor that considers attacking U.S. citizens, forces, or allies with NBC weapons faces enormous risks of punishment. The United States has an unrivaled capacity to punish its international adversaries through the use of force, up to and including nuclear bombardment. Even non-state actors, which usually cannot be directly attacked by military means, face very severe risks, including relentless pursuit by U.S. and allied intelligence and law enforcement agencies. Any group or government competent enough to carry out an NBC attack against the United States is probably intelligent enough to understand that doing so will bring the full weight of the world's only superpower down upon it—assuming, of course, that the United States learns the identity of the attacker. This suggests that if deterrence of an NBC attack fails, it is likely to have failed not because the attacker underestimated the cost of conducting the attack, but because it (a) felt it could escape detection; (b) felt that all alternative courses of action were worse; or (c) for reasons of fanatical motivation or dementia did not care about the prospect of punishment.

The United States should work to maintain the perception that any government or group that used NBC weapons against American interests would suffer enormously. Fortunately, there is little reason to believe that this perception is in jeopardy—at least insofar as it concerns the U.S. willingness and ability to use overwhelming force. There are certain self-imposed constraints on U.S. action, such as the illegality of assassination, the non-use of chemical and biological weapons, and the general principle that individuals should be punished through the judicial process. But even within these constraints—which might not remain sacrosanct in the immediate aftermath of an NBC attack—the United States still has numerous options for conventional and nuclear punishment, and the prospect of criminal prosecution in the United States for mass murder is likely to be regarded by international terrorists as high punishment. U.S. leaders should occasionally state in public that the United States could and would retaliate forcefully against any NBC attacker, but the point is rather obvious. What is not obvious, however, is that the United States would be able to identify the party responsible for a covert NBC attack with sufficient confidence to trigger the effective use of force. This is the issue of attribution, which is primarily a function of the quality of U.S. intelligence, investigative, and forensic capabilities. U.S. leaders should periodically state in public—perhaps even with some deliberate exaggeration—that the United States has these capabilities and is constantly improving them.

The other aspect of deterrence of covert NBC threats that needs work falls into the category of deterrence by denial. The United States is acutely vulnerable to covert NBC attacks, due to the difficulty of detecting these attacks in the first place, and due to its limited ability to mitigate the consequences of attacks that do occur. The recommendations made earlier in this chapter are aimed at correcting these deficiencies. This effort should be motivated in part by the desire to decrease the confidence of potential attackers in their own ability to carry out successful, massively destructive attacks against U.S. targets. As the quality of American preparedness for covert NBC attacks begins to improve, this progress should be subtly advertised, and perhaps even exaggerated, by the U.S. government. . . .

Decision-makers do not rely exclusively on strategic or pragmatic calculation to determine what they should do; most are also influenced by what they, and those around them, believe is right and wrong. U.S. policy should use this fact to advantage by strengthening international norms against all forms of NBC acquisition and use, and by trying to avoid actions that appear hypocritical or that otherwise weaken these norms. . . .

It is sometimes said that norms against NBC acquisition and use are simply irrelevant, since the individuals most likely to present real NBC threats are already beyond the bounds of moral behavior. This assertion represents a fundamental error. U.S. policy does not and should not rely solely on norms to influence the behavior of specific bad actors, such as Saddam Hussein; non-normative policy instruments are available for this purpose. But the existence of a norm, or a law, can contribute to the objectives of U.S. policy by facilitating the formation of international coalitions against these actors. Norms against NBC weapons may also add moral disapprobation to the list of considerations that have discouraged the vast majority of national and non-state leaders from using, and a substantial majority from acquiring, weapons of mass destruction. Moreover, even if individual leaders are unaffected by these normative considerations, the broad delegitimization of NBC weapons may make a state's own citizens, or even the members of a terrorist organization, more inclined to reveal a secret procurement effort to the outside world.

There is no inconsistency between an aggressive program to prepare for the likelihood that state and non-state adversaries will acquire and use NBC weapons, on the one hand, and the delegitimization of these activities, on the other. In fact, the two efforts are strongly reinforcing. . . . Together with its international partners, the United States has made significant contributions to the strengthening of global norms against NBC weapons acquisition and use over the past decades. The United States could do still more, however. These norms are generally embodied in formal international legal agreements, most of which the United States has played an active role in negotiating. Among the most important of these normative agreements are the 1925 Geneva Protocol, which bans the use of chemical weapons in warfare; the 1968 Nuclear Non-Proliferation Treaty (NPT), which permits only five member states to possess nuclear weapons; the 1972 Biological Weapons Convention (BWC), which bans biological weapons programs; and the

1993 Chemical Weapons Convention (CWC), which bans chemical weapons possession and requires the destruction of existing chemical weapons stockpiles. The existence of these agreements has helped establish the principle that the possession and use of chemical and biological weapons is beyond the bounds of civilized behavior, as is the possession of nuclear weapons by states that have voluntarily forsworn this option. The Geneva Protocol and the BWC—neither of which contains effective enforcement or verification provisions—and the NPT have been violated repeatedly, but the level of NBC activity in the international system over the past decades would almost certainly have been higher if there had been no treaties or principles to violate.

Declaratory policy is another instrument that can be used to strengthen international norms against NBC acquisition and use, as well as the perceived disincentives to NBC use, better known as deterrence. U.S. national leaders can and do articulate the arguments—both moral and pragmatic—against NBC weapons. Iraq and North Korea, for example, were strongly condemned in the early 1990s for their violations of their own nonproliferation commitments, as was Iran for its clandestine NBC programs. Ukraine, Belarus, and Kazakstan were persuaded to relinquish the nuclear weapons they inherited from the Soviet Union with a combination of pragmatic and ethical arguments. In general, however, the United States has difficulty making compelling ethical arguments against other states' possession of weapons of mass destruction, since it has never condemned its own massive weapons programs of either the past or present. We argue that the United States should strongly condemn all cases of NBC weapons use, and encourage others to do the same. It has missed opportunities to do so in the past. The Reagan administration, for example, issued only a mild statement against Iraq's use of chemical weapons against Iran and against Iraq's own Kurdish population during the 1980s. Far stronger language, and action, were called for, especially considering that, at the time, the United States was supporting the Iraqi regime.

With respect to terrorist groups and other violent non-state actors, U.S. declaratory policy is clear and sound. First, the United States says that it does not make concessions to terrorist demands, an assertion that has usually (but not always) been true. Second, terrorists have always been strongly condemned by the United States, treated as criminals, and pursued relentlessly. U.S. law allows international terrorists who attack American citizens or property to be prosecuted in the United States even if they committed their crimes abroad, and were captured in a foreign country (even in a country not cooperating in the investigation) and brought forcibly to the United States.

Third, by its own behavior, the United States sets an example for the rest of the world; its example has in many cases strengthened the norms against NBC acquisition and use, but in a few cases has not. The United States renounced its offensive biological weapons program in 1969, clearing the way for the 1972 Biological Weapons Convention. In 1991, the United States similarly agreed, reciprocally with the Soviet Union, to eliminate its chemical weapons stockpile, leading to the signing of the CWC in 1993. Under the terms of the Nuclear Non-Proliferation Treaty, which was extended indefinitely in 1995, non-nuclear weapon states voluntarily forswore the acquisition of nuclear weapons, and accepted the application of international verification measures on their civilian nuclear activities. In return, the five treaty parties that possess nuclear weapons, including the United States, pledged peaceful nuclear cooperation and reductions in their nuclear arsenals, with the goal of the eventual elimination of nuclear weapons. While the United States has reaffirmed its commitment to work toward nuclear disarmament, all indications are that the required international negotiations will be slow, and the nuclear weapon states will retain their nuclear weapons for the near future, albeit in reduced numbers. U.S. policy on peaceful nuclear cooperation has been criticized by some other nations for being unduly discriminatory and for imposing restrictions that were not envisioned in the original NPT bargain. For example, the United States has strongly opposed nuclear cooperation with states that have complied with International Atomic Energy Agency (IAEA) safeguards but that are believed by U.S. intelligence to have clandestine nuclear weapons programs. This situation is clearest in the case of Iran. The United States maintains, correctly in our view, that the NPT does not require nuclear cooperation when there is good evidence to believe that the state in question is seeking nuclear weapons, in violation of the most fundamental purpose of the treaty. With respect to disarmament, the United States and Russia (following the initiatives of the Soviet Union) have made massive reductions in their levels of deployed tactical and strategic nuclear weapons since the late 1980s, and are in the process of dismantling thousands of excess nuclear warheads. The two states should go further still, and should dismantle the thousands of functional detached warheads that both currently intend to keep as a "strategic reserve," but the non-nuclear weapon parties to the NPT can no longer argue that the two nuclear superpowers have disregarded their Article IV commitment to deep and meaningful reductions.

In general, we believe the United States has an appropriate policy posture toward the acquisition and use of weapons of mass destruction by states and non-state actors, and has worked constructively to delegitimize these weapons in the eyes of the world. Where there are deficiencies in this effort, they usually result from recognized policy trade-offs. The United States could, for example, strengthen the norm against nuclear weapons by renouncing and destroying its own nuclear arsenal, but such a step would be precipitous given the existence of large nuclear arsenals in other states, and many would argue that the diffuse benefits of such a step are unlikely to compensate for the specific military and psychological consequences of losing an ultimate deterrent. Likewise, in its nuclear weapons doctrine, the United States, and its NATO allies, have rejected the principle of "no first use" of nuclear weapons, at least against nuclear-armed adversaries, arguing that they must retain the option of initiating nuclear weapon use in order to maintain a strong deterrent. The United States has, however, extended no-first-use pledges to non-nuclear weapon states in a variety of contexts. Examples include the 1978 assurances offered by Secretary of State Cyrus Vance, in which the U.S. government pledged not to use nuclear weapons against non-nuclear weapon states party to the NPT that are not allied with nuclear weapon states; pledges embodied in the Latin American, South Pacific, and African nuclear-weapon-free-zone treaties; and the 1995 pledge that the United States, Britain, France, and Russia made to secure support for the indefinite extension of the Nuclear Non-Proliferation Treaty.

There is an inherent tension between no-first-use pledges, which help strengthen the international norm against nuclear weapons, and the desire to use nuclear threats to deter regional adversaries, such as Iran or Iraq, from using chemical or biological weapons. A degree of ambiguity has already entered into this aspect of U.S. declaratory policy: in 1991, George Bush told Saddam Hussein that he and the Iraqi people would "pay a terrible price" if Iraq used chemical or biological weapons, a statement that was widely interpreted as a veiled nuclear threat. This degree of ambiguity is justified by the needs of regional deterrence, and avoids most of the harm that explicitly abandoning past no-first-use pledges would do to the moral authority of the United States in multilateral nonproliferation diplomacy.

The U.S. government is, however, missing a unique opportunity to strengthen the global norm against weapons of mass destruction, and that is to negotiate a new multilateral convention that would make the production, stockpiling, and use of biological weapons crimes under international law. Such an agreement would make individual participants in a biological weapons program subject to prosecution in other nations or international courts. The existing international legal agreements that ban the production and use of biological weapons apply only to states, while individuals are subject to the laws of the states that have jurisdiction over them. Many, but not all, states have national laws that make the acquisition and use of biological weapons criminal offenses; some that do have such laws lack the ability to enforce them. A powerful state like the United States can assert extra-territorial jurisdiction over individuals that violate U.S. law outside of U.S. borders, but the legitimacy of this position under international law is open to question. Making the possession and use of biological weapons a crime under international law would have two positive effects and virtually no costs. First, the existence of a convention of this kind, if its enforcement seemed credible, might add to the list of pragmatic reasons weighing against a decision to acquire or use biological weapons, since the long-term risks of such an effort might seem greater to the individuals involved. Second, this convention could reinforce the strong position of the international community that the use of disease as a weapon, by anyone and for any purpose, is a basic moral wrong.

# 32

# Dealing with Terrorists

## PAUL R. PILLAR

Sound counterterrorist policy requires a long and broad perspective. Awareness of past efforts to fight terrorism provides a sense of what is—and just as important, what is not—possible to accomplish in that fight. Sensitivity to other current national interests is needed to understand the immediate limits and complications of counterterrorism. An eye aimed at the future helps to prepare for threats yet to develop and possibilities yet to be exploited.

### A PROBLEM MANAGED, NEVER SOLVED

The long history of terrorism is reason enough to expect that it will always be a problem and usually a significant one. It is a product of such basic facts of human existence as the discontent that is sometimes strong enough to impel people toward violence, the asymmetries of the weak confronting the strong, and the vulnerability of almost every facet of civilization to physical harm at the hands of those who find a reason to inflict harm. If there is a "war" against terrorism, it is a war that cannot be won.

Counterterrorism, even though it shares some attributes with warfare, is not accurately represented by the metaphor of *a* war. Unlike most wars, it has neither a fixed set of enemies nor the prospect of coming to closure, be it through a "win" or some other kind of denouement. Like the cold war, it requires long, patient, persistent effort, but unlike it, it will never conclude with the internal collapse of an opponent. There will be victories and defeats, but not big, tide-turning victories. Counterterrorism is a fight and a struggle, but it is not a campaign with a beginning and an end. . . .

A central lesson of counterterrorism is that *terrorism cannot be "defeated"—only reduced, attenuated, and to some degree controlled.* Individual terrorists or terrorist groups sometimes are defeated; terrorism as a whole never will be. Expectations must be kept realistic. Unrealistically high hopes for counterterrorism lead to impatience that in turn leads to sweeping (and thus perhaps satisfying) but not necessarily effective measures, such as some of the legislation enacted in 1996. Such hopes also encourage despair when they cannot be achieved. Each terrorist attack becomes that much more of a discouraging setback, and the dashed hopes assist the terrorist in damaging public morale. Moreover, unrealistic striving for zero terrorist attacks (which might mean retrenchment overseas to reduce exposure to terrorism) would be no better for overall U.S. foreign policy interests than striving for zero unemployment (which would exacerbate inflation) would be for U.S. economic interests. Counterterrorist programs will prevent many terrorist attacks but will not prevent them all. Terrorism happens. It should never be accepted, but it should always be expected.

The impossibility of winning a "war" or inflicting an overall defeat raises the question of what standards to use in assessing the success or failure of counterterrorist programs. Terrorist attacks, and people getting killed or wounded in them, are obvious and quantifiable indications of failure. But as noted, zero attacks would be an impossible standard. One could look at trends as a measure—that is, whether terrorism has been up or down lately—but the sporadic and uneven nature of terrorism means that short-term fluctuations have little significance, and the effects of other factors make longer-term trends only an imperfect gauge of the effectiveness of counterterrorist programs. One might also look at counterterrorist achievements such as renditions, prosecutions, or rolled-up plots, but this can never be more than a partial scorecard.

Although there is no simple standard, any assessment of counterterrorist policies should bear in mind that *the purpose of counterterrorism is to save lives (and limbs and property) without unduly compromising other national interests and objectives.* This principle has two elements, one narrow and one broad. The narrow one is that as far as counterterrorism is concerned, anything other than saving lives is but a means to that end. That goes for everything from prosecuting an individual terrorist to placing sanctions on a state sponsor. Some of those means may have come to be seen as ends in themselves for other reasons (such as the satisfaction of seeing justice done that comes from prosecuting a terrorist), but they are not counterterrorist ends. They are good for counterterrorism only if, given the circumstances in which they are used, they are likely to reduce terrorism and save lives.

The broad element is that counterterrorism constantly and inevitably impinges on other important U.S. interests, and so counterterrorist policy must be judged according not only to how many lives it saves but also to how little damage it does to those other interests. This objective is partly a matter of not letting the fear of terrorism, or measures taken to avoid it, so disrupt the other business of the U.S. government or of U.S. citizens that it constitutes a victory of sorts for the terrorists. This means, for example, not making U.S. elements overseas so preoccupied with protecting themselves against terrorism that what is supposed to be their primary mission becomes secondary. . . .

The integral link between counterterrorism and other aspects of foreign policy suggests an even broader standard for assessing the success or failure of counterterrorist policy. Besides such measures as plots foiled and fugitives caught, the success of any administration's counterterrorist policy should also be measured according to how more—or less—effective it makes that administration's overall foreign policy. It is a counterterrorist success, for example, if the United States elicits more forthright cooperation from a foreign government because effective counterterrorist work has made that government less afraid of terrorist reprisals for doing business with Washington. It is a success if U.S. diplomats feel safe enough in a terrorism-prone area to stay focused on their primary mission of advancing U.S. economic and political interests in the country to which they are accredited. And it is a success if the United States enjoys a positive image in a culture (for example, the Islamic world) because the problem of extremists in that culture has been handled in a deft way that does not antagonize the nonextremists, or if alliances are harmonious because policies toward state sponsors of terrorism are handled in a constructive way that influences the state sponsor's behavior without antagonizing the allies. . . .

## RECOMMENDATIONS

The principal recommendations are summarized in the form of the following precepts.

*Inject the counterterrorist perspective into foreign policy decisionmaking.* Foreign policy should be made with the awareness that many aspects of U.S. foreign relations, although they may not carry the "counterterrorist" label, nonetheless bear on the threat that international terrorism poses to U.S. interests. U.S. initiatives overseas affect the resentments and motivations of those who might resort to terrorism. A U.S. posture overseas may entail increased vulnerability to terrorism (and in the worst case may involve a Lebanon-type trap in which withdrawals cannot be undertaken without the United States appearing to be defeated by terrorism). And the management of relations with many foreign governments whose cooperation is needed in combating terrorism has major consequences for the effectiveness of the whole U.S. counterterrorist effort. Other important U.S. interests—often more important than counterterrorism in any given case—are also at stake, but the question, "What are the implications of this for terrorism?" should at least be posed and analyzed as part of the decisionmaking process for many foreign policy issues. Those issues include any that involve a physical U.S. presence or a significant U.S. initiative overseas and any that have significant bearing on U.S. relations with a state that poses terrorist problems or is an important U.S. partner in combating terrorism. . . .

*Pay attention to the full range of terrorist threats.* International terrorism's impact on U.S. interests covers a very wide range in terms of perpetrators, methods, and the interests affected. The United States cannot afford to focus narrowly on whatever segment of that range currently is in the headlines, given the diversion of attention and resources from other segments (or from terrorism as a whole) that entails. The United States should not become as preoccupied with any one terrorist as it has been with Usama bin Ladin (even given his considerable influence), because in the fractionated world of international terrorism no single individual is responsible for more than a small part of the mayhem. The nation should not be as preoccupied with any one scenario as it has been with mass casualty chemical, biological, radiological, or nuclear (CBRN) terrorism in the United States (even given the calamity that would be, if it occurred), because that is only one of many ways in which international terrorism can seriously affect U.S. interests, and it is not the most likely way. The allocation of counterterrorist attention and resources should be guided not only by the prospect of dead American bodies but also by the harm that international terrorism—by threatening foreigners—does to U.S. interests by wrecking peace processes or by destabilizing or intimidating otherwise friendly regimes. And the United States should look not only for the current bin Ladin but also for the *next* one, and for the circumstances that may cause such a threat to arise.

*Disrupt terrorist infrastructures worldwide.* Counterterrorism needs to be as far reaching, geographically and functionally, as international terrorism itself. With globe-girdling networks of cells, and peripatetic terrorists whom those networks support, most of the activity that could culminate in terrorist attacks on U.S. interests (including attacks in the United States) takes place far from U.S. shores, and most of it consists of such mundane but essential functions as recruitment, finance, and logistics. The United States should therefore devote a major effort to the piece-by-piece disruption of those terrorist infrastructures. It must rely on cooperative foreign governments to do most of this work, and it should take advantage of the enforcement by those governments of their own laws (including laws having nothing to do with terrorism) to make the terrorists' professional life as difficult as possible in as many places as possible. That this work is less visible and less publicly satisfying than the more dramatic counterterrorist measures the United States sometimes takes should not detract from the priority given to it.

*Use all available methods to counter terrorism, while not relying heavily on any one of them.* Even the disruption of terrorist infrastructures has shortcomings as well as advantages. The same is true of every other means available to the United States to combat terrorism. The shortcomings are found in basic elements of counterterrorism (such as attacking capabilities or influencing intentions), functional instruments (such as criminal law or military force), and more specific tools or policies (such as formally designating terrorist groups, or applying sanctions to state sponsors). The limitations may involve practical difficulties in implementation (for example, trying to identify terrorist financial accounts), undesirable side effects (for example, public resentment over a military strike), or the inapplicability of a measure to parts of the terrorist problem (true of many measures taken against state sponsors, which do not curb terrorism by independent groups). Some hoped-for effects may be inherently uncertain, such as the deterrent effect that a criminal prosecution may (or may not) have in the minds of other terrorists. Since no single measure can do the job, the United States must extract whatever advantage it can from each measure. This means the *selective* use of counterterrorist tools and instruments, bearing in mind the applicability—or inapplicability—of an instrument to a particular case. Anyone who promotes a single method or approach as the "key" to counterterrorism is selling not keys but snake oil.

The instrument of criminal law—even though it is enshrined in one of the basic tenets of current U.S. policy—should not automatically be given precedence over other instruments. A prosecution in a U.S. court should be viewed as one possible means rather than an end and should be foregone if in any case the use of other means (including, for example, the continued collection of intelligence on the activities of terrorists at large) seems likely to save more lives. The investigative resources of law enforcement agencies should be used to support not only criminal prosecutions but also other counterterrorist measures (such as administrative actions to interdict flows of money). And the United States should be open to seeing justice served in reliable foreign courts even for some terrorists who may have violated U.S. law.

*Tailor different policies to meet different terrorist challenges.* A foolish consistency is the hobgoblin not only of little minds, as Ralph Waldo Emerson said, but also of insufficiently flexible counterterrorist policy. In some respects consistency in counterterrorism is indeed desirable, such as in upholding a reputation for firmness against terrorist coercion and in opposing terrorism no matter who is the victim (including adversaries of the United States). But beyond basic commitments, differences are at least as significant as similarities. The terrorist threat is not really "a threat" but rather a method used by an assortment of actors who threaten U.S. interests in varying ways and degrees. There are important differences in the roots of terrorism in various countries, the prospects for resolving conflicts with different terrorist organizations, the degree to which state sponsors are still behind terrorism, the salience of other issues in U.S. relations with states that sponsor or enable terrorism, and other pertinent variables. Such differences should form the basis for tailoring what is, in effect, a different counterterrorist policy for each group or state. Foreign terrorist groups are incredibly diverse. . . . The terrorist methods that each has used should be consistently opposed, and a counterterrorist technique or two (such as catching leading members of a group) might be applied to each, but almost everything else about dealing with them needs to be shaped to meet individual circumstances. Such tailoring may be complicated, difficult, and rhetorically unsatisfying (because it defies generalization), but it is necessary to make counterterrorism more effective and to protect other U.S. interests at stake.

*Give peace a chance.* Although the objective regarding most terrorist groups should be to eradicate them, with others the most promising (or least unpromising) path toward ending the bloodshed is to enlist the group in a peace process aimed at resolving the underlying conflict. Determining whether this is so requires a careful assessment of the group's political and military strength, the nature of the issues and whether competing demands are bridgeable, and the availability of more moderate interlocutors to represent interests the terrorists claim to support. If engagement in a peace process seems more feasible than eradication, the United States should encourage the start of such a process or support—even indirectly as an interested outsider—any process that has already begun. . . .

The legacy of a group's past terrorism, the disruptions caused by its more recent attacks, and even the abhorrence of terrorism that touches U.S. interests directly should not lead the United States to reject peacemaking with a group out of hand. Any road to peace that involves organizations that have used terrorism will be rocky. Infractions should be penalized as appropriate but not allowed to kill a process that otherwise still has a chance to succeed. The label "terrorist" should not be a permanent disqualifier for doing business with the United States or for being part of a U.S.-supported political process. Not only were Yasir Arafat and Gerry Adams leaders of terrorist groups; so were Menachem Begin and Yitzhak Shamir. . . .

*Encourage reforming state sponsors to reform even more by engaging them, not just punishing them.* The United States should seize the opportunity provided by the substantial decline in state sponsorship of terrorism during the past several years to nurture even more improvement on this front, as well as to advance other U.S. interests in the states in question. This means not only keeping lists of state sponsors up to date but also using positive and negative techniques to move bilateral relationships in the desired direction. The economic sanctions and other negative measures on which the United States has primarily relied (and the limitations of which have been amply demonstrated) have a role, but their effectiveness as an inducement to better behavior depends on U.S. willingness to change them when the behavior that was the reason for enacting them in the first place has changed. The United States needs to demonstrate this responsiveness to keep the state directly concerned on the right path and to convince others that supporting—or reducing support for—terrorism makes a difference in what kind of relations they will have with Washington.

The United States should try to make it easier, not harder, for regimes trying to clean up their acts to clean them up further. This requires clear communication of what is expected, which is best done through direct dialogue. It also means not expecting the more difficult reforms to be accomplished quickly. And it means incrementally improving the relationship as terrorist-related behavior incrementally improves. Most important, the United States should avoid postures that lead decisionmakers on the other side (or in other countries) to conclude that relations with Washington will remain poisoned no matter how much support for terrorism is reduced. . . .

Of every action (or inaction) regarding relations with state sponsors the question should be asked, "Is this likely to reduce terrorism?" The objective should not be to condemn people for the past but to save lives in the future. Changing a relationship with a foreign leader stained by sins of the past should not require any judgment that he has had a change of heart. What matters is change in his policies, and that might occur (as with Muammar Qadhafi or Fidel Castro) because the circumstances he faces have changed.

*Help other governments to help with counter-terrorism.* The dependence of the United States on a host of foreign governments for much of the counterterrorist work that needs to be done (especially the disruption of terrorist infrastructures) should be recognized in the management of relations with those governments. The needed cooperation often includes measures that are difficult or (from the foreign government's viewpoint) risky, and U.S. assistance and reassurance should be furnished to make the other government willing and able to act. The overall warmth of a bilateral relationship obviously affects willingness, but so do efforts to educate the foreign partner that terrorism is a threat to both countries. Training and other forms of practical assistance to police and security services enhance the ability of many foreign governments (especially in less developed countries) to help, and the United States should be generous in providing such assistance, through Antiterrorism Training Assistance courses and other departmental training programs. The concerns of cooperating governments about terrorist reprisals should be respected by preserving the secrecy of joint operations, even if this means resisting the urge to trumpet counterterrorist successes.

*Work with, not against, allies.* With most Europeans and other close allies, what is needed is not technical assistance and reassurance but rather more comity and coordination. The United States should respect (and even learn something from) different perspectives toward countering terrorism and not try to change allied policies that experience and deeply felt national interests dictate will not be changed. It should exploit ways in which policies that are not uniform may nonetheless be coordinated to mutual benefit, especially regarding state sponsors. The United States should also end the use of secondary economic sanctions—which have been ineffective and damaging to intra-alliance relations—in futile efforts to bend allies to its will. When the counterterrorist operations of allies raise human rights concerns (as they have at times with Israel and Turkey), the United States should work within the framework of continued close counterterrorist cooperation—one of the most effective channels the United States has for influencing human rights practices—to discourage such abuses.

*Use public diplomacy to elucidate terrorism without glamorizing terrorists.* The reaching out for foreign help and cooperation must extend not only to governments but also to their citizens. An active program of public diplomacy should explain why terrorism hurts the interests of those citizens and why U.S. counterterrorist efforts do not. The public diplomacy needs to be adroit, as well as active, to avoid the pitfall of making wanted terrorists appear more like Robin Hood than like malign criminals.

# Acknowledgments

**Chapter 1**
Reprinted by permission from *Security Studies*, Vol. 5, No. 4 published by Frank Cass & Company, 900 Eastern Avenue, Ilford, Essex, England. Copyright © Frank Cass & Co. Ltd.

**Chapter 2**
Reprinted from *The Sources of Military Doctrine: France, Britain and Germany Between the World Wars* by Barry R. Posen. Copyright © 1984 by Cornell University Press. Used by permission of the publisher, Cornell University Press.

**Chapter 3**
Reprinted by permission from *International Security*, Vol. 22, No. 4 published by MIT Press. Copyright © 1998 by the President and Fellows of Harvard College and the Massachusetts Institute of Technology.

**Chapter 4**
Reprinted from *Forceful Persuasion: Coercive Diplomacy as an Alternative to War* by Alexander L. George. Copyright © 1991 by the Endowment of the United States Institute of Peace. Used with permission of the United States Institute of Peace Press, Washington DC, 1991.

**Chapter 5**
Reprinted from David Carlton and Carlo Schaerf, eds., *International Terrorism and World Security* (New York: John Wiley and Sons, 1975), by permission of Croom Helm.

*Chapter 6*
Reprinted by permission from *The Choice: Nuclear Weapons vs. Security*, edited by Gwyn Prins, published by Chatto & Windus. Used by permission of the Random House Group Limited.

*Chapter 7*
Reprinted by permission from *International Security*, Vol. 13, No. 2 (Fall 1988) published by MIT Press, Cambridge, Massachusetts. Copyright © 1988 by the President and Fellows of Harvard College and the Massachusetts Institute of Technology.

*Chapter 8*
Reprinted by permission from *American Political Science Review*, Vol. 84, No. 3 (September 1990) published by the American Political Science Association.

*Chapter 9*
Reprinted by permission from *International Security*, Vol. 9, No. 1 (Summer 1984) published by MIT Press. Copyright © 1984 by the President and Fellows of Harvard College and the Massachusetts Institute of Technology.

*Chapter 10*
Reprinted from John J. Mearsheimer, *Conventional Deterrence*. Copyright © 1983 by Cornell University Press. Used by permission of the publisher, Cornell University Press.

*Chapter 11*
This article first appeared in *International Affairs* (London) Vol. 24, No. 4 (October 1948): 543–55, and is reproduced with permission.

*Chapter 12*
Reprinted by permission of *Foreign Affairs* (January 1957). Copyright © 1956 by the Council on Foreign Relations, Inc.

*Chapter 13*
Reprinted from *Limited War in the Nuclear Age* by Morton H. Halperin by permission of the author.

*Chapter 14*
Reprinted by permission from *International Security*, Vol. 14, No. 3 (Winter 1989/90) published by MIT Press. Copyright © 1989 by the President and Fellows of Harvard College and the Massachusetts Institute of Technology.

# About the Contributors

**Bruce J. Allyn** is a former director of the Kennedy School–Soviet Project on Crisis Prevention, Harvard University, and is now with the Monitor Company.

**Robert J. Art** is professor of politics at Brandeis University.

**James G. Blight** is professor of international relations (research) at the Thomas J. Watson, Jr., Institute of International Studies, Brown University.

**McGeorge Bundy** is a former national security advisor to President Kennedy and professor of history emeritus at New York University.

**Steven L. Burg** is professor of politics at Brandeis University.

**Brahma Chellaney** is professor of security studies at the Center for Policy Research in New Delhi.

**Richard A. Falkenrath** is senior director for policy and programs in the Office of Homeland Security, the White House.

**John Lewis Gaddis** is professor of history at Yale University.

**Alexander L. George** is professor of political science emeritus at Stanford University.

**Morton H. Halperin** is senior fellow at the Council on Foreign Relations and director of the Washington Office of the Open Society Institute.

**G. John Ikenberry** is professor of international relations at the School of Foreign Service, Georgetown University.

**Brian M. Jenkins** is a consultant to the president of the RAND Corporation.

**Robert Jervis** is professor of political science at Columbia University.

**Chaim Kaufmann** is associate professor of international relations at Lehigh College.

**Walter Laqueur** is chairman of the Research Council of the Center for Strategic and International Studies.

**Christopher Layne** is visiting fellow in foreign policy studies at the CATO Institute.

**Louis Morton** was professor of history at Dartmouth College.

**John J. Mearsheimer** is professor of political science at the University of Chicago.

**Robert D. Newman** is an arms control specialist in Washington, D.C.

**Michael E. O'Hanlon** is senior fellow in foreign policy studies at the Brookings Institution.

**Barry R. Posen** is professor of political science at the Massachusetts Institute of Technology.

**Paul R. Pillar** was formerly deputy chief of the Counterterrorism Center at the Central Intelligence Agency and is currently the national intelligence officer for South Asia on the U.S. National Intelligence Council.

**Scott D. Sagan** is professor of political science at Stanford University.

**Sir George Sansom** was a writer and a British diplomat with extensive experience in East Asia.

**Jack Snyder** is professor of political science at Columbia University.

**Bradley A. Thayer** is assistant professor of political science at the University of Minnesota, Duluth.

**Victor A. Utgoff** is deputy director of the Strategy, Forces, and Resource Division of the Institute for Defense Analyses.

**Stephen Van Evera** is professor of political science at the Massachusetts Institute of Technology.

**Barbara F. Walter** is associate professor of political science at the University of California, San Diego.

**Kenneth N. Waltz** is professor emeritus at the University of California, Berkeley, and adjunct professor at Columbia University.

**David A. Welch** is associate professor of political science at the University of Toronto.